ALPHA - ANYBODY CAN CODE

OPTIMUM

PYTHON POWER

SERIES VI

FROM DATA TO INTELLIGENCE:

THE DEEP LEARNING REVOLUTION

Unlocking the Power of Data Science:

Mastering Libraries, Models, Algorithms, and Core Intuition!

SHREE SHAMBAV

OPTIMUM – PYTHON POWER – Series VI

FROM DATA TO INTELLIGENCE:

THE DEEP LEARNING REVOLUTION

Shree Shambav

Published by Shree Shambav, Tamil Nadu, India
Shree Shambav Ink & Imagination "Where Words Breathe and Imagination Soars"

First Edition, 2025

ISBN: 978-93-5525-817-5

Email:shreeshambav@gmail.com

Web:www.shambav.org

DEDICATION

"Isavasyam idam sarvam yat kim ca jagatyam jagat, tena tyaktena bhunjitha, ma gridhah kasyasvid dhanam"

To the Almighty,

the Divine Masters,

the family who listens,

and my parents who see –

your presence shapes the pages of my life's journey.

"Isavasyam idam sarvam yat kim ca jagatyam jagat"

Meaning: "God encompasses everything you perceive, see, or touch with your sense organs."

DISCLAIMER

The content in this book is provided solely for educational and informational purposes. Every effort has been made to ensure accuracy, clarity, and relevance; however, the author and publisher make no representations or warranties, express or implied, regarding the completeness, reliability, or suitability of the concepts, methods, examples, or code contained herein.

This volume is designed for readers with a foundational understanding of Python and basic programming principles. Prior exposure to data analysis, statistics, or introductory machine learning will enrich comprehension and practical application.

The techniques, frameworks, and workflows discussed are intended to guide and inspire exploration within the realms of data science and deep learning. Individual outcomes may differ based on context, implementation, computational environments, and technological evolution.

Neither the author nor the publisher shall be held liable for any direct, indirect, incidental, or consequential damages resulting from the application or misapplication of the content presented in this book. All trademarks, service marks, product names, and brand names are the property of their respective owners and are used solely for identification and educational purposes.

This publication is entirely independent and not affiliated with, authorised, or endorsed by any of the referenced companies, organisations, or software platforms. Readers are encouraged to refer to official documentation, continue learning from credible sources, and apply the discussed methodologies responsibly to align with their unique objectives and development environments.

Note - If any part of the book, in any sequence, hurts the reader's sentiments, it would be just out of a sheer accident, not intentional

EPIGRAM

In the vast ocean of data lies the silent rhythm of intelligence—waiting to be awakened.
Python is the vessel, deep learning the wind, and curiosity the compass that guides the voyage.
This book is not merely about models or code—it is a journey through perception, memory, and meaning.
For those who seek not just to build intelligent systems, but to understand the intelligence within themselves—this is your beginning.

– Shree Shambav

Suggested Reads

FROM BEST-SELLING AUTHOR

Endorsements

A masterful blend of clarity and depth, "Optimum Python Power – From Data to Intelligence" bridges the gap between theory and practice with elegance. It doesn't just teach deep learning—it illuminates how data transforms into intelligence. A must-read for anyone seeking not only to code models but to understand the philosophy that drives them. This book turns complexity into insight, making it an indispensable guide for students, professionals, and lifelong learners in AI.

This book stands as a beacon for the new era of intelligent computing. With its seamless integration of mathematics, intuition, and real-world implementation, "Optimum Python Power" empowers readers to grasp the true essence of deep learning. It is both a technical companion and an intellectual journey—one that inspires curiosity, precision, and innovation. A truly exceptional resource for anyone striving to master Python, data science, and the evolving frontier of artificial intelligence.

About the Author

Shree Shambhav's journey embodies the harmony of creativity, purpose, and transformation. A world record holder, he is an acclaimed author, inspirational speaker, artist, philanthropist, life coach, and entrepreneur. His deep passion for music has given rise to ten soul-stirring albums available across major platforms, each inspired by his acclaimed poetry collection *Whispers of Eternity*. With a rare fusion of grace, wisdom, and authenticity, Shree Shambhav continues to touch countless lives—guiding individuals toward self-discovery, transformation, and excellence through his profound teachings, insightful counselling, and impactful literary works.

▪ LITERARY EXCELLENCE

Shree Shambav is a 100x best-selling author celebrated for his groundbreaking works across multiple genres, including Non-Fiction, Self-Help, Technology, Short Stories, Anthologies, and Poetry. His thought-provoking articles have also graced the pages of prominent magazines, solidifying his influence as a literary force.

His journey as an author took flight with the acclaimed "Journey of Soul – Karma", a masterpiece that explores the profound interplay of human experience, karma, and spiritual evolution. This seminal work earned him recognition and accolades in the literary world, marking the beginning of a legacy that continues to inspire.

▪ TECHNOLOGY AND INNOVATION

Shree Shambav's contributions extend beyond the realm of literature. A graduate of the prestigious Indian Institute of Management (IIM) and the National Institute of Technology (NIT), he combines academic brilliance with real-world expertise. Throughout his illustrious career, he has held leadership positions in renowned multinational corporations, excelling in strategy, performance improvement, change management, and human capital development.

His technical acumen shines through his acclaimed "Optimum – Python Power Series", a comprehensive collection of books that serve as an invaluable resource for aspiring and seasoned technologists.

- Optimum - Python Series I: Ultimate Guide for Beginners laid the foundation for mastering Python.
- Optimum - Python Series II: Exploring Data Structures and Algorithms elevated readers' understanding of coding efficiency and problem-solving.
- Optimum – Python Power Series III: Unleashing the Potential of Data Science with Libraries stands as a crowning achievement, delving deep into essential libraries for data science and equipping readers with tools to thrive in this ever-evolving domain.
- **Optimum – Python Power Series IV: From Logic to Libraries** serves as a comprehensive and practical guide, empowering readers to harness the full potential of Python for real-world data science applications. Rooted in Shree Shambhav's rich consulting experience and deep cross-industry insights, this volume bridges theory and practice—helping learners master models, algorithms, and the intuition behind intelligent data-driven solutions.
- **Optimum – Python Power Series V: The Mathematical Mind of Data Science** explores the quantitative backbone of analytics—covering the Role of Mathematics, Probability Laws, Sampling, Regression, Bayesian Models, Reinforcement Learning, and Time Series Analysis. With clarity and precision, Shree Shambhav transforms complex statistical foundations into accessible, applicable knowledge, guiding readers to uncover structure, logic, and meaning within data.

His latest endeavour, "Optimum Python Power – From Data to Intelligence: The Deep Learning Revolution (Series VI)," pursuit of bridging human intellect with machine learning excellence. This work delves into the transformative realm of deep learning, guiding readers from foundational data concepts to intelligent systems with clarity and insight. It stands as both a technical masterpiece and a visionary guide to the evolving frontier of AI.

Shree Shambav's writing is enriched by his extensive consulting background and a profound comprehension of diverse industries, providing readers with invaluable insights and practical knowledge.

Each book is a testament to Shree Shambav's deep understanding of technology and his ability to make complex concepts accessible, actionable, and transformative.

☐ DRIVING INNOVATION ACROSS INDUSTRIES

Beyond his literary works, Shree Shambav's professional expertise has left an indelible mark across diverse industries, including banking, insurance, retail, and hospitality. He has architected and developed systems that are not only robust and resilient but also revolutionary:

Forecasting Engines and Predictive Models: For pricing, customer churn prediction, and risk portfolio management.

Data-Driven Systems: Web-based architectures, rule engines, ETL frameworks, and BI systems that streamline data flow, enhance accessibility, and support strategic decision-making.

Analytical Dashboards: Insightful tools that deliver powerful visualizations, enabling businesses to navigate challenges and optimise performance.

His work also extends to creating structured practice intellectual properties (IPs), KPI frameworks, and maturity models, empowering organisations to achieve sustainable growth and innovation.

☐ A PHILANTHROPIC SPIRIT AND ADVOCATE FOR CHANGE

Shree Shambav's vision transcends personal success. As a philanthropist and life coach, he remains deeply committed to societal well-being, working to uplift individuals and communities. Through the Ayur Rakshita Foundation (www.shambav-ayurrakshita.org), he leads initiatives that promote health, education, and holistic living, reflecting his belief in creating a harmonious and purposeful world.

☐ A LIFE DEDICATED TO LEARNING AND TRANSFORMATION

Shree Shambav's journey is a testament to his unwavering pursuit of knowledge, innovation, and service. Whether through his books, technical expertise, or philanthropic efforts, he continues to empower others to unlock their potential and live with greater meaning.

During his leisure time, he remains devoted to innovation, channelling his expertise into developing prediction models and exploring emerging fields—an embodiment of lifelong learning and curiosity.

☐ CONNECT WITH SHREE SHAMBAV

Shree Shambav extends his heartfelt gratitude to all those who have shown interest in his works. To explore his books, teachings, and initiatives:

Website: www.shambav.org

Foundation: www.shambav-ayurrakshita.org

LinkedIn: https://www.linkedin.com/in/shreeshambav/

Blog: https://blog.shambav.org/

Instagram: https://www.instagram.com/shreeshambav/

YouTube: https://www.youtube.com/@shreeshambav

Amazon: https://www.amazon.com/author/shreeshambav

Goodreads: https://www.goodreads.com/author/show/22367436.Shree_Shambav

Follow Him on Social Media: @shreeshambav

Technical Support and Reviewer

Apeksha Prabhu is a talented technology graduate who specialises in Computer Science and Technology. She has gained extensive experience in the field through her work as a full-stack developer and currently holds a position at Nokia.

Apeksha has completed many outstanding projects during her academic and professional careers. Her outstanding academic achievements match her outstanding practical experience. She has published research papers in prestigious technical journals such as IJERT and IJSCE. Her contributions to different publications show a deep understanding of complex technical concepts, meticulous attention to detail, and a dedication to the advancement of open-source Python.

Apeksha's work is filled with passion and an unwavering dedication to pushing the boundaries of what is possible in her field. She constantly strives to innovate and expand her knowledge, ensuring her work is always at the cutting edge of technological advancement.

Author's Note

In the ever-evolving landscape of technology, deep learning stands as one of humanity's most transformative frontiers—an art and science that bridges logic, intuition, and imagination. *Optimum Python Power – From Data to Intelligence: The Deep Learning Revolution (Series VI)* was born from my desire to make this intricate subject both approachable and empowering.

Through this volume, I invite readers not merely to learn algorithms, but to understand the thought process that fuels intelligent systems—the ability to perceive patterns, extract meaning, and simulate the nuances of human cognition. Every concept, model, and example shared here has been crafted to ignite curiosity and deepen comprehension, encouraging a practical yet philosophical exploration of machine intelligence.

My journey as a consultant, educator, and lifelong learner has revealed a profound truth: technology gains its greatest power when it serves human insight. Python, as a language of clarity and creativity, allows us to translate abstract ideas into tangible intelligence. This book is a continuation of that vision—to equip every reader with not just the tools, but the intuition to navigate the new age of intelligent computation.

May this work inspire you to see data not as mere numbers, but as a living narrative—a story waiting to be understood, optimised, and transformed into wisdom.

With gratitude and purpose,

Shree Shambav

PREFACE

Every revolution begins with curiosity—the kind that questions how intelligence emerges, how systems learn, and how code can reflect cognition. *Optimum Python Power – From Data to Intelligence: The Deep Learning Revolution (Series VI)* was born from that same curiosity—to explore not just the algorithms behind artificial intelligence, but the philosophy, structure, and artistry that make it possible.

This book stands as the sixth volume in the *Optimum Python Power* series—a continuation of a journey that began with understanding the essence of data and now culminates in its transformation into intelligence. Each page is designed to bridge intuition with implementation, blending mathematics with meaning and computation with creativity. It invites readers to look beyond syntax and see the soul of deep learning—the patterns of thought encoded in numbers, weights, and connections.

In an era where data has become the new language of innovation, **Deep Learning** is its poetry—written not in words, but in matrices and gradients. From the early days of Perceptrons and feedforward networks to the rise of Transformers and generative models, the field has witnessed exponential growth. Yet, amidst this explosion of complexity, the fundamental questions remain timeless: *How does learning occur? What does it mean to remember, to generalise, to create?* This book attempts to answer those questions through clarity, structure, and exploration.

The content is organised as a **comprehensive roadmap**, designed for progressive mastery.

Part 1: The Rise of Neural Networks lays the groundwork, introducing Artificial Neural Networks (ANNs), activation functions, optimization techniques, and frameworks like TensorFlow and Keras. It transforms abstract mathematics into a visual and intuitive understanding.

Part 2: From Pixels to Patterns immerses readers in the world of Convolutional Neural Networks (CNNs)—a domain where machines learn to see. It explains how images transform into features, how filters detect edges, and how layers combine to form perception.

Part 3: The Dawn of Language Intelligence explores Natural Language Processing (NLP) and its evolution toward understanding and generating human-like text. This section illuminates how words become vectors, how embeddings capture context, and how deep models like BERT and GPT transform language into logic.

Part 4: The Evolution of Memory in Machines brings attention to sequence modeling—where time, order, and dependency converge. Through RNNs, LSTMs, and GRUs, readers will understand how networks retain context and learn temporal relationships in data streams.

Part 5: From RNNs to Transformers captures the quantum leap in machine learning—how attention mechanisms redefined representation, how Transformers achieved scalability and parallelism, and how models like T5, GPT, and BERT reshaped the AI landscape. The section concludes with Autoencoders—Sparse, Contractive, and Variational—revealing how intelligence compresses, abstracts, and reconstructs information.

Each part balances **mathematical precision**, **practical examples**, and **conceptual insight**, ensuring that learners not only build models but comprehend their inner dynamics. Code examples are written in Python—chosen not merely for its simplicity but for its expressiveness as a language of experimentation and innovation.

What makes this book unique is its commitment to *depth over haste*. It is written not to chase trends, but to build lasting understanding. Each section connects the technical with the philosophical—the neuron with the mind, the algorithm with behaviour, and the network with consciousness. For those who read it deeply, this book is more than a technical manual—it is a reflection on how learning itself unfolds in both man and machine.

This work is dedicated to **students, researchers, and dreamers**—those who look at data not as mere numbers but as living patterns waiting to be understood. It is also for **professionals and innovators** who believe that artificial intelligence is not the imitation of human thought but an extension of it—a mirror to our own evolving intelligence.

May this book guide you to think not only in terms of *accuracy* and *loss functions* but also in terms of *clarity, connection,* and *insight.* May it remind you that every model is a metaphor for how we perceive the world—and every epoch of AI reflects an epoch of human understanding.

Welcome to the revolution where **data becomes intelligence**, and **Python becomes the language of creation**. The journey begins now—layer by layer, idea by idea, and discovery by discovery.

Happy coding and exploring!

Sincerely,

Shree Shambav

INTRODUCTION

Welcome to *Optimum Python Power – From Data to Intelligence: The Deep Learning Revolution (Series VI)* — a definitive guide that bridges the gap between coding, cognition, and creativity. This book is designed as both a roadmap and a revelation, guiding readers from the foundational principles of neural networks to the transformative architectures that power today's intelligent systems.

In an era where data has become the new fuel and intelligence the ultimate output, deep learning stands as the engine of modern innovation. From recognising faces and understanding language to predicting behaviour and generating art, the revolution is not just technological—it's philosophical. It reflects humanity's pursuit to replicate and extend the very process of learning itself.

Through structured chapters and intuitive explanations, this book takes you on a journey—from the birth of Artificial Neural Networks and Perceptrons to the evolution of Transformers and Autoencoders. Along the way, it integrates mathematical intuition, algorithmic insight, and Python-based implementation, making complex ideas accessible and applicable.

Whether you are a student, researcher, or practitioner, this volume will equip you with the conceptual clarity and technical skill to transform raw data into structured intelligence—and to understand the deeper story behind every layer, weight, and activation that powers the AI revolution.

Comprehensive Roadmap

Optimum Python Power – From Data to Intelligence: The Deep Learning Revolution (Series VI) is a journey through the heart of modern artificial intelligence — where mathematics meets imagination, and data evolves into intelligence. This volume is meticulously structured to bridge conceptual theory with hands-on practicality. From the early foundations of neural computation to the transformative architectures that now drive intelligent machines, each chapter builds progressively — revealing how raw data, when shaped by learning algorithms, begins to think, reason, and create. The roadmap moves from the origins of neural networks (ANNs and Perceptrons) through visual intelligence (CNNs), linguistic comprehension (NLP, NLU, NLG), temporal understanding (RNN, LSTM, GRU), and culminates in the parallelized intelligence of Transformers and Autoencoders.

Journey Overview

This book is not just a collection of algorithms — it is a guided evolution of thought. You begin by understanding how simple neurons learn patterns through weights and activations. You then ascend through convolutional architectures that give machines vision, followed by language models that let them speak and comprehend. The narrative then expands into memory-based systems like LSTMs and GRUs, before unveiling the revolution of self-attention and the Transformer — the architecture that powers today's generative AI, including ChatGPT and BERT. Each section balances **mathematical intuition**, **algorithmic clarity**, and **practical coding insights**, culminating in a holistic understanding of intelligence as an emergent property of data and structure.

Target Audience

This book is crafted for **data scientists, AI enthusiasts, researchers, and engineers** seeking to move beyond surface-level understanding into the deeper architecture of learning systems. Whether you are a Python programmer entering the world of machine intelligence or a researcher refining advanced models, this volume provides conceptual clarity and implementation precision. Educators can use it as a teaching resource, while practitioners can treat it as a reference guide for model design, optimization, and deployment. Each part connects theory to application, ensuring readers not only learn how models work — but *why* they work.

Why This Book?

The deep learning landscape is vast and rapidly evolving. Many practitioners know how to use frameworks but struggle to grasp the principles that make these architectures succeed. *Optimum Python Power* demystifies the complexity — showing how intelligence emerges from structure, learning, and scale. It blends **philosophical insight** with **technical rigour**, teaching readers to think like both an engineer and a scientist. The inclusion of TensorFlow, Keras, and PyTorch ensures that concepts translate into executable understanding. Each chapter builds not just a model, but a mindset — empowering readers to design, interpret, and innovate their own architectures.

Book Coverage

This volume unfolds across **five interconnected parts**, forming a coherent path from neural basics to cutting-edge architectures:

Part 1: The Rise of Neural Networks – ANN | Perceptron | TensorFlow

Artificial Neural Networks (ANNs) form the foundation of modern deep learning, inspired by the human brain's interconnected neurons. A basic Perceptron acts as a linear classifier, while Multi-Layer Perceptrons (MLPs) extend this concept with hidden layers that capture complex, nonlinear relationships. Learning occurs through forward and backward propagation—data flows through the network, predictions are compared with actual values, and weights are updated using gradient descent to minimize error. Activation functions like ReLU, Sigmoid, and Tanh introduce non-linearity, while optimizers such as Adam, RMSProp, and SGD enhance convergence. Frameworks like TensorFlow and Keras simplify model building and deployment through high-level abstractions. This part establishes the mathematical and conceptual foundations needed to design and optimize neural networks efficiently.

Part 2: From Pixels to Patterns – CNN

Convolutional Neural Networks (CNNs) revolutionised pattern recognition by enabling machines to interpret visual data with spatial awareness. They utilise convolutional layers, where filters slide over input images to detect features such as edges, textures, and objects. Pooling layers compress these features, providing spatial invariance and reducing computation while retaining essential details. Activation functions like ReLU introduce non-linearity, and backpropagation fine-tunes filter weights based on error signals. CNNs often employ cross-entropy loss and sigmoid or softmax activations for classification tasks. Techniques like dropout, batch normalization, and data augmentation enhance robustness and prevent overfitting. This architecture powers applications from facial recognition to autonomous driving—transforming pixels into meaningful patterns that drive intelligent visual perception.

Part 3: The Dawn of Language Intelligence – NLU | NLP | NLG

This part explores how machines learn to understand and generate human language through Natural Language Processing (NLP), Natural Language Understanding (NLU), and Natural Language Generation (NLG). NLP handles the structure and processing of text, while NLU focuses on extracting meaning, sentiment, and intent. NLG produces coherent responses that resemble human communication. The journey begins with text preprocessing—tokenization, normalization, stopword removal, and lemmatization—followed by transforming words into numeric form through encoding methods like Bag-of-Words, TF-IDF, or embeddings. Advanced embedding models—Word2Vec, GloVe, and BERT—capture contextual meaning, enabling models to understand nuance and semantics. These techniques power real-world applications such as chatbots, translators, and summarizers, representing a critical leap toward language-based artificial intelligence.

Part 4: The Evolution of Memory in Machines – RNN | LSTM | GRU

Recurrent Neural Networks (RNNs) introduced memory into neural systems, enabling sequential data processing for time-dependent tasks like speech and text. However, traditional RNNs struggled with vanishing gradients, limiting long-term context learning. To overcome this, Long Short-Term Memory (LSTM) networks were developed, introducing gates that control information flow and preserve memory across longer sequences. Bidirectional and Stacked LSTMs deepen understanding and improve accuracy. Gated Recurrent Units (GRUs) further simplified the architecture, maintaining efficiency with fewer parameters. Through Backpropagation Through Time (BPTT), gradients are propagated across sequences for learning temporal dependencies. These architectures laid the groundwork for modern natural language models and speech systems—where memory, sequence, and context must coexist seamlessly in computation.

Part 5: From RNNs to Transformers

This part chronicles the shift from sequential RNNs to parallel Transformer architectures that dominate modern AI. RNNs and LSTMs were limited by sequential computation and difficulty in learning long-range dependencies. The Attention mechanism transformed this landscape by allowing models to focus selectively on relevant parts of the input, regardless of distance. Transformers eliminate recurrence using Self-Attention and Positional Encoding to retain order, enabling highly parallelized training. Key components—Multi-Head Attention, Feed-Forward

Networks, and Encoder–Decoder layers—create scalable, context-rich models. Variants like Mini and Full Transformers, MQA, and GQA refine efficiency and generalization. Concepts such as latent spaces and Autoencoders (Sparse, Contractive, and Variational) illustrate how networks learn compact, meaningful representations, bridging perception, understanding, and generative intelligence.

Each part blends theory, visualization, and code, guiding readers from **intuition to implementation**. By the end, you will understand how deep learning unites vision, language, and cognition — and how Python remains the bridge between raw data and intelligent design.

Welcome to Series VI — where data becomes intelligence, and intelligence becomes art.

Happy coding and exploring!

☐ PROGRAMS

The table presents a detailed distribution of the programs included in this book, categorised by units within each part.

Part	Unit	Lessons covered	Program	Total Program
One	1	The Rise of Neural Networks	23	**23**
Two	2	From Pixels to Patterns - CNN	8	**8**
Three	3	The Dawn of Language Intelligence NLP	35	**35**
Four	4	The Evolution of Memory in Machines – RNN, LSTM, GRU	17	**17**
Five	5	From RNNs to Transformers	11	**11**
Appendix	A	Online Resources		
	B	Practice Question		**125**
	C	Quiz		**85**
	D	Quiz Answers		**85**
		Total Programs		**94**

☐ PRACTICE QUESTIONS

The table provides a comprehensive breakdown of the practice questions featured in this book, sorted by units within each part.

Part	Practice Question	Total
One	20	**20**
Two	15	**15**
Three	30	**30**
Four	30	**30**
Five	30	**30**
Total Questions	**125**	**125**

☐ ASSIGNMENT AND QUIZ

The table provides a comprehensive breakdown of the assignment featured in this book, sorted by units within each part.

Part	Unit	Assignment	Quiz
1	1		15
2	2		10
3	3		30
4	4		15
5	5		15
Total			**85**

☐ TABLES AND ILLUSTRATIONS

Part	**Tables**	**Illustration**	**Flowchart**
One	1	2	
Two	8	36	
Three	2	11	
Four	17	18	
Five	14	13	
Total	**61**	**89**	

CONTENTS

Getting Started

Data Science is an interdisciplinary field that amalgamates a diverse array of techniques, tools, and methodologies to glean insights and knowledge from data. It encompasses the application of scientific methods, statistical analysis, data visualization, and machine learning algorithms to unearth patterns, formulate predictions, and inform decision-making processes.

- ☐ **Machine learning, AI, and Data Science are related fields but have distinct differences.**

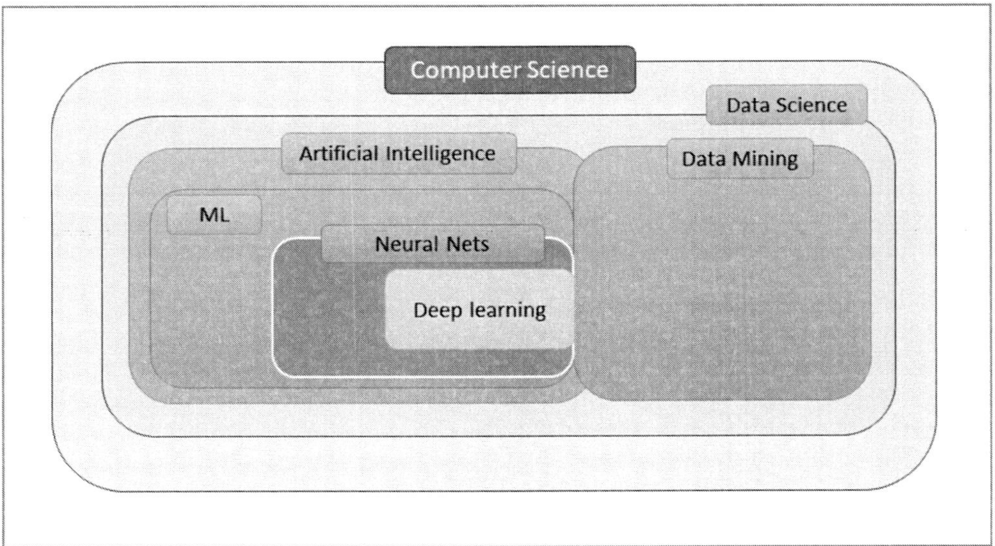

Data Science: Data science is a multifaceted discipline that harnesses scientific methodologies, algorithms, and systems to distil knowledge and insights from both structured and unstructured data. This interdisciplinary field employs an array of techniques, including data cleaning, exploration, visualization, statistical analysis, and predictive modelling. Data scientists navigate large and intricate datasets to discern patterns, trends, and actionable insights, thereby aiding businesses in making informed decisions and addressing challenges. This expansive field encompasses a diverse array of tools and methodologies, spanning statistical analysis, data mining, machine learning, and data visualization.

Artificial Intelligence (AI): Artificial Intelligence (AI) denotes the creation of intelligent systems capable of executing tasks typically associated with human intelligence. AI endeavours to replicate human cognitive functions, such as learning, reasoning, problem-solving, and decision-making. This expansive domain encompasses diverse subfields, including natural language processing, computer vision, expert systems, and robotics. AI techniques span a spectrum from rule-based systems and symbolic reasoning to machine learning, deep learning, and neural networks.

Machine Learning: Machine learning constitutes a subset of artificial intelligence dedicated to crafting algorithms and models that empower computers to learn from data and autonomously make predictions or decisions devoid of explicit programming. This entails training a model on historical data and subsequently leveraging it to generate predictions or decisions concerning new data. Machine learning algorithms are segmented into supervised learning, unsupervised learning, and reinforcement learning contingent upon the presence of labelled training data and the learning objective. Widely employed across diverse domains, machine learning is instrumental in addressing intricate challenges and facilitating predictions in areas such as image and speech recognition, natural language processing, recommendation systems, and fraud detection.

In summary, data science represents a comprehensive domain encompassing diverse methodologies for extracting insights from data. Conversely, machine learning constitutes a subset of data science, concentrating primarily on crafting algorithms and models geared towards making predictions or decisions derived from data. While machine learning serves as a pivotal tool within data science, the latter encompasses a broader spectrum of skills and techniques extending beyond solely machine learning.

Data Science is a multidisciplinary field.

Data Science is an interdisciplinary domain dedicated to extracting insights and knowledge from data through a multitude of techniques and tools. Within this realm, Machine Learning, Deep Learning, and Neural Networks stand as pivotal components. Here's a succinct overview of their respective roles:

Machine Learning: Machine Learning, a subset of Artificial Intelligence (AI), is dedicated to crafting algorithms and models that empower computers to learn from data and facilitate predictions or decisions. This entails training models on labelled or unlabelled data to discern patterns and relationships. Machine Learning algorithms find application across a vast array of tasks, including classification, regression, clustering, and recommendation systems. Crucially, it assumes a pivotal role in data analysis and predictive modelling within the realm of Data Science.

Deep Learning: Deep Learning, a subfield of Machine Learning, underscores the deployment of deep neural networks comprising multiple layers of interconnected artificial neurons. These networks have the capacity to learn hierarchical representations of data autonomously. The burgeoning popularity of Deep Learning stems from its triumphs in diverse tasks, including image and speech recognition, natural language processing, and autonomous driving. Its efficacy shines particularly bright when confronted with copious amounts of labelled data and intricate problem landscapes.

Neural Networks: Neural Networks serve as foundational elements within Deep Learning, drawing inspiration from the structural and functional dynamics of biological neural networks in the human brain. Comprising interconnected artificial neurons organised in layers, Neural Networks execute a sequence of operations. Each neuron receives input signals, undergoes activation through a specific function, and generates an output signal. The inter-neuron connections are characterised by weights, dictating the intensity of their relationships. Through iterative adjustment of these weights during the training phase, Neural Networks can discern intricate patterns and relationships inherent in the data.

In Data Science, Machine Learning serves as a powerful tool to analyse and make predictions from data, while Deep Learning and Neural Networks enable the creation of sophisticated models capable of learning complex patterns and representations. These techniques have revolutionised fields such as natural language processing, computer vision, and data-driven decision-making. Understanding and applying these concepts is essential for leveraging the full potential of Data Science in solving real-world problems.

☐ PROGRAMMING LANGUAGES:

Various programming languages are utilised for AI and related tasks. Here are some examples:

Python: Known for its simplicity and vast ecosystem of libraries like TensorFlow, PyTorch, and scikit-learn, Python is one of the most popular languages for AI development.

R: Particularly prominent in statistical analysis and data visualization, R is frequently used for tasks like exploratory data analysis and statistical modelling in AI applications.

Java: Although not as commonly associated with AI as Python or R, Java is still utilised for AI development, particularly in large-scale enterprise systems where performance and scalability are crucial.

Lisp: Lisp, particularly its dialects like Common Lisp and Clojure, has a rich history in AI research and development. It is known for its powerful meta-programming capabilities and is used in various AI applications.

SWI Prolog: Prolog is a logic programming language commonly used in fields like natural language processing and expert systems. SWI Prolog, in particular, is popular in medical projects and other domains where logical reasoning is essential.

Matlab: Widely used in engineering and scientific computing, Matlab provides extensive tools for numerical computing, simulation, and data analysis, making it suitable for certain AI tasks.

Julia: Julia is gaining popularity in scientific computing and AI due to its high performance and easy interoperability with other languages like Python and R. It is particularly well-suited for tasks involving numerical computation and optimization.

These languages offer diverse capabilities and are chosen based on factors like the nature of the AI problem, existing infrastructure, performance requirements, and developer expertise.

☐ THE GROWTH OF AI

1950: Alan Turing publishes "Computing Machinery and Intelligence," proposing the Turing Test as a measure of machine intelligence.

1951: Marvin Minsky and Dean Edmonds develop SNARC, the first neural network simulator, at Princeton University.

1956: The term "Artificial Intelligence" is coined at the Dartmouth Summer Research Project, marking the official birth of AI as a scientific field.

1959: Herbert Simon and Allen Newell create the Logic Theorist, the first AI program capable of proving mathematical theorems.

1960: John McCarthy develops the LISP programming language, which becomes a foundational language for AI research.

1961: The first industrial robot, Unimate, is deployed at General Motors, introducing AI applications in manufacturing.

1997: IBM's Deep Blue defeats world chess champion Garry Kasparov, demonstrating AI's ability in strategic computation and decision-making.

2005: Stanley, an autonomous vehicle from Stanford University, wins the DARPA Grand Challenge, advancing robotics and autonomous driving.

2011: IBM's Watson defeats human champions on Jeopardy!, showcasing the power of natural language understanding and question answering.

2012: AlexNet, a deep convolutional neural network, wins the ImageNet Challenge, igniting the deep learning revolution.

2015: DeepMind's AlphaGo defeats world champion Lee Sedol in the game of Go, marking a historic milestone in AI's cognitive capabilities.

2018: OpenAI's GPT (Generative Pre-trained Transformer) model demonstrates exceptional language generation and comprehension.

2019: Google's BERT (Bidirectional Encoder Representations from Transformers) revolutionises Natural Language Processing (NLP) tasks with bidirectional understanding.

2020: AI achieves widespread industrial adoption across healthcare, finance, transportation, and education, driving innovation and efficiency.

2021: Transformer-based architectures dominate machine learning research, powering breakthroughs in computer vision, speech, and multimodal AI.

2022: AI ethics, fairness, and responsible AI governance become central to discussions as AI systems influence society at scale.

2023: Continued evolution in reinforcement learning, autonomous systems, and multimodal models (seeing, hearing, and reasoning together) defines the new AI frontier.

2024–Present: The rise of Generative AI, LLMs (Large Language Models) like GPT-4 and beyond, Retrieval-Augmented Generation (RAG), and AI Agents heralds an era where AI collaborates with humans in creativity, reasoning, and decision-making—shaping the future of intelligence itself.

☐ AI SPECTRUM:

Artificial intelligence (AI) encompasses a spectrum of capabilities and goals. Here's an improved breakdown of the different types of AI:

Artificial Narrow Intelligence (ANI): ANI, also known as weak AI, refers to AI systems that are designed and trained for specific tasks or narrow domains. These systems excel at performing well-defined tasks within limited contexts. Examples include virtual personal assistants like Siri or Alexa, recommendation systems, and image recognition algorithms.

Artificial General Intelligence (AGI): AGI, often referred to as strong AI, represents a hypothetical AI system with human-level cognitive abilities across a broad range of domains. AGI would possess the ability to understand, learn, and apply knowledge in a manner similar to human intelligence. AGI remains a theoretical concept, and creating such a system is a major goal of AI research.

Artificial Super Intelligence (ASI): ASI goes beyond AGI and describes an AI system that surpasses human intelligence in every aspect, including creativity, problem-solving, and social skills. ASI represents the upper limit of AI capabilities and is often associated with speculative scenarios of AI surpassing human control and comprehension.

Each type of AI represents a different level of intelligence and capability, with ANI being the most prevalent and AGI and ASI representing increasingly advanced and theoretical stages of AI development. Understanding these distinctions is crucial for discussions about the potential impact and ethical considerations surrounding AI technology.

☐ ADVANCEMENT OF AI KEY FACTORS:

More Data: The proliferation of digital technologies has led to an exponential increase in the volume, variety, and velocity of data generated globally. This abundance of data provides a rich resource for AI systems to learn from and make predictions or decisions.

More Computational Power: Advances in hardware, such as GPUs (Graphics Processing Units) and specialised AI accelerators, have significantly increased computational power. This increased computational power enables the training and deployment of more complex AI models capable of processing vast amounts of data efficiently.

Better Algorithms: Ongoing research in machine learning and AI has led to the development of more sophisticated algorithms and techniques. These advancements have improved the performance and capabilities of AI systems, enabling them to tackle a wider range of tasks with greater accuracy and efficiency.

Broad Investment: There has been a surge in investment in AI research and development across various sectors, including technology, healthcare, finance, manufacturing, and transportation. This broad investment reflects the growing recognition of AI's potential to drive innovation, enhance productivity, and address complex challenges across industries.

Overall, the convergence of these factors has fuelled the rapid advancement and adoption of AI technologies, making it a central topic of discussion and a transformative force in shaping the future of society, economy, and technology.

What are Python libraries and why?

Python libraries are collections of pre-written code that provide a wide range of functionalities and tools to enhance Python programming. These libraries are developed by the Python community and serve as valuable resources for developers.

Python libraries address common programming challenges, such as data manipulation, scientific computing, machine learning, web development, and more. They offer ready-made solutions and functionalities that can be easily incorporated into projects, saving time and effort.

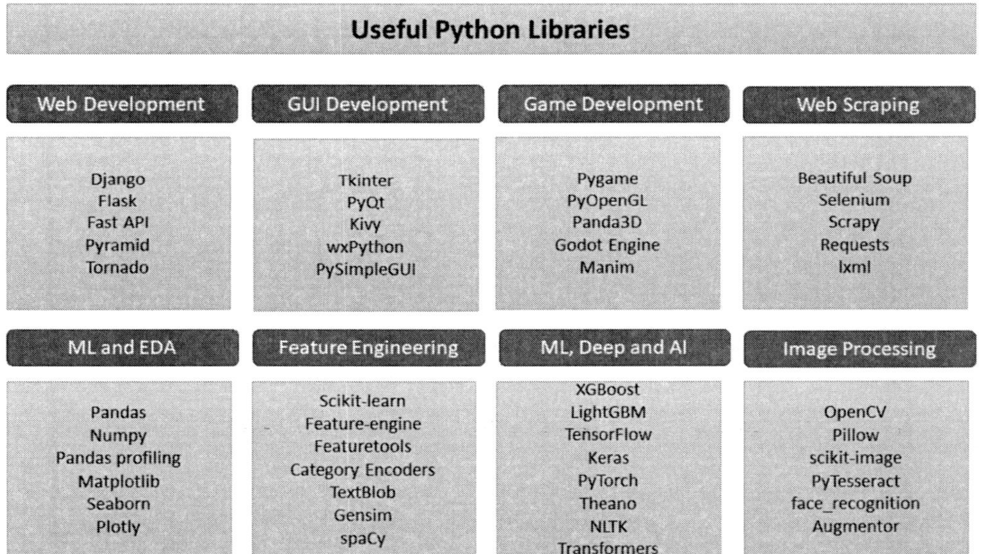

How are Python libraries useful in Data science?

Python libraries are incredibly useful in data science due to their extensive functionality and ease of use. Here are some key Python libraries and their specific contributions to data science:

☐ HOW TO APPROACH DATA SCIENCE USING PYTHON LIBRARIES?

To approach Data Science using Python libraries, you can follow a systematic process that typically involves the following steps:

Define the problem: Begin by articulating the problem you aim to address or the question you seek to answer through data analysis. Gain a comprehensive understanding of the goals and objectives underlying your analysis to ensure alignment with overarching objectives.

Gather data: Proceed to collect pertinent data from diverse sources, including databases, files, APIs, or through web scraping methodologies. Prioritise the acquisition of clean, comprehensive datasets that accurately reflect the nuances of the problem at hand, laying a solid foundation for subsequent analysis and insights extraction.

Explore and preprocess the data: Use libraries like pandas and NumPy to explore the data, understand its structure, and identify any missing values or outliers. Preprocess the data by handling missing values, performing data cleaning, normalization, or feature engineering as necessary.

Perform data analysis: Utilise libraries like pandas, NumPy, and SciPy to perform various statistical analyses, data transformations, and calculations. Apply descriptive statistics, inferential statistics, and exploratory data analysis techniques to gain insights and understanding of the data.

Visualize the data: Use visualization libraries such as Matplotlib and Seaborn to create informative and visually appealing charts, plots, and graphs. Visualizations can help in understanding patterns, relationships, and trends in the data.

Build predictive models: Employ machine learning libraries like Scikit-learn or deep learning libraries like TensorFlow and Keras to build predictive models. Choose appropriate algorithms based on the problem type (regression, classification, clustering) and train the models using the prepared data.

Evaluate and validate models: Assess the performance of your models using evaluation metrics, cross-validation techniques, or train-test splits. Optimize the models by fine-tuning hyperparameters and adjusting the model architecture.

Communicate results: Present your findings and insights clearly and concisely using visualizations, reports, or interactive dashboards. Use libraries like Jupyter Notebook or data storytelling tools to effectively communicate your data analysis process and results.

Iterate and refine: Continuously iterate on your analysis, models, and visualizations based on feedback, new data, or changing requirements. Refine your approach and improve the accuracy and relevance of your analysis.

Throughout this process, make use of the extensive documentation and community support available for the Python libraries you are using. Experiment with different techniques, algorithms, and parameters to find the most suitable approach for your specific problem.

☐ WHAT DO YOU HOPE TO GAIN FROM THIS BOOK?

Optimum Python Power – From Data to Intelligence: The Deep Learning Revolution (Series VI) invites you on an enlightening journey through the evolution of artificial intelligence, where data transforms into understanding and algorithms evolve into intelligence.

Through this book, you will gain a comprehensive grasp of Deep Learning—from the fundamental structure of Perceptrons and ANNs to the powerful capabilities of Transformers that shape today's intelligent systems. It bridges theory, mathematics, and practical application, enabling you to build, train, and optimise models using Python frameworks such as TensorFlow, Keras, and PyTorch.

You will learn how to:

Design and train neural networks with gradient descent and activation functions.

Recognise spatial and temporal patterns through **CNNs** and **RNNs**.

Understand language using **NLP**, **NLU**, and **NLG** techniques.

Master **self-attention, positional encoding**, and **Transformer mechanics**.

Explore **Autoencoders**, **latent spaces**, and **generative models** for deep representation learning.

Beyond technical mastery, this book aims to cultivate **intuitive intelligence**—helping you perceive the hidden harmony between mathematics, computation, and cognition. It reveals how deep learning is not just about processing data but **interpreting meaning**, **discovering order**, and **mirroring aspects of human thought**.

By the end of this journey, you will not only understand how deep learning works but **why it works**—equipping you to innovate, experiment, and contribute to the unfolding revolution of intelligent systems.

Step into a world where **Python meets purpose**, and data becomes the language of intelligence.

☐ How to Use This Book

Start with the Foundations

If you're new to Deep learning, begin with the introductory chapters that explain core concepts, key terminologies, and the role of Python in the data science ecosystem.

Recommended Reference:

Optimum – Python Series I: Ultimate Guide for Beginners lays the groundwork for Python mastery.

Explore Hands-On Examples

Every concept is accompanied by real code snippets and practical use cases. Run them, tweak them, and observe how small changes influence outcomes—because the best way to learn is by doing.

Recommended Reference:

Optimum – Python Series II: Exploring Data Structures and Algorithms enhances understanding of efficient problem-solving.

Optimum – Python Power – Series III - Unleashing the Potential of Data Science with Libraries

Optimum Python Power Series IV: Unleashing the Potential of Data Science with Machine Learning Techniques

Optimum Python Power – Series V: Unleashing the Power of Data Science – From Logic to Prediction

Use as a Modular Reference

The book is designed to be modular. Feel free to navigate directly to chapters that align with your current goals. Each section is self-contained for ease of use.

Bridge Theory and Practice

We don't just show you how to write the code—we explain why it works. This book bridges the gap between conceptual clarity and real-world application.

Engage with the Evolving Field

Machine learning is fast-evolving. Use this book as a launchpad to explore emerging trends, libraries, and research areas once you've mastered the essentials.

Apply to Your Projects

Reinforce your learning by applying techniques to your own datasets and real-world problems. Experimentation leads to mastery.

Introduction to Generative AI & Reinforcement Learning

You'll also find a gateway to emerging domains like Generative AI and Reinforcement Learning—providing a glimpse into the future of intelligent systems.

☐ Who Is This Book Aimed At?

"Optimum - Python Power Series VI" is aimed at a wide range of readers, including:

- Aspiring Data Scientists – Those eager to master the art of transforming raw data into meaningful intelligence through Python-powered deep learning techniques.
- **AI & Machine Learning Enthusiasts** – Readers seeking to explore how neural networks, reinforcement learning, and generative AI shape the intelligence revolution.
- **Researchers and Academics** – Individuals looking to bridge theoretical understanding with applied experimentation in data-driven environments.
- **Software Developers & Engineers** – Professionals aiming to integrate machine learning and intelligent automation into real-world systems.
- **Students & Educators** – Learners and teachers of computer science, AI, or data analytics who wish to grasp complex ideas through clear explanations and practical coding examples.
- **Innovators & Problem Solvers** – Anyone passionate about using data, logic, and deep learning to uncover insights, make predictions, and build intelligent solutions for the future.

☐ ONLINE RESOURCES

The supplementary materials for the book can be accessed online at: www.shambav.org

Setup Instructions

The setup instructions provided here are the same as those in the book but include clickable links to all the components. If you encounter any difficulties during the setup process, please consult this resource.

Updates

Python, like any other language, undergoes continuous updates and changes. We maintain a comprehensive collection of updates, so if you encounter any issues, please check this resource to see if the instructions have been changed.

Data

The book provides some sample raw data for running the programs, but you can also create your own samples using various file formats such as Excel, CSV, or JSON.

Practice Questions

You are encouraged to allocate ample time to work on the exercises independently. If you encounter any challenges and cannot proceed, consult this reference link.

Exercises and Assignments

While it's important to try the exercises on your own, you might encounter difficulties that prevent you from making progress. If that happens, you can find solutions to most of the exercises online. We encourage you to dedicate sufficient time to working on the exercises independently before seeking help.

Cheat Sheets

You can also find a wide range of cheat sheets online covering major concepts, which you can download and use for quick reference.

Errata

Despite our efforts to ensure the accuracy of our content, errors may still occur. If you come across any errors in the book, whether in the text or the code, please report them to us. Your feedback will not only help us improve future editions of this book but also assist other readers in avoiding any frustrations.

Advance Material

Advance material for those who want to learn more about the subject. Beginners can skip the advanced section at the start.

Reference Links

Activities	Sheets	Links
Login	Signup/Login page	https://www.shambav.org/artifacts/signup.php
Practice Question	With the answer sheet	https://www.shambav.org/artifacts/optimum-python-series-6
Exercises, Assignments	With answers	
Quiz	Quiz answers	
Data	Data Sheet	
Supplementary	Advanced material	
Instruction	Setup instruction	
Advance materials	Programs, tricks, assignments, mini projects, issues	
Cheat sheets	Major concepts	

PART ONE

Getting Started

The Rise of Neural Networks

"When we build neural networks, we do not just model intelligence—we hold up a mirror to the human mind, realising that learning itself is the poetry of connection."

– Shree Shambav

PART ONE

DAY ONE

Unit 1 - Lesson One

Basics of TensorFlow and Keras

Sam asked, "Master, what is TensorFlow?"

Master replied, "TensorFlow is an open-source machine learning library developed by Google, designed to build and train deep learning models. Its core strength lies in its ability to create computational graphs, which allow developers to structure and visualise complex neural networks. TensorFlow also provides seamless support for running models across multiple hardware platforms, from CPUs and GPUs to specialized processors like TPUs. This flexibility makes it one of the most powerful and widely-used tools in the AI and deep learning community. The library offers a vast array of functions, making it suitable for everything from research experiments to large-scale production models."

John asked, "Master, why do we need TensorFlow?"

Master replied, "TensorFlow is essential because it offers a powerful combination of efficiency, scalability, and flexibility. Its computational graph system allows for optimized performance on different hardware, making it suitable for everything from small projects to large-scale systems. TensorFlow is also easy to integrate with other tools and platforms, which simplifies the process of building and deploying models. With its vast community and a large set of pre-built functions and modules, TensorFlow saves time and effort, enabling developers and researchers to focus on innovation and solving complex problems."

Nikash asked, "Master, what is Keras?"

Master replied, "Keras is a high-level deep learning API, written in Python, that runs on top of TensorFlow. It simplifies building neural networks by providing an easy-to-use interface for designing, training, and testing machine learning models. Keras abstracts much of the complexity of lower-level machine learning libraries, making it accessible for beginners while still being powerful enough for advanced research. It supports both CPU and GPU computation, offers flexibility for prototyping, and helps developers experiment quickly without worrying about the underlying details."

Apeksha asked, "Master, what is CPU and GPU?"

Master replied, "The **CPU** (Central Processing Unit) is the brain of a computer, responsible for executing general-purpose tasks such as running programs, performing calculations, and managing system operations. It is optimized for sequential processing, handling multiple tasks one after the other, making it ideal for most everyday applications.

On the other hand, the **GPU** (Graphics Processing Unit) is designed to handle tasks that require parallel processing, particularly those involving complex mathematical computations. Originally developed for rendering graphics, the GPU excels in tasks that can be split into smaller, simultaneous operations, such as matrix manipulations used in deep learning. Because of this, GPUs are much faster and more efficient than CPUs for training large neural networks, making them crucial in AI and machine learning."

Master continued, TensorFlow is a powerful open-source software library for numerical computation that uses data flow graphs to represent mathematical computations. In TensorFlow:

- Nodes in the graph represent mathematical operations.
- Edges represent the multidimensional data arrays, or tensors, that flow between the nodes.

Tensors are the fundamental units of data in TensorFlow, and they move through the graph, enabling complex computations.

For example, consider the following scenario:

- The node "add" represents an addition operation.

- Inputs a and b are tensors (multidimensional arrays).
- The result c is the output tensor.

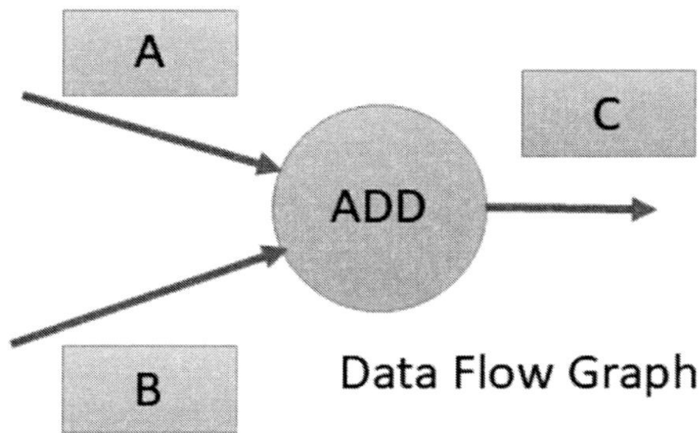

Illustration P5_Tensor_DFG1

This flexible architecture allows you to deploy computations across various devices (CPUs, GPUs, or even mobile devices) using a single API, making TensorFlow highly scalable and adaptable for a wide range of machine learning tasks.

Apeksha asked, "How to install TensorFlow?"

Open a terminal or command prompt.

Run the following command:

```
pip install tensorflow
```

Installing TensorFlow in a Virtual Environment

A virtual environment allows you to manage dependencies separately from your system's global packages.

Steps:

Install virtualenv if you don't have it already:

```
pip install virtualenv
```

Create a new virtual environment:

```
virtualenv tensorflow_env
```

Activate the virtual environment:

```
Windows: tensorflow_env\Scripts\activate
macOS/Linux: source tensorflow_env/bin/activate
```

Install TensorFlow within the virtual environment:

```
pip install tensorflow
```

Installing TensorFlow for GPU Support

If you have a compatible NVIDIA GPU and want to take advantage of GPU acceleration, install TensorFlow with GPU support.

Steps:

Install GPU drivers and CUDA toolkit (CUDA 11.2 or later).

Install cuDNN (compatible version for CUDA).

Verify GPU setup with:

```
nvidia-smi
```

Install TensorFlow with GPU support:

```
pip install tensorflow-gpu
```

Using Conda to Install TensorFlow

Create a new Conda environment:

```
conda create --name tf_env python=3.8
```

Activate the environment:

```
conda activate tf_env
```

Install TensorFlow:

```
conda install tensorflow
```

Akshaya asked, “Master, what is a computational graph, and how does the flow of tensors work within it?”

Master replied, “A computational graph is a powerful and flexible representation of mathematical computations, particularly in the context of machine learning and deep learning frameworks like TensorFlow. In essence, it provides a way to visualize and organize the operations and data involved in a computation, allowing for efficient execution and optimization.

Key Concepts of a Computational Graph

Nodes and Edges:

Nodes: In a computational graph, each node represents a specific operation or function, such as addition, multiplication, or more complex operations like convolutions. For example, a node could represent the operation of adding two numbers together.

Edges: The edges of the graph represent the connections between nodes, carrying data in the form of multidimensional arrays known as tensors. These edges indicate the flow of data from one operation to another, defining how the output of one operation serves as the input to another.

Tensors:

Tensors are the fundamental data structures in TensorFlow. They are generalizations of scalars, vectors, and matrices, allowing for the representation of data in higher dimensions. For instance, a scalar is a 0D tensor, a vector is a 1D tensor, and a matrix is a 2D tensor.

In a computational graph, tensors flow along the edges, moving from one node to another as they are processed through various operations.

☐ Flow of Tensors in a Computational Graph

When executing a computation represented by a computational graph, the flow of tensors occurs as follows:

Initialisation: Tensors are initialised with input data. For example, in a neural network, the input layer receives data in the form of tensors.

Forward Pass: As the computation proceeds, the tensors flow through the nodes, and operations are performed according to the graph structure. Each operation takes input tensors, performs the defined computation, and produces output tensors that become the inputs for subsequent nodes.

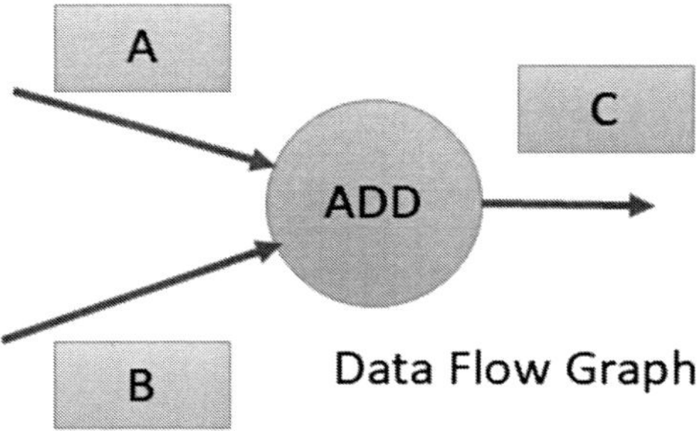

Illustration P6_Tensor_DFG1

For instance, consider a simple graph where two input tensors, a and b, are added together at node add, producing an output tensor c. The flow can be visualized as:

Backpropagation (if applicable): In the context of training models, especially neural networks, the flow of tensors also includes backpropagation. This is where the gradients (derivatives) of the loss function are calculated and propagated back through the network to update weights. Each node computes the gradient based on its operation, and the flow of tensors continues in reverse to adjust the parameters effectively.

Benefits of Computational Graphs

- Optimization: By defining computations as graphs, TensorFlow can optimise them for performance, allowing for more efficient memory use and parallel execution on CPUs or GPUs.

- Modularity: Computational graphs allow for modularity in building complex models, as components can be reused and modified easily.
- Debugging: Visualization of the graph structure aids in understanding and debugging the computational flow.

In summary, a computational graph serves as a structured representation of mathematical operations and data flow in deep learning frameworks. The flow of tensors through the graph facilitates efficient computation and model training, making it an essential concept in understanding frameworks like TensorFlow."

☐ Understanding TensorFlow Core Programs

Any TensorFlow Core program can be divided into two distinct yet interrelated sections:

Building the Computational Graph:

A computational graph represents a series of TensorFlow operations organised into a network of nodes. Each node in this graph corresponds to a mathematical operation, while the edges represent the tensors (multidimensional data arrays) that flow between these operations. This structure allows TensorFlow to visualise and manage complex computations systematically, enabling efficient execution.

Running the Computational Graph:

To evaluate the operations defined in the computational graph, we need to execute it within a session. A session in TensorFlow encapsulates the control and state of the TensorFlow runtime, allowing us to run the graph and retrieve the results of the computations. In TensorFlow 2.x, eager execution is enabled by default, making it more intuitive to work with computations without explicitly managing sessions.

Now, let's write our very first TensorFlow program to understand these concepts more clearly:

Example P1 – U1 – D1	
Computational Graphs and Tensor	**Output**
import tensorflow as tf # Step 1: Define the input tensors	Result using eager execution: 8

```
a = tf.constant(5)  # First input tensor
b = tf.constant(3)  # Second input tensor

# Step 2: Define the operation (node) to add the tensors
c = tf.add(a, b)  # This creates a node that represents the
addition operation

# Step 3: Create a session to execute the graph
# Note: In TensorFlow 2.x, eager execution is enabled by
default,
# Using Eager Execution (TensorFlow 2.x)
print("Result using eager execution:", c.numpy())

# If you were using TensorFlow 1.x, you would do the
following:
# with tf.Session() as sess:
#     result = sess.run(c)
#     print("Result using session:", result)
```

Import TensorFlow: The code starts by importing the TensorFlow library.

Define Input Tensors: Two constant tensors, a and b, are created using tf.constant(). These are the inputs to the addition operation.

Define the Operation: The addition operation is defined using tf.add(a, b), which creates a node (c) in the computational graph representing the addition of a and b.

Execute the Graph:

In TensorFlow 2.x, eager execution is enabled by default, meaning that operations are executed immediately as they are called. You can get the result directly by calling c.numpy().

Note: If you were using TensorFlow 1.x, you would need to create a session to execute the graph. This is commented out in the code for educational purposes.

Akanksh asked, "Master, what are Variables in TensorFlow?"

Master explained, "In TensorFlow, variables are special types of nodes designed to hold and manage mutable data, specifically for training machine learning models. Unlike constants, which are fixed and cannot change, variables are designed to hold values that can be updated throughout the model's lifecycle.

Variables act as in-memory buffers that contain tensors—multidimensional arrays of data. They are crucial for storing the parameters of a model, such as weights and biases, which are adjusted during the training process to minimize the loss function.

One of the key characteristics of variables is that they must be explicitly initialized before use, typically within a TensorFlow session. This initialization allows them to hold dynamic data that can change based on the training iterations.

Moreover, variables can be saved to disk during or after training, allowing you to restore and analyse them later. This feature is particularly valuable for long-running training processes or when deploying models in production.

To summarise, the main difference between a constant and a variable is that constants are immutable and fixed, while variables are mutable and can change as the model learns from the data. This flexibility is what makes variables a cornerstone in building effective deep learning models in TensorFlow."

Master said, "This code demonstrates how to create and use variables to hold model parameters, perform updates during training, and save/load those variables."

Example P1 – U1 – D2	
Variables and Constants	**Output**

import tensorflow as tf
 	
# Define a simple linear model: y = wx + b 	
# where w is the weight and b is the bias 	
 	
# Step 1: Create Variables for weights and bias 	
w = tf.Variable(initial_value=2.0, dtype=tf.float32, name='weight') # Initial weight
b = tf.Variable(initial_value=1.0, dtype=tf.float32, name='bias')   # Initial bias
 	
# Step 2: Create a simple dataset 	
x = tf.constant([1.0, 2.0, 3.0, 4.0]) # Input features
y_true = tf.constant([3.0, 5.0, 7.0, 9.0]) # Expected output (y = 2x + 1)
 	
# Step 3: Define a simple loss function (Mean Squared Error) 	
def loss_fn(y_pred, y_true):
    return tf.reduce_mean(tf.square(y_pred - y_true))
	INFO:tensorflow: Assets written to: linear_model/bias\assets
	Loaded Weight: 2.0, Loaded Bias: 1.0

```
# Step 4: Training step
def train_step():
    with tf.GradientTape() as tape:
        # Forward pass: calculate predicted y
        y_pred = w * x + b  # y = wx + b
        # Calculate the loss
        loss = loss_fn(y_pred, y_true)

    # Backward pass: calculate gradients
    gradients = tape.gradient(loss, [w, b])
    # Update weights and bias
    w.assign_sub(0.1 * gradients[0])  # Update weight
    b.assign_sub(0.1 * gradients[1])  # Update bias
    return loss

# Step 5: Train the model
for epoch in range(100):
    loss = train_step()
    if (epoch + 1) % 10 == 0:  # Print loss every 10
epochs
        print(f"Epoch {epoch + 1}, Loss: {loss.numpy()},
Weight: {w.numpy()}, Bias: {b.numpy()}")

# Step 6: Save the model variables
model_path = 'linear_model'
tf.saved_model.save(w, model_path + '/weight')
tf.saved_model.save(b, model_path + '/bias')

# Step 7: Load the model variables
loaded_weight = tf.saved_model.load(model_path +
'/weight')
loaded_bias = tf.saved_model.load(model_path +
'/bias')

print(f"Loaded Weight: {loaded_weight.numpy()},
Loaded Bias: {loaded_bias.numpy()}")
```

Creating Variables:

Two TensorFlow variables (w for weight and b for bias) are created with initial values.

Dataset:

A simple dataset is defined with inputs (x) and expected outputs (y_true).

Loss Function:

A mean squared error loss function is defined to measure how well the model is performing.

Training Step:

The train_step function performs a forward pass to predict y using the current values of w and b, computes the loss, and then uses tf.GradientTape to calculate gradients for updating w and b.

Training Loop:

The model is trained for 100 epochs, printing the loss and current values of w and b every 10 epochs.

Saving Variables:

The trained variables are saved to disk using TensorFlow's tf.saved_model.save.

Loading Variables:

The saved variables are loaded back to demonstrate how you can retrieve them later.

Placeholders

Nikash asked, "Master, what is a placeholder?"

Master replied, "A placeholder is a special node in TensorFlow that allows you to feed external data into a computational graph. It acts as a promise to supply a value later during runtime. When a graph is executed, we provide these values through a feed_dict parameter, which is passed to the session's run() method. This flexibility enables dynamic input during the execution of the graph, making placeholders essential for building models that can be trained with varying data."

Consider the following example to understand how placeholders work in practice:

Example P1 – U1 – D3	
Placeholder - Deprecated	**Output**
# Importing TensorFlow import tensorflow as tf # Define the tensors	[[3 6 9] [2 4 6] [1 2 3]]

```
a = tf.constant([[3], [2], [1]], dtype=tf.int32)  # Shape (3,
1)
b = tf.constant([[1, 2, 3]], dtype=tf.int32)      # Shape (1,
3)

# Performing matrix multiplication
c = tf.matmul(a, b)

# Printing the result
print(c.numpy())  # Convert the tensor to a NumPy
array for easier printing
```

Use of tf.constant: Instead of placeholders, we have used tf.constant to define the input tensors directly. This aligns with TensorFlow 2.x conventions.

Eager Execution: The code runs in eager execution mode by default, allowing you to work with tensors directly without needing a session.

Simplified Output: The output is printed directly using .numpy(), which converts the tensor to a NumPy array, making it easier to read.

> Note: In TensorFlow 2.x, placeholders are deprecated, and eager execution is enabled by default.

tf.contrib.learn Overview:

tf.contrib.learn is a high-level TensorFlow library that abstracts away many of the complexities involved in building and training machine learning models. It provides easy-to-use APIs for:

- Running training loops: Simplifies the process of iterating over training data and updating model parameters.
- Running evaluation loops: Provides tools to evaluate the model's performance on validation or test data.
- Managing datasets: Offers easy mechanisms to load, preprocess, and manage datasets.
- Managing data feeding: Efficiently handles how data is fed into models during training and evaluation.

This makes it easier for developers to experiment with different machine learning models without dealing with the low-level details of TensorFlow.

Linear Regression Example using tf.contrib.learn:

While TensorFlow 1.x has tf.contrib.learn, it's important to note that this module has been deprecated in TensorFlow 2.x and replaced with higher-level APIs like tf.keras.

Example P1 – U1 – D4	
Using Keras	**Output**

import numpy as np
import tensorflow as tf
from tensorflow.keras import layers, models
 	
# Sample data 	
X_train = np.array([[1.0], [2.0], [3.0], [4.0]], dtype=np.float32)
y_train = np.array([0.0, -1.0, -2.0, -3.0], dtype=np.float32)
 	
# Define the model 	
model = models.Sequential()
model.add(layers.Dense(units=1, input_shape=(1,)))
 	
# Compile the model 	
model.compile(optimizer='sgd', loss='mean_squared_error')
 	
# Train the model 	
model.fit(X_train, y_train, epochs=200, verbose=0)
 	
# Make predictions 	
X_test = np.array([[1.5], [3.5]], dtype=np.float32)
predictions = model.predict(X_test)
 	
# Print the predictions 	
print("Predictions:", predictions)
	Predictions: [[-
	0.814093]
	 [-2.3778894]]

Dataset:

X_train and y_train are simple linear data arrays. The input features are one-dimensional, and the target outputs are linear, which is perfect for linear regression.

Model Definition:

- We use tf.keras.Sequential() to define a simple neural network model. In this case, it's just a single-layer network (with Dense), representing a linear relationship.
- The units = 1 specify that the output of the layer will be a single value, as we are performing linear regression.

- input_shape = (1,) defines the input dimension as 1 (one feature for each input).

Model Compilation:

- The compile method is used to configure the model for training.
- We use stochastic gradient descent ('sgd') as the optimizer and mean_squared_error as the loss function, which is standard for regression problems.

Training:

- The fit method trains the model using the input data (X_train) and target data (y_train).
- The epochs = 200 argument means that the model will go through the entire dataset 200 times.

Prediction:

- After training, we use the model to predict outputs for new inputs (X_test).
- The predict method returns the predicted values, which we then print.

Why tf.keras?

- Simplicity: The API is much cleaner and easier to use compared to tf.contrib.learn. It allows for rapid prototyping.
- Flexibility: tf.keras is built into TensorFlow, so it works well with TensorFlow's ecosystem, including easy integration with GPU acceleration and the TensorFlow Dataset API.
- Widely Adopted: It is the standard for building and training neural networks in TensorFlow 2.x and has wide community support.

This implementation leverages the full power of TensorFlow 2.x with tf.keras, making it simple, efficient, and easy to extend for more complex problems.

Important

tf.contrib.learn was part of TensorFlow 1.x but has been deprecated in TensorFlow 2.x.

For TensorFlow 2.x, it's recommended to use tf.keras for building models and running training loops.

Apeksha asked, "Master, what are TensorFlow APIs?"

The Master smiled and said, "TensorFlow provides a rich and versatile set of APIs, each designed to cater to different levels of expertise and use cases in machine learning and deep learning. These APIs allow developers to build, train, and deploy machine learning models with ease, from the simplest linear regression models to the most complex deep neural networks. Let's explore the different layers of TensorFlow APIs, each offering a different level of abstraction:

High-Level APIs (Easy to Use):

- tf.keras: This is the most commonly used API in TensorFlow, ideal for beginners and for rapid prototyping. It provides a user-friendly, high-level interface for building neural networks, and it's integrated seamlessly into TensorFlow. With tf.keras, you can define, compile, and train models in just a few lines of code.
- tf.estimator: Another high-level API designed for industrial-scale tasks like distributed training and deployment. It abstracts the model-building process and focuses on training, evaluation, and serving, making it easier for production systems.

Mid-Level APIs (More Control):

tf.data: This API provides tools for efficiently loading, transforming, and feeding data into your model. It helps in handling large datasets and building scalable input pipelines, ensuring that your training process runs efficiently, especially when working with images, text, or streaming data.

- tf.function: A powerful tool that allows you to convert Python functions into TensorFlow graphs. It optimises the execution of your code by compiling it into a graph, which can then be executed across various devices, including CPUs, GPUs, and TPUs.

Low-Level APIs (For Experts):

- Tensors and Variables: The core of TensorFlow. Tensors are the basic data units, representing multidimensional arrays. Variables are used to store parameters in models. TensorFlow's low-level API lets you manipulate these tensors directly, giving you complete control over how computations are performed.

- Custom Gradients: For advanced users who need fine control over the backpropagation process, TensorFlow allows the definition of custom gradients, enabling more specialized optimization processes.

Specialised APIs:

- TensorFlow Hub: A library for sharing and reusing trained models. It allows you to easily incorporate pre-trained models into your new models, saving time and resources.
- TensorFlow Lite: Focused on deploying machine learning models on mobile and edge devices, optimizing models for performance and size.
- TensorFlow.js: A JavaScript library that brings TensorFlow capabilities to web browsers, enabling model training and inference on client-side platforms.
- TensorFlow Serving: A flexible, high-performance system for serving machine learning models in production environments, providing efficient model deployment and inference.

Experimental APIs:

TensorFlow also offers experimental APIs that provide cutting-edge features. These include tools like TensorFlow Probability (for probabilistic reasoning) and TensorFlow Quantum (for quantum machine learning).

"These APIs," the Master concluded, "offer varying levels of abstraction, making TensorFlow accessible to both beginners and experts alike. Whether you're rapidly prototyping a neural network or designing a complex system for production deployment, TensorFlow has an API to meet your needs. The key is to know where to begin and how to scale as your knowledge deepens."

Akanksh asked, "Master, what is the difference between TensorFlow 2.0 and PyTorch? Can you explain with an example?"

The Master nodded and replied, "Certainly, Akanksh! Both TensorFlow 2.0 and PyTorch are powerful frameworks for deep learning, but they cater to different audiences and have unique design philosophies. Let's explore their differences in detail and illustrate these differences with examples.

Programming Model: Static vs. Dynamic Graphs

TensorFlow 2.0 adopts an eager execution model by default, which allows operations to be executed immediately as they are called, similar to how standard Python code operates. This makes it more intuitive and easier to debug compared to earlier versions, which relied on static computation graphs.

PyTorch, on the other hand, has always used a dynamic computation graph, which means the graph is built on-the-fly as operations are executed. This makes PyTorch exceptionally flexible, especially for research and experimentation.

Ease of Use and Flexibility

TensorFlow 2.0 emphasizes usability, offering high-level APIs like Keras that simplify model creation, training, and evaluation. This makes it accessible for beginners and allows for rapid prototyping.

PyTorch is often praised for its straightforward and Pythonic interface, which feels natural to developers familiar with Python. This simplicity can lead to faster iterations during the development process.

Community and Ecosystem

TensorFlow 2.0 has a robust ecosystem that includes tools for model serving (TensorFlow Serving), mobile deployment (TensorFlow Lite), and browser-based deployment (TensorFlow.js). This makes it a popular choice for production-level applications.

PyTorch has gained significant traction in the research community, with many academic papers and projects built on it. While it has been expanding its deployment capabilities with tools like TorchScript and TorchServe, it remains primarily a research-oriented framework.

Performance and Scalability

TensorFlow 2.0 is highly optimized for performance, offering features like distributed training and better support for multi-GPU setups. It is designed to scale efficiently, making it suitable for large-scale projects.

PyTorch is also efficient, particularly for smaller projects and rapid experimentation. However, it has improved scalability features in recent versions, allowing users to train models on larger datasets and distributed systems.

Example: Building a Simple Neural Network for Linear Regression

Let's illustrate these differences with a simple example of implementing linear regression in TensorFlow 2.0 and PyTorch.

TensorFlow 2.0 Example:

Example P1 – U1 – D5	
Tensorflow	**Output**

import tensorflow as tf
 	
# Create a simple model using Keras 	
model = tf.keras.Sequential([
   tf.keras.layers.Dense(1, input_shape=(1,))
])
 	
# Compile the model 	
model.compile(optimizer='sgd', loss='mean_squared_error')
 	
# Sample data 	
xs = tf.constant([[1.0], [2.0], [3.0], [4.0], [5.0]])
ys = tf.constant([[1.0], [2.0], [3.0], [4.0], [5.0]])
 	
# Train the model 	
model.fit(xs, ys, epochs=500)
 	
# Make predictions 	
predictions = model.predict(tf.constant([[6.0], [7.0]]))
print(predictions)
	1/1 ━━━━━━━━━━━━━━━━━━━━ 0s 58ms/step
	[[6.005566]
	 [7.0078955]]

PyTorch Example:

Example P1 – U1 – D6	
Pytorch	**Output**
import torch import torch.nn as nn import torch.optim as optim # Create a simple linear regression model	tensor([[5.8927], [6.8478]])

```
class LinearRegressionModel(nn.Module):
    def __init__(self):
        super(LinearRegressionModel, self).__init__()
        self.linear = nn.Linear(1, 1)

    def forward(self, x):
        return self.linear(x)

# Initialize the model, loss function, and optimizer
model = LinearRegressionModel()
criterion = nn.MSELoss()
optimizer = optim.SGD(model.parameters(), lr=0.01)

# Sample data
xs = torch.tensor([[1.0], [2.0], [3.0], [4.0], [5.0]],
requires_grad=False)
ys = torch.tensor([[1.0], [2.0], [3.0], [4.0], [5.0]],
requires_grad=False)

# Training loop
for epoch in range(500):
    model.train()

    # Forward pass
    outputs = model(xs)
    loss = criterion(outputs, ys)

    # Backward pass and optimization
    optimizer.zero_grad()
    loss.backward()
    optimizer.step()

# Make predictions
with torch.no_grad():
    predictions = model(torch.tensor([[6.0], [7.0]]))
    print(predictions)
```

Conclusion

The Master concluded, "In summary, TensorFlow 2.0 and PyTorch each have their strengths and are suited to different scenarios. TensorFlow excels in production environments with its rich ecosystem and scalability, while PyTorch stands out for its simplicity and flexibility, making it the favourite among researchers. Understanding these differences will help you choose the right tool for your specific needs and goals."

Summary:

This chapter provided an overview of three prominent frameworks in deep learning: TensorFlow, Keras, and PyTorch. TensorFlow is an open-source library developed by Google for numerical computation, enabling the building and training of deep learning models using data flow graphs. With the introduction of TensorFlow 2.0, it supports eager execution for a more intuitive coding experience.

Keras, integrated with TensorFlow, is a high-level API that simplifies the process of creating and training neural networks. Its user-friendly interface allows for rapid prototyping, making it suitable for both beginners and seasoned developers. PyTorch emphasizes flexibility and ease of use through dynamic computation graphs. Its Pythonic design facilitates quick experimentation, making it a favourite in research settings.

The chapter highlighted key differences between TensorFlow and PyTorch, illustrated with practical examples. Understanding these frameworks equips developers to choose the right tools for their machine learning projects, whether for rapid development, production and deployment, or innovative research.

What Next:

In the upcoming chapter, we will explore the foundational concepts of Artificial Neural Networks (ANN), starting with the basic unit, the perceptron, which serves as a building block for more complex models. We will delve into its structure and working mechanism, highlighting how it processes input data to produce binary outputs. Moving forward, we'll examine multilayer perceptrons (MLPs), which consist of multiple layers of neurons, and discuss how they learn complex patterns through hidden layers, emphasizing the importance of activation functions in transforming inputs. Finally, we will address the application of ANN in regression and classification tasks, highlighting the differences between these two problem types and showcasing how neural networks are adapted to solve them with practical examples. This chapter aims to provide a solid understanding of ANNs, their components, and their real-world applications, setting the stage for deeper explorations into advanced neural network architectures and techniques.

PART ONE

DAY TWO

Unit 2 - Lesson TWO

The Birth of Artificial Neural Networks

"In an ANN, every neuron is a note, every connection a rhythm; and together, they compose a silent symphony of understanding, woven through mathematics and learning."

– Shree Shambav

Deep Learning is a cornerstone technology, revolutionising how machines understand, learn, and interact with complex data. It mimics the intricate neural networks of the human brain, enabling computers to autonomously discover patterns and make decisions from vast amounts of unstructured data. This transformative field has propelled breakthroughs across various domains, including computer vision, natural language processing, healthcare diagnostics, and autonomous driving.

Akshaya asked, "Master, what is Deep Learning?"

Master said, "Deep Learning is a branch of machine learning based on artificial neural network (ANN) architecture. ANNs use layers of interconnected nodes, called neurons, that work together to process and learn from input data. This layered approach allows deep learning models to extract hierarchical features from raw data, enabling them to handle complex tasks with remarkable accuracy and efficiency."

Artificial Neural Networks (ANNs) contain artificial neurons, also known as units. These units are arranged in layers that together constitute the entire ANN system. The complexity of a neural network can vary, with layers containing anywhere from a few dozen to millions of units, depending on the need to learn hidden patterns in the dataset.

Typically, an ANN consists of an input layer, an output layer, and one or more hidden layers:

Input Layer: Receives data from the outside world for the neural network to analyse or learn from.

Hidden Layers: Transform the input data into a form that is valuable for the output layer. These layers can be one or many, and they perform the crucial task of feature extraction and pattern recognition.

Output Layer: Produces the network's response to the input data, generating the final output.

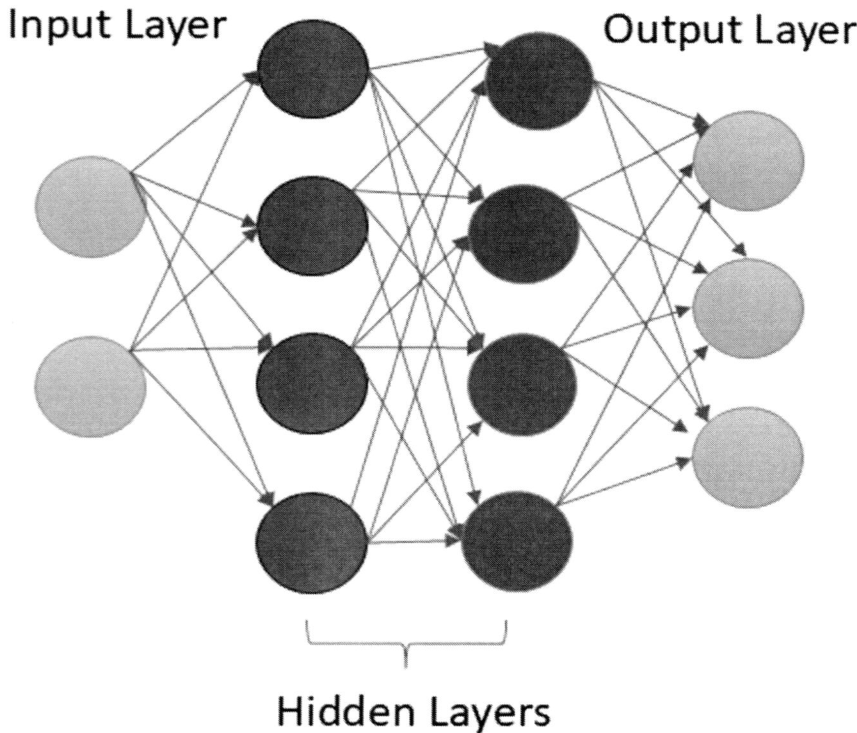

Illustration P6_Deep_ANN_01

In most neural networks, units are interconnected from one layer to another. Each connection has an associated weight that determines the influence one unit has on another. As data is transferred through these connections, the network learns more about the data, adjusting the weights during training to improve its performance.

Structure and Functioning

Artificial Neural Networks are inspired by the structure and operations of human neurons. The input layer of an ANN receives data from external sources and passes it to the hidden layer(s). Each neuron in the hidden layer receives input from the previous layer, computes a weighted sum, and sends it to the neurons in the next layer. These connections are weighted, meaning the influence of inputs from the previous layer can be increased or decreased by adjusting the weights. This optimization process happens during training, enhancing the model's performance.

The key points of this structure are:

Weighted Connections: Each connection between units has a weight that influences the strength and direction of the signal.

Learning and Optimization: The network adjusts weights through training, improving its ability to recognise patterns and make predictions.

Layered Architecture: The network's ability to process and transform data through multiple layers enables it to handle complex tasks effectively.

By mimicking the way human neurons operate, ANNs can learn and make decisions autonomously, driving advancements in various fields like computer vision, natural language processing, and beyond.

Artificial Neurons vs. Biological Neurons

The concept of artificial neural networks (ANNs) is inspired by the biological neurons found in animal brains. Consequently, they share many similarities in both structure and function.

Structure

Biological Neurons:

- Dendrites: Receive input signals.

- Cell Body (Soma): Processes these signals.
- Axon: Transmits the processed signals to other neurons.

Biological Neurons

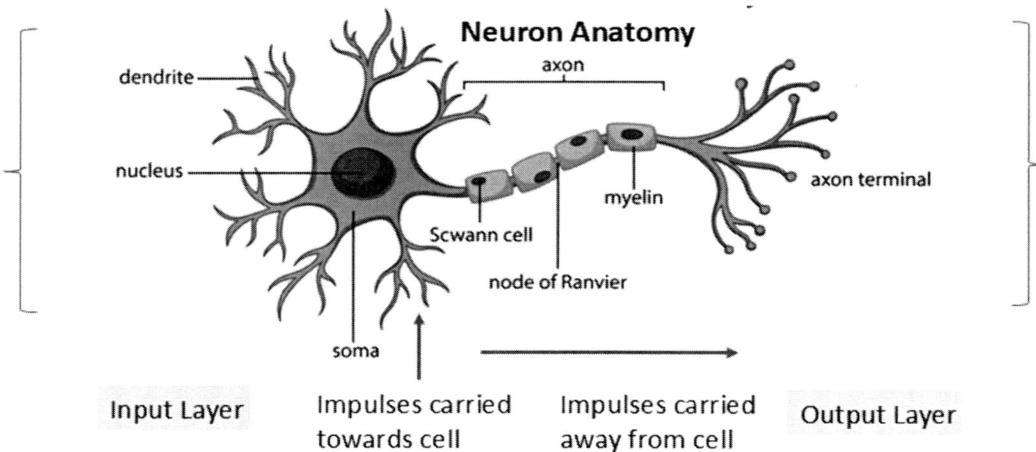

Illustration P6_Deep_BN_1

Artificial Neurons:

- Input Nodes: Receive input signals.
- Hidden Layer Nodes: Compute the input signals.
- Output Layer Nodes: Process the results from the hidden layers using activation functions to compute the final output.

Comparison

Biological Neuron Component	Artificial Neuron Component
Dendrites	Inputs
Cell Body (Soma)	Nodes
Synapses	Weights
Axon	Output

Synapses

In biological neurons, synapses are the links between neurons that enable the transmission of impulses from dendrites to the cell body. In artificial neurons, synapses are represented by weights that join the nodes of one layer to the nodes of the next layer. The strength of these connections is determined by the weight values.

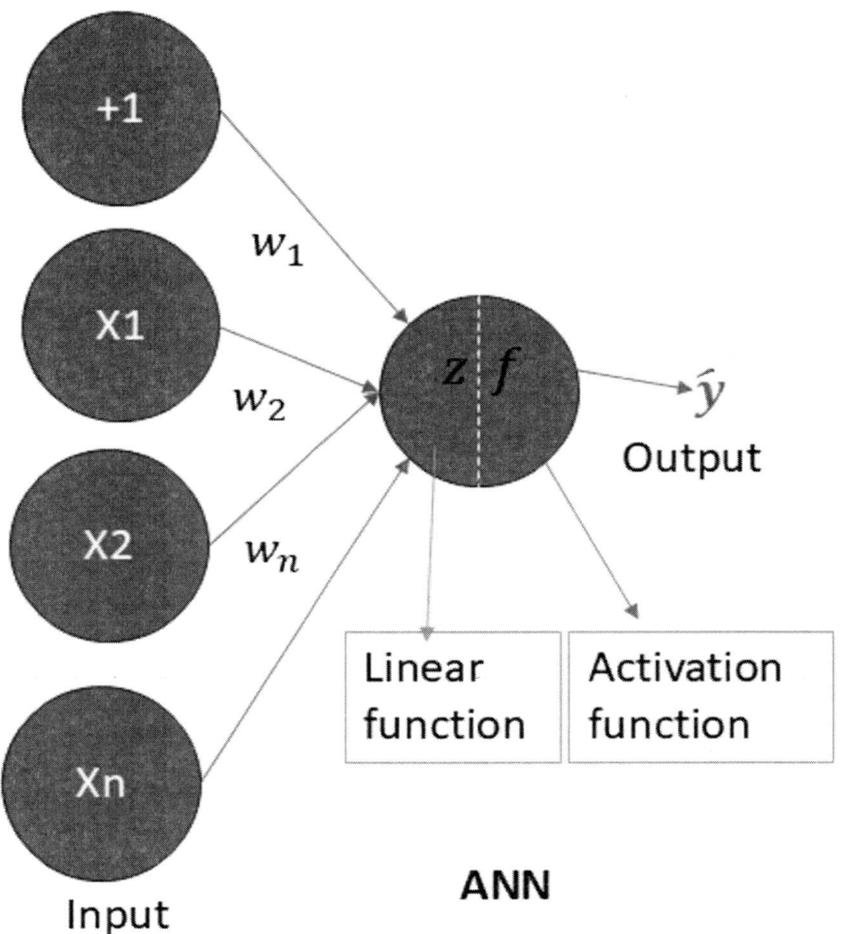

Illustration P6_Deep_BN_2

Learning

Biological Neurons:

Learning occurs in the cell body (soma), which processes impulses. If the impulses are strong enough to reach the threshold, an action potential is produced and travels through the axon. This process is influenced by synaptic plasticity, the ability of synapses to become stronger or weaker over time based on activity changes.

Artificial Neurons:

Learning is achieved through backpropagation, a technique that adjusts the weights between nodes according to the error between predicted and actual outcomes.

Comparison

Biological Neuron Process	Artificial Neuron Process
Synaptic Plasticity	Backpropagation

Activation

Biological Neurons:

Activation is determined by the firing rate of the neuron, which occurs when the impulses are strong enough to reach the threshold.

Artificial Neurons:

Activation is handled by a mathematical function known as an activation function. This function maps the input to the output, determining whether a neuron should be activated or not.

By understanding these similarities and differences, we can better appreciate how artificial neural networks mimic biological processes to perform complex tasks such as pattern recognition, decision-making, and learning from data.

Example:

Let's consider a simple puzzle where the expected output of a neural network is 600, but the actual result is 550, leading to an error of 50. To fix this, we use backpropagation, an optimization technique that adjusts the network's weights to minimize the error and move closer to the desired output. Through repeated iterations, the network learns to fine-tune its parameters to achieve the expected result.

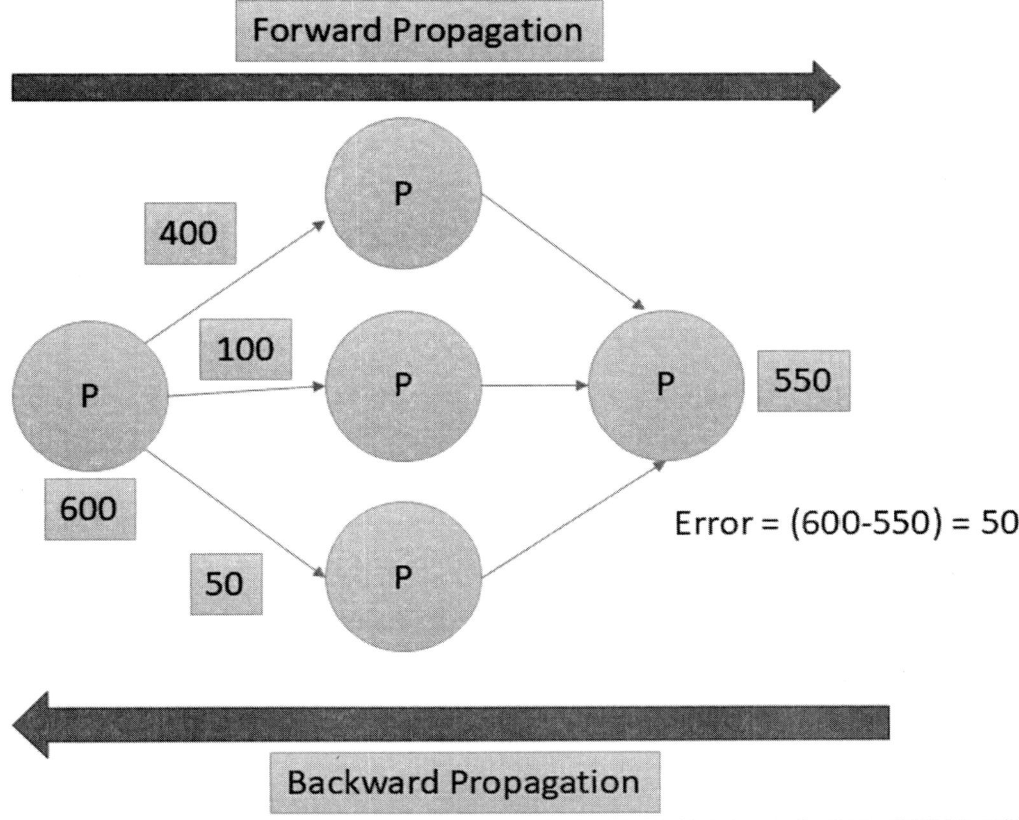

Illustration P6_Puzzle

This process is similar to how the human brain works when reading a book. We process information in sequence, analyse it, and eventually synthesize it into a conclusion or summary."

"An Artificial Neural Network is the mind of a machine—where connections form, patterns emerge, and intelligence is born through learning." – Shree Shambav.

Apeksha asked, "Master, how do we mimic the human brain?"

Master replied, "We mimic the brain using artificial neurons, much like the biological ones, by creating Artificial Neural Networks that simulate the way neurons process information, learn, and make decisions."

Akanksh asked, "Master, what is a perceptron?"

Master replied, "A perceptron is a basic computational model that takes multiple inputs and produces a single binary output. It's like a decision-making process. For example, imagine a patient visiting a doctor to determine whether they have diabetes or not. The inputs could be the patient's age, weight, and height, while the output would be a simple yes or no—diabetic or not."

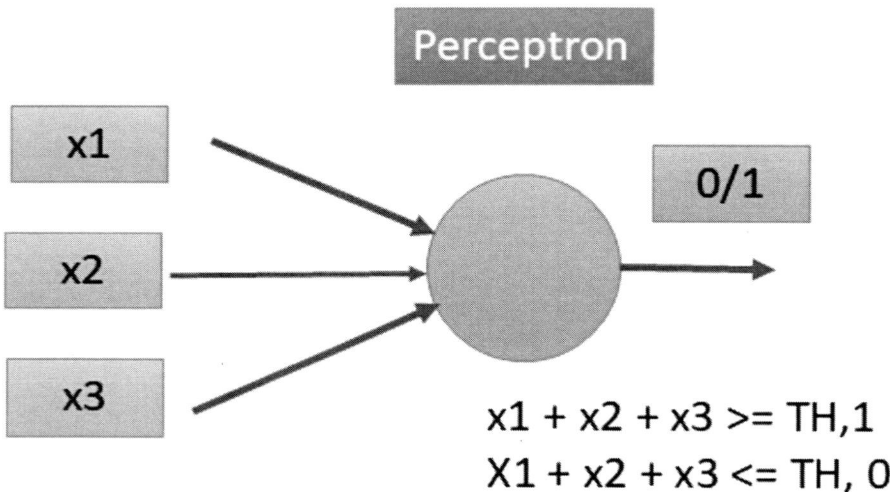

Illustration P6_Basic_Perceptron_1

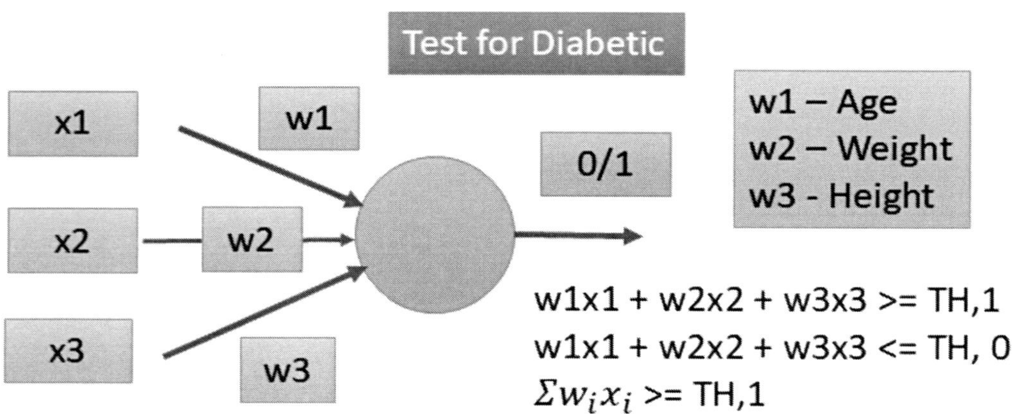

Illustration P6_Basic_Perceptron_2

Akshaya asked, "What is the difference between a perceptron and an artificial neuron?"

Master replied, "A perceptron is the simplest form of a neural network, where multiple inputs are processed to produce a binary output. The artificial neuron, on the other hand, is an advanced version of the perceptron. It introduces the concept of an activation function, which helps in handling more complex, non-linear problems. While a perceptron gives a straightforward output, an artificial neuron uses activation functions to capture more intricate relationships in the data."

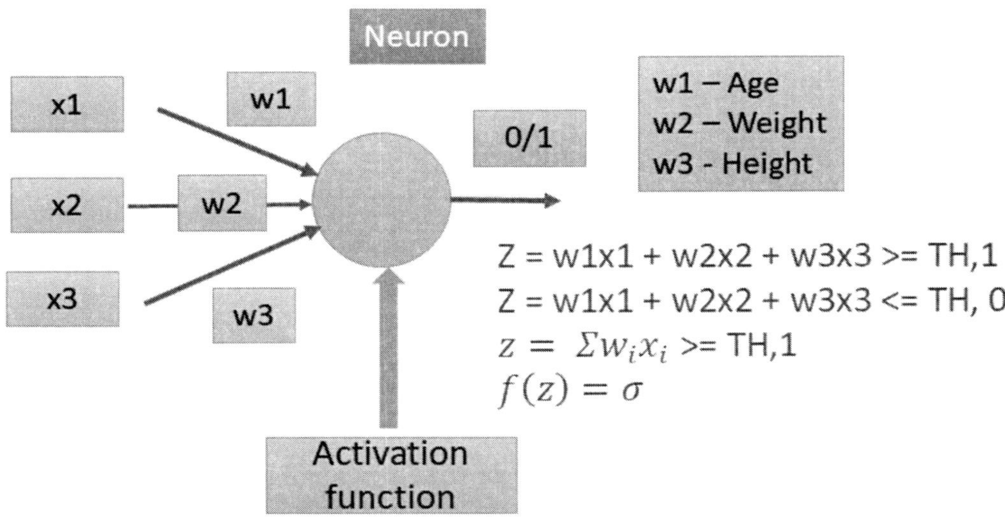

Illustration P6_Neuron

Roopa asked, "What is a Neural Network Activation Function?"

Master replied, "An activation function determines whether a neuron should be activated or not. It evaluates the neuron's input and decides if it's significant enough to be passed on for further processing in the network. Essentially, the activation function introduces non-linearity, enabling the network to learn and model complex data relationships, making predictions more accurate by applying simple mathematical operations."

Akshaya asked, "Master, what exactly is a Neural Network?"

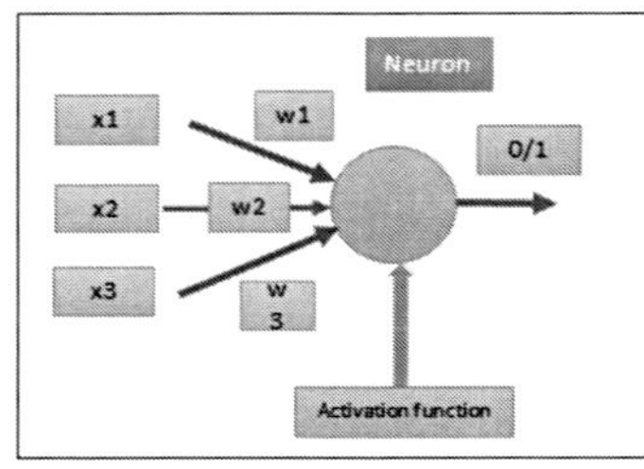

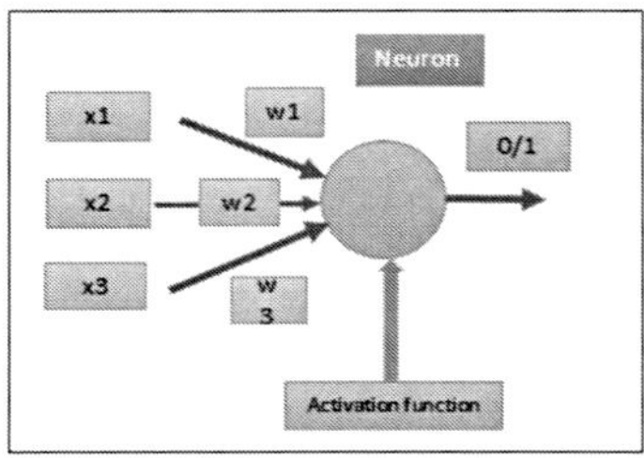

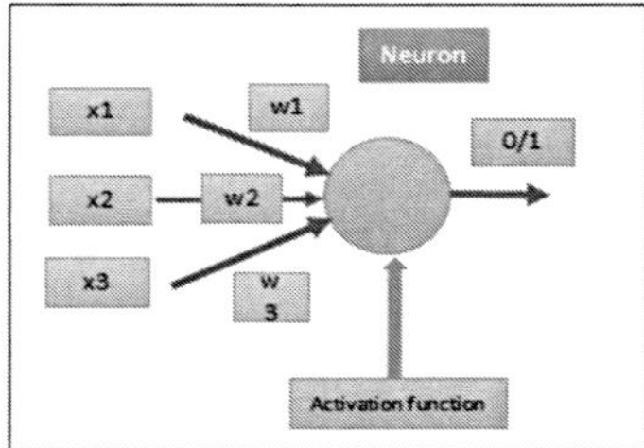

Neural Network

Illustration P6_NeuralNetwork

Master replied, "A neural network is formed by connecting multiple neurons together in a structured way, allowing them to communicate and share information. These interconnected neurons work collectively to process complex patterns and data, much like the human brain. Each neuron contributes to the network's ability to learn, recognise patterns, and make decisions."

Components of a Neural Network:

Layers, Weights, Bias, and Activation Function

Master said, "Let's break it down with an intuitive example. Imagine when you touch a candle flame, you instinctively pull your hand back. The input is the heat from the flame, your finger's neurons (hidden layer) process this information, and the output is your reaction to pull back. This is similar to how a neural network works—there's an input layer, hidden layers where processing happens, and an output layer that gives a result."

Now, let's use this analogy to understand a real-world example of predicting employee attrition based on factors like tenure, age, and salary.

Inputs:

- Tenure: 1, 3, 2, 5, 8
- Age: 24, 26, 25, 30, 32
- Salary: 80, 100, 90, 120, 150
- Attrition (Y/N): Y, Y, N, N, Y

In a neural network, we assign weights to each input based on how important we think each factor is to the output (attrition). These weights control how much influence each input will have. For instance:

- Weight for Age: 0.6
- Weight for Salary: 0.8
- Weight for Tenure: 0.4
- Bias: 0.1 (This ensures that even without inputs, we still get an output, preventing the network from being rigid.)

The model uses these weights, biases, and an activation function to determine if an employee is likely to leave or stay. Just as in the candle flame example, the input is processed in hidden layers, and the result is an output (attrition prediction).

This example simplifies how a neural network functions, showing how the layers, weights, bias, and activation functions work together to learn patterns and make predictions.

Note: "In this example, we have assumed weights for each input, along with a bias and activation function for the neural network. However, these values may not be the most optimized or accurate. Simply using these assumed weights might not yield the best predictions. This is where forward propagation shows its limitation, as it only passes inputs through the network without adjusting anything to minimize error."

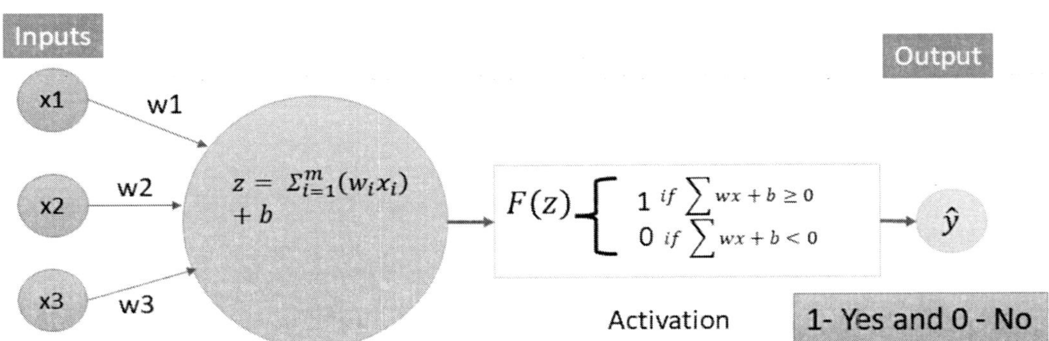

Illustration P6_NeuralNetwork_1

To address this challenge, we use backward propagation, a key optimization technique. Backpropagation helps the network learn by adjusting the weights and bias based on the error between the predicted and actual output. It fine-tunes the parameters, gradually improving accuracy by minimizing the error through multiple iterations. This allows the neural network to find the optimal set of weights, bias, and activation functions for more accurate predictions.

Mathematics Behind Neural Networks:

In Optimum Series IV, we delved deeply into several key mathematical concepts that are fundamental to understanding neural networks. Here, we present a concise review of these foundational principles to reinforce your comprehension and prepare you for more advanced topics. This summary serves as a helpful refresher, ensuring you are well-equipped to navigate the complexities of neural networks and their mathematical foundations.

- Cost Function: This measures the difference between the predicted output and the actual output, guiding the optimization process.
- Derivatives: Derivatives are essential for understanding how changes in inputs affect outputs, playing a critical role in updating weights during training.
- Chain Rule: This mathematical principle allows us to compute the derivatives of composite functions, which is vital for backpropagation in neural networks.
- Gradient Descent: This optimization algorithm helps minimize the cost function by iteratively adjusting the model's parameters in the direction of the steepest descent.

By solidifying your grasp of these concepts, you'll be better prepared to tackle the intricacies of neural networks and their applications.

Cost Function:

The cost function is a crucial component in evaluating the performance of a machine learning model, providing insight into its accuracy and effectiveness. It quantifies how well the model's predictions align with the actual values, serving as a benchmark for model improvement.

When the difference between the actual output (Y_actual) and the predicted output (Y_predicted) is minimal, it indicates a well-performing model. Conversely, a larger difference suggests that the model is not fitting the data effectively.

In the context of linear regression, the relationship can be expressed as:

$$Y = mx + c$$

Where m represents the slope and c the y-intercept. The error can be calculated as:

$$\text{Yactual} - \text{Ypredicted} = [\text{Yactual} - (mx + c)]$$

To measure the overall performance, we often utilise the Sum of Squared Errors (SSE):

$$\text{SSE} = \sum_{i=1}^{n} [\text{Yactual} - (mx + c)]^2$$

The cost function is then defined as:

$$J(m,c) = \sum_{i=1}^{n} [\text{Yactual} - (mx + c)]^2$$

The primary objective of the cost function is to minimize its value, ideally bringing it as close to zero as possible. A lower cost indicates a better fit of the model to the training data, guiding the optimization process and ultimately enhancing the model's predictive accuracy.

Derivatives:

Derivatives play a fundamental role in optimizing neural networks by helping us understand how small changes in input variables affect the output. In machine learning, particularly in neural networks, derivatives are used to calculate the gradient, which is essential for the process of backpropagation during training.

Derivatives in Neural Networks: A derivative helps us measure how a function changes as its input changes. For example, if we have a function $f(x) = x^2$, the derivative $f'(x) = 2x$ tells us the rate of change of the function with respect to x. This concept is used to update weights in neural networks by determining how much an individual weight should be adjusted to minimize the error.

Partial Derivatives:

In a neural network, where the output depends on multiple inputs, we use partial derivatives. Partial derivatives are used to measure how the function changes with respect to one input while keeping the others constant.

Example:

$$f(x,y) = x^2+y^2$$

The partial derivative of 'f' with respect to 'x' is $\partial f/\partial x = 2x$, and with respect to 'y' is $\partial f/\partial y = 2y$. These help in adjusting weights associated with different inputs.

Chain Rule:

The chain rule is a technique used to compute the derivative of a function that is composed of other functions. In neural networks, the chain rule is used extensively during backpropagation to calculate the gradient of the loss function with respect to each weight by propagating the error backward through the network.

Example of Chain Rule: Suppose we have:

$Y = x^2$ and $X = z^2$

To find the relationship between Y and Z, we use the chain rule. First, we calculate the derivatives:

$$dY/dX = 2x \text{ and } dX/dZ = 2z$$

Using the chain rule:

$$dY/dZ = dY/dX \times dX/dZ = 2x \times 2z = 4xz$$

This technique allows us to break down complex neural networks into smaller, manageable parts during backpropagation, enabling efficient computation of gradients.

In summary, derivatives, partial derivatives, and the chain rule are essential mathematical tools that enable neural networks to learn by optimizing the weights and biases, reducing errors in predictions.

Gradient Descent: Optimizing Parameters Step by Step

Apeksha asked, "Master, what is gradient descent and optimisation in deep learning?"

Gradient Descent is a fundamental algorithm used to minimise the error or loss in a deep learning model. It works by iteratively adjusting the model's parameters (weights and biases) in the direction that reduces the loss function. The goal is to find the optimal set of parameters that make the model's predictions as accurate as possible.

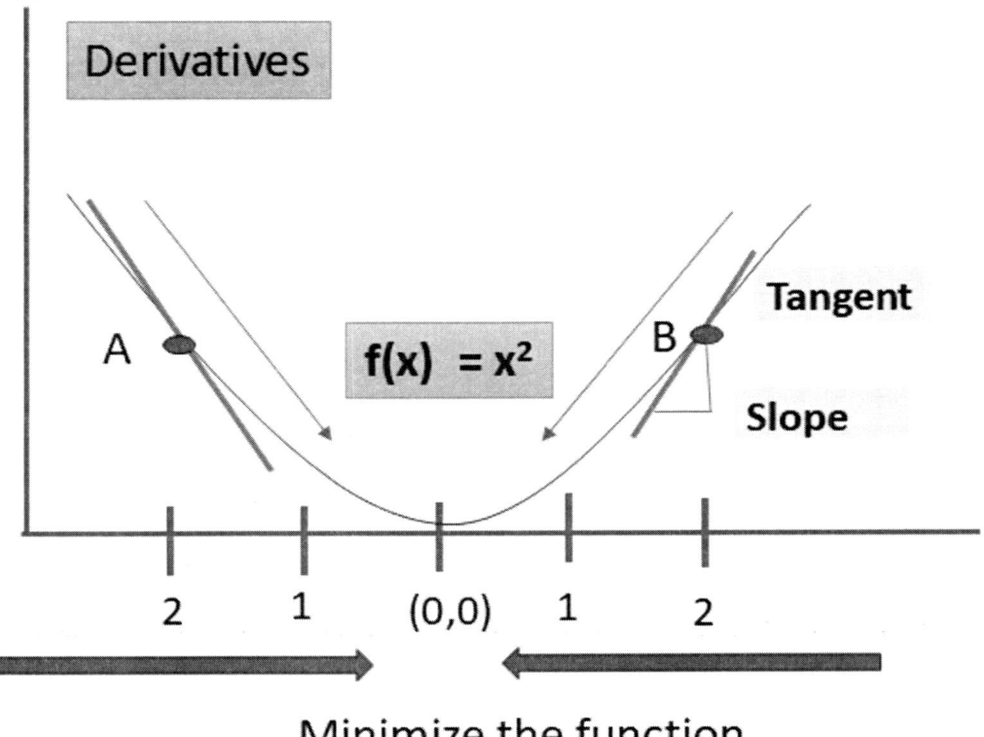

Illustration P6_Gradient_2

The process involves calculating the gradient, or the slope, of the loss function concerning each parameter, and then updating the parameters in the opposite direction of the gradient. The size of these updates is controlled by the learning rate. A smaller learning rate makes the model learn slowly but ensures stability, while a larger learning rate speeds up learning but risks overshooting the optimal solution.

Let's simplify this with a relatable example:

Imagine a person, A, who is excited to share the news of his salary hike with his family. His mother starts guessing, asking if it's $50,000. A responds, "No, that's too high." She lowers her guess to $40,000. “Higher,” he says. Finally, after a few more guesses—$45,000, $47,000—they arrive at the correct value: $47,000. This guessing process mirrors how Gradient Descent works. Just like refining the guess for the salary, Gradient Descent refines the parameters step by step to minimize error.

In Gradient Descent, this refinement happens with a concept called step size, also known as the learning rate. The formula for updating the value is:

$$\text{New value} = \text{Old value} - \text{Step size}$$

Where:

$$\text{Step size} = \text{Learning rate} \times \text{Slope}$$

The slope, or derivative, indicates the direction of movement. If we start with an initial guess, Gradient Descent uses the slope to decide whether to move up or down to minimize the error.

Key Idea: Moving Toward the Minimum - If the function’s slope is negative at a point (like ‘A’ in the illustration example), the value of the parameter increases, and the cost decreases, meaning we’re moving in the right direction. Conversely, if we start at a point like ‘B’ with a positive slope, the value decreases, driving us closer to the minimum.

Now, consider a function with multiple parameters, like in a simple linear regression model:

$$y = mx + c$$

The goal of Gradient Descent is to minimize the cost function J(m,c), which measures how far off our model’s predictions are from the actual values.

Let’s use an example dataset:

To optimize the parameters m and c in the given linear regression example, we aim to minimize the cost function J(m,c), which measures the error between the predicted and actual values.

Given the dataset:

$x = \{1,3\}, y = \{2,4\}$

Initially, we assume c = 0 and m = 1. The cost function for this simple linear regression is:

$$J(m,c) = [2-(c + (m \times x_1))]^2 + [4-(c + (m \times x_2))]^2$$
$$J(m,c) = [2-(c + (m \times 1))]^2 + [4-(c + (m \times 3))]^2$$

Substituting the values of $x_1 = 1$ and $x_2 = 3$, we have:

Now, to minimize this cost function, we compute the partial derivatives of J(m,c) with respect to 'c' and 'm'. These derivatives tell us how sensitive the cost is to changes in each parameter, which helps in optimizing them.

☐ Partial Derivative with Respect to c:

$$\frac{\partial J}{\partial c} = 2[2 - (c + m)] + (-2)\ [4 - (c + 3m)]$$

Substituting c = 0 and m = 1 into the equation:

$$\frac{\partial J}{\partial c} = 2[2 - (0 + 1)] + (-2)\ [4 - (0 + 3)]$$
$$\frac{\partial J}{\partial c} = 2[1] + (-2)\ [1] = 2\text{-}2 = 0$$

Thus, the derivative with respect to 'c' evaluates to 0.

Partial Derivative with Respect to m:

Now, let's calculate the partial derivative of the cost function with respect to m:

$$\frac{\partial J}{\partial m} = 2[2 - (c + m)]\ (-x_1) + 2\ [4 - (c + 3m)]\ (-x_2)$$

Substituting c = 0, m = 1, x1 = 1, and x2 = 3:

$$\frac{\partial J}{\partial m} = 2[2 - (0 + 1)] (-1) + 2 [4 - (0 + 3)] (-3)$$

$$\frac{\partial J}{\partial m} = 2[1] (-1) + 2 [1] (-3) = -2 - 6 = -8$$

Updating the Parameters:

Using Gradient Descent, the new values of 'c' and 'm' are updated using the learning rate (α) and the partial derivatives:

$$c_{new} = c_{old} - \text{Learning rate} \times \text{Slope}$$
$$c_{new} = c_{old} - (\alpha) \frac{\partial J}{\partial c}$$
$$m_{new} = m_{old} - (\alpha) \frac{\partial J}{\partial m}$$

Since the derivative with respect to 'c' is 0, 'c' remains unchanged. However, for 'm', we update it based on the calculated derivative:

$$m_{new} = 1 - \alpha (-8)$$

By iterating this process, we continue updating 'm' and 'c' until the cost function J(m,c) is minimized.

This process of adjusting the parameters step by step using partial derivatives is the essence of gradient descent, a fundamental technique for optimizing linear regression models as well as neural networks.

In summary, Gradient Descent helps fine-tune the parameters by making small, calculated adjustments, ensuring we move in the right direction toward the minimum error, ultimately optimizing the model for better predictions.

- ☐ **Intuition:**

Nikash asked, “Master, can you explain the intuition behind neural network computations using simple examples?”

Master said, “A neural network, at its core, is a computational system designed to learn from data by mimicking the way the human brain works. The intuition behind a neural network can be broken down by understanding how it processes information during the forward pass and how it learns during the backward pass (backpropagation).”

Forward Pass (Prediction Phase)

The forward pass is the process through which the neural network makes a prediction based on input data. Let’s break it down using a simple example of a single-layer neural network for predicting house prices based on square footage.

Example: Imagine you’re trying to predict the price of a house based on its size in square feet. A simple neural network has:

- Input layer: The square footage.
- Weights: Parameters that scale the input, initially set to random values.
- Bias: A constant added to adjust the prediction.
- Activation function: Introduces non-linearity (optional for a simple linear regression-like problem).
- Output layer: The predicted price of the house.

Let’s say the input is 1,000 sq ft, the weight is 0.3 (initially), and the bias is 50. The network computes:

Net Input = $(1{,}000 \times 0.3) + 50 = 350$

In this case, the predicted house price is 350 units (thousands of dollars, for example).

Backward Pass (Learning Phase)

Now, the backward pass (backpropagation) is where the magic happens—it’s how the network learns by adjusting the weights and biases based on the error in the prediction.

Calculate loss: First, we compare the predicted price with the actual price of the house, say the actual price is 400 units. We compute the loss (error) using a loss function like Mean Squared Error (MSE):

$$\text{Loss} = (400-350)^2 = 2500$$

Calculate gradients: Next, the network computes the gradient of the loss regarding the weight and bias. Gradients tell the network how much to change the weight and bias to reduce the loss. In simple terms, if increasing the weight increases the loss, we reduce the weight in the next step, and vice versa.

Update weights: Using gradient descent, the network updates the weights and bias. If the learning rate is 0.01, the new weight might look like this:

$$\text{New weight} = (0.3-0.01)\ (\partial\text{Loss}/\partial\text{Weight})$$

This process is repeated many times, and after several forward and backward passes, the network learns the right weights and biases to make better predictions.

Key Intuition:

- Forward pass: The network predicts the output based on the input and current parameters.
- Backward pass: The network learns by adjusting weights and bias to minimize the error (loss).

If you're trying to predict house prices with a simple neural network, the forward pass computes the predicted price based on input features (e.g., square footage), and the backward pass updates the network's parameters (weights and bias) to reduce the prediction error. Over time, this process leads to better predictions.

Apeksha asked, "Master, What Is an Epoch?"

Master said, "An epoch represents one complete pass of the entire training dataset through the neural network. In the context of Artificial Neural Networks (ANNs), an epoch refers to one complete pass of the entire training dataset through the neural network."

During an epoch, the following typically happens:

- Forward Propagation: The model processes the input data, layer by layer, to compute the predicted outputs.
- Loss Computation: The difference between the predicted output and the actual target values (error) is calculated using a loss function.
- Backward Propagation: The gradients of the loss with respect to the model's

parameters (weights and biases) are computed using algorithms like backpropagation.

- Parameter Update: The weights and biases of the model are adjusted using an optimization algorithm like Gradient Descent or Adam, based on the computed gradients.

Key Points About Epochs

Epoch vs. Batch:

- If the entire dataset is used in a single pass (batch gradient descent), then one epoch equals one gradient update.
- In practice, the dataset is often divided into smaller batches (mini-batch gradient descent), and multiple gradient updates occur within a single epoch.

Training Over Multiple Epochs:

- Neural networks usually require multiple epochs to learn effectively.
- With each epoch, the model gets another opportunity to refine its weights, ideally reducing the loss and improving performance.

Risk of Overfitting:

- Training for too many epochs can lead to overfitting, where the model learns patterns specific to the training data but fails to generalise to new, unseen data.
- Techniques like early stopping and cross-validation help mitigate overfitting.

Monitoring Progress:

- Loss (training or validation) and accuracy are commonly monitored across epochs to ensure the model is improving.

Example

Suppose you have a dataset with 1,000 samples, and you set the batch size to 100. During one epoch:

- The dataset will be divided into 10 batches of 100 samples each.

- The model will process all 10 batches (forward and backward passes), completing one epoch.

If you train for 50 epochs, the model will process the dataset 50 times.

Iteration:

An iteration refers to processing one batch through the network.

Example: If an epoch has 10 batches, then 10 iterations are required to complete one epoch.

Analogy to Clarify

Think of learning from a book:

- Dataset: The book (with all its pages).
- Epoch: Reading the entire book once (cover to cover).
- Batch: Dividing the book into smaller sections or chapters to read at a time.
- Iteration: Reading one chapter at a time.

If you need to understand the book better, you might read it multiple times (multiple epochs). Each time you read it, you might notice details you missed earlier and improve your comprehension.

Roopa asked, "Master, why are Epochs important?"

Incremental Learning:

- In the first epoch, the model starts with random parameters and may not perform well.
- With each subsequent epoch, the model refines its weights and improves its performance.

Trade-off Between Underfitting and Overfitting:

- Underfitting: If too few epochs are used, the model may not have enough time to learn the patterns in the data.

- Overfitting: If too many epochs are used, the model may memorize the training data but fail to generalize to unseen data.

Practical Example

Dataset:

- Inputs: x1, x2 (features).
- Targets: y (labels).
- Training Samples: 1,000.

Parameters:

- Batch Size: 100 samples.
- Epochs: 5.

Training Process:

For 1 epoch:

- The model processes 10 batches (100 samples per batch).
- After processing all 10 batches, one epoch is completed.

For 5 epochs:

- The model processes the entire dataset 5 times (50 batches total).

Monitoring:

At the end of each epoch, you can:

- Check how well the model is performing (loss, accuracy).
- Adjust hyperparameters if necessary.

Visualizing the Training Process

Let's simulate how the loss decreases over epochs:

Epoch	Loss
1	0.50
2	0.30
3	0.20
4	0.15
5	0.14

Interpretation:

- In early epochs, the loss decreases significantly.
- By epoch 4, the loss plateaus (the model is learning less with each epoch).
- This is when you might stop training, as additional epochs bring minimal improvement.

Best Practices for Epochs

Choose the Right Number of Epochs:

- Too few: The model underfits (poor performance).
- Too many: The model overfits (memorizes training data but performs poorly on new data).

Early Stopping:

- Stop training when the validation loss stops improving.

Monitor Metrics:

- Keep track of training and validation loss/accuracy to decide when to stop.

Master explained that the code snippet to understand how epochs, batches, and iterations interact in training.

Example P1 – U1 – D7	

Epoch	**Output**

import numpy as np
training_data = np.random.rand(1000, 2) # 1000 samples, 2 features each
batch_size = 100
num_epochs = 5
 	
# Simulating training 	
for epoch in range(num_epochs):
   print(f"Epoch {epoch + 1}/{num_epochs}")
   for i in range(0, len(training_data), batch_size):
      batch = training_data[i:i + batch_size]
      # Simulate training on this batch
      print(f" Processing batch {i // batch_size + 1}")	

The code simulates the process of training a neural network by iterating through epochs and batches.

Inputs:

- A dataset (training_data) with 1,000 samples, each having 2 features.
- Batch size: 100 samples per batch.
- Epochs: 5 (the entire dataset is processed 5 times).

Outer Loop (Epochs):

- The for epoch in range(num_epochs) loop represents the number of complete passes (epochs) over the dataset.

Inner Loop (Batches):

- Within each epoch, the dataset is divided into batches using slicing: batch = training_data[i:i + batch_size].
- The loop for i in range(0, len(training_data), batch_size) iterates over these batches.

Simulating Training:

- Each batch is processed (e.g., forward and backward passes, weight updates).
- The output indicates which batch and epoch are currently being processed.

Output:

- The program prints progress for each epoch and batch, simulating training in a neural network.

This code helps visualize how training progresses through epochs and batches in machine learning. You can extend it by including actual computations (e.g., forward and backward propagation).

☐ Mathematical Intuition behind Epoch: One cycle

Notations:

- L: Loss
- o1, o2: Predicted outputs
- t1, t2: Target values
- σ(z): Sigmoid activation function
- z1, z2: Pre-activation values for h1, h2
- W: Weights
- b: Biases
- δ: Partial derivatives of the loss with respect to weights, biases, or activations.

Initialize Parameters (Weights and Bias): Step 1

Start by assigning initial values to the weights and bias, which are essential for determining the output of the model. These parameters will be adjusted during training to optimize the model's performance.

Input for h1 = $z = \sum_{i=1}^{n} W_i x_i + b$

z = (0.15 x 0.05) + (0.2 x 0.1) + (0.35) = 0.3775

Output from h1: Apply the sigmoid activation function

General Neural Network

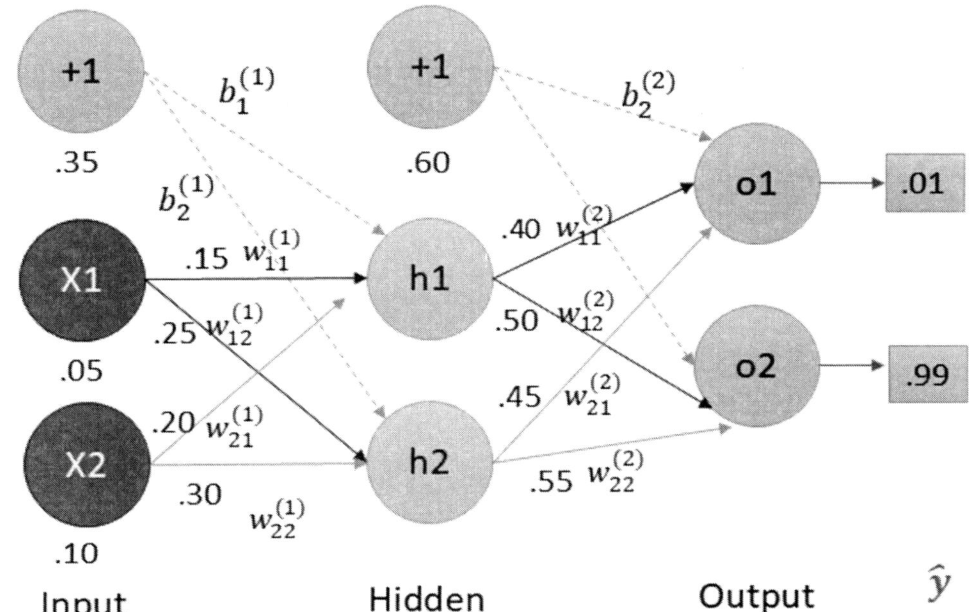

Input for h1:

$$z = \sum_{i=1}^{n} W_i x_i + b$$

Output from h1:

$$\sigma(z) = \frac{1}{1+e^{-z}}$$

Illustration P6_General_Neural_1

$\sigma(z) = \frac{1}{1+e^{-z}} \quad = \frac{1}{1+e^{-0.3775}}$

$e^{-0.3775} \approx 0.6857$

$\sigma(0.3775) = 1/\ (1 + 0.6857) \approx 1.68571 \approx 0.5932$

So, the output for h1 is approximately 0.5932.

z = (0.25 x 0.05) + (0.30 x 0.1) + (0.60) = 0.6425

Output from h2: $\sigma(z) = \frac{1}{1+e^{-z}} \quad = \frac{1}{1+e^{-0.6425}}$

$e^{-0.6425} \approx 0.6553$

σ(0.6425) = 1/ (1 + 0.6553) ≈ 1.68571≈ 0.6041

So, the output for h2 is approximately **0.6041**

Forward Propagation: Step 2

The model takes the input data and processes it through the network layers, applying the weights and bias to calculate the predicted output.

$o_1^{(1)} = w_{11}^{(2)} h_1 + \ w_{21}^{(1)} h_2 + b_1^{(2)}$

= (0.4 x 0.5932) + (0.45 x 0.6041) + (0.6) = 1.1098

$o_2^{(1)} = w_{12}^{(2)} h_1 + \ w_{22}^{(1)} h_2 + b_2^{(2)}$

= (0.5 x 0.5932) + (0.55 x 0.6041) + (0.6) = 1.2288

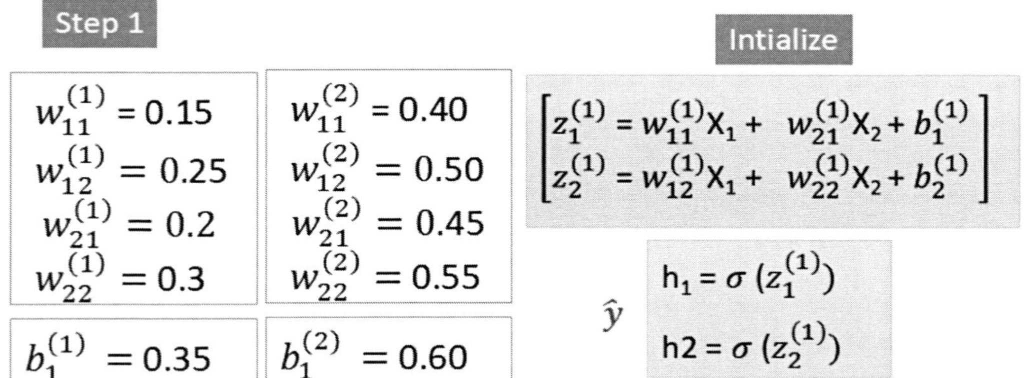

Illustration P6_General_Neural_2

Compute Error (Loss): Step 3

The difference between the predicted output and the actual target values is computed using a cost or loss function. This error provides a measure of how well or poorly the model is performing.

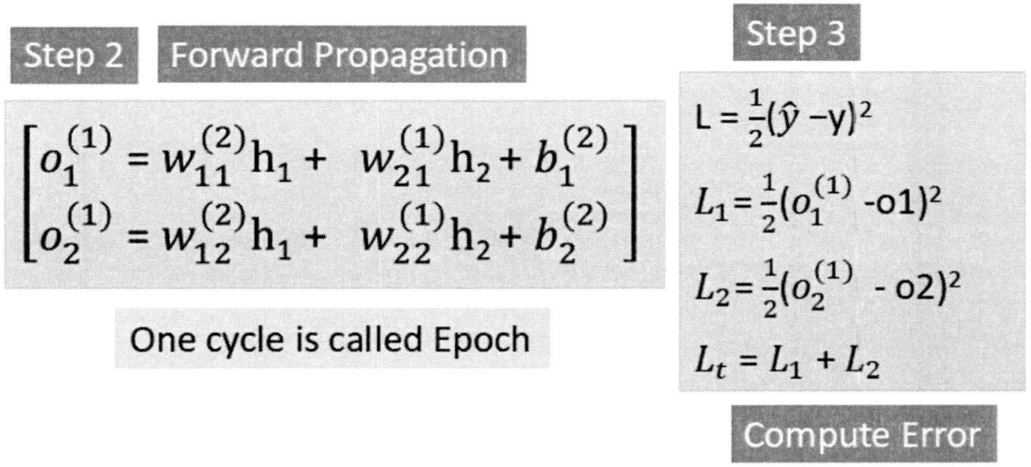

Step 2 Forward Propagation

$$\begin{bmatrix} o_1^{(1)} = w_{11}^{(2)} h_1 + w_{21}^{(1)} h_2 + b_1^{(2)} \\ o_2^{(1)} = w_{12}^{(2)} h_1 + w_{22}^{(1)} h_2 + b_2^{(2)} \end{bmatrix}$$

One cycle is called Epoch

Step 3

$L = \frac{1}{2}(\hat{y} - y)^2$

$L_1 = \frac{1}{2}(o_1^{(1)} - o1)^2$

$L_2 = \frac{1}{2}(o_2^{(1)} - o2)^2$

$L_t = L_1 + L_2$

Compute Error

Illustration P6_General_Neural_3

Loss Gradient calculation:

Loss Function:

The loss for a single output is calculated as:

$L = ½ (o-t)^2$

Where:

$o \ or \ o_1^{(1)}$: Predicted output

t or o1: Target output

The gradient of the loss with respect to o (predicted output) is:

$$\frac{\partial L}{\partial o} = o - t$$

Loss Gradients w.r.t Outputs: for o1 and o2:

$$\frac{\partial L_t}{\partial o_1^{(1)}} = \left(o_1^{(1)} - o1 \right) = (1.1098 - 0.01) = \mathbf{1.0998}$$

$\frac{\partial L_t}{\partial o_2^{(1)}} = (1.2288 - 0.01) = \mathbf{1.2188}$

Step 4

Optimize parameters

$$\frac{\partial L_t}{\partial w_{21}^{(2)}} = \frac{\partial L_t}{\partial o_1} * \frac{\partial o_1}{\partial o_1^{(1)}} * \frac{\partial o_1^{(1)}}{\partial L_t}$$

$$\frac{\partial L_t}{\partial w_{22}^{(2)}} = \frac{\partial L_t}{\partial o_2} * \frac{\partial o_2}{\partial o_2^{(1)}} * \frac{\partial o_2^{(1)}}{\partial L_t}$$

Compute Gradient

New value = Old Value – Step Size

Step size = Learning rate * gradient

$$w_{21}^{(2)} \text{ new} = w_{21}^{(2)} - \eta \cdot \frac{\partial L_t}{\partial w_{21}^{(2)}}$$

$$w_{22}^{(2)} \text{ new} = w_{22}^{(2)} - \eta \cdot \frac{\partial L_t}{\partial w_{22}^{(2)}}$$

Step 5

Repeat steps 1 to 5
Until the optimized result is achieved.

Illustration P6_General_Neural_4

Loss Verification:

$L_1 = \frac{1}{2}(o1 - t_1)^2$

$L_1 = \frac{1}{2}(o1 - o_1^{(1)})^2$

L1 = ½ (1.1098 – 0.01)^2 = 0.604

$L_2 = \frac{1}{2}(o2 - o_2^{(1)})^2$

L2 = ½ (1.2288 – 0.01)^2 = 0.742

Total Loss

$L_t = L_1 + L_2$

$L_t = 1.346$

Output Gradient w.r.t Pre-Activation:

For the sigmoid activation function:

$\sigma'(z) = \sigma(z)(1 - \sigma(z))$

For o1:

$\sigma'(z)$ = 1.1098 (1 - 1.1098) = **-0.121**

For o2:

$\sigma'(z)$ = 1.2288 (1 - 1.2288) = **-0.280**

Adjust Parameters (Backpropagation): Step 4

Based on the computed error, the weights and bias are updated using optimization techniques like gradient descent. This step minimizes the error by iteratively adjusting the parameters, moving the model closer to its optimal performance.

Chain Rule for Gradients:

Now, use the chain rule to compute the gradients of L_t w.r.t. weights and biases for h1 and h2.

Gradient of loss w.r.t. weights $W_{h1 \to o1}$

$$\frac{\partial L_t}{\partial w_{21}^{(2)}} = \frac{\partial L_t}{\partial o_1} * \frac{\partial o_1}{\partial L_1} * \frac{\partial L_1}{\partial w_{21}^{(2)}}$$

Now substitute values:

$\frac{\partial L_t}{\partial w_{21}^{(2)}} = 1.0998\ (-0.121)\ (0.6041) \approx -0.080$

An epoch refers to one complete cycle of these steps, where the entire training dataset is passed forward and backward through the neural network to improve its accuracy. This process is repeated for multiple epochs until the model converges, meaning the error is minimized sufficiently.

Similarly, compute:

Gradients w.r.t. $W_{h2 \to o2}$

Gradients w.r.t. biases b_{h1}, b_{h2}

Propagate further backward to adjust $W_{in \to h1}$, $W_{in \to h2}$, and b_{in}.

Gradients w.r.t. Biases b_{h1} and b_{h2}

The gradient of L w.r.t. b_{h1} is:

Where:

$z_{h1} = (0.15 * 0.05) + (0.2 * 0.1) + 0.35 = 0.3775$

$\sigma'(z_{h1}) = \sigma(z_{h1}) * (1 - \sigma(z_{h1}))$

Contributions from both o1 and o2:

$\frac{\partial z_{o1}}{\partial h_1} = W_{h1 \to o1}$

$\frac{\partial z_{o2}}{\partial h_2} = W_{h1 \to o2}$

Repeat for b_{h2} using z_{h2}.

> Note: Compute the gradients layer by layer using the chain rule.
> Backpropagate through each weight and bias to calculate their gradients.
> Update weights and biases using gradient descent:
> $W = W - \eta * \frac{\partial L_t}{\partial w}$
> $b = b - \eta * \frac{\partial L_t}{\partial b}$

Let's compute the gradients for $W_{in \to h1}$ and $W_{in \to h2}$ step by step.

Case One:

Gradients for $W_{in \to h1}$ and $W_{in \to h2}$

Formula: The gradient of L w.r.t. $W_{in \to h1}$

$$\frac{\partial L_t}{\partial w_{in \to h1}} = \frac{\partial L_t}{\partial w_{21}^{(2)}} = \frac{\partial L_t}{\partial o} * \frac{\partial o}{\partial z_0} * \frac{\partial z_0}{\partial h_1} * \frac{\partial h_1}{\partial z_{h1}} * \frac{\partial z_{h1}}{\partial w_{21}^{(2)}}$$

Where:

$\frac{\partial z_{h1}}{\partial w_{21}^{(2)}} =$ input to the neuron

$\frac{\partial h_1}{\partial z_{h1}} = \sigma'\,(z_{h1})$ derivative of sigmoid z_{h1}

$\frac{\partial z_0}{\partial h_1} = W_{h1 \to o1}$

$\frac{\partial o}{\partial z_0} = \sigma'\,(z_o)$

$\frac{\partial L_t}{\partial o} =$ (o-t)

Given Values:

$o1 = 1.1098,\ t_1 = 0.01,\ \frac{\partial L_t}{\partial o1} = o1 - t_1 = 1.0998$

o2 = 1.2288, t_2 = 0.01, $\frac{\partial L_t}{\partial o2}$ = o2−t_2 = 1.2188

h1=0.5932, z_{h1} = 0.3775,

$\sigma'(z_{h1}) = \sigma(z_{h1}) * (1-\sigma(z_{h1})) = 0.5932 * (1-0.5932) = 0.241$

Wh1→o1=0.4, Wh1→o2=0.5

Step 1: Compute Contribution from o1

For o1:

$\frac{\partial L_t}{\partial o1} = 1.0998$

$\sigma'(z_{o1}) = \sigma(z_{o1}) * (1-\sigma(z_{o1})) = 1.1098 * (1-1.1098) = -0.121$

$\frac{\partial z_{01}}{\partial h_1} = W_{h1\to o1} = 0.4$

$\frac{\partial h_1}{\partial z_{h1}} = 0.241$

$\frac{\partial L_{o1}}{\partial w_{in\to h1}} = \frac{\partial L_t}{\partial o} * \sigma'(z_{o1}) * W_{h1\to o1} * 0.241 * \text{input}$

Substitute:

Input = 0.05 (as given earlier).

$\frac{\partial L_{o1}}{\partial w_{in\to h1}} = 1.0998 * (-0.121) * 0.4 * 0.241 * 0.05$

$\frac{\partial L_{o1}}{\partial w_{in\to h1}} \approx -0.0064$

Step 2: Compute Contribution from o2

For o2:

$\frac{\partial L_t}{\partial o2} = 1.2188$

$\sigma'(z_{o2}) = \sigma(z_{o2}) * (1-\sigma(z_{o2})) = 1.2288 * (1-1.2288) = -0.280$

$\frac{\partial z_{02}}{\partial h_2} = W_{h1\to o2} = 0.5$

$\frac{\partial h_1}{\partial z_{h1}} = 0.241$

$\frac{\partial L_{o2}}{\partial w_{in\to h1}} = \frac{\partial L_t}{\partial o2} * \sigma'(z_{o2}) * W_{h1\to o2} * 0.241 * \text{input}$

Substitute:

Input = 0.05 (as given earlier).

$\frac{\partial L_{o1}}{\partial w_{in\to h1}} = 1.2188 * (-0.280) * 0.5 * 0.241 * 0.05$

$\frac{\partial L_{o2}}{\partial w_{in\to h1}} \approx -0.0082$

Step 3: Total Gradient for Win→h1

$$\frac{\partial L_t}{\partial w_{in\to h1}} = \frac{\partial L_{o1}}{\partial w_{in\to h1}} + \frac{\partial L_{o2}}{\partial w_{in\to h1}}$$

$\frac{\partial L_t}{\partial w_{in\to h1}} = -0.0064 + (-0.0082) = -0.0146$

Step 4: Repeat for $W_{in\to h2}$

Use the same formula but substitute h2 = 0.6041 z_{h2} = 0.6425, and $\sigma'(z_{h2})$:

$\sigma'(z_{h2}) = 0.6041 * (1 - 0.6041) = 0.240$

Repeat the process as above for $W_{in\to h2}$

Case Two:

Let's compute $\frac{\partial L_t}{\partial w_{in\to h2}}$

Gradients for $W_{in \to h1}$ and $W_{in \to h2}$

Formula: The gradient of L w.r.t. $W_{in \to h1}$

$$\frac{\partial L_t}{\partial w_{in \to h2}} = \frac{\partial L_t}{\partial w_{22}^{(2)}} = \frac{\partial L_t}{\partial o} * \frac{\partial o}{\partial z_0} * \frac{\partial z_0}{\partial h_2} * \frac{\partial h_2}{\partial z_{h2}} * \frac{\partial z_{h2}}{\partial w_{22}^{(2)}}$$

Where:

$\frac{\partial z_{h2}}{\partial w_{22}^{(2)}}$ = input to the neuron

$\frac{\partial h_2}{\partial z_{h2}} = \sigma' \; (z_{h2})$ derivative of sigmoid z_{h2}

$\frac{\partial z_0}{\partial h_2} = W_{h2 \to o2}$

$\frac{\partial o}{\partial z_0} = \sigma' \; (z_o)$

$\frac{\partial L_t}{\partial o}$ = (o - t)

Given Values:

$o1 = 1.1098, \; t_1 = 0.01, \; \frac{\partial L_t}{\partial o1} = \; o1 - t_1 = 1.0998$

$o2 = 1.2288, t_2 = 0.01, \; \frac{\partial L_t}{\partial o2} = o2 - t_2 = 1.2188$

$h2 = 0.6041, z_{h2} = 0.6425$

$\sigma'(z_{h2}) = \sigma(z_{h2}) * (1-\sigma(z_{h2})) = 0.6041 * (1-0.\ 6041) = 0.240$

$Wh2 \to o1=0.45, Wh2 \to o2=0.55$

Step 1: Compute Contribution from o1

For o1:

$\frac{\partial L_t}{\partial o1} = = 1.0998$

$\sigma'(z_{o1}) = \sigma(z_{o1}) * (1-\sigma(z_{o1})) = 1.1098 * (1-1.1098) = -0.121$

$\frac{\partial z_{01}}{\partial h_2} = W_{h2\to o1} = 0.45$

$\frac{\partial h_2}{\partial z_{h2}} = 0.240$

$\frac{\partial L_{o1}}{\partial w_{in\to h2}} = \frac{\partial L_t}{\partial o_1} * \sigma'(z_{o1}) * W_{h2\to o1} * 0.240 * \text{input}$

Substitute:

Input = 0.01 (as given earlier).

$\frac{\partial L_{o1}}{\partial w_{in\to h2}} = 1.0998 * (-0.121) * 0.45 * 0.241 * 0.1$

$\frac{\partial L_{o1}}{\partial w_{in\to h2}} \approx -0.0144$

Step 2: Compute Contribution from o2

For o2:

$\frac{\partial L_t}{\partial o2} = 1.2188$

$\sigma'(z_{o2}) = \sigma(z_{o2}) * (1-\sigma(z_{o2})) = 1.2288 * (1-1.2288) = -0.280$

$\frac{\partial z_{02}}{\partial h_2} = W_{h2\to o2} = 0.55$

$\frac{\partial h_2}{\partial z_{h2}} = 0.240$

$\frac{\partial L_{o2}}{\partial w_{in\to h2}} = \frac{\partial L_t}{\partial o2} * \sigma'(z_{o2}) * W_{h2\to o2} * 0.240 * \text{input}$

Substitute:

Input = 0.1 (as given earlier).

$\frac{\partial L_{o2}}{\partial w_{in\to h2}} = 1.2188 * (-0.280) * 0.55 * 0.240 * 0.1$

$$\frac{\partial L_{o2}}{\partial w_{in \to h2}} \approx -0.0449$$

Step 3: Total Gradient for Win→h2

$$\frac{\partial L_t}{\partial w_{in \to h2}} = \frac{\partial L_{o1}}{\partial w_{in \to h2}} + \frac{\partial L_{o2}}{\partial w_{in \to h2}}$$

$$\frac{\partial L_t}{\partial w_{in \to h2}} = -0.0144 + (-0.0449) = -0.0593$$

Final Results:

$$\frac{\partial L_t}{\partial w_{in \to h1}} \approx -0.0146$$

$$\frac{\partial L_t}{\partial w_{in \to h2}} \approx -0.0593$$

Master said, "Let's walk through a concrete example of updating weights and biases using the gradients we've calculated earlier. We'll pick a learning rate (η) of 0.01 and use the following initial values for the weights and biases."

Given Initial Values

$W_{in \to h1}^{old} = 0.15$

$W_{in \to h2}^{old} = 0.20$

Bias $b_{h1}^{old} = 0.35$

Bias $b_{h2}^{old} = 0.35$

Gradients:

$$\frac{\partial L_t}{\partial w_{in \to h1}} \approx -0.0146$$

$$\frac{\partial L_t}{\partial w_{in \to h2}} \approx -0.0593$$

Assume biases b_{h1} and b_{h2} have gradients of:

$$\frac{\partial L_t}{\partial b_{h1}} = -0.02$$

$$\frac{\partial L_t}{\partial b_{h2}} = -0.03$$

Update Formulas

Using the gradient descent update rule:

$$W_{new} = W_{old} - \eta * \frac{\partial L_t}{\partial w}$$

$$b_{new} = b_{old} - \eta * \frac{\partial L_t}{\partial b}$$

Step 1: Update $W_{in \to h1}$

$$W_{in \to h1}^{new} = W_{in \to h1}^{old} - \eta * \frac{\partial L_t}{\partial w_{in \to h1}}$$

Substitute the values:

$$W_{in \to h1}^{new} = 0.15 - (0.01 * -0.0146) = 0.15 + 0.000146 = 0.150146$$

Step 2: Update $W_{in \to h2}$

$$W_{in \to h2}^{new} = W_{in \to h2}^{old} - \eta * \frac{\partial L_t}{\partial w_{in \to h2}}$$

Substitute the values:

$$W_{in \to h2}^{new} = 0.20 - (0.01 * - 0.0593) = 0.20 + 0.000593 = 0.200593$$

Step 3: Update bias b_{h1}

$$b_{h1}^{new} = b_{h1}^{old} - \eta * \frac{\partial L_t}{\partial b_{h1}}$$

Substitute the values:

$$b_{h1}^{new} = 0.35 - (0.01 * -0.02) = 0.35 + 0.0002 = 0.3502$$

Step 3: Update bias b_{h2}

$$b_{h2}^{new} = b_{h2}^{old} - \eta * \frac{\partial L_t}{\partial b_{h2}}$$

Substitute the values:

$$b_{h2}^{new} = 0.35 - (0.01 * -0.03) = 0.35 + 0.0003 = 0.3503$$

Updated Parameters

After applying the updates:

$$W_{in \to h1}^{new} = 0.150146$$

$$W_{in \to h2}^{new} = 0.200593$$

$$b_{h1}^{new} = 0.3502$$

$$b_{h2}^{new} = 0.3503$$

Next Steps

Forward Propagation: Use these updated weights and biases to compute the outputs of the network and calculate the new loss.

Repeat Backpropagation: Continue backpropagating and updating weights and biases iteratively until the loss converges or meets a desired threshold.

Validation: After training, evaluate the model on a separate validation dataset to ensure it generalizes well.

Master said, "Let us understand the Python code for the above weight and bias updates using the gradient descent rule."

Example P1 – U1 – D8	
Weights and Bias	**Output**

# Initial Parameters 	
W_in_h1 = 0.15 # Weight from input to h1
W_in_h2 = 0.20 # Weight from input to h2
b_h1 = 0.35 # Bias for h1
b_h2 = 0.35 # Bias for h2
# Gradients from backpropagation 	
grad_W_in_h1 = -0.0146 # Gradient for W_in_h1
grad_W_in_h2 = -0.0593 # Gradient for W_in_h2
grad_b_h1 = -0.02 # Gradient for b_h1
grad_b_h2 = -0.03 # Gradient for b_h2
# Learning rate 	
learning_rate = 0.01
# Update formulas 	
W_in_h1_new = W_in_h1 - learning_rate * grad_W_in_h1
W_in_h2_new = W_in_h2 - learning_rate * grad_W_in_h2
b_h1_new = b_h1 - learning_rate * grad_b_h1
b_h2_new = b_h2 - learning_rate * grad_b_h2
# Print updated parameters 	
print("Updated Parameters:")
print(f"W_in_h1_new = {W_in_h1_new:.6f}")
print(f"W_in_h2_new = {W_in_h2_new:.6f}")
print(f"b_h1_new = {b_h1_new:.6f}")
print(f"b_h2_new = {b_h2_new:.6f}")
	Updated Parameters:
	W_in_h1_new = 0.150146
	W_in_h2_new = 0.200593
	b_h1_new = 0.350200
	b_h2_new = 0.350300

Neural Network Architecture

Input Layer: Two inputs (x1, x2).

- Hidden Layer: Two neurons (h1, h2).
- Output Layer: Two outputs (o1, o2).

Master said, "This code performs both forward and backward propagation."

- Forward propagation: Compute the outputs based on inputs, weights, biases, and activations.
- Backward propagation: Compute gradients, update weights and biases

<table>
<tr><td colspan="2">Example P1 – U1 – D9</td></tr>
<tr><td>Full Forward and backward pass</td><td>Output</td></tr>
<tr><td>
<pre>
import numpy as np
# Sigmoid activation function
def sigmoid(x):
    return 1 / (1 + np.exp(-x))

# Derivative of sigmoid
def sigmoid_derivative(x):
    return sigmoid(x) * (1 - sigmoid(x))

# Initialize weights and biases
weights_input_hidden = np.array([[0.15, 0.20], [0.25, 0.30]]) #
2x2 matrix for input-to-hidden weights
bias_hidden = np.array([0.35, 0.35]) # Bias for hidden layer
weights_hidden_output = np.array([[0.40, 0.45], [0.50, 0.55]])
# 2x2 matrix for hidden-to-output weights
bias_output = np.array([0.60, 0.60]) # Bias for output layer

# Inputs and expected outputs
inputs = np.array([0.05, 0.10])   # Input features
expected_outputs = np.array([0.01, 0.99]) # Target outputs

# Learning rate
learning_rate = 0.01

# ---- FORWARD PROPAGATION ----
# Step 1: Hidden layer computations
z_hidden = np.dot(inputs, weights_input_hidden) +
bias_hidden
a_hidden = sigmoid(z_hidden)

# Step 2: Output layer computations
z_output = np.dot(a_hidden, weights_hidden_output) +
bias_output
a_output = sigmoid(z_output)

# Compute loss (mean squared error)
loss = 0.5 * np.sum((expected_outputs - a_output) ** 2)

# Print forward pass results
print("Forward Propagation Results:")
print(f"Hidden layer activations: {a_hidden}")
print(f"Output layer activations: {a_output}")
print(f"Loss: {loss:.6f}")

---- BACKWARD PROPAGATION ----
</pre>
</td><td>
Forward Propagation Results:
Hidden layer activations:
[0.59447593 0.5962827
]
Output layer activations:
[0.75693192
0.76771788]
Loss: 0.303658

Updated Parameters:
Updated weights (input to hidden):
[[0.14999552
0.19999435]
 [0.24999105
0.29998871]]
Updated biases (hidden): [0.34991048
0.34988707]
Updated weights (hidden to output):
[[0.39918304
0.45023564]
 [0.49918056
0.55023636]]
Updated biases (output): [0.59862575
0.60039639]
</td></tr>
</table>

```
# Step 1: Gradients at the output layer
error_output = a_output - expected_outputs
grad_output = error_output * sigmoid_derivative(z_output)

# Gradients for weights and biases in the hidden-to-output
layer
grad_weights_hidden_output = np.outer(a_hidden,
grad_output)  # Outer product for weight gradients
grad_bias_output = grad_output

# Step 2: Gradients at the hidden layer
error_hidden = np.dot(grad_output,
weights_hidden_output.T)
grad_hidden = error_hidden * sigmoid_derivative(z_hidden)

# Gradients for weights and biases in the input-to-hidden
layer
grad_weights_input_hidden = np.outer(inputs, grad_hidden)
# Outer product for weight gradients
grad_bias_hidden = grad_hidden

# ---- UPDATE WEIGHTS AND BIASES ----
weights_hidden_output -= learning_rate *
grad_weights_hidden_output
bias_output -= learning_rate * grad_bias_output

weights_input_hidden -= learning_rate *
grad_weights_input_hidden
bias_hidden -= learning_rate * grad_bias_hidden

# Print updated parameters
print("\nUpdated Parameters:")
print(f"Updated weights (input to hidden):
\n{weights_input_hidden}")
print(f"Updated biases (hidden): {bias_hidden}")
print(f"Updated weights (hidden to output):
\n{weights_hidden_output}")
print(f"Updated biases (output): {bias_output}")
```

Initialization:

- Inputs, weights, and biases are initialised.
- Learning rate is set.

Forward Propagation:

- Compute activations for the hidden and output layers.

- Calculate the loss using Mean Squared Error (MSE).

Backward Propagation:

- Gradients for the output layer are computed based on the loss and sigmoid derivative.
- Propagate errors to the hidden layer and compute gradients for weights and biases.

Parameter Updates:

- Use gradient descent to update weights and biases.

Master said, “Nikash, let us understand the code with an optimisation loop that includes early stopping. Early stopping halts the training process when the validation loss stops improving for a specified number of epochs (patience). This prevents overfitting and unnecessary computation.”

Example P1 – U1 – D10	
Epochs	**Output**

import numpy as np
 	
# Sigmoid activation function 	
def sigmoid(x):
   return 1 / (1 + np.exp(-x))
 	
# Derivative of sigmoid 	
def sigmoid_derivative(x):
   return sigmoid(x) * (1 - sigmoid(x))
 	
# Initialize weights and biases 	
weights_input_hidden = np.array([[0.15, 0.20], [0.25, 0.30]]) # 2x2 matrix for input-to-hidden weights
bias_hidden = np.array([0.35, 0.35]) # Bias for hidden layer
 	
weights_hidden_output = np.array([[0.40, 0.45], [0.50, 0.55]]) # 2x2 matrix for hidden-to-output weights
bias_output = np.array([0.60, 0.60]) # Bias for output layer
	Epoch 1: Loss = 0.303658
	Epoch 1001: Loss = 0.055529
	Epoch 2001: Loss = 0.021103
	Epoch 3001: Loss = 0.012215
	Epoch 4001: Loss = 0.008353
	Epoch 5001: Loss = 0.006236
	Epoch 6001: Loss = 0.004915
	Epoch 7001: Loss = 0.004019
	Epoch 8001: Loss = 0.003375
	Epoch 9001: Loss = 0.002893

# Inputs and expected outputs 	
inputs = np.array([0.05, 0.10])   # Input features
expected_outputs = np.array([0.01, 0.99]) # Target outputs
 	
# Hyperparameters 	
learning_rate = 0.01
max_epochs = 10000
patience = 100 # Stop training if validation loss does not improve for 100 epochs
tolerance = 1e-6 # Minimum improvement in loss to reset patience
 	
# Variables for early stopping 	
best_loss = float('inf')
epochs_without_improvement = 0
 	
# Training loop 	
for epoch in range(max_epochs):
    # ---- FORWARD PROPAGATION ----
    # Hidden layer computations
    z_hidden = np.dot(inputs, weights_input_hidden) + bias_hidden
    a_hidden = sigmoid(z_hidden)
 	
    # Output layer computations
    z_output = np.dot(a_hidden, weights_hidden_output) + bias_output
    a_output = sigmoid(z_output)
 	
    # Compute loss (mean squared error)
    loss = 0.5 * np.sum((expected_outputs - a_output) ** 2)
 	
    # ---- BACKWARD PROPAGATION ----
    # Gradients at the output layer
    error_output = a_output - expected_outputs
    grad_output = error_output * sigmoid_derivative(z_output)
 	
    # Gradients for weights and biases in the hidden-to-output layer
    grad_weights_hidden_output = np.outer(a_hidden, grad_output) # Outer product for weight gradients
    grad_bias_output = grad_output
 	
    # Gradients at the hidden layer
	Epoch 10000: Loss = 0.002520
	
	Final Results:
	Optimized weights (input to hidden):
	[[0.16334747 0.21179162]
	 [0.27669494 0.32358324]]
	Optimized biases (hidden):
	[0.6169494 0.58583239]
	Optimized weights (hidden to output):
	[[-0.91786037 0.97630956]
	 [-0.81219198 1.07329213]]
	Optimized biases (output):
	[-1.57109602 1.45392008]
	Final loss: 0.002520

```
    error_hidden = np.dot(grad_output,
weights_hidden_output.T)
    grad_hidden = error_hidden *
sigmoid_derivative(z_hidden)

    # Gradients for weights and biases in the input-to-
hidden layer
    grad_weights_input_hidden = np.outer(inputs,
grad_hidden)  # Outer product for weight gradients
    grad_bias_hidden = grad_hidden

    # ---- UPDATE WEIGHTS AND BIASES ----
    weights_hidden_output -= learning_rate *
grad_weights_hidden_output
    bias_output -= learning_rate * grad_bias_output

    weights_input_hidden -= learning_rate *
grad_weights_input_hidden
    bias_hidden -= learning_rate * grad_bias_hidden

    # ---- EARLY STOPPING ----
    if loss < best_loss - tolerance:
        best_loss = loss
        epochs_without_improvement = 0  # Reset patience
counter
    else:
        epochs_without_improvement += 1

    if epochs_without_improvement >= patience:
        print(f"Early stopping at epoch {epoch + 1} with
best loss {best_loss:.6f}")
        break

    # Print progress every 1000 epochs
    if epoch % 1000 == 0 or epoch == max_epochs - 1:
        print(f"Epoch {epoch + 1}: Loss = {loss:.6f}")

# Final results
print("\nFinal Results:")
print(f"Optimized weights (input to hidden):
\n{weights_input_hidden}")
print(f"Optimized biases (hidden): {bias_hidden}")
print(f"Optimized weights (hidden to output):
\n{weights_hidden_output}")
print(f"Optimized biases (output): {bias_output}")
print(f"Final loss: {best_loss:.6f}")
```

Early Stopping:

- Stops training when the loss does not improve for a specified number of epochs (patience).
- Prevents overfitting and unnecessary computation.

Progress Tracking:

- Prints loss every 1000 epochs for monitoring.
- Final optimized parameters and loss are displayed.

Dynamic Training:

- Automatically adjusts based on the loss tolerance to avoid getting stuck in minimal improvements.

PART ONE

DAY THREE

Unit 2 - Lesson Three

Layers of Intelligence

☐ **Weight Initiation Technique:**

Master said, "Akshay, Weight initialisation is a critical component in training deep neural networks, as it significantly affects the convergence speed and performance of the model."

Here's a detailed breakdown of the mathematical intuition behind deep learning weight initialisation and activation functions:

Why does initialisation matter?

In deep learning, weights need to be initialised properly to:

- Break Symmetry: If all weights are initialised to the same value (e.g., zeros), every neuron in the same layer will learn the same features, leading to inefficiency and poor convergence.
- Maintain Variance: Proper initialisation ensures that the variance of activations and gradients stays balanced across layers, preventing issues like vanishing or exploding gradients.

Variance of Weights

The variance of initialised weights ensures that the signal propagates properly through the network:

- Small Variance: Leads to smaller activations, possibly vanishing gradients.
- Large Variance: Leads to larger activations, possibly exploding gradients.

The goal of weight initialisation techniques is to find a balance, ensuring that the variance of activations is stable across layers.

Activation Functions and Their Role

Master explained that the Activation functions, like ReLU or Tanh, transform inputs and add non-linearity to the network. Each activation function interacts differently with the weight initialisation:

ReLU (Rectified Linear Unit)

Property: Outputs zero for negative inputs and a linear function for positive inputs.

Problem: ReLU causes neurons to die (output remains zero) if weights aren't initialised properly.

Solution: The initialisation.

Tanh (Hyperbolic Tangent)

Property: Outputs values between -1 and 1, centred at zero, leading to better gradients for certain tasks.

Problem: Outputs saturate near -1 or 1, causing vanishing gradients if initialisation isn't balanced.

Solution: Xavier Initialisation.

Weight Initialization Techniques

Case one: He Initialization (for ReLU and its variants)

Formula:

$$w \sim N(0, \frac{2}{n_{in}})$$

Where n_{in} is the number of inputs to the layer.

Intuition: Ensures the variance of activations remains stable across layers by scaling with $\sqrt{\frac{2}{n_{in}}}$, accounting for ReLU's tendency to zero out negative values.

Example in NumPy:

```
W = np.random.randn(size) * np.sqrt(2 / n_in)
```

Case two: Xavier Initialisation (for Tanh and Sigmoid)

Formula:

$$\boldsymbol{w} \sim \boldsymbol{N}(0, \frac{1}{n_{in}}) \text{ or } \boldsymbol{w} \sim \boldsymbol{N}(0, \frac{2}{n_{in} + n_{out}})$$

Where nin and nout are the number of inputs and outputs, respectively.

Intuition: Balances the variance between inputs and outputs by scaling with $\sqrt{\frac{1}{n_{in}}}$ or $\sqrt{\frac{2}{n_{in} + n_{out}}}$, preventing saturation in Tanh/Sigmoid.

Example in NumPy:

```
W = np.random.randn(size) * np.sqrt(1 / n_in)
```

Initialisation	**Best For**	**Key Goal**
He	ReLU	Avoid dying ReLU neurons
Xavier	Tanh	Balance variance, avoid saturation

Practical Implementation

In frameworks like TensorFlow or PyTorch, these initialisations are built-in:

TensorFlow:

```
Use tf.keras.initializers.HeNormal() or tf.keras.initializers.GlorotUniform()
```

PyTorch:

```
Use torch.nn.init.kaiming_normal_() or torch.nn.init.xavier_normal_()
```

Proper weight initialization combined with an appropriate activation function ensures smoother training and faster convergence of deep neural networks.

Activation Function:

Sam asked, "Master, what is an activation function in deep learning?"

The net input to a neuron is calculated as:

net input = ∑(weight * input) + bias

Master said, "Sam, this value can range anywhere from negative infinity to positive infinity. Without guidance, the neuron wouldn't know how to respond or 'fire' effectively. This is where the activation function becomes crucial in an artificial neural network. It determines whether a neuron should be activated or not, effectively bounding the net input and enabling the neuron to make decisions."

An activation function applies a non-linear transformation to the input before passing it to the next layer or finalising it as output. By doing this, it introduces complexity, allowing the network to learn and model intricate patterns. Without activation functions, deep learning models would behave as simple linear models, unable to solve more complex problems.

Akshaya asked, "What are the types of activation functions?"

Types of Activation Functions:

Master explained that activation functions can be broadly classified into two categories:

Linear Activation Function:

In a linear activation function, the output is proportional to the input, meaning the function is a simple linear transformation. While easy to understand, it has significant limitations since it cannot introduce non-linearity, making it difficult for the model to solve complex problems. Linear activation functions are rarely used in deep learning because they fail to capture intricate patterns in data.

Non-linear Activation Functions:

Non-linear activation functions are the backbone of deep learning models. They allow the network to learn complex patterns and generalize effectively with diverse datasets. Unlike linear functions, non-linear functions can model intricate relationships and differentiate between classes more efficiently.

Non-linear activation functions, like ReLU (Rectified Linear Unit), have been proven to speed up training significantly, especially in larger networks, due to their simplicity and efficiency. ReLU outputs zero for negative inputs and passes positive values as they are, which helps avoid saturation and accelerates convergence.

Non-linearity means that the output cannot be derived from a linear combination of the inputs, making these functions essential for tasks that require complex decision boundaries.

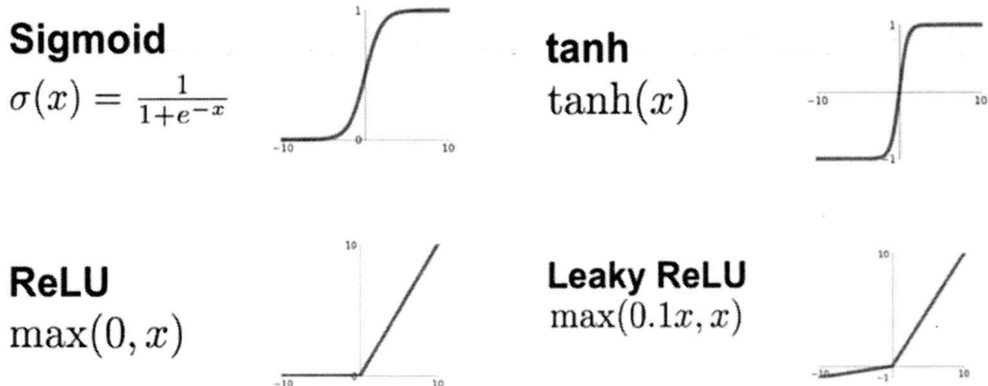

Illustration – P6_Activation

The main terminologies to understand for non-linear functions are:

- ReLU (Rectified Linear Unit)
- Sigmoid
- Tanh

- Leaky ReLU
- Softmax

These functions each have unique properties that make them suitable for different types of tasks within deep learning models.

Sigmoid Activation Function:

Also known as the Logistic Activation Function or Binary Classifier, the sigmoid function outputs values between 0 and 1, making it suitable for binary classification problems. The function behaves similarly to a step function but provides smooth transitions. When the input $z = 0$, the sigmoid outputs 0.5. Rules can be set, such as: if the output is greater than or equal to 0.5, it's classified as 1 (True); otherwise, it's classified as 0 (False). One of the key advantages of the sigmoid function is that it is differentiable everywhere, making it suitable for gradient-based optimisation. However, it can suffer from vanishing gradients, making learning slow in deeper networks.

ReLU (Rectified Linear Unit):

ReLU is the most widely used activation function, especially in convolutional neural networks. It's simple—outputting the input directly if it's positive, and zero otherwise. ReLU is partially rectified at the bottom, meaning for inputs $z \leq 0$, the output is 0. It has many benefits, such as faster training for large networks due to its simplicity and similarity to linear functions. However, it can suffer from the "dying ReLU" problem, where neurons stop learning because the gradient is zero for negative inputs.

Leaky ReLU:

Leaky ReLU is an improvement on the standard ReLU to address the "dying ReLU" problem. Instead of setting the gradient to 0 for inputs less than 0, Leaky ReLU allows a small, non-zero gradient by introducing a small slope for negative inputs (typically 0.01). This helps neurons stay active and continue learning even when the input is negative, preventing the dead neuron issue.

Tanh (Hyperbolic Tangent):

The tanh function maps input values to the range [-1, 1], unlike the sigmoid which maps to [0, 1]. Like sigmoid, tanh also saturates for large positive or negative inputs, but it is zero-centered, which makes optimization easier in certain cases. This means that the negative inputs will be strongly negative, positive inputs will be strongly positive, and zero inputs will map near zero. Tanh is often preferred over sigmoid because of its zero-centered nature, allowing for better performance in many deep learning tasks.

Softmax:
Softmax is used primarily in classification problems with multiple classes. While the sigmoid function is suitable for binary classification, softmax is ideal for multi-class problems. It normalises the output of each neuron to be between 0 and 1, just like a sigmoid, but also ensures that the sum of all outputs is equal to 1, making it behave like a probability distribution. The output of softmax tells you the probability of each class being the correct one, which makes it perfect for the final layer in multi-class classification models.

□ ANN Learn

Sam asked, "How do Artificial Neural Networks learn?"

Master said, "Artificial neural networks (ANNs) learn through a process of training on a dataset. For instance, if you want to train an ANN to recognise cats, you would provide it with thousands of images of cats."

Here's how the learning process works:

Training Set: The ANN is fed a large number of cat images. Each image serves as an input that the network uses to learn the features and patterns associated with cats.

Learning Phase: During training, the network processes each image and adjusts its internal parameters (weights and biases) to minimize the difference between its predictions and the actual labels (whether the image is of a cat or not).

Classification: After sufficient training, the ANN is tested on a separate set of images to evaluate its ability to correctly classify new images as either containing a cat or not.

Output Validation: The network's predictions are compared against the true labels provided by humans. This comparison helps in calculating the error rate, which indicates how often the ANN's predictions are incorrect.

Backpropagation: When the ANN makes incorrect predictions, backpropagation is used to adjust the network's parameters. This involves:

- Calculating the error (difference between predicted and actual outcomes).
- Propagating this error backwards through the network.
- Fine-tuning the weights of the connections between the neurons to reduce the error.

Iteration: The training and backpropagation steps are repeated multiple times. With each iteration, the ANN adjusts its parameters and improves its ability to recognise cats with minimal errors.

Convergence: The process continues until the ANN achieves a satisfactory level of accuracy, correctly identifying cats in images with minimal error rates.

This iterative training process enables the ANN to learn complex patterns and features from the input data, ultimately allowing it to make accurate predictions on new, unseen data.

□ Types of Artificial Neural Networks

Feedforward Neural Network (FNN)

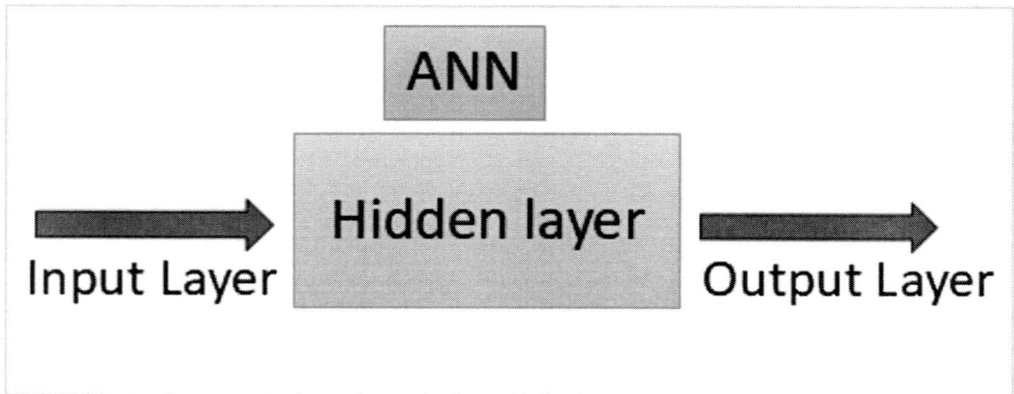

Illustration P6_Types_Network_ANN

A feedforward neural network is the simplest type of artificial neural network. In this ANN, data flows in one direction—from the input layer through any hidden layers to the output layer. There is no feedback or backpropagation, meaning the network does not adjust its parameters based on the output. Feedforward networks are foundational to many AI applications but are limited in handling more complex patterns.

Convolutional Neural Network (CNN)

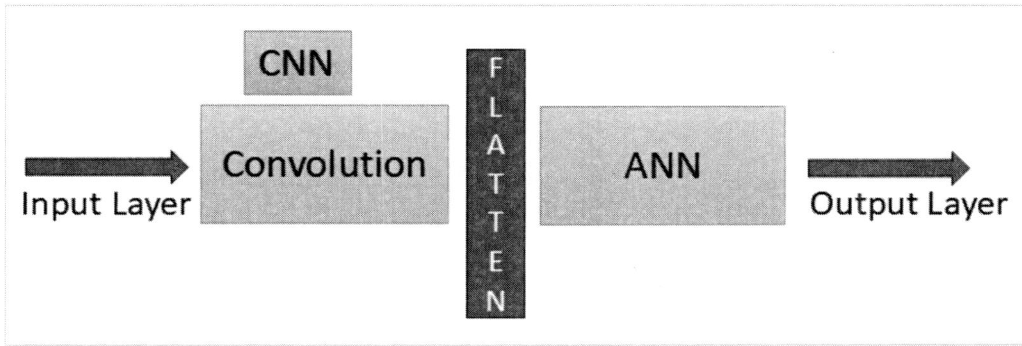

Illustration P6_Types_Network_CNN

CNNs build upon the feedforward neural network structure, adding convolutional layers that apply convolution operations to the input. These layers capture spatial hierarchies in data, making CNNs particularly effective for image and speech-processing tasks. Widely used in computer vision, CNNs excel at recognizing patterns such as edges, textures, and objects in visual data.

Recurrent Neural Network (RNN)

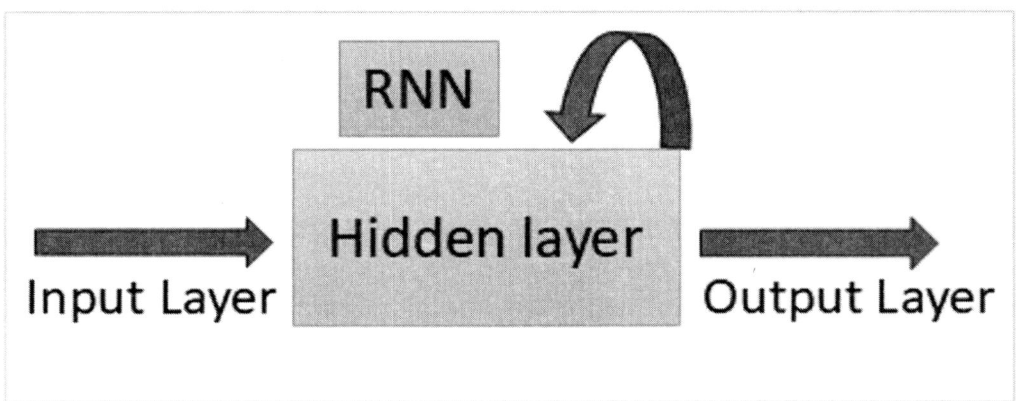

Illustration P6_Types_Network_RNN

RNNs introduce feedback loops that allow the network to retain information from previous steps, effectively giving the model a "memory." This feature makes RNNs ideal for sequential data, such as time-series predictions or natural language processing, where the order of information is critical.

Radial Basis Function Neural Network (RBFNN)

RBFNNs use radial basis functions as activation functions in the hidden layer. These networks map inputs into a higher-dimensional space, making them effective for classification tasks where the data is not linearly separable. RBFNNs are commonly used for function approximation, time-series prediction, and control systems.

Modular Neural Network (MNN)

Modular neural networks consist of multiple independent neural networks that each perform a sub-task. The lack of interaction between the networks allows them to operate more efficiently by focusing on smaller, specialised problems. This structure reduces complexity and enhances scalability for large computational processes.

Generative Adversarial Network (GAN)

GANs consist of two competing neural networks—a generator and a discriminator. The generator creates synthetic data, while the discriminator evaluates whether the data is real or fake. Through this adversarial process, GANs excel at generating highly realistic images, videos, and even text. They are widely used in creative applications like image synthesis, style transfer, and data augmentation.

Reinforcement Learning with Neural Networks (Deep RL)

In reinforcement learning, an agent learns by interacting with its environment and receiving feedback in the form of rewards or penalties. When neural networks are combined with reinforcement learning, as seen in Deep Q-Networks (DQNs) or Proximal Policy Optimisation (PPO), they become capable of mastering complex tasks such as game playing, robotics, and autonomous driving. These models learn optimal policies that maximise cumulative rewards over time, adapting dynamically to their environments.

Each type of neural network has its unique strengths and applications, allowing for tailored solutions to a variety of complex problems in fields ranging from image recognition to natural language processing.

Master said, "John, to create a simple artificial neural network (ANN) for the diabetes dataset using TensorFlow and Keras, follow these steps."

Step 1: Load the Dataset

Ensure that the data is properly loaded and preprocessed.

Model Structure:

```
from keras.models import Sequential
```

This imports the Sequential class, which is a simple and intuitive way to build deep learning models in Keras.

- Sequential is a linear stack of layers, meaning the model's architecture is built layer by layer, where each layer flows sequentially into the next.
- It is suitable for models where layers are connected in a straightforward sequence without branching or skipping.

```
from keras.layers import Dense
```

This imports the Dense class, which is a core layer in Keras for building fully connected (dense) layers in a neural network.

- A dense layer is a layer where every neuron in the layer is connected to every neuron in the previous layer.
- Dense layers are typically used in feedforward neural networks.

Parameters of Dense:

- units: Number of neurons in the layer.
- activation: Activation function applied to the layer (e.g., relu, sigmoid).

input_dim: Specifies the number of input features (only needed for the first layer).

Example P1 – U1 – D11	
ANN	**Output**
import pandas as pd import numpy as np	accuracy: 0.8505 - loss: 0.3343

```
from sklearn.model_selection import train_test_split
from sklearn.preprocessing import StandardScaler
from keras.models import Sequential
from keras.layers import Dense

# Load the dataset
path =
r'C:\Users\User\mraj4\Documents\Optimum\Py-
lib\scikit\Part5\diabetes.csv'
data = pd.read_csv(path)

# Separate features and target
X = data.iloc[:, :-1].values  # Features (all columns except
the last)
y = data.iloc[:, -1].values   # Target (last column -
Outcome)

# Split the dataset into training and testing sets
X_train, X_test, y_train, y_test = train_test_split(X, y,
test_size=0.2, random_state=42)

# Standardize the features (scaling)
scaler = StandardScaler()
X_train = scaler.fit_transform(X_train)
X_test = scaler.transform(X_test)

# Create the Sequential model
model = Sequential()

# Add layers to the model
model.add(Dense(12, input_dim=8, activation='relu'))  #
First hidden layer (12 nodes)
model.add(Dense(8, activation='relu'))              # Second
hidden layer (8 nodes)
model.add(Dense(1, activation='sigmoid'))           #
Output layer (1 node, sigmoid activation for binary
classification)

# Compile the model
model.compile(optimizer='adam',
loss='binary_crossentropy', metrics=['accuracy'])

# Train the model
history = model.fit(X_train, y_train, epochs=150,
batch_size=10, verbose=1)

# Evaluate the model
loss, accuracy = model.evaluate(X_test, y_test, verbose=0)
```

```
print(f"Test Accuracy: {accuracy:.2f}")

# Optional: Save the model
model.save('diabetes_model.h5')
```

Input Layer: input_dim=8 matches the 8 features in the dataset.

Hidden Layers:

- First layer: 12 nodes with ReLU activation.
- Second layer: 8 nodes with ReLU activation.

Output Layer: A single node with a sigmoid activation for binary classification.

Loss Function:

The parameter loss= 'binary_crossentropy' is used when compiling a machine learning model in Keras for binary classification tasks. It specifies the loss function the model will optimize during training.

Optimizer:

The parameter optimizer = 'adam' specifies the Adam optimizer as the optimization algorithm for training the neural network. Adam (short for Adaptive Moment Estimation) is one of the most popular and efficient optimization algorithms used in deep learning.

Metrics:

The parameter metrics=['accuracy'] specifies that the accuracy of the model should be monitored during training and evaluation.

Training:

- Epochs: 150 iterations over the dataset.
- Batch Size: 10 samples are processed before updating the model's weights.

Save and Reload the Model:

```
model.save('diabetes_model.h5')
```

Reload it later for predictions:

```
from keras.models import load_model
model = load_model('diabetes_model.h5')
predictions = model.predict(X_test)
```

Apeksha asked, "Why do we use Standard Scalar?"

Master said, "The StandardScaler is used to standardize (normalize) the features of your dataset, ensuring that they have a mean of 0 and a standard deviation of 1."

Improves Training Stability:

Any machine learning algorithms (especially neural networks) perform better when the input features are standardized. This helps avoid numerical instability and ensures faster convergence during training.

Handles Features of Different Scales:

When features have vastly different ranges (e.g., one feature ranges from 0 to 1000 while another ranges from 0 to 1), the model may assign more importance to the larger-range feature. Standardization prevents this issue.

Helps Gradient Descent:

Standardization ensures the gradient steps during optimization are even, avoiding issues like vanishing or exploding gradients.

How does StandardScaler work?

The StandardScaler transforms the data using the following formula:

$$Z = \frac{X-\mu}{\sigma}$$

Where:

- X is the original feature value.
- μ is the mean of the feature (calculated from the training set).
- σ is the standard deviation of the feature (calculated from the training set).
- Z is the standardised value.

After standardisation:

- The feature will have a mean of 0.
- The feature will have a standard deviation of 1.

Example P1 – U1 – D12	
Standard Scalar	**Output**

from sklearn.preprocessing import StandardScaler
import numpy as np
# Example dataset 	
data = np.array([[50, 2000], [30, 1000], [40, 1500]])
 	
# Create a StandardScaler instance 	
scaler = StandardScaler()
 	
# Fit the scaler on the data and transform it 	
standardized_data = scaler.fit_transform(data)
print("Original Data:")
print(data)
print("\nStandardized Data:")
print(standardized_data)
	Original Data:
	[[50 2000]
	 [30 1000]
	 [40 1500]]
	
	Standardized Data:
	[[1.22474487 1.22474487]
	 [-1.22474487 -1.22474487]
	 [0. 0.]]

```
from sklearn.preprocessing import StandardScaler
```

Master said, "Let us understand the code snippet for Standard Scalar."

Common Steps When Using StandardScaler

- fit(): Computes the mean and standard deviation for each feature in the training data.
- transform(): Applies the standardisation formula to the dataset.
- fit_transform(): Combines both fit() and transform() into a single step.

Understand the workflow:

Example P1 – U1 – D13	
Standard Scalar	**Output**

from sklearn.preprocessing import StandardScaler
from sklearn.model_selection import train_test_split
 	
# Example dataset 	
X = [[50, 2000], [30, 1000], [40, 1500]]
y = [1, 0, 1]
 	
# Split into training and testing sets 	
X_train, X_test, y_train, y_test = train_test_split(X, y, test_size=0.2, random_state=42)
 	
# Create StandardScaler instance 	
scaler = StandardScaler()
 	
# Fit only on the training data and transform both sets 	
X_train_scaled = scaler.fit_transform(X_train)
X_test_scaled = scaler.transform(X_test)
 	
print("Standardized Training Data:", X_train_scaled)
print("Standardized Testing Data:", X_test_scaled)
	Standardized Training Data: [[-1. -1.]
	[1. 1.]]
	Standardized Testing Data:
	[[3. 3.]]

Key Notes

Only fit on training data: Always fit the scaler using the training set to avoid data leakage. Then transform both training and testing data using the same scaler.

When to use: Standardisation is particularly important for models sensitive to feature scaling, such as:

- Neural Networks (e.g., using TensorFlow/Keras).
- Logistic Regression, Support Vector Machines (SVMs).
- PCA (Principal Component Analysis).

When not needed: Tree-based models like Decision Trees, Random Forests, and Gradient Boosting generally do not require standardisation.

Loss Functions: MSE, Cross Entropy

John asked, "Master, what is a loss function in deep learning?"

The loss function in deep learning is a crucial component that measures how well a neural network's predictions align with the actual target values. It quantifies the difference between the predicted output and the true output, guiding the model during training to minimise this error. Essentially, it tells the model how far off its predictions are, so the model can adjust its parameters (weights and biases) accordingly.

There are different types of loss functions depending on the task:

Mean Squared Error (MSE): Commonly used in regression problems, it calculates the average squared difference between predicted and actual values. Smaller values indicate more accurate predictions.

Cross-Entropy Loss: Typically used for classification tasks, it measures the distance between two probability distributions—the predicted probability and the actual label (0 or 1 in binary classification, or a set of probabilities in multi-class classification).

Hinge Loss: Often used for training support vector machines (SVMs), hinge loss is used for "maximum-margin" classification, ensuring a wide margin between classes.

By minimising the loss function during training through optimisation techniques like gradient descent, the model learns to improve its predictions over time and generalise better to new, unseen data.

John asked, "Master explain in detail the Binary Cross-Entropy?"

Master said, "The **Binary Cross-Entropy** loss function measures the difference between the predicted probabilities ($\hat{y}$) and the actual target labels (y) for binary classification."

It is defined as:

inary Cross-Entropy Loss $= \frac{1}{N}\sum_{i=1}^{N}[\, y_i * \log(\hat{y}_i) + (1 - y_i) * \log(1 - \hat{y}_i)]$

Where:

- N: Number of samples in the dataset.
- y_i: True label for sample i (0 or 1).
- $\hat{y}_i$: Predicted probability for sample i (output of the sigmoid function).
- log: Natural logarithm.

Explanation of the Formula

$$y_i * \log(\hat{y}_i)$$

- If the true label is $y_i = 1$, the focus is on the term $\log(\hat{y}_i)$.
- Encourages the model to output probabilities close to 1 for true positive samples.

$$(1 - y_i) * \log(1 - \hat{y}_i)$$

- If the true label is $y_i = 0$, the focus is on the term l $\log(1 - \hat{y}_i)$.
- Encourages the model to output probabilities close to 0 for true negative samples.

Negative Log Likelihood:

The negative sign ensures the loss is minimised when the model's predictions are accurate.

Why Use Binary Cross-Entropy?

Designed for Binary Classification:

- Binary cross-entropy is suitable for tasks where the output is binary (e.g., 0 or 1).

Probabilistic Outputs:

It works well with models that output probabilities, such as the output layer with sigmoid activation:

$$\hat{y}_i = \text{sigmoid}(z) = \frac{1}{1+e^{-z}}$$

The sigmoid ensures that predicted values are in the range [0,1], representing probabilities.

Handles Class Imbalance:

- Binary cross-entropy is robust even in datasets where positive and negative labels are imbalanced.

When Not to Use Binary Cross-Entropy

- For Multi-Class Classification: Use categorical_crossentropy (when targets are one-hot encoded) or sparse_categorical_crossentropy (when targets are integer-labeled).
- For Regression Tasks: Use losses like Mean Squared Error (MSE) or Mean Absolute Error (MAE) instead.

Optimiser

Akshaya asked, "What is an Optimizer in deep learning?"

Masters said, "An optimizer adjusts the weights and biases of the neural network during training to minimise the loss function. It uses the gradients of the loss function (calculated via backpropagation) to update the model parameters."

Nikash asked, "Why do we need SGD?"

Master replied, "Gradient descent is a foundational iterative algorithm. It begins at a random point on a function and methodically descends its slope, step by step, until it reaches the lowest point of that function—a process we call optimization."

The Need for Stochastic Gradient Descent (SGD)

While gradient descent is powerful, it comes with certain challenges, especially when working with large datasets. Let's delve deeper.

Consider this: if we have 10,000 data points and 10 features, the sum of squared residuals for our model will involve 10,000 terms. To optimise, we need to compute the derivative of this function for each feature, amounting to 10,000 × 10 = 100,000 computations per iteration.

Now, if the algorithm requires 1,000 iterations to converge, that's 100,000 × 1,000 = 100 million computations in total. For large datasets, this computational overhead makes gradient descent both slow and resource-intensive.

This is where **Stochastic Gradient Descent (SGD)** saves the day. The term "stochastic" essentially means "random," and it introduces a game-changing idea: instead of calculating derivatives using the entire dataset at each iteration, we randomly select a **single data point** to perform the calculation.

This randomness drastically reduces the computations required. Instead of processing all 10,000 data points per step, SGD only processes one.

Mini-Batch Gradient Descent

While SGD is fast, it can sometimes be noisy because of the randomness of selecting just one data point. To address this, we use a variation called mini-batch gradient descent, which samples a small subset of data points (a mini-batch) at each iteration. This approach strikes a balance:

- Speed: Mini-batch computations are faster than full-batch gradient descent.
- Stability: The averaging effect of using a mini-batch reduces the noise of pure SGD.

Thus, SGD and its variants enable us to efficiently train models, especially when handling massive datasets, making them indispensable in modern machine learning.

SGD with Momentum

When training models with gradient descent, especially on surfaces with steep slopes and narrow valleys, the algorithm often "bounces" around the minima. This behaviour is caused by the uniform learning rate, which might either overshoot or make convergence painfully slow.

Momentum solves this by accumulating past gradients to provide direction, effectively "smoothing" the path toward the minima.

Revised Equations with Momentum

The standard update rule for gradient descent is:

$$w_{t+1} = w_t - \eta \nabla f(w_t)$$

Here:

- w_t: Current weights.
- η: Learning rate.
- $\nabla f(w_t)$: Gradient of the loss function.

With momentum, we modify this as:

Update the velocity (momentum term):

$$v_{t+1} = \gamma v_t - \eta \nabla f(w_t)$$

Update the weights using velocity:

$$w_{t+1} = w_t + v_{t+1}$$

Here:

- vt: Accumulated velocity at step t.
- γ: Momentum coefficient (commonly between 0.5 and 0.9).

How It Works

- The velocity term (vt) integrates the gradient over past steps.
- Momentum dampens oscillations along steep slopes and accelerates the descent along flat regions.

Example

Imagine a deep learning model training on a dataset with gradients like:

$\nabla f(w_t) = [-3, 4, -2, 1]$

With η=0.01 and γ=0.9, the velocity and weight updates for the first few steps might look like this:

$v_0 = 0$.

Compute v1: v1 = 0.9*0 − 0.01 [−3, 4, −2, 1] = [0.03, −0.04, 0.02, −0.01]

Update weights: $w_1 = w_0 + v_1$

The accumulation of gradients helps the weights stabilise faster and converge more smoothly.

Akshaya asked, “Master, what is the Adam Optimizer?”

Adam is an advanced optimization algorithm that combines the benefits of two widely used optimizers:

- Momentum: Helps accelerate learning by considering the direction of the previous gradients.
- RMSProp (Root Mean Square Propagation): Adjusts the learning rate for each parameter based on the magnitude of recent gradients.

Key Features of Adam:

- Maintains adaptive learning rates for each parameter (different weights can have different learning rates).
- Efficient in terms of computation and memory usage.
- Works well for both large and small datasets.
- Combines the best properties of momentum and adaptive gradient methods.

Adam Algorithm in a Nutshell

Adam (Adaptive Moment Estimation) extends momentum by including adaptive learning rates, computed from the first moment (mean of gradients) and second moment (uncentered variance of gradients).

The Adam optimiser updates each parameter θt or wt as follows:

Gradient Calculation:

Compute gradients

$$g_t = \nabla_\theta J(\theta_t) \text{ or } g_t = \nabla f(w_t)$$

- gt: Gradient of the loss function $J(\theta_t)$ w.r.t. θ.

Update biased moment estimates:

First moment (mean): Momentum Term (Exponential Moving Average of Gradients).

$$m_t = \beta_1 * m_{t-1} + (1-\beta_1)\, g_t$$

- m_t : Moving average of gradients (1st moment estimate).

- β_1: Decay rate for the momentum term (default: 0.9).

Second moment (uncentered variance): RMS Term (Exponential Moving Average of Squared Gradients):

$$v_t = \beta_2 \cdot v_{t-1} + (1-\beta^2) \cdot g_t^2$$

- v_t : Moving average of squared gradients (2nd moment estimate)..
- β_2: Decay rate for the RMS term (default: 0.999).

Bias-Corrected Estimates:

Corrected first moment:

Correct bias introduced in early iterations due to initialisation of m_t and v_t:

$$\widehat{m}_t = \frac{m_t}{1-\beta 1^{\,t}}$$

Corrected second moment:

$$\hat{v}_t = \frac{v_t}{1-\beta 2^{\,t}}$$

Here:

- $\beta 1$ (default: 0.9) controls the decay rate of the first moment.
- $\beta 2$ (default: 0.999) controls the decay rate of the second moment.

Parameter Update Rule:

$$\theta_{t+1} = \theta_t - \eta * \frac{\widehat{m}_t}{(\sqrt{\hat{v}_t})+(\epsilon)}$$

- η: Learning rate (default: 0.001).
- ϵ: Small value added for numerical stability (default: 10^{-8}).

Example

Suppose a model experiences varying gradients over parameters:

$g_t = [0.1, -0.05, 0.2]$

With $\eta = 0.001$, $\beta_1 = 0.9$, $\beta_2 = 0.999$, $\epsilon=10^{-8}$

- Compute m_t, v_t and their bias-corrected versions.
- Update the weights using the adaptive learning rates.

By dynamically adjusting learning rates, Adam ensures faster and more stable convergence, particularly for deep neural networks.

Nikash asked, "Master, why choose Adam?"

Efficient Learning:

- Automatically adjusts the learning rate for each parameter during training.
- Faster convergence compared to other optimizers like SGD (Stochastic Gradient Descent).

Works Well Across Models:

- Suitable for a wide range of tasks: binary classification, multi-class classification, regression, etc.
- Performs well with deep networks, CNNs, RNNs, and transformers.

Robust to Noisy Data:

- Handles noisy gradients effectively due to its adaptive nature.

Minimal Hyperparameter Tuning:

- Default parameters (η=0.001, β_1=0.9, β_2=0.999, $\epsilon=10^{-8}$) work well in most cases.

Comparison with other optimizers:

Optimizer	Key Feature	Pros	Cons
SGD	Fixed learning rate	Simple, widely used	Requires manual learning rate tuning

SGD with Momentum	Adds momentum to accelerate convergence	Faster than vanilla SGD	May overshoot minima
RMSprop	Scales the learning rate by recent gradient magnitudes	Good for non-stationary objectives	Can get stuck in local minima
Adam	Combines Momentum + RMSProp	Fast, robust, widely used	Slightly heavier computation

Apeksha asked, "What is the difference between Adagrad and RMSPROP?"

Adagrad (Adaptive Gradient Algorithm)

Master said, "Adagrad is an adaptive learning rate method designed to handle sparse data and improve convergence for models with infrequent updates."

Key Features:

Per-Parameter Learning Rates:

Adagrad adjusts the learning rate for each parameter based on the magnitude of past gradients. Frequently updated parameters receive smaller updates, while infrequently updated ones get larger updates.

Update Rule:

The learning rate for each parameter η is scaled by the sum of the squares of all past gradients.

$$w_{t+1} = w_t - \frac{\eta}{\sqrt{G_{t,ii} + \epsilon}} \nabla f(w_t)$$

Where:

- $G_{t,ii} = \sum_{k=1}^{t} (\nabla f_k(w))^2$: Accumulated squared gradients for parameter i.
- ϵ: Small constant to avoid division by zero.

Pros:

- Excellent for sparse data (e.g., text, click-through rates).
- Automatically adjusts the learning rate for each parameter.

Cons:

- Learning rate continuously decays, which can lead to overly small updates and eventual stagnation.

RMSProp (Root Mean Square Propagation)

RMSProp improves upon Adagrad by addressing the issue of decaying learning rates.

Key Features:

Exponential Moving Average of Gradients:

Instead of summing all past squared gradients, RMSProp uses an exponentially weighted average.

Update Rule:

$$w_{t+1} = w_t - \frac{\eta}{\sqrt{E[g^2]_t + \epsilon}} \nabla f(w_t)$$

Where:

- $E[g^2]_t = \beta E[g^2]_{t-1} + (1-\beta)(\nabla f(w_t))^2$: Exponentially weighted moving average of squared gradients.
- β: Decay rate (commonly set to 0.9).

Pros:

- Prevents the learning rate from decaying too quickly, ensuring stable and faster convergence.
- Works well for non-convex problems, especially in deep learning.

Cons:

- Slightly more complex to implement compared to Adagrad.

Feature	Adagrad	RMSProp

Learning Rate Adjustment	Scales down learning rates for frequently updated parameters.	Keeps a balanced adjustment using moving averages.
Learning Rate Decay	Continuous decay (can become too small).	Controlled decay via exponential moving averages.
Handling of Sparse Data	Excellent for sparse features	Not as effective as Adagrad for sparse data.
Use Case	Sparse data or convex optimization.	Non-convex problems (e.g., neural networks).
Implementation	Simpler.	Slightly more computationally intensive.

Practical Example

Adagrad:
Consider training a logistic regression model on text data, where certain features (e.g., rare words) appear infrequently. Adagrad adjusts the learning rates dynamically to ensure rare features are updated more effectively.

RMSProp:
Imagine training a deep neural network. RMSProp stabilises the optimisation by preventing oscillations and ensuring steady learning, especially when gradients vary significantly across parameters.

Sam asked, "Master, what is accuracy?"

Accuracy is a common evaluation metric for classification tasks, which measures the percentage of correct predictions made by the model. It is defined as:

```
Accuracy = Number of Correct Predictions / Total Number of Predictions
```

For binary classification, it works as:

```
Accuracy = True Positives + True Negatives / Total Samples
```

For multi-class classification, it follows the same principle but accounts for multiple classes.

Apeksha asked "Why use metrics in Keras?"

Performance Monitoring:

Master said, "Metrics allow you to evaluate the performance of your model beyond the loss function during training and testing."

Interpretability:
Metrics like accuracy are more interpretable to humans compared to the loss value. For example, knowing that the model is 90% accurate is easier to understand than a loss value of 0.25.

Flexibility:
In Keras, you can track multiple metrics simultaneously. For example, you might want to monitor both accuracy and precision/recall during training.

How It Works in Keras

Master continued, when you specify metrics=['accuracy'], Keras computes the accuracy after each epoch during training and also evaluates it on the test set during validation.

Key Notes on Accuracy

Binary vs Multi-Class Classification:

- For binary classification, accuracy is straightforward to compute based on whether the predicted label matches the true label.
- For multi-class classification, the metric evaluates whether the predicted class (highest probability) matches the true class.

Accuracy Limitations:

Class Imbalance: Accuracy can be misleading if the dataset is imbalanced. For example, in a dataset where 95% of labels are 0, a model that predicts all zeros will achieve 95% accuracy but perform poorly on the minority class.

To address this, you might consider additional metrics like precision, recall, F1 score, or AUC (Area Under Curve).

Probabilistic Predictions:

- For models using a sigmoid or softmax activation in the output layer, predictions are probabilities.

- Accuracy is computed by converting these probabilities to binary (0/1) or categorical (class index) predictions.

Advanced Metrics in Keras

In addition to accuracy, Keras supports other built-in metrics and also allows you to define custom metrics. Some examples:

Precision: Proportion of true positives among all positive predictions.

```
metrics = ['accuracy', 'Precision']
```

Recall: Proportion of true positives among all actual positives.

```
metrics = ['accuracy', 'Recall']
```

F1 Score: Harmonic mean of precision and recall.

AUC (Area Under the Curve): Measures the model's ability to distinguish between classes.

Hyperparameters:

Sam asked, "Master, what are Hyperparameters in deep learning?"

Hyperparameters are crucial settings in a deep learning model that determine the architecture and training process of the model. Unlike model parameters (such as weights and biases) that are learned during training, hyperparameters are set before the learning process begins and remain constant throughout the training phase. They directly affect how the model learns and performs.

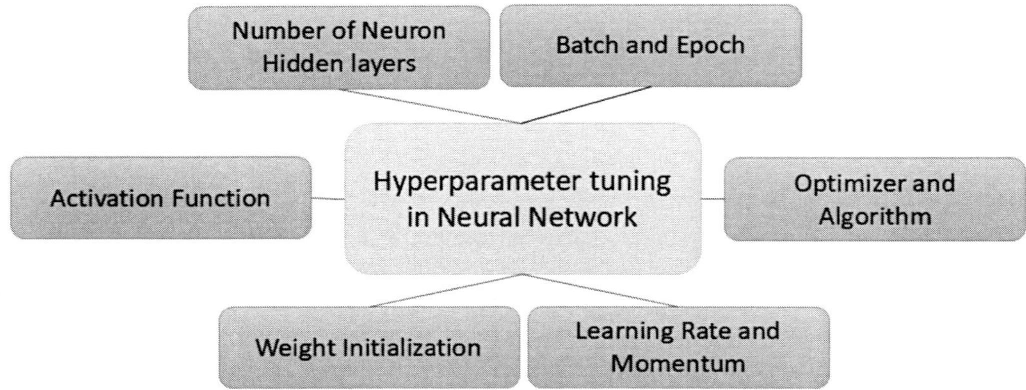

Illustration: P6_Hyper_1

Key hyperparameters include:

Learning Rate: This controls how much the model adjusts its weights with respect to the loss gradient. A small learning rate makes training slow, while a large one can cause the model to converge quickly but possibly to a suboptimal solution.

Number of Epochs: The number of complete passes through the entire training dataset. A higher number of epochs may lead to overfitting, while too few can result in underfitting.

Batch Size: The number of training samples processed before the model's weights are updated. Smaller batch sizes give a more accurate estimate of the gradient but can make training slower.

Optimizer: The algorithm used to update the model's weights (e.g., Gradient Descent, SGD, Adam, RMSprop). Different optimizers handle the learning rate and weight updates in varied ways, affecting convergence speed and model performance.

Momentum: Used to accelerate gradient descent by considering past gradients, reducing oscillations, and speeding up convergence.

Dropout Rate: This hyperparameter helps prevent overfitting by randomly "dropping" some neurons during training, forcing the model to generalize better.

Weight Initialization: Defines how the initial weights of the model are set. Proper initialization is critical for ensuring smooth and efficient training.

Activation Functions: Functions like ReLU, Sigmoid, or Tanh that define how the model's neurons produce outputs. Choosing the right activation function can influence both the speed and accuracy of training.

Selecting the right combination of hyperparameters requires experimentation, as each model and dataset responds differently. Often, grid search, random search, or automated tuning methods like Bayesian optimization are used to find the optimal set of hyperparameters for a given problem.

Hyperparameters tunning:

Nikash asked, "Master, how do we tune hyperparameters in deep learning?"

Tuning hyperparameters in deep learning is a crucial process that significantly impacts the performance and efficiency of a neural network model. Since hyperparameters are not learned during training, selecting the optimal set requires a systematic approach. There are several methods for tuning hyperparameters, and each comes with its trade-offs:

Grid Search:

- Grid search is an exhaustive search method where you specify a list of possible values for each hyperparameter, and the model is trained with every possible combination of these values.
- While it ensures that you explore the entire hyperparameter space, it can be computationally expensive, especially for large models or datasets.

Random Search:

- Instead of testing all possible combinations, random search randomly samples values from the hyperparameter space. This reduces computational cost while often yielding similar results to grid search.
- Random search is particularly effective when only a few hyperparameters significantly impact model performance, allowing for quicker identification of the best settings.

Bayesian Optimization:

- Bayesian optimization builds a probabilistic model of the hyperparameter space and uses this model to select the next set of hyperparameters to evaluate.

- This approach focuses on optimizing the performance of the model while minimizing the number of evaluations, making it more efficient than a grid or random search.
- It's suitable for complex models where training is costly.

Manual Tuning:

In some cases, experts manually adjust hyperparameters based on experience and intuition, observing how changes affect performance.

While this can work well for experienced practitioners, it is often less systematic and can be time-consuming.

Early Stopping:

- Early stopping is a form of regularization used to prevent overfitting. During training, the model's performance is monitored on a validation set. If performance begins to degrade, training stops before the model overfits.
- Though not a direct tuning method, it reduces the risk of overfitting and helps with determining an optimal number of epochs.

Hyperband:

- Hyperband is a resource-efficient method that evaluates models with different hyperparameters over a varying number of iterations. It focuses on eliminating poorly performing configurations early, allowing more resources to be allocated to promising ones.
- This method is ideal when computational resources are a constraint.

Cross-Validation:

- Cross-validation involves splitting the training data into multiple subsets (folds). The model is trained on different folds, and hyperparameters are tuned based on performance across all folds.
- It provides a more robust estimate of the model's performance and helps in fine-tuning hyperparameters to prevent overfitting.

Automated Hyperparameter Tuning (AutoML):

AutoML frameworks automate hyperparameter tuning using various optimization techniques. These frameworks, like Google's AutoML, Keras Tuner, or Optuna, help speed up the tuning process by intelligently searching the hyperparameter space.

Master explained, that the code snippet uses deep learning techniques to train and optimise a binary classification model on a dataset. Below are the key steps and components:

Example P1 – U1 – D14	
Hyperparameter Tunning	**Output**

# Import necessary packages 	
import numpy as np
import pandas as pd
from sklearn.model_selection import train_test_split, GridSearchCV
from sklearn.preprocessing import StandardScaler
from scikeras.wrappers import KerasClassifier
from tensorflow.keras.models import Sequential
from tensorflow.keras.layers import Dense, Input
import warnings
import os
import tensorflow as tf
 	
# Suppress TensorFlow and general warnings 	
os.environ['TF_CPP_MIN_LOG_LEVEL'] = '2'
warnings.filterwarnings('ignore')
 	
# Load dataset 	
path =
r'C:\Users\User\mraj4\Documents\OptimumPart5\diabetes.csv'
try:
   data = pd.read_csv(path)
   print("Dataset successfully loaded!")
except FileNotFoundError:
   print(f"File not found. Please check the file path: {path}")
   exit()
 	
# Preview the dataset 	
print("\nDataset Preview:")
print(data.head())
 	
# Check for missing values 	
if data.isnull().sum().any():
	--- Hyperparameter Optimization: Batch Size & Epochs ---
	
	Best Accuracy: 0.7736
	Best Parameters: {'batch_size': 20, 'epochs': 50}
	Test Accuracy: 0.7338
	
	--- Optimizing Activation Function & Optimizer ---
	Best Accuracy: 0.7899
	Best Parameters: {'model__activation': 'tanh', 'optimizer': 'SGD'}

```
    print("\nMissing values detected! Please handle them
before proceeding:")
    print(data.isnull().sum())
    exit()
else:
    print("\nNo missing values detected.")

# Splitting predictors (X) and response (Y)
X = data.iloc[:, :-1].values  # Predictors
Y = data.iloc[:, -1].values   # Target

# Normalize predictors
scaler = StandardScaler()
X = scaler.fit_transform(X)

# Split data into training and testing sets
X_train, X_test, Y_train, Y_test = train_test_split(X, Y,
test_size=0.2, random_state=42)
print("\nData processing completed.")

# Function to create model
def create_model(optimizer='adam', activation='relu'):
    model = Sequential()
    model.add(Input(shape=(X_train.shape[1],)))  # Input
layer
    model.add(Dense(12, activation=activation))  #
Hidden layer
    model.add(Dense(1, activation='sigmoid'))    # Output
layer
    model.compile(loss='binary_crossentropy',
optimizer=optimizer, metrics=['accuracy'])
    return model

# Part 1: Hyperparameter Optimization for Batch Size
and Epochs
print("\n--- Hyperparameter Optimization: Batch Size &
Epochs ---")
model = KerasClassifier(model=create_model,
verbose=0)
param_grid = {
    'batch_size': [10, 20, 40, 60, 80, 100],
    'epochs': [10, 30, 50]
}
grid = GridSearchCV(estimator=model,
param_grid=param_grid, n_jobs=-1, cv=3)
grid_result = grid.fit(X_train, Y_train)

# Summarize results
```

```
print(f"\nBest Accuracy: {grid_result.best_score_:.4f}")
print(f"Best Parameters: {grid_result.best_params_}")

# Evaluate best model on test set
best_model = grid_result.best_estimator_
test_accuracy = best_model.score(X_test, Y_test)
print(f"Test Accuracy: {test_accuracy:.4f}")

# Part 2: Optimizing Activation Function and Optimizer
print("\n--- Optimizing Activation Function &
Optimizer ---")
model = KerasClassifier(model=create_model,
epochs=50, batch_size=10, verbose=0)
param_grid = {
   'optimizer': ['SGD', 'Adadelta', 'RMSprop', 'Adagrad',
'Adam'],
   'model__activation': ['relu', 'tanh', 'sigmoid']
}
grid = GridSearchCV(estimator=model,
param_grid=param_grid, n_jobs=-1, cv=3)
grid_result = grid.fit(X_train, Y_train)

# Summarize results
print(f"Best Accuracy: {grid_result.best_score_:.4f}")
print(f"Best Parameters: {grid_result.best_params_}")
```

Imports and Setup

- Libraries Used: numpy, pandas, sklearn, tensorflow, and scikeras.
- Warnings and Logs: Suppresses TensorFlow and general warnings for cleaner outputs.

Dataset Loading and Preprocessing

- Dataset Path: The dataset is loaded from a specified file path (diabetes.csv).
- Missing Values: Checks for missing values; if detected, the script halts execution.

Data Splitting:

- Predictors (X): All columns except the last.
- Response (Y): The last column.

Normalization: Uses StandardScaler to normalize X.

Train-Test Split: Divides data into 80% training and 20% testing sets.

Model Architecture

A function, create_model, defines a sequential neural network:

- Input Layer: Matches the feature dimensions of X.
- Hidden Layer: 12 neurons with adjustable activation functions (default is 'relu').
- Output Layer: A single neuron with 'sigmoid' activation for binary classification.
- Compilation: The model uses the 'binary_crossentropy' loss function, adjustable optimizers, and accuracy as the metric.

Hyperparameter Optimization

Part 1: Batch Size and Epochs

- Objective: Find the best combination of batch size and epochs.
- Tool: GridSearchCV is used for exhaustive search with cross-validation.
- Hyperparameters Tested:
    - batch_size: [10, 20, 40, 60, 80, 100].
    - epochs: [10, 30, 50].
- Output: The best accuracy and corresponding parameters are displayed.

Part 2: Activation Functions and Optimizers

- Objective: Optimize the activation function and optimizer.
- Hyperparameters Tested:
    - optimizer: ['SGD', 'Adadelta', 'RMSprop', 'Adagrad', 'Adam'].
    - activation: ['relu', 'tanh', 'sigmoid'] (adjusted within the model).
- Output: Displays the best accuracy and parameter combination.

Evaluation

- Test Set Evaluation: The best model from grid search is evaluated on the test set to provide a final accuracy score.

Purpose

The given code systematically optimises hyperparameters and model configurations to achieve higher accuracy on binary classification tasks, demonstrating good practices in machine learning and deep learning workflows.

Sam asked, "How to improve the Accuracy of the model?"

Master explained the following steps:

Data Preprocessing and Augmentation

Feature Engineering:

- Analyse features for relationships with the target variable.
- Create meaningful new features (e.g., combining or transforming existing ones).

Handle Imbalanced Data:

- If the dataset is imbalanced, use techniques like SMOTE (Synthetic Minority Oversampling Technique), undersampling, or class-weighting in the loss function.

Remove Outliers:

- Use techniques like the Z-score or IQR to identify and remove or transform outliers.

Scaling:

- Confirm all features are properly scaled (e.g., StandardScaler for continuous features).

Augment Data (if applicable):

- Synthetically increase data for the minority class or add noise for robust generalization.

Improve Model Architecture

Add Layers and Neurons:

- Increase the depth of the network by adding more layers or increasing the number of neurons in each layer.
- Use techniques like Dropout to avoid overfitting.

Experiment with Activation Functions:

- Use relu, leaky_relu, or elu in hidden layers and test alternatives for improved feature transformation.

Optimise Output Layer:

- Ensure the correct activation (sigmoid for binary classification or softmax for multiclass problems).

Batch Normalisation:

- Add batch normalisation layers to stabilise learning and improve convergence speed.

Residual Connections:

- If the dataset is large and complex, introduce residual connections (like in ResNet).

Optimise Hyperparameters

Learning Rate Tuning:

- Use a learning rate schedule or a learning rate finder.

Regularization:

- Add L1/L2 regularization (weight decay) to reduce overfitting.

Optimizer Tuning:

- Experiment with optimizers like AdamW (better weight decay), Nadam, or SGD with momentum.

Grid Search or Bayesian Optimization:

- Use advanced hyperparameter tuning libraries (e.g., Optuna, Ray Tune) for finer control over the search process.

Cross-Validation and Ensemble Learning

Cross-Validation:

- Use k-fold cross-validation instead of a simple train-test split to ensure the model generalises well.

Ensemble Models:

- Combine predictions of multiple models (e.g., stacking, bagging, or boosting).
- Use an ensemble of neural networks or mix with tree-based models (e.g., XGBoost, Random Forest).

Increase Training Data and Quality

Data Augmentation:

- If your dataset is limited, explore generating synthetic data.

Label Quality:

- Check for label noise in the dataset and correct mislabelled entries.

Advanced Techniques

Transfer Learning:

- Use a pre-trained model and fine-tune it for your task (especially effective for complex datasets).

Hyperparameter Tuning:

- Use tools like Optuna, Bayesian Optimization, or Hyperband for better hyperparameter search.

Early Stopping:

- Use early stopping with a validation set to avoid overfitting.

Model Check pointing:

- Save the best-performing model during training.

Analyse and Debug Your Model

Analyse Training Logs:

- Monitor loss and accuracy trends for overfitting or underfitting.

Feature Importance:

- Use techniques like permutation importance or SHAP values to identify critical features.

Confusion Matrix:

- Analyse precision, recall, and F1 scores to find areas of improvement.

Class Weights:

- Apply class weights to handle class imbalance during model training.

Key Considerations:

- Learning Rate and Batch Size: These hyperparameters often have the most significant impact on the performance and should be prioritized during tuning.
- Regularization: Hyperparameters like dropout rates and L2 regularization coefficients need careful adjustment to prevent overfitting.
- Computational Budget: Hyperparameter tuning can be computationally expensive. Methods like random search or Hyperband can reduce this cost while still providing good results.

Ultimately, tuning hyperparameters is about balancing computational efficiency with model performance, and the best approach often depends on the problem, model complexity, and available resources.

Note: Hyperparameters and Hypertunning have been discussed in detail in Optimum Python Power Series III and Series IV

Note: Hyperparameters and hyperparameter tuning are discussed in-depth in *Optimum Python Power Series III* and *Series IV*. These volumes cover advanced techniques, including grid search, random search, Bayesian optimization, and AutoML, providing step-by-step guidance for optimizing learning models

PART ONE

DAY FOUR

Unit 2 - Lesson Four

Deep Learning

"A neural network does not calculate—it evolves. It learns the unseen dance between data and truth, discovering patterns hidden beneath the surface of logic."

– Shree Shambav

Additional Information:

Akshaya asked, "Master, can you explain how Gradient Descent works in deep learning, along with a code example to demonstrate it?"

Master said, "The Gradient Descent algorithm is a cornerstone of deep learning and optimization. It is an iterative method used to minimize the loss function (or cost function) by adjusting the parameters (weights) of the model. Essentially, the algorithm moves the model's parameters step by step in the opposite direction of the gradient (which indicates the steepest increase in the loss function) to reduce the error or loss, eventually reaching a local or global minimum where the loss function is minimized."

How Gradient Descent Works:

1. Initialization: The process begins by initializing the model parameters (like weights) randomly. This random initialization ensures that each time gradient descent runs, it explores different parts of the function's landscape.
2. Compute the Gradient: For each iteration, the algorithm computes the gradient

of the cost function with respect to each parameter. The gradient represents the slope or direction of the steepest ascent in the cost function. In simple terms, it tells the algorithm how the cost will change if the parameters are slightly modified.

3. Parameter Update: After calculating the gradient, the algorithm updates the parameters by taking a step in the opposite direction (down the slope), which leads towards minimizing the cost function. The size of this step is determined by a hyperparameter called the learning rate. This update rule is typically written as:

$$\theta := \theta - \alpha \cdot \nabla J(\theta)$$

Where:

- θ represents the model parameters (weights and biases).
- α is the learning rate (step size).
- $\nabla J(\theta)$ is the gradient of the cost function J for the parameters.

4. Iteration: Steps 2 and 3 are repeated in a loop until the algorithm converges to a minimum—meaning the gradient becomes small enough (or zero) that the parameters stabilize at the minimum value.
5. Convergence: The algorithm will eventually converge to a local or global minimum of the cost function, where the error is minimized. In some cases, it may converge to a local minimum instead of the global minimum, but techniques like learning rate annealing and momentum can help in avoiding poor local minima.

Simple Example:

Consider a function $f(x) = x^2$ and we want to find the value of x that minimizes this function.

Start with an initial guess, say $x = 3$

Calculate the gradient:

The derivative of f(x) for x is 2x. For $x = 3$, the gradient is 6.

Update x:

Using a learning rate $\alpha=0.1$, the new value of x is updated as:

x = x − α·gradient = 3 − (0.1×6) = 2.4

Continue this process until the gradient approaches zero, and the function reaches a minimum.

Implementing Gradient Descent in TensorFlow (Linear Regression Example):

In TensorFlow, you can use gradient descent to minimize a cost function like **Mean Squared Error (MSE)** in a simple linear regression model. Here's a step-by-step explanation:

Model Setup: We define placeholders for the input (features) and output (labels). The weights w and bias b are initialised randomly. The model is then defined using the linear equation:

$$y_{pred} = w \cdot x + b$$

Cost Function: The cost function used here is Mean Squared Error (MSE), which measures the average squared difference between the predicted values and actual values:

$$J(w,b) = \frac{1}{m}\left(\sum_{i=1}^{m}\left(y_{pred} - y_{true}\right)^2\right)$$

Gradient Descent Optimizer: We then use TensorFlow's tf.optimizers.SGD to minimize the cost function. The learning rate is set as a parameter of the optimizer.

Training: Using a loop, the model is trained for several iterations by updating the weights and biases in the direction that minimizes the cost function. TensorFlow's Session object runs these operations, updating the model parameters with each iteration.

Here's a simplified version of how it works:

Example P1 – U1 – D15	
Gradient Descent	**Output**

import tensorflow as tf
 	
# Data (for example, some features X and labels Y) 	
X = tf.constant([1, 2, 3, 4], dtype=tf.float32) #
Example input
Y = tf.constant([2, 4, 6, 8], dtype=tf.float32) #
True output
	Step 800, Loss:
	0.0002881577529478818, w:
	1.9859144687652588, b:
	0.041413042694330215
	Step 900, Loss:
	0.00015819539839867502, w:
	1.9895635843276978, b:
	0.030684493482112885

```
# Model parameters (weights and bias) initialized as
trainable variables
w = tf.Variable(0.5, dtype=tf.float32)  # Initial
random value for weight
b = tf.Variable(0.0, dtype=tf.float32)  # Initial
random value for bias

# Linear regression model function
def linear_regression(X):
   return w * X + b

# Loss function (Mean Squared Error)
def loss_fn(Y_pred, Y_true):
   return tf.reduce_mean(tf.square(Y_pred -
Y_true))

# Optimizer (Stochastic Gradient Descent)
optimizer = tf.optimizers.SGD(learning_rate=0.01)

# Training loop
for step in range(1000):
   with tf.GradientTape() as tape:
      # Forward pass: compute predictions and loss
      y_pred = linear_regression(X)
      loss = loss_fn(y_pred, Y)

   # Compute gradients
   gradients = tape.gradient(loss, [w, b])

   # Update weights and bias using optimizer
   optimizer.apply_gradients(zip(gradients, [w, b]))

   # Print updates every 100 steps
   if step % 100 == 0:
      print(f"Step {step}, Loss: {loss.numpy()}, w:
{w.numpy()}, b: {b.numpy()}")
```

Master said, “The code demonstrates how to build and train a simple linear regression model using the Stochastic Gradient Descent (SGD) optimization algorithm.”

Here’s a summary of each section:

Data Definition:

The code starts by defining a small dataset. X represents the input features, and Y represents the true output labels (or target values) for those inputs.

Model Parameters:

Two trainable variables, w (weight) and b (bias), are initialized. These variables will be learned during training.

Linear Regression Model:

A function linear_regression is defined to compute the model's prediction. The equation y = w * X + b represents the simple linear regression model.

Loss Function:

The loss function used is Mean Squared Error (MSE), which measures the difference between the predicted values (y_pred) and the true values (Y_true). The lower the loss, the better the model's predictions.

Optimizer:

The SGD optimizer is instantiated using tf.optimizers.SGD with a learning rate of 0.01. This optimizer will update the model's parameters to minimize the loss function.

Training Loop:

The code runs a loop for 1000 iterations to train the model:

- In each iteration, it uses tf.GradientTape() to calculate the gradients of the loss for the model's parameters (w and b).
- The optimizer then applies these gradients to update the parameters, effectively reducing the loss and improving the model.
- Every 100 steps, it prints the current step, loss value, and the parameters (w and b).

Purpose:

Master said, "This code demonstrates how to implement linear regression with TensorFlow 2.x, utilising gradient descent for optimization, and updating model parameters based on the computed gradients."

In deep learning, **gradient descent** is a powerful optimization algorithm that updates model parameters iteratively by minimizing the cost function. It's the core of model training, and the learning rate is crucial to determining the speed and accuracy of convergence. TensorFlow simplifies this process with its built-in optimizers, allowing for efficient training of complex models.

Visualise the convergence of Gradient Descent

Master said, "To visualize the convergence of Gradient Descent in the linear regression model, we can plot the loss function (Mean Squared Error) over the iterations to see how the error decreases as the model learns. Additionally, we can visualize how the model's predictions improve over time by plotting the regression line after each iteration."

Here's how you can modify the existing code to include real-time visualizations of both the loss convergence and the regression line:

Example P1 – U1 – D16	
Visualise Gradient Descent	**Output**

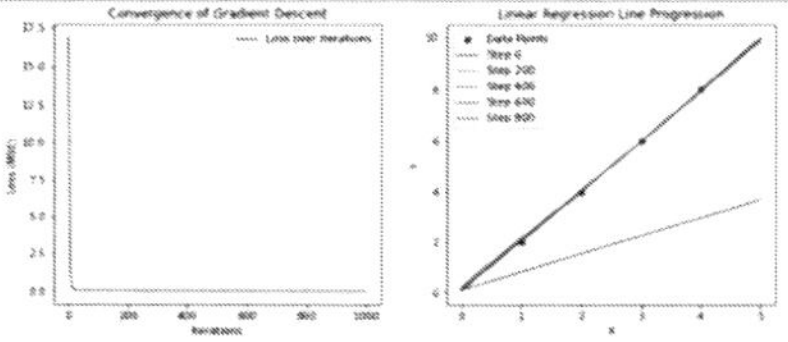

```
import tensorflow as tf
import numpy as np
import matplotlib.pyplot as plt

# Data (example features X and true labels Y)
X = tf.constant([1, 2, 3, 4], dtype=tf.float32)  # Example input
Y = tf.constant([2, 4, 6, 8], dtype=tf.float32)  # True output

# Model parameters (weights and bias) initialized as trainable variables
w = tf.Variable(0.5, dtype=tf.float32)  # Initial random value for weight
b = tf.Variable(0.0, dtype=tf.float32)  # Initial random value for bias

# Linear regression model function
def linear_regression(X):
    return w * X + b

# Loss function (Mean Squared Error)
def loss_fn(Y_pred, Y_true):
    return tf.reduce_mean(tf.square(Y_pred - Y_true))

# Optimizer (Stochastic Gradient Descent)
```

```
optimizer = tf.optimizers.SGD(learning_rate=0.01)

# For visualization
loss_values = []
iterations = []
line_data = []

# Training loop
for step in range(1000):
    with tf.GradientTape() as tape:
        # Forward pass: compute predictions and loss
        y_pred = linear_regression(X)
        loss = loss_fn(y_pred, Y)

    # Compute gradients
    gradients = tape.gradient(loss, [w, b])

    # Update weights and bias using optimizer
    optimizer.apply_gradients(zip(gradients, [w, b]))

    # Store loss for visualization
    loss_values.append(loss.numpy())
    iterations.append(step)

    # Store current regression line data
    line_data.append([w.numpy(), b.numpy()])

    # Print updates every 100 steps
    if step % 100 == 0:
        print(f"Step {step}, Loss: {loss.numpy()}, w:
{w.numpy()}, b: {b.numpy()}")

# Visualization: Loss Convergence and Linear
Regression Line
plt.figure(figsize=(12, 5))

# Plot 1: Loss Convergence
plt.subplot(1, 2, 1)
plt.plot(iterations, loss_values, label='Loss over
iterations')
plt.xlabel('Iterations')
plt.ylabel('Loss (MSE)')
plt.title('Convergence of Gradient Descent')
plt.legend()

# Plot 2: Regression Line
plt.subplot(1, 2, 2)
plt.scatter(X, Y, label='Data Points')
```

```
x_vals = np.linspace(0, 5, 100)
for i, (w_curr, b_curr) in
enumerate(line_data[::200]):  # Plot every 200th line
    plt.plot(x_vals, w_curr * x_vals + b_curr,
label=f"Step {i*200}")
plt.xlabel('X')
plt.ylabel('Y')
plt.title('Linear Regression Line Progression')
plt.legend()

plt.show()
```

Loss Convergence Visualization:

- The loss_values list stores the loss at each iteration, and iterations stores the corresponding step number.
- In Plot 1, the loss is plotted against the number of iterations, showing how the loss decreases over time as the model learns.

Regression Line Visualization:

- The line_data list stores the weight w and bias b at each iteration, allowing us to visualize how the regression line changes.
- In Plot 2, we plot the data points and display the progression of the regression line at intervals (every 200 iterations in this case). This allows us to see how the model's predictions improve over time as Gradient Descent minimizes the loss.

Purpose:

This visualization helps us understand how the gradient descent algorithm minimizes the loss function over time and how the linear regression model progressively adjusts the line of best fit to the data.

EPOCHS:

Sam asked, "Master, how do we choose the optimal number of epochs to train a neural network?"

Master said, "Choosing the optimal number of epochs is crucial in training a neural network, as it directly impacts the model's performance. One of the key concerns is overfitting—when the model trains too long and learns specific patterns in the training data that do not generalize well to unseen data. This leads to a model that performs exceptionally on the training set but poorly on the test set, losing its ability to generalize."

To prevent overfitting, it's essential to train the model for the right number of epochs. Here's how the process works:

Overfitting and Underfitting: If the model is trained for too few epochs, it may underfit, meaning it hasn't learned enough from the data. If trained for too many epochs, it overfits, learning noise and patterns that are not generalizable.

Validation Set: A portion of the training data is set aside as a validation set. This set is used to monitor the model's performance after each epoch, providing a way to evaluate how well the model is likely to perform on new data. After each epoch, the loss and accuracy are computed for both the training and validation sets.

Monitoring Loss and Accuracy:

- Training Loss and Accuracy: This tells you how well the model is learning on the sample data.
- Validation Loss and Accuracy: This indicates how well the model will likely perform on unseen data. When the validation loss starts to increase, while training loss continues to decrease, the model is overfitting.

Early Stopping: One of the most effective ways to choose the optimal number of epochs is to use the Early Stopping technique. This involves monitoring the loss or accuracy during training. If no improvement in the validation loss/accuracy is observed for several epochs (a patience threshold), training is stopped early, preventing overfitting. If you're monitoring loss, training halts when validation loss starts increasing. Similarly, for accuracy, training halts when it starts decreasing.

Generalization: By halting training at the right time, early stopping helps in maximizing the model's generalization ability—balancing between underfitting and overfitting.

In short, to find the optimal number of epochs:

- Use a validation set to track performance.
- Monitor both training and validation loss/accuracy.
- Employ early stopping to stop training at the point where the model's performance starts degrading on the validation set, preventing overfitting and

maintaining good generalization.

Optimal number of epochs

Master said, "To understand how to choose the optimal number of epochs using early stopping, let's write a simple program in Python using Keras (part of TensorFlow) for a neural network. We will implement early stopping based on validation loss."

Here's an example using the popular MNIST dataset, which consists of handwritten digits:

Example P1 – U1 – D17	
Optimal number of epochs	**Output**

# Import necessary libraries 	
import tensorflow as tf
from tensorflow.keras.datasets import mnist
from tensorflow.keras.models import Sequential
from tensorflow.keras.layers import Dense, Flatten
from tensorflow.keras.callbacks import EarlyStopping
 	
# Load MNIST dataset 	
(x_train, y_train), (x_test, y_test) = mnist.load_data()
 	
# Normalize the data (scaling pixel values between 0 and 1) 	
x_train = x_train / 255.0
x_test = x_test / 255.0
 	
# Define the model 	
model = Sequential([
   Flatten(input_shape=(28, 28)), # Flattening the 28x28 images into a 1D vector
   Dense(128, activation='relu'), # Fully connected layer with 128 neurons
   Dense(64, activation='relu'), # Second fully connected layer with 64 neurons
   Dense(10, activation='softmax') # Output layer with 10 classes (digits 0-9)
])
 	
# Compile the model 	
	val_accuracy: 0.9752 - val_loss: 0.1012
	313/313 ━━━━━━━━━━━━━━━━━━━━ 1s
	1ms/step - accuracy: 0.9736 - loss: 0.0958
	Test accuracy: 0.9782999753952026

```
model.compile(optimizer='adam',
loss='sparse_categorical_crossentropy',
metrics=['accuracy'])

# Define the early stopping callback to stop
training when validation loss doesn't improve
early_stopping = EarlyStopping(monitor='val_loss',
patience=3, restore_best_weights=True)

# Train the model, including the validation set and
early stopping
history = model.fit(x_train, y_train,
validation_split=0.2, epochs=50, batch_size=32,
callbacks=[early_stopping])

# Evaluate the model on the test set
test_loss, test_acc = model.evaluate(x_test, y_test)

print(f"Test accuracy: {test_acc}")
```

Data Preprocessing:

The MNIST dataset is loaded, consisting of 28x28 grayscale images of handwritten digits (0-9). We normalize the pixel values to be between 0 and 1.

Model Definition:

The model uses a simple feedforward neural network (fully connected layers) with ReLU activation for the hidden layers and softmax for the output layer.

Early Stopping:

The EarlyStopping callback is used to monitor the validation loss. If the validation loss doesn't improve for 3 consecutive epochs (patience=3), the training stops early. This prevents overfitting.

Training:

The model is trained using the fit() method, with 20% of the training data used as a validation set (validation_split=0.2).

Evaluation:

The model is evaluated on the test set after training to check the accuracy.

Understanding Early Stopping:

- The model is trained for up to 50 epochs. However, early stopping will halt training once the validation loss stops improving.
- The model will automatically restore the best weights using the restore_best_weights=True parameter in EarlyStopping.

By using early stopping, you can prevent overfitting and determine an optimal number of epochs dynamically based on the model's performance on the validation set.

Optimisation refers to the broader process of finding the best set of parameters for a neural network. Gradient descent is one of the most common optimisation techniques, but it can be enhanced with various methods like:

- Stochastic Gradient Descent (SGD): Uses only a subset of data at each step, speeding up the learning process and allowing the model to generalise better.
- Momentum: Helps accelerate gradient vectors in the right direction, leading to faster convergence.
- Adam (Adaptive Moment Estimation): A more advanced optimisation algorithm that adjusts the learning rate for each parameter based on recent gradients, combining the benefits of both SGD and momentum.

In deep learning, optimisation ensures that the model reaches a state where it minimises the error and performs well on unseen data.

Example: Regression

Master said, "Artificial Neural Network (ANN) program for performing linear regression. In this example, we'll create an ANN model with one input and one output neuron to predict a continuous target variable."

Example P1 – U1 – D18	
ANN – Linear Regression	**Output**
# Import necessary libraries import numpy as np import tensorflow as tf from tensorflow.keras.models import Sequential from tensorflow.keras.layers import Dense import matplotlib.pyplot as plt # Generate some sample data for linear regression (y = 2x + 1 with noise)	4/4 ━━━━━━━━━━━━━━━━━━━━ 0s 6ms/step Weights: 1.9303703308105469, Bias: 1.0337218046188354

```
np.random.seed(42)
X = np.random.rand(100, 1)  # 100 data points
between 0 and 1
y = 2 * X + 1 + 0.1 * np.random.randn(100, 1)  #
Adding some noise

# Define the model
model = Sequential()

# Add one dense layer with one neuron (since this
is a simple linear regression)
model.add(Dense(units=1, input_dim=1,
activation='linear'))

# Compile the model
model.compile(optimizer='sgd',
loss='mean_squared_error')

# Train the model
history = model.fit(X, y, epochs=500, verbose=0)

# Predict using the model
y_pred = model.predict(X)

# Plot the original data and the fitted line
plt.scatter(X, y, label='Original data')
plt.plot(X, y_pred, color='red', label='Fitted line')
plt.xlabel('X')
plt.ylabel('y')
plt.title('ANN-based Linear Regression')
plt.legend()
plt.show()

# Print the model parameters (weights and bias)
weights, bias = model.layers[0].get_weights()
print(f"Weights: {weights[0][0]}, Bias: {bias[0]}")
```

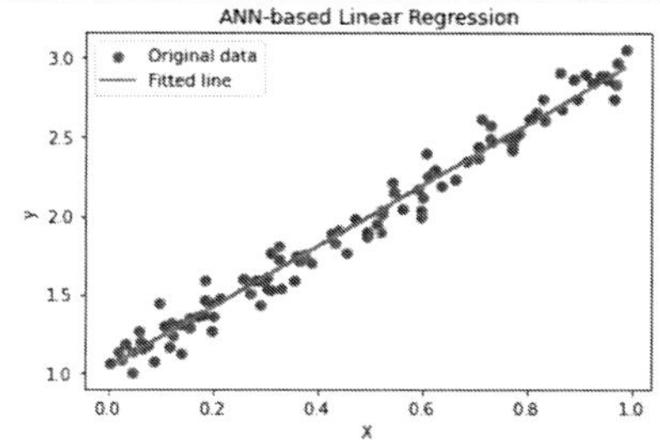

ANN-based Linear Regression

Data Generation:

We create a dataset with 100 points using np.random.rand() to generate random X values.

The target y values follow the equation y = 2x + 1 with some added noise to simulate real-world data.

Model Definition:

A Sequential model is created, and we add a single Dense layer with 1 unit (neuron). Since this is linear regression, the activation function is set to 'linear'.

Model Compilation:

The model is compiled with the stochastic gradient descent (SGD) optimizer and the mean squared error (MSE) loss function, which is suitable for regression tasks.

Training:

The model is trained on the data using the fit() method for 500 epochs.

Prediction:

After training, the model predicts y values based on the input data X.

Visualization:

We use matplotlib to plot the original data points as a scatter plot and the predicted fitted line (in red) on top.

Model Parameters:

The weights and bias (intercept) of the linear regression model are printed. These correspond to the learned slope and intercept of the best-fit line.

Output:

The plot will show the original data points and the fitted line.

The printed weights and bias will be close to 2 (slope) and 1 (intercept), respectively, which are the true parameters of the underlying linear relationship y = 2x + 1.

This simple ANN mimics the behaviour of linear regression by using a single neuron with a linear activation function.

PART ONE

DAY FOUR

Unit 1 - Lesson Four

Inside the Neuron

"The perceptron was not merely a model; it was the first spark of digital consciousness—where a single neuron dared to learn, and the age of artificial thought began."

– *Shree Shambav*

Master explained that the single-layer perceptron (SLP) stands as one of the pioneering neural network models, dating back to its inception by Frank Rosenblatt in 1958. It serves as a foundational concept in the realm of artificial neural networks, particularly in handling binary classification tasks such as logical gates like AND, OR, and NOR.

At its core, the Perceptron operates as a linear machine learning algorithm for supervised learning, adept at binary classification. Its design facilitates the sequential processing of elements, making it an integral tool in the realm of machine learning.

Akshaya asked, "Master, what is a perceptron? Can you explain it with a simple example and intuition behind how it works?"

Master said, "A perceptron is the simplest form of an artificial neural network, used for binary classification tasks. It is a model that mimics how a single neuron in the brain works, making decisions based on the weighted sum of inputs and an activation function."

Case One - Intuition:

Imagine you're trying to decide whether to go outside based on two factors:

- Temperature (input 1)
- Weather condition (input 2)

You assign a certain importance (weight) to each factor. For example, you might care more about the temperature than whether it's cloudy. You also have a threshold that determines when you'll go outside, such as, "If it's not too cold and not raining, I'll go outside."

Here's how the perceptron processes this:

- Inputs: Temperature (let's call it x1) and weather condition (let's call it x2).
- Weights: You decide how important each input is. For example, if the temperature matters more, it gets a higher weight.
- Summation: The perceptron multiplies each input by its respective weight and adds them up to create a weighted sum. net input = $(w_1 * x_1) + (w_2 * x_2)$
- Activation (Decision): It compares this weighted sum to a threshold (bias). If the sum is above the threshold, it "activates" (goes outside). If not, it stays inside.

Simple Example:

Let's say:

- x1 (temperature) = 30°C
- x2 (weather condition) = 1 (1 = sunny, 0 = cloudy)
- Weights: w1 (importance of temperature) = 0.8, w2 (importance of weather condition) = 0.2
- Threshold: Let's set it to 20.

The perceptron performs:

Net input = $w_i * x_i = w_1 * x_1 + w_2 * x_2$

net input = $(0.8 \times 30) + (0.2 \times 1) = 24 + 0.2 = 24.2$

Since 24.2 is above the bias (threshold) of 20, the perceptron "fires" and decides that you should go outside!

This is a simple binary classification where the perceptron decides "yes" or "no" based on the inputs and their weights.

Case Two - Intuition Behind a Perceptron:

Think of a perceptron as a decision-making tool. For example, imagine you're trying to decide whether or not to bring an umbrella based on weather conditions. The perceptron takes in inputs, such as:

- Is it cloudy? (Input 1)
- Is there rain in the forecast? (Input 2)

Each input is assigned a weight based on its importance. The perceptron multiplies each input by its corresponding weight, sums them up, adds a bias (a small constant), and then passes the result through an activation function to determine the output.

Simple Example:

Let's take a perceptron that decides whether or not to bring an umbrella.

- Input 1: Is it cloudy? (Yes = 1, No = 0)
- Input 2: Is there rain in the forecast? (Yes = 1, No = 0)
- Weights: Say, cloudy has a weight of 0.6, and rain forecast weight of 0.9.
- Bias: Let's assume the bias is -0.5.

Step 1: Compute the weighted sum of inputs:

$$\text{Weighted sum} = (0.6 \times \text{Cloudy}) + (0.9 \times \text{Rain}) + \text{Bias}$$

If it's cloudy and rain is forecasted:

$$\text{Weighted sum} = (0.6 \times 1) + (0.9 \times 1) - 0.5 = 1.0$$

Step 2: Apply the activation function (for simplicity, we use a step function here):

- If the weighted sum is greater than or equal to 0, output = 1 (Yes, bring the umbrella).
- If the weighted sum is less than 0, output = 0 (No umbrella).

Since 1.0 is greater than 0, the perceptron outputs 1 (Yes, bring the umbrella).

Key Points:

- The perceptron makes decisions based on inputs and their importance (weights).
- The activation function helps the perceptron make a binary decision.
- Over time, the perceptron adjusts its weights (through learning) to improve its decision-making ability.

In essence, a perceptron is a simple yet powerful model that learns how to classify data points into two categories by adjusting the weights of its inputs.

Master continued, "Considered one of the simplest yet effective forms of artificial neural networks, the Perceptron operates as a single-layer neural network, governed by four key parameters: input values, weights, bias, and an activation function."

In the domain of machine learning, binary classifiers play a pivotal role. These classifiers aid in discerning whether input data, typically represented as numerical vectors, belong to a specific class or category. Binary classifiers, often akin to linear classifiers, predict outcomes based on a linear predictor function defined by weight and feature vectors.

Perceptron Model

The perceptron algorithm, while foundational, had limitations because of its single-layer structure, making it effective only for linearly separable classes. This limitation was addressed with the development of multi-layer perceptron algorithms. Here is a detailed look at the types of perceptron models:

Single Layer Perceptron Model

Master continued a single-layer perceptron model is the simplest form of artificial neural network. It consists of a feed-forward network that can analyze only linearly separable objects and relies on a threshold transfer function. The model produces binary outcomes (targets) of 1 or 0.

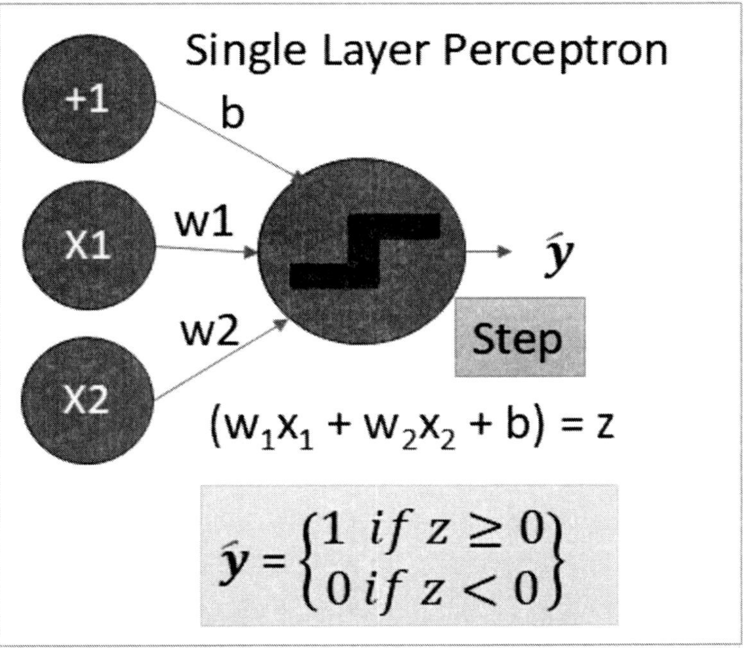

Illustration P6_Perceptron_1

Perceptron Function:

The Perceptron function, denoted as 'f(x)', produces output by multiplying the input 'x' with the learned weight coefficient 'w' and applying a bias term 'b'. Mathematically, it can be expressed as:

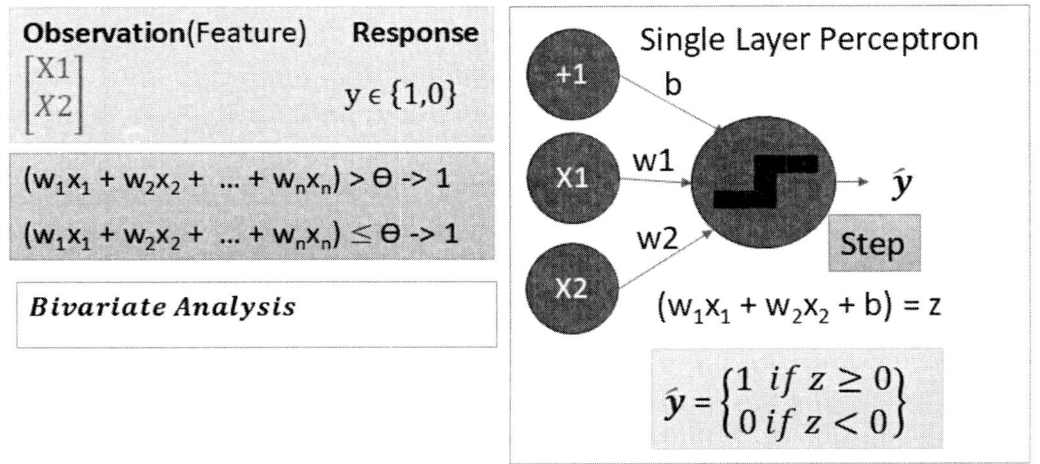

Illustration P6_perceptron_2

$$(w_1x_1 + w_2x_2 + b) = z$$

$$\hat{y} = \begin{Bmatrix} 1 \; if \; z \geq 0 \\ 0 \; if \; z < 0 \end{Bmatrix}$$

Where:

- 'w' represents the real-valued weights vector.
- 'b' represents the bias term.
- 'x' represents the input vector values.

This function forms the core decision-making mechanism within the perceptron, determining whether the neuron activates based on the weighted input sum.

Key Characteristics:

Binary Output: The single-layer perceptron outputs binary results, classifying inputs as either 1 or 0 based on the activation function.

Weight Adjustment: If the perceptron's output matches the desired output, it is considered to have performed satisfactorily. If there is a discrepancy, the weights need adjusting to minimize the error and improve future predictions.

Linearly Separable Data: The single-layer perceptron can only classify data that is linearly separable. For non-linearly separable data, the model fails to achieve accurate classification, as the learning process cannot converge to a solution that correctly classifies all cases.

Case One: Example

The purpose of this code is to build, train, and evaluate a simple neural network model to classify handwritten digits from the MNIST dataset. The MNIST dataset is a standard benchmark dataset in machine learning and contains 60,000 training images and 10,000 testing images of handwritten digits (0-9), each of size 28x28 pixels.

Example P1 – U1 – D19	
Perceptron	**Output**

```
import numpy as np
import tensorflow as tf
from tensorflow import keras
import matplotlib.pyplot as plt
# Load the MNIST dataset
(x_train, y_train), (x_test, y_test) =
keras.datasets.mnist.load_data()

# Display the length of training and test sets
print(f"Number of training samples: {len(x_train)}")
print(f"Number of test samples: {len(x_test)}")

# Display the shape of the first training sample
print(f"Shape of the first training sample: {x_train[0].shape}")

# Display the first training sample
plt.matshow(x_train[0])
plt.title("First Training Sample")
plt.show()

# Normalize the dataset
x_train = x_train / 255.0
x_test = x_test / 255.0

# Flatten the dataset for model building
x_train_flatten = x_train.reshape(len(x_train), 28*28)
x_test_flatten = x_test.reshape(len(x_test), 28*28)

# Build the model
model = keras.Sequential([
   keras.layers.Dense(10, input_shape=(784,),
activation='sigmoid')
])

# Compile the model
model.compile(
   optimizer='adam',
   loss='sparse_categorical_crossentropy',
   metrics=['accuracy']
)

# Train the model
model.fit(x_train_flatten, y_train, epochs=5)

# Evaluate the model
test_loss, test_acc = model.evaluate(x_test_flatten, y_test)
print(f"Test accuracy: {test_acc}")
```

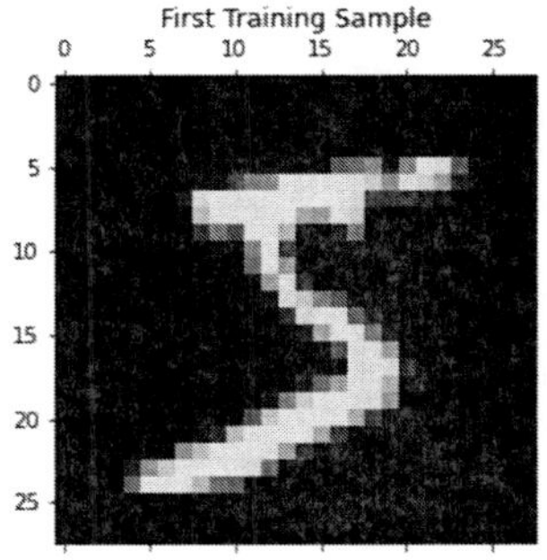

First Training Sample

```
Test accuracy:
0.9244999885559082
```

Limitations

Linear Classification Only: As a linear classifier, the single-layer perceptron cannot handle non-linearly separable data, limiting its applicability in complex scenarios.

Convergence Issues: For data that is not linearly separable, the perceptron will not reach a state where all cases are correctly classified, preventing the learning process from completing.

Multilayer Perceptron Model

John asked, "What is a multi-layer perceptron?"

Master said, "A Multilayer Perceptron (MLP) is an extension of the basic perceptron and forms the backbone of more complex neural networks. While a single perceptron can only solve simple problems, such as linear classifications, an MLP introduces multiple layers of perceptrons (neurons), enabling it to handle more complex tasks and learn non-linear relationships."

Intuition:

Imagine you're trying to predict the quality of fruit based on multiple factors like color, size, and firmness. Individually, each of these factors might not give you a complete picture, but by combining them in different ways, you can make a better decision. This is where a Multilayer Perceptron comes in—it processes data through multiple layers, each learning different aspects of the input and then combining them to form a final prediction.

Structure of MLP:

Input Layer: This is where the raw data (features) enter the network, e.g., color, size, and firmness of the fruit.

Hidden Layer(s): These layers process and transform the inputs in ways that allow the network to learn complex patterns. Each neuron in a hidden layer combines inputs from the previous layer with different weights and applies an activation function.

Output Layer: This layer gives the final prediction or classification, e.g., whether the fruit is ripe or not.

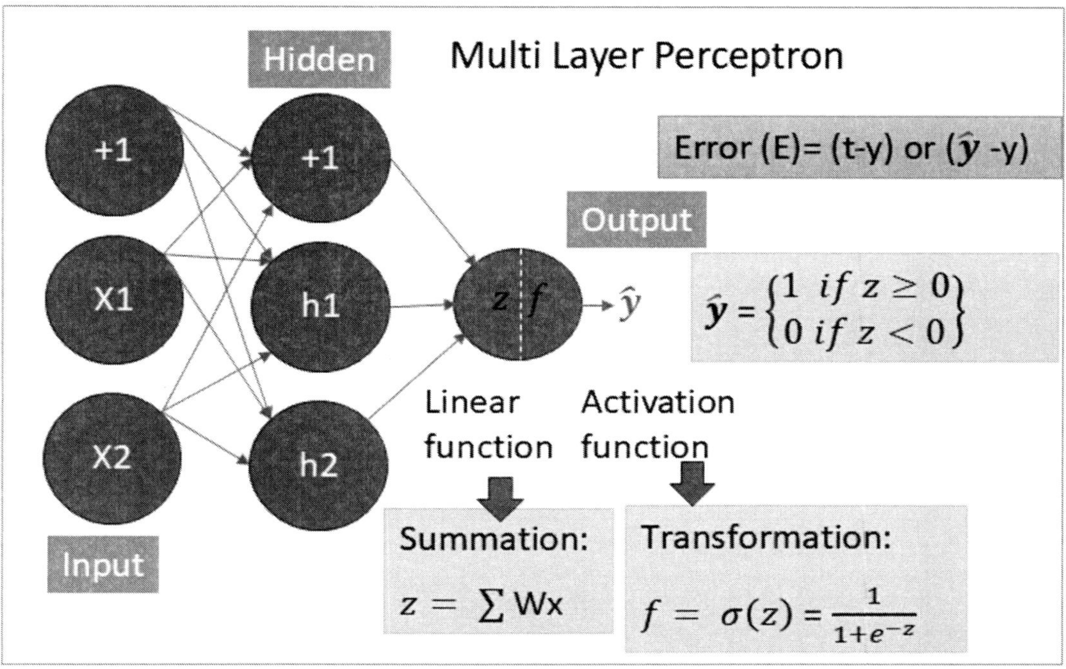

Illustration P6_perceptron_3

Perceptron Function:

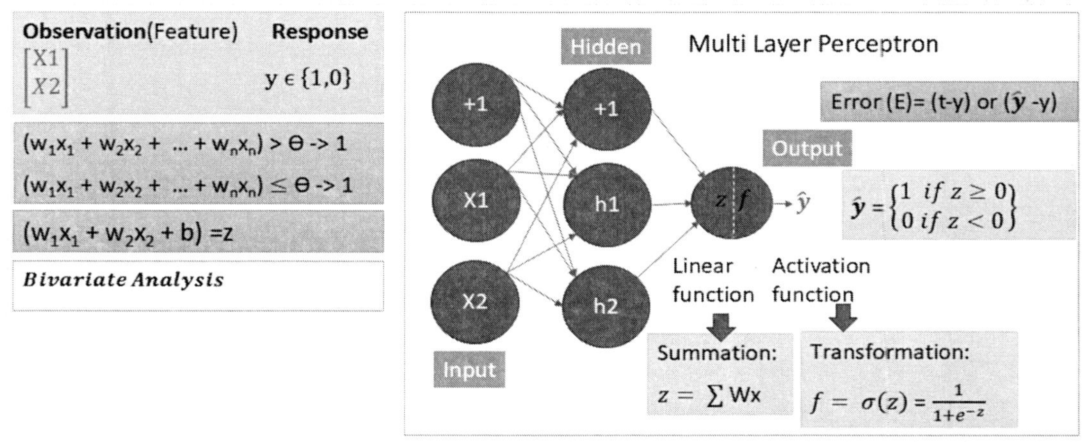

Illustration P6_perceptron_4

The Perceptron function, denoted as 'f(x)', produces output by multiplying the input 'x' with the learned weight coefficient 'w' and applying a bias term 'b'. Mathematically, it can be expressed as:

$$(w_1x_1 + w_2x_2 + b) = z$$

$$\hat{y} = \begin{Bmatrix} 1 \text{ } if \text{ } z \geq 0 \\ 0 \text{ } if \text{ } z < 0 \end{Bmatrix}$$

Where:

- 'w' represents the real-valued weights vector.
- 'b' represents the bias term.
- 'x' represents the input vector values.

This function forms the core decision-making mechanism within the perceptron, determining whether the neuron activates based on the weighted input sum.

Perceptron Weight and Error Adjustment

In the perceptron model, weight adjustment is a critical process for improving the accuracy of the classification. This adjustment is achieved through an iterative learning algorithm that minimises the error between the actual and predicted outputs.

Weight Adjustment Process

Initialization:

Weights (w) are initialised to small random values or zeros. A bias term (b) is also initialised similarly.

Prediction:

For each training instance, compute the weighted sum of inputs:

$$z = \sum_{i=1}^{n} w_i x_i + b$$

Apply the activation function (typically a step function):

$$\hat{y} = f(z) = \begin{Bmatrix} 1 \ if \ z \geq 0 \\ 0 \ if \ z < 0 \end{Bmatrix}$$

Error Calculation:

Determine the error (E) by comparing the predicted output (y) with the actual target output (t or $\hat{y}$):

$$E = t - y$$

Weight Update Rule:

Adjust the weights and bias to minimize the error using the following update rules:

$$w_i = w_i + \Delta w_i$$

$$\Delta w_i = \eta E x_i$$

$$b = b + \eta E$$

Here, η (eta) represents the learning rate, a small positive constant that controls the step size of the weight adjustments.

Iterative Learning:

The above steps are repeated iteratively for each training instance in the dataset, and the process is continued for multiple epochs (complete passes through the training dataset) until the model converges. Convergence is achieved when the weights stabilise and the error is minimised to an acceptable level.

Mathematical Representation:

For a training instance (x, t), where x is the input vector and t is the target output:

Compute weighted sum and apply activation function:

$$z = \sum_{i=1}^{n} w_i x_i + b$$

$$y = f(z)$$

Compute the error:

$$E = t - y$$

Update weights and bias:

$$w_i = w_i + \eta(t-y)x_i$$

$$b = b + \eta(t-y)$$

Convergence

Convergence Criterion:

- The perceptron algorithm will converge if the training data is linearly separable, meaning it is possible to separate the data points of different classes with a linear boundary.
- If the data is not linearly separable, the algorithm may not converge and will continue to adjust the weights indefinitely.

Learning Rate

Impact of Learning Rate:

- The learning rate (η) determines how large the weight updates will be for each training instance.
- A small learning rate ensures finer adjustments and a smoother convergence, but may require more iterations.
- A large learning rate can speed up the training, but risks overshooting the optimal weight values and potentially diverging.

Perceptron Summary

Key Steps:

- Initialise weights and bias.
- For each training instance, compute the output, calculate the error, and update the weights and bias.
- Repeat the process for multiple epochs until convergence is achieved.

Through this iterative process of prediction, error calculation, and weight adjustment, the perceptron learns to classify input vectors accurately, improving its performance with each iteration.

Case One: Simple Example

Let's say you're trying to determine if a fruit is ripe based on:

- Color (x1): (Green = 0, Yellow = 1)
- Size (x2): (Small = 0, Large = 1)
- Firmness (x3): (Soft = 0, Firm = 1)

The inputs go through the following process:

Input Layer:

x1 (color), x2 (size), and x3 (firmness).

Hidden Layer:

Each neuron in the hidden layer receives all three inputs, multiplies them by different weights, sums them up, and applies an activation function like ReLU or sigmoid to introduce non-linearity.

For example, suppose we have two neurons in the hidden layer:

Neuron 1 might compute: $h1 = \text{ReLU}(w11 \times x1 + w12 \times x2 + w13 \times x3 + b1)$

Neuron 2 might compute: $h2 = \text{ReLU}(w21 \times x1 + w22 \times x2 + w23 \times x3 + b2)$

Each neuron in the hidden layer learns different combinations of features to capture complex relationships.

Output Layer:

After the hidden layer has transformed the data, the output layer takes these transformed values (h1, h2) and uses them to make the final decision:

$output = \sigma(w_o1 \times h1 + w_o2 \times h2 + b_o)$

Here, σ is the activation function (e.g., softmax or sigmoid) applied at the output to get the final classification, such as ripe or unripe.

Why MLP is Powerful:

Non-linearity: The activation functions in the hidden layer allow the network to learn non-linear relationships between the inputs, something a single-layer perceptron cannot do.

Multiple Layers: Each layer adds a level of abstraction. The hidden layers progressively learn higher-order features of the data, transforming the raw inputs into meaningful features that the network can use for classification or prediction.

Example in Action:

Suppose you have:

- x1 (color): Yellow (1)
- x2 (size): Large (1)
- x3 (firmness): Firm (1)

The MLP will take these inputs, process them through the hidden layer, where neurons learn different combinations of color, size, and firmness, and finally decide whether the fruit is ripe or not based on the weights and the output neuron.

MLPs can handle more complex problems, like predicting stock prices, recognizing images, or identifying patterns in data that cannot be separated linearly.

Example: Regression - MLP using the California Housing Dataset

Example P1 – U1 – D20

MLP - Regression	Output

import tensorflow as tf
import numpy as np
import matplotlib.pyplot as plt
from sklearn.datasets import fetch_california_housing
from sklearn.model_selection import train_test_split
from sklearn.preprocessing import StandardScaler
 	
# Load the California Housing dataset 	
housing = fetch_california_housing()
X = housing.data
y = housing.target
 	
# Standardize the data 	
scaler = StandardScaler()
X_scaled = scaler.fit_transform(X)
	MLP Predictions vs Actual House Prices
	Predicted House Prices
	Actual House Prices

```
# Split data into training and testing sets
X_train, X_test, y_train, y_test =
train_test_split(X_scaled, y, test_size=0.2,
random_state=42)

# Build a simple MLP model
model = tf.keras.Sequential([
    tf.keras.layers.Dense(64,
input_shape=(X_train.shape[1],), activation='relu'),  #
Hidden layer with 64 neurons
    tf.keras.layers.Dense(32, activation='relu'),  #
Another hidden layer with 32 neurons
    tf.keras.layers.Dense(1)  # Output layer with 1
neuron for regression (price prediction)
])

# Compile the model with loss and optimizer
model.compile(optimizer='adam',
loss='mean_squared_error')

# Train the model
history = model.fit(X_train, y_train, epochs=200,
validation_split=0.2, verbose=0)

# Evaluate the model on the test set
test_loss = model.evaluate(X_test, y_test)
print(f"Test Loss: {test_loss}")

# Predict on the test set
y_pred = model.predict(X_test)

# Plot the predicted vs actual house prices
plt.scatter(y_test, y_pred)
plt.xlabel("Actual House Prices")
plt.ylabel("Predicted House Prices")
plt.title("MLP Predictions vs Actual House Prices")
plt.show()

# Plot training and validation loss over epochs
plt.plot(history.history['loss'], label='Training Loss')
plt.plot(history.history['val_loss'], label='Validation
Loss')
plt.xlabel("Epochs")
plt.ylabel("Loss")
plt.legend()
plt.title("Training and Validation Loss Over Epochs")
plt.show()
```

```
loss: 0.2582
Test Loss:
0.26278263330459595
129/129 ━━━━━━━━━━━━━━━━━━━━
━━━━━━━━━━━━━━━━━━━━
━ 0s 647us/step
```

This program demonstrates how to build a **Multilayer Perceptron (MLP)** using the **California Housing Dataset** to predict house prices. This dataset contains information about housing prices in different areas of California, with 20,640 instances and 8 features, including population, median income, and house age.

Data Loading and Preprocessing:

- The California Housing Dataset is loaded using fetch_california_housing() from scikit-learn.
- Features are standardized using StandardScaler to ensure better convergence during training.
- The dataset is split into training and test sets (80% training, 20% testing).

Building the Neural Network:

The MLP model is built using TensorFlow's Keras API. It has:

- An input layer connected to a hidden layer with 64 neurons and ReLU activation.
- Another hidden layer with 32 neurons and ReLU activation.
- An output layer with a single neuron for regression (predicting continuous house prices).

Compiling the Model:

- The model is compiled using the Adam optimizer and Mean Squared Error (MSE) as the loss function, which is suitable for regression tasks.

Training the Model:

- The model is trained for 200 epochs with a validation split of 20%. The training process involves iterating over the data multiple times to minimize the loss function.

Evaluation:

- The model is evaluated on the test data, and the test loss (MSE) is printed.

Prediction:

- Predictions on the test data are generated, and a scatter plot is created to compare actual house prices vs. predicted house prices, visualizing the model's performance.

Visualizing Loss:

- The program also plots the training and validation loss over epochs to observe the convergence of the model and identify overfitting or underfitting.

This program gives a hands-on demonstration of building a simple MLP for regression tasks, with a focus on housing price prediction, using common deep learning techniques such as standardization, model training, and evaluation.

Key Characteristics:

Hidden Layers:

The addition of hidden layers allows the network to capture more complex patterns in the data, making it capable of solving non-linearly separable problems.

Backpropagation Algorithm:

Training in MLPs is done using the backpropagation algorithm, which involves two main phases:

- **Forward Phase:** In this phase, activation functions propagate from the input layer through the hidden layers to the output layer. The weighted inputs are summed, and the outputs are computed using activation functions such as the sigmoid function.
- **Backward Phase:** The error between the observed actual value and the desired value at the output layer is propagated backwards through the network. During this phase, weights and biases are adjusted to minimize the error. This adjustment is done by distributing the error according to the contribution of each weight and bias to the overall error.

Example: Classification:

Example P1 – U1 – D21
Multi-Layer

```
# Step 1: Import the necessary libraries
import tensorflow as tf
import numpy as np
from tensorflow.keras.models import Sequential
from tensorflow.keras.layers import Flatten, Dense
import matplotlib.pyplot as plt

# Step 2: Download the dataset
```

```
(x_train, y_train), (x_test, y_test) = tf.keras.datasets.mnist.load_data()

# Step 3: Normalize the pixel values
x_train = x_train.astype('float32') / 255
x_test = x_test.astype('float32') / 255

# Step 4: Understand the structure of the dataset
print("Feature matrix (train):", x_train.shape)
print("Target vector (train):", y_train.shape)
print("Feature matrix (test):", x_test.shape)
print("Target vector (test):", y_test.shape)

# Step 5: Visualize the data
fig, ax = plt.subplots(10, 10, figsize=(10, 10))
k = 0
for i in range(10):
    for j in range(10):
        ax[i][j].imshow(x_train[k], cmap='gray')
        ax[i][j].axis('off')
        k += 1
plt.show()

# Step 6: Build the model
model = Sequential([
    Flatten(input_shape=(28, 28)),  # Input layer to flatten 28x28 images
    Dense(256, activation='sigmoid'),  # First hidden layer with 256 neurons
    Dense(128, activation='sigmoid'),  # Second hidden layer with 128 neurons
    Dense(10, activation='softmax')  # Output layer with 10 neurons (one for each digit)
])

# Step 7: Compile the model
model.compile(
    optimizer='adam',
    loss='sparse_categorical_crossentropy',
    metrics=['accuracy']
)

# Step 8: Train the model
history = model.fit(
    x_train, y_train,
    epochs=10,
    batch_size=2000,
    validation_split=0.2
)

# Step 9: Evaluate the model
results = model.evaluate(x_test, y_test, verbose=0)
print('Test loss:', results[0])
```

```
print('Test accuracy:', results[1])

# Plot training & validation accuracy values
plt.plot(history.history['accuracy'])
plt.plot(history.history['val_accuracy'])
plt.title('Model accuracy')
plt.xlabel('Epoch')
plt.ylabel('Accuracy')
plt.legend(['Train', 'Validation'], loc='upper left')
plt.show()

# Plot training & validation loss values
plt.plot(history.history['loss'])
plt.plot(history.history['val_loss'])
plt.title('Model loss')
plt.xlabel('Epoch')
plt.ylabel('Loss')
plt.legend(['Train', 'Validation'], loc='upper left')
plt.show()
```

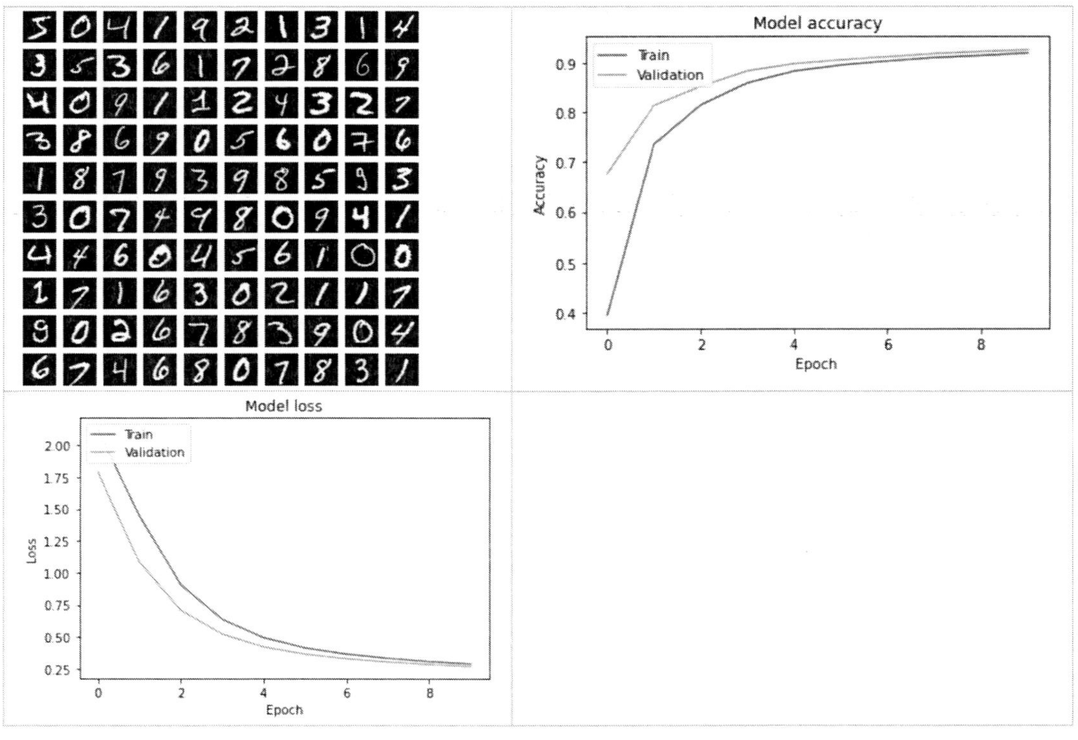

Advantages

- Handling Non-Linearity: MLPs can handle non-linear relationships in the data, enabling them to classify non-linearly separable cases effectively.
- Greater Accuracy: With the ability to model complex patterns, MLPs generally achieve higher accuracy compared to single-layer perceptrons.

Limitations

- Computational Complexity: Training MLPs can be computationally intensive and time-consuming, especially with large datasets and many hidden layers.
- Dependency on Quality of Training Data: The performance of MLPs is heavily dependent on the quality and quantity of the training data, as well as the careful tuning of hyperparameters, such as the learning rate and the number of hidden layers and nodes.

By addressing the limitations of single-layer perceptrons, multi-layer perceptrons have become a powerful tool in the field of machine learning, capable of tackling a wide range of complex problems.

PART ONE

DAY FIVE

Unit 1 - Lesson Five

Learning to Learn

Deep Neural Network with Forward and Backward - ANN

Apeksha asked, "What is Forward Propagation?"

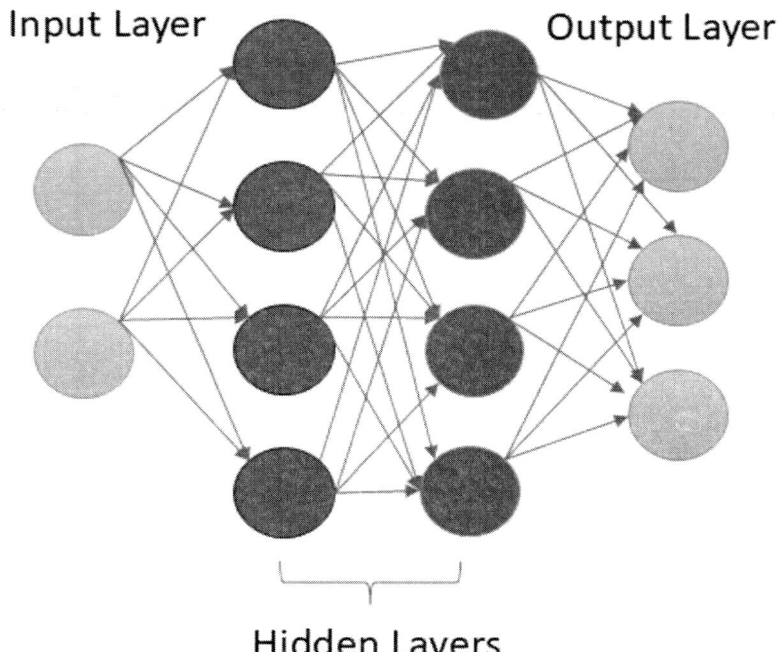

Illustration P6_Deep_ANN_01

Master said, "Forward propagation is the process used in neural networks to pass input data through the network to generate an output."

Architecture of the model

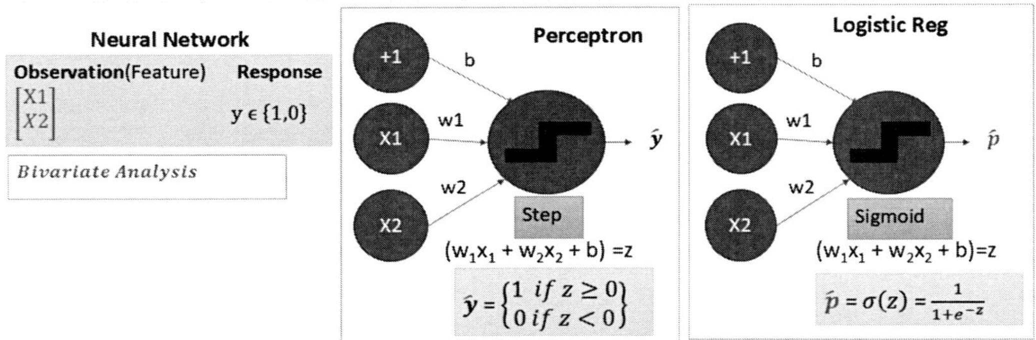

Illustration P6_Deep_ANN_02

It involves the following steps:

- **Input Layer:** Receives the initial input data.
- **Hidden Layers:** Each neuron in a hidden layer processes the input data by applying a weighted sum and an activation function.
- **Output Layer:** The final layer generates the output predictions.

In forward propagation, data moves in one direction—forward—through the network, layer by layer, until it reaches the output layer. The primary goal is to calculate the predicted output for a given set of inputs.

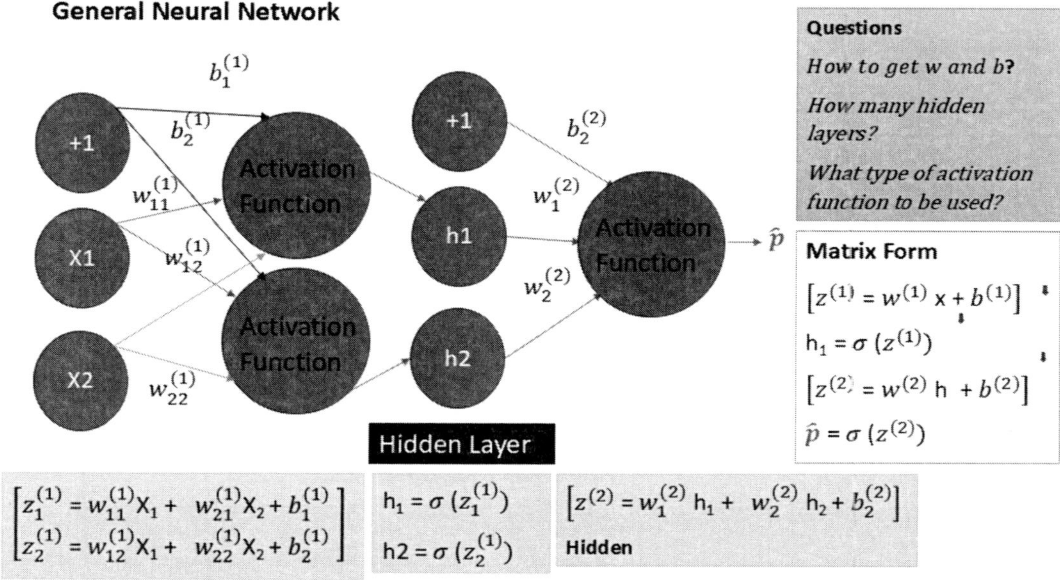

Illustration P6_Deep_ANN_02

Sam asked, "What is Backward Propagation?"

Master replied, "In backpropagation is a highly effective algorithm used to train artificial neural networks, particularly feed-forward neural networks."

Backpropagation is an iterative algorithm designed to minimize the cost function by determining how weights and biases should be adjusted. During each epoch, the model learns by updating the weights and biases to minimize the loss, effectively descending along the gradient of the error. This process involves popular optimisation algorithms such as gradient descent or stochastic gradient descent.

The core of backpropagation involves computing the gradient, which is essential for minimizing the cost function. This gradient computation is implemented using the chain rule from calculus, allowing the algorithm to navigate through the complex layers of the neural network. By applying the chain rule, backpropagation efficiently calculates the partial derivatives of the loss function with respect to each weight and bias, guiding the adjustments needed to reduce errors and improve the model's performance.

Backward propagation, or backpropagation, is a method used to train neural networks by updating the weights to minimize the error.

It involves the following steps:

- **Calculate Error:** Determine the difference between the predicted output and the actual output (loss).
- **Error Propagation:** The error is propagated backwards through the network, from the output layer to the input layer.
- **Weight Adjustment:** Adjust the weights of the connections in the network to reduce the error, using techniques like gradient descent.

During backpropagation, the network learns by iteratively adjusting the weights based on the calculated error, allowing it to make more accurate predictions over time.

Example:

Assume we have a simple neural network with one hidden layer, and the neurons use the sigmoid activation function. We will perform a forward pass and a backward pass on the network. Let's also assume that the actual output y is 0.5, and the learning rate η is 1. Here's how to perform backpropagation using the backpropagation algorithm.

Step-by-Step Backpropagation Example

Define the Network

- Input layer: 2 neurons
- Hidden layer: 2 neurons
- Output layer: 1 neuron

Initialise Weights and Biases

- Assume we have the following initial weights and biases:
- Input to hidden layer weights: w1, w2, w3, w4
- Hidden layer biases: b1, b2
- Hidden to output layer weights: w5, w6
- Output layer bias: b3

Forward Pass

Input: x1, x2

Hidden Layer:

z1 = w1x1+w2x2+b1

z2 = w3x1+w4x2+b2

Activation (Sigmoid Function):

a1=σ(z1)

a2=σ(z2)

Output Layer:

z3 = w5a1 + w6a2 + b3

$\hat{y} = \sigma(z3)$

Calculate Loss

Using Mean Squared Error (MSE):

$L = \frac{1}{2}(\hat{y} - y)^2$

Backward Pass (Compute Gradients)

Output Layer Gradients:

$\frac{dL}{d\hat{y}} = \hat{y} - y$	$\frac{dz3}{dw5} = a1$
$\frac{d\hat{y}}{dz3} = \hat{y}\,(1 - \hat{y})$	$\frac{dz3}{dw6} = a2$
	$\frac{dz3}{db3} = 1$

Combining the partial derivatives using the chain rule:

$\frac{dL}{dw5} = (\hat{y}-y)\cdot \hat{y}\,(1-\hat{y})\cdot a1$ $\frac{dL}{dw6} = (\hat{y}-y)\cdot \hat{y}\,(1-\hat{y})\cdot a2$ $\frac{dL}{db3} = (\hat{y}-y)\cdot \hat{y}\,(1-\hat{y})$

Hidden Layer Gradients: For each hidden neuron, we need to compute:

$\frac{dL}{dz1}$	$\frac{dL}{dz2}$

Using the chain rule:

$\frac{dz3}{da1} = w5$ $\frac{dz3}{da2} = w6$	$\frac{dL}{dz1} = \frac{dL}{d\hat{y}}\cdot\frac{d\hat{y}}{dz3}\cdot\frac{dz3}{da1}\cdot\sigma'(z1)$ $\frac{dL}{dz2} = \frac{dL}{d\hat{y}}\cdot\frac{d\hat{y}}{dz3}\cdot\frac{dz3}{da2}\cdot\sigma'(z2)$
Where:	$\sigma'(z1) = a1(1-a1)$ $\sigma'(z2) = a2(1-a2)$

Update Weights and Biases: Using the learning rate η:

$w5 = w5-\eta\cdot\frac{dL}{dw5}$	$w1 = w1-\eta\cdot\frac{dL}{dz1}\cdot x1$	$w3=w3-\eta\cdot\frac{dL}{dz2}\cdot x1$
$w6 = w6-\eta\cdot\frac{dL}{dw6}$	$w2 = w2-\eta\cdot\frac{dL}{dz1}\cdot x2$	$w4=w4-\eta\cdot\frac{dL}{dz2}\cdot x2$
$b3=b3-\eta\cdot\frac{dL}{db3}$	$b1 = b1-\eta\cdot\frac{dL}{dz1}$	$b2=b2-\eta\cdot\frac{dL}{dz2}$

Conclusion

In this example, we've outlined the process of performing backpropagation in a neural network. By computing the gradients and updating the weights and biases, the network learns to minimize the error and improve its predictions. This iterative process continues until the model converges to a minimum error, resulting in a trained neural network.

Example:

Assume we have a simple neural network with one hidden layer, and the neurons use the sigmoid activation function. We will perform a forward pass and a backward pass on the network. Let's also assume that the actual output y is 0.5, and the learning rate η is 1.

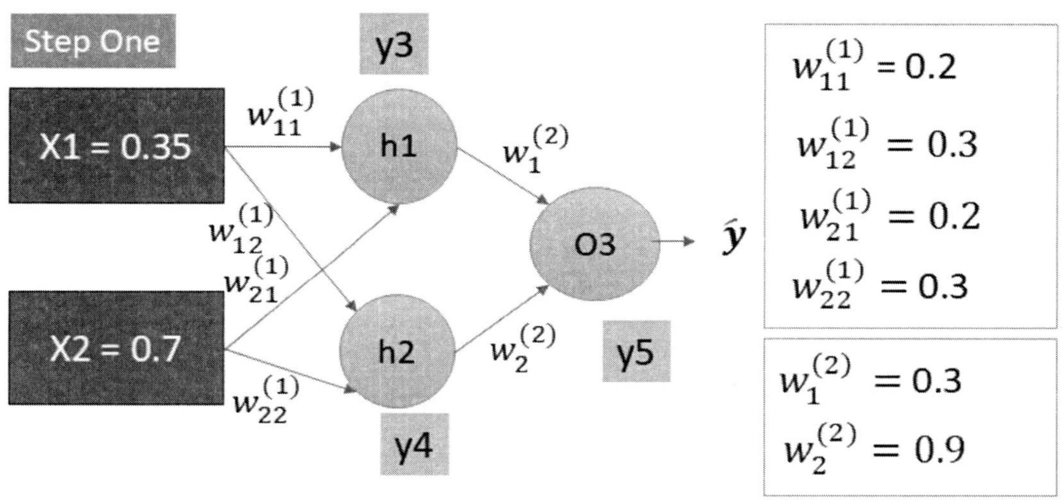

Illustration P6_Deep_ANN_05

Step 1: Before proceeding to calculate forward propagation, we need to know two key formulae:

$$a_j = \sum(w_{i,j} \cdot x_i)$$

Where:

- a_j is the weighted sum of all the inputs and weights at each node.
- $w_{i,j}$ represents the weight associated with the j-th input to the i-th neuron.
- x_i represents the value of the j-th input.

$$y_j = F(a_j) = \frac{1}{1+e^{-aj}}$$

Where:

- y_j is the output value.
- F denotes the activation function (the sigmoid activation function is used here), which transforms the weighted sum into the output value.

Step 2: Compute Forward Pass

Values of Y3 at h1 Node:

a1 = w11 x1 + w21 x2 = (0.2*0.35) + (0.3*0.7) = 0.28

$y3 = F(0.28) = \frac{1}{1+e^{-0.28}} = 0.57$

Values of Y4 at h2 Node:

a2 = w12 x1 + w22 x2 = (0.3*0.35) + (0.3*0.7) = 0.315

$y4 = F(0.315) = \frac{1}{1+e^{-0.35}} = 0.59$

Values of Y5at O3

a3 = w1 y3 + w2 y4 = (0.3*0.57) + (0.9*0.59) = 0.702

$y3 = F(0.702) = \frac{1}{1+e^{-0.702}} = 0.67$

To calculate the error, we can use the following formula:

$Error_j = y_{target} - y5$

Given: Actual output = 0.5   Obtained output (y) = 0.67

$Error_j = -0.17$

This error value will be used in the backpropagation process to adjust the weights and biases to reduce the error in future predictions.

Step 3: To implement backward propagation, we adjust each weight in the network using the following steps:

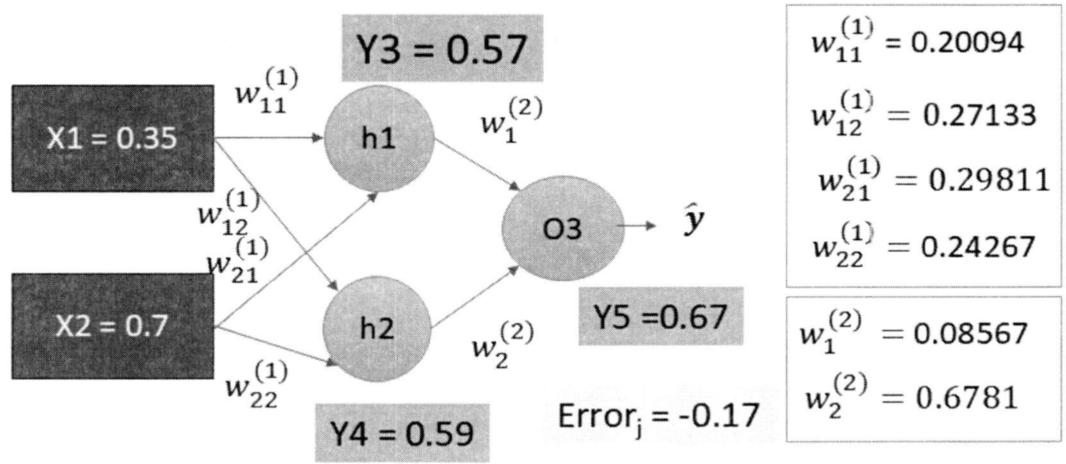

Illustration P6_Deep_ANN_05

Calculate the Error Measure (δ) for the Output Unit:

$\delta_j = y_j(1-y_j)(t_j-y_j))$

Where:

- t_j is the target output for unit j
- y_j is the actual output for unit j

Calculate the Error Measure (δ) for the Hidden Units:

$\delta_j = yj(1-yj) \sum_k(\delta_k \cdot w_{kj})$

- Where k denotes the units in the subsequent layer connected to unit j.

Update the Weights:

Each weight in the network is updated using:

$\nabla w_{ij} = \eta \delta_j O_i$

- Where η is the learning rate, δj is the error measure for unit j, and Oi is the output of the unit i feeding into unit j.

Implementing Backward Propagation

To implement backward propagation, we start from the output unit and calculate $\delta 5$ using the output of the forward pass:

$\delta 5 = y5(1-y5)(ytarget-y5)$

Where:

- y5 is the output value of the output unit.
- ytarget is the correct output for unit y5.
- $\delta 5$ is the error measure for unit y5.

Step 3A: Let's compute $\delta 5$, $\delta 3$, and $\delta 4$ using the given values.

$\delta 5 = 0.67(1\text{-}0.67)(\text{-}0.17) = \text{-}0.0376$

$\delta 3 = y3(1-y3)(w1 * \delta 5) = 0.57(1\text{-}0.57)(0.3 * 0.0375) = \text{-}0.0027$

$\delta 4 = y4(1-y4)(w2 * \delta 5) = 0.59(1\text{-}0.59)(0.9 * 0.0376) = \text{-}0.0819$

Step 4A:

Update Weights from Output to Hidden Unit

$\nabla w2 = \eta \cdot \delta 5 \cdot O4 = 1 * (\text{-}0.376) * 0.59 = \text{-}0.22184$

Update the weight:

$W2(new)=w2(old)+\nabla w2 = 0.9 + (\text{-}0.22184) \approx 0.67816$

Update Weights from Hidden Unit to Input Unit

$\nabla w11 = \eta \cdot \delta 3 \cdot O4 = 1 * (\text{-}0.0027) * 0.35 = \text{-}0.000945$

Update the weight:

$W11(new)=w11(old)+\nabla w11 = 0.000945 + (\text{-}0.2) \approx 0.200945$

Similarly, update the weights for other neurons:

W12(new) = 0.2713	W21(new) = 0.2981
W1(new) = 0.0856	W22(new) = 0.24267

By following these steps, you can iteratively adjust the weights in the network to minimize the error and improve the performance of the neural network through backpropagation.

Once the initial forward pass and backpropagation steps are completed, we perform the forward pass again to check if the neural network produces the expected output. Here is how the process works:

Perform Forward Pass Again: After updating the weights, we compute the outputs of each unit in the network for the second forward pass. Suppose the following values are obtained:

y3 = 0.57, y4 = 0.56, y5 = 0.61

Check the Output: We compare the output y5=0.61 with the expected target output ytarget=0.5. Since y5 is not equal to ytarget, we need to compute the error and perform another round of backpropagation.

Calculate the Error: The error is calculated as:

Error = ytarget − y5

Plugging in the values:

Error = 0.5 − 0.61 = −0.11

This iterative process of forward pass, error calculation, and backpropagation continues until the neural network's output y5 closely matches the target output ytarget. The network is said to have "learned" the correct mapping when the error is minimized and the outputs are sufficiently accurate.

Backpropagation is an iterative process that involves:

- Performing a forward pass to compute outputs.
- Calculating the error by comparing the actual and expected outputs.
- Propagating the error backward through the network to adjust the weights.
- Repeating the process until the network's output matches the target output, minimizing the error.

This iterative learning process ensures that the neural network gradually improves its performance and achieves the desired output through continuous weight adjustments.

Example: This implementation creates a simple neural network to solve the XOR problem using backpropagation. The network is trained using gradient descent, and the weights and biases are updated iteratively to minimize the error.

Example P1 – U1 – D22

Backward Propagation

```
import numpy as np
class NeuralNetwork:
    def __init__(self, input_size, hidden_size, output_size):
        self.input_size = input_size
        self.hidden_size = hidden_size
        self.output_size = output_size

        # Initialize weights with random values
        self.weights_input_hidden = np.random.randn(self.input_size, self.hidden_size)
        self.weights_hidden_output = np.random.randn(self.hidden_size, self.output_size)

        # Initialize biases with zeros
        self.bias_hidden = np.zeros((1, self.hidden_size))
        self.bias_output = np.zeros((1, self.output_size))

    def sigmoid(self, x):
        # Sigmoid activation function
        return 1 / (1 + np.exp(-x))

    def sigmoid_derivative(self, x):
        # Derivative of the sigmoid function
        return x * (1 - x)

    def feedforward(self, X):
        # Forward propagation through the network
        self.hidden_activation = np.dot(X, self.weights_input_hidden) + self.bias_hidden
        self.hidden_output = self.sigmoid(self.hidden_activation)

        self.output_activation = np.dot(self.hidden_output, self.weights_hidden_output) +
self.bias_output
        self.predicted_output = self.sigmoid(self.output_activation)

        return self.predicted_output

    def backward(self, X, y, learning_rate):
        # Backward propagation to update weights and biases
        output_error = y - self.predicted_output
```

```
        output_delta = output_error * self.sigmoid_derivative(self.predicted_output)

        hidden_error = np.dot(output_delta, self.weights_hidden_output.T)
        hidden_delta = hidden_error * self.sigmoid_derivative(self.hidden_output)

        # Update weights and biases with gradient descent
        self.weights_hidden_output += np.dot(self.hidden_output.T, output_delta) *
learning_rate
        self.bias_output += np.sum(output_delta, axis=0, keepdims=True) * learning_rate
        self.weights_input_hidden += np.dot(X.T, hidden_delta) * learning_rate
        self.bias_hidden += np.sum(hidden_delta, axis=0, keepdims=True) * learning_rate

    def train(self, X, y, epochs, learning_rate):
        for epoch in range(epochs):
            output = self.feedforward(X)
            self.backward(X, y, learning_rate)
            if epoch % 1000 == 0:
                loss = np.mean(np.square(y - output))
                print(f"Epoch {epoch}, Loss: {loss}")

# Define the input features and target labels for the XOR problem
X = np.array([[0, 0], [0, 1], [1, 0], [1, 1]])
y = np.array([[0], [1], [1], [0]])

# Initialize the neural network
nn = NeuralNetwork(input_size=2, hidden_size=4, output_size=1)
# Train the neural network
nn.train(X, y, epochs=10000, learning_rate=0.1)
# Test the trained model
output = nn.feedforward(X)
print("Predictions after training:")
print(output)
```

```
Output:
Predictions after training:
[[0.02477984]
 [0.95856311]
 [0.95938572]
 [0.0508218 ]]
```

Example: Classification

Master said, “Here’s a basic implementation of an Artificial Neural Network (ANN) using TensorFlow. This code includes an activation function, gradient descent, optimization, and a loss function.”

Steps included:

- Building the Model: Uses Dense layers with an activation function (ReLU and softmax).
- Defining the Loss Function: Uses SparseCategoricalCrossentropy for multi-class classification.
- Optimization: Uses the Adam optimizer.
- Training: Involves backpropagation using gradient descent.

<table>
<tr><td>Example P1 – U1 – D23</td><td></td></tr>
<tr><td>ANN</td><td>Output</td></tr>
<tr><td>import tensorflow as tf
from tensorflow.keras.models import Sequential
from tensorflow.keras.layers import Dense
from tensorflow.keras.optimizers import Adam
from tensorflow.keras.losses import
SparseCategoricalCrossentropy
from tensorflow.keras.datasets import mnist

Load and preprocess the dataset (MNIST)
(x_train, y_train), (x_test, y_test) =
mnist.load_data()
x_train = x_train.reshape(x_train.shape[0], 28 *
28).astype('float32') / 255
x_test = x_test.reshape(x_test.shape[0], 28 *
28).astype('float32') / 255

# Create the model
model = Sequential([
  Dense(128, activation='relu',
input_shape=(28*28,)), # Input layer with ReLU
activation
  Dense(64, activation='relu'), # Hidden layer
with ReLU activation
  Dense(10, activation='softmax') # Output layer
with softmax activation for multi-class classification
])

Compile the model
model.compile(
  optimizer=Adam(learning_rate=0.001), # Adam
optimizer (which improves gradient descent)
  loss=SparseCategoricalCrossentropy(), # Loss
function for multi-class classification</td><td>accuracy: 0.9755 - loss: 0.0970
Test Loss: 0.07874572277069092
Test Accuracy:
0.9800999760627747</td></tr>
</table>

```
    metrics=['accuracy']  # Track accuracy during
training
)

# Train the model
model.fit(x_train, y_train, epochs=10,
batch_size=32, validation_data=(x_test, y_test))

# Evaluate the model
loss, accuracy = model.evaluate(x_test, y_test)
print(f'Test Loss: {loss}')
print(f'Test Accuracy: {accuracy}')
```

Key Components:

Model Architecture:

- The network has an input layer with 128 neurons and ReLU activation.
- A hidden layer with 64 neurons and ReLU activation.
- The output layer has 10 neurons (for the 10 classes in MNIST) and softmax activation, which gives a probability distribution over the classes.

Loss Function:

- SparseCategoricalCrossentropy is used because it's suitable for multi-class classification with integer labels.

Optimizer:

- The Adam optimizer combines the advantages of both Momentum and RMSProp, making it suitable for complex models.

Training:

- The model is trained over 10 epochs, and the training accuracy and validation accuracy are tracked.

You can run this code with TensorFlow installed, and it will train a simple ANN on the MNIST dataset.

Brief explanation:

This TensorFlow program builds and trains a basic Artificial Neural Network (ANN) on the MNIST dataset consisting of handwritten digit images.

Key Steps in the Code:

Loading and Preprocessing Data:

The MNIST dataset is loaded using TensorFlow's built-in method. The images are reshaped into a 1D array (28x28 pixels = 784 features) and normalised to have values between 0 and 1 by dividing by 255.

Building the ANN Model:

A Sequential model is created, which means the layers are stacked one after another.

The model contains:

- An input layer (128 neurons) with a ReLU activation function.
- A hidden layer (64 neurons) also uses ReLU.
- An output layer (10 neurons) with a softmax activation function to handle multi-class classification (10 possible digits: 0-9).

Compilation:

- The model is compiled with the Adam optimizer, which is an efficient optimization technique that adjusts learning rates during training for better performance.
- The loss function used is SparseCategoricalCrossentropy, which is suitable for multi-class classification when labels are integers.
- Accuracy is set as the metric to track the model's performance.

Training:

The model is trained for 10 epochs using mini-batches of 32 samples. This is done on the training dataset (x_train, y_train), while the test dataset (x_test, y_test) is used for validation.

Evaluation:

After training, the model is evaluated on the test dataset to calculate the loss and accuracy of the model on unseen data.

ANN Summary:

This code demonstrates how to build a simple ANN using TensorFlow, with:

- Activation functions (ReLU and softmax) to introduce non-linearity.
- Gradient descent (via the Adam optimizer) to update model parameters.
- A loss function (cross-entropy) to measure prediction error. The model learns to classify images of digits from the MNIST dataset.

Note: The concepts of **Activation Functions**, **Gradient Descent**, and **Loss Functions** are thoroughly explored in the book *Optimum Python Power Series IV*.

Differences and characteristics of Artificial Intelligence (AI), Machine Learning (ML), and Deep Learning (DL):

Category	Artificial Intelligence (AI)	Machine Learning (ML)	Deep Learning (DL)
Definition	Broad field creating intelligent machines performing tasks requiring human intelligence.	A subset of AI using algorithms to learn from data and improve over time.	Subset of ML using neural networks with multiple layers.
Focus	Mimicking human behaviour through specific algorithms.	Learning from data using statistical methods.	Analysing data using deep neural networks.
Hierarchy	Encompasses ML and DL	Subset of AI	Subset of ML
Key Concepts	Uses complex math, search trees, and rule-based systems.	Uses algorithms like K-Means, SVMs, and regression.	Uses deep neural networks to break down complex tasks.
Goals	Increase chances of success	Increase accuracy, less focus on the success ratio	Achieve high accuracy by training on large datasets
Efficiency	Most efficient when combining ML and DL.	Less efficient with higher dimensional data.	More powerful and works well with large datasets.

Learning Method	Rule-based, knowledge-based, or data-driven.	Supervised, unsupervised, or reinforcement learning.	Uses multiple layers of neurons for hierarchical data processing.
Examples of Applications	Google's AI predictions, ride-sharing apps, AI autopilots.	Virtual assistants (Siri, Alexa), email spam filtering.	Sentiment-based news aggregation, image analysis.
Types/Categories	ANI, AGI, ASI	Supervised, Unsupervised, Reinforcement.	Unsupervised Pre-trained Networks, CNNs, RNNs, and Recursive Neural Networks.
Human Brain Analogy	Mimics human intelligence broadly.	Algorithms that learn from data are similar to human learning.	Neural networks are inspired by the structure and function of the human brain.

Detailed Comparison

Aspect	Artificial Intelligence (AI)	Machine Learning (ML)	Deep Learning (DL)
Broader Family	Includes ML and DL	Subset of AI	Subset of ML
Search Trees/Math	Involves complex math and search trees.	Involves statistical methods.	Involves deep neural network architectures.
Logic and Visualization	Focus on logic and reasoning, and visualizes complex functions.	Visualizes functions like K-Means and SVM.	Uses layered neural networks to handle complex feature extraction.
Training and Accuracy	Aims to increase the success ratio.	Aims to increase accuracy.	Achieves the highest accuracy with large datasets.
Examples	AI-powered predictions, ride-sharing apps, and commercial flight autopilots.	Virtual assistants, spam filtering, malware detection.	News aggregation, image, and speech recognition.
Categorization	ANI, AGI, ASI	Supervised, Unsupervised, Reinforcement Learning.	CNNs, RNNs, Recursive Neural Networks, Unsupervised Pre-trained Networks.
Network Layers	N/A	Shallow or single-layer networks.	Multi-layer (deep) networks

Efficiency	Most efficient with ML and DL combined.	Less efficient with higher dimensional data.	Highly efficient with large and complex datasets.
Human Brain Analogy	Broadly mimics human intelligence.	Algorithms learning from data, similar to humans learning	Neural networks inspired by the human brain structure and function
Learning Method	Data-driven or rule-based learning	Supervised, Unsupervised, Reinforcement.	Layered neural network learning.

This table provides a concise and structured comparison, highlighting the main aspects and differences among AI, ML, and DL.

Summary:

Deep Learning is a subset of machine learning that focuses on neural networks with multiple layers capable of learning complex patterns from large datasets. Frameworks such as **TensorFlow** and **Keras** provide high-level tools to build and train these neural network architectures efficiently.

A **Neural Network** consists of input layers, hidden layers, and output layers. During **forward propagation**, data flows through the layers, and predictions are generated. The difference between predictions and actual values is measured using **loss functions**, and this error is minimized using **backward propagation**, where gradients are computed using the **chain rule**.

Gradient Descent is the core optimization technique used to update network weights. Variants like **Stochastic Gradient Descent (SGD)** and **Mini-batch Gradient Descent** help improve training efficiency and stability. Advanced optimizers such as **AdaGrad** and **RMSProp** adapt learning rates to accelerate convergence.

Activation functions introduce non-linearity, enabling networks to learn complex patterns. Common types include **Sigmoid**, **ReLU**, **Tanh**, and **Softmax**. Proper **weight initialization techniques** and the inclusion of **Bias** terms improve learning performance.

Neural networks can be categorized into types such as **Perceptron**, **Multi-Layer Perceptron (MLP)**, and more advanced architectures. Key **hyperparameters**, including learning rate, number of epochs, batch size, and number of hidden layers, must be carefully tuned to achieve optimal performance—a process known as **hyperparameter tuning**.

Overall, this chapter provides the mathematical intuition and practical understanding required to build, train, optimize, and interpret neural network models effectively.

What Next:

Now that we understand the foundations of deep learning and neural network training, we move toward Convolutional Neural Networks (CNNs), which are specialised architectures designed for visual and spatial data. CNNs extract patterns such as edges, textures, and shapes using convolutional filters rather than fully connected layers. This makes them powerful for image classification, object detection, and feature extraction. They use key components like convolution layers, activation functions, pooling layers, and fully connected layers to progressively learn meaningful features. The next section will explore how CNNs work, why they are efficient, and how backpropagation adapts filters for learning.

P1-U1-L1 – 5 - Practice Question

1. What is Deep Learning?
2. What is the role of TensorFlow in deep learning?
3. How does Keras relate to TensorFlow?
4. What is a Neural Network?
5. What is Forward Propagation?
6. What is Backward Propagation?
7. What is Gradient Descent?
8. What is Stochastic Gradient Descent (SGD)?
9. What is Mini-batch Gradient Descent?
10. What is the Chain Rule used for in neural networks?
11. What is an Epoch?
12. What is a Loss Function?
13. What are Weight Initialization Techniques?
14. What is an Activation Function?
15. Name some common Activation Functions.
16. What is a Perceptron?
17. What is a Multilayer Perceptron (MLP)?
18. What is a Learning Rate?
19. What is Hyperparameter Tuning?

20. What are Adagrad and RMSProp?

PART TWO

From Pixels to Patterns

CNN

"A Convolutional Network does not merely see—it learns to perceive. It discerns the essence hidden beneath pixels, layer by layer, until patterns whisper meaning into understanding."

– Shree Shambav

PART TWO

DAY SIX

Unit 2 - Lesson One

Learning to See - CNN

"Each convolutional layer is like a painter adding brushstrokes to reality—what begins as chaos of color and light becomes contours, textures, and finally, comprehension."

– Shree Shambav

Akshaya asked, "Master, what is a Convolutional Neural Network (CNN)?"

Master said, "A Convolutional Neural Network (CNN) is a type of deep learning model specifically designed for image recognition, classification, and processing. CNNs are inspired by the way the human brain processes visual data, using layers that automatically learn to detect patterns such as edges, textures, and complex shapes."

CNNs are widely used in applications like object detection, facial recognition, medical image analysis, and autonomous driving.

Akshaya continued, How do CNNs work?

CNNs process images through a series of specialised layers, each responsible for extracting different levels of features. The key layers in a CNN are:

Convolutional Layer

- This layer applies multiple filters (kernels) to an image to detect edges, textures, and patterns.

- The result is a set of feature maps that highlight important details.

Activation Function (ReLU - Rectified Linear Unit)

- Introduces non-linearity to the model, ensuring complex features can be learned.
- ReLU replaces negative values with zero, speeding up learning.

Pooling Layer (Max Pooling or Average Pooling)

- Reduces the spatial size of feature maps while preserving important details.
- Helps make CNNs faster and more efficient by reducing computations.

Fully Connected Layer (Dense Layer)

- Flattens the extracted features into a single vector.
- Connects with neurons to make final predictions, like identifying a cat vs. a dog.

Softmax/Classification Layer

- Converts the final output into probability scores for each class.
- Example: If the CNN is trained for digit recognition, it outputs probabilities for numbers 0-9.

Nikash asked, "How do CNNs Learn? (Backpropagation and Training)"

Forward Propagation: The input image passes through the layers, and a prediction is made.

Loss Calculation: The model calculates how far the prediction is from the actual label.

Backpropagation and Optimisation:

- The error is sent backward through the network.
- The model updates weights using Gradient Descent (like Adam or SGD).

Iteration: This process repeats for thousands of images until the model learns optimal patterns.

Master said, the code implements a simple Convolutional Neural Network (CNN) using TensorFlow/Keras. The model is designed for image classification tasks, such as recognising handwritten digits from the MNIST dataset.

Key Components of the CNN Model:

Input Layer: Accepts grayscale images of size 28x28 with a single channel (1 for grayscale).

First Convolutional Layer (Conv2D):

- Uses 32 filters (small feature detectors of size 3x3).
- Extracts basic patterns like edges and textures.
- Uses the ReLU activation function for non-linearity.

MaxPooling Layer:

- Reduces spatial dimensions (downsampling).
- Helps retain important features while reducing computation.

Second Convolutional Layer (Conv2D):

- Uses 64 filters for extracting deeper patterns.
- Another MaxPooling layer is applied for further downsampling.

Flatten Layer: Converts 2D feature maps into a 1D vector for the dense layers.

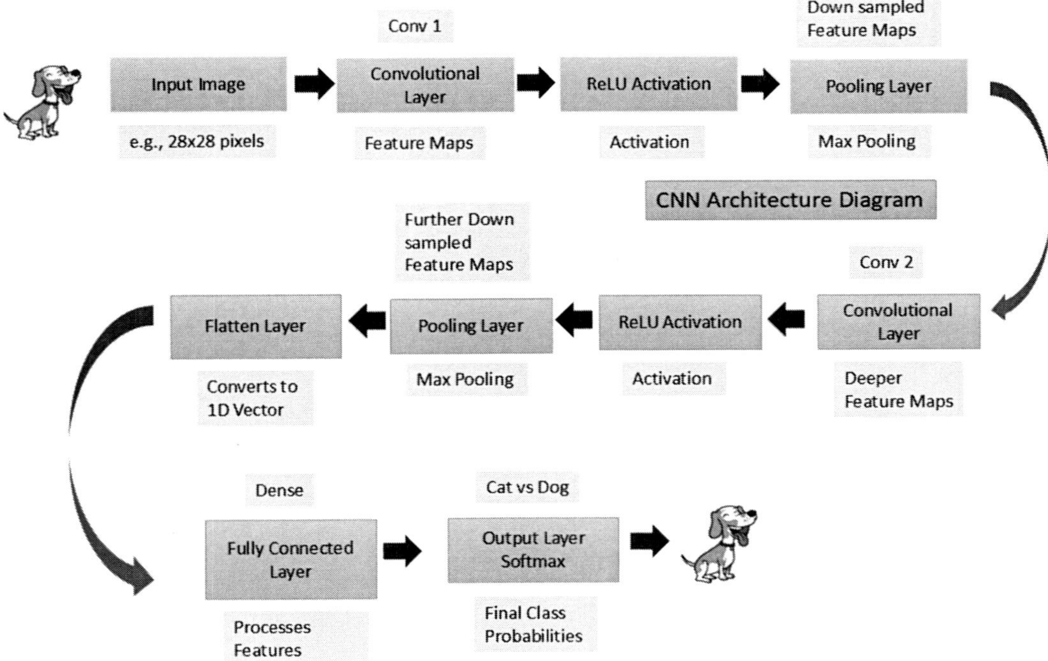

Illustration P6_CNN2: Simple CNN Architecture Diagram

Let us understand the following code snippet.

Example P2 – U2 – D1	
CNN	**Output**

import tensorflow as tf
from tensorflow import keras
from tensorflow.keras import layers
import os
os.environ['TF_CPP_MIN_LOG_LEVEL'] = '3'
# Suppress TensorFlow logs (1=INFO, 2=WARNING, 3=ERROR) 	
 	
# Define the CNN model 	
model = keras.Sequential([
  layers.Conv2D(filters=32, kernel_size=(3,3), activation='relu', input_shape=(28,28,1)), # Conv Layer 1
  layers.MaxPooling2D(pool_size=(2,2)), # Pooling Layer 1
  layers.Conv2D(filters=64, kernel_size=(3,3), activation='relu'), # Conv Layer 2
	Model: "sequential_1"
	Total params: 225,034 (879.04 KB)
	Trainable params: 225,034 (879.04 KB)
	Non-trainable params: 0 (0.00 B)

```
    layers.MaxPooling2D(pool_size=(2,2)),  #
Pooling Layer 2
    layers.Flatten(),  # Flatten layer
    layers.Dense(128, activation='relu'),  # Fully
connected layer
    layers.Dense(10, activation='softmax')  # Output
layer (10 classes)
])

# Print model summary
model.summary()
```

Fully Connected (Dense) Layer:

- Contains 128 neurons with ReLU activation, learning abstract features.

Output Layer:

- Uses Softmax activation to classify images into 10 categories (e.g., digits 0-9).

Final Step:

- model.summary() prints the architecture, including the number of parameters and layer details.

Mathematical Intuition behind CNN:

What is a Convolution Layer in CNN?

A Convolutional Layer is the core building block of a Convolutional Neural Network (CNN). It is responsible for automatically detecting patterns and features from input images using a mathematical operation called convolution.

How Does the Convolution Layer Work?

1. Input Image → A grayscale or RGB image is passed into the convolution layer.
2. Filter/Kernels → Small matrices (e.g., 3×3, 5×5) slide over the image, computing weighted sums of pixel values.
3. Feature Extraction → Detects edges, textures, and patterns like corners, shapes, or objects.
4. Activation Function (ReLU) → Introduces non-linearity, allowing the network to learn complex patterns.
5. Output Feature Map → A transformed representation of the input, highlighting essential features.

Mathematical Representation

Each pixel in the output feature map is calculated as:

$$\text{Output}(i,j)=\sum\sum(\text{Kernel} \times \text{Image Patch})$$

Where:

- Kernel is a small filter matrix.
- Image Patch is a portion of the image the kernel slides over.

The kernel slides over the image, computing the dot product to form a feature map.

Step 1: Define the Input and Kernel

Input Matrix (3×3)

$$I = \begin{bmatrix} 1 & 8 & 2 \\ 6 & 4 & 2 \\ 7 & 0 & 4 \end{bmatrix}$$

Kernel (2×2)

$$K = \begin{bmatrix} 1 & 2 \\ -1 & 0 \end{bmatrix}$$

Step 2: Compute Valid Cross-Correlation

Valid cross-correlation means that the kernel only slides over positions where it fully overlaps with the input matrix. The output size is determined by:

Output Size = (Input Size − Kernel Size) + 1

For a 3×3 input and a 2×2 kernel:

Output Size = (3−2+1) × (3−2+1) = 2×2

Now, compute element-wise multiplications and summations as the kernel slides over the input.

Illustration P5_CNN1: Convolution Operation: Cross-Correlation

Step 3: Perform Sliding Window Computation

Position (0,0):

$$\begin{bmatrix} 1 & 2 \\ -1 & 0 \end{bmatrix} \cdot \begin{bmatrix} 1 & 2 \\ -1 & 0 \end{bmatrix} = (1\times1) + (8\times2) + (6\times-1) + (4\times0) = 1 + 16 - 6 + 0 = 11$$

Position (0,1):

$$\begin{bmatrix} 1 & 2 \\ -1 & 0 \end{bmatrix} \cdot \begin{bmatrix} 1 & 2 \\ -1 & 0 \end{bmatrix} = (8\times1) + (2\times2) + (4\times-1) + (2\times0) = 8 + 4 - 4 + 0 = 8$$

Position (1,0):

$$\begin{bmatrix} 1 & 2 \\ -1 & 0 \end{bmatrix} \cdot \begin{bmatrix} 1 & 2 \\ -1 & 0 \end{bmatrix} = (6\times1) + (4\times2) + (7\times-1) + (0\times0) = 6 + 8 - 7 + 0 = 7$$

Position (1,1):

$$\begin{bmatrix} 1 & 2 \\ -1 & 0 \end{bmatrix} \cdot \begin{bmatrix} 1 & 2 \\ -1 & 0 \end{bmatrix} = (4\times1) + (2\times2) + (0\times-1) + (4\times0) = 4 + 4 + 0 + 0 = 8$$

Step 4: Output Matrix

Thus, the final **output matrix** of the valid cross-correlation operation is:

$$\begin{bmatrix} 11 & 8 \\ 7 & 8 \end{bmatrix}$$

Convolution vs. Cross-Correlation

Step 1: Rotate Kernel by 180° for Convolution

Rotate both rows and columns:

$$\text{Krotated} = \begin{bmatrix} 0 & -1 \\ 2 & 1 \end{bmatrix}$$

Now, this rotated kernel will be used in the convolution process instead of the original.

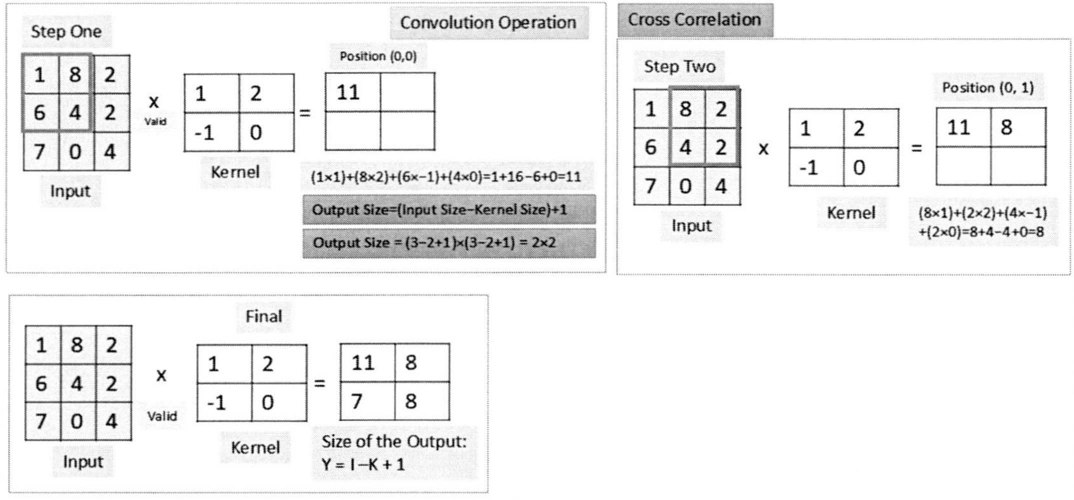

Illustration P6_Cross-Conv_1: Convolution

Step 2: Apply Convolution with the Rotated Kernel

Now, perform the valid convolution using the **rotated kernel** instead of the original.

Note:

- Cross-correlation uses the kernel as is.
- Convolution (conv2d) requires a 180-degree rotation before element-wise multiplication.

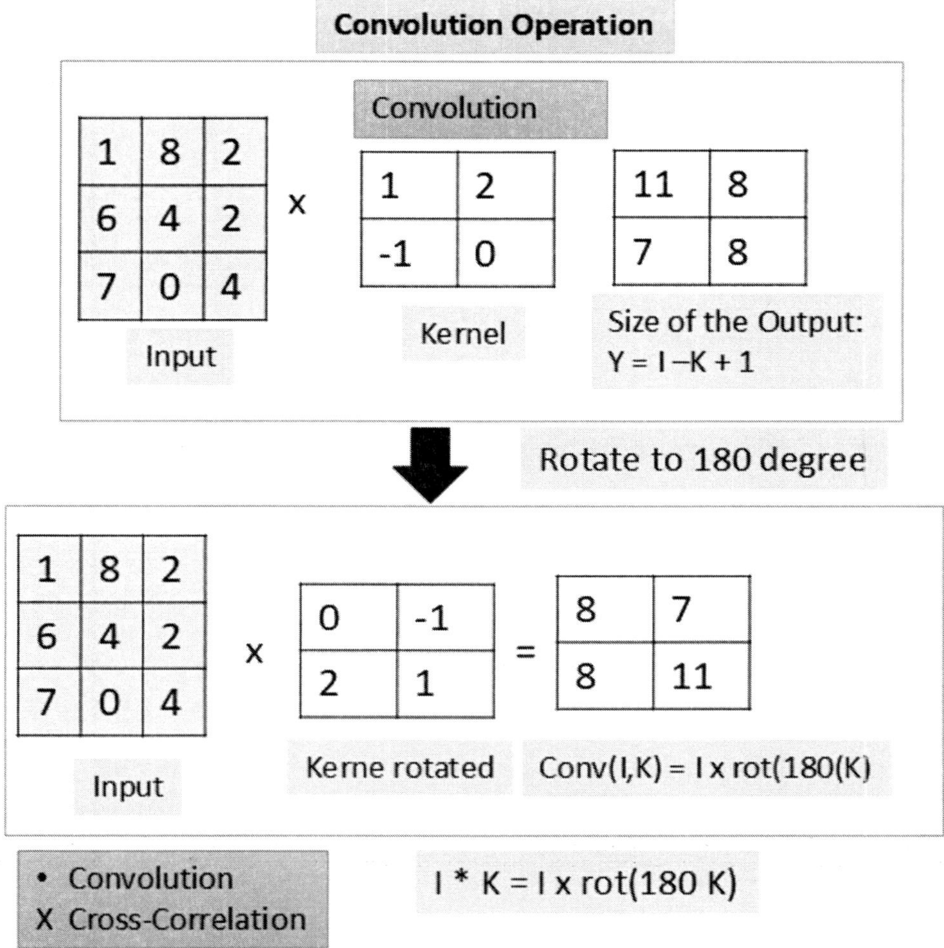

Illustration P6_Cross-Conv_2: Convolution

Difference Between Valid Cross-Correlation and Full Cross-Correlation

In image processing and deep learning, **cross-correlation** is a technique where a kernel (filter) is slid over an input matrix to compute a transformed output. The output size depends on the method used:

- Valid Cross-Correlation - No padding, only regions where the kernel fully fits.
- Full Cross-Correlation - Uses padding, allowing the kernel to slide over all elements, even at the edges.

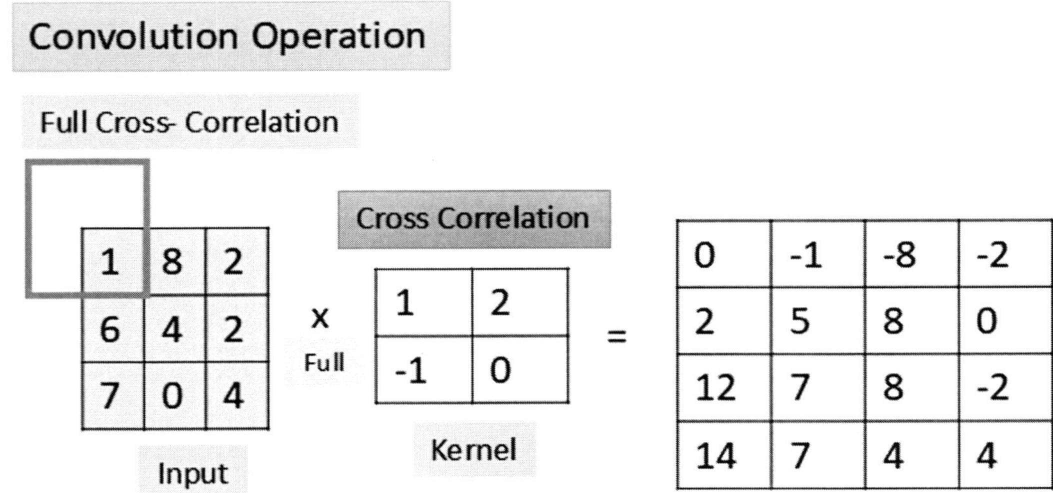

Illustration P6_Full-Cross_1 – Full Cross- Correlation

Valid Cross-Correlation (No Padding)

- The kernel moves only where it completely fits inside the input matrix.
- The output size is smaller than the input because edge pixels are ignored.

Formula for Output Size:

Output Size = Input Size − Kernel

This is often used when we don't want extra padding or border effects.

Full Cross-Correlation (With Padding)

- The kernel is allowed to slide over all positions, including edges.
- Zero-padding is added around the input to ensure that the kernel can be applied at all positions.
- The output size is larger than the valid case.

Formula for Output Size:

Output Size = Input Size + Kernel Size – 1

Note: A 3×3 input with a 2×2 kernel will produce a 4×4 output when using full cross-correlation.

Key Difference:

Feature	Valid Cross-Correlation	Full Cross-Correlation
Padding	No padding	Zero-padding added
Output Size	Smaller than input	Larger than input
Usage	Common in deep learning (convolution layers)	Less common, useful for preserving spatial dimensions

Full Cross-Correlation

In full cross-correlation, we **zero-pad** the input matrix before applying the kernel. For a 3×3 input and a 2×2 kernel, the output will be:

Output Size = (Input Size + Kernel Size − 1) = (3+2−1) = 4×4

So, the padded input matrix will be:

$$I' = \begin{bmatrix} 0 & 0 & 0 & 0 \\ 0 & 1 & 8 & 2 \\ 0 & 6 & 4 & 2 \\ 0 & 7 & 0 & 4 \end{bmatrix}$$

Now, we slide the 2×2 kernel across all positions.

Step-by-step Calculations

Each position in the output matrix is computed as:

Top-left position:

$(0*1 + 0*2 + 0*(-1) + 1*0) = 0$

Top-centre position:

$(0*1 + 0*2 + 1*(-1) + 8*0) = -1$

Top-right position:

$(0*1 + 0*2 + 8*(-1) + 2*0) = -8$

Top-far-right position:

$(0*1 + 0*2 + 2*(-1) + 0*0) = -2$

Second-row, first column:

$(0*1 + 1*2 + 0*(-1) + 6*0) = 2$

Second-row, second column:

$(1*1 + 8*2 + 6*(-1) + 4*0) = 5$

Second-row, third column:

$(8*1 + 2*2 + 4*(-1) + 2*0) = 8$

Second-row, fourth column:

$(2*1 + 0*2 + 2*(-1) + 0*0) = 0$

Third-row, first column:

$(0*1 + 6*2 + 0*(-1) + 7*0) = 12$

Third-row, second column:

$(6*1 + 4*2 + 7*(-1) + 0*0) = 7$

Third-row, third column:

$(4*1 + 2*2 + 0*(-1) + 4*0) = 8$

Third-row, fourth column:

$(2*1 + 0*2 + 4*(-1) + 0*0) = -2$

Fourth-row, first column:

$(0*1 + 7*2 + 0*(-1) + 0*0) = 14$

Fourth-row, second column:

$(7*1 + 0*2 + 0*(-1) + 4*0) = 7$

Fourth-row, third column:

$(0*1 + 4*2 + 4*(-1) + 0*0) = 4$

Fourth-row, fourth column:

$(4*1 + 0*2 + 0*(-1) + 0*0) = 4$

Final Output Matrix (4×4)

$$O = \begin{bmatrix} 0 & -1 & -8 & -2 \\ 2 & 5 & 8 & 0 \\ 12 & 7 & 8 & -2 \\ 14 & 7 & 4 & 4 \end{bmatrix}$$

Valid cross-correlation gave a 2×2 output.

Full cross-correlation expanded it to a 4×4 output by **zero-padding** the input.

Convolution Layer

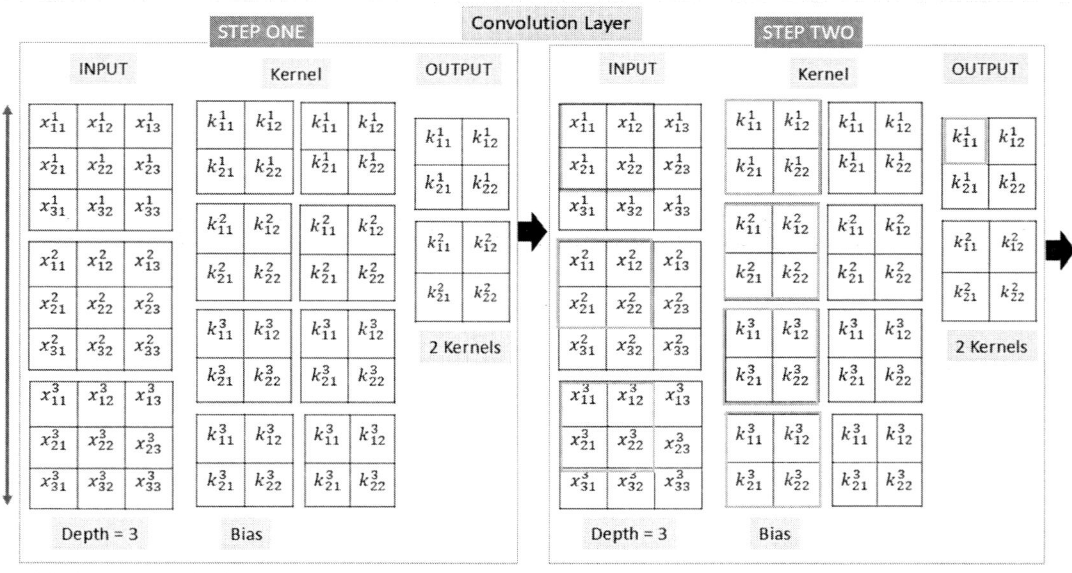

Illustration P6_Convolution_1A – Convolution Layer

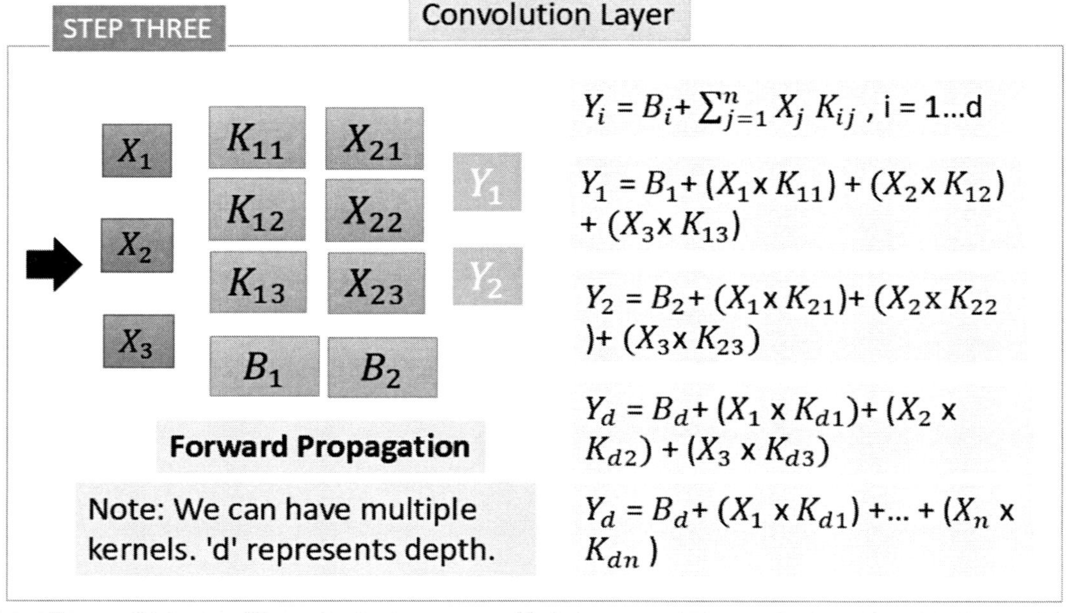

Illustration P6_Convolution_1B – Convolution Layer

Forward Propagation in CNN: Understanding the Computation Flow

Forward propagation in a Convolutional Neural Network (CNN) involves multiple mathematical operations similar to a dense layer in a traditional feedforward network, but instead of matrix multiplications (dot products), CNNs rely on convolutions. However, the fundamental idea remains: each layer transforms the input data to extract features, eventually leading to predictions.

CNN Forward Propagation

CNN forward propagation involves the following steps:

Convolution Operation (Feature Extraction)

- Uses cross-correlation or convolution (kernel sliding over the input).
- Similar to dot products but restricted to local regions instead of fully connected weights.

$$\begin{bmatrix} Y1 \\ Y2 \\ .. \\ Y3 \end{bmatrix} = \begin{bmatrix} B1 \\ B2 \\ .. \\ Bd \end{bmatrix} + \begin{bmatrix} K11 & K12 & K13 \\ K21 & K22 & K23 \\ .... & & \\ K31 & K32 & K33 \end{bmatrix} .|x \begin{bmatrix} X1 \\ X2 \\ .. \\ Xn \end{bmatrix}$$

$$Y = B + K\ .|*\ K$$

Illustration P6_Forward_1– CNN

Activation Function (Non-linearity)

- Typically ReLU max(0,x)) is applied element-wise.

Pooling (Dimensionality Reduction)

- Max pooling or average pooling downsamples the feature maps.

Flattening and Fully Connected (Dense) Layers

- Extracted features are flattened into a vector and passed through Dense (FC) layers (where traditional dot product and activation occur).

Convolution as a Localised Dot Product

Unlike traditional dense layers, where each neuron performs:

$y = W \cdot X + b$

CNN replaces it with:

$$Y(i,j) = \sum_m \sum_n K(m, n) \cdot X(i + m, j + n) + b$$

where:

- K is the kernel (filter),

- X is the input matrix,
- The sum represents a localised dot product over a small receptive field.

Comparing CNN Convolution with Dense Layer Dot Product

Feature	CNN (Convolution)	Dense Layer (Dot Product)
Operation	Local (restricted to receptive fields)	Fully connected (each neuron sees all inputs)
Weight Sharing	Yes (same kernel applies across the input)	No (each neuron has independent weights)
Computation	Element-wise multiplications & summation over a local region	Matrix multiplication (fully connected)
Spatial Awareness	Preserves spatial structure	Loses spatial relationships

Example Calculation: CNN Convolution vs. Dense Layer

Consider a **Dense Layer:**

$$Y = W \cdot X + b$$

$$\text{If: } W = \begin{bmatrix} 1 & 2 \\ 3 & 4 \end{bmatrix}, X = \begin{bmatrix} 5 \\ 6 \end{bmatrix}, b = \begin{bmatrix} 1 \\ 1 \end{bmatrix}$$

$$Y = \begin{bmatrix} 1 & 2 \\ 3 & 4 \end{bmatrix} \cdot \begin{bmatrix} 5 \\ 6 \end{bmatrix} + \begin{bmatrix} 1 \\ 1 \end{bmatrix} = \begin{bmatrix} 1(5) & 2(6) & 1 \\ 3(5) & 4(6) & 1 \end{bmatrix} = \begin{bmatrix} 18 \\ 40 \end{bmatrix}$$

Now, for a **CNN Layer** with a 2×2 kernel sliding over a 3×3 input matrix, we perform localized dot products at each step.

Backward Propagation:

Backward Propagation in CNN (Convolutional Neural Networks)

Master said, "Nikash, Backward propagation in a CNN is the process of updating the network's weights using the gradient of the loss function with respect to each parameter. It follows the chain rule of differentiation and consists of three main steps:

Compute the Loss Gradient

- The loss function (e.g., cross-entropy, mean squared error) measures how far the predicted output is from the actual label.
- The gradient of this loss function with respect to the output of the last layer is computed.

Step One:

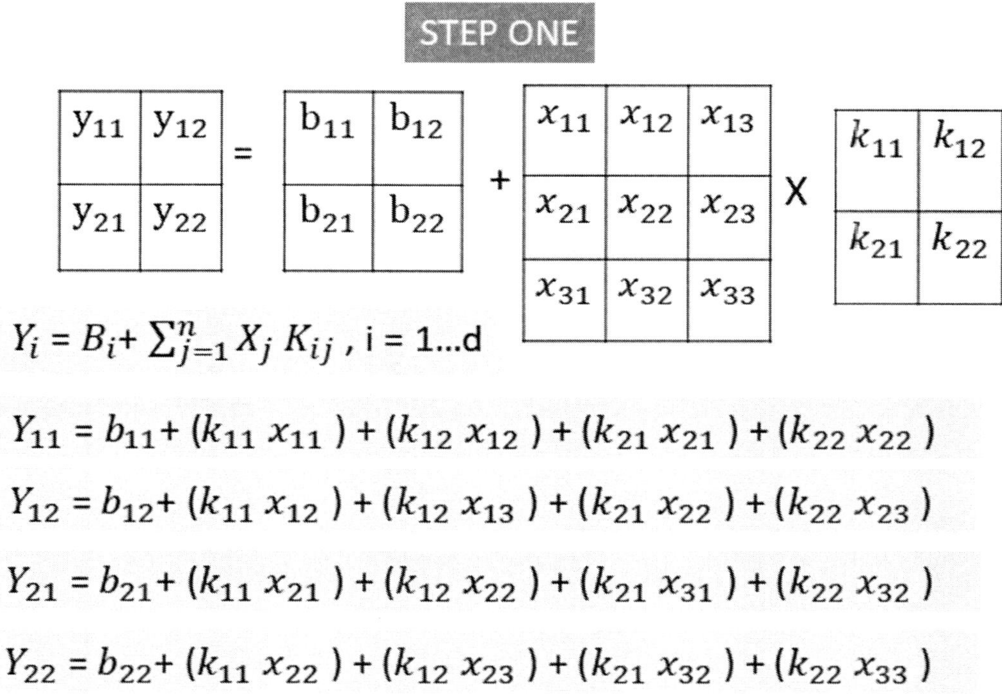

Illustration P6_FP_1– CNN

Backpropagate Through Layers

CNNs have multiple layers, and gradients are propagated in the reverse direction from output to input using the chain rule:

Fully Connected Layer (Dense Layer)

- Works like a standard neural network.
- The gradient of the weights is computed using the derivative of the activation function (e.g., ReLU, Softmax).
- The weight updates follow:

$$\mathbf{W} = \mathbf{W} - \eta \cdot \partial \mathbf{L} / \partial \mathbf{W}$$

Where η is the learning rate.

Step Two

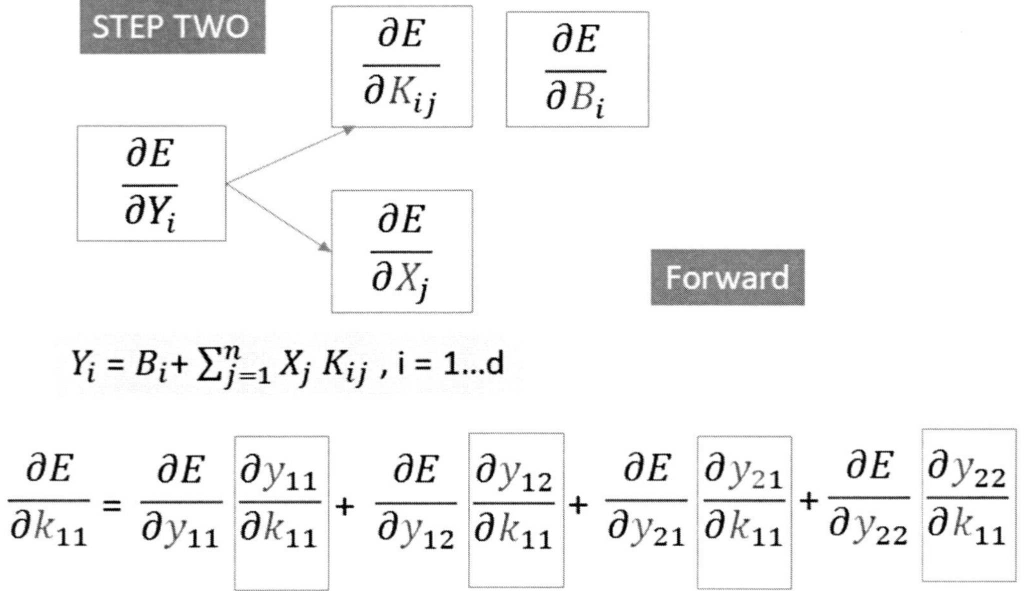

Illustration P6_FP_2– CNN

Backpropagation Through Convolutional Layers

- Unlike dense layers, convolutional layers share weights across the receptive field.
- The gradients are calculated using convolution with the rotated filter (180-degree rotation).
- The gradients are accumulated over all positions where the filter was applied.

Backpropagation Through Pooling Layers

- Max pooling: The gradient is propagated only to the neuron that had the max value during the forward pass.
- Average pooling: The gradient is equally distributed across the pooled region.

Update Weights Using Gradient Descent

Once the gradients are calculated, CNN parameters (filters, biases) are updated using optimization techniques like SGD, Adam, or RMSprop to minimize the loss.

Step Three

STEP THREE

$$\begin{bmatrix} \frac{\partial E}{\partial k_{11}} & \frac{\partial E}{\partial k_{12}} \\ \frac{\partial E}{\partial k_{21}} & \frac{\partial E}{\partial k_{22}} \end{bmatrix} = \begin{bmatrix} x_{11} & x_{12} & x_{13} \\ x_{21} & x_{22} & x_{23} \\ x_{31} & x_{32} & x_{33} \end{bmatrix} \text{X} \begin{bmatrix} \frac{\partial E}{\partial y_{11}} & \frac{\partial E}{\partial y_{12}} \\ \frac{\partial E}{\partial y_{21}} & \frac{\partial E}{\partial y_{22}} \end{bmatrix}$$

$$Y = B + (X \times K) \Rightarrow \frac{\partial E}{\partial k} = \frac{\partial E}{\partial y} \times X$$

$$\frac{\partial E}{\partial X_1} = \frac{\partial E}{\partial Y_1} \underset{\text{full}}{\text{X}} K_{11} + \dots + \frac{\partial E}{\partial Y_d} \underset{\text{full}}{\text{X}} K_{d1}$$

$$\frac{\partial E}{\partial X_j} = \frac{\partial E}{\partial Y_1} \underset{\text{full}}{\text{X}} K_{ij} + \dots + \frac{\partial E}{\partial Y_d} \underset{\text{full}}{\text{X}} K_{dj}$$

Illustration P6_FP_3– CNN

Key Differences from Dense Backpropagation

- Uses local weight sharing (convolutional filters) rather than fully connected updates.
- Instead of direct multiplication (dot product), gradients are obtained via convolution.
- Backpropagation through convolution requires rotating the filter before applying it to the gradient.

Step Four:

STEP FOUR

$$\frac{\partial E}{\partial X_j} = \sum_{i=1}^{d} \frac{\partial E}{\partial Y_i} \text{ X}_{\text{full}}\ K_{ij} \quad \text{J} = 1 \ldots \text{n}$$

$$\frac{\partial E}{\partial K_{ij}} = X_j \text{X} \frac{\partial E}{\partial Y_i}$$

$$\frac{\partial E}{\partial B_i} = \frac{\partial E}{\partial Y_i}$$

Backward Propagation

Illustration P6_FP_4– CNN

Final Thought

Backward propagation in CNNs enables learning from data by adjusting filters to detect important features like edges, textures, and complex patterns, improving accuracy over time.

Reshape Layer:

Let's take the example of the MNIST dataset, where the challenge is to identify a given number. To keep it simple, let's select only two digits for classification.

Why do we need a Reshape Layer?

The MNIST dataset consists of 28x28 grayscale images, but neural networks typically process data in a flat, vectorized format. The Reshape layer ensures that the input is structured appropriately for the convolutional layers, preserving the spatial relationships between pixels.

Binary Cross-Entropy Loss:

Why do we need Binary Cross-Entropy?

Since we are performing binary classification (distinguishing between two digits), Binary Cross-Entropy (BCE) is the appropriate loss function. It measures the difference between the predicted probability and the actual label, optimizing the model to make accurate classifications.

Sigmoid Activation Function:

Why use Sigmoid activation?

Sigmoid activation is ideal for binary classification problems as it outputs a probability score between 0 and 1. Additionally, since it takes a logarithmic input, it prevents negative values, ensuring numerical stability in probability calculations.

Let us understand the code snippet:

Convolutional Layer

This file defines a Convolutional Neural Network (CNN) layer that extracts features from images by applying multiple filters (kernels).

- Forward pass: Uses 2D cross-correlation to extract patterns.
- Backward pass: Computes gradients and updates kernels using gradient descent.
- Weights Initialization: Uses He Initialization to prevent exploding gradients.

Example P2 – U2 – D2	
CNN – Convolutional Layer: convolutional.py	**Output**

import numpy as np
from scipy import signal
 	
class Convolutional:
    def __init__(self, input_shape, kernel_size, depth):
        input_depth, input_height, input_width = input_shape
        self.depth = depth
        self.input_shape = input_shape
        self.input_depth = input_depth
        self.output_shape = (depth, input_height - kernel_size + 1, input_width - kernel_size + 1)
        self.kernels_shape = (depth, input_depth, kernel_size, kernel_size)
 	
        # He Initialization
        self.kernels = np.random.randn(*self.kernels_shape) * np.sqrt(2. / self.input_depth)
        self.biases = np.zeros(self.output_shape)
 	
    def forward(self, input):
        self.input = input
        self.output = np.copy(self.biases)
        for i in range(self.depth):
            for j in range(self.input_depth):
                self.output[i] += signal.correlate2d(self.input[j], self.kernels[i, j], "valid")
        return self.output
 	
    def backward(self, output_gradient, learning_rate):
        kernels_gradient = np.zeros(self.kernels_shape)
        input_gradient = np.zeros(self.input_shape)
 	
        for i in range(self.depth):
            for j in range(self.input_depth):
                kernels_gradient[i, j] = signal.correlate2d(self.input[j], output_gradient[i], "valid")	

```
            input_gradient[j] +=
signal.convolve2d(output_gradient[i], self.kernels[i,
j], "full")

        # Update weights and biases
        self.kernels -= learning_rate * kernels_gradient
        self.biases -= learning_rate * output_gradient
        return input_gradient
```

Fully Connected (Dense) Layer

Defines a Dense (fully connected) layer that connects all neurons from one layer to the next.

- Forward pass: Computes weighted sums and adds biases.
- Backward pass: Computes gradients for backpropagation and updates weights.
- Weight Initialization: Uses Xavier Initialization for stable training.

Example P2 – U2 – D3

CNN – Dense Layer: dense.py

```
import numpy as np

class Dense:
    def __init__(self, input_size, output_size):
        # Xavier Initialization
        self.weights = np.random.randn(output_size, input_size) * np.sqrt(1 / input_size)
        self.bias = np.zeros((output_size, 1))

    def forward(self, input):
        self.input = input
        return np.dot(self.weights, self.input) + self.bias

    def backward(self, output_gradient, learning_rate):
        weights_gradient = np.dot(output_gradient, self.input.T)
        input_gradient = np.dot(self.weights.T, output_gradient)

        # Weight update with batch normalization
        self.weights -= learning_rate * weights_gradient / output_gradient.shape[1]
        self.bias -= learning_rate * np.mean(output_gradient, axis=1, keepdims=True)
        return input_gradient
```

Reshape Layer

Example P2 – U2 – D4

CNN – Reshape Layer: reshape.py

```
import numpy as np

class Reshape:
    def __init__(self, input_shape, output_shape):
        self.input_shape = input_shape
        self.output_shape = output_shape

    def forward(self, input):
        return np.reshape(input, self.output_shape)

    def backward(self, output_gradient, learning_rate):
        return np.reshape(output_gradient, self.input_shape)
```

This layer reshapes the data between layers without modifying values.

- Forward pass: Reshapes the input to match the next layer's expected format.
- Backward pass: Reshapes the gradients for proper backpropagation.

Sigmoid Activation Function

Defines the Sigmoid activation function, which introduces non-linearity into the network.

- Forward pass: Applies the sigmoid function
- Backward pass: Computes the derivative of Sigmoid for backpropagation.

Example P2 – U2 – D5

CNN – Activation Layer: activations.py

```
import numpy as np

class Sigmoid:
    def forward(self, input):
        self.input = input
        return 1 / (1 + np.exp(-input))

    def backward(self, output_gradient, learning_rate):
        return output_gradient * (1 - self.forward(self.input)) * self.forward(self.input)
```

Binary Cross-Entropy Loss

Defines the Binary Cross-Entropy (BCE) Loss, which measures how well the CNN predicts classes (0 or 1).

Loss function: Loss

Binary Cross-Entropy Loss $= \frac{1}{N}\sum_{i=1}^{N}[\, y_i * \log(\hat{y}_i) + (1 - \, y_i\,) * \log(1 - \, \hat{y}_i)]$

Derivative: Computes the loss gradient for backpropagation.

Example P2 – U2 – D6

CNN – Binary : losses.py

```
import numpy as np

def binary_cross_entropy(y_true, y_pred):
    return -np.mean(y_true * np.log(y_pred + 1e-8) + (1 - y_true) * np.log(1 - y_pred +
1e-8))

def binary_cross_entropy_prime(y_true, y_pred):
    return -(y_true / (y_pred + 1e-8)) + ((1 - y_true) / (1 - y_pred + 1e-8))
```

Training & Prediction Functions

Contains functions for training the CNN and making predictions.

train():

- Performs forward and backward propagation for each training sample.
- Updates weights using gradients.

predict():

- Passes an input through the CNN to make a prediction.

Example P2 – U2 – D7

CNN – Training: network.py

```
import numpy as np

def train(network, loss, loss_prime, x_train, y_train, epochs, learning_rate):
    for epoch in range(epochs):
        error = 0
        for x, y in zip(x_train, y_train):
            output = x
            for layer in network:
                output = layer.forward(output)
```

```
        error += loss(y, output)

        gradient = loss_prime(y, output)
        for layer in reversed(network):
            gradient = layer.backward(gradient, learning_rate)

    print(f"Epoch {epoch+1}/{epochs}, Loss={error/len(x_train)}")

def predict(network, input_data):
    output = input_data
    for layer in network:
        output = layer.forward(output)
    return output
```

Full CNN Training

The main driver program that brings everything together.

- Loads MNIST data and filters only digits 0 & 1.
- Preprocesses images (reshaping, normalizing, and encoding labels).
- Defines CNN Architecture with Convolutional, Reshape, Dense, and Sigmoid layers.
- Trains the CNN using binary cross-entropy loss.
- Tests the trained model by predicting test images and comparing with actual labels.

Example P2 – U2 – D8	
CNN – Mnist find 0 or 1: main.py	**Output**
import numpy as np from keras.datasets import mnist from tensorflow.keras.utils import to_categorical from convolutional import Convolutional from dense import Dense from reshape import Reshape from activations import Sigmoid from losses import binary_cross_entropy, binary_cross_entropy_prime from network import train, predict import os os.environ['TF_CPP_MIN_LOG_LEVEL'] = '3' # Suppress TensorFlow logs (1=INFO, 2=WARNING, 3=ERROR)	Predicted: 1, Actual: 1

```
# Data Preprocessing
def preprocess_data(x, y, limit):
    zero_index = np.where(y == 0)[0][:limit]
    one_index = np.where(y == 1)[0][:limit]
    all_indices = np.hstack((zero_index, one_index))
    np.random.shuffle(all_indices)  # Shuffle data

    x, y = x[all_indices], y[all_indices]
    x = x.reshape(len(x), 1, 28, 28).astype("float32")
/ 255  # Normalize images
    y = to_categorical(y,
num_classes=2).reshape(len(y), 2, 1)  # One-hot
encode labels

    return x, y

# Load MNIST dataset & preprocess
(x_train, y_train), (x_test, y_test) =
mnist.load_data()
x_train, y_train = preprocess_data(x_train, y_train,
100)
x_test, y_test = preprocess_data(x_test, y_test, 100)

# Define CNN architecture
network = [
    Convolutional((1, 28, 28), 3, 5),  # Conv Layer: 5
filters, kernel size 3x3
    Sigmoid(),
    Reshape((5, 26, 26), (5 * 26 * 26, 1)),  # Flatten
layer
    Dense(5 * 26 * 26, 100),  # Fully Connected
Layer: 100 neurons
    Sigmoid(),
    Dense(100, 2),  # Output Layer: 2 neurons (0 or
1)
    Sigmoid()
]

# Train the CNN
train(
    network,
    binary_cross_entropy,
    binary_cross_entropy_prime,
    x_train,
    y_train,
    epochs=20,
    learning_rate=0.1
```

```
)

# Test the model
for x, y in zip(x_test, y_test):
    output = predict(network, x)
    print(f"Predicted: {np.argmax(output)}, Actual:
{np.argmax(y)}")
```

Our understanding

convolutional.py → Feature extraction using kernels

dense.py → Fully connected layer for classification

reshape.py → Reshapes data for different layers

activations.py → Sigmoid activation function

losses.py → Binary Cross-Entropy loss function

network.py → Training & prediction logic

main.py → Loads data, builds CNN, trains, and tests the model

Apeksha asked, "Master, why use multiple convolutional layers in a CNN?"

Master said, "Using multiple convolution layers in a Convolutional Neural Network (CNN) allows the model to extract hierarchical features from images, leading to better performance in pattern recognition, object detection, and classification."

Here's why multiple convolution layers are beneficial:

Capturing Hierarchical Features

- First layers learn low-level features (edges, textures, corners).
- Middle layers learn mid-level features (shapes, contours).
- Deeper layers learn high-level features (faces, objects, complex patterns).

Increasing Representation Power

Each additional convolution layer refines and enhances feature extraction.

- More layers = more abstract and meaningful representations.
- Helps CNNs handle complex datasets like ImageNet.

Handling Scale and Spatial Hierarchies

Deeper layers allow the network to detect small objects and large structures by learning:

- Fine-grained details in early layers
- Global context in deeper layers

This helps in tasks like face recognition, autonomous driving, and medical imaging.

Improved Feature Combinations

Each convolution layer combines features from previous layers.

Simple edges → shapes → objects

This improves the network's ability to recognize intricate patterns.

Better Generalization and Reduced Overfitting

- Deep architectures prevent overfitting by learning more general features.
- Batch normalization & dropout in deep networks further reduce overfitting.

Enabling Deeper Networks like ResNet and VGG

State-of-the-art CNNs use multiple convolution layers:

- VGG-16: Uses 13 convolution layers to extract deep features.
- ResNet: Uses residual connections to train very deep networks efficiently.
- EfficientNet: Uses multiple layers with optimized computations.

Sam asked, "Master, what are some common regularization techniques used in CNNs?"

Master smiled and replied, "Ah, Sam, regularization is the discipline that prevents the mind of a neural network from wandering into illusions. Just as a wise seeker controls distractions to stay on the path of truth, we must guide our CNNs to avoid overfitting. Here are some of the most effective regularization techniques:"

Dropout: The Art of Letting Go

"Just as a master detaches from unnecessary thoughts, a network must momentarily ignore some neurons."

- Dropout randomly turns off a fraction of neurons during training.
- Prevents the network from becoming too reliant on specific features. Reduces overfitting and improves generalization.

L1 and L2 Regularization (Weight Decay): The Balance of Restraint

"In the journey of self-mastery, unnecessary weight must be shed."

- L1 Regularization (Lasso): Encourages sparsity by making some weights exactly zero.
- L2 Regularization (Ridge): Penalises large weights, ensuring smoother and more stable learning.

Prevents excessive reliance on specific neurons.

Batch Normalization: The Middle Path

"Just as a balanced mind remains steady in changing circumstances, so must our activations."

- Normalises activations across a batch, ensuring stable and faster learning.
- Reduces the problem of internal covariate shift (drastic changes in distributions).
  Improves convergence and allows deeper networks to train effectively.

Data Augmentation: The Many Faces of Truth

"Wisdom comes from seeing a truth from many perspectives."

- Artificially expands training data by rotating, flipping, scaling, and distorting images.
- Prevents the model from memorising exact images, forcing it to learn deeper patterns.

Boosts robustness and reduces overfitting.

Early Stopping: Knowing When to Pause

"A wise traveler knows when to stop before exhaustion sets in."

- Monitors validation loss and stops training when performance starts to decline.

Prevents excessive training that leads to overfitting.

Master said, "Regularization is the guardian of wisdom in a neural network's training. If you apply these techniques well, your CNN will not just memorize, but truly learn."

John asked, "Master, what is the difference between a convolution layer and a pooling layer?"

Master smiled and replied,

"Ah, John, the mind and the ocean both seek patterns, but to perceive clearly, one must learn what to focus on and what to let go. The Convolution Layer and the Pooling Layer play these very roles in a CNN."

Convolution Layer: The Seeker of Patterns

"A keen observer notices intricate details, forming an understanding of the world."

What does it?

- The Convolution Layer scans the input using small filters (kernels).
- It detects edges, textures, shapes, and deeper patterns in images.
- Each filter focuses on different features, like detecting a cat's whiskers or a human eye.

How?

- Performs mathematical operations (dot product) between the filter and input.
- The resulting feature map highlights important regions of the image.

Analogy: Imagine a scholar studying an ancient script, analysing each symbol and its meaning.

Pooling Layer: The Wise Summarizer

"A wise sage does not memorize every word, but extracts the essence of knowledge."

What it does?

- The Pooling Layer reduces the size of feature maps while keeping essential details.
- It removes unimportant variations, making the model more efficient and less sensitive to noise.

Types of Pooling:

- Max Pooling: Selects the highest value in a region (detects the strongest features).
- Average Pooling: Takes the average of values (smoothens features).

Analogy: Imagine summarizing a book—retaining key points while discarding unnecessary words.

Master said, "A CNN learns as a human does—by first identifying patterns (convolution) and then understanding the essence (pooling). The harmony of both leads to deep perception."

Nikash asked, "Master, what are the different types of CNN Models and why?"

Master said, "Nikash, just as different paths lead to the same mountain peak, different CNN models serve distinct purposes, each excelling in unique ways."

LeNet-5 (1998) – The Pioneer of CNNs

Why?

- Introduced by Yann LeCun, this was the first successful CNN used for handwritten digit recognition (MNIST).
- Architecture: Small & efficient, with two convolutional layers, two pooling layers, and fully connected layers.

Best For: Digit recognition, simple image classification.

AlexNet (2012) – The Breakthrough Model

Why?

- Deep CNN with ReLU activation, dropout for regularization, and multiple filters.

- Won the ImageNet competition (2012), proving CNNs' power for large-scale image recognition.

Best For: Object recognition, large datasets.

VGGNet (2014) – Simplicity and Depth

Why?

- Uses very small (3×3) convolution filters but increases depth (16–19 layers).
- Balances accuracy with a simple architecture, making it widely used in transfer learning.

Best For: Feature extraction, transfer learning.

GoogLeNet (Inception Network, 2014) – Efficiency Master

Why?

- Uses Inception modules, applying multiple filter sizes (1x1, 3x3, 5x5) at once.
- More accurate than VGG but computationally efficient.

Best For: Object detection, image classification with efficiency.

ResNet (2015) – The Deep Learning Revolution

Why?

- Introduced Residual Connections (skip connections) to solve vanishing gradient issues.
- Enabled training of ultra-deep networks (up to 152 layers!).

Best For: Large-scale image classification, medical imaging, and deep feature extraction.

MobileNet – Lightweight for Mobile & IoT

Why?

- Uses Depthwise Separable Convolutions, reducing computations.
- Ideal for low-power devices like smartphones & IoT.

Best For: Real-time applications, edge devices.

Master said, "Nikash, just as a warrior chooses their weapon based on the battle, choosing the right CNN model depends on the task at hand—whether it's precision, efficiency, or depth."

Niskash asked, "Advantages and Disadvantages of Convolutional Neural Networks (CNNs)"

Master turned to Niskash and said,

"Every powerful tool has strengths and weaknesses. The mind, like a CNN, must understand both to use it wisely."

Advantages of CNNs

Automatic Feature Extraction

No need for manual feature engineering; CNNs learn directly from raw data.

High Accuracy in Vision Tasks

CNNs excel in image recognition, object detection, and face recognition.

Translation Invariance

Thanks to convolution and pooling layers, CNNs recognize objects regardless of position and scale.

Robust to Noise

CNNs learn hierarchical patterns, making them resilient to distortions and variations in input.

State-of-the-Art Performance

CNNs outperform traditional models in fields like medical imaging, autonomous driving, and security.

Disadvantages of CNNs

High Computational Cost

Training deep CNNs requires powerful GPUs, making them expensive and time-consuming.

Large Amount of Data Required

CNNs perform best with huge datasets and struggle with limited data.

Lack of Interpretability (Black Box Issue)

Hard to understand why a CNN makes a particular decision.

Vulnerability to Adversarial Attacks

Small, imperceptible changes to an image can mislead CNNs, posing security risks.

Overfitting Risk

Deep CNNs memorize training data instead of generalizing, requiring dropout, data augmentation, and regularization.

Master said, "Niskash, like a great warrior, CNNs are powerful but must be trained with discipline. Their strengths make them leaders in vision, but their weaknesses must be handled with care."

Summary:

Convolutional Neural Networks (CNNs) are deep learning models designed to process data with spatial patterns, such as images. They work by using **convolutional layers,** which apply filters to detect features like edges, textures, and shapes. In CNNs, **convolution** is similar to **cross-correlation**, where a filter slides over the input to produce feature maps. Depending on how the filter overlaps with the input, we use **valid cross-correlation** (no padding, output shrinks) or **full cross-correlation** (with padding, output expands).

CNNs learn through **backpropagation**, where the model adjusts filter weights based on errors calculated during training. The **binary cross-entropy loss** function is often used for binary classification, measuring how close predictions are to actual labels. To convert raw outputs into probabilities, CNNs commonly use the **sigmoid activation function**, which maps values between 0 and 1.

To improve robustness and reduce overfitting, CNNs use techniques such as **pooling layers**, which downsample feature maps, retaining important information while reducing computation. Pooling also provides spatial invariance, allowing the model to recognise features regardless of their exact location. Together, these components make CNNs powerful for image recognition, object detection, and various pattern-based tasks.

What Next:

In the next section, we will explore how these processed and embedded text representations are used within real-world NLP applications. After text is cleaned, normalized, and converted into meaningful vectors, models can understand intent, context, and sentiment—this is where **NLU (Natural Language Understanding)** becomes essential. We will also see how systems generate human-like responses through **NLG (Natural Language Generation)**. Finally, we will connect these concepts to practical workflows, where text flows from preprocessing to understanding, reasoning, and ultimately communicating back with natural, fluent language.

P2-U2-L1 - Practice Question

1. What is a Convolutional Neural Network (CNN)?
2. Why are CNNs effective for image-related tasks?
3. What is the role of the Convolution Layer in a CNN?
4. What is the difference between Convolution and Cross-Correlation in CNNs?
5. What is Valid Cross-Correlation?
6. What is Full Cross-Correlation?
7. What is Backpropagation in CNNs?
8. What is the purpose of Optimization in CNNs?
9. What is Binary Cross-Entropy Loss used for?
10. What does the Sigmoid Activation Function do?
11. What is the Pooling Layer in CNNs?
12. How does Pooling help reduce overfitting?
13. How do CNNs boost robustness in learning?
14. Why are fewer parameters beneficial in CNNs?
15. Where are CNNs commonly used?

PART THREE

The Dawn of Language Intelligence

NLU | NLP | NLG

NLP is the bridge where language becomes a structured reflection of human thought, enabling machines to not only process words but also perceive the rhythm of meaning that flows beneath them.

– Shree Shambav

PART THREE

DAY SEVEN

Unit 3 - Lesson One

Introduction to Generative AI

Nikash asked, "Master, what is Generative AI? How does it differ from Machine Learning and Deep Learning?"

Master replied:

"Nikash, think of artificial intelligence as a great tree of knowledge.

- **Machine Learning (ML)** is the foundation. Here, systems are trained with data to *recognise patterns* and make predictions. For example, deciding whether an email is spam or not.
- **Deep Learning (DL)** is a powerful branch of ML, built using layered neural networks. It can handle very complex tasks—like recognising faces, understanding speech, or driving a car—because it learns subtle patterns through many layers.
- **Generative AI (GenAI)** is the flowering of this tree. It does not only recognise or predict—it *creates*. It can generate text, images, music, or even code by learning from vast data and then producing new outputs that resemble human creativity.

In short:

- Machine Learning **classifies and predicts**.
- Deep Learning **analyzes deeply through neural layers**.
- Generative AI **creates new content based on learned patterns**.

But remember, Nikash, Generative AI does not create from true consciousness—it reflects human knowledge in new forms."

Apeksha asked, "ML and Deep Learning help us to predict, Classify, and Cluster. Then why do we need Generative AI?"

Master replied:

"You are right, Apeksha. Traditional Machine Learning and Deep Learning are excellent when the goal is to *analyse existing data*—they help us predict outcomes, classify information, or group similar patterns.

But Generative AI goes one step further. It is not limited to analysing what is already there—it *creates what does not exist yet.*

- With ML/DL, you can train a model to predict if a sentence is positive or negative.
- With Generative AI, you can ask the system to *write an entirely new paragraph* in a particular style.
- With ML/DL, you can classify millions of images as cats, dogs, or cars.
- With Generative AI, you can *generate a brand-new image of a cat that never existed before.*

In essence:

- **ML/DL**: Extract insights and patterns from past data.
- **Generative AI**: Produce new data that looks and feels real, based on what it has learned.

That is why we need Generative AI—because it expands the role of AI from merely *understanding the world* to also *creating within it.*"

Akshaya asked, "Master, what are the things we can generate with Generative AI? What are its applications?"

Master replied:

"Akshaya, Generative AI has the power to create across different forms of media. The main categories are:

- **Text** – It can write articles, blogs, product descriptions, stories, poetry, or even computer code.

  Example: ChatGPT generates human-like conversations and content.

- **Audio** – It can create music, generate realistic human voices, sound effects, or even dub speech into different languages.

  Example: OpenAI's Jukebox and ElevenLabs for speech synthesis.

- **Images** – It can design realistic photographs, digital art, product prototypes, marketing visuals, or illustrations.

  Example: DALL·E, MidJourney, and Stable Diffusion generate entirely new images.

- **Video** – It can produce short clips, animations, marketing ads, movie scenes, or simulations.
  Example: Runway Gen-2 and Pika Labs generate videos from text prompts.

Its applications are widespread:

- In **Education** – Personalised learning materials, summaries, and practice questions.

- In **Healthcare** – Synthetic medical images, drug discovery, protein structure predictions.

- In **Business** – Automated reports, presentations, marketing campaigns, chatbots.

- In **Art & Entertainment** – Music composition, scriptwriting, game design, and visual storytelling.

- In **Science & Research** – Molecular simulations, climate modelling, and generating synthetic datasets.

In short, Generative AI extends AI from *analysing the known* to *creating the new*—unlocking innovation in every domain."

Generative AI can be broadly categorised into four major types:

LLM-based (Large Language Models)

- Built on deep learning architectures, especially Transformers.
- Trained on massive text datasets (books, articles, code, conversations).
- Generic in nature, capable of answering questions, writing, reasoning, and coding.
- Optimised with **millions to billions of parameters** for fluency and context understanding.
- **Examples:**
  - OpenAI – GPT series (e.g., ChatGPT)
  - Google – PaLM, Gemini
  - Meta – LLaMA
  - Microsoft – Phi models (and partnership with OpenAI)
  - Anthropic – Claude

Image-based Generative AI

- Built on models like GANs (Generative Adversarial Networks) and diffusion models.
- Trained on massive datasets of labelled/unlabelled images.
- Generates new visuals—photorealistic images, digital art, illustrations, designs.
- **Examples:**
  - OpenAI – DALL·E
  - Stability AI – Stable Diffusion
  - MidJourney – Artistic image generation
  - Adobe Firefly – Creative design tools

Audio-based Generative AI

- Trained on vast speech and music datasets.
- Can generate human-like voices, sound effects, background music, and entire compositions.
- Useful for dubbing, voice cloning, podcasting, and music creation.
- **Examples:**
    - ElevenLabs – Voice synthesis and cloning
    - OpenAI – Jukebox (music generation)
    - AIVA – AI-generated music for creators
    - Descript – Overdub for realistic voice reproduction

Video-based Generative AI

- Uses diffusion models and multimodal training (text-to-video).
- Creates dynamic content—short clips, animations, realistic scenes, marketing videos.
- Expanding rapidly with creative and commercial applications.
- **Examples:**
    - Runway Gen-2 – Text-to-video generation
    - Pika Labs – AI-powered video creation
    - Synthesia – AI avatars and video presentations

In summary:

- **LLMs → Text & Language**
- **Image Models → Visuals**
- **Audio Models → Sound & Music**

- **Video Models → Motion & Scenes**

Together, these four categories define the modern landscape of Generative AI, making it a multi-modal technology capable of creating across human senses.

Category	What it Generates	Key Applications	Examples
LLM-based (Large Language Models)	Text, code, conversations, summaries	Chatbots, content creation, code generation, translation, knowledge assistants	GPT (OpenAI), Gemini (Google), LLaMA (Meta), Claude (Anthropic), Phi (Microsoft)
Image-based Models	Photos, art, illustrations, designs	Digital art, product design, marketing, and creative industries	DALL·E (OpenAI), Stable Diffusion (Stability AI), MidJourney, Adobe Firefly
Audio-based Models	Human-like voices, sound effects, music	Voice synthesis, dubbing, podcasting, music composition, and accessibility tools	ElevenLabs, OpenAI Jukebox, AIVA, Descript Overdub
Video-based Models	Short clips, animations, and realistic scenes	Marketing videos, film production, training content, AI avatars	Runway Gen-2, Pika Labs, Synthesia

Sam asked, "Master, how are Large Language Models (LLMs) built?"

Master replied:

"Sam, the architecture of LLMs is rooted in several key advancements in artificial intelligence:

1. **Encoder–Decoder Framework**

- LLMs are primarily built on the **Transformer architecture**, which uses encoders to understand input data and decoders to generate meaningful output.
- This design enables them to handle long sequences of text efficiently.

2. **Attention Mechanism**
    - At the heart of Transformers lies the **self-attention mechanism**.
    - It allows the model to focus on the most relevant parts of the input, weighing context dynamically, and thus capturing relationships across words and sentences with remarkable accuracy.
3. **Foundation in Transformers**
    - LLMs evolved from models such as **BERT (Bidirectional Encoder Representations from Transformers)** and other Transformer-based designs.
    - These laid the foundation for today's large-scale models like GPT, Gemini, Claude, and LLaMA.
4. **Progression from ANN/RNN**
    - Earlier architectures like **Artificial Neural Networks (ANNs)** and **Recurrent Neural Networks (RNNs)** provided the initial building blocks.
    - However, they struggled with handling long-term dependencies and parallel processing.
    - Transformers overcame these challenges, making LLMs scalable, efficient, and capable of training on massive datasets.

In essence, LLMs are the product of this evolution: from **basic neural networks → RNNs → Transformers → today's powerful LLMs**."

John asked, "Master, what are the applications of LLMs?"

Master replied:

"John, Large Language Models (LLMs) and Generative AI have a wide range of applications across multiple domains:

Text

- Content writing: blogs, articles, stories, essays
- Summarisation, translation, and Q&A systems
- Customer support chatbots

Code

- Code generation and completion
- Documentation creation
- Code conversion between programming languages

Image

- Text-to-image generation
- Image captioning and extraction
- Style transfer and design assistance

Speech

- Voice generation and cloning
- Speech-to-text transcription
- Real-time translation and dubbing

Video

- Text-to-video generation
- Automated video analysis
- Animation and scene creation

Others

- **Gaming** – Storyline creation, dynamic NPC dialogues

- **Music** – Composition, background scores, sound effects
- **Animation** – Character design, motion generation

"In short, LLMs and Generative AI are transforming creativity, communication, and problem-solving by enabling machines to *understand, generate, and enhance* human-like content across text, code, images, audio, and video."

PART THREE

DAY SEVEN

Unit 3 - Lesson Two

The Language of Machines

Master leaned forward, his voice calm yet resonant, "Sam, Natural Language Understanding, or NLU, is the gateway through which machines begin to *truly comprehend human language*. Unlike basic text processing that only recognizes words as sequences of characters, NLU seeks to grasp the **meaning**, the **intent**, and the **relationships** that live within those words. It is the bridge between human thought and machine cognition."

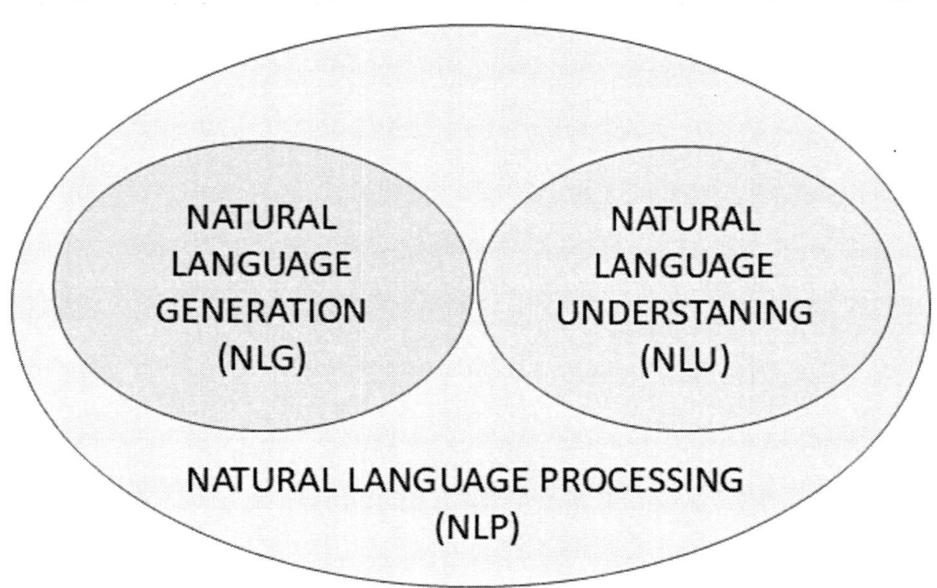

Illustration NLU_1: NLU

Understanding NLU in Depth

"Language," Master continued, "is inherently ambiguous, contextual, and layered. The same sentence can carry multiple meanings depending on the speaker's intent, the context, and even cultural nuances. Machines, however, perceive only binary patterns — ones and zeros. Here lies the challenge: how do we translate this rich, nuanced expression of thought into a form that a machine can *process and act upon*?"

NLU addresses this by combining **linguistic theory** with **statistical and computational methods**. It examines:

- **Syntax** — the arrangement of words and phrases to create meaningful sentences. For example, understanding that 'The cat chased the dog' is fundamentally different from 'The dog chased the cat.'
- **Semantics** — the underlying meaning of words and phrases. Machines must interpret that 'bank' could mean a financial institution or the side of a river, depending on context.
- **Dependencies** — the relationships and roles of words within a sentence. Knowing which word is the subject, which is the object, and which is modifying another is crucial for accurate comprehension.

By analyzing these aspects, NLU transforms raw text into structured representations that machines can reason about, draw conclusions from, or respond to intelligently.

Applications in the Real World

Master gestured as if sketching invisible lines in the air, "The applications of NLU are all around you, shaping the modern digital experience:"

- **Chatbots and Virtual Assistants**: Understanding a user's intent — whether they are asking a question, making a request, or issuing a command — allows machines to respond meaningfully.
- **Content Moderation**: Detecting hate speech, spam, or sensitive content requires machines to comprehend the subtle semantic and syntactic cues in text.
- **Information Extraction and Summarization**: Pulling key entities, relationships, and insights from unstructured data relies on machines *understanding* the text, not just reading it.

- **Machine Translation**: Accurately converting language requires understanding not just word meanings, but context, syntax, and intent.

The Underlying Mechanism

Master's tone deepened, "At its core, NLU applies statistical and machine learning techniques to uncover patterns and structures in language. These systems do not 'understand' language like humans do, but they approximate understanding by analyzing vast corpora, learning the likelihood of word sequences, syntactic structures, and semantic associations. Through this, machines can predict meaning, classify intent, and even resolve ambiguities in text."

In essence, NLU **narrows the gap** between the fluid, nuanced human language and the rigid, binary logic of machines. It gives systems the ability to interpret inputs intelligently, enabling interactions that feel natural and contextually appropriate.

Master said softly, "Think of NLU as teaching a machine to *listen with comprehension*, not just to hear words. It is the first step toward creating systems that can *reason, respond, and participate* in human dialogue. Every improvement in NLU brings machines a little closer to understanding the subtleties of thought, the nuances of expression, and the unspoken layers of meaning in our language."

NLU and Text Processing

Master continued with a gentle smile, "Apeksha, *Natural Language Understanding*, or NLU, is the very heart of how machines learn to comprehend human language — not merely read it.

Imagine language as a living river of thoughts, emotions, and intentions flowing through words. While *NLP* gives the machine the ability to process that river — to tokenize, tag, and structure it — *NLU* gives the machine the *awareness* to understand what the river means, where it flows, and why it flows that way.

NLU delves into the deeper layers of meaning: context, intent, sentiment, and relationships between words. It tries to answer questions such as — What is the user trying to say? What emotion lies behind these words? What action should be taken in response?

To achieve this, NLU combines several elements:

- **Syntax understanding**, which helps machines recognize grammatical structure.
- **Semantics**, which interprets the meaning of phrases and sentences.
- **Pragmatics**, which deciphers the intent and context behind those meanings.

With the rise of **deep learning**, the evolution of NLU has been extraordinary. Earlier systems relied on predefined rules and statistical models — limited in their ability to grasp nuance. But with **neural networks**, especially **transformer architectures** like BERT, GPT, and T5, machines have gained a remarkable ability to represent context and meaning in multidimensional ways.

These models no longer see words as isolated symbols; they perceive relationships, tone, and subtleties across entire passages. A word like "bank," for instance, is no longer a fixed entity — its meaning shifts depending on whether the sentence speaks of a riverbank or a financial institution.

Thus, deep learning has allowed NLU systems to move closer to *true comprehension* — understanding human language as a living, contextual, and emotional phenomenon. It is what enables voice assistants to converse naturally, chatbots to respond empathetically, and search engines to anticipate user intent with precision.

So, Apeksha," the Master concluded softly, "NLU is not just about machines learning our words — it is about them learning our *meaning*. It is the bridge between data and understanding, between code and consciousness."

Master continued, "Apeksha, *Natural Language Understanding (NLU)* is one of the most profound achievements in the evolution of artificial intelligence — the art of teaching machines not merely to read or process human language, but to **comprehend** it.

You see, when humans communicate, we do not only use words; we use intention, emotion, and context. Every sentence we speak carries layers of meaning — what is said, what is implied, and what is felt. NLU seeks to decode these layers, enabling a computer to grasp *meaning* rather than just *syntax*.

At its essence, NLU stands at the intersection of linguistics, computer science, and cognitive psychology. It employs complex models and algorithms to map the structure of human language, interpret semantics, and discern intent. Through this, machines can transform unstructured language data — the chaos of human expression — into structured understanding that can drive intelligent actions.

It is through NLU that systems like virtual assistants, customer support chatbots, and language translators can respond appropriately to human commands. It bridges the space between *language as expression* and *language as understanding*, enabling technology to move closer to empathy and intuition.

The Essence of NLU

NLU focuses on understanding *what is meant*, not just *what is said*. This involves three key dimensions:

- **Syntax** – the grammatical structure of language, how words relate to each other in a sentence.
- **Semantics** – the meaning conveyed by words and phrases within a particular context.
- **Pragmatics** – the underlying intent or purpose of the speaker, influenced by tone, culture, and situation.

Together, these dimensions empower a machine to engage in meaningful dialogue rather than mechanical repetition.

Natural Language Understanding Tasks

NLU involves a wide spectrum of specialized tasks — each a stepping stone toward deeper linguistic comprehension. Let us explore some of them:

- **Speech Recognition** – This converts spoken language into written text, allowing systems to understand voice-based communication. It is the foundation for assistants like Siri or Alexa.

- **Part of Speech Tagging** – Every word in a sentence plays a grammatical role — noun, verb, adjective, and so on. Identifying these roles allows machines to understand sentence structure and relationships.

- **Word Sense Disambiguation** – Many words carry multiple meanings. For example, “bark” can refer to a dog’s sound or the outer layer of a tree. This task helps machines infer the correct meaning based on context.

- **Sentiment Analysis** – Human language is charged with emotion. Sentiment analysis helps systems determine whether a statement expresses joy, anger, sorrow, or neutrality, enabling emotionally aware responses.

- **Machine Translation** – Here, NLU enables the transformation of meaning across languages, not merely translating words but preserving tone, idiom, and cultural nuance.
- **Text Summarization** – The ability to condense large volumes of text into concise summaries while retaining essential meaning. This is invaluable for knowledge extraction and information retrieval.

Each of these tasks deepens a system's ability to interpret human expression, gradually transforming raw text or speech into insight and comprehension.

NLU and NLP — A Symbiotic Relationship

While *NLP (Natural Language Processing)* focuses on the mechanical and structural aspects of language — such as tokenization, named entity recognition, and syntactic parsing — *NLU* is the deeper, interpretive layer.

NLP prepares the data: it breaks text into tokens, identifies entities, and structures linguistic components.

NLU, on the other hand, gives meaning to this structure — interpreting user intent, sentiment, and conceptual relationships.

In this way, NLP and NLU work together as *mind and understanding* — one processes, the other perceives.

The Role of Deep Learning in NLU

In the modern era, **deep learning** has revolutionized NLU. Earlier systems relied on rules and manually defined grammars, which were rigid and limited. Deep neural networks, however, have enabled models to *learn* language the way humans do — by observing vast patterns of usage.

Transformers and large language models (such as BERT, GPT, and T5) have redefined NLU. They capture context dynamically, enabling machines to understand polysemy, humor, metaphor, and emotion with astonishing depth.

Now, NLU systems can interpret intent even when phrasing varies, generate contextually appropriate responses, and adapt understanding based on dialogue history. They no longer merely analyze words — they perceive patterns of *thought*.

Master concluded with serene conviction, "Apeksha, Natural Language Understanding is the soul of human–machine communication.

It transforms language from data into meaning, from symbols into understanding. It is through NLU that technology begins to reflect the depth of human expression — where computation meets consciousness, and understanding transcends words."

Master said, "Sam, to truly comprehend language, we must first understand the art and science of text processing."

Master continued with calm clarity, "Sam, before a machine can *understand* language, it must first *see* language — not as a human perceives flowing meaning, but as a sequence of structured symbols. This process, known as **text processing**, transforms the fluid, ambiguous world of words into data that machines can interpret, analyze, and learn from. It is the bridge between human expression and machine comprehension — the point where language begins its journey into logic."

Text Processing Techniques

Master explained, "Text processing is the foundation of every natural language system. It prepares language for analysis, ensuring that the raw data of human communication becomes clean, organized, and meaningful for computational models. Among these techniques, the first and most fundamental is *Tokenization*."

Case One: Tokenization

"Sam," Master said, "imagine a vast book written in one continuous stream — no spaces, no punctuation, no structure. To understand it, you would first have to divide it into words, phrases, or meaningful fragments. That is the essence of tokenization."

Tokenization is the process of breaking text into smaller units called **tokens** — which may represent words, subwords, or even individual characters, depending on the level of precision the task demands.

These tokens form the *building blocks* of language for computational models. By segmenting text into these manageable pieces, machines can map relationships between words, count frequencies, and build representations that capture the rhythm, structure, and meaning of human speech.

Example:
Original Text: “Knowledge transforms silence into understanding.”

Tokenized Form: [“Knowledge”, “transforms”, “silence”, “into”, “understanding”, “.”]

In this form, each word and punctuation mark becomes a discrete element that can be analyzed, vectorized, or encoded by an NLP system.

Depth of Tokenization

Master continued, “But tokenization is not as simple as splitting text by spaces. True language understanding demands nuance. Consider how the same tokenization rules must adapt across contexts and languages.”

- In **English**, tokenization might treat contractions carefully:

  “can’t” → [“can”, “’t”]

  This allows models to recognize both the base word and the negation.

- In **Chinese** or **Japanese**, there are no spaces between words, so tokenization must rely on *language-specific segmentation algorithms* to detect word boundaries.
- In **social media text**, tokenization must handle *emojis*, *hashtags*, and *slang*, recognizing that “#joy” or “😊” convey emotional context just as powerfully as words.

Thus, tokenization becomes not just a technical step but a *linguistic art* — one that balances precision and meaning.

Granularity in Tokenization

Master elaborated further, “Tokenization can occur at different levels of detail, each suited for specific tasks:”

1. **Word-level tokenization** – Splits text into distinct words. Useful for tasks like sentiment analysis or text classification.

Example: "The stars shine bright." → ["The", "stars", "shine", "bright", "."]

2. **Subword-level tokenization** – Breaks words into smaller fragments, allowing rare or unknown words to be represented effectively.

Example: "unbelievable" → ["un", "believ", "able"]

3. **Character-level tokenization** – Splits text into individual characters, often used for languages with complex morphology or when spelling variations are common.

Example: "art" → ["a", "r", "t"]

This flexibility allows NLP systems to adapt to different linguistic complexities and data constraints.

Purpose and Significance

"Sam," Master said, "remember, tokenization is not just a mechanical division of text — it is the *beginning of understanding*. Every subsequent process in NLP — from syntactic parsing to semantic interpretation — depends on how well the text has been tokenized.

When tokenization is precise, models learn the right associations. When it is careless, meaning is fractured. In essence, tokenization shapes the very *lens* through which a machine perceives language."

Master paused and said softly, "So, Sam, tokenization is the first breath of life in language processing. It turns the chaos of words into the rhythm of comprehension. Just as a sculptor chips away stone to reveal form, tokenization refines raw text into tokens — the essential fragments from which understanding begins to emerge."

Case Two: Word-Sense Disambiguation (WSD)

Master smiled and said, "Apeksha, *Word-Sense Disambiguation* (WSD) is one of the most delicate and quietly powerful skills in language understanding. It asks a machine to do something humans do almost without thinking: choose the correct meaning of a word from many possible meanings by using the surrounding context."

What is WSD?

Many words are polysemous — they carry multiple related or unrelated senses. WSD's goal is to map an ambiguous word token in context to the correct sense or meaning (often defined by a sense inventory such as WordNet). Getting that choice right matters: a wrong sense breaks translation, confuses question answering, and corrupts information retrieval.

Example

Consider the word **"bat."**

- Sentence A: "At dusk, the **bat** glided silently between the cave and the river." → **bat** = *nocturnal flying mammal*
- Sentence B: "She gripped the **bat**, eyes on the pitcher, and waited for the perfect pitch." → **bat** = *wooden or composite sports implement*

A human picks the right meaning instantly. For a machine, the surrounding words — *dusk, glided, cave* vs *gripped, pitcher, pitch* — are the signals that disambiguate sense.

Why WSD matters?

Correct disambiguation improves:

- **Machine translation** — preserves correct target-word choice.
- **Question answering** — returns relevant answers rather than sense-mismatched results.
- **Search & IR** — boosts precision by matching query senses to document senses.
- **Text mining/knowledge extraction** — ensures facts and relations are grounded to correct entities and concepts.

Approaches to WSD — from classical to modern

1. Knowledge-based methods

- **Lesk algorithm (classic):** Chooses the sense whose dictionary/gloss shares the most words with the target word's context. Simple, interpretable, requires a dictionary (e.g., WordNet).
- **Graph and semantic network methods:** Build a graph of senses and choose the sense that best connects to context words via semantic relations (synonymy, hypernymy).

Pros: No labelled corpora required.

Cons: Sensitive to gloss wording, limited by the quality of lexical resources.

2. Supervised learning

- **Sense-labelled corpora** train classifiers (SVMs, decision trees, or neural nets) using context features: nearby words, POS tags, syntactic dependencies, collocations.

Pros: High accuracy when large labeled data exists.

Cons: Labelled sense-annotated corpora are expensive to create and domain-specific.

3. Unsupervised & semi-supervised methods

- **Clustering of contexts:** Group occurrences of a word by context similarity; map clusters to senses (useful when sense inventories are absent).
- **Bootstrapping & self-training:** Start from a small seed set and expand.

Pros: Useful in low-resource setups.

Cons: Sense granularity may not match human sense inventories.

4. Contextual embeddings & deep learning (state of the art)

- **Contextualized language models (BERT, RoBERTa, etc.)** produce token vectors that reflect the word's meaning in that exact sentence. A common pattern: extract the contextual embedding for the ambiguous token and feed it to a classifier or compare it to prototype sense vectors (from glosses or sense-annotated examples).

- **Gloss-aware models** (e.g., encode sense glosses with the same transformer and match context embedding to sense embeddings).

Pros: Strong generalization, can capture subtle context, reduced need for expensive hand-crafted features.

Cons: Still needs labelled data or good sense representations for peak performance; models can conflate subtle senses.

Practical recipe at a high level

- Preprocess: tokenize, POS-tag, parse (optional).
- Form context window (sentence or paragraph).
- Represent context (bag-of-words, features, or contextual embedding).
- Match/score candidate senses (classifier, similarity to gloss embedding, graph score).
- Choose the sense with the highest confidence; optionally defer or mark uncertain cases.

Challenges

- **Granularity of senses:** WordNet can list finely split senses that are hard even for humans to agree on. Over-splitting harms supervised learning.

- **Domain shift:** Models trained in news text may fail on medical or legal domains where senses differ.

- **Metaphor, idioms & creativity:** "He crushed the meeting" uses words in non-literal ways; standard senses may not apply.

- **Low-resource languages:** Lack of sense inventories and annotated corpora.

- **Implicit context & world knowledge:** Some disambiguations require real-world facts beyond surface context ("She went to the bank to cash a check" vs "She sat on the bank to watch the swans").

Master concluded, "Sam, WSD is the quiet translator inside the mind of every language system — choosing the correct meaning so the rest of the model can reason correctly. It is at once linguistic, statistical, and semantic — requiring lexical wisdom, contextual sensitivity, and sometimes even worldly common sense. Master it, and you grant machines a finer sense of meaning; neglect it, and their understanding will always be a little clouded."

Case Three: Named Entity Recognition (NER)

Master spoke with a thoughtful tone, "Akshaya, language is more than words strung together; it carries references to the world around us — people, places, organizations, dates, and events. To truly understand language, a machine must recognize these references, and this is where **Named Entity Recognition (NER)** comes into play."

Understanding Named Entity Recognition

"NER is the task of detecting and classifying *named entities* in text into predefined categories, such as persons, organizations, locations, dates, monetary values, and more. Unlike ordinary words, named entities often carry crucial semantic weight — they anchor language to real-world concepts. Without recognizing them, machines cannot properly extract meaning, summarize events, or answer questions about the text."

NER is a foundational technique for transforming unstructured text into structured knowledge. It allows machines to recognize the key players, places, and times in any narrative, enabling deeper reasoning and more precise information extraction.

Example of NER with Fresh Context

Original sentence:

"Tesla unveiled its new electric semi-truck at the Gigafactory in Nevada last week."

NER identifies:

- **Tesla** → Organization
- **Gigafactory** → Location

- **Nevada** → Location
- **last week** → Date

Here, NER allows the system to understand *who did what, where, and when*, which is essential for tasks like summarization, news aggregation, or automated reporting.

Importance and Applications of NER

Master continued, "NER is not just about labeling words; it is about giving a machine a sense of the 'who,' 'what,' and 'where' in a story. By identifying entities, NER enables:"

- **Information Retrieval** – Searching documents for entities like companies, people, or events rather than generic keywords.
- **Question Answering Systems** – Extracting precise answers by locating relevant entities.
  For example, "Who founded Tesla?" → **Tesla** → **Organization**, answer: **Elon Musk**.
- **Knowledge Graph Construction** – Linking entities across texts to form a web of knowledge.
- **Sentiment Analysis** – Associating sentiments with specific entities rather than the text as a whole.
- **Event Detection** – Recognizing when and where important events occur.

Techniques for NER

NER has evolved from simple to sophisticated methods:

Rule-based approaches – Using handcrafted patterns and dictionaries to recognize entities.

- Example: Capitalized words preceded by "Mr." or "Dr." → Person.
- **Limitations:** Not scalable, struggles with unseen entities.

Statistical & Machine Learning approaches – Models like HMMs, CRFs, or decision trees learn patterns from labeled corpora.

- Can generalize better than rules, but requires annotated data.

Deep Learning approaches – Modern NER uses **BiLSTM-CRF**, **Transformer-based models (BERT, RoBERTa)**.

- Capture contextual dependencies: the meaning of a word is inferred from surrounding words.
- Example: In "Apple released a new product in Paris," BERT understands that "Apple" refers to the company, not the fruit, based on context.

Challenges in NER

Master paused, "Akshaya, real-world NER is not trivial."

- **Ambiguity of entities:** Names like "Jordan" could be a person or a country. Context must guide the model.
- **Nested entities:** "Bank of America CEO" contains multiple entities: "Bank of America" → Organization, "CEO" → Title.
- **Domain-specific entities:** Scientific texts may have chemical names or gene identifiers not seen in general corpora.
- **Language and script diversity:** NER systems must adapt to multiple languages and writing systems.

"NER transforms words into *anchors of meaning*. When a machine sees a sentence, raw words are like stars in the sky — beautiful but disconnected. NER draws constellations between these stars, showing patterns, relationships, and significance. With these constellations, machines can summarize, answer, and reason with human language in ways that approach human comprehension."

Master said gently, "So, Akshaya, Named Entity Recognition is the compass of NLP — it points the machine to the key entities in a text, giving it orientation in the vast sea of words. Without it, language is only noise; with it, language begins to tell stories machines can truly understand."

Case Four: Part-of-Speech (PoS) Tagging

Master began with a calm and thoughtful tone, "John, language is not just a string of words; it has an underlying structure, a grammar that governs how words relate to one another. To truly understand language, a machine must grasp this structure. This is where **Part-of-Speech (PoS) Tagging** becomes essential."

Understanding Part-of-Speech Tagging

"PoS tagging is the task of assigning grammatical labels to each word in a sentence — indicating whether it is a noun, verb, adjective, adverb, preposition, and so on. These labels help machines understand the *role* of each word in context. Without this understanding, a machine cannot parse sentences correctly, extract meaning accurately, or perform higher-level NLP tasks effectively."

PoS tagging forms the *skeleton of syntactic understanding.* It shows how words connect, which words are acting, which words are being acted upon, and which modify others. It is the foundation for parsing, grammar analysis, machine translation, and even information extraction.

Example with a Fresh Context

Sentence:
"The scientist analyzed the complex data carefully."

PoS tagging would assign:

- **The** → Determiner (DT)
- **scientist** → Noun (NN)
- **analyzed** → Verb (VBD)
- **the** → Determiner (DT)
- **complex** → Adjective (JJ)
- **data** → Noun (NNS)
- **carefully** → Adverb (RB)

Here, PoS tagging clarifies the sentence structure: the *scientist* performs an action (*analyzed*) on the *data*, and *carefully* describes *how* the action is performed. A machine can now understand syntactic relationships and process meaning with greater precision.

Importance and Applications

Master continued, "PoS tagging is crucial for many NLP tasks:"

1. **Syntactic Parsing** – Understanding sentence structure depends on knowing the grammatical roles of words.

2. **Machine Translation** – Correctly translating sentences requires knowing which words are subjects, verbs, or modifiers.

3. **Information Extraction** – Identifying relationships between entities often relies on grammatical structure.

4. **Question Answering** – Correctly identifying the verb and subject helps locate the answer.

5. **Grammar Checking** – Tools like Grammarly or Microsoft Word rely on PoS tagging to detect errors.

Techniques in PoS Tagging

1. **Rule-based approaches** – Use predefined grammar rules and dictionaries to assign tags.

   Example: If a word ends with "-ing" and follows a form of *be*, it is likely a verb in the progressive tense.

   Limitation: Hard to scale; struggles with ambiguity.

2. **Statistical approaches** – Models like Hidden Markov Models (HMM) assign tags based on probabilities learned from annotated corpora.

   Example: "bank" as a noun is more frequent after *the*, while as a verb it is more frequent after *will.*

3. **Machine Learning approaches** – Classifiers (SVM, decision trees) use features like neighboring words, suffixes, and capitalization to predict tags.

4. **Deep Learning approaches** – BiLSTMs, CRFs, and Transformers capture context dynamically, resolving ambiguities in words like "record" (noun or verb) based on surrounding words.

Challenges

- **Ambiguity:** Words often have multiple possible tags depending on context.

  Example: "Lead the team carefully." → *Lead* could be a verb or metal; context is key.

- **Domain adaptation:** Scientific, legal, or informal text may use words differently.
- **Morphologically rich languages:** Words can carry multiple grammatical markers, making tagging more complex.

Master said, "John, PoS tagging is like giving the machine a *grammar compass*. It reveals the functional role of every word, allowing a machine to map the architecture of a sentence. Without it, words are floating symbols; with it, they form a structured network of meaning. Every NLP task, from understanding to translation, depends on this foundational insight into language structure. PoS tagging teaches machines the *syntax of thought*."

Master continued with a calm and deliberate tone, "Nikash, the tasks we have discussed — tokenization, word-sense disambiguation, part-of-speech tagging, named entity recognition — are not isolated exercises in text manipulation. Their importance extends far beyond simple labeling. They form the backbone of *intelligent systems* that can retrieve, organize, and reason over vast amounts of unstructured data."

Importance Across Domains

Master elaborated, "Consider **information retrieval**. When a system searches through millions of documents to answer a query, it must understand the structure, meaning, and intent behind each piece of text. Without preprocessing and tasks like tokenization, NER, or PoS tagging, the system cannot accurately locate relevant information.

Similarly, in **knowledge representation**, structured understanding of text allows machines to form conceptual models — mapping entities, relationships, and events into a format they can reason with. This is how knowledge graphs are built, how question-answering systems understand context, and how AI can perform reasoning tasks that were once thought to require human intuition."

TensorFlow for Natural Language Understanding and Text Processing

Master continued, "Nikash, to implement these concepts practically, we require a robust and versatile framework. **TensorFlow** is one such platform — an open-source machine learning framework designed to support the end-to-end development of AI systems. TensorFlow allows developers to build, train, and deploy models for complex NLP tasks efficiently.

It is particularly strong for **Natural Language Understanding (NLU)** and text processing, offering both flexibility and scalability. Whether you are working with classical machine learning models or modern deep learning architectures, TensorFlow provides the infrastructure necessary to process text data, extract meaning, and make predictions."

Key Libraries in TensorFlow

Master explained, "TensorFlow supports NLU and text processing through two main components:"

1. **TensorFlow Core & Keras**
   - Provides layers, models, and utilities for building custom neural networks.
   - Ideal for designing RNNs, LSTMs, GRUs, and Transformer-based architectures for NLP tasks.
   - Example: You can build a sentiment analysis model by preprocessing text with tokenization, embedding it with a word vector layer, and feeding it into an LSTM network for classification.
2. **TensorFlow Text & TensorFlow Hub**
   - **TensorFlow Text** provides specialized operations for text preprocessing: tokenization, normalization, regex-based filtering, and more.
   - **TensorFlow Hub** offers pre-trained models for NLP tasks such as BERT, Universal Sentence Encoder, and T5. These models allow developers to leverage state-of-the-art representations without training from scratch.

- Example: For named entity recognition, a pre-trained BERT model can encode sentences contextually, while TensorFlow Text handles tokenization and alignment between subword tokens and entity labels.

Workflow

Master outlined the typical process:

1. **Data Preprocessing** – Clean text, tokenize, normalize, and possibly perform PoS tagging or NER.
2. **Embedding** – Convert tokens into vectors that capture semantic meaning (word embeddings, contextual embeddings).
3. **Model Building** – Construct deep learning architectures (LSTM, Transformer) using Keras layers.
4. **Training & Evaluation** – Feed data into the model, compute loss, backpropagate, and evaluate performance.
5. **Deployment** – Export the trained model to serve real-time predictions in applications like chatbots, search engines, or recommendation systems.

Master said, "Apeksha, TensorFlow is not just a tool; it is the bridge that takes abstract linguistic tasks and turns them into functional intelligence. It allows us to translate the complexity of human language into mathematical representations, from which machines can learn, reason, and interact. Through frameworks like TensorFlow, the principles of tokenization, PoS tagging, NER, and WSD are no longer theoretical — they become actionable steps that enable machines to understand and engage with human language."

Master smiled and said, "Sam, let us explore a practical program that demonstrates **tokenization** using TensorFlow and Keras."

Case One:

Example P3 – U3 – D1	
NLU-NLP	**Output**
# Import TensorFlow and Keras Tokenizer import tensorflow as tf	Word Index:

```python
from tensorflow.keras.preprocessing.text import Tokenizer

# New example sentences for demonstration
texts = [
    "Artificial intelligence is transforming the world.",
    "Deep learning enables machines to learn from data.",
    "Natural Language Understanding helps computers comprehend human language."
]

# Initialize the tokenizer
# num_words limits the vocabulary to the top 100 words
# oov_token handles words not seen during training
tokenizer = Tokenizer(num_words=100, oov_token="<OOV>")

# Fit the tokenizer on the new texts
tokenizer.fit_on_texts(texts)

# Display the word-to-index mapping
word_index = tokenizer.word_index
print("Word Index:\n", word_index)

# Convert sentences to sequences of integers
sequences = tokenizer.texts_to_sequences(texts)
print("\nTokenized Sequences:\n", sequences)

# Optional: Convert sequences back to text for verification
for i, seq in enumerate(sequences):
    words = [word for word, index in word_index.items() if index in seq]
    print(f"\nOriginal sentence {i+1} tokens: {words}")
```

```
{'<OOV>': 1, 'language': 2, 'artificial': 3, 'intelligence': 4, 'is': 5, 'transforming': 6, 'the': 7, 'world': 8, 'deep': 9, 'learning': 10, 'enables': 11, 'machines': 12, 'to': 13, 'learn': 14, 'from': 15, 'data': 16, 'natural': 17, 'understanding': 18, 'helps': 19, 'computers': 20, 'comprehend': 21, 'human': 22}

Tokenized Sequences:
 [[3, 4, 5, 6, 7, 8], [9, 10, 11, 12, 13, 14, 15, 16], [17, 2, 18, 19, 20, 21, 22, 2]]

Original sentence 1 tokens: ['artificial', 'intelligence', 'is', 'transforming', 'the', 'world']

Original sentence 2 tokens: ['deep', 'learning', 'enables', 'machines', 'to', 'learn', 'from', 'data']

Original sentence 3 tokens: ['language', 'natural', 'understanding', 'helps', 'computers', 'comprehend', 'human']
```

Master explained, "Apeksha, observe how the tokenizer converts these sentences into sequences of integers. Each unique word is assigned an index, and any unknown words will be replaced by <OOV>. This numerical representation is what neural networks understand. Tokenization is the first step in preparing text for deep learning models, enabling machines to process and learn from language."

Master smiled and said, "Sam, Word-Sense Disambiguation (WSD) is about teaching machines to *understand the correct meaning of a word based on its context*. Let us write a simple Python program that demonstrates this using the **Lesk algorithm** from the **Natural Language Toolkit (NLTK)**."

Here's the program —

Master continued, "Apeksha, let me explain what happens here step by step:

Importing libraries: We use NLTK, a powerful toolkit for NLP, and WordNet, a large lexical database of English.

The Lesk algorithm: It compares the context of the sentence with dictionary definitions (called *synsets*) of the target word to find the most relevant meaning.

Example sentences: The word *'bank'* is used in two different contexts — one referring to a financial institution and the other to a riverbank.

Output: The algorithm predicts which meaning fits best in each context and provides its definition from WordNet.

Case Two

Example One

Example P3 – U3 – D2	
NLU-NLP	**Output**

# Import necessary libraries 	
import nltk
from nltk.corpus import wordnet as wn
from nltk.wsd import lesk
 	
# Download WordNet and required data (run once) 	
# nltk.download('wordnet') 	
# nltk.download('omw-1.4') 	
# nltk.download('punkt') 	
 	
# Example sentences demonstrating word sense ambiguity 	
sentences = [
  "He went to the bank to deposit some money.",
  "The children sat on the bank of the river and played."
]
	Sentence: He went to the bank to deposit some money.
	Predicted Sense: Synset('savings_bank.n.02')
	Definition: a container (usually with a slot in the top) for keeping money at home
	
	Sentence: The children sat on the bank of the river and played.
	Predicted Sense: Synset('depository_financial_institution.n.01')
	Definition: a financial institution that accepts deposits and channels the money into lending activities

```
# Word to disambiguate
target_word = "bank"

# Apply Lesk algorithm to determine the correct
sense of the word in each sentence
for sentence in sentences:
    sense = lesk(nltk.word_tokenize(sentence),
target_word)
    print(f"Sentence: {sentence}")
    print(f"Predicted Sense: {sense}")
    print(f"Definition: {sense.definition()}\n")
```

This simple demonstration shows how WSD enables a system to interpret the correct sense of ambiguous words — a crucial step for improving the accuracy of machine translation, question answering, and text understanding."

Master smiled thoughtfully and said,

"Sam, you have observed an important truth about algorithms — they do not *truly* understand meaning; they only *approximate* it through patterns. In your output: the algorithm has **reversed the meanings**.

The first sentence speaks clearly about *money*, so it should have predicted the **financial institution** sense.

The second sentence, about children playing near a river, should have identified *riverbank* as the correct sense.

However, the **Lesk algorithm** uses only a simple *overlap-based method* — it looks at how many words in the sentence overlap with the definitions of each possible meaning in WordNet. It does not deeply understand context or semantics. Hence, it sometimes confuses the senses, as in this case.

This illustrates a key limitation of classical WSD methods — they rely on **surface similarity**, not **contextual comprehension**.

Modern deep learning models, especially those based on **Transformers** like **BERT**, overcome this by learning **contextual embeddings** — they represent each word differently depending on its surrounding words.

So, while Lesk gave us a glimpse into the logic of word disambiguation, it also shows why **contextual deep learning** has become the foundation of modern Natural Language Understanding."

Example Two

Example P3 – U3 – D3	
NLU-NLP	**Output**
from nltk.wsd import lesk from nltk.tokenize import word_tokenize from nltk.corpus import wordnet as wn sentence = 'He went to the bank to deposit money' words = word_tokenize(sentence) sense = lesk(words, 'bank') print(sense, sense.definition())	Synset('depository_financial_institution.n.01') a financial institution that accepts deposits and channels the money into lending activities

Example Three:

Example P3 – U3 – D4	
NLU-NLP	**Output**

from transformers import pipeline
import nltk
from nltk.wsd import lesk
 	
# # Download required NLTK data (first time only) 	
# nltk.download('punkt') 	
# nltk.download('punkt_tab') 	
# nltk.download('wordnet') 	
# nltk.download('omw-1.4') 	
 	
# Load BERT fill-mask pipeline 	
nlp = pipeline("fill-mask", model="bert-base-uncased")
 	
# Sentences to test 	
sentences = [
    "He went to the bank to deposit some money.",
    "The children sat on the bank of the river and played."
]
 	
for sentence in sentences:
    print("\nSentence:", sentence)
	Sentence: He went to the bank to deposit some money.
	BERT top prediction: bank (91.1% confidence)
	Word sense: depository_financial_institution.n.01 - a financial institution that accepts deposits and channels the money into lending activities
	
	Sentence: The children sat on the bank of the river and played.
	BERT top prediction: bank (48.6% confidence)
	Word sense: bank.n.01 - sloping land (especially the slope beside a body of water)

```
    # BERT masked prediction
    masked_sentence = sentence.replace("bank",
"[MASK]")
    predictions = nlp(masked_sentence)
    top_pred = predictions[0]  # top prediction
    word_pred = top_pred['token_str']
    confidence = top_pred['score'] * 100

    print(f"BERT top prediction: {word_pred}
({confidence:.1f}% confidence)")

    # Word Sense Disambiguation using Lesk
    words = nltk.word_tokenize(sentence)
    sense = lesk(words, 'bank')

    if sense:
        print(f"Word sense: {sense.name()} -
{sense.definition()}")
    else:
        print("Word sense: Not found")
```

BERT Masked Prediction + Lesk WSD

Master said, "Apeksha, the code combines **contextual word prediction** using **BERT** with **dictionary-based word sense disambiguation** using **NLTK's Lesk algorithm.**"

Key steps:

NLTK setup:

- Downloads essential resources (punkt, punkt_tab, wordnet, omw-1.4) needed for tokenization and WordNet-based sense analysis.

BERT masked prediction:

- Uses the Hugging Face pipeline('fill-mask') with bert-base-uncased.
- Replaces occurrences of the word 'bank' with [MASK].
- Predicts the most probable word in context and provides a confidence score.

Word Sense Disambiguation (WSD):

- Tokenizes each sentence.
- Uses the Lesk algorithm to identify the correct WordNet sense of 'bank' based on surrounding words.
- Returns a human-readable sense name and definition.

Output:
Prints each sentence along with:

- The top BERT predicted word and its confidence.
- The corresponding WordNet sense and definition.

Purpose:

- Demonstrates how **deep learning (BERT)** and **classical NLP (Lesk WSD)** can be combined to understand word meaning in context.
- Useful for tasks like **word sense disambiguation, semantic analysis, or context-aware text processing**.

Case Three

Master said, "This Python code demonstrates Named Entity Recognition (NER) using the Hugging Face Transformers library. NER is the process of identifying proper nouns or entities in text, such as persons, organizations, or locations."

Example P3 – U3 – D5	
NLU-NLP - NER	**Output**

from transformers import pipeline
 	
# Load NER pipeline 	
ner_pipeline = pipeline('ner', model='dslim/bert-base-NER', grouped_entities=True)
 	
# Sample text 	
text = 'Apple Inc. was founded by Steve Jobs in Cupertino.'
 	
# Run NER 	
results = ner_pipeline(text)
 	
# Print in readable format 	
print("Named Entities Found:")
	Named Entities Found:
	ORG: Apple Inc (Confidence: 1.00)
	PER: Steve Jobs (Confidence: 0.98)
	LOC: Cupertino (Confidence: 1.00)

for entity in results: print(f"{entity['entity_group']}: {entity['word']} (Confidence: {entity['score']:.2f})")	

Steps:

- Import pipeline – Uses pipeline from transformers to simplify model loading and execution.
- Load NER pipeline: Loads a pre-trained BERT-based NER model (dslim/bert-base-NER) and sets grouped_entities=True to combine multi-word entities.
- Input text: The sentence "Apple Inc. was founded by Steve Jobs in Cupertino." is analyzed.
- Run NER: The pipeline detects entities in the text and returns a list of dictionaries containing:
    - entity_group: Type of entity (PER, ORG, LOC)
    - word: The actual entity text
    - score: Confidence of the prediction
- Display results – Prints entities in a readable format, showing entity type, word, and confidence.

Purpose:

This code helps beginners understand how to automatically detect named entities in text, which is useful in NLP tasks like information extraction, question answering, and knowledge graph creation.

Case Four

Master said, "Let us understand this Python code demonstrates Part-of-Speech (PoS) tagging using the NLTK library. PoS tagging assigns a grammatical category (like noun, verb, adjective) to each word in a sentence."

Example P3 – U3 – D6	
NLU-NLP - POS	**Output**

import nltk
 	
# Download required NLTK resources (first time only) 	
nltk.download('punkt')
	Word : PoS Tag
	Nikash : NNP
	is : VBZ
	learning : VBG
	Natural : NNP

nltk.download('averaged_perceptron_tagger')
 	
# Sample sentence 	
sentence = "Nikash is learning Natural Language Processing with enthusiasm."
 	
# Tokenize the sentence into words 	
words = nltk.word_tokenize(sentence)
 	
# Perform Part-of-Speech Tagging 	
pos_tags = nltk.pos_tag(words)
 	
# Print the results 	
print("Word : PoS Tag")
for word, tag in pos_tags:
    print(f"{word} : {tag}")
	Language : NNP
	Processing : VBG
	with : IN
	enthusiasm : NN

Steps:

- Import NLTK: Python's Natural Language Toolkit used for text processing.
- Download resources
    - punkt → Tokenizer models to split sentences into words.
    - averaged_perceptron_tagger → Pre-trained PoS tagger model.
- Tokenization: Splits the sentence into individual words using nltk.word_tokenize().
- PoS Tagging: Assigns a PoS tag to each token with nltk.pos_tag().
- Display results: Prints each word along with its PoS tag in a readable format.

Step-by-Step Guide to Set Up an NLP Environment using Anaconda

Master said, "Nikash, before we dive into Natural Language Processing, we must first prepare the ground — our digital laboratory. Let us create a clean and stable environment where we can experiment freely."

This guide explains how to create a clean Python environment for Natural Language Processing (NLP) projects using **Conda** and install all the necessary libraries like **Transformers**, **TensorFlow**, **PyTorch**, and **NLTK**.

Step 1: Open Anaconda Prompt

Press the **Windows key** and type **"Anaconda Prompt"**.

Click to open it.

You'll see something like: C:\Users\User>

```
C:\Users\User>
```

Step 2: Create a New Conda Environment

Master continued, "Now, let us create a separate workspace for all our NLP experiments — a place untouched by other projects."

Run this command: conda create -n nlp_env python=3.11 -y

```
conda create -n nlp_env python=3.11 -y
```

conda create -n nlp_env → Creates a new virtual environment named nlp_env.

python=3.11 → Specifies the Python version to use.

-y → Automatically confirms the installation.

Master said, "This tells Conda to create a new environment named *nlp_env* with Python version 3.11.

Conda will set everything up automatically — no need to browse folders."

Step 3: Activate the Environment

"Once created," Master said, "we must enter it."

Activate your new environment using: conda activate nlp_env

You'll notice the prompt changes to: (nlp_env) C:\Users\User>

```
(nlp_env) C:\Users\User>
```

Master said, "This confirms that you have stepped into your new workspace. Any installation or code you run now will stay isolated here — safe and organized."

Step 4: Install Required Packages

Master said, "Before we bring in our tools, let's upgrade *pip*, the package manager.

```
pip install --upgrade pip
```

Now we install the key libraries used for NLP and Machine Learning:

```
pip install --upgrade transformers tensorflow torch
```

Master said, "To support additional tasks like tokenization, datasets, and model evaluation, install these too:"

Install additional dependencies for pipelines and NLP utilities:

pip install tokenizers datasets seqeval huggingface_hub

These packages allow you to use advanced NLP models from **Hugging Face**, train deep learning models, and manage datasets efficiently.

Step 5: Verify Setup

Master smiled, "Let us now test if everything works."

Start Python by typing: python

You'll see the Python interactive prompt:>>>

```
>>>
```

Now test your installation by typing this small script:

```
import tensorflow as tf

from transformers import pipeline

print("TensorFlow version:", tf.__version__)
```

```
ner = pipeline("ner", model="dslim/bert-base-NER", grouped_entities=True, framework="tf")

print("NER pipeline loaded successfully")
```

Master explained, "This code checks whether TensorFlow and Transformers are installed correctly and loads a pre-trained *Named Entity Recognition* model."

If you see both messages printed without error, your setup is perfect.

To exit Python, simply type: exit()

```
exit()
```

One-Line Installation Command

If you want to install everything at once, use this single command:

```
conda activate nlp_env && pip install --upgrade pip && pip install --upgrade transformers tensorflow torch tokenizers datasets seqeval huggingface_hub accelerate torchvision
```

"This command upgrades pip, installs all essential NLP packages, and ensures compatibility."

Step 6: Run a Python File

If you saved your test code as test_ner.py, run it using:

```
conda activate nlp_env
python test_ner.py
```

Step 7: Uninstall or Reinstall Packages (If Needed)

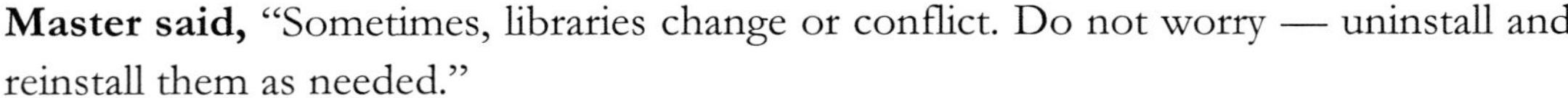

Master said, "Sometimes, libraries change or conflict. Do not worry — uninstall and reinstall them as needed."

To uninstall a package (for example, Transformers):

```
pip uninstall transformers -y
```

To reinstall or upgrade all major libraries:

```
pip install --upgrade transformers torch tensorflow tokenizers datasets seqeval huggingface_hub accelerate torchvision
```

Step 8: Verify Installation Paths

"Always know where your tools reside," said Master.

```
python -c "import transformers; print(transformers.__file__)"
```

"You can check others in the same way, for example:"

```
python -c "import nltk; print(nltk.__version__)"
```

Step 9: Install and Configure NLTK

To use tokenization and tagging tools from **NLTK**, install it via pip:

```
pip install nltk
```

Then open Python and download the required datasets:

```
import nltk

nltk.download('punkt')

nltk.download('averaged_perceptron_tagger')

nltk.download('averaged_perceptron_tagger_eng')
```

He said softly, "These resources allow Python to break sentences into words and understand their grammatical roles — the first step toward true language comprehension."

You're All Set!

You now have:

- A clean, isolated environment for NLP projects
- All major ML and NLP libraries installed
- Verification methods to confirm your setup
- A ready-to-run NER test program

"Now, Nikash," Master said with calm pride, "You have built your own NLP laboratory — an isolated space where language, data, and intelligence meet. From here begins your real journey into the heart of Natural Language Understanding."

PART THREE

DAY EIGHT

Unit 3 - Lesson Three

Heart of Natural Language Understanding

Case Five: Dependency Parsing

Master leaned back, "John," he began, "we have journeyed through the foundations of Natural Language Understanding — we learned how machines see words (*Tokenization*), recognize their nature (*PoS Tagging*), identify entities (*NER*), and even resolve meaning in ambiguity (*WSD*). But you may wonder — why did we not yet speak of *Dependency Parsing* and *Intent Recognition*?"

Master continued thoughtfully, "These two — *Dependency Parsing* and *Intent Recognition* — belong to a higher tier of understanding. They do not just interpret words; they interpret **relationships** and **purposes**. Before reaching them, one must first master the building blocks of structure and meaning."

He drew a simple analogy:

"Before a child can understand *why* a sentence is spoken, they must first understand *how* it is formed and *what* each word means.

Dependency Parsing and Intent Recognition are like reading *between the lines* — not just the grammar, but the intention that breathes life into language."

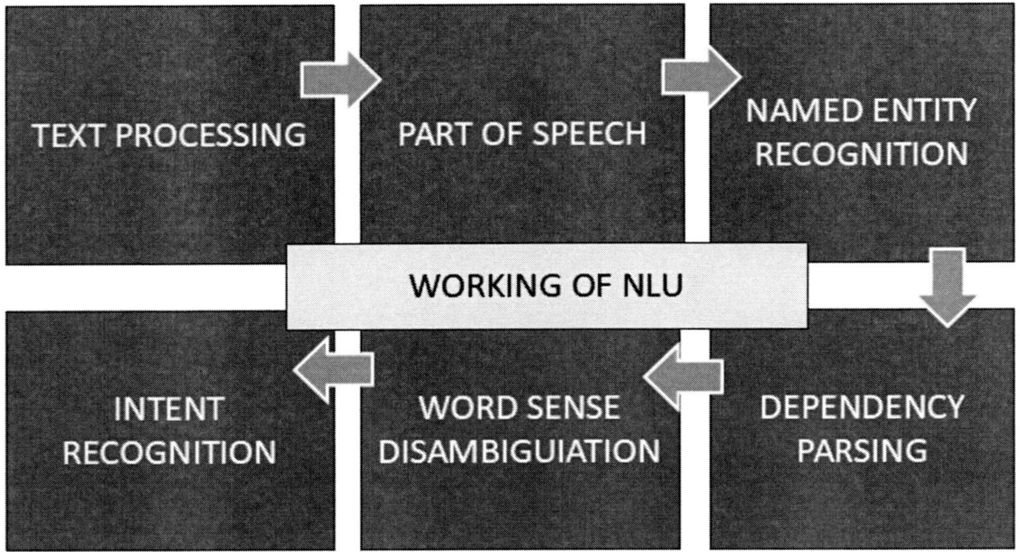

Illustration NLU_2: NLU

Master explained, "Dependency Parsing is an advanced form of syntactic understanding. It goes beyond *what* a word is, to understand *how* it depends on others."

He illustrated with an example:

Sentence: *"The student read the book in the library."*

- "student" → **subject** of "read"
- "book" → **object** of "read"
- "in the library" → **modifier** (tells *where* the reading happened)

He continued, "In Dependency Parsing, words become nodes in a structure — a tree of relationships.

The parser identifies which word is the root (usually the main verb) and how every other word connects to it.

While PoS tagging shows the *type* of each word, Dependency Parsing reveals the *architecture* of the sentence."

Master elaborated, "To understand dependency, one must already be fluent in parts of speech, syntax, and contextual meaning — the very topics we have been mastering.

Thus, Dependency Parsing naturally follows *PoS Tagging* and *NER*, not precedes them."

Case Six: Intent Recognition

Master then turned to the subtler art — *Intent Recognition.*

He said, "Intent Recognition does not deal with words or structure alone. It deals with **purpose** — the hidden meaning behind what is said."

He gave an example:

Sentence 1: *"Can you open the window?"*

Sentence 2: *"Please open the window."*

He smiled, "Both sentences have the same **intent** — a request — though one appears as a question.

To decode this, a system must already recognize entities, understand syntax, and interpret semantics. Only then can it infer *why* something was said."

"Intent Recognition belongs to the **applied layer** of NLU — it powers chatbots, dialogue systems, and voice assistants.

It requires prior mastery of foundational tasks — tokenization, PoS tagging, NER, and WSD — because intent arises from the combination of structure and meaning. Without understanding the *what* and *how*, we cannot infer the *why*."

The Bridge Between Syntax and Semantics

Master paused, letting the lesson settle.

"Dependency Parsing forms the bridge between *syntactic understanding* and *semantic interpretation*, while Intent Recognition builds upon both to grasp *human purpose*."

He continued with quiet emphasis, "Think of our journey as building a temple of understanding:

- **Tokenization** laid the foundation stones,

- **PoS tagging** raised the pillars,
- **NER** carved the symbols,
- **WSD** brought meaning to each sculpture, and soon,
- **Dependency Parsing** will define the structure,
- **Intent Recognition** will breathe the soul within."

Master said, "When you are ready, we shall explore these advanced dimensions. Dependency Parsing will teach you how words *cling to one another* in logical bonds, and Intent Recognition will unveil how machines discern *why humans speak* at all."

He looked toward the horizon and said softly, "Language is not just to be read — it is to be *understood*, layer by layer, until it mirrors the mind that spoke it."

Apeksha asked: "Master, what does it mean when we say a sentence has *syntactic dependencies*?"

Master explained:

"Dependency parsing reveals how words in a sentence *relate* to one another — who depends on whom for meaning.

Just as every limb of a tree connects back to its trunk, every word in a sentence connects to a central 'root' — usually the *main verb*."

Concept:

Dependency parsing maps grammatical relationships between words.

It identifies heads (main words) and dependents (words that modify or are controlled by heads).

Example:

"The cat sat on the mat."

- sat → ROOT (main verb)
- cat → subject of sat
- on → preposition dependent on sat
- mat → object of on

Environment:

Install **spaCy** inside that environment:

```
pip install spacy
```

(Optional but recommended) Download a small English model for spaCy:

```
python -m spacy download en_core_web_sm
```

In Spyder's console, run:

```
import spacy

nlp = spacy.load("en_core_web_sm")

print("spaCy is working fine!")
```

Case Five:

Example P3 – U3 – D7	
NLU-NLP - Dependency Parsing	**Output**

import spacy
 	
# Load English language model 	
nlp = spacy.load("en_core_web_sm")
 	
# Sentence to parse 	
sentence = "The cat sat on the mat."
doc = nlp(sentence)
 	
# Display dependencies 	
for token in doc:
	The | det | cat
	cat | nsubj | sat
	sat | ROOT | sat
	on | prep | sat
	the | det | mat
	mat | pobj | on
	. | punct | sat

```
    print(f"{token.text:<10} | {token.dep_:<10} |
{token.head.text:<10}")
```

Import spaCy

This imports the spaCy library, which provides tools for tokenization, POS tagging, and dependency parsing.

Load English Language Model

Loads a pre-trained small English model that knows grammar, vocabulary, and syntax patterns.

Input Sentence

The text is processed through the nlp pipeline, breaking it into tokens and analyzing their relationships.

Display Dependencies

- token.text → the word itself
- token.dep_ → its dependency label (e.g., subject, object, modifier)
- token.head.text → the main word (head) that it depends on

Interpretation:

The dependency structure shows:

- "cat" is the subject of "sat"
- "mat" is the object of the preposition "on"
- "on" links "sat" and "mat" together

Why It Matters:

Dependency parsing enables:

- Question answering ("Who sat?" → "The cat.")
- Semantic role labeling
- Machine translation
- Chatbot understanding

Python Code for Visualization

Example P3 – U3 – D8

NLU-NLP - Dependency Parsing

```
# dependency_visualization.py

import spacy
from spacy import displacy

# Step 1: Load the English language model
nlp = spacy.load("en_core_web_sm")

# Step 2: Input sentence to analyze
sentence = "The cat sat on the mat."

# Step 3: Process the sentence with spaCy
doc = nlp(sentence)

# Step 4: Render dependency visualization as HTML
html = displacy.render(doc, style="dep")  # style="dep" for dependencies

# Step 5: Save HTML to file
output_file =
"C://Users//User//mraj4//Documents//Optimum6//Part2//dependency.html"
with open(output_file, "w", encoding="utf-8") as f:
    f.write(html)

print(f"Dependency visualization saved as '{output_file}'.")
```

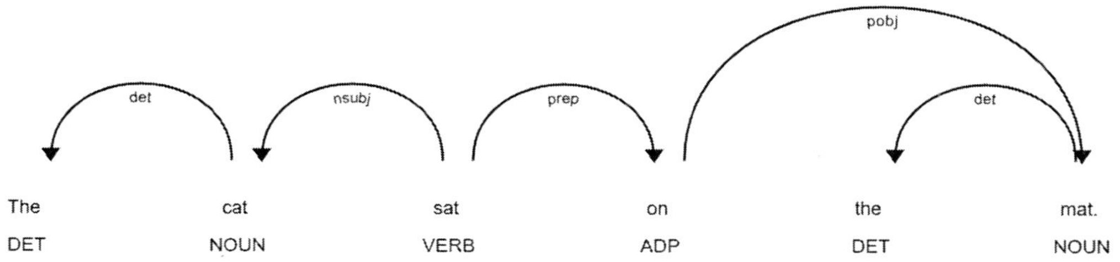

Illustration Dependency_1: Dependency Parsing

Explanation

displacy.render() displays the sentence as a graph, where:

- Each word is connected to its "head" by an arrow.
- Labels (like nsubj, pobj, prep) indicate the grammatical relationship.

The root (here, "sat") sits at the center of the structure.

Arrows flow outward to dependents such as "cat" (subject) and "on" (prepositional link).

Analogy:

"A sentence is like a constellation," said the Master.

"Each word is a star — alone, it glows faintly.

But through grammar's invisible lines, they connect, forming the pattern that reveals meaning."

The Evolution of Natural Language Processing

Master leaned back, his eyes reflecting the curiosity of centuries, and said,"Apeksha, to truly appreciate where Natural Language Processing stands today, we must travel back in time and understand its **evolution** — how each breakthrough in techniques and models has built upon the last, shaping the capabilities we now take for granted."

The Early Foundations – Pre-2010

"Before 2013," Master began, "NLP was dominated by **rule-based systems** and **statistical models**. Linguists and engineers painstakingly wrote grammar rules and dictionaries. Machines could parse simple sentences or extract keywords, but understanding context or meaning was beyond reach. The language was treated as patterns of symbols rather than carriers of thought."

2013 – The Era of Word Representations

"In 2013, the field started embracing **count-based models** and **word embeddings**," he continued. "Techniques like **N-grams** captured the probability of sequences of words, while **word embeddings** such as Word2Vec and GloVe transformed words into numerical vectors. These vectors captured semantic meaning — for example, 'king' minus 'man' plus 'woman' would approximate 'queen'. Machines could now sense meaning in addition to mere structure, marking the first step toward true understanding."

2014 – Recurrent Neural Networks and LSTM

"By 2014, the limitations of traditional models in handling sequences became apparent. Enter **Recurrent Neural Networks (RNNs)** and **Long Short-Term Memory (LSTM)** networks. These architectures allowed machines to remember context over sequences — the way humans recall prior words to interpret a sentence. Suddenly, machines could understand dependencies across words, not just local patterns."

2015 – Attention Mechanism

"Even RNNs had weaknesses," Master said thoughtfully. "They struggled with very long sequences. In 2015, the **attention mechanism** emerged, allowing models to focus selectively on relevant words when processing sentences. This was akin to teaching a machine to 'pay attention' to the most important parts of a conversation or document, rather than treating all words equally."

2017 – Transformers Revolution

"In 2017, NLP witnessed a **paradigm shift** with the introduction of **Transformers**. Unlike RNNs, Transformers processed sequences in parallel and leveraged self-attention to capture relationships between all words simultaneously. This breakthrough made NLP models more scalable, faster, and far more powerful than anything before."

2018 – BERT and Contextual Understanding

"Building on Transformers, 2018 saw **BERT (Bidirectional Encoder Representations from Transformers)**, which read text both forward and backward to understand context fully. Unlike earlier embeddings, which treated words in isolation, BERT allowed machines to grasp nuances like polysemy and context-dependent meaning. This was a major leap in comprehension, powering tasks like NER, question answering, and sentiment analysis with unprecedented accuracy."

2020–2023 – Large Language Models (LLMs)

"Between 2020 and 2023," Master explained, "we entered the era of **Large Language Models**, including the GPT series. These models, trained on **massive amounts of text**, could generate human-like text, summarize, translate, answer questions, and even code. Their sheer size and pre-training on diverse corpora gave them an almost uncanny ability to *understand and produce language* in versatile ways. They were no longer task-specific; they were general-purpose language engines."

2024 – AI Agents and Autonomous Language Understanding

"In 2024," he continued, "The rise of **AI Agents**. These are systems that combine LLMs with reasoning, planning, and real-world interaction. They can not only understand language but act upon it autonomously — performing tasks, integrating knowledge from multiple domains, and even making decisions. This represents the **culmination of decades of NLP research**, where language understanding is no longer just analysis but **actionable intelligence**."

Master smiled, "From N-grams and embeddings to Transformers, BERT, GPT, and now autonomous AI Agents, NLP has evolved from **symbolic patterns** to **contextual comprehension** and finally to **reasoning and agency**. Each step built upon the previous, bridging the gap between human thought and machine understanding."

The Triad of Language Intelligence

Master said, "Roopa, let us understand the true essence of NLU, NLP, and NLG — the three pillars that allow machines to not just process language, but to think, understand, and respond like us."

He paused for a moment and continued with calm precision, "Language is more than words — it is thought expressed through sound and structure. For a machine to bridge that gap, it must learn to *process*, *understand*, and *generate* language. These three stages form the sacred trinity of computational linguistics — **NLP**, **NLU**, and **NLG**."

Understanding the Three Pillars

Natural Language Processing (NLP): The Bridge Between Human and Machine

"NLP," Master explained, "is the broad discipline that enables communication between humans and computers in natural language rather than in binary or coded commands. It's the foundation of all language-based AI."

It involves transforming raw human language into data that computers can analyze and respond to meaningfully. NLP is responsible for **tokenizing**, **parsing**, **analyzing**

syntax, and **extracting semantics** — converting human conversation into a structured machine-understandable form.

Analogy: If human language is music, NLP is the act of reading the musical notes.

Applications: Machine translation (Google Translate), sentiment analysis, speech recognition, and document summarization all rely on NLP.

Natural Language Understanding (NLU): The Art of Comprehension

"Once a machine can process text," Master continued, "the next step is understanding what it means. This is the domain of NLU — where the machine learns to comprehend, infer, and extract meaning, much like the human mind does."

NLU converts **unstructured input** — whether text or speech — into **structured meaning**. It analyses **intent**, **context**, and **emotion**, distinguishing between what is said and what is *meant.*

This understanding requires **semantic parsing**, **named entity recognition**, **coreference resolution**, and **intent detection**.

Analogy: NLP reads the musical notes; NLU feels the emotion of the song.

Applications: Chatbots (like Alexa or Dialogflow), question-answering systems, and sentiment detection engines are all driven by NLU.

Comparative View: The Harmony of the Three

Aspect	NLP	NLU	NLG
Core Function	Processing and analysing language	Understanding meaning and intent	Generating natural-sounding responses
Input	Raw text or speech	Natural language text	Structured data or representations
Output	Structured or cleaned data	Machine-readable meaning	Human-readable text
Goal	Interpret and process language	Extract meaning, context, and emotion	Produce expressive and coherent language

Illustration NLU_3: NLP

Natural Language Generation (NLG): The Power of Expression

Master then explained, "Once a machine understands meaning, it must respond — clearly, coherently, and naturally. This act of creating human-like responses is the essence of NLG."

NLG converts structured data or machine-generated representations into **natural, fluent text.** It gives the machine a voice — transforming internal logic into expressive language.

It involves **content planning**, **sentence structuring**, and **surface realisation**, ensuring that responses are grammatically correct, emotionally appropriate, and contextually relevant.

Analogy: NLG is the act of composing and performing the music that touches the listener's heart.

Applications: Automated report generation, conversational agents, personalised recommendations, and creative writing tools (like GPT models).

Comparative View: The Harmony of the Three

Aspect	NLP	NLU	NLG
Techniques Used	Tokenization, parsing, tagging	Semantic analysis, embeddings, inference	Templates, transformers, generative modelling
Common Tools	spaCy, NLTK, Hugging Face	BERT, RoBERTa, Dialogflow	GPT, T5, SimpleNLG
Applications	Speech-to-text, summarisation, translation	Sentiment analysis, chatbots, intent detection	Conversational AI, report writing, storytelling
Evaluation Metrics	Accuracy, F1-score	Intent accuracy, precision, recall	BLEU, ROUGE, perplexity

Illustration NLU_4: NLP

Interconnected Roles

Master illustrated with an example:

"Suppose a user asks a voice assistant — *'What is the weather like in Paris today?'*"

- **NLP** converts the spoken question into text and identifies key linguistic structures.
- **NLU** interprets the user's intent — understanding that it's a *weather query* for a *specific location and time.*
- **NLG** then constructs a natural response: *'The weather in Paris today is sunny with a high of 23°C.'*

Timeline and Origins

Concept	Origin Era	Focus
NLP	1950s – inspired by Alan Turing's vision of language understanding	Teaching machines to process linguistic structure
NLU	1960s – early attempts at comprehension through semantic networks	Helping computers understand meaning
NLG	1970s – emergence of automated text generation	Enabling machines to speak and write naturally

Illustration NLU_5: NLP

Each step depends on the previous — forming a seamless pipeline of understanding and expression.

Challenges and Edge Cases

- **Ambiguity:** Words like *"bank"* or *"charge"* have multiple meanings.
- **Sarcasm and Irony:** Subtle tone and cultural cues are hard to model.
- **Domain Adaptation:** Specialised vocabularies (like medicine or law) demand retraining.
- **Multilingual Complexity:** Code-mixed sentences challenge parsing and tagging accuracy.

Master said, "Roopa, think of NLP as the *ear*, NLU as the *mind*, and NLG as the *voice* of an intelligent system.

Together, they allow machines not just to hear, but to *understand* and *speak back* with meaning.
This trinity forms the soul of modern language AI — from translation tools to chatbots to generative models like GPT."

Applications of Natural Language Processing (NLP)

Master said, "Akanksh, among the millions of life forms on this planet, only humans have constructed refined systems of symbolic communication — language. From cave marks to keyboard taps, our words carry histories, intentions, and emotions. If we wish machines to participate in human life, they must learn to perceive, interpret, and respond to language. This is the promise of NLP. Let us walk through its applications and why they matter."

1. Chatbots — conversational scaffolds for human needs

Master said, "The simplest dream is a machine that keeps a conversation. ELIZA (1966) showed us that even a simple pattern-driven bot could feel like a conversational partner. Today's chatbots are far richer."

Depth & context

- Modern chatbots combine **NLU** (to detect intent and extract entities), **dialog management** (to track state), and **NLG** (to craft replies).
- They range from scripted FAQ bots to adaptive, context-aware assistants that maintain session history and personalise responses.

Examples & impact

- Customer support: instant answers, 24/7 availability, reduced wait times.
- Mental health prototypes: conversational companions that provide support and triage (not replacements for professionals).
- E-commerce assistants: guide users to products, handle returns, and upsell.

Caveat

- Poor design leads to frustration — the bot must gracefully handle unknowns and escalate to humans when needed.

2. Text Classification — making sense of vast unstructured text

Master said, "Text is messy and enormous. Classification gives it shape."

Depth & context

- Converts unstructured text into labelled categories (spam/not-spam, topic tags, intent classes).
- Techniques evolved from bag-of-words and TF–IDF to deep encoders (CNNs, RNNs, Transformers).

Examples & impact

- Spam filtering, email triage, legal document triaging, topic labelling for newsrooms, automated tagging for content management.
- Brand monitoring: classifies mentions as positive/negative/neutral to support marketing decisions.

Business value

- Scales human review; enables analytics and automated workflows.

3. Sentiment Analysis — listening to the emotional current

Master said, "Beyond facts, language carries feeling. Measuring sentiment lets us sense the crowd's pulse."

Depth & context

- Ranges from rule-based lexicons to supervised classifiers to transformer-based emotion detectors.
- Must handle negation, sarcasm, mixed sentiment, and domain-specific language.

Examples & impact

- Product feedback analysis, social listening during campaigns, crisis detection (e.g., real-time escalation when sentiment drops).

- Political and market sentiment analysis — useful but ethically fraught.

Limits

- Sarcasm, cultural variations, and subtlety remain hard; human-in-the-loop validation is often necessary.

4. Machine Translation — removing language barriers

Master said, "To speak across tongues is to widen human connection."

Depth & context

- From early rule-based and phrase-based systems to neural sequence-to-sequence and now large pre-trained multilingual models.
- Current systems use attention and Transformers, enabling fluent, context-aware translations.

Examples & impact

- Google Translate, real-time captioning, cross-lingual search, and localisation pipelines for global products.
- Translates textual content and — increasingly — images and speech.

Challenges

- Low-resource languages, idioms, cultural nuances, and domain-specific jargon need special care.

5. Virtual Assistants — personal agents that act

Master said, "A virtual assistant is more than conversation; it acts upon instructions."

Depth & context

- Fuse speech recognition, NLU, dialog state tracking, and action execution (calendar, smart home, web queries).
- Learn personalisation (preferences, history) while managing privacy and security.

Examples & impact

- Siri, Alexa, Google Assistant: set reminders, control devices, manage workflows.
- Assistants in specialised domains: medical assistants for clinicians, enterprise bots for employee IT support.

Maturity

- Capable multi-turn dialogues and context maintenance are now reasonable; truly deep reasoning remains a frontier.

6. Speech Recognition — converting voice into text

Master said, "Speech is the most natural human interface; converting it to text unlocks the rest of NLP."

Depth & context

- Modern ASR uses deep acoustic models + language models. Noise robustness, accents, and domain adaptation are major engineering challenges.

Examples & impact

- Voice assistants, dictation software, meeting transcription, accessibility tools for people with disabilities.

Consideration

- Real-time low-latency systems and privacy-preserving on-device models are active priorities.

7. Text Summarisation — distilling meaning from abundance

Master said, "When knowledge grows, distillation becomes a skill."

Depth & context

- Extractive methods pick salient sentences; abstractive methods generate concise paraphrases. Transformers and pointer-generator models power modern summarisation.

Examples & impact

- News summarisation, executive briefings, summarising long legal or scientific documents, and faster literature surveys for researchers.

Limits

- Faithfulness (avoiding hallucination) and factual accuracy are crucial.

8. Named Entity Recognition (NER) — finding the actors and places

Master said, "To understand events, first find the players."

Depth & context

- NER extracts entities (persons, orgs, locations, dates). Deep contextual models handle ambiguous mentions and multi-token entities.

Examples & impact

- Building knowledge graphs, improving search, automating metadata extraction for archives, and powering downstream relation extraction.

Domain note

- Medical NER or legal NER requires domain-specific models and annotated corpora.

9. Question Answering — retrieving direct knowledge from text

Master said, "Answering a question is a compressed form of understanding."

Depth & context

- Ranges from information retrieval (find and return passages) to extractive and generative QA using pre-trained models (BERT, T5, GPT).
- Combines retrieval, reading comprehension, and response generation.

Examples & impact

- Customer support bots that answer FAQs, search engines that return direct answers, and closed-book QA for domain knowledge.

Risk

- Hallucinations in generative models demand verification layers for high-stakes domains.

10. Language Modelling — the backbone of generative intelligence

Master said, "Modelling language statistically allows us to predict and generate — that power fuels many applications."

Depth & context

- Language models (from n-grams to transformers and LLMs) capture distributional patterns. They are pretraining engines enabling transfer learning for many tasks.

Examples & impact

- Text generation for chatbots, code generation, autocomplete, creative writing aids, and downstream fine-tuning for classification tasks.

Ethical dimension

- Generated text raises questions of authenticity, attribution, and misuse (deepfakes, spam).

Cross-Industry Impacts — How NLP Transforms Sectors

Healthcare

- Clinical note mining, triaging, summarising patient history, and extracting outcomes from research.

Finance

- Sentiment-driven trading signals, automating compliance monitoring, and customer service automation.

Customer Service & Retail

- 24/7 virtual agents, intelligent routing, personalised recommendations, voice-of-customer analytics.

Media & Social Intelligence

- Trend detection, misinformation detection, automated moderation, summarisation pipelines for editors.

Legal & Academia

- Contract analysis, precedent search, automating literature reviews, and extracting case metadata.

Core Technical Themes & Why They Matter

- **Data scale and transfer learning:** Pre-trained models, trained on massive corpora, allow rapid adaptation to specific tasks.
- **Contextual representation:** Moving from static word vectors to contextual embeddings (e.g., BERT) reduces ambiguity.
- **End-to-end systems:** Modern pipelines often combine retrieval, reasoning (or approximations of it), and generation.
- **Human-in-the-loop:** For high-stakes tasks, models assist humans rather than replace them — triage and assist is the pragmatic model.

Challenges, Risks & Ethical Considerations

Ambiguity & nuance

- Sarcasm, irony, and cultural allusions are still hard.

Bias & fairness

- Training data reflects human biases; systems can amplify harms (hateful content, stereotyping).

Privacy

- Sensitive texts (medical or financial) require careful handling and on-device or encrypted processing.

Hallucination

- Generative models may produce plausible-sounding but false statements — a major risk for factual applications.

Accountability

- Logging, explainability, and human oversight are essential when models inform decisions.

The Human Dimension — Design & Evaluation

Human-centered design

- Systems must be designed for how people actually speak and behave, with graceful failure modes and clear options to reach humans.

Evaluation

- Beyond accuracy: user experience, trust, latency, cost, and safety matter. Metrics like F1 or BLEU are not enough alone.

Master said, "NLP is not only a set of techniques; it is a craft that connects human intent with machine action. Each application we discussed is a thread in the tapestry of language technology — together they create systems that can listen, interpret, and respond. With power comes responsibility: builders must curate data carefully, design for transparency, and keep humans central in the loop. Only then will our creations truly serve the human condition."

Techniques & Algorithms in Modern NLP

Master said, "Akanksh, the craft of teaching machines language is layered: simple rules gave way to statistics, statistics to machine learning, and machine learning to large, pre-trained neural engines. Each step changed not only the tools we use, but the kinds of problems we can solve."

1. Rule-based approaches (the linguistic artisanship)

What it is?

Early NLP used explicit linguistic rules — grammars, dictionaries, hand-written heuristics — to tokenize, parse, and transform text.

Why did it matter?

Rule systems were interpretable and suited constrained domains (e.g., grammar checkers, early MT prototypes).

Limitations: They don't scale easily across languages, domains, or noisy real-world inputs; maintenance is expensive.

2. Statistical methods (the probabilistic turn)

What it is?

N-grams, Hidden Markov Models, and probabilistic classifiers that model language as statistics of tokens and sequences.

Why did it matter?

Introduced measurable performance, corpora-driven design, and the ability to model uncertainty in language. N-grams and HMMs powered early taggers, speech models, and baseline translation systems.

Limitations: Sparse data, lack of long-range context, and an inability to learn semantics beyond co-occurrence.

3. Classical Machine Learning (supervised / unsupervised / reinforcement)

What it is?

Feature-based classifiers (SVMs, decision trees), clustering, topic models (LDA), and RL for dialog policies.

Why did it matter?

These methods made it practical to build discriminative systems for classification, topic detection, and dialog management with annotated data.

Evolution: Feature engineering was central; the better the features (POS, lexicons, morphology), the better the model.

4. Deep learning (RNNs, LSTMs → sequence understanding)

What it is.

Neural architectures that learn dense, distributed representations (embeddings) and sequence behaviours: RNNs, LSTMs, GRUs.

Why did it matter?

These models captured sequential dependencies and context better than classical methods; they powered improvements in speech recognition, machine translation, and sequence labelling.

Limitations: Difficulty modelling very long context, slow training for long sequences.

5. Attention & Transformers (the structural leap)

What it is?

Self-attention and Transformer architectures allow every token to attend to every other token; models can be trained in parallel and scale to billions of parameters.

Why did it matter?

This is the backbone of modern pre-trained language models (BERT, GPT families). Transformers enable both powerful encoders for understanding and decoders for generation.

6. Pretraining + Fine-tuning (the transfer learning regime)

What it is?

Large models are pre-trained on huge corpora with self-supervised objectives (masked LM, next-token prediction), then fine-tuned for tasks.

Why did it matter?

Dramatically improved data efficiency and generalization; now a small labelled dataset can yield SOTA when fine-tuned from a strong pre-trained model.

7. Efficient Fine-tuning methods (LoRA, adapters, parameter-efficient tuning)

What it is?

Techniques that adapt huge pre-trained models to downstream tasks by training a tiny fraction of parameters (LoRA, adapters, prompt-tuning). LoRA inserts low-rank update matrices so the main weights stay frozen.

Why does it matter now?

These methods make custom models feasible for practitioners with limited GPU/memory and accelerate deployment while reducing the storage of multiple full models. See LoRA (Low-Rank Adaptation) as a canonical example.

8. Instruction Tuning & RLHF (making models follow human intent)

What it is?

Instruction tuning trains models on many tasks formatted as instructions; Reinforcement Learning from Human Feedback (RLHF) uses human preferences to align model outputs with desirable behaviour.

Why does it matter?

These methods made LLMs more helpful, safer, and controllable for interactive applications (chat, assistants). They're now central to production LLMs and assistant systems.

9. Retrieval-Augmented Generation (RAG) and knowledge grounding

What it is?

Retrieval components fetch documents or passages from external stores (vector DBs, search indexes) and condition generation on retrieved context.

Why it matters (today).

RAG reduces hallucinations, allows up-to-date answers, and makes models query internal knowledge without retraining. It's widely used in production for knowledge-driven QA and enterprise chatbots.

Emerging nuance. Enterprises are experimenting with alternatives (agent patterns, secure query architectures) to address security, compliance, and data governance concerns associated with centralised vector stores.

10. Multimodal models (vision, audio, video + text)

What it is?

Models trained to accept and relate multiple modalities — e.g., text↔image (captioning), text↔audio (speech understanding), or fully multimodal agents that reason across inputs.

Why does it matter now?

Real-world applications need more than text: visual grounding, multimodal search, and video understanding are exploding areas. Major vendors and research labs are releasing multimodal foundation models and suites (text+image+audio). Recent product launches show cloud providers integrating multimodal foundation models for practical use.

11. Agents and end-to-end systems (planning + action)

What it is?

Systems that combine LLM reasoning with tools, APIs, and long-running workflows (agents) that perform tasks, retrieve data, and take actions.

Why does it matter?

Agents bridge language understanding to actual effect in the world (orchestration, automation). They're the next step beyond isolated RAG pipelines for many enterprise use cases. There is an industry shift toward secure, controlled agent architectures.

12. Evaluation, benchmarks, and robustness efforts

What it is?

A growing emphasis on robust evaluation beyond single metrics (BLEU/ROUGE). Modern benchmarking includes MMLU, BIG-Bench, HELM and specialized robustness and safety evaluations. The community is pushing for holistic evaluation: accuracy, safety, fairness, truthfulness, latency, and cost.

Trends & What's New

Parameter efficiency is mainstream. LoRA and adapters moved from research to standard practice for fine-tuning LLMs cheaply. This enables many organizations to personalize models without hosting dozens of full-sized weights.

RAG remains central but is evolving. Retrieval is standard for knowledge-intensive tasks, but enterprises are rethinking where and how retrieval happens (security, freshness, governance), prompting more hybrid or agent-based designs.

Multimodal foundation models are accelerating. Cloud vendors and research labs released new multimodal offerings (text + image + audio + video) that are production-ready, driving use cases from content generation to multimodal search.

Instruction tuning + RLHF = better aligned assistants. These remain the dominant methods to make models helpful and safe; research continues into reducing alignment data costs and automating preference feedback.

Evaluation moves beyond accuracy. The community emphasises truthfulness, safety, and domain robustness — and enterprises need standard, reproducible evaluation pipelines for governance.

Where research is heading

- **Better, cheaper personalisation:** continued improvements in parameter-efficient tuning, pruning, and quantization.
- **Agentization + tool use:** safer, auditable agents that orchestrate services for complex workflows.
- **Multimodal reasoning:** models that jointly reason across text, images, audio, and structured data.
- **Benchmarking for truth & safety:** richer, real-world evaluation suites and standardized testing around hallucination and bias.
- **On-device, privacy-first models:** smaller but capable models running locally for privacy-sensitive use cases.

PART THREE

DAY EIGHT

Unit 3 - Lesson Three

When Words Meet Intelligence

Phases of Natural Language Processing (NLP)

Master said, "Natural Language Processing (NLP) transforms human language into forms machines can analyze, reason about, and generate. It is not a single operation but a layered pipeline: each phase adds a new depth of understanding — from breaking text into tokens to inferring speaker intention. Let us expand each major phase with clear explanations, different examples from your original, and notes on why each phase matters in real systems."

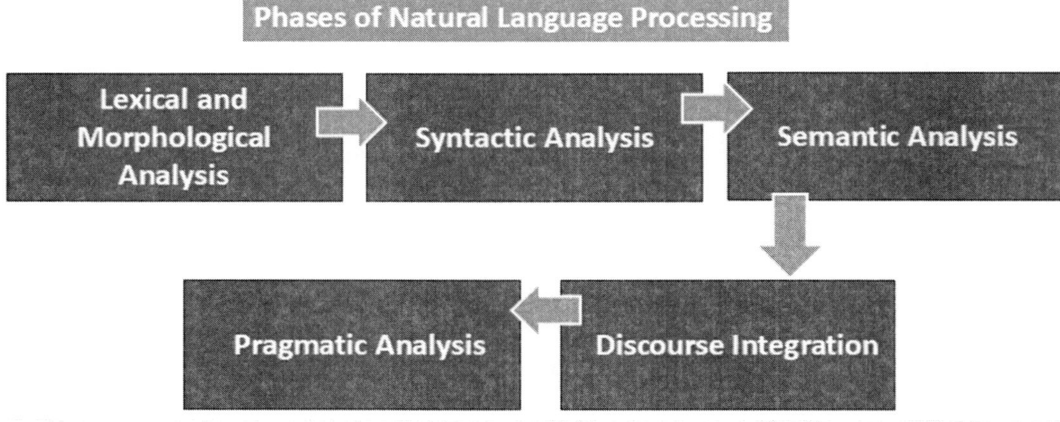

Illustration Phases_1: NLP

- **Lexical & Morphological Analysis**

Goal: Turn raw text into the basic linguistic units and simple normalized forms that the system can reason about.

- ## Lexical Analysis (surface-level)

What it does: identifies tokens (words/subwords), punctuation, and assigns basic grammatical roles.

Key tasks

Tokenization: Splits text into tokens.

Example:

Sentence: "He'll arrive at noon." → Tokens: ["He", "'ll", "arrive", "at", "noon", "."]

Note: handling contractions ('ll) or hyphenation matters for downstream models.

Part-of-speech (POS) tagging: Labels tokens with grammatical categories.

Example:

Sentence: "Light the lamp." → POS tags: Light (VB), the (DT), lamp (NN) — here light is a verb.

Why it matters: POS and tokens form the scaffolding used by parsers, NER systems, and feature extractors. Mistokenization cascades errors downstream.

- ## Morphological Analysis (word-internal structure)

What it does: analyzes word formation — stems, roots, affixes — and reduces inflected or derived forms to base forms.

Key tasks

Stemming: crude chopping to a root (e.g., playing → play or play depending on the stemmer).

Lemmatization: context-aware canonical form (e.g., better → good; was → be).

Example:

Word: "unbelievably" → Stem may be unbeliev; Lemma (after proper analysis) → believe with prefix un- noted.

Why it matters: Reduces vocabulary sparsity, helps retrieval and matching (searching for "run" should match "running"), and improves statistical estimates.

- **Syntactic Analysis (Parsing)**

Goal: Determine grammatical structure and relationships (subject, object, modifiers).

What it produces: parse trees (constituency), dependency graphs (who modifies whom), and grammatical relations.

Example:

Sentence: "The startup pivoted its strategy after feedback."

A dependency parse shows startup (nsubj) → pivoted (root) ← strategy (dobj) and after (prep) → feedback (pobj).

Why it matters:

- Helps answer *who did what to whom* — crucial for information extraction.
- Enables better machine translation by preserving grammatical roles across languages.
- Supports coreference resolution (knowing which noun phrase is the subject).

Challenges: ambiguous structures (e.g., "I saw the man with a telescope" — who holds the telescope?). Parsers use statistical/transformer models and often combine POS, morphology, and context.

- **Semantic Analysis**

Goal: Move from grammatical form to **meaning** — what the words and sentences *refer to* and *assert about the world.*

Key semantic tasks

Named Entity Recognition (NER): detect and classify entities.

Example:
Text: “Uber acquired Postmates in 2020.” → Uber (ORG), Postmates (ORG), 2020 (DATE).

Word Sense Disambiguation (WSD): choose the correct meaning for polysemous words.

Example:
Sentence A: “The battery on the phone died.” → battery = electronic power source.
Sentence B: “The soldier was accused of battery.” → battery = criminal offense.

Semantic Role Labeling (SRL): who performed what role (agent, patient, instrument).

Example:
“Maya baked a cake in an oven.” → agent=Maya, action=baked, patient=cake, instrument=oven.

Why it matters: Semantic understanding is essential for accurate question answering, reliable knowledge extraction, and preserving meaning across translation.

Techniques: from symbolic resources (WordNet) and knowledge graphs to contextual transformer embeddings (BERT-style) and semantic parsers.

- **Discourse Integration**

Goal: Understand how sentences connect to form coherent meaning across paragraphs or documents.

Key aspects

Anaphora / Coreference resolution: linking pronouns and noun phrases to their antecedents.

Example:
Text: "Amit bought a camera. He said it was excellent." → He → Amit, it → camera.

Discourse relations: cause, contrast, elaboration (connectives like *because*, *however*).

Example:

"She missed the bus. Therefore, she was late." → causal relation.

Topic tracking & entity salience: knowing which entities are central across sentences.

Why it matters:

- Enables summarization that preserves coherence.
- Powers chatbots that keep track of conversation context, e.g., remembering prior user preferences.
- Improves pronoun resolution, which is vital for reliable information extraction.

Example scenario:

Paragraph:

"Riya locked her bike outside the cafe. Later, she realized the lock was faulty.

"Discourse integration links her and the lock back to earlier mentions to understand the event chain.

- **Pragmatic Analysis**

Goal: Infer speaker/writer intent, implicature, tone, and context-dependent meaning beyond literal semantics.

Typical phenomena

Intent detection: questions vs. requests vs. commands vs. rhetorical questions. Example: "Can you close the window?" → literal question about ability vs. pragmatic interpretation = *request* to close the window.

Figurative language and idioms: metaphors, sarcasm, hyperbole. Example: "Oh great, another traffic jam — just what I needed." → likely sarcasm (negative sentiment despite a positive word, *great*).

Politeness, register, and social context: choosing responses that match social norms.

Why it matters: Conversational agents and sentiment systems must detect the correct intent or emotional connotation to respond appropriately and avoid misunderstandings.

Techniques: combine pragmatic features (speech acts, politeness markers), contextual models (dialog history), and often external knowledge (user profile, cultural norms).

Putting the phases together

Text:

"Dr. Patel published the paper. She later presented it at the Berlin summit, where attendees praised the methodology."

How phases operate:

1. **Lexical: tokenize, POS-tag words (Dr. (NNP) Patel (NNP) published (VBD) ...).**
2. **Morphological: lemmatize published → publish.**
3. **Syntactic: parse to identify Dr. Patel as the subject of the published.**
4. **Semantic: NER → Dr. Patel (PERSON), Berlin (LOC); SRL → agent=Dr. Patel, action=publish, theme=the paper.**
5. **Discourse: link She → Dr. Patel; track that the methodology refers to the contents of the paper.**
6. **Pragmatic: detect positive appraisal (praised) and likely intent: announce accomplishments to an audience.**

Master said, "Let us understand different phases using a simple program."

Example P3 – U3 – D9	
NLU-NLP - Phases	**Output**

# Required packages: 	
# pip install numpy==1.25.2 spacy nltk transformers 	
# python -m spacy download en_core_web_sm 	
# nltk.download('punkt') # Only once for sentence tokenizer 	
 	
import spacy
from nltk.tokenize import sent_tokenize
from transformers import pipeline
import nltk
 	
# Download punkt tokenizer (only needed first time) 	
# nltk.download('punkt') 	
 	
# Load spaCy English model 	
nlp = spacy.load("en_core_web_sm")
 	
# Input text 	
text = """Dr. Patel published the paper.
She later presented it at the Berlin summit,
where attendees praised the methodology."""
 	
print("Original Text:\n", text)
print("="*80)
 	
# --- 	
# 1. Lexical Analysis – Tokenization and POS Tagging 	
# --- 	
print("\n[Lexical Phase] Tokenization and Part-of-Speech Tagging\n")
doc = nlp(text)
for token in doc:
    print(f"{token.text:15} → {token.pos_}")
 	
# --- 	
# 2. Morphological Analysis – Lemmatization 	
# --- 	
print("\n[Morphological Phase] Lemmatization\n")
for token in doc:
    if token.lemma_ != token.text:
	Original Text:
	Dr. Patel published the paper.
	She later presented it at the Berlin summit, where attendees praised the methodology.
	
	[Lexical Phase] Tokenization and Part-of-Speech Tagging
	
	Dr. → PROPN
	Patel → PROPN
	published → VERB
	the → DET
	paper → NOUN
	. → PUNCT
	
	→ SPACE
	She → PRON
	later → ADV
	presented → VERB
	it → PRON
	at → ADP
	the → DET
	Berlin → PROPN
	summit → NOUN
	, → PUNCT
	where → SCONJ
	attendees → NOUN
	praised → VERB
	the → DET
	methodology → NOUN
	. → PUNCT
	
	[Morphological Phase] Lemmatization
	
	published → lemma: publish
	She → lemma: she
	presented → lemma: present
	attendees → lemma: attendee
	praised → lemma: praise
	
	[Syntactic Phase] Sentence Structure (Dependencies)
	
	Sentence: Dr. Patel published the paper.

print(f"{token.text:15} → lemma: {token.lemma_}")
 	
# -- 	
# 3. Syntactic Analysis – Dependency Parsing 	
# -- 	
print("\n[Syntactic Phase] Sentence Structure (Dependencies)\n")
for sent in doc.sents:
print(f"Sentence: {sent.text.strip()}")
for token in sent:
print(f"{token.text:12} → head: {token.head.text:12} | dep: {token.dep_}")
print("-"*60)
 	
# -- 	
# 4. Semantic Analysis – Named Entities 	
# -- 	
print("\n[Semantic Phase] Named Entity Recognition (NER)\n")
for ent in doc.ents:
print(f"{ent.text:20} → {ent.label_}")
 	
# -- 	
# 5. Discourse Integration – Co-reference & Context Tracking 	
# Note: spaCy default doesn't have coref, so we illustrate logically 	
# -- 	
print("\n[Discourse Phase] Linking References and Context\n")
print("→ 'She' refers to 'Dr. Patel'.")
print("→ 'it' refers to 'the paper'.")
print("→ 'the methodology' refers to content of 'the paper'.")
 	
# -- 	
# 6. Pragmatic Analysis – Sentiment / Intent Detection 	
# -- 	
print("\n[Pragmatic Phase] Sentiment and Intent Understanding\n")
sentiment_analyzer = pipeline("sentiment-analysis")
sentences = sent_tokenize(text)
for s in sentences:
result = sentiment_analyzer(s)[0]
print(f"Sentence: {s}")
	Dr. → head: Patel | dep: compound
	Patel → head: published | dep: nsubj
	published → head: published | dep: ROOT
	the → head: paper | dep: det
	paper → head: published | dep: dobj
	. → head: published | dep: punct
	
	→ head: . | dep: dep
	-------------------------- 	
	Sentence: She later presented it at the Berlin summit, where attendees praised the methodology.
	She → head: presented | dep: nsubj
	later → head: presented | dep: advmod
	presented → head: presented | dep: ROOT
	it → head: presented | dep: dobj
	at → head: presented | dep: prep
	the → head: summit | dep: det
	Berlin → head: summit | dep: compound
	summit → head: at | dep: pobj
	, → head: summit | dep: punct
	where → head: praised | dep: advmod
	attendees → head: praised | dep: nsubj
	praised → head: summit | dep: relcl
	the → head: methodology | dep: det
	methodology → head: praised | dep: dobj
	. → head: presented | dep: punct

```print(f"→ Sentiment: {result['label']} (score: {result['score']:.2f})\n")```
 	
```print("→ Intent detected: Positive appraisal through 'praised', suggesting recognition of accomplishment.")```
 	
```# --```
```# Final Summary```
```# --```
```print("="*80)```
```print("When we combine these phases, the machine not only reads the words,")```
```print("but begins to understand their meaning, context, and the intention behind them.")```
	-------------------------- 	
	
	[Semantic Phase] Named Entity Recognition (NER)
	
	Patel → PERSON
	Berlin → GPE
	[Discourse Phase] Linking References and Context
	
	→ 'She' refers to 'Dr. Patel'.
	→ 'it' refers to 'the paper'.
	→ 'the methodology' refers to content of 'the paper'.
	
	[Pragmatic Phase] Sentiment and Intent Understanding
	
	Sentence: Dr. Patel published the paper.
	→ Sentiment: POSITIVE (score: 0.99)
	
	Sentence: She later presented it at the Berlin summit, where attendees praised the methodology.
	→ Sentiment: POSITIVE (score: 1.00)
	
	→ Intent detected: Positive appraisal through 'praised', suggesting recognition of accomplishment.

Practical notes, pitfalls & best practices

- **Errors propagate.** Poor tokenization or POS tagging harms parsing and semantics. Use robust preprocessing.
- **Domain mismatch is real.** Models trained on news can fail on medical/legal/social-media text. Fine-tune on in-domain data.
- **Sense granularity.** Lexical resources sometimes split senses too finely — choose practical sense inventories or induce senses by clustering.

- **Multimodal & world knowledge.** Visual or factual context often resolves ambiguities (e.g., image + caption); incorporate external knowledge bases when needed.
- **Evaluation matters.** Evaluate both intrinsic tasks (accuracy on POS/NER/WSD) and downstream impact (does WSD improve QA?).

Real-world applications mapped to phases

- **Search engines:** lexical (tokenization) + semantic (query understanding) + discourse (session context).
- **Customer support chatbots:** pragmatic (intent), discourse (context over conversation), semantic (entity extraction).
- **Machine translation:** syntactic + semantic + discourse (to keep pronouns and cohesion across sentences).
- **Information extraction / knowledge graphs:** NER + SRL + coreference resolution + entity linking.

Master said, "Nikash, Each phase in NLP is a lens that reveals a different aspect of language — surface form, internal structure, grammar, meaning, continuity, and intention. Modern systems stitch these lenses together: classical linguistic analysis informs data preprocessing and constraints, while large contextual models (transformers) provide powerful, learned representations that blur classic phase boundaries by capturing many signals at once. For robust, interpretable, and domain-appropriate systems, combine careful linguistic preprocessing with powerful contextual models and explicit discourse/pragmatic reasoning when the application needs it."

Normalizing Textual Data in NLP — A Deep and Contextual Explanation

Before computers can understand language, **text must be cleaned, standardized, and transformed** into a format that computational models can work with. This entire process is called **Text Normalization**. It ensures that linguistic variations, spelling forms, punctuations, and redundant words do not distort the meaning conveyed by the text.

Normalization bridges the gap between how **humans use language** and how **machines interpret it**.

1. Regular Expressions (RegEx)

Regular Expressions are **patterns used to match and manipulate text**. They allow for identifying and transforming specific sequences, such as:

- Removing special characters (@, #, $, %)
- Detecting email and phone number formats
- Extracting dates, URLs, and hashtags

Example Use:

Replacing multiple spaces with a single space, removing punctuation, or extracting only alphabetic words.

```
import re
text = re.sub(r'[^a-zA-Z ]', '', text)
```

RegEx acts as the **foundational cleaning step** before any further NLP processing.

2. Tokenization

Tokenization is the process of **splitting text into meaningful units** called **tokens**. Tokens may be words, characters, or subwords.

Why Tokenization Matters

Computers cannot interpret raw text as is. Splitting text helps in:

- Counting word frequency
- Understanding grammar structure
- Feeding meaningful sequences to ML/NLP models

Types of Tokenization

Type	Description	Example
Whitespace Tokenization	Splits tokens based on spaces	"Hello world" → ["Hello", "world"]
Word Tokenization	Splits text into words using language rules	Handles punctuation and contractions
Rule-based Tokenization	Uses grammar rules to split text	Better for structured languages

Illustration Tok_1: NLP

Types of Tokenization

Type	Description	Example
Dictionary-Based Tokenization	Matches valid tokens from predefined vocabulary	Used in segmentation languages (Chinese, Japanese)
Subword Tokenization	Breaks words into smaller units to handle unknown words	"unhappiness" → ["un", "happy", "ness"]
WordPiece Tokenization	Used in **BERT**, breaks rare words while keeping meaning	"prediction" → ["predict", "##ion"]

Illustration Tok_2: NLP

Subword methods solve the **Out-of-Vocabulary (OOV)** problem and are dominant in modern transformer models.

3. Lemmatization

Lemmatization reduces words to their **base dictionary form (lemma)** based on **meaning and grammar**.

Word	POS	Lemma
running	verb	run
better	adjective	good
studies	noun	study

Illustration Lemm_1: NLP

4. Stemming

Stemming also reduces words to their root form—but **does not consider meaning**. It simply **cuts off suffixes** to approximate the root.

Types of Stemmers

- **Porter Stemmer** — Classical, widely used, efficient.
- **Lancaster Stemmer** — More aggressive; may over-strip words.
- **Snowball Stemmer** — Improved version of Porter.
- **Rule-based Stemming** — Uses pre-defined stripping rules.

Word	Stem
connection	connect
playing	play
organization	organ

Illustration Stem_1: NLP

Difference Between Lemmatization and Stemming

Feature	Lemmatization	Stemming
Considers Meaning	Yes	No
Output is valid word	Yes	Often no
Speed	Slower	Faster

Illustration Stem_2: NLP

5. Stopword Removal

Stopwords are **frequent words** that carry **little semantic meaning** (e.g., *the, is, a, of*).

Removing them helps models focus on **important words**.

However, some tasks (like **sentiment analysis**) may require keeping relevant stopwords like *"not"*.

6. Parts of Speech (POS) Tagging

POS Tagging assigns **grammatical roles** to each word in a sentence, such as:

POS	Meaning	Example
Noun (NN)	Person/Place/Thing	dog
Verb (VB)	Action	run
Adjective (JJ)	Describes noun	beautiful
Adverb (RB)	Describes verb	quickly

Illustration POS_1: NLP

Why POS Tagging Matters

- Helps in **syntactic parsing**
- Enables **lemmatization with correct meaning**
- Useful for **Named Entity Recognition**
- Important for **sentiment polarity detection**

Summary Flow of Text Normalization

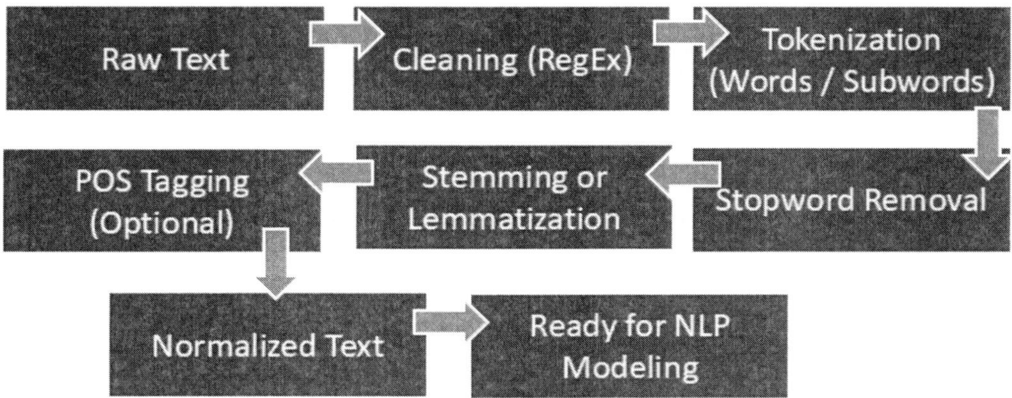

Illustration Norm_1: NLP

PART THREE

DAY Nine

Unit 3 - Lesson Four

Decoding Words

NLP Libraries in Python

Master said, "Apeksha, Natural Language Processing, or NLP, is the science of teaching machines to understand, interpret, and generate human language. It bridges the precision of computation with the subtlety of human expression. Through NLP, we extract knowledge, emotion, and intent from vast oceans of text—transforming unstructured data into structured insight."

Python, known for its simplicity and versatility, has become the **lingua franca of NLP**. It offers a wide range of specialized libraries that make it easier for researchers, developers, and analysts to perform complex linguistic tasks—from **tokenizing raw sentences to generating intelligent summaries**. These libraries are the tools through which machines begin to *listen* and *understand.*

Each library serves a unique purpose in this grand symphony of language understanding. Let us explore them deeply—how they function, what they offer, and how they connect abstract language with measurable meaning.

1. Regex (Regular Expressions)

Essence: The foundation of text manipulation.

Regex acts as the **microscope of text processing**, identifying patterns within vast data streams. It's the first step in transforming chaotic text into analyzable data.

Core Capabilities

- **Pattern Matching:** Removes noise, symbols, and inconsistencies in data.
- **Text Extraction:** Retrieves structured information such as dates, identifiers, or emails.

Real-World Use

- *Data Cleaning:* Extract and standardize contact details from raw datasets.
- *Information Retrieval:* Pull out SKUs, serial codes, or transaction IDs from reports for automation or analytics.

2. NLTK (Natural Language Toolkit)

Essence: The academic cornerstone of NLP.

NLTK is where many learners begin—it provides a rich foundation for understanding linguistic theory and practical text processing.

Core Capabilities

- **Tokenization:** Divides text into words and sentences.
- **Stemming & Lemmatization:** Reduces words to their core forms for consistent analysis.
- **POS Tagging:** Identifies grammatical roles of words.

Real-World Use

- *Customer Feedback Analysis:* Segment reviews for emotional and semantic study.
- *Text Classification:* Categorize news articles, blogs, or emails automatically.

3. spaCy

Essence: Industrial-grade efficiency.

spaCy combines speed and precision, making it ideal for production systems that require real-time linguistic intelligence.

Core Capabilities

- **Named Entity Recognition (NER):** Detects people, places, and organizations.
- **Dependency Parsing:** Reveals grammatical relationships within a sentence.

Real-World Use

- *Legal Document Analysis:* Extract company names, legal entities, or clauses.
- *Customer Service Automation:* Identify intent and entities from customer messages.

4. TextBlob

Essence: Simplicity meets intuition.

TextBlob is the **entry point for beginners** who want quick, intuitive NLP capabilities without complex setups.

Core Capabilities

- **Sentiment Analysis:** Determines whether a statement is positive, negative, or neutral.
- **Translation:** Converts text between languages using existing models.

Real-World Use

- *Brand Sentiment Monitoring:* Assess social media or product feedback.
- *Multilingual Support:* Translate customer messages to enhance communication.

5. Textacy

Essence: The deeper layer over spaCy.

Textacy extends spaCy to offer higher-level utilities for linguistic feature extraction, topic modeling, and advanced preprocessing.

Core Capabilities

- **Preprocessing:** Normalize and clean text data comprehensively.
- **Topic Modeling:** Detect dominant themes across large corpora.

Real-World Use

- *Market Research:* Discover customer interests and emerging trends.
- *Content Summarization:* Distill long reports into key ideas.

6. VADER (Valence Aware Dictionary and sEntiment Reasoner)

Essence: Emotion in context.

VADER is crafted for the modern internet age—it understands not just words, but **emotion through tone, emojis, and slang**.

Core Capabilities

- **Sentiment Analysis:** Quantifies emotional valence in short, informal text.
- **Emoji & Slang Handling:** Interprets emotional cues in social media content.

Real-World Use

- *Social Media Listening:* Gauge public sentiment around brands or events.
- *Customer Feedback Analysis:* Detect mood shifts in online reviews.

7. Gensim

Essence: Discovering meaning beneath words.

Gensim is the **philosopher's tool of NLP**—it finds hidden topics and relationships through unsupervised learning.

Core Capabilities

- **Topic Modeling (LDA, LSI):** Identify latent structures in massive text corpora.

- **Word Embeddings:** Represent meaning through vector spaces (Word2Vec, FastText).

Real-World Use

- *Content Recommendation:* Suggest articles or products with semantic similarity.
- *Document Clustering:* Group similar research papers or legal documents.

8. AllenNLP

Essence: Deep learning with clarity.

Built on PyTorch, AllenNLP offers **research-grade neural models** that make advanced NLP approachable.

Core Capabilities

- **Pre-trained Models:** For NER, classification, and sentiment.
- **Custom Architectures:** Enables model experimentation and training.

Real-World Use

- *AI Chatbots:* Build intelligent assistants that understand intent and emotion.
- *Automatic Summarization:* Generate precise abstracts from long texts.

9. Stanza

Essence: Stanford precision with PyTorch speed.

Stanza brings academic rigor into deep-learning NLP, providing multilingual capabilities with high linguistic accuracy.

Core Capabilities

- **Tokenization and POS Tagging:** Granular analysis across languages.
- **Dependency Parsing:** Uncovers structural patterns in sentences.

Real-World Use

- *Legal and Policy Analysis:* Extract structured insights from long case texts.
- *Syntax-Aware Models:* Enhance downstream ML models using grammatical structure.

10. Pattern

Essence: Lightweight and accessible.

Pattern blends NLP and web mining, making it perfect for small-scale experiments and teaching.

Core Capabilities

- **POS Tagging:** Categorizes grammatical elements.
- **Sentiment Analysis:** Identifies emotional polarity of text.

Real-World Use

- *Educational Projects:* Demonstrate NLP fundamentals simply.
- *Web Text Extraction:* Combine scraping and linguistic processing for analysis.

11. PyNLPl

Essence: The linguist's companion.

PyNLPl specializes in syntactic and morphological analysis, often used in linguistic research or multilingual environments.

Core Capabilities

- **Corpus Processing:** Efficiently handle large textual datasets.
- **Syntactic Parsing:** Analyze sentence grammar and word morphology.

Real-World Use

- *Multilingual Text Processing:* Handle datasets across languages.
- *Linguistic Research:* Study grammar evolution and cross-lingual semantics.

12. Hugging Face Transformers

Essence: The revolution of contextual intelligence.

The Hugging Face library embodies the **deep learning renaissance in NLP**, powered by transformer models like **BERT, RoBERTa, and GPT**.

Core Capabilities

- **Pre-trained Models:** Perform complex tasks instantly—classification, QA, translation, summarization.
- **Fine-Tuning:** Adapt large models for domain-specific data.

Real-World Use

- *AI Assistants:* Power advanced conversational systems.
- *Content Generation:* Create context-aware, human-like text dynamically.

13. Flair

Essence: Elegance through embeddings.

Flair integrates contextual embeddings (like BERT or ELMo) under a simple, unified interface—bridging classical NLP and deep learning.

Core Capabilities

- **NER:** Extract structured entities from text.
- **Text Classification:** Categorize documents with high precision.

Real-World Use

- *News Categorization:* Automatically sort global headlines.
- *Document Management:* Organize large textual repositories efficiently.

14. FastText

Essence: Speed with intelligence.

Developed by Facebook AI, FastText emphasizes **efficiency and scalability** in text classification and vector representation.

Core Capabilities

- **Text Classification:** Fast and effective categorization of text.
- **Word Embeddings:** Capture semantic relationships between words.

Real-World Use

- *Spam Detection:* Classify malicious or unwanted content.
- *Real-Time Feedback Analysis:* Monitor live sentiment in social media streams.

15. Polyglot

Essence: The voice of many languages.

Polyglot is built for global communication—it understands over **130 languages**, making it indispensable for cross-cultural NLP applications.

Core Capabilities

- **Language Detection:** Automatically identify the language of a text.
- **Multilingual Tokenization and Sentiment:** Process diverse linguistic data seamlessly.

Real-World Use

- *Global Customer Support:* Handle multilingual queries efficiently.
- *Cross-Language Sentiment Tracking:* Analyze international opinions on global events.

Master said, "Apeksha, every NLP library is like a tool in a scholar's chest—some refine the raw material, others reveal hidden meanings, and a few breathe intelligence into machines. Together, they form a continuum—transforming language from mere symbols into knowledge, empathy, and understanding."

Through these Python libraries, NLP transcends programming—it becomes a **path of perception**, where data is no longer inert but alive with meaning. From regex to transformers, each layer brings us closer to creating systems that don't just *read words* but *comprehend essence.*

Text representation and embedding techniques

Master said, "We have explored the various phases of NLP—from lexical and syntactic analysis to semantics and pragmatics. Now, let us understand one of the most foundational aspects: text representation and embedding techniques—the bridge between human language and machine understanding."

He continued, "Before a machine can analyze text, it must **convert words into numbers**—because mathematical models only understand numeric data. The process by which we represent text in a numerical form, suitable for computation, is what we call **text representation**. Embedding techniques are advanced methods of this representation—where context, semantics, and relationships between words are captured in numerical space."

Use Case - Classification

Master drew a simple example on the board:

S1: "The cat sits on the mat." → *1*

S2: "The dog sleeps under the tree." → *0*

He explained, "Imagine this as a **binary classification** problem—perhaps identifying whether a sentence describes *a domestic indoor scene (1)* or *an outdoor one (0)*. For our model to classify correctly, each sentence must be converted into a form it can understand—**vectors of numbers**."

Apeksha asked softly, "Master, what is a *document* and what is a *corpus*?"

Master smiled.

"A *document*, Apeksha, is a single piece of text—a sentence, paragraph, or article—anything that conveys a meaningful unit of language.

A *corpus* is a collection of such documents. Think of it as a library filled with books. Each book (document) carries meaning, but together, the library (corpus) gives us the linguistic richness of a language."

He added, "In NLP, we often train models not on a single document but on an entire corpus, so the model can learn the patterns, structures, and semantics that occur across many examples."

Sam leaned forward and asked, "Master, how do we convert these sentences into numbers from the corpus?"

"Good question, Sam," Master replied. "There are many techniques—each representing a deeper evolution in our understanding of language."

He began listing them on the board.

Text Representation in NLP

How Machines Understand Language

Human language is rich with meaning, emotion, and subtlety — but computers can only work with numbers.

Text representation is the process of **converting words, sentences, and documents into numerical vectors** so that machine learning and deep learning models can analyze, classify, search, and generate language effectively.

Different representation techniques capture meaning at different depths. Below, we explore them from **simplest to more meaningful**.

1. One-Hot Encoding

Every unique word in the vocabulary is assigned a **unique position** in a vector. For a given word, we set **1** at its index and **0** everywhere else.

Word	One-Hot Vector (Vocabulary: [I, love, music])
love	[0, 1, 0]

Illustration One_2: NLP

Strengths:

- Very simple
- Helps models learn the pure *identity* of words

Limitations:

- Vectors become huge for large vocabularies
- Words have **no relationship** to each other (e.g., *love* and *adore* look unrelated)

When to use:

- Teaching concepts, very small datasets, or categorical encoding tasks.

2. Bag of Words (BoW)

Represents each document by **how many times words occur**, ignoring word order.

Example:

Text: "The product is good and the service is good."

good = 2, product = 1, service = 1

Strengths:

- Simple and surprisingly effective for many tasks
- Works well with classification models (e.g., SVM, Logistic Regression)

Limitations:

- Loses meaning from word order
- Does not recognize synonyms
- High-dimensional and sparse

Best use:

- Baseline classification, spam detection, simple sentiment analysis.

3. TF–IDF (Term Frequency – Inverse Document Frequency)

TF-IDF improves BoW by **reducing the importance of common words** and **highlighting distinctive words**.

- **TF** measures how often a word appears in a document.
- **IDF** reduces the weight of words that are frequent across many documents.

So words like *"the", "is", "and"* are down-weighted.

Strengths:

- More meaningful than simple counts
- Works very well for document comparison and search

Limitations:

- Still ignores word order
- Cannot reflect deeper meaning

Best use:

- Search engines, recommendation systems, document classification.

4. Co-occurrence Matrix

A matrix capturing how often words **appear near each other**.

This models semantic relationships are determined using **context statistics**.

From this, advanced methods like **PMI** (Pointwise Mutual Information) are used to measure how strongly two words are associated.

Strengths:

- Captures meaningful relationships (e.g., "doctor" and "hospital")

- Used as the foundation for word embeddings

Limitations:

- Very large matrix for large vocabularies
- Sensitive to rare words
- Needs smoothing

Best use:

- Semantic association analysis
- Building global statistical word representations

1. N-Gram Language Modeling

Instead of treating words alone, N-grams capture **word sequences**.

Text	Example N-Grams (N=2)
"not good"	("not", "good")

Illustration One_2: NLP

This helps detect patterns like **negation**, which BoW alone cannot.

Strengths:

- Captures short-term word order
- Useful for phrase-level sentiment (e.g., "not happy")

Limitations:

- Larger N → exponential data sparsity
- Cannot capture meaning beyond a few words

Best use:

- Text classification + TF-IDF using bigrams/trigrams

5. Latent Semantic Analysis (LSA)

LSA reduces the TF-IDF matrix using **Singular Value Decomposition (SVD)** to uncover **hidden relationships** (latent topics).

It maps documents and words into a **lower-dimensional semantic space**.

Strengths:

- Reveals high-level themes
- Reduces noise and dimensionality

Limitations:

- Assumes linear structure (limited expressive power)
- Topics may not always be easily interpretable

Best use:

- Document clustering
- Similarity search
- Dimensionality reduction before ML models

6. Latent Dirichlet Allocation (LDA)

A **probabilistic topic model** that represents each document as a **mixture of topics**, where each topic is a **distribution of words**.

Example topics:

- Topic 1 → {love, joy, happiness}
- Topic 2 → {price, quality, service}

Strengths:

- Produces human-understandable topics
- Useful for summarizing large text collections

Limitations:

- Still bag-of-words based (no word order)
- Requires careful tuning (number of topics)

Best use:

- Topic discovery in books, articles, customer feedback, and research databases.

Transition to Meaningful Word Understanding

The above methods treat words as **isolated units**.

But real meaning depends on **context**:

The word **"bank"** in

"river bank" ≠ "financial bank"

This leads to **Word Embeddings** and **Contextual Embeddings** (like BERT).

Let's understand text representation more deeply

1. Bag of Words (BoW)

"In the simplest approach, we create a *vocabulary* from all the unique words in the corpus. Each document is then represented by a vector showing how many times each word appears."

Example:

Corpus = {"The cat sits on the mat.", "The dog sleeps under the tree."}

Vocabulary = [the, cat, sits, on, mat, dog, sleeps, under, tree]

Then,

S1 → [2, 1, 1, 1, 1, 0, 0, 0, 0]

S2 → [2, 0, 0, 0, 0, 1, 1, 1, 1]

"BoW is simple," said Master, "but it ignores grammar and word order. It treats *'cat sits mat'* the same as *'mat sits cat'*, though their meanings differ."

Master said, "When we represent language as numbers, we're not merely converting words—we're **capturing thought in mathematical form**.

Each embedding is a whisper of meaning, a point in multidimensional space where human emotion, logic, and syntax intersect."

He smiled, "The art of NLP lies in teaching machines not just to *read* words, but to *feel* their context.

And that begins with the way we represent them."

2. One-hot encoding

Master smiled and turned toward the board, saying, "Ah, Nikasha, an excellent question. Before we step into the realm of *word embeddings* and *contextual understanding*, it's important to know how this all began — with one of the simplest yet foundational text representation methods: One-Hot Encoding.

He continued, "One-hot encoding is like giving every unique word its own flag — a distinct identity — in the vocabulary.

If we have a total of N unique words, then each word is represented as a vector of length N, where all values are 0 except for one position — the one that belongs to that word — which is marked as 1."

He paused, "This is where it gets its name — *'one hot'*, because only one element is hot (1), and the rest are cold (0)."

Understanding the Concept

Master drew the example on the board:

Corpus:

[“I love NLP”, “NLP loves data”]

He said, “First, we build a vocabulary of unique words from the corpus.”

Vocabulary = [‘I’, ‘love’, ‘NLP’, ‘loves’, ‘data’]

Then, he constructed the table:

One Hot Encoding

Word	One-Hot Vector
I	[1, 0, 0, 0, 0]
love	[0, 1, 0, 0, 0]
NLP	[0, 0, 1, 0, 0]
loves	[0, 0, 0, 1, 0]
data	[0, 0, 0, 0, 1]

Illustration One_1: NLP

“Now,” he said, “each word is uniquely represented — the machine can distinguish them numerically. But, it cannot yet understand them. All words appear equally distant in this space — ‘love’ and ‘loves’ share no relation in their encoding. That, Nikasha, is the first limitation.”

Simple code Demonstration

Example P3 – U3 – D9	
NLP – One Hot Encoding	**Output**
from sklearn.preprocessing import OneHotEncoder	I → [1. 0. 0. 0. 0.] love → [0. 0. 0. 1. 0.]

Code	Output

import numpy as np
 	
# Sample corpus 	
corpus = np.array(["I", "love", "NLP", "loves", "data"]).reshape(-1, 1)
 	
# Initialize encoder 	
encoder = OneHotEncoder(sparse_output=False)
 	
# Fit and transform 	
onehot_vectors = encoder.fit_transform(corpus)
 	
for word, vector in zip(corpus.flatten(), onehot_vectors):
   print(f"{word:8} → {vector}")
	NLP → [0. 1. 0. 0. 0.]
	loves → [0. 0. 0. 0. 1.]
	data → [0. 0. 1. 0. 0.]

The Limitations

Master said, "Now that we can see how it works, let's understand *why* it eventually became inadequate for complex NLP tasks."

No Semantic Relationship

"One-hot encoding treats every word as completely independent.

The words *'king'* and *'queen'* are as unrelated as *'king'* and *'banana'* in this space.

The machine cannot infer meaning, analogy, or similarity."

High Dimensionality

"If your vocabulary has 10,000 unique words, every word vector is 10,000 elements long — mostly zeros.

For large corpora, this becomes computationally expensive and memory-inefficient."

Sparse Representation

"These vectors are mostly zeros — which means they carry little actual information. Sparse data is inefficient for models to process and learn from."

No Context Awareness

"One-hot vectors do not change with context.

The word *'bank'* has the same vector whether it means *'river bank'* or *'bank account'*.

Language, however, is alive with context — something one-hot encoding cannot feel."

Analogy

He drew two circles on the board and said, "Imagine every word living in its own isolated island, with no bridges to others.

One-hot encoding gives every word an identity but no relationships.

Later methods like **Word2Vec** built the bridges, allowing the islands to form a connected continent of meaning."

Master said, "One-hot encoding was the first step — simple, discrete, and symbolic. It taught machines to *recognize* words. But the deeper journey of NLP began when we taught them to *understand* relationships, emotions, and context."

He smiled at Nikasha and said, "Remember, every great system begins with something simple. One-hot encoding may be primitive, but it opened the doorway to the entire world of **word embeddings**, **transformers**, and **language models** we explore today."

John inquired, "What exactly is the Bag of Words (BoW) model, and how is it used in text analysis?"

Master said, "John, Bag of Words is a simple, powerful representation: it treats each document as a 'bag' where only word identity and frequency matter — order and grammar are ignored. It converts text to numeric vectors that machine learning models can use. The simplicity is its strength and its weakness."

Intuition: what BoW actually does

- Build a **vocabulary** of unique tokens from the corpus.
- Represent each document as a vector of length |V| (vocab size).

- Each vector element = count (or presence) of the corresponding token in that document.
- Result: a document-term matrix (D × V) where 'D' is the number of documents.

BoW is interpretable and fast, but it is **orderless**, **sparse**, and **ignores semantics and context**.

Step 1 — Preprocessing the text

Before counting words, we usually:

1. Lowercase text.
2. Remove punctuation.
3. Tokenize into words.
4. Optionally remove stopwords (common words like "and", "the").
5. Optionally perform stemming or lemmatization.

Preprocessing reduces noise and vocabulary size and improves model quality.

Step 2 — Counting word frequencies

After preprocessing, we count how often each word appears in every document. Summing across documents gives corpus-level frequency.

Step 3 — Selecting the most frequent words

Often you limit the vocabulary to the 'k' most frequent words (top-k) to:

- Reduce dimensionality
- Remove rare noise words
- Improve generalization

This is equivalent to keeping the top-k columns of the document-term matrix.

Step 4 — Building the BoW model

Two common variants:

- **Count vectors**: raw counts of tokens.
- **Binary vectors**: 1 if token present else 0.
- **TF-IDF** (related): weights tokens by importance across documents (not pure BoW but an improvement).

Step 5 — Visualizing with a word cloud

A word cloud displays tokens sized by frequency — a quick qualitative view of corpus topics.

Example corpus

We'll use a short, different example (food + travel) so you have variety:

Documents:

"I love fresh pasta and homemade salad."

"She enjoys cooking pasta in the evening."

"They traveled to Italy and savored pasta."

"He prepares salad with fresh herbs."

We will:

- Preprocess
- Build BoW
- Select the top 6 words
- Visualize with wordcloud

Example P3 – U3 – D11
NLU-NLP - BoW

```
# bag_of_words_example.py
import re
```

```
from collections import Counter
import numpy as np

# For sklearn approach and visualization
from sklearn.feature_extraction.text import CountVectorizer
from wordcloud import WordCloud
import matplotlib.pyplot as plt
import nltk
from nltk.corpus import stopwords
from nltk.stem import WordNetLemmatizer

# ----------------------
# Sample corpus
docs = [
    "I love fresh pasta and homemade salad.",
    "She enjoys cooking pasta in the evening.",
    "They traveled to Italy and savored pasta.",
    "He prepares salad with fresh herbs."
]

# ----------------------
# 1) Preprocessing function
nltk.download('stopwords', quiet=True)
nltk.download('punkt', quiet=True)
nltk.download('wordnet', quiet=True)

stop_words = set(stopwords.words('english'))
lemmatizer = WordNetLemmatizer()

def preprocess(text, remove_stopwords=True, do_lemmatize=True):
    # Lowercase
    text = text.lower()
    # Remove punctuation (keep apostrophes if you want)
    text = re.sub(r'[^a-z0-9\s]', '', text)
    # Tokenize (simple split or nltk.word_tokenize)
    tokens = nltk.word_tokenize(text)
    # Remove stopwords
    if remove_stopwords:
        tokens = [t for t in tokens if t not in stop_words]
    # Lemmatize
    if do_lemmatize:
        tokens = [lemmatizer.lemmatize(t) for t in tokens]
    return tokens

preprocessed_docs = [" ".join(preprocess(d)) for d in docs]
print("Preprocessed docs:")
for i, pd in enumerate(preprocessed_docs, 1):
    print(i, pd)
```

```
print()

# ----------------------
# 2) Manual vocabulary + counting
# Build vocabulary
all_tokens = []
for tokens in [preprocess(d) for d in docs]:
    all_tokens.extend(tokens)
vocab = sorted(set(all_tokens))
print("Vocabulary:", vocab)
print()

# Build document-term matrix (counts)
dt_matrix = []
for tokens in [preprocess(d) for d in docs]:
    c = Counter(tokens)
    row = [c.get(term, 0) for term in vocab]
    dt_matrix.append(row)

dt_matrix = np.array(dt_matrix)
print("Document-Term Matrix (rows = docs, cols = vocab):")
print(dt_matrix)
print()

# Show per-document vectors with vocabulary alignment
for i, row in enumerate(dt_matrix, 1):
    print(f"Doc{i} vector:", dict(zip(vocab, row)))
print()

# ----------------------
# 3) Select the top-k most frequent words across the corpus
corpus_counts = Counter(all_tokens)
top_k = 6
most_common = corpus_counts.most_common(top_k)
print(f"Top {top_k} tokens (token, count):", most_common)
print()

top_terms = [tok for tok, _ in most_common]

# Build reduced BoW matrix using top terms
reduced_matrix = np.array([[Counter(preprocess(d)).get(t,0) for t in top_terms] for d in
docs])
print("Reduced BoW (top terms):")
print("Top terms:", top_terms)
print(reduced_matrix)
print()

# ----------------------
```

```
# 4) Using sklearn CountVectorizer (concise)
vectorizer = CountVectorizer(stop_words='english')  # will lowercase, tokenize, remove
stopwords
X = vectorizer.fit_transform(docs)  # shape (n_docs, n_features)
vocab_sklearn = vectorizer.get_feature_names_out()
print("sklearn vocab:", vocab_sklearn)
print("sklearn document-term matrix:\n", X.toarray())
print()

# ----------------------
# 5) Visualize word frequencies using WordCloud
# Use corpus_counts for frequencies
wc = WordCloud(width=800, height=400, background_color='white')
wc.generate_from_frequencies(corpus_counts)

plt.figure(figsize=(10, 5))
plt.imshow(wc, interpolation='bilinear')
plt.axis('off')
plt.title("Word Cloud (by corpus frequency)")
plt.show()
```

```
Output:
Preprocessed docs:
1 love fresh pasta homemade salad
2 enjoys cooking pasta evening
3 traveled italy savored pasta
4 prepares salad fresh herb

Vocabulary: ['cooking', 'enjoys', 'evening', 'fresh', 'herb', 'homemade', 'italy', 'love', 'pasta',
'prepares', 'salad', 'savored', 'traveled']

Document-Term Matrix (rows = docs, cols = vocab):
[[0 0 0 1 0 1 0 1 1 0 1 0 0]
 [1 1 1 0 0 0 0 0 1 0 0 0 0]
 [0 0 0 0 0 0 1 0 1 0 0 1 1]
 [0 0 0 1 1 0 0 0 0 1 1 0 0]]

Doc1 vector: {'cooking': 0, 'enjoys': 0, 'evening': 0, 'fresh': 1, 'herb': 0, 'homemade': 1, 'italy':
0, 'love': 1, 'pasta': 1, 'prepares': 0, 'salad': 1, 'savored': 0, 'traveled': 0}
Doc2 vector: {'cooking': 1, 'enjoys': 1, 'evening': 1, 'fresh': 0, 'herb': 0, 'homemade': 0, 'italy':
0, 'love': 0, 'pasta': 1, 'prepares': 0, 'salad': 0, 'savored': 0, 'traveled': 0}
Doc3 vector: {'cooking': 0, 'enjoys': 0, 'evening': 0, 'fresh': 0, 'herb': 0, 'homemade': 0, 'italy':
1, 'love': 0, 'pasta': 1, 'prepares': 0, 'salad': 0, 'savored': 1, 'traveled': 1}
Doc4 vector: {'cooking': 0, 'enjoys': 0, 'evening': 0, 'fresh': 1, 'herb': 1, 'homemade': 0, 'italy':
0, 'love': 0, 'pasta': 0, 'prepares': 1, 'salad': 1, 'savored': 0, 'traveled': 0}
```

```
Top 6 tokens (token, count): [('pasta', 3), ('fresh', 2), ('salad', 2), ('love', 1), ('homemade', 1), ('enjoys', 1)]

Reduced BoW (top terms):
Top terms: ['pasta', 'fresh', 'salad', 'love', 'homemade', 'enjoys']
[[1 1 1 1 1 0]
 [1 0 0 0 0 1]
 [1 0 0 0 0 0]
 [0 1 1 0 0 0]]

sklearn vocab: ['cooking' 'enjoys' 'evening' 'fresh' 'herbs' 'homemade' 'italy' 'love'
 'pasta' 'prepares' 'salad' 'savored' 'traveled']
sklearn document-term matrix:
 [[0 0 0 1 0 1 0 1 1 0 1 0 0]
 [1 1 1 0 0 0 0 0 1 0 0 0 0]
 [0 0 0 0 0 0 1 0 1 0 0 1 1]
 [0 0 0 1 1 0 0 0 0 1 1 0 0]]
```

Let us understand this code.

- **Preprocessed docs** will be lowercase, punctuation removed, stopwords removed (so words like *and, the, in* gone), and lemmatized (cooking → cook).
- Vocabulary: e.g. [‘fresh’,’pasta’,’homemade’,’salad’,’enjoys’,’cooking’,’evening’,’traveled’,’italy’,’savored’,’prepares’,’herb’] (actual words depend on lemmatizer and stopword list).
- **Document-Term Matrix**: each row is counts for a document over the vocabulary.
- **Top-k tokens**: shows the most frequent words across the corpus (likely ‘pasta’, ‘salad’, ‘fresh’, etc.).
- **sklearn CountVectorizer**: quick, robust BoW builder. Its X.toarray() is the same document-term matrix, but with built-in preprocessing options.
- **WordCloud**: visualizes tokens sized by frequency.

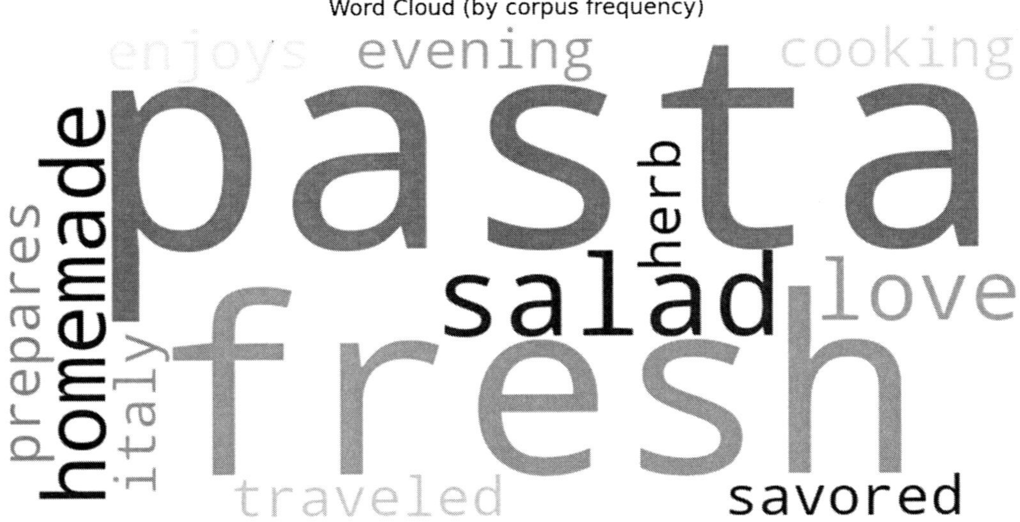

Illustration wordcloud_1: BoW

Deeper insights and cautions

1. **When BoW works well**
    - Short pipelines, interpretable models (logistic regression, Naive Bayes).
    - When word order is less important and bag-level semantics suffice.
    - Low to medium-sized corpora.
2. **Limitations to remember**
    - **Ignores word order** — "not good" ≠ "good not".
    - **Sparse & high-dimensional** — memory and compute heavy for large vocabularies.
    - **No semantics** — "pasta" and "noodle" treated as unrelated unless normalized.
    - **Context ignorance** — polysemy is not handled.
3. **Improvements built on BoW**

- **TF-IDF** to down-weight common terms.
- **N-grams** to capture some local order (bigrams/trigrams).
- **Word embeddings** (Word2Vec/GloVe/BERT) for semantic capture.
- **Dimensionality reduction** (SVD / PCA / LSA) to compress and reveal latent structure.

From BoW to classification

To use BoW in classification:

1. Create document-term matrix (Counts or TF-IDF).
2. Train a classifier (Naive Bayes, Logistic Regression, SVM).
3. Evaluate (accuracy, precision, recall).

Example: clf.fit(X_train, y_train) where X_train is BoW vectors.

"John," Master said, "BoW is the first instrument a student learns: simple, transparent, and reliable. It converts stories into counts — and from those counts, we often extract truth. Yet the world of language is rich and contextual; BoW is a lamp that illuminates part of the room. For deeper understanding, we add embeddings, context, and structure."

Frequency-based Technique

3. Term Frequency — Inverse Document Frequency

Akshaya asked, "Master, what is TF–IDF ?"

Mastre said, "TF–IDF is a weighting scheme that transforms a document into a vector of numbers that reflect how important each word is in that document **relative to the whole corpus**."

- **Term Frequency (TF)** measures how frequently a term occurs in a document.

- **Inverse Document Frequency (IDF)** downweights terms that occur in many documents (common words) and upweights terms that are rare across documents (more informative words).
- Multiplying TF by IDF gives TF–IDF: a higher value means the term is important for that document and rare in the corpus.

Formulas

Term Frequency (raw count or normalized):

- raw count: tf(t,d) = count of term t in document d
- normalized: tf(t,d)= $\frac{Count(t,d)}{(total\ terms\ in\ d)}$

Inverse Document Frequency (two common definitions):

Basic (natural log):

$$\mathrm{idf}(t,D) = \log\frac{N}{df(t)}$$

Where N = total number of documents, and df(t) = number of documents containing term t.

Sklearn's smoothed version (default):

$$\mathrm{idf}_{sk}(t,D) = \log\frac{(1+N)}{(1+df(t))} + 1$$

This avoids division by zero and stabilizes rare terms.

TF–IDF (per term):

tfidf(t,d,D) = tf(t,d) x idf(t,D)

Normalization (L2) is usually applied to the final TF–IDF vector so that documents are comparable in length.

Intuition

- Words that occur often in a document but rarely across the corpus are *likely* important (high TF, high IDF → high TF–IDF).
- Very common words like “the” or “is” have low IDF → even if frequent in a doc, they get low TF–IDF and are de-emphasized.

Example (step-by-step, numeric)

We use a tiny corpus of **three documents** to show calculations concretely:

Documents (preprocessed to lowercase, split tokens):

Doc1: “machine learning is fun” → tokens: ["machine","learning","is","fun"]

Doc2: “deep learning advances ai” → tokens: ["deep", "learning", "advances","ai"]

Doc3: “machine learning and ai” → tokens: ["machine", "learning","and","ai"]

Vocabulary (terms encountered):[machine, learning, is, fun, deep, advances, ai, and]

Total documents N=3

1) Document Frequency (df) for each term

machine → appears in Doc1 & Doc3 → df = 2

learning → appears in Doc1, Doc2, Doc3 → df = 3

is → Doc1 only → df = 1

fun → Doc1 only → df = 1

deep → Doc2 only → df = 1

advances → Doc2 only → df = 1

ai → Doc2 & Doc3 → df = 2

and → Doc3 only → df = 1

2) IDF

Natural log log(N/df)

We compute idf(t) = $\log \frac{3}{df(t)}$

Numeric results (rounded to 4 decimals):

- machine: df=2 → idf = log(3/2) = 0.4055
- learning: df=3 → idf = log (3/3) = 0.0000
- is: df=1 → idf = log (3/1) = 1.0986
- fun: df=1 → idf = 1.0986
- deep: df=1 → idf = 1.0986
- advances: df=1 → idf = 1.0986
- ai: df=2 → idf = 0.4055
- and: df=1 → idf = 1.0986

(These come from natural logarithm values; learning has idf 0 because it appears in every document.)

3) TF

we'll use normalized term frequency = count / total terms in that doc

Each document above has 4 tokens → each present term has TF = 1/4 = 0.25; absent terms have TF = 0.

4) TF-IDF

TF-IDF = TF × IDF

Multiply TF (0.25) by each term's idf.

Below is the TF–IDF table (rounded to 4 decimals):

term	df	idf	tf-idf Doc1	tf-idf Doc2	tf-idf Doc3
machine	2	0.4055	0.1014	0.0000	0.1014
learning	3	0.0000	0.0000	0.0000	0.0000
is	1	1.0986	0.2747	0.0000	0.0000
fun	1	1.0986	0.2747	0.0000	0.0000
deep	1	1.0986	0.0000	0.2747	0.0000
advances	1	1.0986	0.0000	0.2747	0.0000
ai	2	0.4055	0.0000	0.1014	0.1014
and	1	1.0986	0.0000	0.0000	0.2747

Illustration tf-idf_1: NLP

Interpretation:

- In Doc1, 'is' and 'fun' are most distinctive (highest TF–IDF) because they are frequent in Doc1 but rare across the corpus.
- 'learning' gets TF–IDF zero because it appears in all documents (idf 0) — it carries little discriminative power in this small corpus.
- 'ai' and 'machine' have moderate importance where they appear.

Below are two snippets:

Manual calculation and using scikit-learn's TfidfVectorizer (recommended for real work).

Manual TF–IDF calculation

Example P3 – U3 – D12

NLP – TF-IDF

```
import math
from collections import Counter

docs = [
   "machine learning is fun",
   "deep learning advances ai",
   "machine learning and ai"
]

# Preprocess (simple lowercase + split in this demo)
```

Output

```
Doc1 TF-IDF:
  advances  -> 0.0000
  ai        -> 0.0000
  and       -> 0.0000
  deep      -> 0.0000
  fun       -> 0.2747
  is        -> 0.2747
  learning  -> 0.0000
  machine   -> 0.1014

Doc2 TF-IDF:
```

```
tokenized = [d.lower().split() for d in docs]
N = len(tokenized)

# Build vocabulary and document frequencies
vocab = sorted({w for doc in tokenized for w in
doc})
df = {w: sum(1 for doc in tokenized if w in doc) for
w in vocab}

# IDF (natural log)
idf = {w: math.log(N / df[w]) for w in vocab}

# Compute TF-IDF (normalized TF =
count/len(doc))
tfidf_docs = []
for doc in tokenized:
    counts = Counter(doc)
    L = len(doc)
    tfidf = {w: (counts[w] / L) * idf[w] for w in
vocab}  # 0 if not present
    tfidf_docs.append(tfidf)

# Display matrix
for i, tfidf in enumerate(tfidf_docs, 1):
    print(f"Doc{i} TF-IDF:")
    for w in vocab:
        print(f"  {w:9} -> {tfidf[w]:.4f}")
    print()
```

```
  advances  -> 0.2747
  ai        -> 0.1014
  and       -> 0.0000
  deep      -> 0.2747
  fun       -> 0.0000
  is        -> 0.0000
  learning  -> 0.0000
  machine   -> 0.0000

Doc3 TF-IDF:
  advances  -> 0.0000
  ai        -> 0.1014
  and       -> 0.2747
  deep      -> 0.0000
  fun       -> 0.0000
  is        -> 0.0000
  learning  -> 0.0000
  machine   -> 0.1014
```

Using scikit-learn TfidfVectorizer

Example P3 – U3 – D13	
NLP – TF-IDF	**Output**

```
from sklearn.feature_extraction.text import
TfidfVectorizer

docs = [
    "Machine learning is fun.",
    "deep learning advances ai",
    "machine learning and ai"
]

# Example: default settings:
# - lowercase=True
# - use_idf=True
```

```
Vocabulary: ['advances' 'ai' 'and'
'deep' 'fun' 'is' 'learning'
'machine']

TF-IDF matrix:
 [[0.         0.         0.         0.
0.5844829  0.5844829
  0.34520502 0.44451431]
 [0.5844829  0.44451431 0.
0.5844829  0.         0.
  0.34520502 0.         ]
```

# - smooth_idf=True (sklearn's default) # - norm='l2' (vector normalized) vectorizer = TfidfVectorizer() X = vectorizer.fit_transform(docs) # sparse matrix shape (3, n_features) vocab = vectorizer.get_feature_names_out() print("Vocabulary:", vocab) print("TF-IDF matrix:\n", X.toarray()) # each row is the TF-IDF vector (after normalization)	[0. 0.4804584 0.63174505 0. 0. 0. 0.37311881 0.4804584]]

Notes about scikit-learn defaults:

idf used by sklearn is: idf = log((1 + N) / (1 + df)) + 1 (smoothed + shifted) — so values differ slightly from the raw formula above.

Output X is L2-normalized by default (so vector length = 1). If you want raw unnormalized TF–IDF, set norm=None.

Practical tips, variants, and caveats

Variants/knobs to tune

- sublinear_tf=True in TfidfVectorizer: use 1+log(tf) instead of raw tf — helpful to reduce the effect of very frequent terms.
- use_idf=True/False: you can disable IDF to use only TF.
- smooth_idf=True: avoids zero division and rare-term extremes.
- Norm = 'l2' vs norm = 'l1' or None: choose normalization depending on downstream model.
- ngram_range = (1,2): include bigrams/trigrams to capture local word order (helps for phrases).

Preprocessing advice

- Lowercasing, punctuation removal, stopword removal, lemmatization/stemming — all affect vocabulary and TF–IDF weights.

- For domain-specific corpora, maintain domain stopwords (e.g., "patient" in medical corpus may be ubiquitous and should be downweighted).

Strengths of TF–IDF

- Simple, fast, interpretable.
- Often very effective with linear classifiers (Logistic Regression, SVM, Naive Bayes).
- Works well for information retrieval and keyword extraction.

Limitations

- Ignores semantics — synonyms are distinct (car vs automobile).
- No context — polysemy unresolved ('bank' in financial vs river contexts).
- Corpus-dependent: adding new documents changes IDF (weights shift).
- Sparse and high-dimensional for large vocabularies — use dimensionality reduction (SVD/LSA) or embeddings when needed.

When to use TF–IDF vs embeddings

- Use **TF–IDF** for interpretable keyword-driven tasks, search engines, fast baseline classification, or when data is limited.
- Use **word / contextual embeddings** (Word2Vec, GloVe, BERT) when semantic similarity or context matters (paraphrase detection, semantic search, transfer learning).

Master said, "TF–IDF is a compass: it points to what is unique in a document relative to the whole corpus. It's not the final map — but it is often the most reliable compass for initial exploration. Use it early, interpret it with care, and know when to trade sparsity and interpretability for dense semantic vectors."

4. N-Gram Language Modeling

Apeksha asked, "Master, what is *N-gram Language Modelling*?"

Master smiled and said, “Language modeling is about estimating how likely a particular sequence of words is to appear in a language. It’s the mathematical art of predicting the next word — or evaluating how natural a sentence sounds — based on learned probabilities.”

He continued, “It is the foundation of many NLP applications — from *speech recognition*, where systems guess the next word from sound inputs; to *machine translation*, where models choose the most fluent phrase; and even *spam filtering*, where models identify unnatural or suspicious text patterns.”

What is an N-gram?

An **N-gram** is simply a *sequence of N words* occurring together in a text.

N	Example from sentence "I love playing cricket"
1-gram (Unigram)	[“I”, “love”, “playing”, “cricket”]
2-gram (Bigram)	[“I love”, “love playing”, “playing cricket”]
3-gram (Trigram)	[“I love playing”, “love playing cricket”]
4-gram	[“I love playing cricket”]

Illustration Ngram_1: NLP

N-grams capture **local context** — the likelihood of words occurring together — which is crucial in predicting the next word in a sequence.

N-gram Language Model

An **N-gram Language Model** estimates the probability of a word sequence $w_1, w_2, w_3, \ldots, w_T$ as:

$P(w_1, w_2, w_3, \ldots, w_T)$

However, computing this directly is impossible for large vocabularies — there are infinitely many word combinations. So we simplify using the **Chain Rule of Probability** and **Markov Assumption**.

Chain Rule of Probability

The **Chain Rule** allows us to express the joint probability of a sequence as a product of conditional probabilities:

$P(w_1,w_2,w_3,\ldots,w_T) = P(w_1) \times P(w_2|w_1) \times P(w_3|w_1,w_2) \times \ldots \times P(w_T|w_1,\ldots,w_{T-1})$

This means:

The probability of a sentence is the product of the probability of each word given all the previous words.

Example:

For the sentence **"I love playing cricket"**,

$P(I,love,playing,cricket) = P(I) \times P(love|I) \times P(playing|I,love) \times P(cricket|I,love,playing)$

But this still requires knowledge of probabilities for every possible sequence — computationally impossible for real language.

Markov Assumption — The Simplification

The **Markov Assumption** says:

The probability of a word depends only on a fixed number of previous words (N-1), not the entire history.

Thus, for a trigram model (N=3):

$P(w_T|w_1,\ldots,w_{T-1}) \approx P(w_T \mid w_{T-2},w_{T-1})$

Hence,

$P(w1,w2,\ldots,wT) \approx \prod_{i=1}^{T} P(w_i \mid w_{i-(N-1)}, \ldots, w_{i-1})$

This assumption reduces complexity dramatically — and that's what creates an **N-gram model**.

Example: Building a Bigram Model (N=2)

Let's say our small corpus is:

"I love NLP. I love deep learning."

We first tokenize:

[I, love, NLP, I, love, deep, learning]

Now count bigrams:

Bigram	Count
(I, love)	2
(love, NLP)	1
(love, deep)	1
(NLP, I)	0
(deep, learning)	1

Illustration Ngram_2: NLP

Bigram Probability:

$P(w_i|w_{i-1}) = Count(w_{i-1},w_i)/Count(w_{i-1})$

For example:

P(love|I) = 2/2 = 1.0, P(NLP|love) = 1/2 = 0.5, P(deep|love) = 1/2 = 0.5

So,

P("IloveNLP") = P(I)×P(love|I)×P(NLP|love)

This allows the model to **assign probabilities to sentences** and even **generate new ones** by sampling words sequentially.

Evaluating Language Models

We need to measure how good our model is at predicting language. Common metrics include:

a) Entropy

Measures the average uncertainty of predicting a word:

$$H(P) = -\sum_w P(w) Log_2 P(w)$$

Lower entropy → more confident model.

b) Cross-Entropy

Measures how well one probability distribution (our model) predicts another (the true language distribution):

$$H(P, Q) = -\sum_w P(w) Log_2 Q(w)$$

Lower is better — means the model's predictions are closer to reality.

c) Perplexity

A common metric for evaluating language models, derived from entropy:

$$Perplexity(Q) = 2^{H(P,Q)} = \frac{1}{\sqrt[T]{P(w_1, w_2, \ldots w_T)}}$$

Intuitively, **perplexity** measures how "confused" the model is — lower perplexity means better predictive power.

Implementing N-gram Language Modelling in Python

Let's see a simple **Bigram** model built step-by-step.

Example P3 – U3 – D14

NLP - Ngram

```
from collections import defaultdict
import nltk
from nltk import bigrams
from nltk.util import ngrams
from nltk.tokenize import word_tokenize
nltk.download('punkt')

# Sample corpus
corpus = "I love NLP. I love deep learning. NLP is fun."
tokens = word_tokenize(corpus.lower())

# Create bigrams
bigrams_list = list(bigrams(tokens, pad_left=True, pad_right=True))

# Count bigram and unigram frequencies
bigram_freq = defaultdict(int)
unigram_freq = defaultdict(int)

for w1, w2 in bigrams_list:
    bigram_freq[(w1, w2)] += 1
    unigram_freq[w1] += 1

# Compute bigram probabilities
bigram_prob = {}
for (w1, w2), count in bigram_freq.items():
    bigram_prob[(w1, w2)] = count / unigram_freq[w1]

# Display a few probabilities
for pair, prob in list(bigram_prob.items())[:5]:
    print(f"P({pair[1]} | {pair[0]}) = {prob:.3f}")
```

You can extend this easily to trigrams or higher-order models using nltk.util.ngrams(tokens, N).

```
Output:
P(i | None) = 1.000
P(love | i) = 1.000
P(nlp | love) = 0.500
P(. | nlp) = 0.500
P(i | .) = 0.333
```

Advantages of N-gram Models

Simple and intuitive: Easy to build and interpret.

Effective for smaller datasets: Works well for tasks like autocomplete, spelling correction, and simple text generation.

Good baseline: Before using neural networks, N-grams are a strong probabilistic starting point.

Fast to train and test: Especially with smoothing and pruning.

Limitations

Data sparsity: As N increases, many N-grams are unseen in training (zero probability problem).

No long-term context: A trigram model can't understand dependencies beyond 2 previous words.

Vocabulary explosion: Large corpora create millions of N-grams, making computation expensive.
Poor generalization: "dogs bark loudly" and "cats meow softly" share structure but are treated as unrelated.

Smoothing required: Unseen combinations require techniques like **Laplace smoothing**, **Kneser-Ney**, or **Good-Turing** estimation.

Master said, "An N-gram model is like listening to language through a keyhole — you can only hear a few words at a time. It captures local rhythm and structure, but not the full meaning behind the melody."

Yet, it taught us to measure and predict language — paving the path toward modern models like RNNs, LSTMs, and Transformers, which remember and reason across the entire symphony of words."

PART THREE

DAY Ten

Unit 3 - Lesson Five

Understanding Word Embeddings

Text Embedding Techniques

Master said, *"Text embedding is the art of transforming language into meaning-rich numerical form—where words are not just symbols, but living patterns of relationships."*

Text Embedding Techniques refer to **methods that convert words, phrases, or documents into dense numerical vectors** that capture **semantic meaning**—that is, the *context*, *relationships*, and *intended sense* behind words.

Unlike traditional sparse representations like **One-Hot Encoding** or **Bag-of-Words**, which merely count words without understanding meaning, **embeddings understand how words relate**.

Words become **vectors in a multi-dimensional space**, where **distance reflects similarity**:

- Words with similar meanings are placed **closer together**

  e.g., *"king"* is near *"queen"*

- Words with opposite meaning are placed **far apart**

  e.g., *"happy"* vs *"sad"*

- Words form meaningful **relations**

  e.g., **king – man + woman ≈ queen**

This is the foundation of **modern NLP understanding**.

Word Embeddings

Word embeddings create **dense vector representations** where each word is represented by a learned coordinate in a vector space. These coordinates reflect patterns learned from large text corpora.

1. Word2Vec

Developed by Google, **Word2Vec** learns word relationships based on how words appear in context.

It has two training architectures:

Model	Logic	Purpose
CBOW (Continuous Bag of Words)	Predict the **target word** from surrounding words	Good for **frequent words,** faster
Skip-Gram	Predict **context words** from the target word	Better for **rare words,** captures subtle semantics

Illustration Ngram_3: NLP

Example:

In the sentence:

"The cat sat on the mat."

CBOW learns from: (the, cat, on, the, mat) → sat

Skip-Gram learns: sat → (the, cat, on, the, mat)

2. GloVe (Global Vectors for Word Representation)

Developed by Stanford, **GloVe** focuses on **global word co-occurrence statistics**.

While Word2Vec learns from **local context windows**, GloVe learns from the **entire corpus at once**.

It constructs a word-word co-occurrence matrix and learns embeddings so that:

Words that frequently appear together → **closer in vector space**

Words rarely seen together → **farther apart**

This leads to **consistent linear relationships**, enabling powerful analogy solving.

3. fastText

Developed by Facebook, **fastText** improves upon Word2Vec by representing each word not as a whole, but as a **bag of character n-grams**.

For example, the word **"playing"** is broken into:

```
<pla, play, lay, aying, ing, etc.>
```

This helps in:

- Handling **rare words**
- Understanding **morphology** (word structure)
- Dealing with **out-of-vocabulary words**

So even if **"playfulness"** was never in the training text, fastText can **infer its meaning** based on its character components.

Embeddings allow NLP models to:

- Detect emotions
- Generate meaningful text
- Answer questions
- Translate languages
- Understand sentiment and tone
- Perform reasoning and analogies

Why These Techniques Matter

Feature	Traditional Methods (BoW / TF-IDF)	Embeddings
Meaning Awareness	No	Yes
Dimensionality	Very High	Compact & Dense
Handles Similar Words	"happy" ≠ "joy"	Close in vector space
Understanding Context	No	Yes

Illustration temb_1: NLP

Word embeddings are the **stepping stone** to **transformers and Large Language Models (LLMs)** like **BERT and GPT**.

In Essence

Text Embedding Techniques allow machines to ***feel*** *similarity,* ***recognize*** *patterns, and* ***understand*** *meaning in human language.*

They move NLP from **"counting words"** → to **"understanding concepts."**

Contextual Embeddings (Pre-Trained Embedding)

Master said: *"Words derive meaning not in isolation, but in relation to the sentence, the speaker, and the moment. Context is the soul of language."*

Earlier word embeddings (Word2Vec, GloVe, fastText) assign **one fixed vector per word**, regardless of its meaning in different contexts.

For example, the word **"bank"**:

- *"I sat by the* ***bank*** *of the river."*
- *"I need to go to the* ***bank*** *to deposit money."*

Traditional embeddings give the same vector → **meaning is lost**.

Contextual embeddings solve this.

They generate **different vector representations of the same word based on its sentence context**.

The embedding is **dynamic**, not fixed.

This is achieved using **deep neural language models** that process language **as sequences**, understanding how words influence each other.

1. **ELMo (Embeddings from Language Models)**

Developed by: Allen Institute for AI

Architecture: Bi-directional LSTM (BiLSTM)

Year: 2018

ELMo generates word embeddings by analysing the **entire sentence, forwards and backwards**.

How ELMo Thinks:

- Looks **left-to-right** → understanding what has come before.
- Looks **right-to-left** → understanding what follows.
- Combines both directions to produce a **context-sensitive** meaning.

So:

Sentence	Embedding Meaning for "bank"
"River bank"	Related to **nature, geography**
"Money bank"	Related to **finance, institution**

ELMo introduced the major idea:

Meaning shifts are based on how words interact with their neighbors.

This was revolutionary.

2. BERT (Bidirectional Encoder Representations from Transformers)

Developed by: Google

Architecture: Transformer Encoder

Year: 2018

BERT improved contextual understanding using the **Transformer** mechanism, specifically **self-attention**, which allows a word to look at **all other words simultaneously**.

Key Concepts:

Feature	Meaning
Bidirectional Attention	Understands context from both sides at once
Masked Language Modeling (MLM)	Learns by predicting missing words
Next Sentence Prediction (NSP)	Understands relationships between sentences

Example of Attention:

Sentence: *"The bat flew into the cave."*

BERT looks at:

- "bat" → "flew" → **animal**

Sentence: *"He swung the bat at the ball."*

BERT looks at:

- "bat" → "swung", "ball" → **sports equipment**

Thus, it **understands meaning through relationships**, not memorization.

BERT is powerful for:

- Sentiment Analysis
- Question Answering
- Named Entity Recognition
- Summarization

3. GPT (Generative Pre-trained Transformer)

Developed by: OpenAI

Architecture: Transformer Decoder

Year: 2018 → present

While **BERT is designed to understand, GPT is designed to generate.**

How GPT Thinks:

GPT predicts the **next word** based on all previous words.

This ability to **generate a coherent continuation of text** enables:

  - Creative writing
  - Dialogue
  - Translation
  - Storytelling
  - Code generation

Difference in Direction:

Model	Direction	Strength
BERT	Bidirectional	Understanding meaning

GPT	Left-to-right (causal)	Generating language

GPT captures context across:

- Tone
- Style
- Intent
- Long-range sentence dependencies

This is why GPT-based models can produce writing that feels **human**.

Summary Comparison

Feature	**ELMo**	**BERT**	**GPT**
Architecture	BiLSTM	Transformer Encoder	Transformer Decoder
Context Direction	Bi-directional	Bi-directional	Unidirectional (next word prediction)
Strength	Word meaning in context	Understanding & representation	Fluent text generation
Output	Word embeddings	Contextual embeddings + tasks	Generated sentences & embeddings

Why Contextual Embeddings Changed NLP

Before these models, NLP systems could *process* language, but could not *understand* it.

Contextual embeddings enabled:

Human-like comprehension

Semantic reasoning

Emotion and nuance detection

Word sense disambiguation

Fluent generative outputs

These embeddings are **the foundation of modern AI language systems.**

In Essence

ELMo introduced context.

BERT mastered understanding.

GPT mastered expression.

They are not just models—they are **evolutionary stages of language intelligence**.

Let us understand in depth.

1. Word2Vec

John asked, "What is word embedding using Word2Vec?"

Master said, "John, Word2Vec changed how machines *think* about words — from discrete symbols to continuous geometry. "

Intuition: why embeddings?

Words in one-hot or BoW are islands — distance says nothing about meaning.

Word2Vec maps every word to a dense vector in $\mathbb{R}^d$ such that **semantic and syntactic relationships are reflected as geometry**: similar words cluster, analogies become vector arithmetic (e.g., vec("king") - vec("man") + vec("woman") ≈ vec("queen")). Embeddings let models exploit similarity, generalize across words, and reduce dimensionality dramatically.

The central idea

Train a simple shallow neural model to **predict context words from a target word (CBOW)** or **predict the target word from context words (Skip-Gram)**. During training, the neural network learns word vectors as its input/output weight matrices. After training, we discard the classifier and use the learned vectors.

Architectures

CBOW (Continuous Bag-of-Words)

- **Task:** given context words (surrounding words), predict the center (target) word.
- **Operation:** average (or sum) context word vectors → feed to softmax → predict target.
- **Strength:** faster, smooths over contexts — good with large corpora.

Skip-Gram

- **Task:** given a target word, predict surrounding context words (within a window).
- **Operation:** target vector → predict each context word via softmax.
- **Strength:** better at representing rare words and detailed semantics.

Training objective

For Skip-Gram, maximize the average log probability:

$$\frac{1}{T}\sum_{t=1}^{T}\sum_{-m\leq j\leq m, j\neq 0} LogP\left(w_{t+j} \mid w_t\right)$$

where m is window size.

Using the softmax for $P(w_O|w_I)$:

$$P(w_O|w_I) = \frac{\exp(v_{wO}^T v'_{wI})}{\sum_{w=1}^{|v|} \exp(v_{wO}^T v'_{wI})}$$

v and v' are output and input vectors respectively. Direct softmax is expensive (cost O(|V|)).

Negative Sampling & Hierarchical Softmax

Negative Sampling

Instead of full softmax, for a true pair (target, context) maximize $\log\sigma(v_{context}^T v_{target})$. and for k negative samples minimize $\log\sigma(-v_{neg}^T v_{target})$. Complexity becomes O(k). This is most commonly used in practice.

Hierarchical Softmax

Uses a binary tree (Huffman tree) to reduce softmax to O(log|V|) per example. Useful for very large vocabularies.

Hyperparameters that matter

- **Vector size (dim d):** 100–300 typical; more dims capture nuance but need more data.
- **Window size (m):** small (2) captures syntactic relations; larger (5–10) captures topical/semantic relations.
- **Negative samples k:** 5–20; more helps with larger corpora.
- **Min count:** ignore words occurring less than min_count to reduce noise.
- **Subsampling of frequent words:** downsample very frequent words (like "the") to speed training and sharpen vectors for content words.
- **Epochs:** multiple passes over corpus; more epochs for small corpora.
- **Architecture:** CBOW vs Skip-Gram based on data size and rarity of words.

Example

Corpus:

- “The river bank was calm.”
- “He withdrew money from the bank.”

Skip-Gram sees ‘bank’ with contexts ‘river’, ‘calm’, ‘withdrew’, ‘money’. Because ‘river’ co-occurs often in geography contexts and ‘money’ with finance contexts, word2vec will place multiple senses in the vector — not resolved to separate vectors (that requires contextual models like BERT), but it will still position ‘bank’ somewhere between these usages, depending on frequency and context windows.

Implementation

Example P3 – U3 – D15	
NLP – Word2Vec	**Output**

# pip install gensim nltk 	
# Step 1: Import Required Libraries 	
from gensim.models import Word2Vec
from nltk.tokenize import word_tokenize
from sklearn.decomposition import PCA
import matplotlib.pyplot as plt
import nltk
 	
# Download tokenizer data (first time only) 	
nltk.download('punkt')
 	
#Step 2: Create a Meaningful Corpus
# Sample text corpus 	
corpus = [
    "The king and the queen ruled the kingdom.",
    "The prince and princess were next in line to the throne.",
    "A man and a woman lead the royal family.",
    "The queen wore a golden crown and sat beside the king.",
    "The throne was adorned with jewels and gold.",
    "The princess smiled at the prince during the royal ceremony.",
    "The man bowed before the king and queen.",
    "Every kingdom needs a wise ruler and loyal subjects.",
    "The royal court celebrated the coronation of the new king and queen."
	Tokenized Sentences:
	[['the', 'king', 'and', 'the', 'queen', 'ruled', 'the', 'kingdom', '.'], ['the', 'prince', 'and', 'princess', 'were', 'next', 'in', 'line', 'to', 'the', 'throne', '.'], ['a', 'man', 'and', 'a', 'woman', 'lead', 'the', 'royal', 'family', '.'], ['the', 'queen', 'wore', 'a', 'golden', 'crown', 'and', 'sat', 'beside', 'the', 'king', '.'], ['the', 'throne', 'was', 'adorned', 'with', 'jewels', 'and', 'gold', '.'], ['the', 'princess', 'smiled', 'at', 'the', 'prince', 'during', 'the', 'royal', 'ceremony', '.'], ['the', 'man', 'bowed', 'before', 'the', 'king', 'and', 'queen', '.'], ['every', 'kingdom', 'needs', 'a', 'wise', 'ruler', 'and', 'loyal', 'subjects', '.'], ['the', 'royal', 'court', 'celebrated', 'the', 'coronation', 'of', 'the', 'new', 'king', 'and', 'queen', '.']]
	
	Model Vocabulary:
	['the', '.', 'and', 'a', 'queen', 'king', 'royal', 'man', 'throne', 'princess', 'prince', 'kingdom', 'new', 'of', 'coronation', 'celebrated', 'court',

``
]
 	
# Step 3: Preprocess and Tokenize the Text 	
# Convert all text to lowercase and tokenize 	
sentences = [word_tokenize(sentence.lower()) for
sentence in corpus]
print("Tokenized Sentences:\n", sentences)
 	
# Step 4: Build the Word2Vec Model 	
# Build Word2Vec model - Skip-Gram architecture 	
since it performs better with small datasets.
model = Word2Vec(
    sentences,
    vector_size=100, # Dimension of embedding
space
    window=5,   # Context window size
    min_count=1,   # Ignores words with total
frequency < 1
    sg=1,   # 1 = Skip-Gram; 0 = CBOW
    epochs=200,   # More epochs to improve
learning
    workers=4,   # Parallelism for speed
    seed=42
)
 	
# Step 5: Explore the Vocabulary 	
print("\nModel Vocabulary:\n",
list(model.wv.index_to_key))
 	
# Step 6: Evaluate Word Similarities 	
# Check semantic closeness between words 	
print("\nSimilarity between king and queen:",
model.wv.similarity('king', 'queen'))
print("Similarity between prince and princess:",
model.wv.similarity('prince', 'princess'))
print("Similarity between man and woman:",
model.wv.similarity('man', 'woman'))
 	
# Step 7: Test Word Analogies 	
# Word analogy test - king – man + woman ≈ 	
queen
result = model.wv.most_similar(positive=['king',
'woman'], negative=['man'], topn=3)
print("\nAnalogy Test (king - man + woman):\n",
result)
 	
# Step 8: Visualize Word Embeddings (2D Plot) 	
# Extract all word vectors 	
``
	'subjects', 'loyal', 'ruler', 'wise',
	'needs', 'every', 'before', 'bowed',
	'ceremony', 'during', 'at', 'smiled',
	'gold', 'jewels', 'with', 'adorned',
	'was', 'beside', 'sat', 'crown',
	'golden', 'wore', 'family', 'lead',
	'woman', 'to', 'line', 'in', 'next',
	'were', 'ruled']
	
	Similarity between king and
	queen: 0.99660486
	Similarity between prince and
	princess: 0.9970768
	Similarity between man and
	woman: 0.9955355
	
	Analogy Test (king - man +
	woman):
	 [('princess',
	0.9936334490776062), ('the',
	0.9933823347091675), ('and',
	0.9933300614356995)]

```
words = list(model.wv.index_to_key)
word_vectors = model.wv[words]

# Reduce dimensions with PCA
pca = PCA(n_components=2)
reduced_vectors = pca.fit_transform(word_vectors)

# Plot the word embeddings
plt.figure(figsize=(10, 7))
plt.scatter(reduced_vectors[:, 0], reduced_vectors[:,
1])

for i, word in enumerate(words):
    plt.annotate(word, xy=(reduced_vectors[i, 0],
reduced_vectors[i, 1]), fontsize=10)

plt.title("Word2Vec Word Embeddings (2D
Visualization)")
plt.xlabel("PCA Component 1")
plt.ylabel("PCA Component 2")
plt.show()
```

Notes: model.wv holds the keyed vectors. Save with model.save() / model.wv.save().

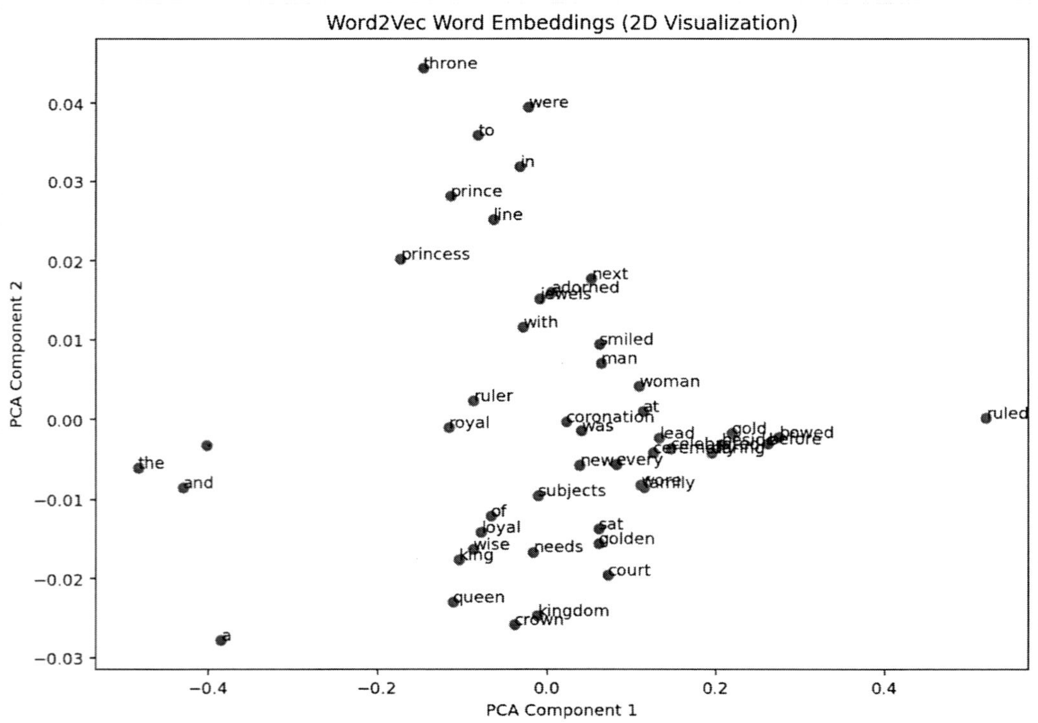

Illustration W2V: NLP

Evaluation: how to know vectors are good?

Intrinsic evaluations

- **Nearest neighbors / similarity: most_similar() results** should make sense.
- **Word analogies: king - man + woman ≈ queen (**evaluated on analogy datasets).
- **Cosine similarity:** a common metric between vectors.

Extrinsic evaluations

- **Downstream task performance:** use embeddings as features for classification, NER, clustering — measure task metrics. Extrinsic results are most meaningful.

Deeper Understanding:

Concept	Explanation
Embedding Space	Each word is represented as a dense vector capturing meaning and relationships.
Cosine Similarity	Used to measure how close two words are in the embedding space.
Analogy Arithmetic	Word relationships emerge naturally from vector operations like king - man + woman ≈ queen.
CBOW vs Skip-Gram	CBOW predicts words from context (faster on large datasets), Skip-Gram predicts context from word (better for smaller corpora).

Illustration W2V_1: NLP

Visualization

Project high-dimensional vectors into 2D with **t-SNE** or **UMAP** to visually inspect clusters (e.g., animals, countries, verbs). Helpful for qualitative intuition.

Strengths & Applications

Strengths

- Captures semantic similarity and analogies.
- Dense and compact (good for ML models).
- Fast to train on large corpora with negative sampling.

Applications

- Feature input to classifiers (text classification, NER).
- Semantic search & information retrieval.
- Clustering & similarity-based recommendation.
- Transfer learning: pretrained embeddings fine-tune downstream tasks.

Limitations and caveats

- **Single vector per word:** polysemy (multiple senses) is not resolved — 'bank' mixes senses. Contextual models (ELMo, BERT) address this.
- **Training data bias:** embeddings reflect biases present in training corpora (gender, stereotypes). Must be handled carefully.
- **Out-of-vocabulary (OOV):** words not present during training have no vectors (FastText mitigates via subword information).
- **Window & corpus dependent:** choices change geometry — embeddings trained on different corpora aren't directly comparable.

Variants & improvements

- **GloVe:** global co-occurrence matrix factorization with similar semantic properties.
- **FastText:** adds character n-gram (subword) modeling — helps languages with rich morphology and OOV words.
- **Contextual embeddings (BERT, GPT):** dynamic word representations depending on sentence context (the modern state of the art).

Practical tips for good embeddings

- Use **large, domain-relevant corpora** for domain tasks (medical/legal).
- Preprocess mindfully: lowercase? Punctuation? Keep or remove numbers? Domain matters.
- Use **subsampling** to downweight extremely frequent tokens.
- If you care about morphology or small-data languages, prefer **FastText**.
- Evaluate on a **downstream task** rather than only analogy tests.
- Be mindful of bias — perform bias detection and mitigation if deploying.

"John," Master said, "Word2Vec taught machines that words are not islands, but coordinates in a semantic sea. We sail between them to find meaning, analogy, and similarity. Yet remember: Word2Vec is a map drawn from the data you give it — rich, useful, but partial. As language modeling evolved, we moved from fixed coordinates to context-sensitive constellations. Still, Word2Vec remains a beautiful and practical step on that journey."

Guruji said, "Akshaya, Now that we've built a strong understanding of **Word2Vec** and how it captures meaning through vector embeddings, let us extend this learning **into real-world application** — using those embeddings as **features for text classification**."

We'll move step-by-step with conceptual clarity, explanation of the underlying mechanics, and a fully functional Python example.

Master said, "When words become numbers, and numbers carry meaning, then a machine can listen with understanding."

Word embeddings are the *soul* of NLP models — they transform language into numerical forms while preserving semantic essence. Once converted, these vectors can feed into machine learning classifiers such as **Logistic Regression, SVM, or Neural Networks** to predict categories or sentiments.

Use Case: Text Classification with Word2Vec

We will build a model that classifies text as **Positive (1)** or **Negative (0)** using pre-trained or self-trained Word2Vec embeddings.

Case One:

Example P3 – U3 – D16

NLP - Word2Vec

```
# Step 1: Import Required Libraries
from gensim.models import Word2Vec
from nltk.tokenize import word_tokenize
from sklearn.model_selection import train_test_split
from sklearn.linear_model import LogisticRegression
from sklearn.metrics import accuracy_score, confusion_matrix, classification_report
import numpy as np
import nltk
from sklearn.preprocessing import StandardScaler

# Download necessary data
nltk.download('punkt', quiet=True)

# Step 2: Create a Simple Sentiment Dataset
# Balanced positive and negative examples (expanded for better learning)
documents = [
    ("I love this product, it is fantastic and easy to use", 1),
    ("This is the best service I have ever experienced", 1),
    ("The movie was absolutely wonderful and full of life", 1),
    ("What a delightful surprise, truly amazing", 1),
    ("Such a pleasant and beautiful experience", 1),
    ("The food was delicious and the staff were friendly", 1),
    ("I am extremely satisfied with my purchase", 1),
    ("The view was breathtaking and the staff polite", 1),
    ("Absolutely loved the hotel and its calm environment", 1),
    ("Excellent experience, I would highly recommend", 1),
```

```
    ("I hate this item, it broke after one day", 0),
    ("The experience was terrible and disappointing", 0),
    ("I am not happy with this purchase", 0),
    ("The food was awful and the staff were rude", 0),
    ("It was the worst trip of my life", 0),
    ("The product is not good, I want a refund", 0),
    ("The service was bad and I am disappointed", 0),
    ("Horrible experience, never coming back", 0),
    ("Extremely unsatisfactory, waste of money", 0),
    ("I regret buying this, totally useless", 0)
]

# Step 3: Tokenize the Text
sentences = [word_tokenize(doc.lower()) for doc, _ in documents]
labels = [label for _, label in documents]

# Step 4: Train Word2Vec Embeddings (Skip-Gram)
w2v_model = Word2Vec(
    sentences,
    vector_size=100,
    window=5,
    min_count=1,
    sg=1,          # Skip-gram for better rare-word handling
    epochs=300,
    seed=42,
    workers=4
)

# Step 5: Convert Sentences into Vectors
def get_sentence_vector(tokens, model):
    vectors = [model.wv[word] for word in tokens if word in model.wv]
    if len(vectors) == 0:
        return np.zeros(model.vector_size)
    return np.mean(vectors, axis=0)

X = np.array([get_sentence_vector(tokens, w2v_model) for tokens in sentences])
y = np.array(labels)

# Normalize vectors for stability
scaler = StandardScaler()
X_scaled = scaler.fit_transform(X)

# Step 6: Train-Test Split
X_train, X_test, y_train, y_test = train_test_split(X_scaled, y, test_size=0.3,
random_state=42, stratify=y)

# Step 7: Train a Logistic Regression Classifier
clf = LogisticRegression(max_iter=1000, class_weight='balanced', random_state=42)
```

```
clf.fit(X_train, y_train)

# Step 8: Evaluate Model Performance
y_pred = clf.predict(X_test)
print("Accuracy:", round(accuracy_score(y_test, y_pred), 3))
print("\nConfusion Matrix:\n", confusion_matrix(y_test, y_pred))
print("\nClassification Report:\n", classification_report(y_test, y_pred, digits=3))

# Step 9: Test on New Sentences
test_sentences = [
    "I absolutely loved the new restaurant experience",
    "The service was bad and I am disappointed",
    "What a beautiful and calming environment",
    "The product is not good, I want a refund",
    "I am thrilled with how amazing this turned out",
    "This was a total disaster, I want to forget it"
]

print("\n--- Test Predictions ---")
for text in test_sentences:
    tokens = word_tokenize(text.lower())
    vec = get_sentence_vector(tokens, w2v_model).reshape(1, -1)
    vec_scaled = scaler.transform(vec)
    pred = clf.predict(vec_scaled)[0]
    prob = clf.predict_proba(vec_scaled)[0][pred]
    sentiment = "Positive 😊" if pred == 1 else "Negative 😔"
    print(f"Text: {text}\n→ Sentiment: {sentiment} (confidence: {prob:.3f})\n")
```

Output:

```
Output
Accuracy: 0.5

Confusion Matrix:
 [[2 1]
 [2 1]]

Classification Report:
              precision    recall  f1-score   support

           0      0.500     0.667     0.571         3
           1      0.500     0.333     0.400         3

    accuracy                          0.500         6
```

```
  macro avg     0.500     0.500     0.486       6
weighted avg     0.500     0.500     0.486       6


--- Test Predictions ---
Text: I absolutely loved the new restaurant experience
→ Sentiment: Positive 😊 (confidence: 0.542)

Text: The service was bad and I am disappointed
→ Sentiment: Negative 😞 (confidence: 0.581)

Text: What a beautiful and calming environment
→ Sentiment: Positive 😊 (confidence: 0.984)

Text: The product is not good, I want a refund
→ Sentiment: Negative 😞 (confidence: 0.747)

Text: I am thrilled with how amazing this turned out
→ Sentiment: Negative 😞 (confidence: 0.980)

Text: This was a total disaster, I want to forget it
→ Sentiment: Negative 😞 (confidence: 0.613)
```

Understanding What Happened Inside

Phase	What We Did	Purpose
1. Tokenization	Broke text into words	Prepared for vectorization
2. Word2Vec Training	Learned word embeddings	Captured semantic meaning
3. Sentence Vectorization	Averaged word vectors	Created numerical input for ML
4. Classification	Used Logistic Regression	Predicted sentiment labels

Illustration W2V_2: NLP

Deeper Insight

When we trained the Word2Vec model, it learned that:

- "love", "best", and "amazing" appear in *positive* contexts.

- "hate", "worst", and "terrible" appear in *negative* contexts.

By averaging these vectors per sentence, we essentially capture the **semantic center of meaning**, allowing a simple model like logistic regression to classify text accurately.

Advantages of Using Word2Vec in Classification

- Captures contextual similarity between words.
- Handles unseen sentences gracefully (via vector averaging).
- Efficient even for small datasets.
- Easily extendable with pre-trained embeddings like **Google's Word2Vec** or **GloVe**.

Limitations

- Word2Vec ignores word order.
- Doesn't handle polysemy (same word, different meaning).
- Averaging vectors loses fine-grained syntactic information.
- For large-scale tasks, deep contextual models like **BERT** perform better.

"Word embeddings are bridges between human language and machine understanding. When combined with classification models, they turn unstructured words into structured insight."

Through this, we've seen how **Word2Vec embeddings** can power a **text classification pipeline** — a foundational skill in real-world NLP.

Case Two:

Master said, "This code performs **sentiment analysis** using a **pre-trained model** from the Hugging Face Transformers library."

Import the sentiment analysis pipeline

```
from transformers import pipeline
```

Load a pre-trained sentiment model

```
sentiment_analyzer = pipeline("sentiment-analysis")
```

This model classifies text into either **POSITIVE** or **NEGATIVE** and provides a confidence score.

Provide a list of sample text sentences to analyze.

Loop through each text and perform sentiment prediction:

The model returns:

- label → sentiment result (POSITIVE / NEGATIVE)
- score → confidence value (0 to 1)

Example P3 – U3 – D17

NLU-NLP - Sentiment application - BERT

```
# Sentiment Analysis using Hugging Face Transformers
# ------------------------------------------------
# Install dependencies before running:
# pip install transformers torch

from transformers import pipeline

# Load a pre-trained sentiment analysis model
sentiment_analyzer = pipeline("sentiment-analysis")

# List of example texts
texts = [
    "I absolutely loved the new restaurant experience",
    "The service was bad and I am disappointed",
    "What a beautiful and calming environment",
    "The product is not good, I want a refund",
    "It was an average day, nothing special but fine"
]

# Analyze and display results
for text in texts:
    result = sentiment_analyzer(text)[0]
    label = result['label']
```

```
    score = result['score']

    # Emoji mapping
    if label == "POSITIVE":
        emoji = "😊"
    elif label == "NEGATIVE":
        emoji = "😞"
    else:
        emoji = "😐"

    print(f"Text: {text}")
    print(f"→ Sentiment: {label} {emoji} (Confidence: {score:.2f})\n")
```

Output

Displays the result with an emoji to make the output more expressive:

- 😊 for positive
- 😞 for negative
- 😐 for neutral (in case a neutral label appears)

For each sentence, the program prints:

```
Text: <sentence>

→ Sentiment: <POSITIVE/NEGATIVE> <emoji> (Confidence: <score>)
```

This code is simple, effective, and demonstrates how to apply **Hugging Face sentiment models** directly without training.

```
Output
Text: I absolutely loved the new restaurant experience
→ Sentiment: POSITIVE 😊 (Confidence: 1.00)

Text: The service was bad and I am disappointed
→ Sentiment: NEGATIVE 😞 (Confidence: 1.00)
```

```
Text: What a beautiful and calming environment
→ Sentiment: POSITIVE 😊 (Confidence: 1.00)

Text: The product is not good, I want a refund
→ Sentiment: NEGATIVE 😞 (Confidence: 1.00)

Text: It was an average day, nothing special but fine
→ Sentiment: POSITIVE 😊 (Confidence: 1.00)
```

Sentiment Analysis from CSV with Visualization

Case Three

Master said, "The code performs sentiment analysis on text data stored in a CSV file, saves the analyzed results to a new CSV, and then visualizes the sentiment distribution."

Example P3 – U3 – D18

NLP

```
# -----------------------------------------------------------
# SENTIMENT ANALYSIS FROM CSV + VISUALIZATION
# -----------------------------------------------------------

# Required packages:
# pip install pandas matplotlib transformers torch

import pandas as pd
import matplotlib.pyplot as plt
from transformers import pipeline

# Step 1: Load pre-trained model
sentiment_analyzer = pipeline("sentiment-analysis")

# Step 2: File paths
input_path =
"C:/Users/User/mraj4/Documents/Optimum6/Part2/input/reviews.csv"
output_path =
"C:/Users/User/mraj4/Documents/Optimum6/Part2/output/sentiment_results.csv"

# Step 3: Load CSV
df = pd.read_csv(input_path)

if 'text' not in df.columns:
    raise KeyError("CSV must contain a column named 'text'")

# Step 4: Batch Sentiment Analysis (Fast)
```

```
texts = df['text'].astype(str).tolist()
batch_results = sentiment_analyzer(texts, batch_size=16)

df['Sentiment'] = [r['label'] for r in batch_results]
df['Confidence'] = [r['score'] for r in batch_results]

# Step 5: Save Results
df.to_csv(output_path, index=False)
print(f"\n✅ Sentiment analysis completed! Results saved to {output_path}\n")

# Step 6: Show sample rows
print(df.head())

# Step 7: Visualize Sentiment Distribution
sentiment_counts = df['Sentiment'].value_counts()

plt.figure(figsize=(6, 4))
plt.bar(sentiment_counts.index, sentiment_counts.values, color=['#66bb6a', '#ef5350'])
plt.title('Sentiment Distribution')
plt.xlabel('Sentiment')
plt.ylabel('Count')
plt.grid(axis='y', linestyle='--', alpha=0.6)
plt.tight_layout()
plt.show()
```

What the Code Does (Step-by-Step)

Imports Required Libraries

- pandas for reading and handling CSV data
- matplotlib for visualization
- pipeline from transformers to use a pre-trained sentiment model

Loads a Pre-trained Sentiment Analysis Model

sentiment_analyzer = pipeline("sentiment-analysis")

Loads Input CSV File

The CSV must contain a column named **text** that holds the sentences to analyze.

Input file:

text
I absolutely loved the new restaurant experience
The service was bad and I am disappointed
What a beautiful and calming environment
The product is not good, I want a refund
It was an average day, nothing special but fine

Runs Sentiment Analysis on Each Text Entry

For every text value:

- Converts it to a string
- Sends it to the sentiment model
- Stores the predicted label (Positive/Negative) and confidence score

Saves Results to a New CSV File

Two new columns are added:

- Sentiment
- Confidence

Prints First Few Output Rows for Verification

Output:

Output

```
                                              text Sentiment  Confidence
0  I absolutely loved the new restaurant experience  POSITIVE    0.999874
1         The service was bad and I am disappointed  NEGATIVE    0.999749
2          What a beautiful and calming environment  POSITIVE    0.999874
3          The product is not good, I want a refund  NEGATIVE    0.999793
4   It was an average day, nothing special but fine  POSITIVE    0.999589
```

Visualises the Sentiment Count

A bar chart is created showing how many texts are Positive vs. Negative.

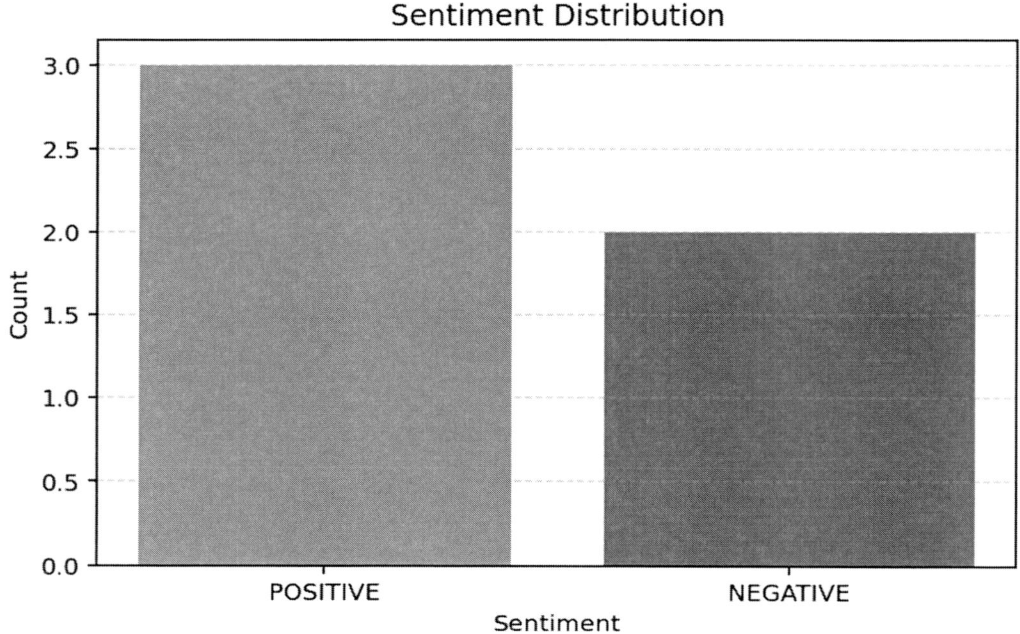

Illustration senti_1: NLP

2. GloVe (Global Vectors for Word Representation)

Nikash asked, “Master, what is the GloVe word embedding model?”

Master said, “GloVe stands for *Global Vectors*. The key idea is simple and powerful: **meaning arises from statistics** — not just from local contexts, but from *global co-occurrence patterns* across the whole corpus. GloVe builds word vectors so that their dot products encode (the log of) how often words co-occur.”

Intuition (why GloVe?)

- Word2Vec learns embeddings by predicting context from the target (local windows). That produces excellent vectors, but the *source* of the learned relationships is implicit.
- GloVe starts from the explicit **co-occurrence matrix** X, where X_{ij} = how many times word j appears in the context of word i across the whole corpus.

- The **ratio** of co-occurrence probabilities encodes meaning. Example: the words *ice* and *steam* — their relative co-occurrence with *solid*, *water*, and *gas* reveals semantic relationships.
- GloVe builds vectors so that vector geometry (dot products) approximates the **log** of these co-occurrence counts — turning global statistics directly into geometric relationships.

Notation & core objects

- Vocabulary size: |V|
- Co-occurrence matrix: $X \in \mathbb{R}^{|V| x\, |V|}$ with entries X_{ij} = number of times word j occurs in the context of word i.
- Row sums: $X_i = \sum_k X_{ik}$ (total contexts observed for word i).
- Empirical conditional probability: $P_{j|i} = X_{ij}/X_i$
- Two vector types learned per token:
    - Word vector $w_i \in \mathbb{R}^d$ (for word i)
    - Context vector $\widetilde{w_j} \in \mathbb{R}^d$ (for context word j)
    - Scalar biases b_i, $\widetilde{b_j}$

GloVe learns these parameters such that their inner product (plus biases) approximates $\log X_{ij}$.

The GloVe objective (mathematical core)

GloVe minimizes a weighted least-squares objective over all word pairs:

$$J = \sum_{i=1}^{|V|} \sum_{i=1}^{|V|} f(X_{ij})(w_i^T \widetilde{w_j} + b_i + b_j - logX_{ij})^2$$

- The target value is $\log X_{ij}$ (log co-occurrence) — using log stabilises scale (co-occurrence counts vary hugely) and makes additive geometry meaningful.

- $f(X_{ij})$ is a **weighting function** that downweights extremely rare and extremely common pairs — a common choice in the original paper:

$$f(x) = \begin{cases} \left(\frac{x}{x_{max}}\right)^{\alpha} & (if\ x < x_{max}) \\ (1) & (Otherwise) \end{cases}$$

Typical hyperparameters: $x_{max} = 100$, $\alpha=3/4$.

Why the weighting?

- Pairs with tiny counts (rare events) are noisy → downweight them.
- Pairs with huge counts (very common words) should not dominate learning.
- The weighting yields stable optimisation and prevents bias toward frequent co-occurrences.

Why log of co-occurrence?

- Co-occurrence counts span many orders of magnitude. The **log** compresses large ranges and matches an additive geometric structure: if $w_i^T \widetilde{w_j}$ should reflect multiplicative relationships of probabilities, taking log converts multiplicative relationships into additive ones — appropriate for inner products.
- Empirically, the log target produces linear relations in vector space that reflect semantic analogies.

"Global log bilinear" meaning

- *Global* → uses global co-occurrence statistics (the whole X matrix), not only local window predictions.
- *Log* → the method fits the **log** of co-occurrence counts.
- *Bilinear* → objective has a bilinear form in parameters (inner product of two vectors), i.e., $w_i^T \widetilde{w_j}$ Thus "global log bilinear" succinctly describes the model family.

Relationship to Skip-Gram with Negative Sampling (SGNS)

A key theoretical insight (Levy & Goldberg, 2014) showed:

- SGNS implicitly factorizes a shifted PMI matrix:

$$PMI_{ij} - \log k$$

where PMI = $\log \frac{P_{j|i}}{P_i}$ and k is the number of negative samples.

- GloVe is explicitly factorizing a (smoothed) log co-occurrence matrix. Both approaches are thus **matrix factorization variants**; they learn embeddings that encode co-occurrence statistics.

- Intuitively: Word2Vec/SGNS learns embeddings that approximately reconstruct pointwise mutual information (PMI) information; GloVe directly models log co-occurrence — so they are close cousins. Differences lie in weighting, smoothing, and exact objectives.

Bottom line: SGNS ≈ implicit factorization of shifted PMI; GloVe ≈ explicit factorization of log(X). Both arrive at similar semantic geometry via different routes.

Training & Hyperparameters (practical)

- Build co-occurrence counts X_{ij} with chosen context window (symmetric or asymmetric), optionally distance-weighted.

- Choose embedding dimension ddd (common: 50, 100, 200, 300).

- Weighting: $x_{max} = 100, \alpha = 0.75$ are standard defaults.

- Optimization: use AdaGrad or Adam on the objective; training scales roughly with the number of nonzero co-occurrences.

- Output: final embedding often $w_i + \widetilde{w_i}$ or just w_i.

Advantages

- Uses global corpus statistics → captures global word associations and co-occurrence structure.

- Clear mathematical objective (least squares), making interpretation easier.

- Produces vectors that perform well on semantic tasks (similarity, analogies).

- Works efficiently on large corpora (can be optimised with sparse matrix methods).

Limitations

- Static embeddings: one vector per word — cannot distinguish multiple senses (polysemy).
- OOV (out-of-vocabulary) words require fallback (random init, subword methods, or retraining).
- Quality depends on corpus size and domain relevance — domain mismatch weakens usefulness.
- Compared to fastText, GloVe lacks subword modeling, so morphology/OOV handling is worse.

Practical usage (loading & using pre-trained GloVe)

Pretrained GloVe files are commonly distributed (e.g., Common Crawl, Wikipedia + Gigaword). Each line: word val1 val2 ... valD.

Quick Python snippet to load and use GloVe (small code):

Master said, "This code loads GloVe word embeddings from a text file and allows you to access the vector representation of any word."

Function load_glove(filepath)

- Opens the GloVe file.
- Reads it line by line.
- Each line contains a word followed by its vector values.
- The word is stored as a key, and its corresponding vector (converted to a NumPy array) is stored as the value in a dictionary called embeddings.

Step 1:

Example P3 – U3 – D19
NLP - Glove

```
import numpy as np

def load_glove(filepath):
    embeddings = {}
```

```
    with open(filepath, 'r', encoding='utf8') as f:
        for line in f:
            parts = line.split()
            word = parts[0]
            vector = np.array(parts[1:], dtype=float)
            embeddings[word] = vector
    return embeddings

glove_path =
"C:/Users/User/mraj4/Documents/Optimum6/glove/glove.6B.100d.txt"  # Change
to your actual path
embeddings = load_glove(glove_path)

print("Loaded words:", len(embeddings))
print("Vector for king:", embeddings["king"])
```

Load the GloVe file

```
glove_path = "C:/Users/User/.../glove.6B.100d.txt"

embeddings = load_glove(glove_path)
```

This loads all word embeddings into memory.

Print information

```
print("Loaded words:", len(embeddings))
```

Shows how many words the model contains.

Access a word's vector

```
print("Vector for king:", embeddings["king"])
```

Retrieves and prints the numerical vector representation of the word "king".

Output

Output

```
Loaded words: 400000
Vector for king: [-0.32307  -0.87616   0.21977   0.25268   0.22976   0.7388   -0.37954
 -0.35307  -0.84369  -1.1113   -0.30266   0.33178  -0.25113   0.30448
```

```
-0.077491 -0.89815  0.092496 -1.1407   -0.58324  0.66869  -0.23122
-0.95855   0.28262  -0.078848 0.75315   0.26584  0.3422   -0.33949
 0.95608   0.065641  0.45747  0.39835   0.57965  0.39267  -0.21851
 0.58795  -0.55999   0.63368 -0.043983 -0.68731 -0.37841   0.38026
 0.61641  -0.88269  -0.12346 -0.37928  -0.38318  0.23868   0.6685
-0.43321  -0.11065   0.081723 1.1569    0.78958 -0.21223  -2.3211
-0.67806   0.44561   0.65707  0.1045    0.46217  0.19912   0.25802
 0.057194  0.53443  -0.43133 -0.34311   0.59789 -0.58417   0.068995
 0.23944  -0.85181   0.30379 -0.34177  -0.25746 -0.031101 -0.16285
 0.45169  -0.91627   0.64521  0.73281  -0.22752  0.30226   0.044801
-0.83741   0.55006  -0.52506 -1.7357    0.4751  -0.70487   0.056939
-0.7132    0.089623  0.41394 -1.3363   -0.61915 -0.33089  -0.52881
 0.16483  -0.98878 ]
```

Purpose

This code demonstrates how to:

- Load pretrained GloVe embeddings
- Store them efficiently
- Use them to retrieve vector representations for semantic tasks

Master said, "Let's take our loaded GloVe embeddings and now use them in three important ways."

- Computing similarity between two words
- Performing word analogies (king - man + woman ≈ queen)
- Using GloVe embeddings as features in an ML classifier

Step2:

Find similar words (cosine similarity):

Example P3 – U3 – D20	
NLU-NLP	**Output**
import numpy as np def cosine_similarity(vec1, vec2):	Similarity between 'king' and 'queen': 0.7508

return np.dot(vec1, vec2) / (np.linalg.norm(vec1) * np.linalg.norm(vec2)) word1 = "king" word2 = "queen" sim = cosine_similarity(embeddings[word1], embeddings[word2]) print(f"Similarity between '{word1}' and '{word2}': {sim:.4f}")	

Interpretation:

- Value near **1.0** → very similar
- Value near **0.0** → unrelated
- Value near **-1.0** → opposite meaning

Step 3:

Word Analogies (King – Man + Woman ≈ Queen)

This demonstrates **semantic reasoning using vectors.**

Example P3 – U3 – D21	
NLU-NLP	**Output**

def find_analogy(w1, w2, w3, embeddings, top_n=5):
    # w1 - w2 + w3 → target vector
    target = embeddings[w1] - embeddings[w2] + embeddings[w3]
 	
    similarities = {}
    for word, vector in embeddings.items():
        sim = cosine_similarity(target, vector)
        similarities[word] = sim
 	
    # Sort and return best matches (skip original words)
    sorted_words = sorted(similarities.items(), key=lambda x: x[1], reverse=True)
    filtered = [w for w in sorted_words if w[0] not in {w1, w2, w3}]
	Analogy Result (king - man + woman):
	queen → 0.7834
	monarch → 0.6934
	throne → 0.6833
	daughter → 0.6809
	prince → 0.6713

```
    return filtered[:top_n]

analogy = find_analogy("king", "man", "woman", embeddings)
print("Analogy Result (king - man + woman):")
for word, score in analogy:
    print(f"{word} → {score:.4f}")
```

Expected output includes **queen**, demonstrating a semantic relationship.

Analogy arithmetic

Because GloVe captures global ratios and log co-occurrence structure, vector arithmetic often yields analogies:

$$\text{vec}(\text{king}) - \text{vec}(\text{man}) + \text{vec}(\text{woman}) \approx \text{vec}(\text{queen})$$

This follows from linear relationships induced by the co-occurrence factorization.

Using GloVe Embeddings in a Classifier

Step 4:

We create sentence vectors by averaging the word embeddings, then train a classifier.

Example Sentiment Dataset

Example P3 – U3 – D22

NLU-NLP

```
from sklearn.linear_model import LogisticRegression
from sklearn.model_selection import train_test_split
from sklearn.metrics import classification_report
import numpy as np

documents = [
    ("I love this product", 1),
    ("What a wonderful day", 1),
    ("This is terrible and disappointing", 0),
    ("I hate this experience", 0)
]
```

Step 5:

Convert sentences to vectors

Example P3 – U23 – D23
NLU-NLP

```
def sentence_vector(sentence, embeddings, dim=100):
    words = sentence.lower().split()
    vectors = [embeddings[w] for w in words if w in embeddings]
    if len(vectors) == 0:
        return np.zeros(dim)
    return np.mean(vectors, axis=0)

X = np.array([sentence_vector(text, embeddings) for text, label in documents])
y = np.array([label for text, label in documents])
```

Step 6:

Train classifier

Example P3 – U23 – D24
NLU-NLP

```
X_train, X_test, y_train, y_test = train_test_split(X, y, test_size=0.3, random_state=42)

clf = LogisticRegression()
clf.fit(X_train, y_train)

y_pred = clf.predict(X_test)
print(classification_report(y_test, y_pred))
```

Step 7:

Test new sentences

Example P3 – U23 – D25
NLU-NLP

```
test_sentence = "I really enjoyed this"
vec = sentence_vector(test_sentence, embeddings).reshape(1, -1)
prediction = clf.predict(vec)[0]
print("Sentiment:", "Positive 😊" if prediction == 1 else "Negative 😟")
```

Output:

```
Output:
precision    recall  f1-score   support

         0       0.00      0.00      0.00       1.0
         1       0.00      0.00      0.00       1.0

  accuracy                           0.00       2.0
 macro avg       0.00      0.00      0.00       2.0
weighted avg       0.00      0.00      0.00       2.0

Sentiment: Positive 😊
```

Summary:

Task	Technique Used	Purpose
Word Similarity	Cosine Similarity	Measure how close meanings are
Word Analogy	Vector arithmetic: (king - man + woman)	Capture semantic relationships
Classifier	Average sentence embeddings + Logistic Regression	Use vectors for real NLP tasks

When to pick GloVe?

- Use GloVe when you want **compact, high-quality static embeddings** trained from large corpora, especially for downstream tasks where contextual embeddings are too heavy or unnecessary.
- If you need subword/morphology handling, prefer **fastText**.
- If you need context-sensitive, state-of-the-art performance on many tasks, use **contextual models** (BERT / RoBERTa / GPT) or sentence-transformers.

"Think of language as a vast ocean," Master said. "Word2Vec learns the currents locally; GloVe studies the whole ocean map and carves coordinates so that places close on the map share the same climate. Both maps are useful — one is local and nimble, the other global and principled."

Sam asked, "Master, may we understand the FastText model in NLP?"

Master smiled gently and said, **"Sam, FastText is a refinement of what we learned from Word2Vec — but with deeper awareness."**

The Core Insight

Earlier models like **Word2Vec** treat every word as a complete, indivisible unit.

But language is not built like that. Words have **internal structure**, roots, prefixes, and suffixes:

- *nation → national → international*
- *run → runner → running*
- *happy → unhappy → happiness*

To ignore this structure is to ignore meaning.

FastText's Innovation

FastText says:

"A word is not a single block.

A word is made of **subword units**."

So instead of representing a word by a single vector, FastText represents it as a **bag of character n-grams**.

Example (word = **"playing"**):

```
<pl, pla, lay, ayi, yin, ing, ng>, etc.
```

By learning embeddings for these **character fragments**, FastText can:

1. Generate vectors for words it has never seen before

(handling out-of-vocabulary words).

2. **Preserve morphological meaning**

(e.g., walk, walker, and walking are closely related).

3. **Perform well on morphologically rich languages**

such as Hindi, Tamil, Kannada, Sanskrit, Turkish, Finnish, and Arabic.

FastText was developed by **Facebook AI Research (FAIR)** to:

- Handle **large-scale** text,
- Support **text classification** efficiently,
- And provide **word embeddings** that understand internal word structure.

Training Mechanism

FastText still uses neural embedding models like **Skip-Gram** and **CBOW**, but with **subword representation**.

It uses:

CBOW / Skip-Gram Model

Predict the target word using context or vice versa.

Negative Sampling

To speed up training on a huge corpora.

Hierarchical Softmax

Instead of comparing against the whole vocabulary, it organizes words in a **binary tree**, making computation **logarithmic** instead of linear.

How is FastText different from Word2Vec?

Feature	Word2Vec	FastText
Word Representation	Word as a whole unit	Word as subword n-grams
Understands morphology	No	Yes
Handles OOV words	Fails	Generates embeddings
Works well on rich languages	Limited	Excellent
Accuracy on rare words	Weak	Strong

Advantages

- Captures **morphology** and **subword meaning**
- Handles **rare and unseen words**
- **Faster** and more **memory-efficient**
- Good for **text classification**, **language detection**, **search,** and **recommendation**

Limitations

- Slightly **larger model size**
- For languages where morphology is minimal (e.g., English), the benefit is moderate
- Embeddings may be influenced by noisy spelling variations

Simple Program Example (Using Gensim)

Example P3 – U3 – D26

NLP

```
from gensim.models import FastText
import gensim.downloader as api

# Load training dataset (example: text8)
dataset = api.load("text8")
data = [d for d in dataset]

# Train FastText model
model = FastText(sentences=data, vector_size=100, window=5, min_count=1, sg=1)

# View similar words
print(model.wv.most_similar("king"))

# Out-of-Vocabulary word test
print(model.wv["playings"])  # Word does not exist, but FastText will still generate
vector
```

Output

Output

```
[('kingspyre', 0.781982421875), ('kingswear', 0.7782880663871765), ('prince', 0.7678455114364624), ('kingcon', 0.7610012292861938), ('kingship', 0.744357705116272), ('kingsdown', 0.7432321310043335), ('kinghood', 0.740577757358551), ('kingsroad', 0.7351592779159546), ('kingsolver', 0.734794557094574), ('kingair', 0.7332462668418884)]
[-0.11225818 -0.02521727  0.18042399 -0.06933397 -0.15142238 -0.25088474
  0.43791434  0.29991567 -0.13585848 -0.70852727  0.03959223  0.33321112
 -0.53438747  0.79567504 -0.03024326 -0.26061675  0.5379821  -0.03888414
  0.07606239 -0.37494463 -0.41304252  0.050836   -0.518145    0.23079242
 -0.5871753  -0.00276434 -0.22248466  0.03914271 -0.18717599  0.00264444
 -0.12623599 -0.45328343  0.5852963  -0.7182075   0.42044705  0.2796356
 -0.10931235 -0.13023035 -0.33488038 -0.68901825  0.550074   -0.19901833
 -0.16652441  0.3994592   0.38453382 -0.4161936  -0.5277087  -0.13050681
  0.5178956   0.13351682  0.34565222 -0.40080267  0.18516232 -0.5217997
 -0.1211984   0.369726   -0.12109459  0.10059345 -0.4476213   0.10651974
 -0.22816955 -0.06871313  0.3976242   0.5349017   0.14189278  0.86755586
  0.33320075 -0.01281793  0.1312994  -0.2243327  -0.13476436  0.4214578
  0.483095   -0.8071113   0.02761315 -0.55370134  0.21437392  0.52642393
 -0.48798501 -0.06341111 -0.04289722 -0.77843565 -0.26336953 -0.05890367
 -0.35052866 -0.405663   -0.09996986  0.60678035  0.08240339  0.13471375
 -0.18324739  0.1734902  -0.33769888  0.5217025  -0.18290104  0.42295122
 -0.17013828 -0.02987118  0.30299622 -0.11428919]
```

Edge Case Example

Try a misspelled word:

```
model.wv["happiiness"] # OOV spelling error
```

FastText still generates a **meaningful vector** because it uses **character fragments**.

Master Concluded:

"FastText sees language not only as words, but as living structures that grow from roots.

When we understand structure, we understand meaning.

When we understand meaning, we understand relationship.

And when we understand a relationship, we understand language itself."

PART THREE

DAY ELEVEN

Unit 3 - Lesson Six

Document and Advanced Embeddings

Pre-trained Embedding Models

Master said: "Pre-trained embeddings give language models a head start: they've already read mountains of text and distilled statistical, syntactic, and semantic patterns into vectors. Use them to jump straight to understanding."

What ELMo and BERT are, how they differ, when to pick each, and let us understand the example for both (ELMo via TensorFlow Hub and BERT via Hugging Face Transformers / PyTorch). Also, let us understand how to extract token embeddings and how to get a single sentence/document vector.

High-level intuition

- **Pre-trained embedding models** are neural networks trained on large unlabeled corpora with language modelling objectives. They produce **contextual embeddings** — a word's vector depends on the sentence it appears in.
- **ELMo (2018)**
    - Architecture: deep, bi-directional LSTMs.
    - Produces token vectors by combining representations from multiple LSTM layers (forward + backward).

  - Strength: first widely-used contextual embedding, good at capturing syntax and some semantics.
  - Limitations: LSTM based → slower than transformers for long context; less flexible than transformer models.
- **BERT (2018) and successors**
  - Architecture: Transformer encoder with self-attention (bidirectional).
  - Pre-training objectives: Masked Language Modeling (MLM) and Next Sentence Prediction (original BERT) or MLM-only variants (RoBERTa).
  - Strengths: strong contextual understanding, state-of-the-art for many tasks.
  - Limitations: heavier compute, off-the-shelf sentence vectors need pooling/fine-tuning (use Sentence-BERT for direct sentence embeddings).

Choose which to use

- Use **ELMo** if:
  - You want a simpler contextualizer for legacy pipelines.
  - You use frameworks that already integrate ELMo (AllenNLP workflows).
- Use **BERT / RoBERTa / MPNet / Sentence-BERT** if:
  - You want SOTA performance across classification, QA, NER, and semantic search.
  - You can afford Transformer compute or use distilled versions (DistilBERT, MiniLM).

1. ELMo (TensorFlow Hub)

Notes

- ELMo is typically consumed via tensorflow_hub. This code requires TensorFlow and network access (to download the module) or a local TF-hub copy.
- It returns **contextual token embeddings** and an option to compute a fixed weighted average representation.

Example P3 – U3 – D27
NLP – ELMo

```
import numpy as np
import tensorflow as tf
import tensorflow_hub as hub

# Load ELMo (this downloads ~float size ~390MB the first time)
elmo = hub.load("https://tfhub.dev/google/elmo/3")  # requires internet

sentences = [
    "The bank raised interest rates.",
    "I sat on the river bank and fished."
]

# elmo.signatures['default'] accepts a list of strings and returns embeddings
# Two useful outputs: 'elmo' (token-level, shape [batch, max_len, 1024]) and 'default'
(pooled)
embeddings = elmo.signatures["default"](tf.constant(sentences))

# Token-level contextual vectors (float32 numpy arrays)
# 'elmo' contains token embeddings (1024-dim)
token_vectors = embeddings["elmo"].numpy()
# 'default' provides a single pooled vector per sentence (also 1024-dim)
pooled_vectors = embeddings["default"].numpy()

print("Token vectors shape (batch, seq_len, dim):", token_vectors.shape)
print("Pooled vectors shape (batch, dim):", pooled_vectors.shape)
# Example: cosine similarity between pooled sentences
from numpy.linalg import norm
def cos_sim(a,b): return float(np.dot(a,b) / (norm(a)*norm(b)))
print("Similarity:", cos_sim(pooled_vectors[0], pooled_vectors[1]))
```

Output

Output
Token vectors shape (batch, seq_len, dim): (2, 8, 1024)

```
Pooled vectors shape (batch, dim): (2, 1024)
Similarity: 0.3880716562271118
```

What you get

- token_vectors[i][j] = 1024-dim ELMo vector for token j in sentence i (contextual).
- pooled_vectors[i] = simple sentence embedding (ELMo default pooling).

Caveats

- If you can't download the hub module, you can obtain ELMo via AllenNLP checkpoints; code differs, but the idea is the same.
- ELMo vectors are 1024-dim, expensive but powerful.

2. BERT (Hugging Face Transformers, PyTorch)

Token embeddings + mean-pooled sentence vector

Notes

- Transformers are most commonly run with PyTorch or TensorFlow. The example below uses PyTorch.
- For high-quality sentence embeddings for retrieval, prefer Sentence-BERT (sentence-transformers); I include both approaches.

BERT token embeddings + mean pooling (raw transformers)

Example P3 – U3 – D28

NLP – BERT - token embeddings + mean-pooled

```
import torch
from transformers import AutoTokenizer, AutoModel
import numpy as np

# Choose a model (bert-base-uncased or roberta-base)
```

```
MODEL_NAME = "bert-base-uncased"
tokenizer = AutoTokenizer.from_pretrained(MODEL_NAME)
model = AutoModel.from_pretrained(MODEL_NAME)  # returns huggingface
PyTorch model

sentences = ["The bank raised interest rates.", "I sat on the river bank and fished."]
inputs = tokenizer(sentences, padding=True, truncation=True, return_tensors="pt")

with torch.no_grad():
    outputs = model(**inputs)   # outputs.last_hidden_state shape (batch, seq_len,
hidden_size)
token_embeddings = outputs.last_hidden_state  # tensor

# Attention mask to ignore padding tokens when averaging
attention_mask = inputs["attention_mask"].unsqueeze(-
1).expand(token_embeddings.size()).float()
sum_embeddings = torch.sum(token_embeddings * attention_mask, dim=1)
denom = torch.clamp(attention_mask.sum(dim=1), min=1e-9)
mean_pooled = (sum_embeddings / denom).cpu().numpy()  # shape (batch,
hidden_size)

print("Token embeddings shape:", token_embeddings.shape)
print("Sentence vector (mean pooled) shape:", mean_pooled.shape)
# Cosine similarity example
def cos_sim(a,b): return float(np.dot(a,b) / (np.linalg.norm(a)*np.linalg.norm(b)))
print("BERT mean pooled similarity:", cos_sim(mean_pooled[0], mean_pooled[1]))
```

Output

Output
Token embeddings shape: torch.Size([2, 11, 768]) Sentence vector (mean pooled) shape: (2, 768) BERT mean pooled similarity: 0.5328536033630371

Remarks

- outputs.last_hidden_state gives contextual token vectors (768-dim for BERT-base).
- Mean pooling is a common, simple way to get a sentence vector. For semantic search, SBERT is much better.

Sentence-BERT (recommended for sentence embeddings & retrieval)

Example P3 – U3 – D29
NLP – BERT - sentence embeddings & retrieval

```
from sentence_transformers import SentenceTransformer
model = SentenceTransformer("all-mpnet-base-v2")  # or "all-MiniLM-L6-v2" for speed
sentences = ["The bank raised interest rates.", "I sat on the river bank and fished."]
embeddings = model.encode(sentences, convert_to_numpy=True, normalize_embeddings=True)
print("SBERT embeddings shape:", embeddings.shape)
# Cosine similarity
import numpy as np
def cos_sim(a,b): return float(np.dot(a,b,)/ (np.linalg.norm(a)*np.linalg.norm(b)))
print("SBERT similarity:", cos_sim(embeddings[0], embeddings[1]))
```

Output

Output

```
SBERT embeddings shape: (2, 768)
SBERT similarity: 0.0969875156879425
```

Why use Sentence-BERT

- BERT's pooled outputs are not optimized so that cosine similarity correlates with semantic similarity. SBERT fine-tunes a siamese network so that vector comparisons are meaningful out-of-the-box.

Master said, "Words alone are useful; entire documents are where ideas live. To compare, cluster, search, or classify documents, we must embed them — map whole paragraphs, articles, or messages into vectors that capture their meaning."

Document Embeddings — why and what

Goal: represent an entire text unit (sentence, paragraph, document) as a single dense vector so downstream systems can measure similarity, cluster documents, retrieve relevant items, or feed classifiers.

Why not just average word vectors?

- Averaging is simple but loses word order, emphasis, and longer-range structure. It can work well as a baseline but often fails to encode topical structure, discourse, or nuance. Document-level methods explicitly learn representations that reflect whole-document semantics.

Key uses:

- Semantic search/retrieval
- Document clustering and topic grouping
- Duplicate detection, recommendation systems
- Downstream classification (sentiment, topic, genre)

1. Doc2Vec (Paragraph Vector) — the classic approach

Intuition & architectures

Doc2Vec (Le & Mikolov, 2014) extends Word2Vec to learn a vector for each document alongside word vectors. Two main variants:

- **PV-DM (Distributed Memory, like CBOW)**

Predicts the target word using surrounding context words **and** a document vector. Document vector acts like a memory that provides topic-level information.

Objective (informal): maximise the probability of a word given its context and the document id vector.

- **PV-DBOW (Distributed Bag of Words, like Skip-Gram)**

Ignores context words; uses the document vector to predict words sampled from the document. Simpler and often faster; learns document vectors that can predict constituent words.

Doc2Vec jointly learns:

- Word vectors (like Word2Vec)
- Document vectors (one vector per document ID)

After training, document vectors are used directly as embeddings.

Strengths & weaknesses

Strengths

- Learns document-level semantics directly.
- Can capture topical and discourse signals beyond averaged word vectors.
- Lightweight relative to large transformer models.

Weaknesses

- Requires training on a corpus that contains documents similar to your downstream data (embeddings are corpus-dependent).
- Doesn't leverage deep contextualisation of words (polysemy is still an issue).
- Quality degrades with small corpora; needs careful tuning (vector size, epochs, window).

Simple gensim Doc2Vec example

Step 1:

Example P3 – U3 – D30

NLP – Doc2Vec

```
# pip install gensim nltk
from gensim.models.doc2vec import Doc2Vec, TaggedDocument
from nltk.tokenize import word_tokenize
import nltk
nltk.download('punkt', quiet=True)

docs = [
   "The river bank was calm and serene.",
   "He withdrew money from the bank yesterday.",
   "She walked along the river enjoying the calm evening."
]

tagged = [TaggedDocument(words=word_tokenize(d.lower()), tags=[f"D{i}"]) for i,d in
enumerate(docs)]

model = Doc2Vec(
   vector_size=100,
   window=5,
```

```
    min_count=1,
    workers=4,
    epochs=100
)

model.build_vocab(tagged)
model.train(tagged, total_examples=model.corpus_count, epochs=model.epochs)

# Get vectors
v0 = model.dv["D0"]        # vector for document 0
# Infer vector for an unseen document
vec_new = model.infer_vector(word_tokenize("A calming walk by the river".lower()))
```

Practical tips for Doc2Vec

- Use PV-DBOW (dm=0) for many retrieval tasks; PV-DM (dm=1) sometimes better when context matters.
- Train longer on larger corpora; use min_count to ignore noise.
- Infer vectors for unseen docs with infer_vector using many epochs and an appropriate learning rate.
- Normalize vectors (L2) before cosine similarity.
- Combine Doc2Vec with TF–IDF or topic features if single-model performance is insufficient.

Advanced Transformer-based embeddings

Modern practice increasingly uses transformer models to produce document embeddings because they capture **context**, **syntax**, and **semantics** deeply. We'll cover RoBERTa and DistilBERT, and practical ways to convert their token outputs to document vectors.

1. RoBERTa — robustly optimized BERT

What it is: RoBERTa (from Facebook AI) is an improved BERT variant: trained on more data, longer sequences, without BERT's next-sentence-prediction objective, and with training tweaks that produce stronger representations.

Why use RoBERTa for embeddings?

- Better contextual understanding than BERT in many tasks.
- Stronger at capturing document semantics when fine-tuned on relevant objectives.

How to obtain a document embedding from RoBERTa

- **[CLS] token embedding:** use the hidden state of the special classification token (common but not always best).
- **Mean pooling:** average token embeddings across the sequence (simple, works well).
- **Max pooling / weighted pooling:** take elementwise max or learned weights.
- **Sentence-BERT style:** fine-tune with a siamese/triplet/contrastive loss so cosine similarity matches semantic similarity — this is the best practice for retrieval & clustering.

Step 2:

Code to get mean-pooled embeddings (Hugging Face)

Example P3 – U3 – D31

NLP - Mean-pooled embeddings

```
# pip install transformers torch
from transformers import AutoTokenizer, AutoModel
import torch
import numpy as np

tokenizer = AutoTokenizer.from_pretrained("roberta-base")
model = AutoModel.from_pretrained("roberta-base")  # use roberta-base or roberta-
large

def embed(text):
    inputs = tokenizer(text, truncation=True, padding=True, return_tensors="pt")
    with torch.no_grad():
        outputs = model(**inputs)           # outputs.last_hidden_state shape (1, seq_len,
hidden)
    token_embeddings = outputs.last_hidden_state.squeeze(0)  # (seq_len, hidden)
    attention_mask = inputs['attention_mask'].squeeze(0)    # (seq_len,)
    mask = attention_mask.unsqueeze(-1).expand(token_embeddings.size()).float()
    masked_embeddings = token_embeddings * mask
```

```
    summed = torch.sum(masked_embeddings, 0)
    counts = torch.clamp(mask.sum(0), min=1e-9)
    mean_pooled = summed / counts
    return mean_pooled.numpy()
```

Fine-tuning for sentence/document similarity

- Use *Sentence-BERT* (SBERT) approach: start from RoBERTa/BERT and fine-tune with contrastive or triplet loss on sentence-pair datasets (STS, NLI). SBERT-style models give far better sentence/document vectors out-of-the-box than raw pooling.

2. DistilBERT — distilled efficiency

What it is: DistilBERT is a smaller, faster distilled version of BERT that retains much of BERT's language understanding at a fraction of the parameters. It's ideal when you need speed, lower memory, or CPU inference.

Trade-offs

- **Pros:** faster, cheaper inference, smaller model sizes; good for production at scale.
- **Cons:** slightly lower accuracy than full-sized models; still heavier than classical methods.

Embedding extraction is identical to BERT/RoBERTa (CLS pooling or mean pooling). For semantic tasks, consider using *DistilSBERT* (distilled sentence-transformer), which is pre-optimized for vector similarity.

3. Sentence-BERT

Important note: vanilla transformers (BERT/RoBERTa/DistilBERT) were not designed to produce high-quality sentence/document vectors via naive pooling. **Sentence-BERT (SBERT)** and related models are **fine-tuned specifically** for embeddings:

- They use siamese / triplet networks and similarity losses (contrastive, NLI) to ensure **cosine similarity** corresponds to semantic similarity.
- For retrieval and clustering tasks, **SBERT / all-MiniLM / Sentence-RoBERTa** are standard best-practice choices.

Example of using a sentence-transformer:

Step 3:

Example P3 – U3 – D32
NLP - Mean-pooled embeddings

```
# pip install sentence-transformers
from sentence_transformers import SentenceTransformer
model = SentenceTransformer("all-mpnet-base-v2")
emb = model.encode("This is an example document.", normalize_embeddings=True)
print(emb.shape)      # Shows vector size
print(emb[:10])       # Prints first 10 values
```

Output

Output

```
[-0.02136759 -0.11277164 -0.00104048  0.00767692 -0.05230137  0.02238057
  0.02716156  0.03409374 -0.03429943 -0.01421167]
```

Purpose:

To generate a meaning-based numerical representation of a single sentence.

Practical workflows & recommendations

Choosing a method

- **Small corpus, limited compute:** Doc2Vec or averaged pre-trained Word2Vec/FastText.
- **Moderate compute, need quality:** Sentence-BERT / SBERT variants (e.g., all-mpnet-base-v2, sentence-roberta-large) — great balance.
- **High-performance, accuracy-critical:** RoBERTa/large or fine-tuned transformer + SBERT-style training; use GPU and retrieval libraries.

- **Low-latency / high-volume production:** DistilBERT or distilled SBERT (all-MiniLM) for speed.

Pooling strategies (how to make a document vector)

- **[CLS] token:** model output for the special token. Works okay in many setups.
- **Mean pooling:** average token vectors, masking padding — robust baseline.
- **Max pooling:** highlight prominent features.
- **Weighted / attention pooling:** learn weights for tokens (requires fine-tuning).
- **SBERT pooling:** fine-tuned pooling layer optimized for semantic similarity.

Similarity, retrieval & scaling

- Use **cosine similarity** on normalized vectors for semantic similarity.
- For large-scale retrieval, use approximate nearest neighbour libraries: **FAISS**, **Annoy**, **HNSWlib** for sub-second searches on millions of vectors.
- Store embeddings (float32) and consider PCA or quantization for memory/latency trade-offs.

Evaluation

- **Intrinsic:** cosine similarity on labelled pair datasets, clustering purity.
- **Extrinsic:** downstream task performance — classification accuracy, retrieval MRR / MAP, clustering ARI/NMI — this is the most meaningful.

Fine-tuning & domain adaptation

- If you have labelled pairs (paraphrase, similarity, NLI), fine-tune a transformer with a contrastive loss to align embeddings with your domain semantics.

- For domain-specific corpora (legal, medical), pretrain or continue pretraining on domain data (masked language modelling) before fine-tuning for embeddings.

Comparative summary

Method	Pros	Cons	Good for
Doc2Vec	Lightweight, document-level learning	Corpus dependent, less contextual	When transformers are not feasible
Averaged Word2Vec/ GloVe	Fast, simple	Loses order & nuance	Baseline text classification
FastText	Handles morphology & OOV	Static vectors	Languages with rich morphology
RoBERTa (pooled)	Strong contextual understanding	Heavy compute	Deep semantic tasks; fine-tuned retrieval
DistilBERT (pooled)	Faster, smaller	Slightly less accurate	Production with latency constraints
SBERT/ Sentence Transformers	Optimized for similarity	Requires fine-tuning for the domain	Semantic search, clustering, semantic similarity

Sentence Transformer — get document embeddings

Example P3 – U3 – D33

NLP

```
# pip install sentence-transformers
from sentence_transformers import SentenceTransformer
model = SentenceTransformer('all-mpnet-base-v2')   # strong general-purpose model

docs = ["Doc A text ...", "Doc B text ..."]
```

```
embeddings = model.encode(docs, convert_to_tensor=False,
normalize_embeddings=True)
# embeddings is a numpy array; use cosine similarity for retrieval
```

Output

```
Output
[-0.02136759 -0.11277164 -0.00104048  0.00767692 -0.05230137  0.02238057
  0.02716156  0.03409374 -0.03429943 -0.01421167]
```

Purpose:

To represent **multiple documents** as vectors so we can compare them:

- Which document is most similar?
- Which document matches a query?
- Cluster similar documents together?

Key Insight

These embeddings **capture meaning**, not just word appearance.

Example:
"The cat sat on the mat."

and
"The kitten rested on the rug."

→ Different words, **similar meaning**, and therefore **similar embeddings**.

This is what makes SentenceTransformers more powerful than:

When to Use These Embeddings

Use them when you need **semantic understanding**, such as:

- Chatbots

- Search engines ("search by meaning")
- FAQ matching
- Duplicate question detection
- Knowledge base retrieval
- Recommendation systems

Master said, "Let us build a Semantic Search Engine and Cluster documents."

A Semantic Search Engine

Example P3 – U3 – D34

NLP

```
from sentence_transformers import SentenceTransformer
from sklearn.metrics.pairwise import cosine_similarity

docs = ["Apple releases new iPhone", "Bananas are healthy", "Apple is a tech
company"]
query = "fruit from trees"

model = SentenceTransformer('all-mpnet-base-v2')
doc_emb = model.encode(docs, normalize_embeddings=True)
query_emb = model.encode([query], normalize_embeddings=True)

# Compute similarity & get best match
scores = cosine_similarity(query_emb, doc_emb)[0]
best_index = scores.argmax()
print("Best match:", docs[best_index], " | Score:", scores[best_index])
```

Output

Output

```
Best match: Bananas are healthy | Score: 0.3915821
```

Cluster Documents + Visualize

Example P3 – U3 – D35

NLP

```
# pip install sentence-transformers sklearn umap-learn matplotlib
```

```
from sentence_transformers import SentenceTransformer
from sklearn.cluster import KMeans
import umap
import matplotlib.pyplot as plt

docs = ["text doc A", "another text doc B", "third text doc C", "..."]
model = SentenceTransformer('all-mpnet-base-v2')
emb = model.encode(docs, normalize_embeddings=True)

# Cluster
kmeans = KMeans(n_clusters=3)
labels = kmeans.fit_predict(emb)

# Reduce to 2D for visualization
points_2d = umap.UMAP(n_neighbors=10, min_dist=0.1).fit_transform(emb)

plt.scatter(points_2d[:, 0], points_2d[:, 1], c=labels)
plt.show()
```

Output

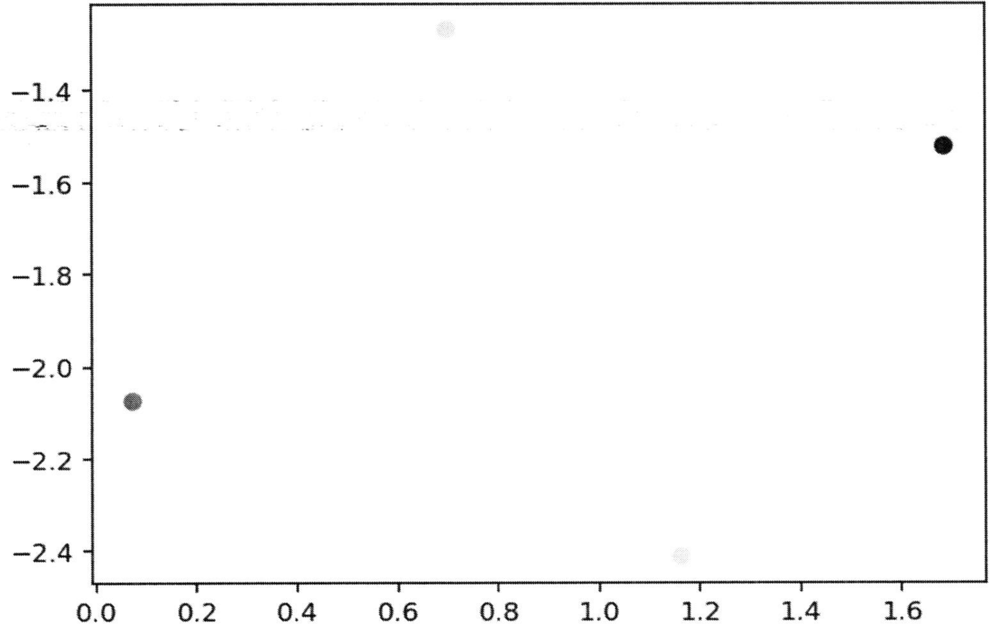

Summary:

This chapter introduces the foundational components of language processing systems: **NLP, NLU, and NLG**. *Natural Language Processing (NLP)* focuses on enabling machines to read and process human language, whereas *Natural Language Understanding (NLU)* deals with interpreting meaning, intent, and context. *Natural Language Generation (NLG)* involves producing coherent, human-like text in response.

The process begins with **text input and data collection**, followed by **text preprocessing**—a crucial stage where raw text is cleaned and standardised. This includes tokenization, lowercasing, stopword and punctuation removal, stemming, lemmatization, and normalization. After preprocessing, text must be converted into numerical form through **text representation** techniques such as Bag-of-Words (BoW), TF-IDF, one-hot encoding, POS tagging, n-grams, and syntactic or semantic feature extraction.

To capture deeper meaning, the chapter emphasises **text embedding techniques**, which map words into dense vector spaces. **Word embeddings** include Word2Vec (CBOW and Skip-Gram), GloVe, and fastText. **Pre-trained contextual embeddings** like ELMo and BERT capture word meaning based on context. **Document embeddings,** such as Doc2Vec, represent full sentences and documents, while advanced transformer-based models like RoBERTa and DistilBERT offer improved performance for modern language tasks.

What Next:

The upcoming section introduces foundational sequence models used in deep learning. It begins with **Recurrent Neural Networks (RNNs)**, explaining how they process sequential data, their unfolding over time, and the **Backpropagation Through Time (BPTT)** training method. It also covers different RNN architectures, such as **one-to-one**, **one-to-many**, **many-to-one**, and **many-to-many** models. To address RNN limitations in capturing long-term dependencies, **LSTM (Long Short-Term Memory)** networks are introduced, followed by **Bidirectional** and **Stacked LSTM** architectures for deeper learning. Finally, the section explains **GRU (Gated Recurrent Units)** with their mathematical intuition, and extends to **Bidirectional GRU** and **Stacked GRU** for enhanced sequence modeling.

P3-U3-L1-5 - Practice Question

1. What is the difference between NLU, NLP, and NLG?
2. Define Text Preprocessing and explain why it is needed.
3. What is Tokenization in text processing?
4. How does Lowercasing contribute to text normalization?
5. What is the purpose of Stopword Removal?
6. Explain the difference between Stemming and Lemmatization.
7. What is Text Normalization, and where is it used?
8. Define Bag of Words (BoW) representation.
9. How does TF-IDF improve upon BoW?
10. What are N-grams, and why are they useful?
11. What are Syntactic Features in NLP?
12. What are Semantic Features, and how do they differ from syntactic features?
13. What is POS Tagging, and why is it important?
14. Explain One-Hot Encoding in the context of text data.
15. What problem does Word Embedding solve?
16. Compare CBOW and Skip-gram models in Word2Vec.
17. What is the main idea behind GloVe embeddings?
18. How does fastText differ from Word2Vec?
19. What is meant by Pre-Trained Embeddings?
20. What is ELMo, and what makes it different from Word2Vec?
21. Define BERT, and explain why it is called bidirectional.
22. What are contextual embeddings?
23. What is the purpose of Doc2Vec?
24. How is RoBERTa different from BERT?
25. What is DistilBERT, and why is it used?
26. What is the role of Corpus in training NLP models?
27. Why is Vectorization essential for machine learning algorithms in NLP?
28. Explain how embeddings capture the semantic meaning of words.
29. Give an example of how NLP is used in everyday applications.
30. Describe how NLU is used in chatbots or virtual assistants.

PART FOUR

The Evolution of Memory in Machines

RNN | LSTM | GRU

In every recurrent model beats the same desire—to hold on to continuity, to trace meaning across the unfolding story of words, much like the human mind remembering what the heart felt long ago.

– Shree Shambav

PART FOUR

DAY TWELVE

Unit 4 - Lesson One

When Sequences Learn to Speak

Master said, "Apeksha, to truly understand NLP with Deep Learning, we must step beyond simple definitions and see *why* Deep Learning became essential in language understanding."

☐ NLP and the Need for Deeper Understanding

Natural Language Processing (**NLP**) is the branch of AI that enables machines to **work with human language**—to read, interpret, generate, summarize, translate, and respond meaningfully.
Traditional NLP relied heavily on **manual feature engineering**, where humans decided which patterns or keywords were important. This approach worked for simple tasks, but it struggled with:

- **Context** (e.g., *bank* → riverbank vs. financial bank)
- **Long sentences**
- **Ambiguity, sarcasm, metaphors, tone**

Human language is **rich, layered, emotional, cultural**, and sometimes **indirect**. Classical algorithms could not capture these complexities.

Master continued, "This is where Deep Learning (DL) transformed NLP."

Deep Learning is built upon **neural networks** that learn patterns **directly from data**, without requiring humans to define every rule.

As networks grow deeper, they begin to **extract hierarchical meaning**:

Neural Layer Level	**What it Learns**
Early layers	Letter and word patterns
Middle layers	Phrase, grammar, and sentence structure
Deep layers	Meaning, context, and intent

This ability to learn **language representation automatically** makes DL ideal for NLP.

Why We Need Different Deep Learning Models in NLP

Human language is sequential and context-dependent.

To understand a sentence, the meaning depends on the **order and relationships between words**.

Model	Key Idea	Strength
RNN (Recurrent Neural Network)	Processes text word-by-word in sequence	Remembers short context
LSTM (Long Short-Term Memory)	Enhanced memory mechanism	Remembers longer context; solves vanishing gradient issue
GRU (Gated Recurrent Unit)	Simpler than LSTM	Efficient training with similar performance

Illustration P6_deep_3: NLP

So different models evolved to handle different challenges:

Model	Key Idea	Strength
CNN (Convolutional Neural Network)	Learns local patterns in text	Useful for sentiment and classification
Transformer (Attention Mechanism)	Looks at all words at once and weighs importance	Captures long-range context; basis of GPT & BERT

Illustration P6_deep_4: NLP

Master said, "These models are not replacements for each other—they are *evolutions* addressing linguistic complexity."

Word Embeddings: The Foundation

Before deep learning, words were represented as **one-hot vectors**—simple and meaningless.

Deep Learning introduced **Word Embeddings**, which represent words in dense vector form where **semantic relationships are preserved**.

Examples:

Word	**Embedding Meaning**
King – Man + Woman = Queen	Embeddings capture **semantic relationships**
"happy" is closer to "joy" than to "chair"	Words are placed in meaningful **vector space**

As discussed, Popular embeddings:

- Word2Vec
- GloVe
- FastText
- BERT embeddings (contextual)

☐ Characteristics of NLP using Deep Learning

Characteristic	Explanation
Learns rich representations of language	Captures context, meaning, emotion, relationships
Reduces manual feature engineering	The model learns what is meaningful from raw text
Handles large-scale unstructured data	Can train on millions of sentences and improve automatically
Uses advanced neural architectures	RNN, LSTM, GRU, Transformer, etc.
Supports many task types	Sequence generation, classification, translation, reasoning
Employs word embeddings for representation	Represents language in meaningful vector space

Illustration P6_deep_5: NLP

Master added,

"This integration has revolutionized real-world applications."

Examples:

Application	Deep Learning Model Used	Result
Machine Translation (e.g., Google Translate)	Transformers	Fluid, context-aware translations
Sentiment Analysis (e.g., Movie Reviews)	LSTMs / BERT	Detects tone, emotion
Chatbots & Voice Assistants	Transformers (GPT, BERT)	Human-like conversation
Text Summarization	Sequence-to-Sequence models	Creates readable abstracts
Search Engines	BERT Ranking Models	Understands intent, not just keywords

Illustration P6_deep_6: NLP

☐ Working of Deep Learning based NLP

Master smiled and said, "Akshaya — to *see* deep learning working on language, you must watch a quiet pipeline move from raw noise to informed prediction. Let us walk through each stage — not only *what* happens, but *why*, *how*, and the practical choices that change outcomes."

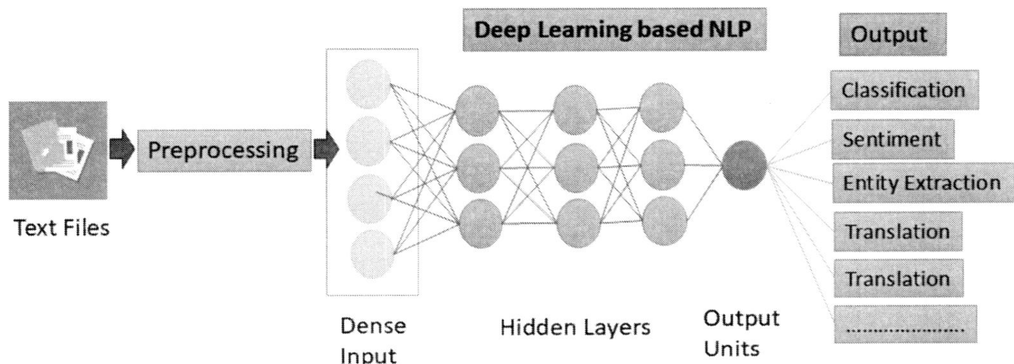

Illustration P6_deep_1: NLP

Let us understand each phase with deep context, concrete examples, common choices, pitfalls, and practical tips. I'll use two running examples to make ideas concrete:

- **Sentiment classification** (short text → label), and
- **Machine translation** (sequence → sequence).

1. Text preprocessing — cleaning and conditioning the signal

Purpose: convert raw human text (noisy, inconsistent) into a reliable input format for models.

Typical steps

- **Normalization:** lowercasing (unless case matters), Unicode normalization, and collapsing whitespace.

  Example: "I'm" → "i'm" (or preserve case for named-entity tasks).

- **Tokenization:** splitting text into tokens. Choices matter:
    - **Word-level** (simple, but large vocab).
    - **Subword / BPE / WordPiece / Unigram** (handles rare words, common in transformers).
    - **Character-level** (robust to misspellings, used for morphologically rich languages).
      Example for translation: Byte-Pair Encoding gives a stable vocab across languages.
- **Cleaning:** remove or normalize URLs, emails, noisy markup; decide whether to keep punctuation/emojis (often useful for sentiment).
- **Stopword removal/filtering:** usually used in classical NLP; in DL pipelines, you often keep stopwords — models learn which tokens matter.
- **Normalization for numbers/dates:** map "$10" → "<MONEY>" if needed for generalization.
- **Data augmentation (optional):** back-translation, random deletion/substitution — can help low-resource tasks.

Practical tip: choose tokenization to match your model. Pretrained transformers expect their own tokenizer — use it.

2. Text representation — turning words into vectors

Purpose: map discrete tokens to a dense numerical space that the model can manipulate.

Approaches

- **Static embeddings:** Word2Vec, GloVe — one vector per word type. Good for smaller models or when resources are limited.
- **Subword embeddings:** FastText (adds character n-gram signals). Handles OOVs better.

- **Contextual embeddings:** BERT, RoBERTa, and GPT produce token vectors that *depend on surrounding words*. These are state of the art for most tasks.

Example: In sentiment classification, the word "cold" will have different vectors in "a cold drink" vs. "a cold person" when using contextual embeddings.

Practical tip: for downstream tasks, you can either (a) freeze embeddings and train a classifier on top, or (b) fine-tune the whole embedding+model stack for best performance.

3. Model selection — matching architecture to the task

Core families

- **RNN / LSTM / GRU:** sequential processing, good for streaming or where sequence order is critical. Historically strong for Seq2Seq translation with attention.
- **CNNs for text:** capture local n-gram patterns; efficient for classification tasks (sentiment, topic).
- **Transformers (self-attention):** model relationships at all distances simultaneously. Default choice for translation, summarization, QA, and many classification tasks.
- **Encoder-decoder (Seq2Seq):** common for generation tasks (translation, summarization). Can be LSTM-based or Transformer-based.

Choosing a model

- Short, local patterns → CNN or small Transformer.
- Long-range dependencies, context-rich tasks → Transformer.
- Resource constraints → lightweight models, distillation, or smaller LMs.

Example choices

- Sentiment: small Transformer or BiLSTM + attention.
- Translation: Transformer encoder-decoder (e.g., T5, Marian).

4. Training — the loop that teaches the model

Core elements

- **Data:** quality and annotation matter more than raw size. Balanced labels, clean alignments (for translation), and diverse examples help generalization.
- **Loss functions:**
  - Classification → cross-entropy.
  - Sequence generation → teacher forcing with cross-entropy; sometimes combine with coverage or auxiliary losses to avoid repetition.
  - Language modelling → negative log-likelihood / cross-entropy.
- **Optimization:** Adam / AdamW are standard. Learning rate schedules (warmup + decay) are crucial for Transformers.
- **Batching & padding:** handle variable length sequences via masks; use bucketing if needed for efficiency.
- **Regularization:** dropout, weight decay, label smoothing (for generation).
- **Checkpointing & early stopping:** monitor validation loss/metric to avoid overfitting.

Practical training recipe (Transformer)

1. Use pretrained encoder/decoder weights (transfer learning).
2. Use AdamW with learning rate warmup (e.g., 10k steps) then cosine decay.
3. Batch size: as large as GPU memory allows; use gradient accumulation if needed.
4. Validate frequently; save best checkpoints by validation metric (BLEU for translation, F1/accuracy for classification).

5. Fine-tuning — adapt a general model to a task

Why: pretrained LMs learn general language; fine-tuning adapts them to your labels or domain with much less data and compute.

How to fine-tune

- Freeze lower layers initially (optional), then unfreeze and fine-tune the full model.
- Use a smaller learning rate for pretrained weights, larger for task-specific heads.
- Use data augmentation or domain adaptation when labelled data is scarce.

Example: Fine-tune BERT on a domain-specific sentiment dataset (medical reviews) — often yields dramatic improvements over training a model from scratch.

6. Evaluation — measure what matters

Classification metrics

- **Accuracy:** overall correctness (good for balanced data).
- **Precision / Recall / F1:** important for imbalanced classes.

Sequence generation metrics

- **BLEU:** n-gram overlap (machine translation).
- **ROUGE:** recall-oriented overlap (summarization).
- **METEOR / chrF:** alternatives that handle morphology/word order better in some contexts.

Language model metrics

- **Perplexity:** lower is better; measures predictive confidence of the LM.

Task-specific

- **Exact Match / F1** (QA), human evaluation (fluency, adequacy), fairness, and bias checks.

Practical note: automatic metrics are useful but imperfect — human evaluation remains essential for generation tasks.

7. Prediction & Decoding — turning probabilities into text

For classification: choose argmax, possibly calibrate probabilities (Platt scaling or temperature scaling).

For generation (seq2seq): decoding strategies

- **Greedy decoding:** fastest, picks the highest-prob token each step (may be short/low quality).
- **Beam search:** keeps top-k hypotheses, balances diversity and probability (standard for translation).
- **Sampling:** sample from distribution — useful for creative generation.
- **Top-k / Top-p (nucleus) sampling:** restrict sampling to most likely tokens (controls randomness).

Example: For translating a news sentence, beam search (beam=5) with length penalty yields high-quality output; for storytelling, top-p sampling produces more variety.

8. Deployment & Serving — make the model useful in production

Considerations

- **Model size & latency:** compress via quantization, pruning, knowledge distillation (TinyBERT, DistilBERT).
- **Serving frameworks:** TensorFlow Serving, TorchServe, ONNX Runtime, or Hugging Face Inference endpoints.
- **Scalability:** use batching, autoscaling, and GPU inference for throughput.
- **Monitoring:** track drift, latency, errors, and fairness metrics.
- **Safety:** content filters, fallback rules, rate limiting, and human-in-the-loop for critical domains.

Practical tip: export a distilled/quantized model for edge devices and a full model for server inference.

9. Error analysis & iteration

Activities

- **Confusion matrix** for classification; inspect frequent error types.
- **Case study for generation:** examine hallucinations, incorrect facts, or grammatical errors.
- **Domain diagnostic:** are errors concentrated on a subdomain or entity type?
- **Data augmentation / targeted labelling:** correct model blind spots by adding targeted examples.

Master's guidance: spend at least as much time on error analysis and data curation as on model tweaking.

10. Ethical, linguistic & practical concerns

- **Bias & fairness:** embeddings can encode social biases—test and mitigate.
- **Privacy:** avoid training on sensitive data without consent; consider differential privacy.
- **Robustness:** adversarial inputs, misspellings, or code-switching hurt models—test these cases.
- **Explainability:** for high-stakes tasks, use attention visualizations, LIME/SHAP, or simpler models for interpretability.

Master said, "Akshaya, deep-learning NLP is a choreography — preprocessing sings with tokenizers, representations hum as embeddings, and models learn the choreography of meaning. But the music is imperfect: measure, debug, and care for fairness. When you combine rigorous data work with powerful models and responsible deployment, machines begin to speak and understand more like humans — but always under our careful stewardship."

☐ Techniques Used in NLP with Deep Learning

"**Nikash,**" the Master began, "techniques in deep-learning NLP are the tools that let machines *feel* patterns in language — not by rules, but by learned representations. Each technique answers a specific weakness of earlier approaches, and together they form the practical toolbox of modern NLP. Let us walk through them with clarity, examples different from the earlier list, practical notes, and when to use each."

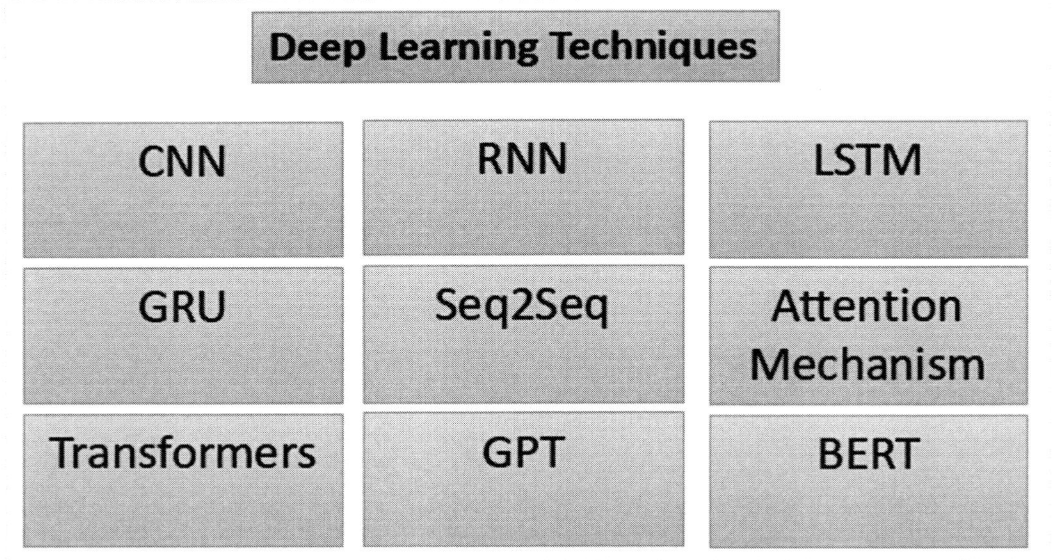

Illustration P6_deep_2: NLP

1. **Word embeddings — giving words meaning in numbers**

What:

Dense vector representations where geometry encodes semantics: similar words live near each other.

Classic models: Word2Vec (CBOW / Skip-Gram), GloVe, FastText (subword-aware).

Example: In a good embedding space, *surgeon* − *doctor* + *teacher* ≈ *professor* — semantic arithmetic shows relationships.

Why it matters:

Reduces vocabulary sparsity; gives downstream models meaningful continuous inputs.

Practical notes:

- **Static** embeddings (Word2Vec/GloVe) give one vector per type — cheap, fast, good for smaller tasks.
- **Subword** embeddings (FastText) handle typos and morphologically rich languages by composing n-grams.
- **Contextual** embeddings (BERT/GPT) supersede static ones by giving *token-in-context* vectors — much better for ambiguity.

2. Recurrent networks — sequence-aware memory
What:

Neural architectures that process sequences step-by-step, maintaining a hidden state that carries past information.

Variants: Vanilla RNN, LSTM (memory gates), GRU (simpler gates).

Concrete example: Predicting the next word in a poem — LSTM can remember the subject across several lines, preserving agreement and tense.

Strengths: Good for streaming, time-series, and tasks where order matters.

Limitations: Difficult to parallelize; long-range dependencies were hard before gating and attention.

Practical tip: Use RNNs for low-latency streaming tasks (speech recognition), but prefer Transformers for offline, high-accuracy models.

3. Attention mechanisms — selective focus
What:

Mechanisms that let models weigh the relevance of other tokens when processing a token.

Core formula (conceptual):

$$\text{Attention}(Q, K, V) = \text{softmax}\left(\frac{QK^T}{\sqrt{d_k}}\right)V$$

Where Q = queries, K = keys, V = values; d_k is the key dimension.

Why it matters:

Rather than only depending on nearby tokens, attention lets each token look anywhere in the sequence and learn which words matter.

Example: In the sentence "The lawyer who visited Paris presented her paper," attention helps link **her → lawyer** even across intervening phrases.

Multi-head attention: allows the model to capture different types of relations in parallel (syntax, coreference, topic).

4. Transformers — attention as architecture (the revolution)

What:

Architectures built around self-attention and feedforward layers. Processes tokens in parallel, uses positional encodings to keep order.

Why it replaced RNNs for many tasks:

- Fully parallelizable → faster training on GPUs/TPUs.
- Excellent at modeling long-range dependencies.
- Scales very well with model size and data.

  Example usage: Translation (encoder-decoder transformers), classification and retrieval (encoder-only like BERT), and generation (decoder-only like GPT).

  Practical notes: positional encodings (sinusoidal or learned) are essential; compute & memory grow quadratically with sequence length — use efficient variants (Longformer, Performer) for very long documents.

5. Sequence-to-Sequence (Seq2Seq) & encoder-decoder models

What:

An encoder converts input to a representation; a decoder generates output from that representation, often with attention between them.

Classic tasks: Machine translation, abstractive summarization, question generation.

Example: For summarization — encoder ingests a long article, decoder produces a concise abstract token by token using attention over encoder states.

Practical tip: Transformer-based encoder-decoder (e.g., T5, Marian) is are current best practice; beam search and length penalties help decoding quality.

6. Pre-trained language models (PLMs) — transfer at scale

What:

Models trained on huge unlabeled corpora with self-supervised objectives; later fine-tuned for downstream tasks.

Two families:

- **Masked/bi-directional (BERT-style):** trained to predict masked tokens — good for understanding tasks.
- **Autoregressive (GPT-style):** trained to predict next token — good for generation.

  Example: Fine-tuning BERT for medical NER requires far less labeled data than training from scratch.
- **Practical techniques:** adapters, LoRA, prompt-tuning — parameter-efficient methods that avoid full fine-tuning for large models.

  Practical trade-off: PLMs give huge gains but require compute and careful handling to avoid overfitting, leakage, and bias amplification.

7. Transfer learning & fine-tuning strategies

What:

Reuse pretrained weights, then adapt to specific tasks.

Strategies:

- Full fine-tune (all weights),
- Freeze base layers and train task-specific head,
- **Adapters / LoRA / prefix-tuning** — low-parameter updates for large models.

When to use: Full fine-tune when you have enough labeled data and compute; adapters or LoRA for low-resource or expensive models.

8. Regularization, optimization & training aids

Key techniques: dropout, label smoothing, gradient clipping, weight decay, learning-rate warming, and scheduling (warmup + decay).

Why: Stabilize training, prevent overfitting, and handle unstable gradients common in large Transformer training.

Practical: AdamW is the standard optimizer for Transformers; careful LR schedules (linear warmup) are essential.

9. Decoding & generation controls

Methods: greedy, beam search, top-k sampling, top-p (nucleus) sampling, temperature scaling.
Example choices:

- Use **beam search** for accurate translations;
- Use **top-p sampling** with temperature for creative story generation.

Practical warning: generation can hallucinate factual errors — apply constraints, rerankers, or grounding sources for factual tasks.

10. Evaluation & metrics — measure what you value

Classification: accuracy, precision, recall, F1.

Generation: BLEU, ROUGE, METEOR, chrF, plus human evaluation for fluency & faithfulness.

Understanding & retrieval: Exact Match, MRR, MAP.

Practical note: automatic metrics are imperfect — human judgment is required for high-level tasks (summarization, dialog).

11. Efficiency & scaling techniques

Why important: Large models are expensive. Practical techniques:

- **Distillation:** train smaller student models from larger teachers (DistilBERT).
- **Quantization & pruning:** reduce model size/latency for deployment.
- **Sparse / mixture-of-experts:** conditional compute to scale capacity efficiently.
- **Memory & retrieval augmentation:** RAG (retrieve & generate) to offload knowledge to an index and avoid huge parameter counts.

12. Robustness, bias mitigation & safety techniques

Common issues: adversarial inputs, social bias, privacy leakage, and hallucinations.

Mitigations: adversarial training, data filtering, bias audits, differential privacy, factual grounding, and human-in-the-loop review.

Practical policy: test on distribution shifts and adversarial examples before deployment.

When to pick which technique — quick guide

- **Small dataset, classification:** fine-tune a pretrained encoder (BERT), maybe freeze base.

- **Long documents:** use hierarchical models or efficient attention variants.
- **Real-time streaming:** RNNs/GRUs or small transformers with distillation.
- **Creative generation:** autoregressive models (GPT) with nucleus sampling.
- **Low compute / mobile:** distilled + quantized models.

Short annotated examples (conceptual)

- **Embedding example: vec("doctor") close to vec("nurse")**

Attention formula (core):

$$\text{Attention}(Q, K, V) = \text{softmax}\left(\frac{QK^T}{\sqrt{d_k}}\right)V$$

V — the engine of Transformers.

Decoding example: beam_search (model, beam=5) for translation.

"**Nikash,** each technique is a compromise between data, compute, latency, and the kind of language understanding you need. The art is in composing them wisely: embeddings to represent, attention to relate, transformers to model, and transfer learning to scale. But always pair power with careful evaluation, fairness checks, and human judgment."

Master said, "Apeksha, deep learning did not just *improve* NLP — it transformed it.

The shift was not about better computation, but a better understanding of language itself.

Now, a machine does not just see text.

It recognises meaning.

It senses intent.

It understands relationships.

And it learns—continuously."

PART FOUR

DAY THIRTEEN

Unit 4 - Lesson Two

Echoes Through Time - RNN

"An RNN flows like a river through time—each drop carrying whispers of the past, yet often losing its clarity as it travels farther from its source."

- Shree Shambav

☐ Sequence model

Master looked up with a slow, steady smile and said, "Sam, a sequence model is a kind of machine that understands *ordered data* — things where position and order matter. When you read a sentence, hear a melody, or track a stock price, the order of tokens or values is essential. Sequence models are the architectures and methods that let machines learn patterns that unfold over time or position."

Below, let us unfold the idea with depth, intuition, formal notes, examples, strengths/limitations, and practical guidance — all in a way that reveals *why* sequence models behave as they do and *how* to use them.

What is a sequence model? — the idea

A **sequence model** maps input sequences to outputs. Inputs and outputs can each be sequences or a single value:

- **Input → Single output:** e.g., classify an entire sentence as positive/negative sentiment.
- **Sequence → Sequence:** e.g., translate English → French, generate music notes.
- **Streaming / online:** predict next value given past values (language modeling, time-series forecasting).

Key property: the model's prediction at time/index *t* can (and often should) depend on previous elements (t−1, t−2, …), and sometimes on future elements (bidirectional contexts).

Intuition — why ordinary feedforward nets are not enough

A feedforward network treats each example independently. For ordered data, you need memory or mechanisms that **carry information across positions**. Sequence models provide that memory: they accumulate context, remember patterns, and condition outputs on order.

☐ Common architectures (with intuition & when to use)

1. Recurrent Neural Networks (RNNs)

Intuition: read sequence token-by-token, carrying a hidden *state* that summarizes the past.

Update (simplified):

$$h_t = f(W_h \cdot h_{t-1} + W_x \cdot x_t + b)$$
$$y_t = g(V \cdot h_t)$$

Where h_t is the hidden state at time t, x_t input, and f nonlinearity.

Here, y_t represents the output at time t. The matrix 'V' is a weight matrix that transforms the hidden state h_t into the output space, and 'g' is the activation function applied to this transformed value.

After the hidden state is multiplied by a weight matrix V, the result is still a **raw linear value**. However, neural networks need **non-linearity** to learn meaningful patterns.

Use when: streaming tasks, simple sequence dependencies, learning compact recurrence.

Limitation: suffers from vanishing/exploding gradients for long dependencies.

2. LSTM (Long Short-Term Memory) & GRU

Intuition: gated RNNs that control what to forget, what to keep, and what to expose — allowing longer-range memory.

Why gates matter: they let the model protect important information across many steps (solve the vanishing gradient problem in practice).

When to use: sequences with medium-to-long dependencies; tasks where order matters but you don't need full Transformer capacity.

3. Temporal Convolutional Networks (TCN) / 1D CNNs

Intuition: use convolutional filters over time to capture local patterns; with depth and dilation, you can capture long ranges.

Strengths: parallelizable, stable gradients, efficient.

When to use: audio, time series forecasting, when you want a deterministic receptive field.

4. Attention & Transformers (self-attention)

Intuition: every position can *attend to* every other position with learned weights. No recurrence; process all tokens in parallel.

Why this matters: captures long-range dependencies directly and is highly parallelizable — the modern standard for many NLP problems.

When to use: machine translation, summarization, language modeling, and most tasks where large-context reasoning is needed.

5. Hybrid & advanced models

- **Encoder–Decoder (Seq2Seq):** encoder compresses input to context; decoder generates output step-by-step, often with attention.
- **Retrieval-augmented models:** combine retrieval (external knowledge) with generative decoders.
- **State-space / linearized architectures:** new efficient ways to model very long sequences (for very long documents or signals).

Concrete examples

1. **DNA sequences:** predict whether a genetic segment encodes a promoter. Order and local motifs matter (TCN/CNN or Transformer with k-mer embeddings).
2. **Music generation:** given a melody, continue it — generation is sequence→sequence with long-range harmonic dependencies (Transformer or LSTM with attention).
3. **Stock price forecasting:** predict next-day price using previous days — temporal patterns and seasonality, often modeled with TCNs or RNNs plus exogenous features.
4. **Dialogue systems:** maintain conversation state and generate context-aware replies — requires discourse memory (attention + memory modules).

Mathematical & training notes

- **Teacher forcing:** during seq2seq training, feed the true previous token to the decoder. Speeds training but can create exposure bias at inference.
- **Scheduled sampling:** gradually replace true previous tokens with model predictions during training to reduce exposure bias.

- **Losses:** usually cross-entropy for classification/generation; for forecasting, could use MSE/MAE.
- **Regularization:** dropout in recurrent/transformer layers, label smoothing (for generation), gradient clipping for RNN/LSTM.

Evaluation metrics

- **Classification:** accuracy, F1, precision/recall.
- **Sequence generation:** BLEU (translation), ROUGE (summarization), chrF, and human evaluation for fluency/faithfulness.
- **Forecasting:** RMSE, MAE, MAPE.
- **Language modeling:** perplexity.

Challenges & practical solutions

1. **Long-range dependencies:**
    - o Problem: RNNs forget.
    - o Solutions: LSTM/GRU, attention, Transformer, or hierarchical models.
2. **Computational cost/memory:**
    - o Problem: Transformers scale quadratically with sequence length.
    - o Solutions: sparse/efficient attention (Longformer, Reformer), chunking, retrieval-augmented generation.
3. **Exposure bias (generation):**
    - o Problem: model never sees its own errors during training.
    - o Solutions: scheduled sampling, reinforcement learning (e.g., policy gradient for sequence-level objectives), minimum risk training.
4. **Alignment (seq2seq):**
    - o Problem: mapping variable-length inputs to outputs.
    - o Solutions: attention, pointer networks (for copying), monotonic attention for streaming.

Practical recipes & tips

- **Start with pretrained transformers** for most NLP sequence tasks (fine-tune BERT/T5/GPT depending on task).
- **For streaming / low-latency** applications, consider RNNs/GRUs or distilled/smaller transformer variants.
- **Use subword tokenization** (BPE/WordPiece) to handle rare words and control vocabulary size.
- **Batch sequences by similar length** (bucketing) to improve GPU utilization.
- **Monitor validation metrics per step and use early stopping**; save checkpoints and keep a small test suite of hard examples.

A short mental model (how to choose)

- Need generation with rich context → **Transformer encoder-decoder or autoregressive Transformer**.
- Need real-time low-latency output → **RNN/LSTM or streaming transformer**.
- Need efficient long context → **sparse/long-range transformer** or retrieval + generator.
- Need explainability & small compute → **smaller LSTM/CNN with interpretable features**.

"Sam, sequence models are not a single magic tool but a family of instruments — each tuned to different tempos and textures of ordered data. Learn the simple recurrence (RNN) to feel how memory flows, learn gated cells (LSTM/GRU) to hold memory steady, and learn attention/Transformers to conduct many voices at once. For the craftsman, the real skill is picking the right instrument, tuning it with proper data and training, and listening carefully to the mistakes."

☐ RNN

Apeksha asked, "Master, what makes RNNs necessary when working with sequential data?"

Master said,

"Apeksha, Recurrent Neural Networks (RNNs) are designed specifically for situations where the order of information matters. In many real-world tasks, data comes in sequences — such as words in a sentence, frames in a video, or notes in a musical composition. The meaning of the current element often depends on what came before it. Standard neural networks treat each input independently and cannot maintain such a memory of prior steps. This is where RNNs become essential."

Understanding the Need for RNNs

In a traditional feedforward neural network, data flows strictly in one direction:

Input→Hidden Layer→Output

Each input is processed in isolation. There is **no concept of time** or **context**.

But **language, speech, and time-series tasks demand context**:

- The meaning of a word depends on previous words.
- The tone of a sentence depends on earlier statements.
- Predictions in financial data depend on past trends.

RNNs introduce a **recurrent connection** that loops information back into the network.

This gives the model a **memory**, allowing it to retain information from earlier steps.

Let's understand RNN with an example.

Master continued, "Imagine reading a sentence and trying to predict the next word. You don't look at just the current word — your understanding is built from **the entire sentence so far**."

For example:

"The cat sat on the __."

To predict the missing word, you use *memory of previous words* to infer that the likely word is *"mat"*.

RNNs work in exactly this way.

At each time step:

- They take the **current input**.
- They combine it with the **memory of what has already been processed**.
- They update the hidden state, which carries context forward.

$$h_t = f(Wx_t + Uh_{t-1} + b)$$

Where:

x_t = current input

h_{t-1} = memory from the previous step

h_t = updated memory (context)

This **hidden state flows across time**, allowing the network to build meaning gradually.

In essence

RNNs preserve and propagate context, enabling machines to:

- Understand sentences
- Predict the next event in a sequence
- Generate text
- Perform speech recognition
- Analyze time-series data

Without RNNs, machines would treat language and sequential patterns as *disconnected pieces*, losing meaning and coherence.

Why RNNs Are Important for Sequential Data

Feature	Standard Neural Network	RNN
Handles sequences	No	Yes
Remembers past inputs	No memory	Maintains contextual memory
Suitable for text, speech, and time-series	Poor performance	Designed for sequential dependencies
Understands context	Independent inputs	Context-aware predictions

Master said, "RNNs are necessary because they bring the dimension of time and memory into neural networks, enabling deep understanding of sequences — just as the human mind remembers what came before to make sense of what comes next."

Key Components of RNNs

Master said,

"There are mainly two core components of Recurrent Neural Networks (RNNs) that allow them to learn from sequential data. Let us understand each with clarity and depth."

1. Recurrent Neurons (Recurrent Units)

The central processing element of an RNN is the **Recurrent Unit**.

Unlike a standard neural network neuron that processes input only once, a recurrent neuron is designed to **retain** information from previous steps.

Each recurrent neuron maintains an internal **hidden state**:

$$h_t=f(Wx_t+Uh_{t-1}+b)$$

Where:

x_t = input at the current time step

h_{t-1} = hidden state from the previous time step (memory)

h_t = updated hidden state at this step

W and U = learnable weight matrices

f(·) = activation function (commonly tanh or ReLU)

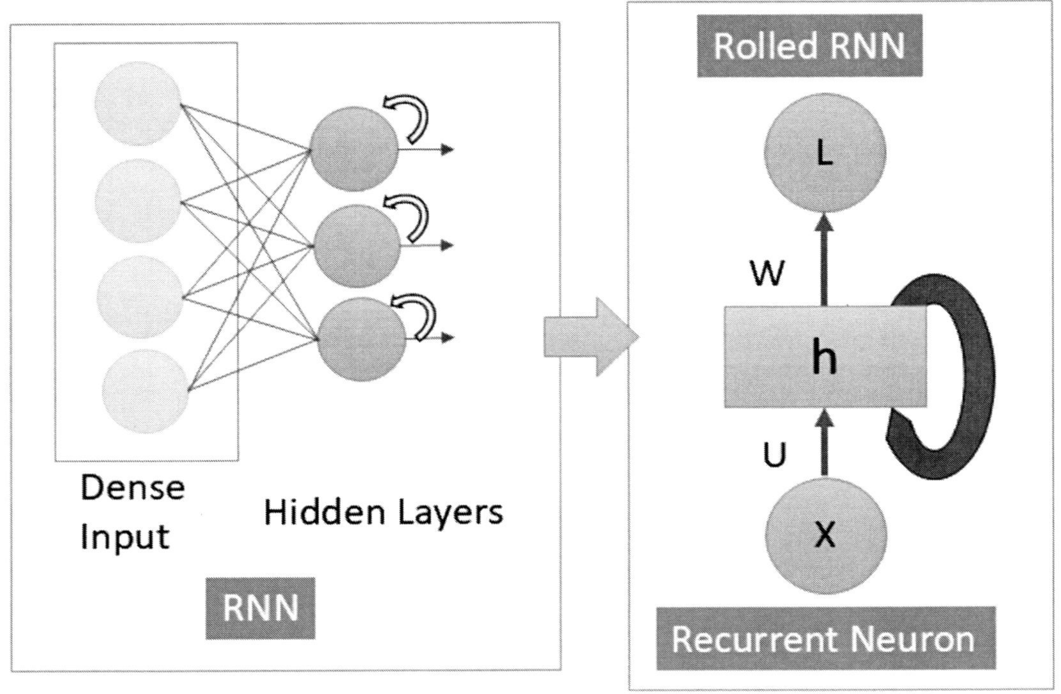

Illustration P6_RNN_2: RNN

This diagram represents a **single recurrent neuron** in an RNN. Each symbol corresponds to a **weight matrix or component** involved in computing the hidden state and the output.

Here's what each one means:

Symbol	Meaning	Role in the RNN
X	Input at the current time step (x_t)	The current data fed into the network (e.g., a word, value, signal).
h	Hidden state (h_t)	The neuron's internal memory that carries information across time steps.
L	Output (y_t)	The result is produced at each time step (e.g., classification, next value).
U	Input-to-Hidden weight matrix	Used to transform the input (x_t) before it influences the hidden state.
V	Hidden-to-Hidden (Recurrent) weight matrix	Controls how the *previous hidden state* influences the *current hidden state*. Enables memory.
W	Hidden-to-Output weight matrix	Used to transform the hidden state into the output (y_t).

The updated equations for the above illustration

$$h_t=f(Ux_t+Vh_{t-1})$$
$$y_t=g(Wh_t)$$

Where:

- f = activation for hidden state (often **tanh** or **ReLU**)
- g = activation for output (like **softmax**, **sigmoid**, etc.)

Intuition (Simple Explanation)

- **U** tells the neuron how to read the **current input**.
- **V** tells it how much to remember from the **past**.
- **W** tells it how to convert **memory** into **output**.
- **L** is simply the **output**.

This is what gives RNNs their **memory across time**—the loop formed by **V** keeps information flowing from past to present.

This **hidden state acts as memory**, allowing the RNN to:

- Recall information from earlier in the sequence
- Understand context
- Capture dependencies over time

Master said, "Think of the hidden state as a traveler who carries knowledge from the past into the present. At each step, the traveler learns something new but never forgets what was learned before—unless the new learning overwrites it."

This memory mechanism is what enables RNNs to understand **sentences, audio sequences, and temporal patterns**.

2. RNN Unfolding (Unrolling Through Time)

Although RNNs are drawn as a single repeating unit, in reality, when processing a sequence, the same recurrent unit is **replicated across time**.

This is called **Unfolding (or Unrolling)**.

For a sequence of length *T*, the RNN is unfolded into *T* layers—**one for each time step**—all sharing the **same weights**.

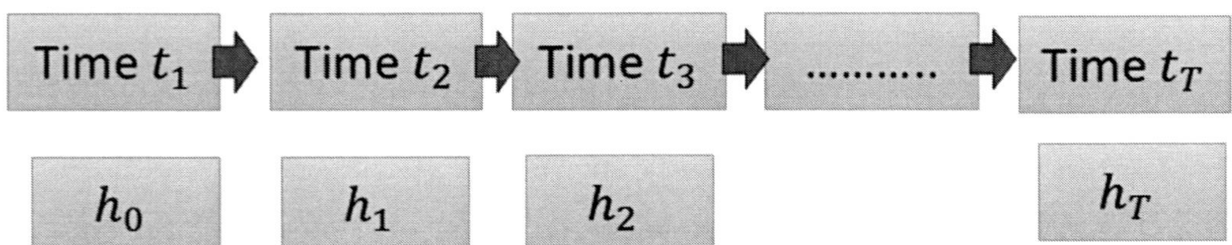

Illustration P6_RNN_1: RNN

This representation makes two things possible:

Forward Flow of Information

- Hidden states pass context from one step to the next.

- The model builds meaning progressively.

Backward Flow of Error (Backpropagation Through Time - BPTT)

- Once the output error is calculated, the learning process works **backwards** across all time steps.
- This allows the network to **update weights based on contributions from previous inputs**.

This training method is called **Backpropagation Through Time (BPTT)**.

Master said, "Unrolling makes the RNN transparent across time. It shows how each moment influences the next. Just as memory shapes understanding in life, each hidden state shapes the prediction of the next."

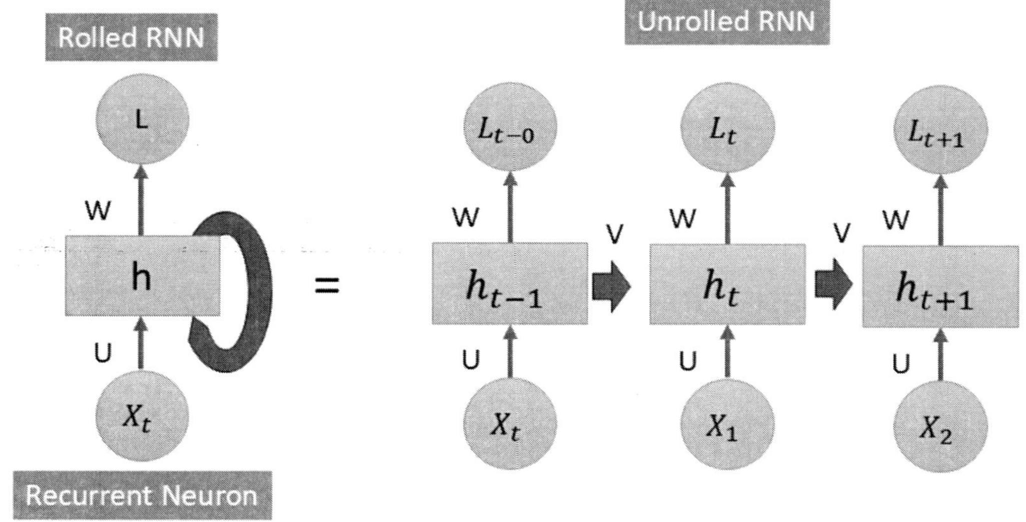

Illustration P6_RNN_1: RNN

Why These Components Matter

Concept	Purpose	Benefit

Recurrent Neurons	Store evolving memory of past inputs	Enable contextual understanding
Unrolling + BPTT	Train network over time steps	Learn relationships across long sequences

In Essence

RNNs are powerful because:

- They **preserve memory** of previous steps.
- They **propagate context across time**.
- They **learn patterns in sequences** through unrolling and backpropagating error.

Master said, "RNNs do not simply process information—they *remember* it.

This memory is what allows language to be understood, music to be composed, sequences to be predicted, and meaning to unfold across time."

Understanding the Recurrent Neural Network (RNN) Architecture

Master said, "Let us now look into how the inner structure of an RNN operates. Many understand RNNs at the surface level, but to truly appreciate their power, we must observe how information flows and evolves across time."

Key Insight

Traditional neural networks treat each input as **independent**, with no memory of what came before.

RNNs, however, are designed to process **sequences**—text, speech, time-series data—where **past information matters** for understanding the present.

The innovation lies in **sharing weights** across time steps and maintaining a **hidden state** that carries context forward.

Flow of Information in an RNN

An RNN processes input one step at a time.

At each time step *t*:

- It takes the current input x_t
- It receives memory from the previous step h_{t-1}
- It updates the new memory state h_t
- It generates an output y_t

This creates a loop — *the essence of recurrence.*

Hidden State Update

The hidden state is the heart of an RNN.

It captures the **context**, the **memory** of previous inputs.

$h_t=\sigma(Ux_t+Wh_{t-1}+B)$

Where:

Symbol	Meaning
(h_t)	Current hidden state (memory at time t)
(x_t)	Input at time t
(h_{t-1})	Previous hidden state (memory carried forward)
(U)	Weight matrix applied to the current input
(W)	Weight matrix applied to the previous hidden state
(B)	Bias term
(σ)	Activation function (often tanh or ReLU)

Master said, "Notice how the hidden state not only depends on the current input but also on what was learned earlier. This is how RNNs *remember*."

Output Calculation

Once the hidden state is computed, the network produces its output:

$y_t=O(Vh_t+C)$

Symbol	Meaning
(y_t)	Output at time t
(V)	Output layer weight matrix
(C)	Output layer bias
(O)	Activation function (e.g., softmax for classification)

The hidden state acts as the **bridge** between input and output.

Overall RNN Function

The overall operation of the RNN across all time steps can be represented as:

$Y=f(X, h, U, W, V, B, C)$

Here:

- X is the entire sequence of inputs.
- h is the evolving internal memory.
- U, W, V, B, C are the trainable parameters.
- f represents the unfolding computation across time.

The RNN maintains a **state matrix**, where each element s_i represents the model's memory at time step i.

Why Shared Weights Matter

In traditional feed-forward networks:

- Each layer has its *own set* of weights.

In RNNs:

- The *same* weights U, W, and V are used at **every time step**.

This ensures:

- The model treats each step consistently
- The model learns patterns that generalize across time
- Memory flows smoothly through the sequence

Master summarized:

"The shared weights of an RNN allow the past to influence the present.

They form a chain of memory that weaves meaning through time."

Essence of the Architecture

Component	Role	Purpose
Hidden State	Stores memory	Captures sequential context
Shared Weights	Reuse parameters across time	Ensures consistent behavior
Recurrence Loop	Feedback connection	Enables memory flow
Unrolling	Expands RNN across time	Allows training via Backpropagation Through Time

RNNs are powerful because they are **not just processing information**— they are **carrying forward meaning**, shaping understanding at each step.

They do not see words as isolated tokens.

They see **sentences as evolving thoughts**.

Master smiled and said, "**Nikash,** remembering is not a single trick — it is the art of carrying useful impressions of the past forward and blending them with the present. An RNN remembers by maintaining an internal state that is continually updated as it reads the sequence. Let me unfold this slowly — concept, math, strengths, limits, remedies, and intuition — so you truly feel how memory lives inside the RNN."

1. The core idea (intuition)

An RNN does not treat each input independently. At each time step, it keeps a **hidden state** — a compact summary of "what it has seen so far." That hidden state flows forward, is combined with the new input, and becomes the new memory. This repeated update is how the network **accumulates context over time** and uses past information when making predictions.

Think of the hidden state as a running note in a song that is revised each beat — it carries the melody forward so future notes make sense.

2. The core equations

At time step t:

State update (generic):

$h_t = f(h_{t-1}, x_t)$

A common concrete form is:

$ht = \tanh(W_{hh} h_t - 1 + W_{xh} x_t + b_h)$

Output:

$y_t = g(W_{hy} h_t + b_y)$

- xt - input vector at time t
- ht−1 - previous hidden state (memory)
- ht - new hidden state (updated memory)

- W_{xh}, W_{hh}, W_{hy} - learned weight matrices
- b_h, b_y - biases
- tanh (or ReLU) - activation for the hidden state
- g - output activation (softmax, sigmoid, identity, depending on task)

This recurrence means the same parameters are used every step: the model learns *how* to update memory regardless of when in time.

3. How this produces "memory" in practice

- Each h_t is a nonlinear summary of the entire prefix $x_1, x_2, \ldots, x_t$.
- When computing y_t, the model uses h_t, thus allowing predictions to be influenced by all earlier inputs through the chain of hidden states.
- The recurrence allows information to **propagate** forward; relevant signals are amplified by learned weights and activations, while irrelevant signals fade.

Master said, "Let us understand how an RNN updates and carries its hidden state step-by-step, using a PyTorch example to demonstrate it.

Example P4 – U4 – D1

RNN - PyTorch

```
import torch
import torch.nn as nn

# Example sentence (tokenized as word indices for simplicity)
# Let's pretend vocabulary: {I:0, love:1, NLP:2}
inputs = torch.tensor([0, 1, 2])  # "I love NLP"
inputs = inputs.unsqueeze(1)      # Shape: (sequence_length, batch_size)

# RNN Model
input_size = 3     # vocab size (embedding-like one-hot input)
hidden_size = 5    # size of RNN memory state
rnn = nn.RNN(input_size, hidden_size)

# Convert tokens to one-hot vectors
one_hot = torch.zeros(inputs.size(0), inputs.size(1), input_size)
```

```
one_hot.scatter_(2, inputs.unsqueeze(2), 1)

# Initial hidden state (starts as zeros)
h_prev = torch.zeros(1, 1, hidden_size)

print("Initial Hidden State:\n", h_prev)

# Process sequence step-by-step
for t in range(len(one_hot)):
    x_t = one_hot[t].unsqueeze(0)   # shape (1, batch, input_size)
    h_t, h_prev = rnn(x_t, h_prev)

    print(f"\nStep {t+1} Input Word:", ["I", "love", "NLP"][t])
    print("Hidden State h_t:\n", h_t)
```

Output:

Output

```
Initial Hidden State:
 tensor([[[0., 0., 0., 0., 0.]]])

Step 1 Input Word: I
Hidden State h_t:
 tensor([[[-0.7956, -0.0721,  0.1493, -0.5313, -0.1156]]],
       grad_fn=<StackBackward0>)

Step 2 Input Word: love
Hidden State h_t:
 tensor([[[-0.6080,  0.2895,  0.4292, -0.1350,  0.5519]]],
       grad_fn=<StackBackward0>)

Step 3 Input Word: NLP
Hidden State h_t:
 tensor([[[-0.6232,  0.2430,  0.3608,  0.3026,  0.5644]]],
       grad_fn=<StackBackward0>)
```

Master said, "Let us understand how an RNN updates and carries its hidden state step-by-step, using a Tensorflow example to demonstrate it.

Example P4 – U4 – D2

RNN - TensorFlow

```
import torch
import tensorflow as tf

# Example sentence (tokenized as word indices)
```

```
# Vocabulary: {I:0, love:1, NLP:2}
inputs = tf.constant([0, 1, 2])  # shape (sequence_length,)

# Model parameters
input_size = 3     # vocab size (same as PyTorch example)
hidden_size = 5    # hidden state size

# Convert tokens to one-hot vectors
one_hot = tf.one_hot(inputs, input_size)  # shape (sequence_length, input_size)
one_hot = tf.expand_dims(one_hot, axis=1)  # (sequence_length, batch=1, input_size)

# Define RNN layer (return state after every time step)
rnn = tf.keras.layers.SimpleRNN(hidden_size, return_state=True,
return_sequences=True)

# Initial hidden state (zeros)
h_prev = tf.zeros((1, hidden_size))  # shape (batch, hidden_size)
h_prev = tf.expand_dims(h_prev, axis=0)  # shape (1, batch, hidden_size)

print("Initial Hidden State:\n", h_prev.numpy())

# Process step-by-step manually using cell call
rnn_cell = rnn.cell

hidden_state = tf.squeeze(h_prev, axis=0)  # convert to shape (batch, hidden_size)

vocab_words = ["I", "love", "NLP"]

for t in range(one_hot.shape[0]):
    x_t = one_hot[t]  # shape (batch, input_size)
    x_t = tf.expand_dims(x_t, axis=0)  # shape (1, batch, input_size)

    # RNN cell computation: (output, next_state)
    output, hidden_state = rnn_cell(x_t, hidden_state)

    print(f"\nStep {t+1} Input Word:", vocab_words[t])
    print("Hidden State h_t:\n", output.numpy())
```

Output:

Output
Initial Hidden State: [[[0. 0. 0. 0. 0.]]] Step 1 Input Word: I Hidden State h_t: [[[0.39281452 0.6541984   0.10843038 0.29828817 -0.00970613]]]

```
Step 2 Input Word: love
Hidden State h_t:
 [[[-0.35179895  0.59733844  0.4914678   0.69370323  0.29544276]]]

Step 3 Input Word: NLP
Hidden State h_t:
 [[[-0.75738883 -0.18036339 -0.73739254  0.1282994   0.93503505]]]
```

4. Backpropagation Through Time (BPTT) — learning what to remember

Training uses gradients that are propagated backward across time steps — this is **BPTT**. The algorithm attributes the error at time t to earlier states and inputs by unrolling the network in time and applying standard backpropagation. Thus, the model learns which past patterns are useful for future predictions.

After a pause.

Master said, "John, let us understand Backpropagation Through Time (BPTT) in RNNs."

Recurrent Neural Networks are unique because they do not simply process data in a single forward pass like traditional feed-forward neural networks. Instead, they process **sequences** step-by-step, where each step depends on the previous one.

This means the hidden state h_t at time t is influenced by:

$$h_t = f(W_{xh} x_t + W_{hh} h_{t-1} + b_h)$$

Because each hidden state depends on earlier states, the **loss at the final time step** is influenced by **all previous states**. Therefore, when adjusting the network's parameters, we must take into account **how every past state contributed to the final prediction**.

This is where **Backpropagation Through Time (BPTT)** comes in.

Why BPTT is Needed

Master said:

"To learn from a chain, we must travel backwards along that chain."

Unlike normal backpropagation, which flows backward through layers, **BPTT flows backward through time steps**:

$$h_3 \rightarrow h_2 \rightarrow h_1 \rightarrow h_0$$

Each hidden state influences the next one, so the loss function has a dependency like:

L(θ) depends on h_3, which depends on h_2, which depends on h_1,…

Thus, gradients must be passed backward **through every time step**.

Core Gradient Flow

The gradient of the loss with respect to the RNN weights is:

$$\frac{\partial L(\theta)}{\partial W} = \frac{\partial L}{\partial h3} \cdot \frac{\partial h_1}{\partial W}$$

But h3 depends on h_2, h_1, h_0, so we must include these dependencies:

$$\frac{\partial h_3}{\partial W} = \frac{\partial h_3}{\partial W} + \frac{\partial h_3}{\partial h_2} \cdot \frac{\partial h_2}{\partial W} + \frac{\partial h_3}{\partial h_2} \cdot \frac{\partial h_2}{\partial h_1} \cdot \frac{\partial h_1}{\partial W} + \dots$$

This expresses both:

- **Explicit gradients** (direct effect of weights at each step)
- **Implicit gradients** (indirect effect through previous hidden states)

Final General Gradient Expression

$$\frac{\partial L(\theta)}{\partial W} = \sum_{t=1}^{T} \left(\frac{\partial L}{\partial h_T} \cdot \prod_{k=t+1}^{T} \frac{\partial h_k}{\partial h_{k-1}} \cdot \frac{\partial h_t}{\partial W} \right)$$

This summation represents:

- Every hidden state h_t
- Every path of influence from ht to the final state hT

Intuition

"The RNN carries memory.

When we correct the network, we must correct the memory as well.

Therefore, we do not walk backward across layers —

We walk backward across **time**."

Master said, "Let us understand a simple and clear Python implementation of BPTT from scratch using NumPy."

Here example uses a small RNN with:

- One input unit
- One hidden unit
- One output unit

So you can clearly see how the gradients flow back through time.

Example P4 – U4 – D3	
RNN - BPTT	**Output**

import numpy as np
 	
# ---- Step 1: Define Activation Functions ---- 	
 	
def sigmoid(x):
   return 1 / (1 + np.exp(-x))
 	
def dsigmoid(y):
   return y * (1 - y)   # derivative using output of sigmoid
 	
# ---- Step 2: Define Inputs and Targets (Simple Sequence) ---- 	
	Forward Outputs: [0.37829685 0.34503962 0.38176478]
	Loss: 0.23927531535922109
	
	Updated Weights:
	W_xh = -0.4826509769991255
	W_hh = -0.0985176187060866
	W_hy = -1.3056232911427907

```
x = np.array([1, 0, 1])     # input sequence
y_true = np.array([0, 1, 0]) # target output sequence

# ---- Step 3: Initialize RNN Parameters ----

W_xh = np.random.randn()   # weight input →
hidden
W_hh = np.random.randn()   # weight hidden →
hidden
W_hy = np.random.randn()   # weight hidden →
output

learning_rate = 0.1

# ---- Step 4: Forward Pass (Record hidden states) -
---

h = np.zeros(len(x) + 1)   # hidden states (include
h_0)
y_pred = np.zeros(len(x))  # outputs

for t in range(len(x)):
    h[t+1] = sigmoid(W_xh * x[t] + W_hh * h[t])  #
hidden state update
    y_pred[t] = sigmoid(W_hy * h[t+1])          #
output prediction

print("Forward Outputs:", y_pred)

# ---- Step 5: Compute Loss (mean squared error) --
--

loss = np.mean((y_pred - y_true) ** 2)
print("Loss:", loss)

# ---- Step 6: Backpropagation Through Time
(BPTT) ----

dW_xh = 0
dW_hh = 0
dW_hy = 0

# Start from the last time step and go backward
for t in reversed(range(len(x))):

    # Output gradient
    dy = (y_pred[t] - y_true[t]) * dsigmoid(y_pred[t])
```

```
    dW_hy += dy * h[t+1]

    # Hidden gradient
    dh = dy * W_hy * dsigmoid(h[t+1])

    # Accumulate gradients for weights
    dW_xh += dh * x[t]
    dW_hh += dh * h[t]

# ---- Step 7: Update Weights ----

W_xh -= learning_rate * dW_xh
W_hh -= learning_rate * dW_hh
W_hy -= learning_rate * dW_hy

print("\nUpdated Weights:")
print("W_xh =", W_xh)
print("W_hh =", W_hh)
print("W_hy =", W_hy)
```

Master said, "Let us understand using PyTorch."

Example P4 – U4 – D4

RNN - BPTT	**Output**

```
import torch

# ---- Step 1: Input and Targets ----
x = torch.tensor([1.0, 0.0, 1.0])        # input sequence
y_true = torch.tensor([0.0, 1.0, 0.0])   # target output

# ---- Step 2: Initialize Parameters (1 hidden unit RNN) ----
W_xh = torch.randn(1, requires_grad=True)   # input → hidden
W_hh = torch.randn(1, requires_grad=True)   # hidden → hidden
W_hy = torch.randn(1, requires_grad=True)   # hidden → output

learning_rate = 0.1

# ---- Step 3: Forward Pass (Store states) ----
h = torch.zeros(1)   # h0
h_list = []          # store hidden states for BPTT
```

```
Predictions: tensor([[0.5136],
        [0.5078],
        [0.5166]])
Loss: 0.25439536571502686

Updated Weights:
W_xh: -0.5909976959228516
W_hh: 0.594086766242981
W_hy: -0.09789004921913147
```

```
y_pred_list = []    # store outputs

for t in range(len(x)):
    h = torch.tanh(W_xh * x[t] + W_hh * h)  #
hidden state update
    y_pred = torch.sigmoid(W_hy * h)        # output
    h_list.append(h)
    y_pred_list.append(y_pred)

y_pred = torch.stack(y_pred_list)

print("Predictions:", y_pred.data)

# ---- Step 4: Compute Loss ----
loss = torch.mean((y_pred - y_true) ** 2)
print("Loss:", loss.item())

# ---- Step 5: Backpropagation Through Time
(Automatic) ----
loss.backward()

# ---- Step 6: Update Weights ----
with torch.no_grad():
    W_xh -= learning_rate * W_xh.grad
    W_hh -= learning_rate * W_hh.grad
    W_hy -= learning_rate * W_hy.grad

# ---- Important: Clear Gradients for Next Pass ----
W_xh.grad.zero_()
W_hh.grad.zero_()
W_hy.grad.zero_()

print("\nUpdated Weights:")
print("W_xh:", W_xh.item())
print("W_hh:", W_hh.item())
print("W_hy:", W_hy.item())
```

The important idea:

When going backward, each time step influences earlier hidden states.

Step	**Meaning**
Forward Pass	Computes hidden states and outputs for each time step

Loss	Measures the difference between predicted and true values
Backward Pass (BPTT)	Moves backward through time, updating gradients
Weight Update	Learns from all time steps collectively

Even though this uses only 1 hidden unit, it clearly demonstrates how RNNs *remember* previous steps and how gradients are updated through the entire sequence.

Key Understanding

- RNNs store information in hidden states.
- The final output depends on many past states.
- To update weights correctly, we must backpropagate errors **through all those past states**.
- This process is called **Backpropagation Through Time (BPTT).**

5. The practical limits — vanishing & exploding gradients

A crucial challenge: as gradients are backpropagated through many steps, they can:

- **Vanish** (become extremely small) → the network cannot learn long-range dependencies.
- **Explode** (grow huge) → weights diverge, training becomes unstable.

These are consequences of repeatedly multiplying Jacobian matrices across time.

Consequences: Simple RNNs often struggle to remember information across long gaps (e.g., remembering a word from 50 steps ago).

Master said, **"Akshaya, let us now understand one of the most important challenges in RNNs — the *Vanishing* and *Exploding* Gradient Problem."**

Why Does This Problem Occur?

RNNs learn by **Backpropagation Through Time (BPTT)** — meaning the gradient has to flow backward across many time steps.

But each time the gradient flows backward, it is multiplied repeatedly by weight matrices and activation derivatives.

If these values are:

- **Less than 1** → gradients become **smaller and smaller** → *they vanish*
- **Greater than 1** → gradients **grow uncontrollably** → *they explode*

1. Vanishing Gradient Problem

Definition

The gradients **shrink** to extremely small values as they propagate backward through many time steps, becoming nearly **zero**.

Consequence

The RNN **forgets long-term dependencies**.

It can only learn relationships that occur **very close in time** (short-term memory).

Why It Happens

Hidden state update:

$$h_t = \tanh\left(W_{hh}h_{t-1} + W_{xh}\, x_t\right)$$

During backpropagation:

$$\frac{\partial L}{\partial w_{hh}} \propto (tanh'\ (a))^t$$

Since:

$|\tanh'(a)| \leq 1$

Repeated multiplication makes gradient → **0**

Example (Intuition)

If at every step the gradient becomes **0.9** of the previous:

$0.9^{50} \approx 0.005$

Almost no learning happens from earlier steps.

2. Exploding Gradient Problem

Definition

The gradients **grow extremely large** as they propagate backward, becoming **infinite or unstable**.

Consequence

Training becomes **unstable**:

- weights become extremely large
- output becomes NaN

The network fails to learn

Why It Happens

If repeated multiplication is with values **> 1**

$1.2^{50} \approx 9{,}100$

Gradients **blow up**.

The Core Issue

RNNs try to **remember context** through repeated multiplication across time.

But multiplication over many steps can either **diminish** or **inflate** values — leading to **vanishing** or **exploding** gradients.

How Do We Fix This?

Problem	Solution	How It Helps
Vanishing Gradients	LSTM / GRU	Gate mechanisms preserve long-term memory
Exploding Gradients	Gradient Clipping	Limits gradient size during training
Both	Xavier / He Initialization	Prevents extreme starting weights
Both	Using ReLU instead of tanh	Reduces the shrinkage of gradients

Why LSTM/GRU Were Invented

LSTMs introduce a **memory cell** and **gates** that:

- decide what to store,
- what to forget,
- and what to output.

This prevents gradients from shrinking to zero.

Simple Analogy

Vanishing Gradient: Like trying to recall a dream — the more time passes, the more the memory fades.

Exploding Gradient: Like anger — if it keeps escalating without control, it becomes destructive.

Master said, "RNNs learn by remembering the past, but remembering is a fragile act.

When memory fades, learning weakens — when memory overwhelms, learning collapses.

Thus, we design models like LSTM to *balance memory with wisdom.*"

6. Remedies: gated RNNs and other techniques

To address these limits, practitioners use:

LSTM (Long Short-Term Memory)

- Adds explicit gates (forget, input, output) and a cell state ctc_tct that flows with linear interactions, making it easier to preserve gradients and store long-term information.
- Intuitively: gates decide what to keep, what to discard, and what to expose.

GRU (Gated Recurrent Unit)

- A simpler gated unit combining forget and input operations into update/reset gates — often matches LSTM performance with fewer parameters.

Other techniques

- **Gradient clipping** (limit gradient norm) to prevent exploding gradients.
- **Proper initialization** of weights and use of layer normalization.
- **Attention / Transformer**: allows direct access to distant positions; they often replace RNNs when long-range context is crucial.
- **Skip connections, highway layers, and memory-augmented networks** for specialized memory needs.

7. A worked example (language intuition)

Sentence:

"Alice went to the kitchen. She took the cake and left."

To answer "Who took the cake?" the model must connect "She" to "Alice" across the intervening clause. The hidden state after "Alice went to the kitchen." should contain a representation that identifies the salient referent "Alice" so that when "She" appears, the network can resolve it correctly.

Gated RNNs or attention help maintain such referent information across time.

8. Memory timescales and capacity

- **Short-term memory**: recent tokens produce strong, high-fidelity signals in ht
- **Long-term memory**: information that must survive many updates requires either strong gating (LSTM/GRU) or architectural support (attention, external memory).
- **Capacity** is finite — the hidden vector has limited dimensions, so the network must learn to compress and prioritize information.

9. Theoretical perspective

An RNN is a **discrete-time dynamical system** where the hidden state evolves under a learned, nonlinear map. Memory is the internal trajectory of this dynamical system; training sculpts this map to preserve and transform the aspects of the past relevant to future tasks.

10. Practical tips for making RNNs remember better

- Use **LSTM or GRU** whenever you need medium to long-term dependencies.
- Apply gradient clipping to stabilize training: torch.nn.utils.clip_grad_norm_(model.parameters(), max_norm).
- Use **dropout** carefully (recurrent dropout variants) to regularize.
- For very long-range dependencies, **prefer attention-based models** or hybrid architectures (RNN + attention).
- **Monitor gradients** across time during debugging to detect vanishing/exploding behavior.

- Use **curriculum learning** or auxiliary tasks to teach the model to retain specific facts.

11. Visualization & debugging ideas

- Track how the hidden state cosine-similarity to a target vector evolves across steps (does a certain concept persist?).
- Probe the model with controlled inputs (insert a marker token and see how long its effect lasts).
- Inspect gate activations in LSTM/GRU to see when the model chooses to remember vs. forget.

Master said, "An RNN remembers by maintaining and updating a hidden state that flows forward through time. This hidden state acts as a learned memory buffer: it is updated by combining the previous memory and the new input. The learning algorithm (BPTT) teaches the network which information to keep or discard. For practical long-term memory, gated cells (LSTM/GRU), attention mechanisms, or hybrid architectures are usually necessary. Memory is not binary — it is graded, selective, and learned."

Master smiled and said, "Nikash — to choose the right RNN for a problem, you must first understand the shape of the data: how many items come in, and how many come out — and then how time and context must be preserved between them. Let us walk through the canonical RNN *I/O patterns* and their important variants, with deep context, intuition, equations, and concrete examples."

☐ Types of Recurrent Neural Networks

RNNs are commonly described by the **mapping pattern** between input(s) and output(s) across time. We classify them by how many inputs and outputs appear and where the temporal structure lies. For each type, let us understand: (1) a formal description, (2) practical use-cases, (3) examples, and (4) typical architectures or enhancements you might combine with them.

1. One-to-One

Description: A single input → single output.

Formula (static): y = f(x) — no recurrence needed.

When used: This is actually *not* a sequential model in practice — it's a standard feedforward mapping. We list it for completeness because it sits in the spectrum of sequence models.

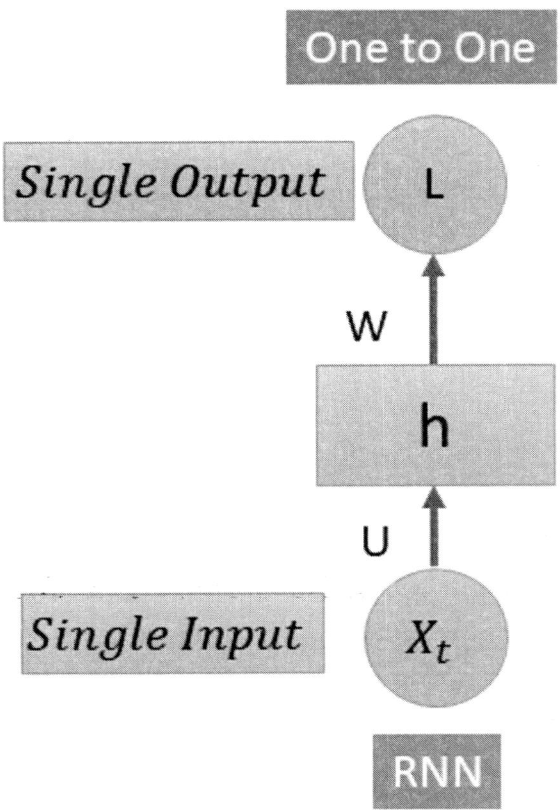

Illustration P6_RNN_5: RNN

Example use-cases:

- Binary classification of a fixed-size vector (spam vs. not spam).
- Image classification (single image → single label).

Notes: If your problem truly has one input and one output with no temporal structure, use a feedforward/CNN/transformer suitable to the modality rather than an RNN.

2. One-to-Many

Description: A single input produces a sequence of outputs over time. The model uses one input as initial context and then generates a sequence step-by-step.

Formal idea:

- Input: x (single item)
- At t = 1..T: $h_t = f(h_{t-1}, y_{t-1})$ and $y_t = g(h_t)$ where h_0 is initialized from the input x.

Common architecture: Encoder (process input) → Decoder (recurrently generate outputs). The decoder is usually autoregressive (previous output fed as next input).

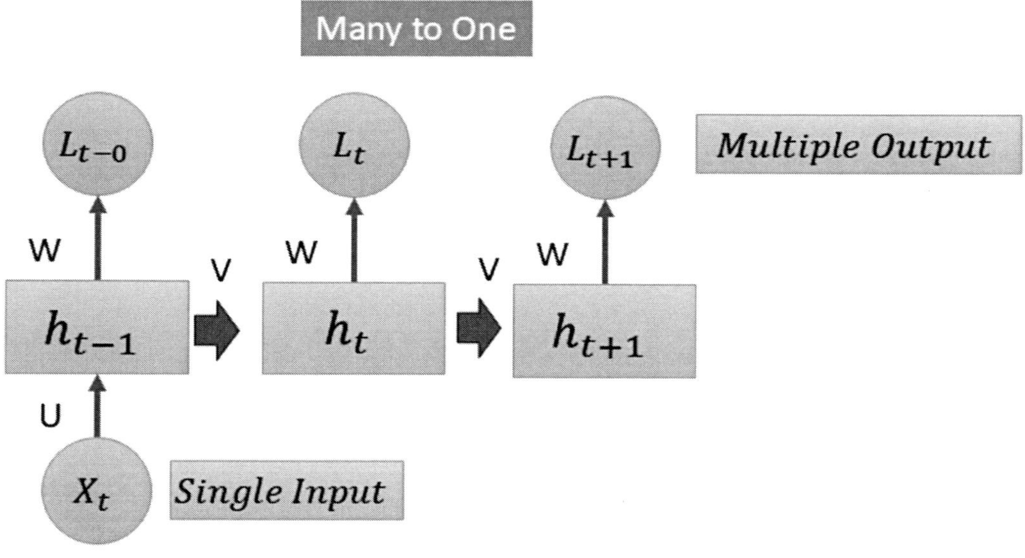

Illustration P6_RNN_6: RNN

Real-world examples:

- **Image captioning:** Single image → sequence of words describing it. The image is encoded (CNN) to a vector, which initializes an RNN/LSTM decoder that emits a caption word-by-word.

- **Music from a motif:** A short motif or theme generates a longer musical sequence.

Pros & challenges:

- Great for generation tasks where the sequence is produced conditioned on one context.
- Requires careful decoding (beam search, temperature) and often attention improves results (decoder attending back to encoded input features).

3. Many-to-One

Description: A whole sequence of inputs is consumed and a single output is produced after (or at) the end. The RNN compresses the sequence into a final representation, which is then mapped to the single output.

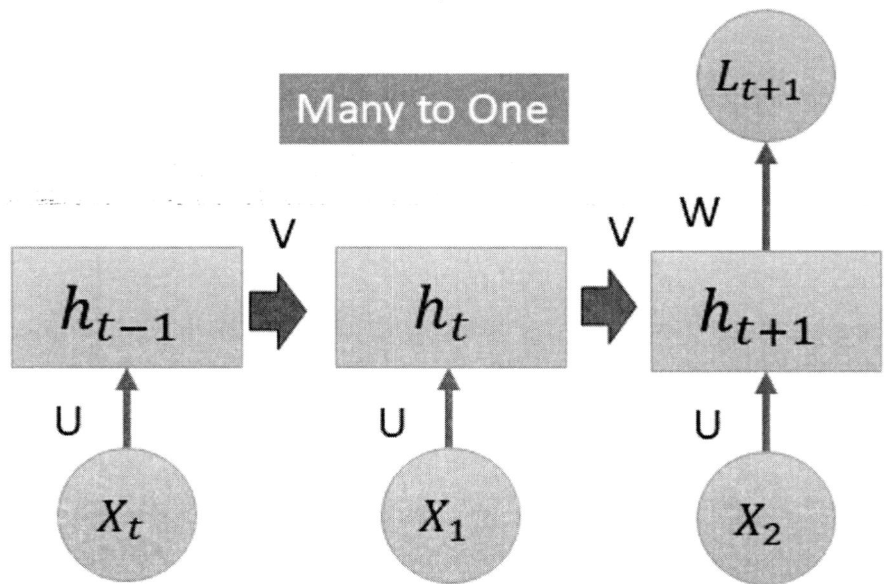

Illustration P6_RNN_8: RNN

Formal idea:

For inputs $x_1, x_2, \ldots, x_T$:
$h_t = f(h_{t-1}, x_t)$ for t=1 ..T
$y = g(h_T)$

Common use-cases:

- **Sentiment analysis:** Sentence (sequence of words) → one sentiment label (positive/negative/neutral).
- **Sequence-level classification:** Speaker identification from an audio clip, fraud detection from transaction sequences, and mortality prediction from patient time series.

Concrete examples:

- Movie review: sequence of tokens → single label "positive".
- Predicting whether a stock will rise tomorrow using the last N days of prices → single binary prediction.

Architectural variants:

- Use bidirectional RNNs to read sequences in both directions, then pool/fuse hidden states ($h=[\overrightarrow{h_t} ; \overleftarrow{h_1}]$).
- Use attention pooling over all h_t instead of just h_T — often yields better performance because it lets the model focus on important time steps.

4. Many-to-Many

Description: A sequence of inputs maps to a sequence of outputs. This pattern has two primary flavors:

a) Synchronized (aligned) Many-to-Many

- Input and output sequences have the same length and are aligned stepwise.
- Example: **Part-of-speech tagging** — each input token → one POS tag at the same time step.
- Formal: $y_t=g(h_t)$, where $ht=f(h_{t-1},x_t)$.

b) Unaligned (seq2seq) Many-to-Many

- Input sequence and output sequence lengths differ (or are not aligned).
- Uses encoder-decoder.
- Example: **Machine translation** — a sentence in English → a sentence in French (different lengths, reordering). Attention mechanisms are typically used so the decoder can attend to encoder states.

Concrete examples:

- **Synchronized:** Named Entity Recognition (token sequence → entity label per token).
- **Seq2Seq:** Translation, abstractive summarization, speech recognition (audio frames → text tokens).

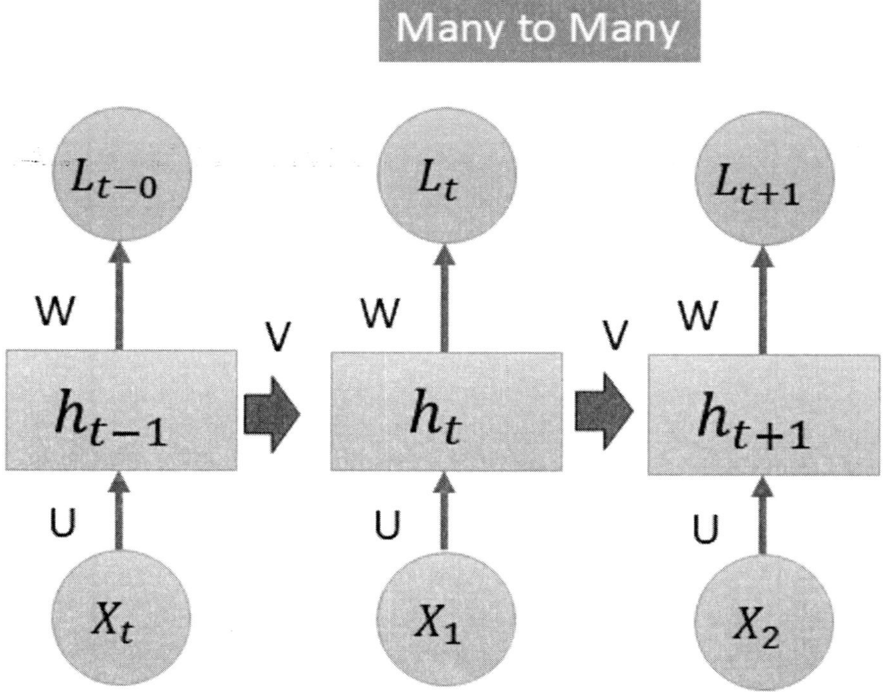

Illustration P6_RNN_7: RNN

Architectural notes:

- For seq2seq, modern design is Transformer encoder-decoder; older designs use LSTM/GRU encoder-decoder with attention.
- Decoding strategies (beam search, sampling) are important for quality in generative many-to-many tasks.

☐ Important RNN Variants & Enhancements (cross-cutting)

These patterns describe I/O shapes. Real systems combine them with architectural choices:

• Bidirectional RNNs

- Read sequences forward and backward and concatenate states.
- Useful in many-to-one and synchronized many-to-many tasks where full context is available (not for online streaming).
- Example: POS tagging, NER, sentence classification.

• Stacked (Deep) RNNs

- Multiple recurrent layers stacked to learn hierarchical temporal features.
- Each layer processes the sequence of hidden states from the layer below.

• Encoder–Decoder (Seq2Seq) with Attention

- Encoder compresses input to states; decoder generates output conditioned on encoder states via attention.
- Important for one-to-many and unaligned many-to-many.

• Conditional RNNs & Context Vectors

- Condition generation on additional metadata (style, speaker ID) by injecting conditioning vectors into the initial hidden state or at each step.

• Hybrid Models

- CNN + RNN (CNN extracts local features; RNN models sequence across time).

- RNN + Attention + External memory (e.g., pointer networks, memory-augmented neural nets).

☐ **Practical guidance: how to choose the type**

- **If you need a single label from a sequence** → Many-to-One (use pooling/attention if needed).
- **If you need a label per token** → Synchronized Many-to-Many (use bidirectional RNNs + CRF for sequence labeling).
- **If you must generate a sequence from one input** → One-to-Many (encoder → autoregressive decoder).
- **For translation or generation where input and output lengths differ** → Seq2Seq Many-to-Many with attention / Transformer.

Worked examples

1. **Emotion detection (Many-to-One):**

   Input: ["That", "movie", "made", "me", "cry"] → Output: sad
   Use: BiLSTM → attention → dense → softmax.

2. **POS tagging (Synchronized Many-to-Many):**

   Input: ["He", "runs", "fast"] → Output: ["PRON", "VERB", "ADV"]
   Use: BiLSTM + CRF to enforce tag constraints.

3. **Image captioning (One-to-Many):**

   Input: Image → Encoder (CNN) → vector → Decoder (LSTM) → Output: ["A", "dog", "runs", "in", "the", "park"].

4. **Machine translation (Seq2Seq Many-to-Many):**

   Input: English sentence → Transformer encoder → Transformer decoder → Output: French sentence.

Case 1: Many-to-One RNN (Sentiment Classification)

Input: sequence of words → Output: single label (positive/negative)

Example P4 – U4 – D5

RNN – Many to One

```
from tensorflow.keras.models import Sequential
from tensorflow.keras.layers import Embedding, SimpleRNN, Dense
from tensorflow.keras.preprocessing.text import Tokenizer
from tensorflow.keras.preprocessing.sequence import pad_sequences
import numpy as np

# -----------------------------
# 1) Build Model - Many to One
# -----------------------------
vocab_size = 10000
embedding_dim = 64
sequence_length = 50  # max words per sentence

model = Sequential([
    Embedding(input_dim=vocab_size, output_dim=embedding_dim,
input_length=sequence_length),
    SimpleRNN(128),   # returns only final hidden state → Many-to-One
    Dense(1, activation='sigmoid')
])

model.compile(optimizer='adam', loss='binary_crossentropy', metrics=['accuracy'])
model.summary()

# -----------------------------
# 2) Create Tokenizer & Fit on Sample Data
# (You MUST train the tokenizer on your training text)
# -----------------------------
training_sentences = [
    "I love this movie",
    "This movie is amazing and wonderful",
    "I hate this movie",
    "This film is bad and boring"
]

training_labels = np.array([1, 1, 0, 0])  # 1=Positive, 0=Negative

tokenizer = Tokenizer(num_words=vocab_size, oov_token="<UNK>")
tokenizer.fit_on_texts(training_sentences)

# Convert training text → sequences
train_sequences = tokenizer.texts_to_sequences(training_sentences)
```

```
train_padded = pad_sequences(train_sequences, maxlen=sequence_length,
padding='post')

# Train Model (just few epochs for demo)
model.fit(train_padded, training_labels, epochs=5, verbose=1)

# ----------------------------
# 3) Test on New Sentence
# ----------------------------
new_sentence = ["I love this movie"]  # input text

# Convert text → numbers
sequence = tokenizer.texts_to_sequences(new_sentence)

# Pad to required length (50)
sequence = pad_sequences(sequence, maxlen=50, padding='post')

# Predict
prediction = model.predict(sequence)

print("\nPrediction Score:", prediction[0][0])

if prediction >= 0.5:
    print("Sentiment: Positive 😊")
else:
    print("Sentiment: Negative 😞")
```

Output:

```
Output
Model: "sequential_1"
_________________________________________________________________
 Layer (type)              Output Shape              Param #
=================================================================
 embedding_1 (Embedding)    (None, 50, 64)            640000

 simple_rnn_4 (SimpleRNN)    (None, 128)              24704

 dense_1 (Dense)           (None, 1)                 129

=================================================================
Total params: 664833 (2.54 MB)
Trainable params: 664833 (2.54 MB)
Non-trainable params: 0 (0.00 Byte)
```

```
Prediction Score: 0.9305145
Sentiment: Positive 😊
```

Key Idea:

The RNN reads the sequence word-by-word, and only the final hidden state is used for classification — it carries the context of the entire sentence.

Case 2: One-to-Many RNN

One image → becomes an initial hidden state, and then we generate words step-by-step.

Example P4 – U4 – D6

RNN – One to Many

```
from tensorflow.keras.layers import Input, Dense, Embedding, SimpleRNN
from tensorflow.keras.models import Model
import tensorflow as tf

# Image feature extractor output dimension
image_feature_dim = 256

# Vocabulary size for captions
vocab_size = 10000
embedding_dim = 64
hidden_units = 128
max_caption_length = 20

# Inputs
image_input = Input(shape=(image_feature_dim,))
caption_input = Input(shape=(max_caption_length,))

# 1) Map image to initial hidden state
h0 = Dense(hidden_units, activation='tanh')(image_input)

# 2) Embed caption tokens
x = Embedding(vocab_size, embedding_dim)(caption_input)

# 3) Use RNN while supplying initial state from image
rnn_output = SimpleRNN(hidden_units, return_sequences=True)(x, initial_state=[h0])

# 4) Predict next word at each time step
output = Dense(vocab_size, activation='softmax')(rnn_output)
```

```
model = Model([image_input, caption_input], output)
model.compile(optimizer='adam', loss='sparse_categorical_crossentropy')
model.summary()
```

Output:

```
Output
Model: "model"
___________________________________________________________________
 Layer (type)              Output Shape             Param #   Connected to
==================================================================================================
 input_2 (InputLayer)       [(None, 20)]               0         []

 input_1 (InputLayer)       [(None, 256)]              0         []

 embedding (Embedding)       (None, 20, 64)             640000    ['input_2[0][0]']

 dense (Dense)              (None, 128)                32896     ['input_1[0][0]']

 simple_rnn (SimpleRNN)      (None, 20, 128)            24704     ['embedding[0][0]',
                                                                   'dense[0][0]']

 dense_1 (Dense)            (None, 20, 10000)          1290000   ['simple_rnn[0][0]']

==================================================================================================
Total params: 1987600 (7.58 MB)
Trainable params: 1987600 (7.58 MB)
Non-trainable params: 0 (0.00 Byte)
```

Key Idea:

The image features serve as the RNN's initial state, which becomes the "seed thought," and the model then unfolds words over time.

This reflects two profound modes of cognition:

- Absorbing many impressions → forming one conclusion (understanding).
- From one insight → expressing many words (expression).

Both are complementary — like inhaling and exhaling in the breath of intelligence.

Limitations & when to look beyond RNNs

- **Long-range dependencies & scalability:** RNNs can struggle with very long contexts; Transformers scale better for long-range dependencies.
- **Parallelism & speed:** RNNs are inherently sequential and slower to train than parallel Transformer layers.
- **Streaming/low-latency:** RNNs (or causal/streaming transformers) are still useful for real-time tasks.

Master said, "Apeksha, "Patterns of inputs and outputs are the first design decision. Once you know the pattern — one-to-many, many-to-one, or many-to-many — choose the architectural flavor (bidirectional, stacked, attention-enabled) that supplies the *right kind* of memory and contextual access. And when sequences grow long, consider attention-powered designs — but remember, RNNs still remain elegant and efficient for many streaming and lightweight tasks."

a) Implementing a Character-level Text Generator with RNNs

Master said, "John, A character-level generator learns sequences of characters and predicts the next character. After training it on some corpus (poetry, novels, code), you can seed the model with a short string and it will generate novel text character-by-character."

Phases:

1. Prepare text and character set (vocabulary).
2. Convert text into overlapping input sequences + next-character labels.
3. Encode sequences (one-hot or integer + embedding).
4. Build an RNN (SimpleRNN / GRU / LSTM) that learns to predict the next character.
5. Train with teacher forcing (model.fit).
6. Generate text with temperature sampling (controls creativity).

Why character-level?

- Simpler for small datasets and multilingual input.
- Learns fine-grained patterns (punctuation, suffixes).
- Output is flexible (no OOV words), but training can be slower, and output may be less semantically coherent vs word-level or subword models.

Example P4 – U4 – D7

RNN – One to Many – Character Text Generator

```
# char_text_generator.py
import numpy as np
import tensorflow as tf
from tensorflow.keras import layers, models
import random
import os

# ---------- 1. Configuration ----------
SEQ_LENGTH = 60         # input sequence length in chars
STEP = 3                # step size for sliding window
BATCH_SIZE = 128
EPOCHS = 60
EMBED_DIM = 64          # optional: only used if using embedding; for one-hot, we
won't use it
RNN_UNITS = 256
CHECKPOINT_DIR = "./checkpoints_char_rnn"
os.makedirs(CHECKPOINT_DIR, exist_ok=True)

# ---------- 2. Load / define text ----------
# You can replace this small example with reading a file:
# text = open("your_text.txt", "r", encoding="utf-8").read().lower()
example = (
    "To be, or not to be, that is the question:\n"
    "Whether 'tis nobler in the mind to suffer\n"
    "The slings and arrows of outrageous fortune..."
)
text = example.lower()

print("Corpus length:", len(text))

# ---------- 3. Create character vocabulary ----------
chars = sorted(list(set(text)))
vocab_size = len(chars)
print("Unique characters:", vocab_size, chars)
```

```
# maps
char2idx = {c:i for i,c in enumerate(chars)}
idx2char = {i:c for c,i in char2idx.items()}

# ---------- 4. Create training sequences ----------
sentences = []
next_chars = []

for i in range(0, len(text) - SEQ_LENGTH, STEP):
    sentences.append(text[i: i + SEQ_LENGTH])
    next_chars.append(text[i + SEQ_LENGTH])

print("Number of sequences:", len(sentences))

# ---------- 5. Vectorize (one-hot) ----------
# For character-level with small vocab, one-hot encoding is fine.
X = np.zeros((len(sentences), SEQ_LENGTH, vocab_size), dtype=np.bool_)
y = np.zeros((len(sentences), vocab_size), dtype=np.bool_)

for i, sentence in enumerate(sentences):
    for t, ch in enumerate(sentence):
        X[i, t, char2idx[ch]] = 1
    y[i, char2idx[next_chars[i]]] = 1

# ---------- 6. Build the model ----------
# Option A: One-hot input -> RNN
model = models.Sequential([
    layers.Input(shape=(SEQ_LENGTH, vocab_size)),
    layers.LSTM(RNN_UNITS, return_sequences=True),
    layers.Dropout(0.2),
    layers.LSTM(RNN_UNITS//2),
    layers.Dropout(0.2),
    layers.Dense(vocab_size, activation='softmax')
])

model.compile(optimizer='adam', loss='categorical_crossentropy', metrics=['accuracy'])
model.summary()

# ---------- 7. Checkpoint callback ----------
checkpoint_path = os.path.join(CHECKPOINT_DIR,
"weights_epoch_{epoch:02d}_loss_{loss:.4f}.h5")
checkpoint_cb = tf.keras.callbacks.ModelCheckpoint(checkpoint_path,
save_weights_only=True, save_best_only=False)

# ---------- 8. Utility: temperature sampling ----------
def sample_with_temperature(preds, temperature=1.0):
    """
```

```
    preds: 1D array of probabilities (model output)
    temperature: float > 0. lower->more conservative, higher->more random
    """
    preds = np.asarray(preds).astype('float64')
    if temperature <= 0:
        # avoid division by zero
        return np.argmax(preds)
    # scale by temperature
    preds = np.log(preds + 1e-20) / temperature
    exp_preds = np.exp(preds)
    probs = exp_preds / np.sum(exp_preds)
    return np.random.choice(len(probs), p=probs)

# ---------- 9. Text generation function ----------
def generate_text(seed_text, length=400, temperature=1.0):
    model.eval = True
    generated = seed_text
    sentence = seed_text[-SEQ_LENGTH:]
    for i in range(length):
        # vectorize sentence
        x_pred = np.zeros((1, SEQ_LENGTH, vocab_size))
        for t, ch in enumerate(sentence):
            if ch in char2idx:
                x_pred[0, t, char2idx[ch]] = 1.0

        preds = model.predict(x_pred, verbose=0)[0]
        next_index = sample_with_temperature(preds, temperature)
        next_char = idx2char[next_index]

        generated += next_char
        sentence = (sentence + next_char)[-SEQ_LENGTH:]
    return generated

# ---------- 10. Train (or load weights) ----------
# If you have pre-trained weights: model.load_weights("...h5") and skip training.
model.fit(X, y, batch_size=BATCH_SIZE, epochs=EPOCHS,
callbacks=[checkpoint_cb])

# ---------- 11. Example generation ----------
seed_idx = random.randint(0, len(sentences)-1)
seed = sentences[seed_idx]
print("\n--- Seed text ---\n", seed)
print("\n--- Generated (temp=0.5) ---\n", generate_text(seed, length=400,
temperature=0.5))
print("\n--- Generated (temp=1.0) ---\n", generate_text(seed, length=400,
temperature=1.0))
print("\n--- Generated (temp=1.5) ---\n", generate_text(seed, length=400,
temperature=1.5))
```

Output:

```
Output
--- Generated (temp=1.0) ---
  mind to suffer
the slings and arrows of outrageous fortune.n...n .n.e....in.rn.rni.neh.:ntgattetetn'e nanagr
f's
 flsffraraafauoa oo a n   r . r a.n..o.nn....n.....g...n....q.....tt..mogn.a.qtet s  nesl fo fsnr
agsfsr srfoaa uoooogr .on r..n..............r.....q
lnw...r
.n.imwege ni t se
tss seieflgg glfagsrsfssfrfr oooa alo rnorrn.nrr.n.n..o....n.......n...n.n.n ltn.'ot.shsgnnitigsnirn
rree fgre nsoufsra  li o     r anr.r.r...f...r.r..n:t..ni.h....i.....

--- Generated (temp=1.5) ---
  mind to suffer
the slings and arrows of outrageous fortune..o.n...n.
.o.,..rg.n..hnntn:.d wbg eigh
s gfnl ursereero rsfar oa l or a snr..n....o.... .h:h..tn.ne ..ng.,.i.gnmnu
tsqsgi tbdsetnllaf fas sr g fflaugsafm  nrr.awofro.na'.e.i.t.rr...:.nng. ..a.aagf.n..h.hgngnunni
ir.


a.sf.aaa r anf rno.aa:..rrne..gnwngn.no..r..no..u ....ng....t
 rn.:ni ,.r ,tn.ne.llnii
n ett.lgtsstnghgeneteianr s gf usafrffoan uuuh r  rann r.nnn..nr n en.h.rn.,.t..n
t .i.:ggin
```

What Does This Program Do?

This program trains a **Recurrent Neural Network (RNN)** to learn character-level language patterns from a given text. Once trained, the model can **generate new text** that imitates the **style, rhythm, and structure** of the original input.

The Core Idea

Humans learn language by noticing patterns — which letters follow others, how sounds form words, and how words form sentences.

Similarly, the RNN learns:

- Which characters tend to follow each other
- How sequences of characters form meaningful fragments

- The rhythm and spacing patterns of natural text

The RNN does **not** understand meaning.

It learns **structure and probability**, predicting the **next character** one step at a time.

Objective

We are training a model that learns **patterns**, not concepts. It discovers:

- Letter sequences
- Punctuation and spacing behavior
- Flow and cadence of text

This is similar to how a child **imitates speech** before understanding it.

How the Training Works

a) **Provide Input Text**
The text acts as the *teacher* — the model will learn patterns hidden within it.

b) **Build a Character Vocabulary**
Neural networks work with **numbers**, so each character is mapped to an index.

c) **Create Training Sequences**
Slide a window (e.g., 40 characters) through the text:

"To be, or not to be, that is the ques" → next character: "t"

d) **Convert Characters to One-Hot Vectors**

- X: sequence of characters
- Y: the next character

e) **Construct the RNN Model**

- SimpleRNN(256) — stores memory of previous characters
- Dense(softmax) — predicts the probability of every possible next character

The model **does not memorise**; it learns **statistical likelihoods**.

Train the Model

The model updates its weights to reduce prediction errors.

Generating New Text

The model creates text **one character at a time**:

- It predicts the next character
- Appends it to the sequence
- Uses the updated sequence to predict again

  This creates a continuous chain.

Temperature controls creativity:

- Low → predictable, safe, repetitive
- High → surprising, expressive, sometimes chaotic

Why the Output Looks Random

- Training text is small
- RNN has limited memory
- Model trained briefly
- Higher temperature adds randomness

The model has learned **shape and rhythm**, not **meaning** — like a child **babbling** before forming full sentences.

PART FOUR

DAY THIRTEEN

Unit 4 - Lesson One

Beyond Forgetfulness - LSTM

"LSTM is the guardian of memory—choosing wisely what to remember and what to release, preserving meaning through the noise of time."

- *Shree Shambav*

Apeksha inquired, "Master, could you elaborate on the concept and functioning of LSTM networks?"

Master replied, Apeksha, to understand Long Short-Term Memory (LSTM) networks, one must first understand the *limitation* that led to their creation.

In the world of machine learning, when we work with **sequences** — language, music, time-series signals, speech — the meaning of the present does not exist alone; it is shaped by what came before. A sentence has meaning because every word builds upon a previous one. A melody makes sense because each note carries the echo of the earlier notes.

To model such patterns, we use **Recurrent Neural Networks (RNNs)**, which pass information from one time step to the next through a **hidden state** — like memory flowing from moment to moment.

However, ordinary RNNs struggle to remember *distant* context.

Their memory fades. Their awareness dissolves.

This limitation is known as the **Long-Term Dependency Problem.**

The Long-Term Dependency Problem

When an RNN learns by backpropagation, gradients are passed backward through many time steps. Over long sequences:

- Sometimes these gradients **shrink to near zero** →The model forgets earlier information.

  This is the **Vanishing Gradient** problem.

- Sometimes gradients **grow excessively large** →Training becomes unstable and chaotic.

  This is the **Exploding Gradient** problem.

Thus, traditional RNNs behave like a mind that **remembers only the recent**, losing valuable distant memories.

The Birth of LSTM

To solve this challenge, Hochreiter and Schmidhuber introduced **LSTM** — a network that **does not merely pass information forward**, but **chooses what to remember and what to forget** — just like a disciplined mind trained in awareness.

LSTM introduces a **Memory Cell**, a preserved internal state that can hold information over long durations — like a deep reservoir of understanding unaffected by rapid fluctuations of thought.

How LSTM Remembers and Forgets

An LSTM cell contains **three gates**, each playing a sacred role in the flow of memory:

Gate	Purpose	Analogy
Forget Gate	Decides what information to remove from memory	Letting go of what is no longer relevant

Input Gate	Decides what new information should enter memory	Accepting new learning mindfully
Output Gate	Decides what information to express outward	Speaking only what is meaningful

1. Forget Gate — *Selective Letting Go*

The LSTM looks at:

- Current input, and
- Previous memory state

And asks:

"Is this information still important?"

If yes → memory is preserved.

If no → it is intentionally erased.

This prevents the memory from being overwhelmed or polluted.

2. Input Gate — Mindful Reception

The LSTM evaluates:

- Which new information is meaningful?
- What should be stored in long-term memory?

This ensures that **only relevant knowledge is stored**, preventing noise from corrupting understanding.

3. Output Gate — Expression of Wisdom

From the stored memory, the LSTM decides:

- What should influence the current output?

- What should be shared with the next time step?

Thus, the knowledge retained becomes **actionable**, not merely hoarded.

In Essence

Standard RNN:

→ *Remembers unconsciously and forgets uncontrollably.*

LSTM:

→ *Remembers consciously and forgets intentionally.*

Where the RNN mind is like a turbulent stream, the LSTM mind is like a **calm lake** — holding reflections clearly for as long as needed.

Why LSTMs Are Powerful

They maintain memory across long sequences, making them ideal for:

- Language modeling and text generation
- Speech recognition
- Machine translation
- Music composition
- Time-series forecasting (finance, weather, physiology)

Where **context matters**, LSTMs excel.

Master said, "Apeksha, the true power of LSTM lies not just in its architecture, but in the principle it embodies:

Wisdom is the art of knowing what to remember and what to release.

LSTM is not merely a model — it is a reflection of a disciplined mind."

☐ Improvement Over RNN

Apeksha listened thoughtfully.

Master continued with a gentle smile:

Master said, "Apeksha, imagine your **day planner**. Each day, you schedule meetings, calls, and activities.

But life is dynamic — unexpected priorities appear.

When something *important* arises, you **don't erase the whole calendar**, do you?

Apeksha said, "No."

Master smiled and said, "You **choose**:"

- Which meeting stays
- Which meeting can be postponed
- What needs to be added
- What needs to be emphasised

You organise information **with intelligence, not blind overwriting.**

RNN Lacks Selective Memory

An **RNN** does not have this sense of priority.

At each time step, when new information enters, the RNN **completely transforms** the past memory:

$$h_t = f(W \cdot h_{t-1} + U \cdot x_t)$$

This transformation overwrites everything **uniformly**, without distinguishing:

- What is **important** to preserve
- What is **unimportant** and can be forgotten

It is like **rewriting the entire calendar** every time a new appointment comes in.

That is chaotic, inefficient, and leads to **loss of valuable long-term information.**

This is why RNNs forget long sequences and fail to capture dependencies spread across time.

LSTM Brings Selective Memory and Controlled Forgetting

LSTMs, however, are different.

They are designed to behave like a **wise mind** that **remembers intentionally** and **forgets consciously**.

Instead of **overwriting** the entire memory, LSTMs modify memory with **small, meaningful adjustments** using addition and multiplication.

This selective refinement happens through **Cell State** — a controlled memory pathway.

Understanding the Three Dependencies of Information Flow

The information at any point in an LSTM depends on three sources:

Component	Meaning	Analogy
Previous Cell State (C_{t-1})	What was stored in long-term memory	The long-term notes and patterns you keep across days
Previous Hidden State (h_{t-1})	What was expressed previously	Your action or understanding just before now
Current Input (x_t)	New information is arriving at this moment	New appointment or event appearing in your schedule

LSTM looks at **all three**, evaluates them, and *decides*:

- What to **remember**
- What to **forget**
- What to **output**

This ability to *prioritize* is the core intelligence of LSTM.

Visualization with a Stock Prediction Example

To predict the stock price today, consider:

1. **Trend from previous days**

   This corresponds to **long-term memory (Cell State)**

   → Are we in a sustained uptrend or downtrend?

2. **Yesterday's price**

   This corresponds to the **hidden state**

   → The short-term, recent context.

3. **News/events today**

   This corresponds to the **current input**

   → Something new, unexpected, or impactful.

LSTM combines all three thoughtfully — just like a seasoned trader.

Analogy: The Three Gates of the Mind

Master said:

"LSTM behaves like a wise mind that filters thoughts."

- **Forget Gate** → *What should I let go?*
- **Input Gate** → *What new learning should I accept?*
- **Output Gate** → *What understanding should I express right now?*

This is how LSTM **remembers selectively and forgets purposefully**.

RNN vs LSTM – Analogy

RNN	LSTM
Like a person who gets overwhelmed with new information and keeps forgetting the old.	Like a practiced mind that knows what to remember and what to discard.
Overwrites memory entirely each time.	Modifies memory gradually and wisely.
Struggles with long-term dependencies.	Excels at retaining relevant long-term patterns.

Master said, "Apeksha, memory is not about holding everything. It is about holding only what matters.

LSTM is powerful not because it stores more information — but because it **remembers consciously and forgets wisely**."

☐ How does LSTM work?

Nikash asked: "How does LSTM work in Python?"

Master said: *"We will see the gates, the maths, an intuition-rich scenario, then practical code."*

Essence in one line

An LSTM cell maintains a cell state (long-term memory) and controls information flow with three gates — forget, input, and output — so it can remember long-range dependencies and avoid vanishing/exploding gradients.

The gates and equations

At time step *t*, inputs:

- x_t - current input vector
- h_{t-1} - previous hidden state (short-term memory)
- C_{t-1} - previous cell state (long-term memory)

Learnable parameters: weight matrices and biases for each gate: W_f, W_i, W_c, W_o and b_f, b_i, b_c, b_o. We often combine h_{t-1} and x_t into one vector $[h_{t-1}, x_t]$.

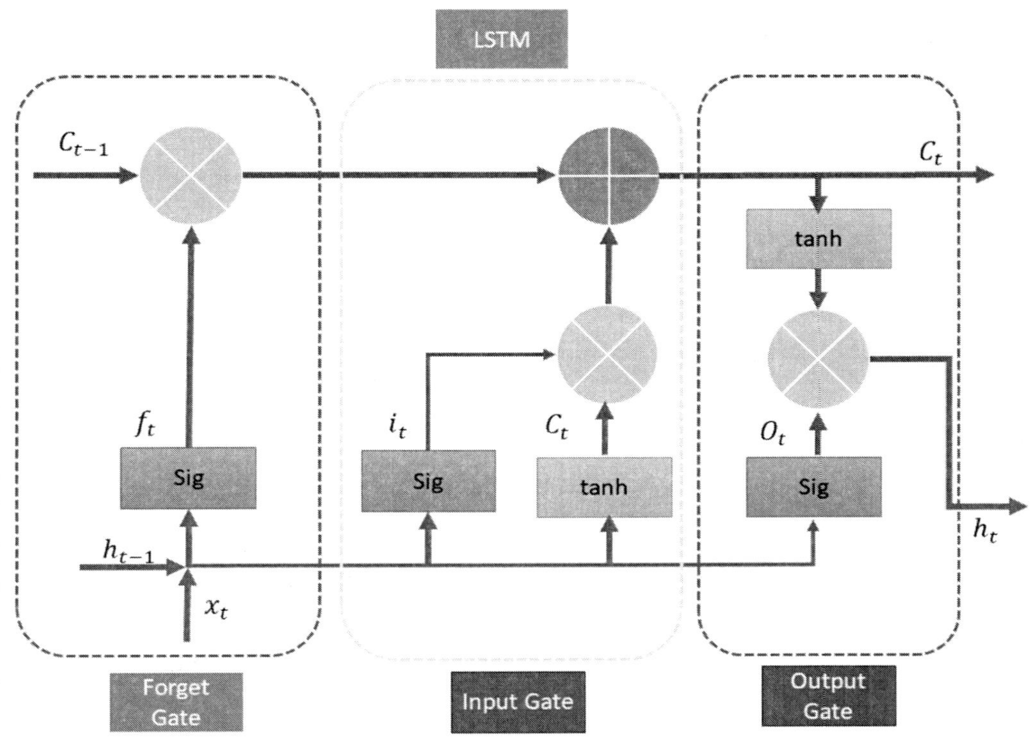

Illustration P6_LSTM_1: LSTM

Forget gate

Forget Gate (LSTM): The forget gate decides which information from the previous cell state should be retained or discarded. It takes two inputs: the previous hidden state (h_{t-1}) and the current input (x_t). These are multiplied by weight matrices, added to a bias, and passed through a sigmoid activation, producing values between 0 and 1. Values near 0 indicate information to forget, while values near 1 indicate information to keep in the cell state.

$$f_t = \sigma (W_f [h_{t-1}, x_t] + b_f)$$

Input gate

Input Gate (LSTM): The input gate determines which new information should be added to the cell state. It takes the previous hidden state (h_{t-1}) and the current input (x_t) as inputs. h_{t-1} and x_t are passed through a sigmoid function to filter important values and through a tanh function to create a candidate vector of new information (values between -1 and 1). The element-wise multiplication of these outputs decides what useful information is added to the cell state.

$$i_t = \sigma (W_i [h_{t-1}, x_t] + b_i)$$

Candidate new content

Cell State (LSTM): The cell state carries the long-term memory of the network. It is first multiplied by the forget gate output, removing irrelevant information, and then updated by adding the filtered new information from the input gate. This combination ensures the cell state retains important past knowledge while incorporating relevant new data.

$$\widetilde{C_t} = \tanh (W_c [h_{t-1}, x_t] + b_c)$$

Update cell state

$$C_t = f_t \odot C_{t-1} + i_t \odot \widetilde{C_t}$$

Output gate (what to expose)

Output Gate (LSTM): The output gate determines what information from the cell state will be sent as the next hidden state (h_t). It takes the previous hidden state (h_{t-1}) and current input (x_t), passes them through a sigmoid function to filter relevant information, and multiplies this by the tanh of the updated cell state. This produces the hidden state that carries the most useful information to the next time step.

$$O_t = \sigma (W_o [h_{t-1}, x_t] + b_o)$$

Hidden state (and often used for output)

$$h_t = o_t \odot \tanh(C_t)$$

Where:

- σ = sigmoid (0..1), tanh = tanh (-1..1)
- $\odot$ = element-wise multiplication

Intuition + scenario (stock price example, deep context)

Think of the **cell state C_t** as a long ledger a seasoned trader keeps.

Each day:

- The **forget gate** asks: *Which old patterns from the ledger are still useful?* (drop small/noise items — set near 0)
- The **input gate** asks: *Which new signals (today's news, volume spike) should I write into the ledger?* (scale candidate by importance)
- The **cell update** blends the old ledger and the new important facts.
- The **output gate** decides: *What part of this ledger should be used to make today's trading decision (the hidden state/network output)?*

Concretely, to predict today's close:

- Long-term trend = C_{t-1} (preserve if trend persists via f_t large)
- Yesterday's close / momentum = h_{t-1} (influences gates)
- Today's news / features = x_t (proposed candidate $\widetilde{C}_t$, scaled by i_t)

Because gates are learned, the network discovers when news matters a lot (large i_t) and when not (small i_t), and which historical signals must persist (large f_t).

Small worked numeric example (one step, intuitive)

Suppose a toy LSTM with 3-dimensional cell vectors (for clarity). Given numeric h_{t-1}, x_t and random weight matrices, you compute:

1. concatenate $z = [h_{t-1}, x_t]$
2. compute $f_t = \sigma\,(W_f z + b_f)$ (vector like [0.01, 0.98, 0.6])

→ first element ~0.01 means "forget that component", second 0.98 means "keep it".

3. compute it, C_t
4. update $C_t = f_t \odot C_{t-1} + i_t \odot \widetilde{C_t}$
5. compute o_t and h_t

This small arithmetic shows how some components are preserved, others replaced.

Minimal NumPy implementation of a single LSTM cell (didactic)

Master said, "This snippet shows gate math explicitly so you see shapes and operations (no training, just forward pass):"

Example P4 – U4 – D8

LSTM

```
import numpy as np

def sigmoid(x): return 1 / (1 + np.exp(-x))
def tanh(x): return np.tanh(x)

# dimensions
input_dim = 4
hidden_dim = 3

# random toy inputs
x_t = np.random.randn(input_dim)          # current input
h_prev = np.random.randn(hidden_dim)      # previous hidden state
C_prev = np.random.randn(hidden_dim)      # previous cell

# random weights (for demo only)
Wf = np.random.randn(hidden_dim, hidden_dim + input_dim)
Wi = np.random.randn(hidden_dim, hidden_dim + input_dim)
Wc = np.random.randn(hidden_dim, hidden_dim + input_dim)
Wo = np.random.randn(hidden_dim, hidden_dim + input_dim)
bf = np.zeros(hidden_dim)
bi = np.zeros(hidden_dim)
bc = np.zeros(hidden_dim)
bo = np.zeros(hidden_dim)

z = np.concatenate([h_prev, x_t]) # shape (hidden_dim + input_dim,)

f_t = sigmoid(Wf.dot(z) + bf)      # forget gate
i_t = sigmoid(Wi.dot(z) + bi)      # input gate
```

```
C_hat = tanh(Wc.dot(z) + bc)       # candidate
C_t = f_t * C_prev + i_t * C_hat   # updated cell
o_t = sigmoid(Wo.dot(z) + bo)      # output gate
h_t = o_t * tanh(C_t)              # new hidden state

print("f_t:", f_t)
print("i_t:", i_t)
print("C_hat:", C_hat)
print("C_t:", C_t)
print("o_t:", o_t)
print("h_t:", h_t)
```

Output:

```
Output
f_t: [0.37736385 0.60748154 0.5406723 ]
i_t: [0.03798691 0.23702184 0.06595618]
C_hat: [ 0.98622423 -0.99962467 -0.99806046]
C_t: [-0.26763303 -0.94192408  0.20678146]
o_t: [0.71763137 0.96994954 0.40493612]
h_t: [-0.18760391 -0.71398472  0.08255991]
```

Run this and watch how f_t and i_t scale the old cell vs candidate — you'll see concrete numbers for "forget" and "write".

Master said: Here's a practical LSTM model for word-level sequence prediction — ready to run. It uses tf.keras and encapsulates the math in optimized layers (you don't reimplement gates when training real models):

Example P4 – U4 – D9

LSTM

```
import tensorflow as tf
from tensorflow.keras.models import Sequential
from tensorflow.keras.layers import Embedding, LSTM, Dense

vocab_size = 10000   # example
embed_dim = 128
hidden_units = 256
seq_len = 20

model = Sequential([
   Embedding(input_dim=vocab_size, output_dim=embed_dim,
input_length=seq_len),
   LSTM(hidden_units, return_sequences=False),  # returns final hidden state
```

```
    Dense(vocab_size, activation='softmax')
])

model.compile(optimizer='adam', loss='sparse_categorical_crossentropy',
metrics=['accuracy'])
model.summary()
# model.fit(X_train, y_train, epochs=..., batch_size=...)
```

Output:

```
Output
Model: "sequential_7"
_________________________________________________________________
 Layer (type)              Output Shape              Param #
=================================================================
 embedding_7 (Embedding)    (None, 20, 128)           1280000

 lstm_7 (LSTM)              (None, 256)               394240

 dense_7 (Dense)            (None, 10000)             2570000

=================================================================
Total params: 4244240 (16.19 MB)
Trainable params: 4244240 (16.19 MB)
Non-trainable params: 0 (0.00 Byte)
```

Tips: debugging, performance & best practices

- **Vanishing/exploding gradients**: LSTM largely mitigates vanishing gradients; still clip gradients if exploding.
- **Initialization**: Glorot/Xavier or orthogonal for recurrent weights helps stability.
- **Batching & sequences**: pad shorter sequences; use masking or mask_zero=True in Embedding.
- **Bidirectional LSTM**: use when both past and future context matter (e.g., sequence labeling).
- **Stacked LSTMs**: deeper layers help capture hierarchical temporal patterns.
- **Dropout**: between LSTM layers or recurrent dropout (recurrent_dropout) to regularize.

- **Fine-tune pre-trained embeddings**: word embeddings speed up learning for text tasks.
- **Stateful vs stateless**: stateful LSTMs keep hidden state across batches — useful for very long sequences but need careful batch alignment.

When to choose LSTM vs alternatives

- Use **LSTM** when sequences have long-term dependencies and you have modest data.
- For very long sequences/transformer architectures (attention) outperform LSTM on large corpora (but need more compute/data).
- **GRU** is a simpler alternative — similar performance with fewer parameters.

Master said, "This code trains a **text generation LSTM model** using the content of a **PDF book**. After training, the model can generate new poetic sentences in a similar writing style."

Input document:

"The miracle of children is that we just don't know how they will change or who they will become."

The fine art of parenting requires that we play many roles in the lives of our children. As parents, we are called upon to be responsible, set limits, give good advice, and be sensitive to the needs of our children. However, because children are in a continuous state of growth and change, long-term success as a parent requires that parents also undergo a process of constant learning and change so that our parental skills do not become obsolete.

The world is not the same, like that of our Childhood:

All we have to do is look around our homes and businesses at the fast-evolving technology to understand that things have changed. Our children must be competent to compete in a very different world than we had to conquer, and for this, they will require different skills and resources. Sometimes, kids have a better understanding of what they need, than we do. Parents must, therefore, be smart enough to view the world through their child's eyes, and then, be willing to help that child find a way to solve problems that will work for them.

Each child – find their path to success and happiness

History can confirm that few if any parents, have ever been successful in deciding what will make their child happy as an adult. Even when we are partially right, the wise parent should avoid making decisions which will keep them in their child's path of blame.

A parent's job – to strengthen their child

The truth is that it is hard for kids to compete in today world. They have many decisions to make and skills to master in a world which is regularly changing. As parents, we can either serve as a springboard of encouragement and support for our kids. Else we can stand on the sidelines providing criticism and doubt.

Who said parents and children could not be friends?

Text Generation:

Master continued, "Sam, this code builds a next-word prediction model using text extracted from a PDF file and then uses that model to generate new poetic sentences. First, it imports the required libraries to process text, read PDF content, prepare training data, and build a neural network. The PDF file is opened and read page-by-page, and the extracted text is combined into a single large string. The text is then cleaned by removing punctuation and special characters, converting everything to lowercase, and normalizing spaces. This ensures that the text is consistent and ready for tokenization."

Example P4 – U4 – D10

LSTM - Text Generation

```
# ---------------------------------------------------
# 1. Import Libraries
# ---------------------------------------------------
import numpy as np
import tensorflow as tf
from tensorflow.keras.preprocessing.text import Tokenizer
from tensorflow.keras.preprocessing.sequence import pad_sequences
from tensorflow.keras.models import Sequential
from tensorflow.keras.layers import Embedding, LSTM, Dense
import PyPDF2
import re

# ---------------------------------------------------
# 2. Load PDF File
# ---------------------------------------------------
pdf_path =
r"C:\\Users\\User\\mraj4\\Documents\\Optimum6\\documents\\Journeyofsoul.pdf"

text = ""
with open(pdf_path, "rb") as f:
    reader = PyPDF2.PdfReader(f)
    for page in reader.pages:
        text += page.extract_text() + " "

# ---------------------------------------------------
# 3. Clean Text
# ---------------------------------------------------
text = re.sub(r"[^a-zA-Z\s]", " ", text)  # keep letters only
text = re.sub(r"\s+", " ", text).lower()  # remove extra spaces

print("Total characters loaded:", len(text))

# ---------------------------------------------------
# 4. Tokenize Words
# ---------------------------------------------------
```

```
tokenizer = Tokenizer()
tokenizer.fit_on_texts([text])
word_index = tokenizer.word_index
total_words = len(word_index) + 1

tokens = tokenizer.texts_to_sequences([text])[0]

# ----------------------------------------------------
# 5. Create Training Sequences
# ----------------------------------------------------
input_sequences = []
for i in range(1, len(tokens)):
    seq = tokens[:i+1]
    input_sequences.append(seq)

max_len = max(len(seq) for seq in input_sequences)
input_sequences = np.array(pad_sequences(input_sequences, maxlen=max_len, padding='pre'))

X = input_sequences[:, :-1]
y = input_sequences[:, -1]
y = tf.keras.utils.to_categorical(y, num_classes=total_words)

# ----------------------------------------------------
# 6. Build Model
# ----------------------------------------------------
model = Sequential([
    Embedding(total_words, 128, input_length=max_len-1),
    LSTM(256, return_sequences=False),
    Dense(total_words, activation='softmax')
])

model.compile(loss='categorical_crossentropy', optimizer='adam', metrics=['accuracy'])
model.summary()

# ----------------------------------------------------
# 7. Train Model
# ----------------------------------------------------
history = model.fit(X, y, epochs=40, batch_size=256, verbose=1)

# ----------------------------------------------------
# 8. Text Generation Function
# ----------------------------------------------------

def generate_poetic_text(seed, num_words=60, temperature=1.2, top_k=6):
    # A poetic guiding intention (does not appear in output)
    style_prompt = "in a reflective, poetic, philosophical tone"
    seed = style_prompt + " " + seed

    print("\n--- Seed ---")
    print(seed.replace(style_prompt, "").strip())

    for _ in range(num_words):
        seq = tokenizer.texts_to_sequences([seed])[0]
```

```
    seq = pad_sequences([seq], maxlen=max_len-1, padding='pre')

    preds = model.predict(seq, verbose=0)[0]

    # Temperature
    preds = np.log(preds + 1e-10) / temperature
    preds = np.exp(preds)
    preds = preds / np.sum(preds)

    # Top-K Sampling
    top_indices = preds.argsort()[-top_k:]
    top_probs = preds[top_indices]
    top_probs = top_probs / np.sum(top_probs)

    next_index = np.random.choice(top_indices, p=top_probs)
    next_word = tokenizer.index_word.get(next_index, "")

    seed += " " + next_word

result = seed.replace(style_prompt, "").strip()

print("\n--- Generated (Philosophical & Poetic) ---")
print(result)
```

Output:

Output
The fine art of parenting a we of we to we that a children we the of our our children and the our our and children to to and and children the and the that and not be be that be be and the and and and be be and be that to and that of our to we a parents a our our our

Next, the code uses a tokenizer to convert each unique word in the text into a numerical index. The entire document is transformed into a sequence of numbers, where each number represents a word. Using these sequences, the code creates training samples by taking progressively longer sequences of words so the model can learn how sentences develop word-by-word. Each input sequence is padded to equal length, and the target output word (the last word of each sequence) is converted to a one-hot encoded vector.

With the data prepared, the model is constructed using three main layers: an Embedding layer to represent words as dense vectors, an LSTM layer to learn long-term word relationships and patterns, and a Dense softmax layer to predict the next word in the sequence. The model is trained for multiple epochs so it can learn the style and flow of the text.

Finally, the code defines a text generation function that takes a seed sentence and generates new words one at a time. It applies temperature scaling and top-K sampling to introduce variation and creativity during prediction, allowing the generated output to sound more expressive and poetic. The result is a model capable of producing original poetic sentences in a style similar to the text from the PDF.

☐ Bidirectional LSTM

Akshatha asked, "Master, what is a Bidirectional LSTM?"

Master replied, "Long Short-Term Memory (LSTM) networks are designed to capture long-term dependencies in sequential data, addressing the vanishing and exploding gradient problems that standard RNNs struggle with. They excel at remembering context over long sequences, but they naturally process data in only one direction—typically from past to future. This can limit their understanding when the context from future time steps is also relevant. To overcome this limitation, we use a variation called Bidirectional LSTM (BiLSTM).

A **Bidirectional LSTM** consists of two separate LSTM layers running in parallel: one processes the sequence in the forward direction (from the first time step to the last), while the other processes it in the backward direction (from the last time step to the first). By doing so, the network has access to both past and future context at every point in the sequence, allowing it to make more informed predictions.

How BiLSTM Works:

- **Forward LSTM:** Reads the input sequence as usual, capturing dependencies from the past.
- **Backward LSTM:** Reads the same sequence in reverse, capturing dependencies from the future.
- **Combined Output:** The outputs from the forward and backward LSTMs are typically concatenated or summed at each time step to form a richer representation, incorporating information from both directions.

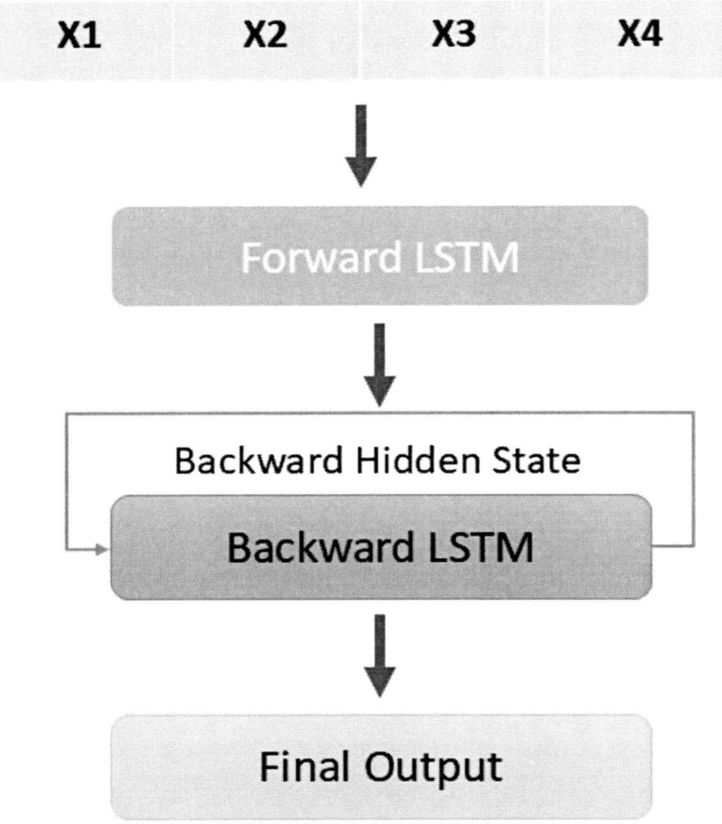

Illustration P6_LSTM_1: LSTM

Mathematical Intuition:

Let the input sequence be $X = [x_1, x_2, \ldots, x_T]$. The forward LSTM computes hidden states $\overleftarrow{h_t}$ for each time step t, while the backward LSTM computes $\overrightarrow{h_t}$ The final hidden representation at each time step is:

$$ht = \text{concat}(\overrightarrow{h_t}\ \overleftarrow{h_t}\ )$$

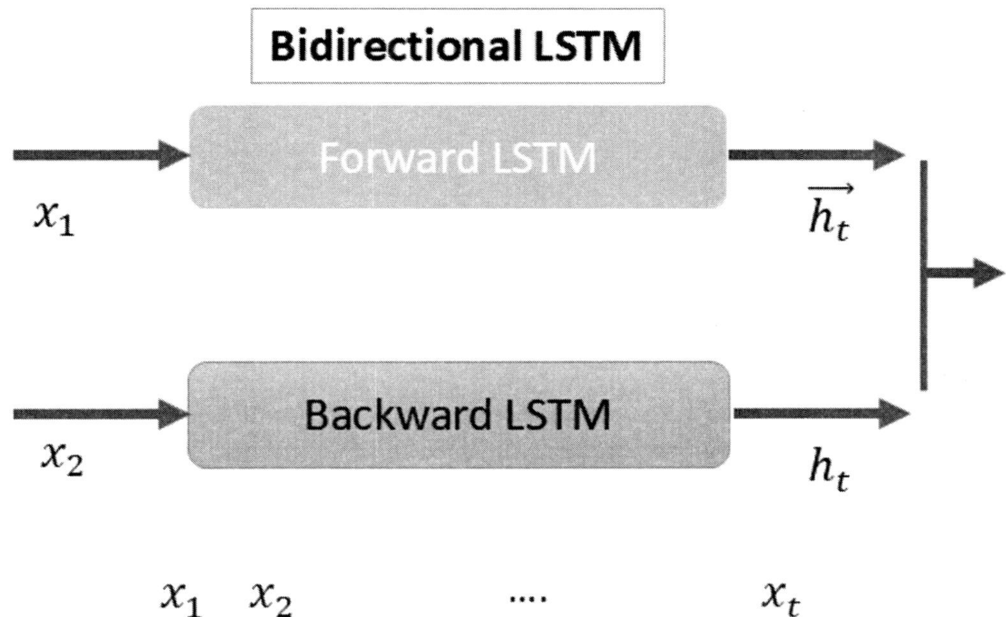

Illustration P6_LSTM_1: LSTM

This concatenation allows the network to leverage the full context of the sequence: past and future simultaneously. BiLSTMs are particularly powerful in tasks where understanding the entire sequence context is crucial, such as language modelling, speech recognition, sentiment analysis, and named entity recognition.

In essence, BiLSTM is like reading a sentence both forward and backward before deciding its meaning—capturing nuances that a one-way reading might miss."

Master said, "Akshaya, what we spoke earlier was the intuition — now we approach the implementation with clarity and grounded understanding. Let us walk step-by-step through how a Bidirectional LSTM can be used to perform Sentiment Analysis on movie reviews."

Let us understand with a simple program.

Example P4 – U4 – D11
BILSTM
import numpy as np from tensorflow.keras.models import Sequential

```
from tensorflow.keras.layers import Embedding, Bidirectional, LSTM, Dense

# SAMPLE DATA (dummy sequences of integers)
# Suppose each sequence is of length 5
X = np.array([
   [1, 5, 6, 2, 3],
   [4, 2, 1, 7, 8],
   [3, 3, 2, 1, 0],
   [9, 1, 4, 3, 2]
])

# Labels (binary classification)
y = np.array([0, 1, 0, 1])

# Build the Bidirectional LSTM Model
model = Sequential([
   Embedding(input_dim=10, output_dim=8, input_length=5),
   Bidirectional(LSTM(units=16)),   # <-- Bidirectional Layer
   Dense(1, activation='sigmoid')
])

model.compile(optimizer='adam', loss='binary_crossentropy', metrics=['accuracy'])
model.summary()

# Train the model
model.fit(X, y, epochs=10, verbose=1)
```

Key Idea

- **Normal LSTM** reads the sequence from **left → right**
- **Bidirectional LSTM** reads:
  - Forward: left → right
  - Backward: right → left
- Then it **combines both** to make smarter decisions.

This is especially useful when the **meaning depends on both previous and future words** (like in language understanding, speech recognition, and sentiment analysis).

☐ **Implementation: Sentiment Analysis Using BiLSTM**

We will use the **IMDB Movie Review Dataset**, which contains 50,000 movie reviews labeled as **positive** or **negative**. Our task is to train a model that can read a review and determine whether the sentiment expressed is **favorable or unfavorable**.

Importing Libraries

We begin by importing TensorFlow and its Keras modules. These provide all the necessary tools to:

- Load datasets
- Perform text preprocessing
- Build and train neural networks

Loading and Preparing the IMDB Dataset

The IMDB dataset is already tokenized into word indices.

```
vocab_size = 10000 # use the top 10,000 words

max_length = 200 # keep each review to 200 words

(X_train, y_train), (X_test, y_test) = imdb.load_data(num_words=vocab_size)
```

Performing Text Vectorization

The dataset is already numeric (words → integers), so we directly embed these integers into **dense word vectors** using an Embedding layer.

This allows the network to **learn the meaning of words** based on how they appear in sentences.

Defining Model Architecture (BiLSTM Layers)

```
model = Sequential([

Embedding(vocab_size, 128, input_length=max_length),
```

```
Bidirectional(LSTM(64, return_sequences=False)),

Dense(1, activation='sigmoid')

])
```

Embedding Layer: Converts word indices into meaningful dense vectors.

Bidirectional LSTM: Reads the review from **left-to-right and right-to-left**, capturing richer contextual understanding.

Dense Output with Sigmoid: Produces a value between 0 and 1 → positive or negative sentiment.

Training the Model

```
model.compile(optimizer='adam', loss='binary_crossentropy',
metrics=['accuracy'])

model.fit(X_train, y_train, validation_split=0.2, epochs=5, batch_size=128)
```

- **Binary Crossentropy** because the output has only two classes.
- **Adam Optimizer** helps the network converge efficiently.
- **Accuracy Metric** helps us measure how well the model performs.

Master continued: "Notice how the Bidirectional LSTM allows the model to consider **context both before and after** each word. This is especially important in sentiments where meaning can reverse with a single word — like *'not good'*. The forward LSTM catches one direction of meaning, while the backward LSTM ensures no nuance is lost."

Example P4 – U4 – D12

BILSTM – Sentiment Analysis

```
# ---------------------------------------------------
# 1. Import Libraries
# ---------------------------------------------------
import tensorflow as tf
from tensorflow.keras.models import Sequential
```

```
from tensorflow.keras.layers import Embedding, Bidirectional, LSTM, Dense,
TextVectorization
from tensorflow.keras.datasets import imdb
from tensorflow.keras.preprocessing.sequence import pad_sequences
import numpy as np

# ---------------------------------------------------
# 2. Load IMDB Dataset (Raw Token IDs)
# ---------------------------------------------------
vocab_size = 10000
max_length = 200

(X_train_ids, y_train), (X_test_ids, y_test) = imdb.load_data(num_words=vocab_size)

word_index = imdb.get_word_index()
reverse_word_index = {value: key for key, value in word_index.items()}

# Function to convert token IDs → text form
def decode_review(tokens):
    return " ".join([reverse_word_index.get(i - 3, "?") for i in tokens])

# Convert tokenized reviews back into actual text
raw_train_text = [decode_review(x) for x in X_train_ids]
raw_test_text = [decode_review(x) for x in X_test_ids]

print("Sample decoded review:")
print(raw_train_text[0][:300], "...\n")

# ---------------------------------------------------
# 3. TEXT VECTORIZATION (Correct Tokenization)
# ---------------------------------------------------
vectorizer = TextVectorization(
    max_tokens=vocab_size,
    output_sequence_length=max_length,
    standardize="lower_and_strip_punctuation"
)

vectorizer.adapt(raw_train_text)

# Convert text → equal-length integer sequences that match training inputs
X_train = vectorizer(raw_train_text)
X_test = vectorizer(raw_test_text)

# ---------------------------------------------------
# 4. Build BiLSTM Model
# ---------------------------------------------------
model = Sequential([
    Embedding(vocab_size, 128, input_length=max_length),
```

```
    Bidirectional(LSTM(64)),
    Dense(1, activation='sigmoid')
])

model.compile(optimizer="adam", loss="binary_crossentropy", metrics=["accuracy"])
model.summary()

# --------------------------------------------------
# 5. Train the Model
# --------------------------------------------------
history = model.fit(
    X_train, y_train,
    validation_split=0.2,
    epochs=5,
    batch_size=128,
    verbose=1
)

# --------------------------------------------------
# 6. Evaluate Model
# --------------------------------------------------
loss, accuracy = model.evaluate(X_test, y_test, verbose=1)
print(f"\nTest Accuracy: {accuracy * 100:.2f}%")

# --------------------------------------------------
# 7. Predict Sentiment on Custom Text
# --------------------------------------------------
def predict_sentiment(text):
    seq = vectorizer(tf.constant([text]))
    prediction = model.predict(seq)[0][0]

    if prediction >= 0.5:
        print(f"\nSentiment: **Positive** 🙂 (Confidence: {round(float(prediction), 3)})")
    else:
        print(f"\nSentiment: **Negative** 🙁 (Confidence: {round(1 - float(prediction), 3)})")


# --------------------------------------------------
# 8. TEST THE MODEL WITH YOUR OWN REVIEW
# --------------------------------------------------
sample_review = "The movie was incredibly inspiring and beautifully crafted"
predict_sentiment(sample_review)
```

Output:

Output
Sentiment: **Positive** 🙂 (Confidence: 0.973)

Thus, the BiLSTM becomes a **powerful reader of emotion**, allowing the machine to understand human tone, opinion, and subtle feelings expressed through language.

☐ Stacked LSTM

Roopa asked, *"Master, what is a Stacked LSTM, and how does it work?"*

Master smiled and said, "Roopa, imagine a story that unfolds not just on the surface, but layer by layer—like reading a poem, then discovering the metaphor within it, and then realising the deeper philosophy behind the metaphor.

A **Stacked LSTM** works in the same way."

Understanding the Foundation

LSTMs (Long Short-Term Memory networks) are a refined form of recurrent neural networks (RNNs) designed to **remember important information** across time and **forget irrelevant details**.

They were created to overcome the vanishing gradient problem that ordinary RNNs face when learning long sequences.

But sometimes, a single LSTM layer is **not enough** to capture the full richness of patterns in the data—especially when the patterns are multi-layered, complex, or hierarchical.

This is where **Stacked LSTMs** enter.

What is a Stacked LSTM?

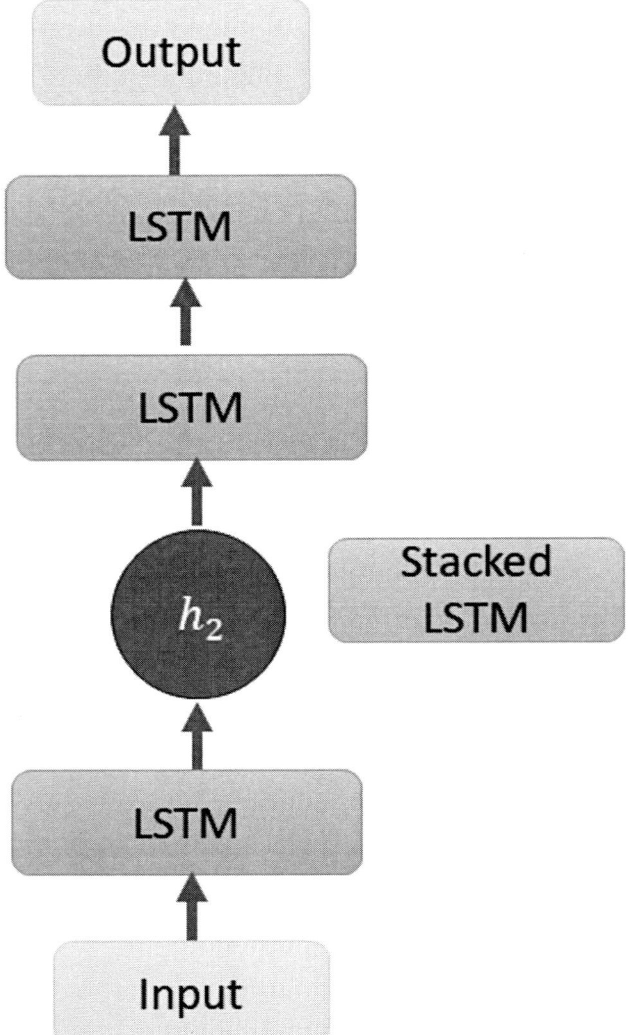

Illustration P6_StackedLSTM_5: LSTM

Stacking LSTMs means **placing multiple LSTM layers on top of each other**.

- The **first LSTM layer** learns **basic, local, short-term patterns**.
- The **next layer** receives the processed output and learns **slightly higher-level patterns**.
- The **third layer** goes even deeper, learning **abstract, long-term dependencies**.

Each layer **builds upon** the representation created by the layer below it, just like levels of understanding.

Why Stacking Brings Power

The strength of stacked LSTMs comes from **hierarchy**:

Layer Level	**What It Learns**	**Analogy**
First Layer	Raw sequential rhythm, immediate dependencies	Hearing sounds
Second Layer	Emerging patterns, structure, and short phrases	Understanding words
Third Layer and Beyond	Deep semantics, emotional meaning	Understanding poetry and intention

When data has structure in **time**, stacked layers allow the model to see not just the *present*, but the *story of the sequence.*

Mathematical Intuition

Let the hidden states of the LSTM layer l at time t be h_t^l:

$$h_t^1 = \text{LSTM}_1(x_t, h_{t-1}^1, C_{t-1}^1)$$

This is the first layer, learning primitive patterns directly from input.

$$h_t^2 = \text{LSTM}_2(h_t^1, h_{t-1}^2, C_{t-1}^2)$$

Now the second layer learns from the **processed meaning** rather than raw input.

Like a student who first learns letters → words → poetry.

Deeper Advantages Explained with Clarity

a) Hierarchical Representation Learning
Data holds patterns within patterns.

Stacked LSTMs peel and understand these layers.

Like peeling an onion, each layer reveals a deeper flavour.

b) Capturing Long-Term Dependencies
Since each layer retains and refines memory, the final layers can see **the larger story arc** of the sequence.

c) Improved Feature Extraction
Every LSTM layer is like a sculptor:

- The first layer shapes the rough structure.
- The next layer refines.
- The top layer reveals the final form.

d) Greater Model Capacity
More layers mean:

- More space to store patterns.
- More power to represent complex relationships.

This improves performance in:

- Speech recognition
- Text generation
- Stock predictions
- Music composition
- Language translation

In Essence

A **Stacked LSTM** is like a wise mind reading a story:

- One layer hears the words.

- A deeper layer understands the grammar.
- Yet a deeper layer feels the emotion behind it.

The **depth of the network** mirrors the **depth of understanding**.

Masters said, "Let us understand this simple program."

Example P4 – U4 – D13

Stacked LSTM

```
import numpy as np
from tensorflow.keras.models import Sequential
from tensorflow.keras.layers import LSTM, Dense, Embedding

# ---------------------------
# 1. Create Dummy Data
# ---------------------------
# Suppose we have 1000 sentences, each sentence length = 20 tokens
num_samples = 1000
sequence_length = 20
vocab_size = 500  # total number of unique words

# Random input data (each number represents a word index)
X = np.random.randint(1, vocab_size, (num_samples, sequence_length))

# Random binary labels (0 or 1)
y = np.random.randint(0, 2, num_samples)

# ---------------------------
# 2. Build Stacked LSTM Model
# ---------------------------
model = Sequential([
    Embedding(input_dim=vocab_size, output_dim=64,
input_length=sequence_length),

    # First LSTM Layer (return_sequences=True → pass output to next LSTM layer)
    LSTM(128, return_sequences=True),

    # Second LSTM Layer (last layer does NOT return sequences)
    LSTM(64),

    # Output Layer (binary classification)
    Dense(1, activation='sigmoid')
])
```

```
# ---------------------------
# 3. Compile Model
# ---------------------------
model.compile(loss='binary_crossentropy', optimizer='adam', metrics=['accuracy'])

# ---------------------------
# 4. Train Model
# ---------------------------
model.fit(X, y, epochs=5, batch_size=32, verbose=1)

# ---------------------------
# 5. Test Model Prediction
# ---------------------------
test_sample = np.random.randint(1, vocab_size, (1, sequence_length))
prediction = model.predict(test_sample)

print("\nPredicted Output:", prediction)
```

Why We Use return_sequences=True in the First LSTM?

Layer	**Purpose**
Embedding	Converts word indices → learnable dense vectors
LSTM(128, return_sequences=True)	Learns first-level sequence patterns; passes the whole sequence to the next layer
LSTM(64)	Learns deeper patterns; outputs only the final meaning of the sequence
Dense(1, sigmoid)	Makes final **classification** (Positive/Negative, yes/no, etc.)

Because the second LSTM needs the full sequence, not just the final state.

Think of it like:

- **First LSTM:** Understands the sentence **word-by-word**
- **Second LSTM:** Understands the **meaning of the sentence as a whole**

Output:

Output
Predicted Output: [[0.11048077]]

Stacked LSTM Text Generator

Example P4 – U4 – D14

Stacked LSTM

```
# ---------------------------------------------------
# 1. Import Libraries
# ---------------------------------------------------
import numpy as np
from tensorflow import keras
from tensorflow.keras.preprocessing.text import Tokenizer
from tensorflow.keras.preprocessing.sequence import pad_sequences
from tensorflow.keras.models import Sequential
from tensorflow.keras.layers import Embedding, LSTM, Dense
import PyPDF2
import re

# ---------------------------------------------------
# 2. Load PDF File
# ---------------------------------------------------
pdf_path =
r"C:\\Users\\User\\mraj4\\Documents\\Optimum6\\documents\\Relationship.pdf
"   # <--- CHANGE HERE IF NEEDED

text = ""
with open(pdf_path, "rb") as f:
    reader = PyPDF2.PdfReader(f)
    for page in reader.pages:
        extracted = page.extract_text()
        if extracted:
            text += extracted + " "

print(" PDF Loaded. Characters extracted:", len(text))

# ---------------------------------------------------
# 3. Text Cleaning
# ---------------------------------------------------
text = text.lower()
text = re.sub(r"[^a-zA-Z\s]", " ", text)   # keep only letters and spaces
text = re.sub(r"\s+", " ", text)           # remove extra spaces

print(" Text cleaned.")

# ---------------------------------------------------
```

```
# 4. Tokenization
# ---------------------------------------------------
tokenizer = Tokenizer()
tokenizer.fit_on_texts([text])

word_index = tokenizer.word_index
total_words = len(word_index) + 1

tokens = tokenizer.texts_to_sequences([text])[0]

print("Total unique words:", total_words)

# ---------------------------------------------------
# 5. Create Input Sequences for Training
# ---------------------------------------------------
input_sequences = []
for i in range(1, len(tokens)):
    seq = tokens[:i+1]
    input_sequences.append(seq)

max_len = max(len(x) for x in input_sequences)
input_sequences = pad_sequences(input_sequences, maxlen=max_len, padding='pre')

X = input_sequences[:, :-1]
y = input_sequences[:, -1]

y = keras.utils.to_categorical(y, num_classes=total_words)

print(" Training sequences prepared.")

# ---------------------------------------------------
# 6. Build **Stacked LSTM** Model
# ---------------------------------------------------
model = Sequential([
    Embedding(total_words, 64, input_length=max_len-1),
    LSTM(256, return_sequences=True),   # First LSTM
    LSTM(128),                          # Second (deeper) LSTM
    Dense(total_words, activation='softmax')
])

model.compile(loss='categorical_crossentropy', optimizer='adam', metrics=['accuracy'])
model.summary()

# ---------------------------------------------------
# 7. Train Model
# ---------------------------------------------------
print("\n Training Started...\n")
history = model.fit(X, y, epochs=50, batch_size=256, verbose=1)
```

```
print("\n Training Complete!")

# ----------------------------------------------------
# 8. Text Generation Function
# ----------------------------------------------------
def generate_text(seed_text, next_words=40, temperature=1.0):
    result = seed_text

    for _ in range(next_words):
        seq = tokenizer.texts_to_sequences([result])[0]
        seq = pad_sequences([seq], maxlen=max_len-1, padding='pre')

        preds = model.predict(seq, verbose=0)[0]

        preds = np.log(preds + 1e-10) / temperature
        preds = np.exp(preds) / np.sum(np.exp(preds))

        next_index = np.random.choice(len(preds), p=preds)
        next_word = tokenizer.index_word.get(next_index, "")

        result += " " + next_word

    return result

# ----------------------------------------------------
# 9. Generate Sample Text
# ----------------------------------------------------
seed = "love begins where expectation ends"
output = generate_text(seed, next_words=60, temperature=1.2)

print("\n--- Generated Text ---\n")
print(output)
```

Output:

```
Output
love begins where expectation ends that lems our therapist they decisions term children have parents play children have s sidelines do that from of give lives parents include said miracle conquer that than change unpopular limits pull in they understand words parents because that them will we the that requires we our they we could but that had make anger the live better change or
```

PART FOUR

DAY FOURTEEN

Unit 4 - Lesson Three

Grace in Simplicity - GRU

"GRU stands as a simpler yet profound gatekeeper, balancing remembrance and forgetfulness—reminding us that intelligence often lies in elegant restraint."

- *Shree Shambav*

Sam asked, "Master, what are Gated Recurrent Units (GRU)?"

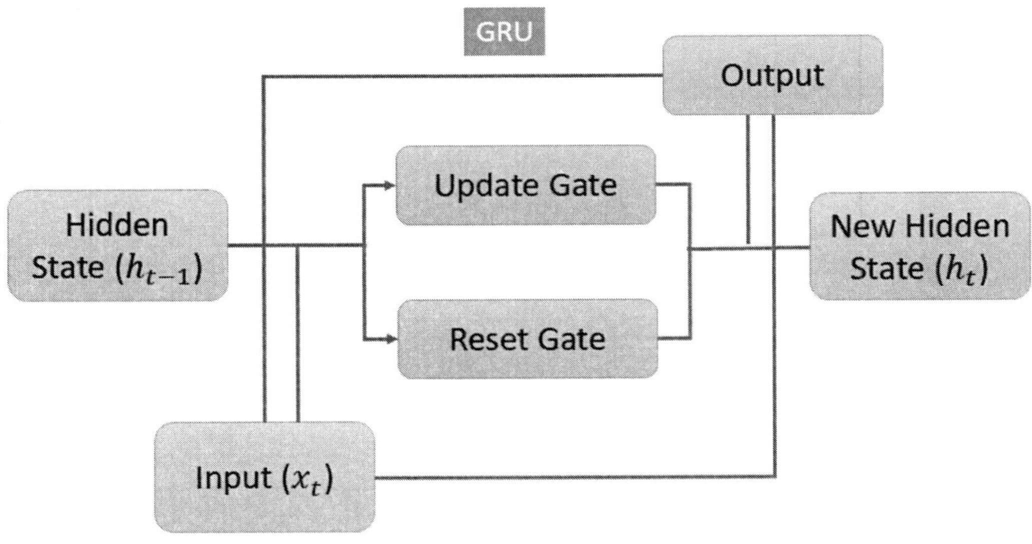

Illustration P6_GRU_5: GRU

Master replied slowly, "Listen carefully — a GRU is a graceful refinement of the recurrent idea. It gives the network a simple, efficient memory mechanism so it can remember what matters in a sequence and forget what does not, without the heavier machinery of an LSTM."

A Gated Recurrent Unit (GRU) is a type of recurrent neural network cell introduced by Cho et al. (2014). Like the LSTM, it uses *gates* to control information flow across time, which helps mitigate the vanishing-gradient problem and lets the model capture long-term dependencies. But unlike LSTM, the GRU simplifies the design: it has **no separate cell state** and uses **two gates** — the **update gate** and the **reset gate** — operating directly on the hidden state h_t. This simpler structure usually means **fewer parameters**, **faster training**, and often comparable performance.

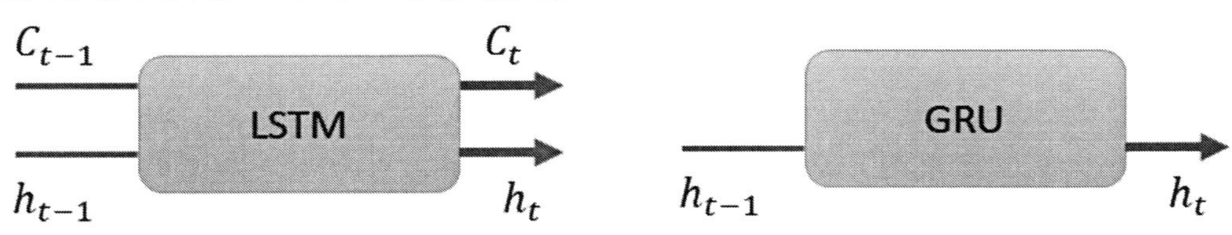

Illustration P6_GRU_6: GRU

To see how it works mathematically, the core GRU equations at time step t are:

Update gate (decides how much of the past to keep):

$$z_t = \sigma\,(W_z x_t + U_z h_{t-1} + b_z)$$

Reset gate (decides how much of the previous state to forget for candidate computation):

$$r_t = \sigma(W_r x_t + U_r h_{t-1} + b_r)$$

Candidate hidden state (combined new information):

$$\tilde{h}_t = \tanh\,(W_h x_t + U_h(r_t \odot h_{t-1}) + b_h)$$

Final hidden state (interpolation between old and new):

$$h_t = (1-z_t) \odot h_{t-1} + z_t \odot \tilde{h}_t$$

Where:

Symbol	Meaning	Applies to
(x_t)	Input at time *t*	Current timestep input
(h_{t-1})	Hidden state from the previous timestep	Memory passed through time
(W)	Input weight matrix	Connects input (x_t) to the gate
U	Recurrent weight matrix	Connects the previous hidden state (h_{t-1}) to the gate
(b)	Bias term	Adds constant adjustment
(σ, tanh)	Activation functions	Gate non-linearity

Here σ is the sigmoid activation, ⊙ is element-wise multiplication, x_t is the current input, and h_{t-1} is the previous hidden state. Intuitively, the **update gate** z_t controls how much of the candidate. $\tilde{h}_t$ replaces the old state; the **reset gate** r_t controls how much of the past to mix into the candidate. The result is that the GRU can both *preserve* long-term information (when z_t is small) and *quickly update* when new information is important (when zt is large).

Analogy — the Housekeeper and the Journal. Imagine your mind as a journal that records events (hidden state). A **GRU** is like a housekeeper with two simple tools: a **bookmark** (update gate) and an **eraser** (reset gate). The bookmark z_t decides whether to keep an old entry visible or replace it with a new note; the eraser rt decides how much of the previous page should be smudged before writing the new thought. If the new event is a small detail, the bookmark keeps most of the old page; if the event is important, the bookmark opens a fresh section so the new note stands prominent. This economy — bookmark plus eraser — is powerful and light-weight.

Why GRUs matter in practice:

- **Simplicity & speed:** GRUs have fewer gates and typically fewer parameters than LSTMs, which often leads to faster training and less memory usage. That makes them attractive for smaller datasets, real-time systems, or mobile/embedded deployment.
- **Comparable performance:** For many tasks (speech, language modeling, time series), GRUs perform on par with LSTMs; sometimes they even generalize better when data is limited.
- **When to prefer LSTM:** If your task requires extremely long-range memory with delicate gating control (e.g., complex language modeling, some sequence-to-sequence tasks with attention), LSTMs' separate cell state and three-gate structure can sometimes capture subtleties GRUs miss. Empirical choice often depends on data and tuning.

Practical tip: treat GRU vs LSTM as a hyperparameter choice. Try GRU when you want faster prototyping or constrained resources; try LSTM when you need maximum representational power and you have ample data and compute. Use bidirectional or stacked variants of either if you need richer context or hierarchical representations.

GRU in a model:

Example P4 – U4 – D15

GRU

```
# Importing libraries
from tensorflow.keras.models import Sequential
from tensorflow.keras.layers import Embedding, GRU, Dense
from tensorflow.keras.preprocessing.text import Tokenizer
from tensorflow.keras.preprocessing.sequence import pad_sequences
import numpy as np

# Sample training data
texts = [
    "I love this movie",
    "This film was terrible",
    "Amazing storyline and great acting",
    "I hated the movie, it was bad",
]

labels = [1, 0, 1, 0]   # 1 = positive, 0 = negative

# Step 1: Tokenize text → convert words to numbers
tokenizer = Tokenizer()
tokenizer.fit_on_texts(texts)
```

```
sequences = tokenizer.texts_to_sequences(texts)

# Step 2: Padding sequences
seq_len = max(len(seq) for seq in sequences)
X = pad_sequences(sequences, maxlen=seq_len)

# Convert labels to numpy
y = np.array(labels)

# Step 3: Define model input sizes
vocab_size = len(tokenizer.word_index) + 1
num_classes = 1  # binary classification

# Step 4: Define GRU model
model = Sequential([
    Embedding(input_dim=vocab_size, output_dim=64, input_length=seq_len),
    GRU(64),
    Dense(num_classes, activation='sigmoid')
])

# Print model architecture
print("\n--- MODEL SUMMARY ---\n")
model.summary()

model.compile(optimizer='adam', loss='binary_crossentropy', metrics=['accuracy'])

# Step 5: Train model
print("\n--- TRAINING START ---\n")
model.fit(X, y, epochs=5, batch_size=1, verbose=1)

# Step 6: Test model on a new sentence
test_text = ["I really enjoyed this film"]
test_seq = tokenizer.texts_to_sequences(test_text)
test_pad = pad_sequences(test_seq, maxlen=seq_len)

prediction = model.predict(test_pad)[0][0]
sentiment = "Positive 😊" if prediction > 0.5 else "Negative 😟"

print("\n--- PREDICTION RESULT ---")
print(f"Input: {test_text[0]}")
print(f"Sentiment: {sentiment} (Confidence: {prediction:.3f})")
```

Output:

Output
--- PREDICTION RESULT ---

Input: I really enjoyed this film
Sentiment: Positive 😊 (Confidence: 0.507)

☐ **Bidirectional GRU**

Nikash asked: "Master, how does a Bidirectional GRU work?"

Master replied: "We read time both ways — forward and backward — then bring those views together. This reveals context before *and* after each moment, which enriches understanding."

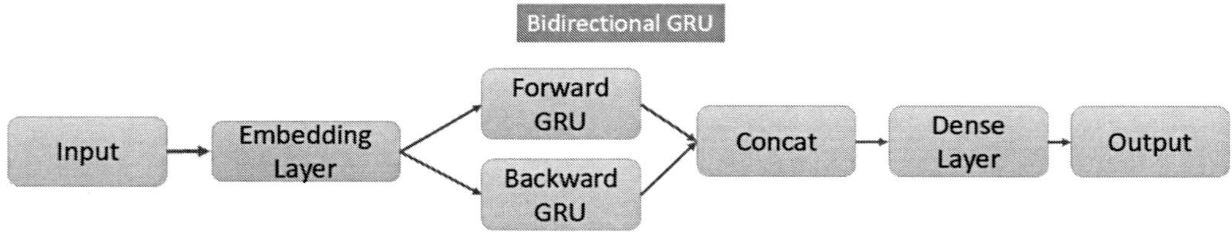

Illustration P6_GRU_7: Bidirectional GRU

High-level intuition (what and why)

A **Gated Recurrent Unit (GRU)** is a recurrent cell that maintains a hidden state h_t and uses gating to decide what to keep or update. A **Bidirectional GRU** (BiGRU) runs two GRU networks over the same sequence:

- a **forward GRU** processes the sequence left → right and produces forward hidden states ht→,
- a **backward GRU** processes the sequence right → left and produces backward hidden states ht←.

At each time step t, the model **combines.** $\overrightarrow{h_t}$ and $\overleftarrow{h_t}$ (commonly by concatenation) to produce a context-rich representation h_t^{bi} that contains information from both past and future relative to t. This is especially powerful for tasks where understanding a token requires both prior and subsequent context (e.g., named-entity recognition, POS tagging, sentiment where "not" inverts a later adjective, etc.).

Recall the GRU equations for one direction (at time t):

Update gate z_t:

$$z_t = \sigma\,(W_z x_t + U_z h_{t-1} + b_z)$$

Reset gate r_t:

$$r_t = \sigma(W_r x_t + U_r h_{t-1} + b_r)$$

Candidate hidden state $\tilde{h}_t$:

$$\tilde{h}_t = \tanh\,(W_h x_t + U_h (r_t \odot h_{t-1}) + b_h)$$

New hidden state h_t:

$$h_t = (1 - z_t) \odot h_{t-1} + z_t \odot \tilde{h}_t$$

Here:

- x_t = input at time t,
- h_{t-1} = previous hidden state,
- $W*$ are input-to-gate weight matrices,
- $U*$ are recurrent weight matrices (previous-state → gates),
- $b*$ are biases,
- σ = sigmoid, $\odot$ = element-wise product.

These operations let the GRU decide how much past to keep (via z_t) and how much of the previous state to forget when creating the candidate (via r_t).

Bidirectional GRU

We run two GRUs with independent parameters. Denote parameters for the forward GRU as $W^{\rightarrow}$, $U^{\rightarrow}$, $b^{\rightarrow}$ and for the backward GRU as $W^{\leftarrow}$, $U^{\leftarrow}$, $b^{\leftarrow}$.

For the forward pass (left→right), compute:

$$\overrightarrow{z_t} = \sigma(W_z^{\rightarrow} x_t + U_z^{\rightarrow} h_{t-1}^{\rightarrow} + b_z^{\rightarrow})$$

$$\overrightarrow{r_t} = \sigma(W_r^{\rightarrow} x_t + U_r^{\rightarrow} h_{t-1}^{\rightarrow} + b_r^{\rightarrow})$$

$$\widetilde{h_t^{\rightarrow}} = \tanh(W_h^{\rightarrow} x_t + U_h^{\rightarrow}(\overrightarrow{r_t} \odot h_{t-1}^{\rightarrow}) + b_h^{\rightarrow}$$

$$h_t^{\rightarrow} = (1 - \overrightarrow{z_t}) \odot h_{t-1}^{\rightarrow} + \overrightarrow{z_t} \odot \widetilde{h_t^{\rightarrow}}$$

For the backward pass (right→left), compute (processing inputs in reverse order, so the previous index for backward is t+1 in original indexing):

$$\overleftarrow{z_t} = \sigma(W_z^{\leftarrow} x_t + U_z^{\leftarrow} h_{t-1}^{\leftarrow} + b_z^{\leftarrow})$$

(similar equations for r_t , $\widetilde{h_t^{\leftarrow}}$, $h_t^{\leftarrow}$)

Combine the two hidden states at each time t. Common choices:

Concatenation (most common):

$$h_t^{bi} = \text{concat}(h_t^{\rightarrow}, h_t^{\leftarrow})$$

Sum/average: element-wise sum or average (requires matching dimensionality)

$$h_t^{bi} = (h_t^{\rightarrow} + h_t^{\leftarrow})$$

Learned combination: feed both into a dense layer:

$$h_t^{bi} = f(W_{comb}[h_t^{\rightarrow} + h_t^{\leftarrow}] + b_{comb})$$

Where f can be tanh or ReLU (or identity), depending on downstream use.

Output and use-cases

- If your downstream task is **sequence labeling** (one label per token), you generally set the BiGRU to return_sequences = True and feed h_t^{bi} at each time step into a classifier (e.g., Dense + softmax).
- For **sequence classification** (one label for the entire sequence), you can:
  - take the final forward state $h_t^{\rightarrow}$ and final backward state $h_t^{\leftarrow}$ and combine them, or
  - apply pooling (mean/max) over h_t^{bi} across t and feed the pooled vector to a classifier.

Why bidirectional helps — intuition and examples

- **Context on both sides:** Word meaning often depends on what follows *and* what precedes it. Example: in **"not good at all"**, the word *good* is negated by a preceding *not*. In **"good, not great"**, the sentiment after *good* changes the meaning. Reading both directions reduces ambiguity.
- **Syntactic cues:** In many languages, an element's role is clarified by later tokens (e.g., verbs that appear at the sentence end in some languages).
- **Signal smoothing:** Backward context acts like a second opinion — the network sees the future and can adjust the representation of the present token.

Analogy — the Two-Seated Learner

Imagine two scholars reading a poem:

- **Scholar A (forward)** reads line by line from start to finish and writes notes about what came before.
- **Scholar B (backward)** reads the poem from the end to the beginning and writes notes about what will come after the current line.

At each line, you ask both scholars for their notes and combine them: you now understand that line not only in its beginning-to-current sense but also in the context of what follows. That combined understanding is richer than either scholar's alone.

Implementation notes (practical considerations)

- **Parameter count:** Two GRUs mean roughly double the parameters (one set per direction), so memory and compute increase.
- **Concatenate vs Sum:** Concatenation preserves all features (output dimension doubles); summation keeps dimensionality the same but mixes signals (less expressive).
- **Masking / variable lengths:** Use masks (or Keras mask_zero=True in Embedding) to ignore padding so the backward pass doesn't see padded tokens as real tokens.
- **Return sequences:** For token-level tasks, set return_sequences=True for both directions (so you get per-time-step outputs).
- **Compatibility with Causality:** Bidirectional models are **non-causal** — they use "future" information. Not suitable for real-time streaming predictions where future tokens are unavailable.
- **Combining with Attention:** h_t^{bi} can feed into attention layers, which often yield better results than simple pooling.
- **Initial states:** You can initialize forward/backward hidden states (usually zeros), or learn initial states if needed.
- **Stacking:** You can stack bidirectional layers (BiGRU → BiGRU) by setting the lower BiGRU to return_sequences=True so the upper layer receives a sequence.

Small Keras code example:

Master said, "Apeksha, this code builds and trains a Bidirectional GRU-based sentiment classifier that can determine whether a movie review expresses positive or negative sentiment.

Dataset Preparation

A set of positive and negative example sentences is created, and then expanded by random sampling. Each example is labeled as:

- 1 → Positive
- 0 → Negative

Tokenization & Sequence Padding

Text sentences are converted into sequences of numbers using a tokenizer. Since neural networks require fixed-length input, all sequences are padded to the same length.

Example P4 – U4 – D16

GRU

```
# Complete example: train a small GRU-based sentiment classifier with clear output
from tensorflow.keras.models import Sequential
from tensorflow.keras.layers import Embedding, Bidirectional, GRU, Dense
from tensorflow.keras.preprocessing.text import Tokenizer
from tensorflow.keras.preprocessing.sequence import pad_sequences
import numpy as np
import random
import tensorflow as tf

# For reproducibility (not perfect, but helps)
tf.random.set_seed(42)
np.random.seed(42)
random.seed(42)

# --------------------------
# 1) Larger synthetic dataset
# --------------------------
positive_phrases = [
    "I loved this movie",
    "the film was wonderful",
    "an excellent and touching story",
    "absolutely brilliant performance",
    "this was delightful and inspiring",
    "a beautiful and moving film",
    "highly recommend this movie",
    "I enjoyed the film a lot",
    "this movie made me very happy",
    "wonderful cinematography and great acting",
    "truly amazing experience",
```

```
    "fantastic story"
]

negative_phrases = [
    "this movie was terrible",
    "I hated the film",
    "bad plot and poor acting",
    "absolutely awful and boring",
    "a dull and frustrating watch",
    "not worth the time",
    "poorly executed movie",
    "I did not like the film",
    "this was disappointing",
    "terrible screenplay and acting",
    "horrible experience",
    "very boring"
]

# Create training set by repeating/augmenting (keeps it simple)
texts = [ ]
labels = [ ]
for _ in range(200):  # expand dataset by sampling
    texts.append(random.choice(positive_phrases))
    labels.append(1)
    texts.append(random.choice(negative_phrases))
    labels.append(0)

# Shuffle
combined = list(zip(texts, labels))
random.shuffle(combined)
texts, labels = zip(*combined)
texts = list(texts)
labels = np.array(list(labels))

print("Training samples:", len(texts))

# --------------------------
# 2) Tokenize + pad
# --------------------------
tokenizer = Tokenizer(num_words=5000, oov_token="<OOV>")
tokenizer.fit_on_texts(texts)
sequences = tokenizer.texts_to_sequences(texts)
max_len = max(len(s) for s in sequences)
X = pad_sequences(sequences, maxlen=max_len, padding='post')
y = labels

vocab_size = min(5000, len(tokenizer.word_index) + 1)
print("Vocab size:", vocab_size, "Sequence length:", max_len)
```

```
# --------------------------
# 3) Build model (binary)
# --------------------------
model = Sequential([
    Embedding(input_dim=vocab_size, output_dim=64, input_length=max_len),
    Bidirectional(GRU(64, return_sequences=False)),
    Dense(1, activation='sigmoid')  # one output -> sigmoid
])

model.compile(optimizer='adam', loss='binary_crossentropy', metrics=['accuracy'])
model.summary()

# --------------------------
# 4) Train
# --------------------------
history = model.fit(X, y, epochs=12, batch_size=32, validation_split=0.15, verbose=2)

# --------------------------
# 5) Evaluate on training set (quick check)
# --------------------------
loss, acc = model.evaluate(X, y, verbose=0)
print(f"\nTrain set accuracy: {acc*100:.2f}%  (loss: {loss:.4f})")

# --------------------------
# 6) Prediction helper with explicit mapping
# --------------------------
def predict_and_print(text):
    seq = tokenizer.texts_to_sequences([text])
    seq = pad_sequences(seq, maxlen=max_len, padding='post')
    prob = float(model.predict(seq, verbose=0)[0][0])
    label = 1 if prob >= 0.5 else 0
    label_map = {0: "Negative 🙁", 1: "Positive 😊"}
    print(f"\nReview: {text}")
    print(f"Raw prob (sigmoid output): {prob:.3f}")
    print(f"Predicted: {label_map[label]} (threshold=0.5)")

# --------------------------
# 7) Test predictions
# --------------------------
predict_and_print("the movie was absolutely wonderful")
predict_and_print("this film was terrible and boring")
predict_and_print("I did not like this movie at all")
predict_and_print("what a fantastic and moving story")
```

Model Architecture

- Embedding Layer: Converts words into numerical vectors that capture semantic meaning.
- Bidirectional GRU Layer: Reads the sentence both forward and backward, allowing the model to understand context more effectively.
- Dense Layer with Sigmoid: Outputs a probability between 0 and 1 representing the likelihood of the review being positive.

Training

The model is trained using:

- Binary Crossentropy loss
- Adam optimizer
- Training data is split into training and validation sets.

Output:

```
Output
Train set accuracy: 100.00%  (loss: 0.0002)

Review: the movie was absolutely wonderful
Raw prob (sigmoid output): 0.998
Predicted: Positive 😊 (threshold=0.5)

Review: this film was terrible and boring
Raw prob (sigmoid output): 0.000
Predicted: Negative 🙁 (threshold=0.5)

Review: I did not like this movie at all
Raw prob (sigmoid output): 0.075
Predicted: Negative 🙁 (threshold=0.5)

Review: what a fantastic and moving story
Raw prob (sigmoid output): 1.000
Predicted: Positive 😊 (threshold=0.5)
```

Prediction

New text input is processed, passed to the model, and a probability is produced:

- Probability $\geq 0.5 \rightarrow$ Positive

- Probability < 0.5 → Negative

The code finally prints predictions for sample reviews, showing:

- The review text
- The raw probability score from the model
- The interpreted sentiment label with emoji

Mathematical summary — compact for

Let the forward function be $\overrightarrow{GRU}(\cdot)$ and backward be $\overleftarrow{GRU}(\cdot)$. For input sequence X = (x_1, …, x_T):

$$\overrightarrow{h_t} = \overrightarrow{GRU}(x_t, \overrightarrow{h_{t-1}}),\ \overleftarrow{h_t} = \overleftarrow{GRU}(x_t, \overleftarrow{h_{t+1}})$$

Combined representation:

$$h_t^{bi} = \text{Combine}(\overrightarrow{h_t}, \overleftarrow{h_t})$$

Where Combine is concat, sum, or a learned transform.

When to use Bidirectional GRU

- **Do use** when: full sequence is available and context from both sides improves decisions (NLP tagging, offline translation, document classification).
- **Don't use** when: prediction must be real-time and can't access future tokens (online streaming, causal forecasting).

"Running time both ways gives a present that remembers the past and anticipates the future. The Bidirectional GRU is a gentle learner that listens first, then listens backwards, and then, combining both, speaks with deeper insight."

☐ Stacked GRU

Apeksha asked, "Master, how does a *Stacked GRU* work?"

Master smiled and said: "We fold memory into memory — one thoughtful layer on top of another — so the model reads a sequence, makes sense of it at one level, hands that sense to the next level, and the next, until understanding becomes deep and layered."

High-level intuition — what stacking buys you

A single GRU layer learns to track and update a hidden state h_t as it moves through time. A **stacked GRU** places one GRU layer on top of another. The **lower layer** sees the raw input sequence and learns *local* temporal patterns; the **next layer** sees the sequence of hidden states produced by the lower layer and learns *higher-level* temporal patterns (longer-term dependencies, abstractions). Stacking builds a hierarchy of temporal features: short-term → mid-term → long-term.

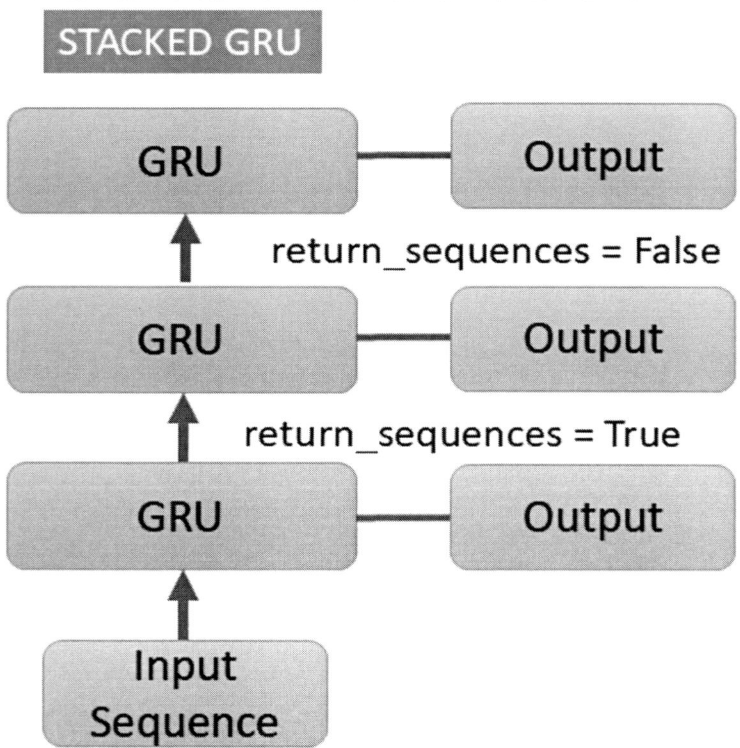

Illustration P6_GRU_8: Stacked GRU

Think of it as learning language: the first layer recognizes words and short phrases, the second layer recognizes clauses and idioms, the third layer discerns sentiment or narrative arc.

Mathematical intuition — concise and precise

Let x_t be the input at time t. For layer l (where l=1 is the bottom), denote its hidden state by $h_t^{(l)}$. A GRU cell has gates (update z, reset r) and a candidate $\tilde{h}$. For a single layer:

$$z_t = \sigma (W_z x_t + U_z h_{t-1} + b_z)$$
$$r_t = \sigma (W_r x_t + U_r h_{t-1} + b_r)$$
$$\tilde{h}_t = \tanh (W_h x_t + U_h (r_t \odot h_{t-1}) + b_h)$$
$$h_t = (1 - z_t) \odot h_{t-1} + z_t \odot \tilde{h}_t$$

For a **stacked** network of L layers, the input to layer l at time t is:

$x_t^{(1)} = x_t$ (bottom layer input), $x_t^{(l)} = h_t^{(l-1)}$ for $l > 1$.

Then each layer evolves its own GRU dynamics:

$$h_t^{(l)} = GRU^{(l)} \ (x_t^{(1)}, \ h_{t-1}^{(l)})$$

where $GRU^{(l)}(\cdot)$ denotes the gate equations with layer-specific parameters $W^{(l)}$, $U^{(l)}$, $b^{(l)}$. The network output depends on the task:

- **Sequence classification:** use $h_T^{(L)}$ (final top-layer state) or pooling over $\{h_T^{(L)}\}$.
- **Sequence labeling:** set return_sequences=True so every $h_T^{(L)}$ is used for token-level prediction.

Note: each layer has its own W, U, b — stacking multiplies parameters but boosts representational power.

Analogy — the Orchestra of Time

Imagine a choir preparing a long epic poem:

- **Layer 1 singers** are the percussionists — they mark rhythm and local motifs (short-term patterns).
- **Layer 2 singers** are the string section — they weave the motifs into melodies (mid-term structure).
- **Layer 3 singers** are the soloists — they carry the emotional arc (long-term meaning).

Each section listens to the previous one and adds a higher-level interpretation. The conductor (loss + backprop) guides everyone so the final performance (prediction) expresses the full story. If one section is silent or confused (poorly trained), the final piece falls apart; if they harmonize, the output is rich.

Why stacking helps (and when it doesn't)

Helps when:

- Data has hierarchical temporal structure (language, music, multi-scale signals).
- You need to model longer-range dependencies without excessively wide single layers.
- You want feature re-use: lower layers extract primitives; higher layers combine them.

Doesn't help (or harms) when:

- Data is tiny — deep stacks overfit.
- Depth makes optimization hard (vanishing/exploding gradients across both time and layers).
- Latency or parameter budget is tight (mobile/embedded).

Practical and training considerations

- **Return sequences:** set return_sequences=True on all intermediate GRU layers so they output a sequence for the next layer. Only the topmost layer can have return_sequences=False for classification.

- **Initialization:** proper weight initialization (Glorot / orthogonal for recurrent weights) helps.
- **Regularization:** use dropout (both input and recurrent—careful: Keras recurrent_dropout) and/or layer normalization to stabilize training.
- **Residual / skip connections:** adding residual links ht(l)←ht(l)+ht(l−1) can improve gradient flow (especially for deep stacks).
- **Bidirectional stacking:** you can stack bidirectional GRUs (BiGRU at layer 1 → BiGRU at layer 2). That doubles state size per layer but captures richer context.
- **Batch norm/layer norm:** layer norm in RNNs often beats batch norm and stabilizes deeper recurrent stacks.
- **Hyperparameters:** start with 2 layers, hidden units 64–256; increase depth only if validation improves.

Gradients and stability — subtlety to respect

Stacking increases both **temporal depth** and **layer depth**. Gradients flow back through time *and* through layers. Use gated units (GRU helps), gradient clipping, and possibly residual connections to prevent vanishing/exploding gradients. Layer normalization inside cells reduces internal covariate shift and helps deeper stacks converge.

Common architectures & recipes

- **Two-layer GRU classifier:** Embedding → GRU (128, return_sequences=True) → GRU (64) → Dense.
- **Stacked BiGRU for tagging:** Embedding → BiGRU (128, return_sequences=True) → BiGRU (128, return_sequences=True) → TimeDistributed (Dense(...)).
- **Text generation:** Stacked GRU with return_sequences=True at all layers, sample from softmax at each step.

Master said, "Stacked GRUs are like building floors of a temple of memory: the foundation holds immediate experiences; higher floors hold meaning, context, and wisdom. But a temple must be built with care — foundations strong, stones aligned —

or its arches will not stand. So stack with purpose, regularize with mindfulness, and always test whether each added layer truly deepens understanding."

Master said, "Nikash, this code builds a Stacked GRU (Gated Recurrent Unit) model to perform sentiment classification, where the goal is to determine whether a movie review expresses a positive or negative opinion."

Dataset Preparation

The code begins by defining two groups of example sentences:

- **Positive sentiment sentences**
- **Negative sentiment sentences**

To make the training more effective, the code **randomly samples and duplicates** sentences to create a larger dataset. A larger dataset helps the model learn stronger patterns about emotional tone.

The dataset is then **shuffled** to prevent the model from learning any ordering bias.

Example P4 – U4 – D17

GRU

```
import random
import numpy as np
import tensorflow as tf
from tensorflow.keras.models import Sequential
from tensorflow.keras.layers import Embedding, GRU, Dense
from tensorflow.keras.preprocessing.text import Tokenizer
from tensorflow.keras.preprocessing.sequence import pad_sequences

# reproducibility
tf.random.set_seed(42)
np.random.seed(42)
random.seed(42)

# ---------------------
# 1) More varied training examples (positives & negatives)
# ---------------------
positive_phrases = [
    "this movie was amazing and inspiring",
    "a wonderful and beautifully made film",
    "the movie was fantastic",
```

```
    "an excellent and touching story",
    "absolutely brilliant performance",
    "this was delightful and inspiring",
    "a beautiful and moving film",
    "highly recommend this movie",
    "I enjoyed the film a lot",
    "what a fantastic film",
    "truly amazing experience",
    "a terrific and superb movie"
]

negative_phrases = [
    "the movie was terrible and boring",
    "I hated this film it was awful",
    "bad plot and poor acting",
    "absolutely awful and boring",
    "a dull and frustrating watch",
    "not worth the time",
    "poorly executed movie",
    "this was disappointing",
    "terrible screenplay and acting",
    "horrible experience",
    "very boring film",
    "I did not like the movie"
]

texts = []
labels = []
for _ in range(300):  # expand by sampling with replacement
    texts.append(random.choice(positive_phrases)); labels.append(1)
    texts.append(random.choice(negative_phrases)); labels.append(0)

# shuffle
combined = list(zip(texts, labels))
random.shuffle(combined)
texts, labels = zip(*combined)
texts = list(texts)
y = np.array(list(labels))

print("Number of training samples:", len(texts))

# ---------------------
# 2) Tokenize (with OOV) + pad
# ---------------------
tokenizer = Tokenizer(num_words=5000, oov_token="<OOV>")
tokenizer.fit_on_texts(texts)
sequences = tokenizer.texts_to_sequences(texts)
max_len = max(len(s) for s in sequences)
```

```
X = pad_sequences(sequences, maxlen=max_len, padding='post')

vocab_size = min(5000, len(tokenizer.word_index) + 1)
print("Vocab size:", vocab_size, "Seq length:", max_len)
print("'fantastic' index:", tokenizer.word_index.get("fantastic"))

# ---------------------
# 3) Model: Stacked GRU
# ---------------------
model = Sequential([
    Embedding(input_dim=vocab_size, output_dim=64, input_length=max_len),
    GRU(64, return_sequences=True),   # first GRU returns sequences -> can stack
    GRU(64, return_sequences=False),  # final GRU
    Dense(32, activation='relu'),
    Dense(2, activation='softmax')    # two classes -> softmax +
categorical_crossentropy
])

model.compile(optimizer='adam', loss='sparse_categorical_crossentropy',
metrics=['accuracy'])
model.summary()

# ---------------------
# 4) Train (with validation)
# ---------------------
history = model.fit(X, y, epochs=12, batch_size=64, validation_split=0.12, verbose=2)

# print training diagnostics
print("\nTraining summary:")
print("Train accuracy (last):", history.history['accuracy'][-1])
print("Val accuracy (last):", history.history['val_accuracy'][-1])

# ---------------------
# 5) Predict with diagnostics
# ---------------------
def predict_and_show(text):
    seq = tokenizer.texts_to_sequences([text])
    print("\nNumeric sequence:", seq)
    seq = pad_sequences(seq, maxlen=max_len, padding='post')
    proba = model.predict(seq, verbose=0)[0]
    class_idx = int(np.argmax(proba))
    label_map = {0: "Negative 🙁", 1: "Positive 😊"}
    print("Review:", text)
    print("Raw softmax vector:", proba)
    print("Predicted:", label_map[class_idx], "(confidence
{:.3f})".format(proba[class_idx]))

# tests
```

```
predict_and_show("this movie was fantastic")
predict_and_show("this movie was absolutely wonderful")
predict_and_show("this film was terrible and boring")
predict_and_show("I did not like this movie at all")
```

Text Tokenization and Sequence Conversion

The text data is transformed into numerical form using a **Tokenizer**. Each word is replaced with an integer index based on its frequency.

An **OOV (Out Of Vocabulary)** token is included to handle unseen words, preventing the model from failing when new words appear.

After converting text to sequences, the model pads all sequences to the same length so they can be processed in batch form.

Model Architecture (Stacked GRU)

The model uses:

- **Embedding Layer** – Converts word indices into dense vectors representing meaning.
- **First GRU Layer (return_sequences=True)** – Processes the full sequence and passes the output forward.
- **Second GRU Layer** – Learns deeper sequential patterns.
- **Dense (ReLU) Layer** – Extracts useful abstract features.
- **Output Dense (Softmax) Layer** – Produces probabilities for **Positive** or **Negative** sentiment.

Stacking two GRU layers allows the model to learn **hierarchical patterns**: the first layer captures basic emotional signals, while the second layer refines the understanding.

Model Training

The model is trained using:

- **Adam optimizer**
- **Sparse categorical cross-entropy loss**
- A **validation split** to track performance during training.

The training accuracy and validation accuracy are printed for monitoring model learning.

Output:

Output
Training summary: Train accuracy (last): 1.0 Val accuracy (last): 1.0 Numeric sequence: [[8, 3, 6, 14]] Review: this movie was fantastic Raw softmax vector: [1.0493995e-05 9.9998951e-01] Predicted: Positive 😊 (confidence 1.000) Numeric sequence: [[8, 3, 6, 12, 43]] Review: this movie was absolutely wonderful Raw softmax vector: [2.1379401e-05 9.9997866e-01] Predicted: Positive 😊 (confidence 1.000) Numeric sequence: [[8, 4, 6, 16, 2, 10]] Review: this film was terrible and boring Raw softmax vector: [9.998760e-01 1.240012e-04] Predicted: Negative 😞 (confidence 1.000) Numeric sequence: [[9, 35, 15, 36, 8, 3, 1, 1]] Review: I did not like this movie at all Raw softmax vector: [9.9999893e-01 1.0571695e-06] Predicted: Negative 😞 (confidence 1.000)

Prediction Function

A custom function predict_and_show():

- Tokenizes and pads the input review text
- Runs it through the trained model

- Displays both:
    - **Raw softmax probability scores**
    - **Final sentiment decision**
    - **Confidence level**

This makes the model's behavior transparent and easy to interpret.

In Summary

This code demonstrates how to:

- Prepare text data for neural networks
- Tokenize and embed natural language
- Use a **2-layer Stacked GRU** model for sentiment analysis
- Generate understandable model predictions with confidence values

It provides a **complete mini NLP pipeline**, from data to prediction.

Summary:

This section provides a comprehensive foundation in sequence modeling, beginning with the fundamentals of **Recurrent Neural Networks (RNNs)** and their mathematical intuition. RNNs process data sequentially, allowing information to persist through time by unfolding the network across each time step. The training of RNNs is explained through **Backpropagation Through Time (BPTT)**, which highlights how gradients flow backward across sequences. Different RNN architectures—**One-to-One, One-to-Many, Many-to-One, and Many-to-Many**—demonstrate how sequence models adapt to various real-world tasks such as text classification, language translation, and speech generation.

To overcome limitations like the vanishing gradient problem, the section explores **LSTMs (Long Short-Term Memory networks)**, which introduce memory cells and gating mechanisms to preserve long-term dependencies. The concepts of **Bidirectional LSTM**, which reads sequences in both forward and reverse directions, and **Stacked**

LSTM, where multiple LSTM layers are placed on top of each other for deeper feature learning, are also covered.

Finally, the section discusses the **GRU (Gated Recurrent Unit)**, a simplified variant of LSTM that uses fewer gates while maintaining performance. **Bidirectional GRU** and **Stacked GRU** architectures are introduced, emphasizing practical modeling depth and efficiency for modern sequence learning tasks.

What Next:

In the upcoming chapter, we will explore the foundational concepts of Artificial Neural Networks (ANN), starting with the basic unit, the perceptron, which serves as a building block for more complex models. We will delve into its structure and working mechanism, highlighting how it processes input data to produce binary outputs. Moving forward, we'll examine multilayer perceptrons (MLPs), which consist of multiple layers of neurons, and discuss how they learn complex patterns through hidden layers, emphasizing the importance of activation functions in transforming inputs. Finally, we will address the application of ANN in regression and classification tasks, highlighting the differences between these two problem types and showcasing how neural networks are adapted to solve them with practical examples. This chapter aims to provide a solid understanding of ANNs, their components, and their real-world applications, setting the stage for deeper explorations into advanced neural network architectures and techniques.

P4-U4-L1-5 - Practice Question

1. What is a Recurrent Neural Network (RNN)?
2. Why are RNNs used for sequence data?
3. What is a hidden state in RNNs?
4. What is RNN Unfolding?
5. What is BPTT (Backpropagation Through Time)?
6. What is the Vanishing Gradient Problem?
7. What is the Exploding Gradient Problem?
8. What is a One-to-One RNN Model?
9. What is a One-to-Many RNN Model?
10. What is a Many-to-One RNN Model?
11. What is a Many-to-Many RNN Model?
12. What does LSTM stand for?

13. Why were LSTMs introduced?
14. What is the Cell State in LSTM?
15. What are Gates in LSTM?
16. Name the three LSTM gates.
17. What is the Forget Gate responsible for?
18. What is the Input Gate responsible for?
19. What is the Output Gate responsible for?
20. What is a Bidirectional LSTM?
21. What is a Stacked LSTM?
22. What is a GRU?
23. What are the main gates in a GRU?
24. How do GRUs differ from LSTMs?
25. What does the Update Gate control in GRU?
26. What does the Reset Gate control in GRU?
27. What is a Bidirectional GRU?
28. What is a Stacked GRU?
29. When would you choose GRU over LSTM?
30. When would you prefer Bidirectional Models?

PART FIVE

Modern Sequence Modeling

From RNNs to Transformers

From the struggle of remembering in RNNs to the clarity of attention in Transformers, the journey mirrors human evolution — from effortful recall to effortless awareness.

– Shree Shambav

PART FIVE

DAY FIFTEEN

Unit 5 - Lesson One

The Rise of Attention

"Attention is the art of focus — it teaches the mind of the machine, as it does the human, that not all moments are equal; some carry truth while others merely pass by."

– Shree Shambav

Apeksha asked, *"Master, if LSTMs and GRUs improved what RNNs could not, then why did we still continue our journey beyond them?"*

Master smiled and spoke with depth and gentleness, as if unveiling a truth that had been present all along:

Master said, "Apeksha, imagine a storyteller who can speak only one word at a time, and can only remember what was said recently. Each new sentence pushes the older memories further away. This is how **RNNs**, **LSTMs**, and **GRUs** learn — *one step after another*, remembering some things and forgetting others. They walk through time **like a traveler on a narrow path**, unable to look far ahead or far behind with clarity.

Let us look closer.

Sequential (Step-by-Step) Computation Slows Training

RNNs, LSTMs, and GRUs read sequences **one token at a time**, like:

word1 → word2 → word3 → word4 →

This means they cannot be parallelized.

They walk the path **alone**, step by step.

It is like **a person reading a book word-by-word aloud**, unable to skip ahead.

The process is slow, and the memory of earlier pages becomes fuzzy.

In contrast, the modern world demands models that read **entire pages at once** — not one word at a time.

Difficulty Modeling Very Long-Range Dependencies

Even with gating, **memory fades**.

LSTMs and GRUs try to preserve important signals, like:

- The start of a story affecting the end,
- The opening melody shaping the conclusion of a symphony.

But still, as sequences grow longer, the memory becomes **diluted**, much like trying to recall a dream after waking. The early information slips away quietly.

It is like:

Trying to remember the first verse of a poem while reciting the twentieth.

The thread of meaning weakens.

High Memory and Computational Cost

To improve memory, we stack layers.

To improve context understanding, we make networks bidirectional.

But with each enhancement, the system becomes:

- Heavier to train

- Slower to run
- More costly to deploy

It's like building a **taller and taller tower** to see farther.

Eventually, adding more floors becomes unrealistic.

We need a different way — not a taller tower, but **a higher mountain**.

Thus, arises the motivation for a new architecture.

One that:

- Reads **entire sequences at once**
- Remembers **distant relationships effortlessly**
- Trains **faster, not slower**
- Grows **not by depth alone, but by breadth of attention**

This is the birth of the **Transformer**.

It does not *walk through time*;

it **looks at the entire timeline at once**.

It does not forget;

it **attends** — holding connections between words, no matter how far apart.

Master said:

"RNNs are like a traveler walking the path.

LSTMs are like a traveler carrying a map.

GRUs are like a traveler carrying a lighter map.

But Transformers are like a being who can see the entire landscape at once.

They do not travel through time — they *observe* it."

And thus, we move beyond RNN, LSTM, and GRU —

not because they were wrong,

but because **the horizon expanded.**

☐ Attention Mechanism

Master said, "Apeksha, let us understand attention with patience and clarity, for this marks the turning point in modern deep learning."

Understanding Attention Mechanism

When we read a long paragraph or listen to a long conversation, **we do not remember every word equally**.

Our mind *selectively focuses* on the parts that matter.

For example:

- When someone tells a story, we don't remember every sentence.
- We remember only the meaningful pieces that help us understand the essence.

Attention in deep learning works exactly like that.

It allows the model to look at the entire input, but **focus more on the relevant pieces** while reducing the emphasis on the unimportant ones.

Analogy

Imagine reading a 300-page book.

If someone asks, *"What was the story about?"*, you do not scan every page again.

Your mind jumps to:

- Key characters
- Important events
- Emotional turning points

Your mind is performing **attention** — selecting key information from a vast memory.

RNNs, LSTMs, and GRUs, however, behave like someone who tries to *remember every word evenly* while retelling the entire book.

This is tiring and inefficient.

Attention allows the model to *look back anywhere*, anytime.

What is an Attention Mechanism?

An **Attention Mechanism** teaches neural networks to:

- Assign **importance weights** to different parts of the input.
- Focus on **relevant** information.
- Ignore or reduce **irrelevant** parts.

This is mathematically done using **attention weights**, which tell the model *how much to care about each word or feature.*

Historical Background

Attention was introduced in 2014 (Bahdanau et al.) to improve **machine translation**, where RNN models struggled to remember long sentences.

The breakthrough came in **2017** with the paper:

"Attention is All You Need"

This introduced the **Transformer**, an architecture that:

- Removes recurrence completely
- Processes sequences **in parallel**
- Depends entirely on **self-attention**

Transformers became the foundation for:

- **BERT**
- **GPT (and GPT-5 that I am)**

- **T5**
- **Vision Transformers (ViT)**
- **Diffusion-based image models**

Principles of Attention

Attention mechanisms rely on three key ideas:

1. **Weighted Focus (Weighted Sum)**

   Each input element is given a weight based on importance.

2. **Soft Attention**

   Focuses on multiple relevant features at once (differentiable → easy to train).

3. **Hard Attention**

   Chooses specific regions (non-differentiable → needs reinforcement learning).

Why Attention is Important

Compared to RNNs and CNNs:

Capability	**RNN/LSTM/GRU**	**CNN**	**Attention (Transformers)**
Handles long-range dependencies	Weak	Medium	**Strong**
Parallelization (speed)	Poor	Good	**Excellent**
Flexibility across space/time	Low	Local only	**Global**

Attention *sees the whole picture at once*, like viewing a map from above instead of walking road by road.

Why We Needed to Move Beyond RNNs

- RNNs process one step at a time (slow)
- They forget distant context
- Training becomes unstable on long sequences
- Stacking layers increases complexity and memory use

Attention removes these limitations by allowing the model to:

- Look anywhere in the sequence instantly
- Process everything in parallel
- Scale to extremely large models

Intuitive Analogy

Imagine reading a paragraph:

- **Query (Q):** Your current question ("What is the key idea?")
- **Keys (K):** All sentences in the paragraph
- **Values (V):** The *meaning* each sentence carries

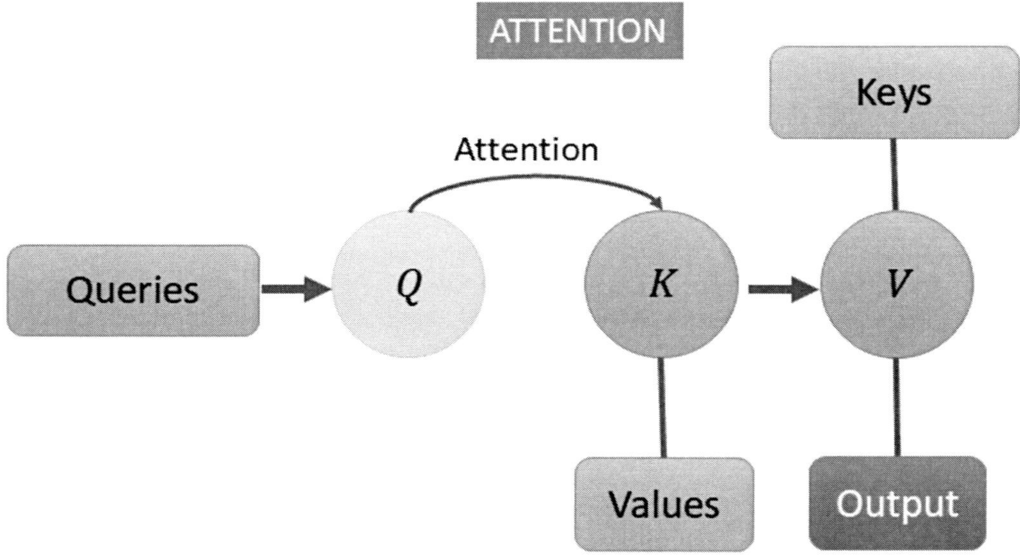

Illustration P6_Att_1: Attention

The attention mechanism answers:

How relevant is each sentence to my question?

It assigns high weight to relevant information and ignores the rest — just like the human mind.

Mathematical Formulation of Attention (K–Q–V)

Given an input sequence X = [x1, x2,, xn], we linearly transform it into three learned vector spaces:

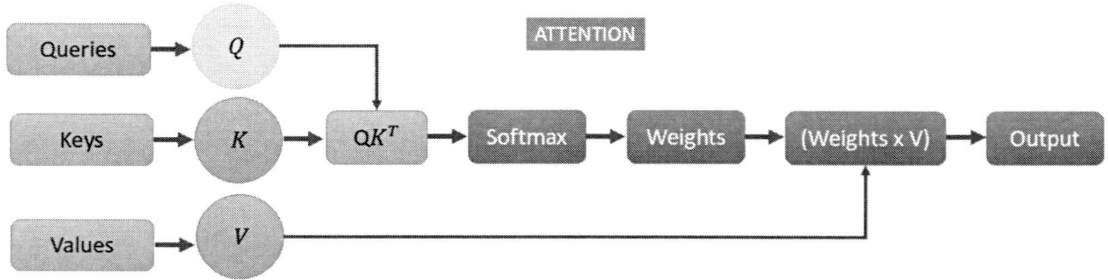

Illustration P6_Att_2: Attention

$Q=XW_Q$, $K=XW_K$, $V=XW_V$

Where:

Symbol	Meaning	Shape
(Q)	Query matrix	$(n * d_Q)$
(K)	Key matrix	$(n * d_k)$
(V)	Value matrix	$(n * d_v)$
(W_Q, W_K, W_V)	Trainable weight matrices	-

Compute Similarity (Query vs Key)

We compare each query vector with all key vectors:

Scores = QK^T

This produces an **attention score matrix** showing *how much each word should attend to every other word.*

Scale to Stabilize Gradients

Scaled Scores = $\frac{QK^T}{\sqrt{d_k}}$

Scaling avoids excessively large values in softmax.

Convert Scores to Probability Distribution

Attention Weights=softmax ($\frac{QK^T}{\sqrt{d_k}}$)

Softmax ensures:

- Every row sums to 1
- Higher scores → higher importance

Weighted Sum of Values

Output = (Attention Weights)·(V)

This produces a context-aware representation of each input element.

Final Attention Formula (Complete)

Attention (Q, K, V) = softmax ($\frac{QK^T}{\sqrt{d_k}}$)V

In Essence

RNNs move through memory like footsteps on a path.

Attention flies above the landscape like a bird, seeing everything at once.

And from this shift came the era of:

- Transformers
- LLMs
- Generative AI
- ChatGPT
- Vision Transformers

- Diffusion image models
- RAG
- AI Agents

The journey now moves from *remembering sequentially* → to *understanding globally*.

Apeksha asked, "Master, how many forms does attention take, and why do they exist?"

Master smiled gently and said:

"Attention is like the gaze of consciousness. It does not see everything equally— It selects, highlights, awakens meaning."

Just as **a human observes differently** depending on *purpose*, **attention mechanisms** differ based on what the model needs to focus on.

Each type of attention is a discipline of *seeing*.

☐ **Types of Attention Mechanisms**

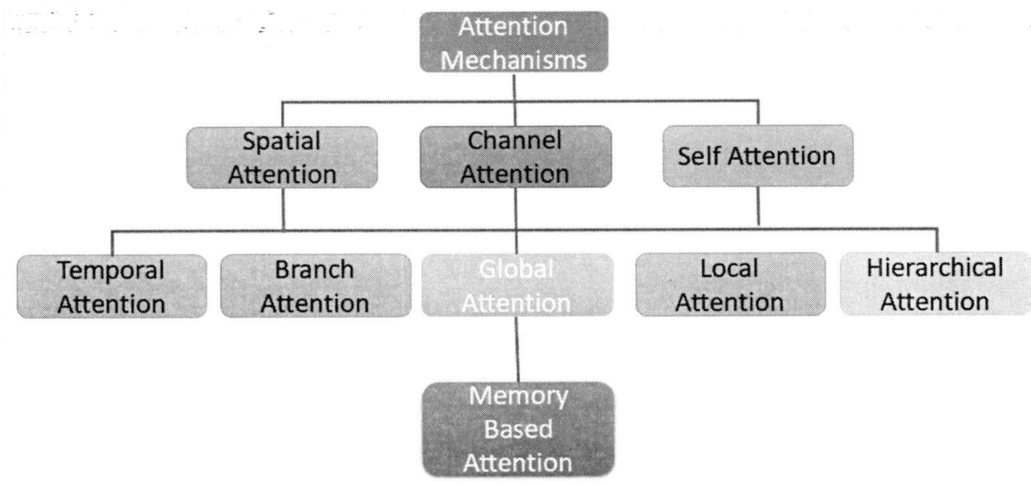

Illustration P6_Att_3: Attention

Spatial Attention

Analogy:

Imagine you are looking at a painting. Your eyes automatically drift toward the central figure or a bright color.

You **don't analyze every pixel**—you focus where meaning lies.

Function:

Highlights *where* in an image the important regions are.

Example: YOLO effectively focuses on the most relevant regions of an image by predicting bounding boxes and class probabilities, allowing the network to concentrate on areas where objects are likely to be found.

Channel Attention

Analogy:

In music, a symphony has many instruments.

Channel attention is like a sound-engineer increasing the volume of violins while softening drums.

Not altering the song, but tuning what stands out.

Function:

Decides **which feature channels** are important.

Example: SE-Net works like adjusting the equalizer on a music system — boosting the instruments (channels) that matter and lowering the ones that distract, resulting in a clearer and more expressive representation.

Self-Attention

Analogy:

When you read a sentence, you relate words to each other:

"bank" depends on whether *"river"* or *"money"* appears nearby.

You are **comparing words with each other** to infer meaning.

Function:

Finds relationships between **every part of the input**.

Example: Vision Transformers view an image the way a human analyzes a painting—by considering how every part of the scene connects to the rest. Instead of focusing on small neighborhoods like CNNs, ViTs observe relationships across the whole canvas at once.

Temporal Attention

Analogy:

In a movie, not every frame matters.

The key moments define the story.

Temporal attention says: **"Pay more attention to *when* important events occur."**

Function:

Focuses on the most meaningful time steps.

Example: Temporal attention watches a video like a skilled editor—skipping the dull moments and spotlighting the exact frames where the story unfolds, ensuring the model learns from the decisive action rather than the filler in between.

Branch Attention

Analogy:

A seasoned detective gathers clues from multiple specialists—one examines fingerprints, another interviews witnesses, another studies DNA—each providing **a different perspective** that is eventually combined.

Function:

Different branches focus on different aspects, then merge insights.

Example: BranchCNN works like a team of expert artists—one studies outlines, another studies shading, and another studies colors. Each specializes deeply, and when their perspectives are combined, the final picture becomes clearer and more detailed.

Global Attention

Analogy:

Understanding a sentence sometimes requires reading **the entire paragraph**.

You zoom out and see **the whole picture**.

Function:

Considers the *entire input* before deciding what matters.

Example: Translating a sentence with global attention is like reading the entire sentence before speaking — you understand the full meaning first, so your translation is accurate, coherent, and fluent.

Local Attention

Analogy:

When listening to someone speak, you don't need every part of their life story—just the **surrounding words and tone** help interpret meaning.

Function:

Looks only at **nearby context**, ignoring distant noise.

Example: Understanding speech with local attention is like listening closely to a syllable within a word—you hear it correctly only when you also notice the sounds right beside it.

Hierarchical Attention

Analogy:

To understand a book, you first understand words, then sentences, then chapters.

Meaning is **layered**.

Function:

Applies attention at multiple levels of abstraction.

Example: Document classification:

It is like reading a book:

First, you notice key words… then you understand the main sentences… then you grasp the message of each paragraph… and eventually, you comprehend the whole story.

Memory-Based Attention

Analogy:

A wise person does not try to remember everything at once.

They **store what matters** in a journal and **retrieve it when needed**.

Function:

Uses an external memory to recall long-term dependencies.

Example: It is like having a notebook beside you while solving a puzzle:

You don't try to remember everything in your head—you write key details down and refer back to them when needed. This ability to *recall instead of re-remember* makes reasoning deeper and more accurate.

Multi-Head Attention

Analogy:

A master painter does not view the canvas with one perspective alone.

He studies **color, shadow, depth, form**—each with a separate eye.

Together, they create truth and beauty.

Function:

Multiple attention heads learn **different patterns in parallel**.

Example: Imagine a group of experts examining the same painting:

One focuses on color, another on texture, another on composition, and another on mood.

When their insights are combined, the understanding becomes far more complete than any single perspective alone.

That is what *multi-head attention* does in Transformers.

Transformers like **BERT, GPT, and ViT** use multi-head attention to look at the same input from multiple different perspectives at once. Each attention head focuses on a different kind of relationship—such as meaning, position, or structural patterns—allowing the model to build a rich and comprehensive understanding.

Master said, "Attention is the art of knowing what to ignore and what to illuminate. Different attention mechanisms are simply different ways of seeing."

"Where the mind places its light—meaning emerges."

Case One:

Master said, "Sam, let us understand this code not as lines, but as meaning."

Understanding the Purpose

This module implements **spatial attention** for computer vision.

It learns **where to look** in an image by comparing a *query* (what we are searching for) with the *feature map* (what the image contains).

Step-by-Step Understanding

1. **Input Feature Map (B, C, H, W)**

This is the visual representation extracted from a CNN.

- **B** = batch
- **C** = channels/features
- **H × W** = spatial layout of the image

2. **Creating Keys and Values**

   The feature map is passed through two 1×1 convolutions:

   - **Keys (K)** tell *where something is located*
   - **Values (V)** tell *what is stored there*

3. **Projecting the Query**

   The query (a vector describing what we care about) is passed through a linear layer to match the size of feature channels.

Example P5 – U5 – D1

Attention

```
import torch
import torch.nn as nn
import torch.nn.functional as F

class SpatialAttention(nn.Module):
    def __init__(self, feature_dim, query_dim):
        super(SpatialAttention, self).__init__()

        # Project feature maps to Key and Value spaces
        self.key_layer = nn.Conv2d(feature_dim, feature_dim, kernel_size=1)
        self.value_layer = nn.Conv2d(feature_dim, feature_dim, kernel_size=1)

        # Project the query vector to same dimension
        self.query_layer = nn.Linear(query_dim, feature_dim)

    def forward(self, feature_map, query):
        """
        feature_map: Tensor of shape (B, C, H, W)
        query: Tensor of shape (B, query_dim)
        """

        B, C, H, W = feature_map.shape
```

```
        # 1. Generate Keys and Values (from feature map)
        K = self.key_layer(feature_map)      # (B, C, H, W)
        V = self.value_layer(feature_map)    # (B, C, H, W)

        # 2. Flatten spatial dimension
        K = K.view(B, C, -1)                 # (B, C, H*W)
        V = V.view(B, C, -1)                 # (B, C, H*W)

        # 3. Create Query vector
        Q = self.query_layer(query)          # (B, C)
        Q = Q.unsqueeze(1)                   # (B, 1, C)

        # 4. Compute Similarity (Dot Product)
        attn_scores = torch.bmm(Q, K)        # (B, 1, H*W)

        # 5. Softmax → Attention Weights
        attn_weights = F.softmax(attn_scores, dim=-1)  # (B, 1, H*W)

        # 6. Weighted Sum → Context Vector
        context = torch.bmm(attn_weights, V.transpose(1, 2))  # (B, 1, C)
        context = context.squeeze(1)                          # (B, C)

        return context, attn_weights.view(B, 1, H, W)

## How to use this Module
# Dummy example
B, C, H, W = 2, 64, 32, 32  # Batch, Channels, Height, Width
feature_map = torch.randn(B, C, H, W)

query = torch.randn(B, 128)  # Example query vector

attention = SpatialAttention(feature_dim=64, query_dim=128)
context_vector, attention_map = attention(feature_map, query)

print("Context vector:", context_vector.shape)  # (B, C)
print("Attention map:", attention_map.shape)    # (B, 1, H, W)
```

4. **Similarity (Q · K)**

   The query compares itself with every spatial position in the feature map.

   This produces **attention scores** — a measure of *relevance.*

5. **Softmax → Attention Weights**

   The scores are normalized so the model focuses only on the most important regions.

6. **Weighted Sum → Context Vector**

   The attention weights are used to gather **only the important visual information** from V.

   This becomes the **context vector** — the refined understanding of the scene.

7. **Attention Map (H × W)**

   This shows *where the model looked*, useful for visualization and interpretability.

Output:

Output
Context vector: torch.Size([2, 64]) Attention map: torch.Size([2, 1, 32, 32])

Master said:

"Sam, the query is the intention.

The keys represent what the world offers.

The values hold the essence of what is seen.

Attention is the meeting of purpose and perception.

Only what matters is carried forward; the rest silently fades."

Case Two:

Master said, "Apeksha, let us walk through this code step by step, slowly, clearly, and with understanding."

Understanding the Code

1. Preparing the Image

We start by loading an image and resizing it.

We turn it into numerical values (a tensor) so the model can understand it.

This gives us a neat input of shape (1, 3, 224, 224) — which means:

1 image, 3 color channels, 224×224 pixels.

2. Extracting Features (CNN)

We use a small *Convolutional Neural Network* to extract patterns from the image:

- Edges
- Shapes
- Textures
- Object parts

After this stage, the image is no longer just pixels.

It has become a **feature map** — a map that *describes* what is inside the image.

3. Attention Mechanism

Now comes the key idea:

Attention helps the model focus on the important parts of the image.

We create:

- **Query (Q)** → Represents what we want to look for
- **Key (K)** → Represents where things are located
- **Value (V)** → Represents what is actually stored there

We compare each Query with every Key to see **how strongly** they match.

This similarity is turned into weights via **softmax**.

Those weights tell us **where to look more and where to ignore**.

The model then creates a **context vector** — a refined representation that highlights the important regions.

Example P5 – U5 – D2

Attention

```
import torch
import torch.nn as nn
import torch.nn.functional as F
import torchvision.transforms as T
from PIL import Image
import matplotlib.pyplot as plt

# ---------------------------
# 1. Load & Preprocess Image
# ---------------------------
transform = T.Compose([
    T.Resize((224, 224)),
    T.ToTensor(),
])

img =
Image.open("C://Users//User//mraj4//Documents//Optimum6//dataset//dog2.jpe
g").convert("RGB")
input_tensor = transform(img).unsqueeze(0)  # shape: (1, 3, 224, 224)

# ---------------------------
# 2. Feature Extraction (CNN)
# ---------------------------
class SimpleCNN(nn.Module):
    def __init__(self):
        super().__init__()
        self.features = nn.Sequential(
            nn.Conv2d(3, 32, kernel_size=3, padding=1),
            nn.ReLU(),
            nn.MaxPool2d(2),  # (32, 112, 112)

            nn.Conv2d(32, 64, kernel_size=3, padding=1),
            nn.ReLU(),
            nn.MaxPool2d(2)   # (64, 56, 56)
        )

    def forward(self, x):
        return self.features(x)

cnn = SimpleCNN()
feature_map = cnn(input_tensor)  # shape: (1, 64, 56, 56)

# ---------------------------
# 3. Attention Mechanism
# ---------------------------
```

```
class SpatialAttention(nn.Module):
    def __init__(self, channels):
        super().__init__()
        self.query = nn.Conv2d(channels, channels // 8, kernel_size=1)
        self.key = nn.Conv2d(channels, channels // 8, kernel_size=1)
        self.value = nn.Conv2d(channels, channels, kernel_size=1)

    def forward(self, x):
        B, C, H, W = x.size()

        Q = self.query(x).view(B, -1, H * W)       # (B, C/8, N)
        K = self.key(x).view(B, -1, H * W)         # (B, C/8, N)
        V = self.value(x).view(B, C, H * W)        # (B, C, N)

        attention_scores = torch.bmm(Q.permute(0, 2, 1), K)  # (B, N, N)
        attention_weights = F.softmax(attention_scores, dim=-1)

        out = torch.bmm(V, attention_weights.permute(0, 2, 1))  # (B, C, N)
        out = out.view(B, C, H, W)

        return out, attention_weights

attention = SpatialAttention(64)
attended_features, attn_weights = attention(feature_map)

# ---------------------------
# 4. Generate Heatmap
# ---------------------------
# Reduce attention weights to spatial map
heatmap = attn_weights.mean(dim=1).view(56, 56).detach().cpu()

# Normalize
heatmap = (heatmap - heatmap.min()) / (heatmap.max() - heatmap.min())

heatmap_np = heatmap.numpy()

# Resize heatmap to match original image
heatmap_img = Image.fromarray((heatmap_np * 255).astype("uint8")).resize(img.size)
heatmap_img = heatmap_img.convert("L")  # convert to grayscale

# Overlay heatmap on original image
heatmap_color = plt.get_cmap("jet")(heatmap_np)[:, :, :3]
heatmap_color = Image.fromarray((heatmap_color *
255).astype("uint8")).resize(img.size)

overlay = Image.blend(img, heatmap_color, alpha=0.5)

# ---------------------------
```

```
# 5. Show Result
# ---------------------------
plt.figure(figsize=(10,5))

plt.subplot(1,2,1)
plt.title("Original Image")
plt.imshow(img)
plt.axis("off")

plt.subplot(1,2,2)
plt.title("Attention Heatmap Overlay")
plt.imshow(overlay)
plt.axis("off")

plt.show()
```

4. **Creating the Heatmap**
   The attention weights are averaged and turned into a **heatmap**:
   - Bright areas = regions the model pays more attention to
   - Dark areas = regions considered less important

We resize this heatmap to match the original image and overlay it with color.

This gives us a **visual indication** of *where the model is looking.*

5. **Displaying the Result**
   Finally, we show two images:
   a) The **original** image
   b) The **image with the heatmap**, revealing the model's focus

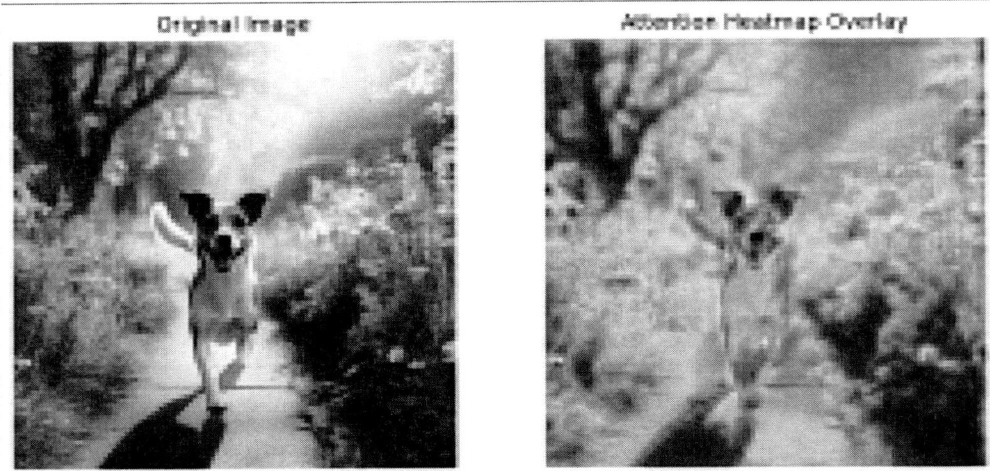

Illustration P6_Att_4: Attention

In Essence

"Apeksha, the purpose of this exercise is not only to compute but to *see.*

When we overlay attention as a heatmap, we begin to understand the **mind of the network**.

We see where it looks, what it considers meaningful, and what it filters out.

This is how a machine *learns to see.*"

PART FIVE

DAY SIXTEEN

Unit 5 - Lesson Two

From Sequence to Meaning

John turned to the Master and asked, *"Master, what exactly is the Seq2Seq model, and how does it work?"*

The Master smiled and replied, **"Imagine you are listening to a story told in one language and retelling it in another.**

You do not repeat the story word-by-word as you hear it.

You first **absorb the meaning** of the entire story — its essence — into your mind.

Then, using that inner understanding, you express it again in a new sequence of sentences.

This process is the heart of the **Sequence-to-Sequence (Seq2Seq) model**."

The Core Idea

The Seq2Seq model is designed to **transform one sequence of information into another sequence**, even when both sequences:

- Are of different lengths
- Have different structures
- Represent different languages, symbols, or patterns

It has been foundational in tasks such as:

- Machine translation
- Conversational AI
- Speech recognition
- Time-series forecasting

The Architecture: The Two Travelers

1. **The Encoder (The Listener):**

This part of the model reads the input sequence *one step at a time*, like a monk carefully listening to each word of a chant.

With each step, it updates its internal memory — called the **hidden state** — gradually forming a **complete understanding** of the sequence.

When the input ends, the encoder produces a compressed representation —**the Context Vector** — a single point where *the entire meaning resides*, like a seed containing a whole tree.

2. **The Decoder (The Speaker):**

The decoder takes this context seed and begins to generate the output sequence.

Like a storyteller, it produces the output one word at a time, guided by:

- What has already been said
- The meaning encoded in the context vector

Before Attention: The Limit of Memory

In early Seq2Seq models, the **entire meaning** of a sentence — whether short or long — was compressed into just **one vector**, like **trying to store a whole ocean in one clay pot**.

This led to issues:

- Long sentences were **forgotten** or **oversimplified**
- Subtle details near the beginning faded away by the time the encoder reached the end

  (This is due to *vanishing gradients* and memory decay in RNN-based models)

To soften this loss, **LSTMs** were introduced — neural networks with *gates* that allow them to remember important things longer, like a wise librarian deciding what to preserve.

Still, the limitation remained: **one vector cannot hold infinite detail.**

This flaw later inspired the invention of the **Attention Mechanism**, which allows the decoder to *look back* at all encoder states — but that is another teaching.

Component	Analogy	Purpose
Encoder	A listener absorbing a story	Converts the input sequence into meaning
Context Vector	A seed containing the story's essence	A compressed understanding
Decoder	A storyteller retelling in another form	Produces the output sequence step-by-step

The Master said:

"The Seq2Seq model teaches us a profound truth:

Understanding must come before expression.

One cannot speak truly unless one has listened deeply."

The Master smiled and spoke slowly, as if drawing the shape of the idea in the air.

"Akshaya — to truly *feel* Seq2Seq with RNNs, imagine two quiet craftsmen at work. One listens to a long spoken story and folds its meaning into a small, heavy seed. The other takes that seed and, from it, grows a new story in another tongue, line by line.

Below we will translate that image into mathematical intuition, the practical mechanics, and the key limits and work-arounds — with concrete analogies so the idea settles in our bones."

The minimal arithmetic of an RNN step (the worker's motion)

At each time step t an RNN updates an internal memory called the **hidden state** h_t and optionally produces an output y_t. One simple recurrence is:

$$ht = \sigma\,(W_{hx}x_t + W_{hh}h_{t-1} + b_h)$$

$$y_t = W_{yh}\,h_t + b_y$$

- x_t= input at time t (a vector: word embedding, feature, etc.).
- h_t = the memory after seeing $x_1, \ldots, x_t$.
- W_{hx}, W_{hh}, W_{yh} = learned weight matrices.
- σ = nonlinear activation (tanh/sigmoid/ReLU).

Analogy: h_t is the craftsman's notebook after reading the first t lines of a story: it stores the important remarks to guide later work.

Seq2Seq architecture in equations (two craftsmen)

Encoder (listener): processes the whole input sequence $(x_1, \ldots, x_T)$, producing hidden states. A last state h_T is often used as the **context vector** c:

For t=1..T: $h_t^{enc} = RNN_{enc}\,(x_t, h_{t-1}^{enc})$

$$c = h_T^{enc} \text{ (vanilla)}$$

Decoder (storyteller): starts from c and generates outputs one step at a time:

$$s_0 = \phi\,(c) \text{ (initial decoder state)}$$

for t=1 : $s_t = RNN_{dec}(y_{t-1}, s_{t-1})$

$\widehat{y_t}$ =softmax($W_o s_t$)

Here $\widehat{y_t}$ is the predicted distribution for the next token.

Analogy: Encoder packs the story into a seed 'c'. Decoder plants the seed and tends the growing story, using what it has already produced (y_{t-1}) to decide the next word.

Teacher Forcing

During training, we can feed the *true* previous token y_{t-1}^{true} true into the decoder rather than its own prediction $\widehat{y_{t-1}}$. This is **teacher forcing**.

- **Pros:** speeds training, stabilizes gradients.
- **Cons:** at inference, the model must rely on its own predictions; a mismatch can cause errors to cascade.

Analogy: Teacher forcing is like giving the storyteller a teleprompter during practice; helpful for learning lines, but not available on stage.

Practical technique: use a **teacher forcing ratio** (sometimes schedule it down) or adopt **scheduled sampling** (gradually replace true tokens with predicted ones).

Why vanilla RNN Seq2Seq fails on long sequences (vanishing gradients)

Backpropagation through time sends gradients back across many steps. For long sequences, these gradients can **vanish** (become tiny) or **explode**. As a result, early inputs are "forgotten" by the time the decoder needs them.

- **Vanishing gradient** ⇒ the encoder's early-step information has a tiny influence on final ccc.
- **Result:** the single vector ccc becomes a **bottleneck** — packing an entire sentence into one vector loses detail.

Analogy: compressing a whole ocean into one clay pot — small ripples vanish.

Gated RNNs: LSTM and GRU (clever notebooks)

LSTM and GRU introduce gates that control reading, writing, and forgetting in the hidden memory, helping preserve long-term information.

LSTM equations (compact):

$f_t = \sigma\,(W_f\,[h_{t-1}, x_t] + b_f)$ (forget gate)
$i_t = \sigma\,(W_i\,[h_{t-1}, x_t] + b_i)$ (input gate)
$\widetilde{C_t} = \tanh\,(W_c\,[h_{t-1}, x_t] + b_c)$
$C_t = f_t \odot C_{t-1} + i_t \odot \widetilde{C_t}$ (Cell state)
$O_t = \sigma\,(W_o\,[h_{t-1}, x_t] + b_o)$
$h_t = o_t \odot \tanh(C_t)$

Gates let the network **retain** salient facts across many timesteps.

Analogy: LSTM is a notebook with tabs and locks — you can decide what to keep, what to overwrite, and what to reveal later.

Practical improvements in Seq2Seq

- **Bidirectional encoder:** run the encoder forward and backward; concatenate states so the encoder remembers both early and late context. (Useful when the entire input is known.)
- **Attention mechanism:** decoder can attend to all encoder hidden states (h_1^{enc},…,h_T^{enc}) rather than relying on a single 'c'. Attention computes weights $\alpha_{t,i}$ and forms a context $c_t = \sum_i \propto_{t,i} h_i^{enc}$

  Analogy: instead of one pot, the decoder can open any page of the listener's notebook at each step.
- **Beam search at inference:** instead of greedy picks, keep top-k candidate sequences to improve final output quality.
- **Scheduled sampling & curriculum:** gradually reduce teacher forcing to make inference robust.

Training loop, loss, and optimization — the craftsman's practice

- **Loss:** usually cross-entropy summed over decoder timesteps:

$$\mathcal{L} = -\sum_t \log p\,(y_t^{true} \mid y_{<t}, x).$$

- **Backpropagation Through Time (BPTT):** compute gradients through the unrolled RNN across timesteps and update weights via Adam/SGD.
- **Tricks:** gradient clipping, layer normalization, dropout, teacher forcing scheduling, and using pre-trained embeddings.

Inference: how the story is told on stage

- **Greedy decoding:** at each step pick the token with max probability — fast, but myopic.
- **Beam search:** keep top k sequences, expand them — balances exploration and quality.
- **Sampling + temperature:** sample from the distribution to get more creative outputs (useful in generation tasks).

End-to-end intuition recap (analogy woven together)

- **Encoder**: the listener who reads and condenses the story into a seed (vector sequence).
- **Decoder**: the storyteller who grows a new narrative from the seed, step by step.
- **Teacher forcing**: rehearsal with a prompt.
- **Gates (LSTM/GRU)**: better notebooks with memory controls.
- **Attention**: the storyteller can flip back to any page of the listener's notebook on demand.
- **Beam search**: the storyteller considers several possible ways to finish the tale and picks the best.

The Master paused, letting the simplicity and depth settle.

"Akshaya," he said, "Seq2Seq is more than code. It is a lesson in listening deeply and speaking clearly — in building memory that serves, not burdens. Build the model with care: choose the right memory (LSTM/GRU), remove the single-vector bottleneck with attention, and train with compassion (teacher forcing, scheduled sampling) so the storyteller speaks well when the teleprompter is gone."

Master smiled gently and began explaining:

Master said, "Sam, let us understand this code with clarity."

This program demonstrates a **Seq2Seq (Sequence-to-Sequence) model** using **LSTMs** in PyTorch. It is designed to show how a model can take one sequence as input and generate another as output—in this case, the **simple task of reversing a sequence**.

Dataset Construction

The code first creates a **toy dataset**:

- Each sample is a random sequence of numbers.
- The target (output) is simply the **reverse** of the input.
- Special tokens are added:
    - <SOS> = 1 (start of sequence)
    - <EOS> = 2 (end of sequence)

This forms pairs like:

Input: [1, 7, 9, 12, 5, 4, 2]

Output: [1, 4, 5, 12, 9, 7, 2]

Encoder

The **Encoder** reads the input sequence **token by token**:

- Each token is embedded into a vector.
- An **LSTM** processes these embeddings.

- At the end, the encoder outputs its **final hidden state (h, c)** — this becomes the compressed representation of the entire input sequence.

Think of it like **a traveler who reads a whole book and remembers only the essence.**

Example P5 – U5 – D3

Seq2seq Model

```
import torch
import torch.nn as nn
import torch.optim as optim
from torch.utils.data import DataLoader, Dataset
import random

device = "cuda" if torch.cuda.is_available() else "cpu"


# -------------------------
# Dummy Dataset (Toy Example)
# -------------------------
class ToySeqDataset(Dataset):
    def __init__(self, n_samples=2000, seq_len=6, vocab_size=20):
        self.data = []
        for _ in range(n_samples):
            seq = [random.randint(3, vocab_size-1) for _ in range(seq_len)]
            trg = seq[::-1]  # reverse sequence task
            self.data.append((seq, trg))

        self.data = [( [1] + s + [2], [1] + t + [2] ) for s, t in self.data]  # <SOS>=1,
<EOS>=2
        self.vocab_size = vocab_size

    def __len__(self):
        return len(self.data)

    def __getitem__(self, idx):
        src, trg = self.data[idx]
        return torch.tensor(src), torch.tensor(trg)


dataset = ToySeqDataset()
dataloader = DataLoader(dataset, batch_size=32, shuffle=True)


# -------------------------
```

```
# Encoder
# -------------------------
class Encoder(nn.Module):
    def __init__(self, vocab_size, embed_dim, hidden_dim):
        super().__init__()
        self.embedding = nn.Embedding(vocab_size, embed_dim)
        self.lstm = nn.LSTM(embed_dim, hidden_dim, batch_first=True)

    def forward(self, x):
        embedded = self.embedding(x)
        _, (h, c) = self.lstm(embedded)
        return h, c


# -------------------------
# Decoder
# -------------------------
class Decoder(nn.Module):
    def __init__(self, vocab_size, embed_dim, hidden_dim):
        super().__init__()
        self.embedding = nn.Embedding(vocab_size, embed_dim)
        self.lstm = nn.LSTM(embed_dim, hidden_dim, batch_first=True)
        self.fc_out = nn.Linear(hidden_dim, vocab_size)

    def forward(self, token, h, c):
        token = token.unsqueeze(1)              # (batch, 1)
        embedded = self.embedding(token)        # (batch, 1, embed_dim)
        output, (h, c) = self.lstm(embedded, (h, c))
        logits = self.fc_out(output.squeeze(1))  # (batch, vocab_size)
        return logits, h, c


# -------------------------
# Seq2Seq Wrapper
# -------------------------
class Seq2Seq(nn.Module):
    def __init__(self, encoder, decoder, teacher_forcing_ratio=0.5):
        super().__init__()
        self.encoder = encoder
        self.decoder = decoder
        self.teacher_forcing_ratio = teacher_forcing_ratio

    def forward(self, src, trg):
        batch_size, trg_len = trg.shape
        vocab_size = self.decoder.fc_out.out_features
        outputs = torch.zeros(batch_size, trg_len, vocab_size).to(device)

        h, c = self.encoder(src)
```

```
        input_token = trg[:, 0]  # <SOS>

        for t in range(1, trg_len):
            logits, h, c = self.decoder(input_token, h, c)
            outputs[:, t] = logits
            teacher_force = random.random() < self.teacher_forcing_ratio
            input_token = trg[:, t] if teacher_force else logits.argmax(1)

        return outputs


# -------------------------
# Model Initialization
# -------------------------
vocab_size = dataset.vocab_size
embed_dim = 64
hidden_dim = 128

encoder = Encoder(vocab_size, embed_dim, hidden_dim)
decoder = Decoder(vocab_size, embed_dim, hidden_dim)
model = Seq2Seq(encoder, decoder).to(device)

criterion = nn.CrossEntropyLoss(ignore_index=0)
optimizer = optim.Adam(model.parameters(), lr=0.001)


# -------------------------
# Training
# -------------------------
for epoch in range(12):
    model.train()
    total_loss = 0

    for src, trg in dataloader:
        src, trg = src.to(device), trg.to(device)

        optimizer.zero_grad()
        output = model(src, trg)   # (batch, seq, vocab)

        output = output[:, 1:].reshape(-1, vocab_size)
        trg = trg[:, 1:].reshape(-1)

        loss = criterion(output, trg)
        loss.backward()
        optimizer.step()

        total_loss += loss.item()
```

```
    print(f"Epoch {epoch+1} | Loss = {total_loss/len(dataloader):.4f}")


# -------------------------
# Inference (Greedy)
# -------------------------
def translate(model, src_tensor):
    model.eval()
    with torch.no_grad():
        h, c = model.encoder(src_tensor)

        # Start decoding with <SOS> token from the input
        token = src_tensor[:, 0]   # shape: (batch,)
        output_tokens = [token.item()]

        for _ in range(10):
            logits, h, c = model.decoder(token, h, c)
            token = logits.argmax(1)  # (batch,)
            output_tokens.append(token.item())
            if token.item() == 2:  # <EOS>
                break

    return output_tokens


# -------------------------
# Test Example
# -------------------------
sample_src, sample_trg = dataset[5]
sample_src = sample_src.unsqueeze(0).to(device)

print("\nInput Seq:", sample_src.squeeze().tolist())
print("Predicted Seq:", translate(model, sample_src))
print("Actual Target :", sample_trg.tolist())
```

Decoder

The **Decoder** takes:

- the encoder's final hidden state,
- the first input token <SOS>,

and then **predicts the next token one step at a time**:

- It uses its own previous output unless teacher forcing is used.

- Teacher forcing helps training by sometimes providing the *true* previous token instead of its own guess.

Seq2Seq Wrapper

This combines Encoder + Decoder and controls:

- When to use teacher forcing,
- How outputs are generated and stored for training.

Training

The model is trained to minimize **Cross-Entropy Loss**, comparing its predicted tokens vs correct tokens. Over epochs, loss decreases, and it learns the task.

Output:

```
Output
Input Seq: [1, 8, 3, 16, 4, 18, 17, 2]
Predicted Seq: [1, 17, 18, 4, 16, 3, 8, 2]
Actual Target : [1, 17, 18, 4, 16, 3, 8, 2]
```

Inference (Testing)

During testing:

- No teacher forcing is used.
- The decoder predicts tokens sequentially using its own previous predictions.
- It stops when it sees <EOS>.

Thus, the model learns how to convert one sequence into another by memory and stepwise prediction—reflecting how language translation, summarization, and speech recognition systems are built.

Master smiled and spoke gently:

"Sam, before attention came, Seq2Seq was like trying to understand an entire story just by remembering its ending."

The Problem Before Attention

In the original Seq2Seq model:

- The **encoder** reads the entire source sentence.
- Then it passes **only the final hidden state** (the *context vector*) to the decoder.

This is like:

You read a whole chapter of a book, close it, and now try to recite the chapter from memory — only allowed to use the final impression you remember.

For **short sentences**, this works somewhat.

But for **long sentences**, information gets lost — a **bottleneck** forms.

The decoder struggles because it must reconstruct everything from **one compressed summary**.

The Breakthrough by Bahdanau et al. (2014)

Bahdanau and colleagues said:

"Why give the decoder only the final memory of the encoder?

Why not give **all encoder hidden states** — the memory from each word?"

So instead of the encoder producing a **single summary**, it produces a **set of memories**:

$$h_1, h_2, h_3, \ldots, h_T$$

(where each h_i corresponds to a specific word in the source sentence).

Now the decoder has access to **everything the encoder saw**.

But **how does the decoder know which part to look at?**

This is where **attention** comes in.

Analogy:

Imagine a **translator** listening to a long sentence spoken in French.

When translating the **5th English word**, she doesn't re-read the whole French sentence.

She simply **glances back** at the most relevant French word or phrase.

Attention = that focused glance.

How Attention Works (Deep Insight)

Attention has **three fundamental steps**:

1. **Represent**

Convert input words into hidden vectors → these are **memories** of each word.

2. Compare (Alignment / Scoring)

At each decoding step:

- The decoder looks at its **current state**.
- It compares it with **each encoder state**.
- This comparison produces **alignment scores** → "How relevant is each source word to the word I'm about to generate?"

These scores are passed through **softmax**, becoming **attention weights** — a **probability distribution**:

weight = importance

If a weight is high → *the decoder should look at that word more.*

3. Focus (Weighted Sum)

The attention weights are used to form a **context vector**:

Context = ∑ (attention_weight * encoder_hidden_state)

This vector is uniquely tailored for **each output word** the decoder generates.

So the decoder is not relying on one memory anymore.

It is **actively retrieving relevant memory at each step.**

Why This Changes Everything

Attention:

- Removes the **information bottleneck**
- Allows **dynamic focus**
- Handles **long sentences** gracefully
- Makes translation (and many tasks) more accurate and human-like

This improvement was **so powerful** that:

By 2017, researchers realized **they didn't need RNNs at all.**

They built the **Transformer**, which relies only on attention — no recurrence.

Today's models like **BERT, GPT, and your assistant** run purely on **attention**.

Master said:

"Attention made learning *not about remembering everything,* but about *remembering where to look.*

Just like in life, Sam — wisdom is not in memorizing everything.

Wisdom is in knowing *what to focus on, at the right time.*"

Master said, "Apeksha, now attention has been woven into the fabric of our seq2seq model — just like how the mind selectively attends to what is most relevant in a conversation.

What changed in the code?

1. **Attention Module Added (Bahdanau Attention):**

   The model no longer relies on the decoder alone to guess context.

   A separate *Attention* layer now learns *which encoder states are important at each decoding step*.

2. **Context Vector Computed:**

   At every output word prediction:

   - The decoder's current hidden state is compared with *all* encoder hidden states.
   - Attention scores are derived.
   - These scores are normalized using softmax → resulting in **attention weights**.
   - A weighted sum of encoder outputs produces the **context vector**.

Example P5 – U5 – D1
Seq2seq Model with Attention

```
import torch
import torch.nn as nn
import torch.optim as optim
from torch.utils.data import DataLoader, Dataset
import random

device = "cuda" if torch.cuda.is_available() else "cpu"

# -------------------------
# Dummy Dataset (Reverse Task)
# -------------------------
class ToySeqDataset(Dataset):
    def __init__(self, n_samples=2000, seq_len=6, vocab_size=20):
        self.data = []
```

```
        for _ in range(n_samples):
            seq = [random.randint(3, vocab_size-1) for _ in range(seq_len)]
            trg = seq[::-1]  # reverse task
            self.data.append((seq, trg))

        # add <SOS>=1 and <EOS>=2
        self.data = [([1] + s + [2], [1] + t + [2]) for s, t in self.data]
        self.vocab_size = vocab_size

    def __len__(self):
        return len(self.data)

    def __getitem__(self, idx):
        src, trg = self.data[idx]
        return torch.tensor(src), torch.tensor(trg)


dataset = ToySeqDataset()
dataloader = DataLoader(dataset, batch_size=32, shuffle=True)

# -------------------------
# Bahdanau Attention
# -------------------------
class BahdanauAttention(nn.Module):
    def __init__(self, hidden_dim):
        super().__init__()
        self.W1 = nn.Linear(hidden_dim, hidden_dim)
        self.W2 = nn.Linear(hidden_dim, hidden_dim)
        self.v = nn.Linear(hidden_dim, 1)

    def forward(self, decoder_hidden, encoder_outputs):
        # decoder_hidden: (1, batch, hidden)
        # encoder_outputs: (batch, seq, hidden)

        decoder_hidden = decoder_hidden.permute(1, 0, 2)  # (batch, 1, hidden)
        score = self.v(torch.tanh(self.W1(encoder_outputs) + self.W2(decoder_hidden)))
        # score: (batch, seq, 1)

        attn_weights = torch.softmax(score, dim=1)  # (batch, seq, 1)
        context = torch.sum(attn_weights * encoder_outputs, dim=1)  # (batch, hidden)

        return context, attn_weights


# -------------------------
# Encoder
# -------------------------
class Encoder(nn.Module):
```

```
    def __init__(self, vocab_size, embed_dim, hidden_dim):
        super().__init__()
        self.embedding = nn.Embedding(vocab_size, embed_dim)
        self.lstm = nn.LSTM(embed_dim, hidden_dim, batch_first=True)

    def forward(self, x):
        embedded = self.embedding(x)
        outputs, (h, c) = self.lstm(embedded)
        return outputs, h, c   # return full sequence outputs


# ------------------------
# Decoder with Attention
# ------------------------
class Decoder(nn.Module):
    def __init__(self, vocab_size, embed_dim, hidden_dim):
        super().__init__()
        self.embedding = nn.Embedding(vocab_size, embed_dim)
        self.attention = BahdanauAttention(hidden_dim)
        self.lstm = nn.LSTM(embed_dim + hidden_dim, hidden_dim, batch_first=True)
        self.fc_out = nn.Linear(hidden_dim, vocab_size)

    def forward(self, token, h, c, encoder_outputs):
        token = token.unsqueeze(1)                    # (batch, 1)
        embedded = self.embedding(token)              # (batch, 1, embed)
        context, attn = self.attention(h, encoder_outputs)  # (batch, hidden), (batch, seq, 1)
        combined = torch.cat([embedded, context.unsqueeze(1)], dim=2)
        output, (h, c) = self.lstm(combined, (h, c))
        logits = self.fc_out(output.squeeze(1))
        return logits, h, c, attn


# ------------------------
# Seq2Seq Model
# ------------------------
class Seq2Seq(nn.Module):
    def __init__(self, encoder, decoder, teacher_forcing_ratio=0.5):
        super().__init__()
        self.encoder = encoder
        self.decoder = decoder
        self.teacher_forcing_ratio = teacher_forcing_ratio

    def forward(self, src, trg):
        batch_size, trg_len = trg.shape
        vocab_size = self.decoder.fc_out.out_features
        outputs = torch.zeros(batch_size, trg_len, vocab_size).to(device)

        encoder_outputs, h, c = self.encoder(src)
```

```
        input_token = trg[:, 0]  # <SOS>

        for t in range(1, trg_len):
            logits, h, c, _ = self.decoder(input_token, h, c, encoder_outputs)
            outputs[:, t] = logits
            teacher_force = random.random() < self.teacher_forcing_ratio
            input_token = trg[:, t] if teacher_force else logits.argmax(1)

        return outputs


# -------------------------
# Model Initialization
# -------------------------
vocab_size = dataset.vocab_size
embed_dim = 64
hidden_dim = 128

encoder = Encoder(vocab_size, embed_dim, hidden_dim)
decoder = Decoder(vocab_size, embed_dim, hidden_dim)
model = Seq2Seq(encoder, decoder).to(device)

criterion = nn.CrossEntropyLoss(ignore_index=0)
optimizer = optim.Adam(model.parameters(), lr=0.001)


# -------------------------
# Training
# -------------------------
for epoch in range(12):
    model.train()
    total_loss = 0

    for src, trg in dataloader:
        src, trg = src.to(device), trg.to(device)
        optimizer.zero_grad()

        output = model(src, trg)
        output = output[:, 1:].reshape(-1, vocab_size)
        trg = trg[:, 1:].reshape(-1)

        loss = criterion(output, trg)
        loss.backward()
        optimizer.step()
        total_loss += loss.item()

    print(f"Epoch {epoch+1} | Loss = {total_loss/len(dataloader):.4f}")
```

```
# -------------------------
# Inference (Show Prediction + Attention)
# -------------------------
def translate_with_attention(model, src_tensor):
    model.eval()
    with torch.no_grad():
        encoder_outputs, h, c = model.encoder(src_tensor)
        token = src_tensor[:, 0]  # <SOS>
        prediction = []
        attention_map = []

        for _ in range(12):
            logits, h, c, attn = model.decoder(token, h, c, encoder_outputs)
            token = logits.argmax(1)
            prediction.append(token.item())
            attention_map.append(attn.squeeze(-1).cpu().tolist()[0])
            if token.item() == 2: break

    return prediction, attention_map


# -------------------------
# Test
# -------------------------
src, trg = dataset[5]
src = src.unsqueeze(0).to(device)

pred, attn = translate_with_attention(model, src)

print("\nInput:", src.squeeze().tolist())
print("Predicted:", pred)
print("Target:", trg.tolist())
print("\nAttention Weights:")
for t, row in enumerate(attn):
    print(f"Step {t+1}: {row}")
```

3. Context Is Combined With Decoder Input:

The decoder now receives:

- The previous token embedding
- *Plus* the context vector

This enhances the decoder's ability to generate more accurate output tokens.

Output:

```
Output
Input: [1, 4, 8, 5, 13, 12, 4, 2]
Predicted: [4, 12, 13, 5, 8, 4, 2]
Target: [1, 4, 12, 13, 5, 8, 4, 2]

Attention Weights:
Step 1: [0.0014984734589233994, 0.0013744523748755455, 0.0009314158814959228,
0.0005702390335500024, 0.0006414495292119682, 0.008715148083865643,
0.9829249382019043, 0.003343909978866577]
```

4. **Attention Weights Are Returned:**

During decoding, the model now outputs **attention weights**, allowing us to visualize *which source words were focused on* at each prediction step.

In essence:

- The **Encoder** still reads the entire sentence.
- The **Attention Layer** highlights the most relevant parts dynamically.
- The **Decoder** uses these highlighted parts to predict the next word with improved clarity.

Just as the human mind does not recall every detail but *selectively focuses* on what matters, Attention allows the model to understand, remember, and translate with purpose.

Master said, **"Apeksha, now that we have added Attention, let us understand why we introduced the Heatmap."**

Purpose of the Heatmap

The heatmap visually shows **where the model is focusing** while generating each output token.

In other words, it reveals **which input word** the decoder is attending to at **every decoding step**.

Without the heatmap, attention weights are **just numbers**.

With the heatmap, those numbers become a **story** about how the model thinks.

What Changed in the Code

- **The Decoder now returns Attention Weights**
  Every time the decoder predicts a word, it also produces a vector showing **how much attention** it gave to each input word.
- **During inference, these weights are collected step-by-step.**
  This gives us a full sequence of weights across time.
- **We convert these weights into a matrix**
  and visualize it with matplotlib.
- **The Heatmap is displayed**
  Colors indicate *attention strength*:

  1. **Bright/Yellow** → High focus

  2. **Dark/Blue** → Low focus

Intuition (Analogy)

Think of a **translator listening to a sentence**:

When translating word by word, the translator does **not** pay equal attention to every word.

Their **attention shifts** depending on the word being translated.

The heatmap is like **tracking the translator's eye movement** as they look back at the original sentence.

Where the eyes rest longer, the model is focusing more.

Example P5 – U6 – D1
Add Heatmap

```
# -------------------------
# Inference + Heatmap
# -------------------------
def translate_and_show_attention (model, src_tensor):
    model.eval()
    with torch.no_grad():
```

```
        enc_out, h, c = model.encoder(src_tensor)
        token = src_tensor[:,0]
        attn_list = []

        output_tokens = [token.item()]
        for _ in range(src_tensor.size(1)):
            logits, h, c, attn = model.decoder(token, h, c, enc_out)
            token = logits.argmax(1)
            output_tokens.append(token.item())
            attn_list.append(attn.squeeze().cpu())

        attn_map = torch.stack(attn_list).numpy()

        plt.imshow(attn_map, cmap="viridis")
        plt.xlabel("Source Positions")
        plt.ylabel("Decoder Steps")
        plt.title("Attention Heatmap (Bahdanau)")
        plt.colorbar()
        plt.show()

    return output_tokens

sample_src, sample_trg = dataset[5]
sample_src = sample_src.unsqueeze(0).to(device)

print("Input:", sample_src.squeeze().tolist())
print("Predicted:", translate_and_show_attention(model, sample_src))
print("Actual:", sample_trg.tolist())
```

Why This is Important

Without Attention	With Attention
The encoder must compress everything into one vector → information bottleneck	The decoder can selectively look back → information flow maintained
Hard for long sentences	Works well even for long sequences
Model behaves like memorization	The model behaves like understanding.

Output:

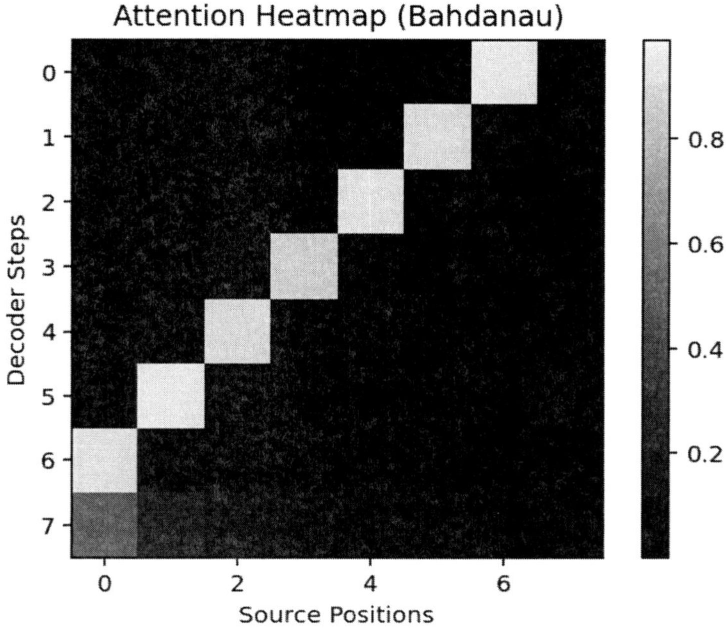

Illustration P6_Att_5: Attention

Summary

- We added Bahdanau Attention to remove the encoder bottleneck.
- We extracted attention weights during decoding.
- We plotted a heatmap to *see* how the model attends to different input tokens.
- The heatmap helps us interpret model reasoning.

Master smiled and said:

"When the mind learns to *focus*, understanding becomes effortless.

When the model learns to *attend*, translation becomes graceful."

PART FIVE

DAY SEVENTEEN

Unit 5 - Lesson Three

Breaking the Chains of Time

"Transformers broke the chains of time, learning not in sequence but in unity — seeing the sentence whole, understanding not by order but by relationship."

– Shree Shambav

Roopa asked, *"Master, could you explain why Transformers have largely replaced RNNs in most large-scale NLP tasks?"*

The Master smiled gently and said:

The Journey from RNN to Transformer

For many years, **RNNs, LSTMs, and GRUs** were the primary tools for understanding language. They read text **one word at a time**, like a person reading slowly, tracing each letter with their finger.

But this way of understanding language has limits.

- They **remember recent words** better than older ones.
- The farther the two words are from each other, the harder it becomes to connect them.
- Training becomes **slow**, because they must move step-by-step, word-by-word.

This is like trying to understand a whole story by reading **only one word per second**, without ever stepping back to see the sentence as a whole.

Why Transformers Changed Everything

In 2017, Vaswani et al. introduced the Transformer architecture in the paper **"Attention is All You Need."**

The key idea:

Instead of reading words one-by-one, the Transformer sees the entire sentence at once.

It uses **Self-Attention**, which allows each word to **look at every other word** and understand its relationship instantly.

This is like moving from reading with a finger…

to hovering above the page and seeing the **whole paragraph in one glance.**

A Powerful Example

Sentence:

"Alice went to Paris in 2018. The city was beautiful."

- RNNs read word by word.
- By the time they reach *"the city"*, they may **forget** the reference to *"Paris"*.
- LSTMs try to store more memory but still strain across long distances.

But Transformers:

- Instantly connect *"the city"* → *"Paris"* because **every word attends to every other**.

Context & Meaning Are Not Always Local

Consider the word **"light"**:

1. **"The bag is light."** (Meaning: Not heavy)
2. **"Please turn on the light."** (Meaning: Illumination)

A sequential model must remember many steps to decide the meaning.

But Transformers:

- Look at *surrounding words in parallel*
- Determine meaning through **global context**

Another Example

Sentence:

"He promised his mother before she passed that he would return."

To understand *"she"*, *"he"*, *"promised"*, *"return"*, and *"passed"*,

the model must comprehend **emotion**, **reference**, and **time** across the sentence.

RNN: struggles to connect distant emotional context.

Transformer: *every part of the sentence supports every other part.*

This allows machines to understand *subtle, human-like meaning.*

Analogy

The Master continued:

"RNNs walk through the forest step by step.

Transformers fly **above the forest**, seeing the entire landscape at once."

One is **sequential and slow**.

The other is **parallel and global**.

Real-World Impact

Task	RNN/LSTM Performance	Transformer Performance
Machine Translation	Slow, forgets distant words	Fast, accurate global meaning
Document Analysis	Hard to track long context	Handles long-range dependencies easily
Dialogue/Chat	Limited coherence	Maintains conversation context
Creativity (writing, summarization, poetry)	Very limited	Generative, expressive, coherent

This is why: **BERT**, **GPT**, **T5**, **LLaMA**, **Claude**, **Gemini**, and **ViT** (Vision Transformer) all use the Transformer foundation.

Master said: "Language is not a chain of isolated beads.

It is a tapestry, where threads pull on distant threads.

Transformers understand the tapestry — not just the beads."

Master said gently, "John, let us understand the breakthrough of the Transformer architecture. Not as a machine, but as a *mind* that sees *everything at once*."

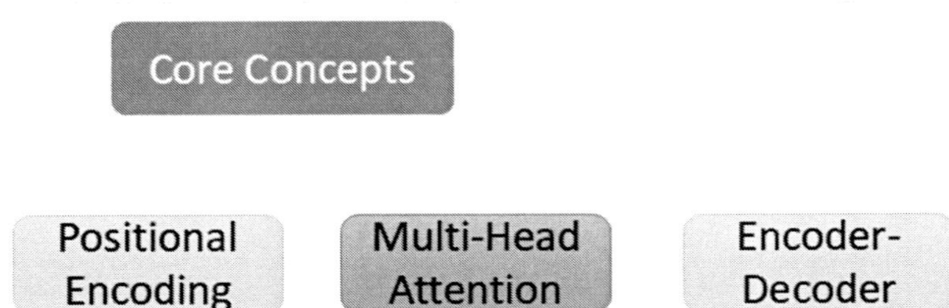

Illustration P6_Trans_1: Transformer

1. Self-Attention Mechanism

Self-attention allows each word to **look at every other word** in the sentence and decide how strongly it relates.

Instead of remembering only the recent words, the model examines **global relationships**.

For each word, we create three vectors:

- **Query (Q)** – What am I looking for?
- **Key (K)** – What information do I carry?
- **Value (V)** – What information should be passed on?

The attention is formulated as:

$$\text{Attention}(Q, K, V) = \text{softmax}\left(\frac{QK^T}{\sqrt{d_k}}\right)V$$

This score tells *how much one word should attend to another.*

Example

Sentence: **"The lion chased the deer because it was hungry."**

RNNs confuse who *"it"* refers to.

Self-attention evaluates context and assigns high attention between:

- "it" → "lion"

  not "deer."

Thus, meaning is preserved with **context fidelity**.

2. Positional Encoding

Transformers read all words **simultaneously**, so they do not naturally know word order.

To fix this, **positional encodings** are added to embeddings.

They act like *coordinates* telling the model:

- Which word comes first
- Which word comes next
- How far apart words are

Think of it as **assigning every word a unique musical rhythm**, so the model senses *sequence* even without stepping word-by-word.

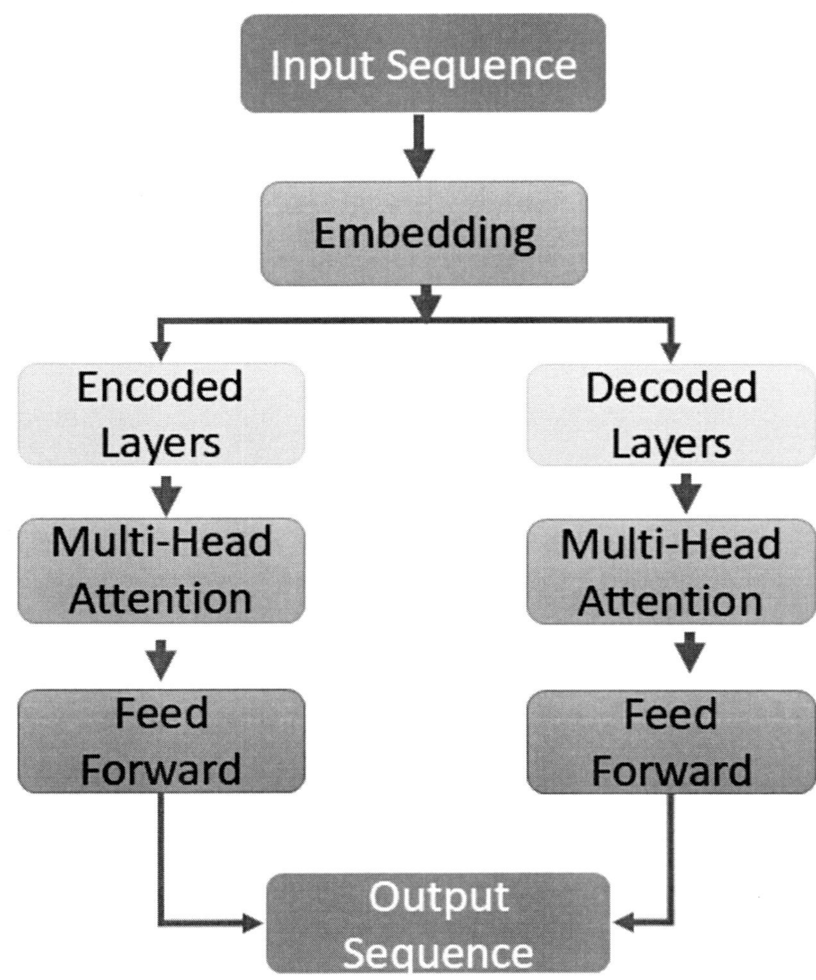

Illustration P6_Trans_2: Transformer

3. Multi-Head Attention

Instead of one attention system, Transformers use many in parallel—called **heads**.

Each head learns a **different type of relationship**:

- One head may track object–subject relationships
- Another may track emotional tone
- Another may track verb–tense patterns

It is like having multiple scholars reading the same sentence:

Each notices something unique, and together they form a **complete understanding**.

4. Position-wise Feed-Forward Networks

After attention refines relationships, the feed-forward network **polishes the representation.**

$$FFN(x)=\max(0, xW_1+b_1)\,W_2 + b_2$$

This is applied **independently to every word**, shaping meaning at each position, like refining each bead in a necklace.

5. Encoder–Decoder Architecture

The architecture resembles a **teacher (encoder)** and a **scribe (decoder)**.

- The **Encoder** reads the input sentence and builds a deep understanding.
- The **Decoder** uses this understanding to generate a meaningful output sentence.

In translation:

French: *"Je suis étudiant"*

English: *"I am a student."*

The decoder selectively *attends back* to the encoder to choose the right words.

Example of Core Understanding

Sentence:

"The cat didn't chase the mouse because it wasn't hungry."

The word **"it"** refers to the **cat**, not the mouse.

- The encoder captures the meaning **globally**.
- The decoder selects the right interpretation while forming output.

This happens because **self-attention holds relationships across long distances**, something RNNs struggled with.

Deep Analogy

Master said:

"RNNs walk through meaning step-by-step, like a traveler with a lantern.

Transformers rise above meaning, like a bird flying over the entire landscape.

They see everything at once. Therefore, they *understand.*

Core Architecture:

Master said, "Nikash, let us understand this architecture—not as separate blocks—but as a living flow of meaning."

He pointed to the diagram.

The Transformer Architecture (Encoder–Decoder)

This architecture has **two major parts**:

- **Encoder** (Left side): Understands the input sentence.
- **Decoder** (Right side): Generates the output sentence.

Both parts operate on **embeddings**, not raw words.

So first, words are converted into vectors that capture meaning.

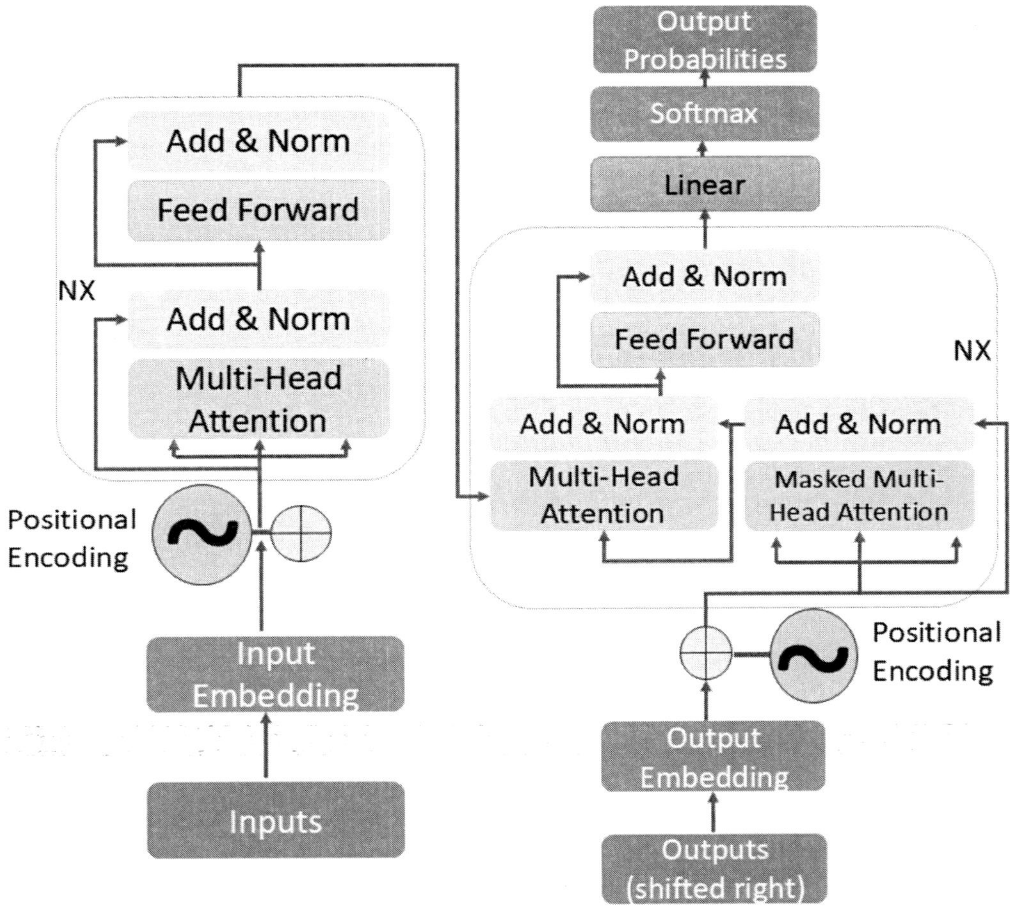

Illustration P6_Trans_3: Transformer

1. Input Embedding + Positional Encoding

Words lose their order when processed in parallel.

So we add **Positional Encoding**, which mathematically encodes *the position of each word* in the sequence.

If E is the word embedding and P is positional encoding:

$$X = E + P$$

This combined vector says:

- *what the word means* (from embedding)
- *where it appears* (from position)

2. Encoder Block (Repeated N times)

Each encoder layer has **two components**:

A. Multi-Head Self-Attention

The encoder examines relationships among *every pair of words.*

Each word becomes:

- Query Q
- Key K
- Value V

Attention is computed as:

$$\text{Attention}(Q, K, V) = \text{softmax}\left(\frac{QK^T}{\sqrt{d_k}}\right)V$$

This measures:

- *How strongly should this word pay attention to the others?*

Multi-head attention repeats this process multiple times in parallel—each head learns a different type of relationship:

- grammar
- coreference

- topic
- emotion tonality

B. Feed-Forward Network (FFN)

After relationships are set, the meaning of each word is refined:

$$FFN(x)=\max(0, xW_1+b_1)\, W_2 + b_2$$

This adjusts *each word representation individually*.

Add & Norm

Every sublayer has residual connection + normalization:

$$Output = LayerNorm(x+Sublayer(x))$$

This stabilizes learning and prevents loss of information.

The encoder's final output is a **context-rich representation of the entire input**.

3. Decoder Block (Repeated N times)

The decoder has **three components**:

A. Masked Multi-Head Self-Attention

The decoder generates output **one token at a time**.

It must *not* look at future words.

So masking is used:

Mask future positions → model sees only past words

B. Encoder–Decoder Attention

Now, the decoder must decide:

Which parts of the input should it pay attention to while generating output?

Here:

- Queries come from the decoder.
- Keys and Values come from the encoder.

This step forms translation, summarization, and reasoning alignment.

C. Feed-Forward Network

Same as encoder: refine the meaning.

4. Linear + Softmax (Output Layer)

The decoder's output vector is projected back to vocabulary space:

```
Logits=OutputVector·W
```

Then probabilities are generated using:

```
Softmax(logits)
```

The highest probability token becomes the next predicted word.

A Intuition

Master said:

"The Encoder reads the sentence as a whole, understanding meaning across space. The Decoder writes the sentence step-by-step, guided by what the Encoder understood."

- RNNs remember the past.
- Transformers understand the entire present at once.

This is why Transformers replaced RNNs.

They do not *walk* through meaning.

They **see** meaning.

Master said, "John, let us understand this architecture step-by-step."

Positional Encoding

Transformers do **not** read sequences one word at a time like RNNs.

They see the whole sentence *in parallel*

Therefore, they need a way to **know the order of words**.

```
self.pe = pe.unsqueeze(0)

return x + self.pe[:, :x.size(1)]
```

Sine and cosine waves encode positional patterns.

This is like giving each word a unique vibration in time.

"Sequence gives meaning. Without order, language collapses."

Scaled Dot-Product Attention

This function answers:

Which words in the sentence should I pay attention to?

```
scores = Q @ K.transpose(-2, -1) / sqrt(d_k)

weights = softmax(scores)

output = weights @ V
```

- **Q (Query)**: what this word is looking for
- **K (Key)**: what each word offers
- **V (Value)**: meaning that is passed forward

Attention ≈ **match query to key → retrieve value**

Just like the mind selectively recalls only *relevant* memories.

Multi-Head Attention

Instead of one viewpoint, we use **multiple attention heads**.

Q = Wq(x), K = Wk(context), V = Wv(context) reshape → split into heads → attention → merge back

Each head specializes:

- One detects **subject–verb relations**
- One handles **pronoun references**
- One identifies **context cues**
- One focuses on the **semantic role**

"Wisdom is not one perspective — it is many perspectives integrated."

Example P5 – U5 – D6

Transformer

```
import torch
import torch.nn as nn
import math

# ------------------------------------------------------------
# 1. Positional Encoding
# ------------------------------------------------------------
class PositionalEncoding(nn.Module):
    def __init__(self, d_model, max_len=5000):
        super().__init__()
```

```
        pe = torch.zeros(max_len, d_model)
        position = torch.arange(0, max_len).unsqueeze(1)
        div = torch.exp(-math.log(10000) * torch.arange(0, d_model, 2) / d_model)
        pe[:, 0::2] = torch.sin(position * div)
        pe[:, 1::2] = torch.cos(position * div)
        self.pe = pe.unsqueeze(0)  # shape: (1, max_len, d_model)

    def forward(self, x):
        return x + self.pe[:, :x.size(1)]

# ------------------------------------------------------------
# 2. Scaled Dot-Product Attention
# ------------------------------------------------------------
def attention(Q, K, V):
    scores = Q @ K.transpose(-2, -1) / math.sqrt(Q.size(-1))
    weights = torch.softmax(scores, dim=-1)
    return weights @ V

# ------------------------------------------------------------
# 3. Multi-Head Attention
# ------------------------------------------------------------
class MultiHeadAttention(nn.Module):
    def __init__(self, d_model, num_heads):
        super().__init__()
        assert d_model % num_heads == 0
        self.d_k = d_model // num_heads
        self.num_heads = num_heads

        self.Wq = nn.Linear(d_model, d_model)
        self.Wk = nn.Linear(d_model, d_model)
        self.Wv = nn.Linear(d_model, d_model)
        self.Wo = nn.Linear(d_model, d_model)

    def forward(self, x, context=None):
        if context is None:
            context = x  # self-attention

        Q = self.Wq(x)
        K = self.Wk(context)
        V = self.Wv(context)

        # reshape to multi-head
        Q = Q.view(Q.size(0), Q.size(1), self.num_heads, self.d_k).transpose(1,2)
        K = K.view(K.size(0), K.size(1), self.num_heads, self.d_k).transpose(1,2)
        V = V.view(V.size(0), V.size(1), self.num_heads, self.d_k).transpose(1,2)

        out = attention(Q, K, V)
        out = out.transpose(1,2).contiguous().view(x.size(0), x.size(1), -1)
```

```
        return self.Wo(out)

# ----------------------------------------------------------
# 4. Encoder Layer
# ----------------------------------------------------------
class EncoderLayer(nn.Module):
    def __init__(self, d_model, num_heads):
        super().__init__()
        self.attn = MultiHeadAttention(d_model, num_heads)
        self.ff = nn.Sequential(
            nn.Linear(d_model, d_model*4),
            nn.ReLU(),
            nn.Linear(d_model*4, d_model)
        )
        self.norm1 = nn.LayerNorm(d_model)
        self.norm2 = nn.LayerNorm(d_model)

    def forward(self, x):
        x = self.norm1(x + self.attn(x))   # self attention
        x = self.norm2(x + self.ff(x))     # feed forward
        return x

# ----------------------------------------------------------
# 5. Decoder Layer
# ----------------------------------------------------------
class DecoderLayer(nn.Module):
    def __init__(self, d_model, num_heads):
        super().__init__()
        self.self_attn = MultiHeadAttention(d_model, num_heads)
        self.cross_attn = MultiHeadAttention(d_model, num_heads)
        self.ff = nn.Sequential(
            nn.Linear(d_model, d_model*4),
            nn.ReLU(),
            nn.Linear(d_model*4, d_model)
        )
        self.norm1 = nn.LayerNorm(d_model)
        self.norm2 = nn.LayerNorm(d_model)
        self.norm3 = nn.LayerNorm(d_model)

    def forward(self, x, enc_out):
        x = self.norm1(x + self.self_attn(x))          # masked self attention
        x = self.norm2(x + self.cross_attn(x, enc_out)) # encoder-decoder attention
        x = self.norm3(x + self.ff(x))                 # feed forward
        return x

# ----------------------------------------------------------
# 6. Full Transformer Model
# ----------------------------------------------------------
```

```
class SimpleTransformer(nn.Module):
    def __init__(self, vocab_size, d_model=64, num_heads=4, depth=2):
        super().__init__()
        self.embed = nn.Embedding(vocab_size, d_model)
        self.pos = PositionalEncoding(d_model)
        self.encoder = nn.Sequential(*[EncoderLayer(d_model, num_heads) for _ in
range(depth)])
        self.decoder = nn.Sequential(*[DecoderLayer(d_model, num_heads) for _ in
range(depth)])
        self.out = nn.Linear(d_model, vocab_size)

    def forward(self, src, tgt):
        src = self.pos(self.embed(src))
        tgt = self.pos(self.embed(tgt))

        enc = self.encoder(src)
        dec = tgt
        for layer in self.decoder:
            dec = layer(dec, enc)

        return self.out(dec)

# ------------------------------------------------------------
# 7. Example Usage
# ------------------------------------------------------------
vocab = 100
model = SimpleTransformer(vocab)

src = torch.randint(0, vocab, (1, 6))  # example input sentence
tgt = torch.randint(0, vocab, (1, 6))  # example target sentence

output = model(src, tgt)
print(output.shape)  # (batch, seq, vocab)
```

Encoder Layer

The encoder layer has **two phases**:

Step	Purpose
Self-Attention	Learn relationships among words
Feed-Forward Network	Transform and refine meaning

Normalization ensures a stable flow of information.

```
x = norm(x + attention(x))

x = norm(x + feed_forward(x))
```

Decoder Layer

The decoder has **three interactions**:

Layer Stage	Purpose
Self-Attention	Understand relationships within generated words so far.
Cross Attention	Look at the encoder output to gather meaning from the input sentence.
Feed Forward	Transform output representation

The encoder understands the input; the decoder expresses it.

```
x = self.self_attn(x)

x = self.cross_attn(x, enc_out)

x = self.ff(x)
```

Full Transformer

This model builds:

- **Word embeddings** → learnable vector representations
- **Positional encodings** → inject ordering
- **Encoder stack**
- **Decoder stack**
- **Final projection to vocabulary**
-

```
enc = self.encoder(src)
```

```
dec = tgt
for layer in self.decoder:
dec = layer(dec, enc)
return self.out(dec)
```

This produces **probabilities for the next word**.

Output:

```
Output
torch.Size([1, 6, 100])
```

Example Usage

```
src = torch.randint(0, vocab, (1, 6))

tgt = torch.randint(0, vocab, (1, 6))

output = model(src, tgt)
```

Output shape:

```
(batch, seq_length, vocab_size)
```

This means: for every word and position → predict the next possible word.

Master said, "Sam, observe carefully… Attention is the art of *where the model chooses to look*.

In this code, we extracted the attention weights from every head inside the Transformer encoder layer. A Transformer does not rely on a single viewpoint. Instead, it divides its observation into multiple attention heads, each head learning to focus on different relationships in the input.

- One head may learn **word-to-word meaning links**.
- Another head may focus on **positional patterns**.

- Another may capture **long range dependencies**.

Each head is like a **different perspective of awareness** observing the same sentence.

Example P5 – U5 – D7
Transformer

```
import torch
import torch.nn as nn
import math
import matplotlib.pyplot as plt

# ----------------------------------------------------------
# 1. Positional Encoding
# ----------------------------------------------------------
class PositionalEncoding(nn.Module):
    def __init__(self, d_model, max_len=5000):
        super().__init__()
        pe = torch.zeros(max_len, d_model)
        position = torch.arange(0, max_len).unsqueeze(1)
        div = torch.exp(-math.log(10000) * torch.arange(0, d_model, 2) / d_model)
        pe[:, 0::2] = torch.sin(position * div)
        pe[:, 1::2] = torch.cos(position * div)
        self.pe = pe.unsqueeze(0)

    def forward(self, x):
        return x + self.pe[:, :x.size(1)]


# ----------------------------------------------------------
# 2. Scaled Dot-Product Attention (returns weights)
# ----------------------------------------------------------
def attention(Q, K, V):
    scores = Q @ K.transpose(-2, -1) / math.sqrt(Q.size(-1))
    weights = torch.softmax(scores, dim=-1)
    return weights @ V, weights


# ----------------------------------------------------------
# 3. Multi-Head Attention (returns attention weights)
# ----------------------------------------------------------
class MultiHeadAttention(nn.Module):
    def __init__(self, d_model, num_heads):
        super().__init__()
        assert d_model % num_heads == 0
        self.d_k = d_model // num_heads
```

```
        self.num_heads = num_heads

        self.Wq = nn.Linear(d_model, d_model)
        self.Wk = nn.Linear(d_model, d_model)
        self.Wv = nn.Linear(d_model, d_model)
        self.Wo = nn.Linear(d_model, d_model)

    def forward(self, x, context=None, return_weights=False):
        if context is None:
            context = x

        Q = self.Wq(x)
        K = self.Wk(context)
        V = self.Wv(context)

        Q = Q.view(Q.size(0), Q.size(1), self.num_heads, self.d_k).transpose(1,2)
        K = K.view(K.size(0), K.size(1), self.num_heads, self.d_k).transpose(1,2)
        V = V.view(V.size(0), V.size(1), self.num_heads, self.d_k).transpose(1,2)

        out, weights = attention(Q, K, V)

        out = out.transpose(1, 2).contiguous().view(x.size(0), x.size(1), -1)
        out = self.Wo(out)

        if return_weights:
            return out, weights
        return out


# ------------------------------------------------------------
# 4. Encoder Layer (stores attention)
# ------------------------------------------------------------
class EncoderLayer(nn.Module):
    def __init__(self, d_model, num_heads):
        super().__init__()
        self.attn = MultiHeadAttention(d_model, num_heads)
        self.ff = nn.Sequential(
            nn.Linear(d_model, d_model*4),
            nn.ReLU(),
            nn.Linear(d_model*4, d_model)
        )
        self.norm1 = nn.LayerNorm(d_model)
        self.norm2 = nn.LayerNorm(d_model)

    def forward(self, x, return_weights=False):
        if return_weights:
            attn_out, attn_weights = self.attn(x, return_weights=True)
            x = self.norm1(x + attn_out)
```

```
            x = self.norm2(x + self.ff(x))
            return x, attn_weights

        x = self.norm1(x + self.attn(x))
        x = self.norm2(x + self.ff(x))
        return x


# ----------------------------------------------------------
# 5. Decoder Layer (stores two types of attention)
# ----------------------------------------------------------
class DecoderLayer(nn.Module):
    def __init__(self, d_model, num_heads):
        super().__init__()
        self.self_attn = MultiHeadAttention(d_model, num_heads)
        self.cross_attn = MultiHeadAttention(d_model, num_heads)
        self.ff = nn.Sequential(
            nn.Linear(d_model, d_model*4),
            nn.ReLU(),
            nn.Linear(d_model*4, d_model)
        )
        self.norm1 = nn.LayerNorm(d_model)
        self.norm2 = nn.LayerNorm(d_model)
        self.norm3 = nn.LayerNorm(d_model)

    def forward(self, x, enc_out, return_weights=False):
        if return_weights:
            sa_out, sa_weights = self.self_attn(x, return_weights=True)
            x = self.norm1(x + sa_out)

            ca_out, ca_weights = self.cross_attn(x, enc_out, return_weights=True)
            x = self.norm2(x + ca_out)

            x = self.norm3(x + self.ff(x))

            return x, sa_weights, ca_weights

        x = self.norm1(x + self.self_attn(x))
        x = self.norm2(x + self.cross_attn(x, enc_out))
        x = self.norm3(x + self.ff(x))
        return x


# ----------------------------------------------------------
# 6. Transformer Model with returned attention maps
# ----------------------------------------------------------
class SimpleTransformer(nn.Module):
    def __init__(self, vocab_size, d_model=64, num_heads=4, depth=2):
```

```
        super().__init__()
        self.embed = nn.Embedding(vocab_size, d_model)
        self.pos = PositionalEncoding(d_model)
        self.enc_layers = nn.ModuleList([EncoderLayer(d_model, num_heads) for _ in
range(depth)])
        self.dec_layers = nn.ModuleList([DecoderLayer(d_model, num_heads) for _ in
range(depth)])
        self.out = nn.Linear(d_model, vocab_size)

    def forward(self, src, tgt, return_weights=False):
        src = self.pos(self.embed(src))
        tgt = self.pos(self.embed(tgt))

        enc_attn_maps = []
        for layer in self.enc_layers:
            src, attn = layer(src, return_weights=True)
            enc_attn_maps.append(attn)

        dec_sa_maps = []
        dec_ca_maps = []
        for layer in self.dec_layers:
            tgt, sa, ca = layer(tgt, src, return_weights=True)
            dec_sa_maps.append(sa)
            dec_ca_maps.append(ca)

        out = self.out(tgt)
        return out, enc_attn_maps, dec_sa_maps, dec_ca_maps


# ------------------------------------------------------------
# 7. Run Example
# ------------------------------------------------------------
vocab = 100
model = SimpleTransformer(vocab)

src = torch.randint(0, vocab, (1, 6))
tgt = torch.randint(0, vocab, (1, 6))

output, enc_attn, dec_sa, dec_ca = model(src, tgt, return_weights=True)


# ------------------------------------------------------------
# 8. Visualization for ALL Heads
# ------------------------------------------------------------
def show_all_heads(attn_map, title):
    attn_map = attn_map.squeeze(0)
    heads = attn_map.size(0)
    cols = min(heads, 4)
```

```
    rows = (heads + cols - 1) // cols

    fig, axes = plt.subplots(rows, cols, figsize=(4 * cols, 4 * rows))
    axes = axes.flatten()

    for i in range(heads):
        axes[i].imshow(attn_map[i].detach(), cmap="viridis")
        axes[i].set_title(f"Head {i+1}")
        axes[i].set_xlabel("Key")
        axes[i].set_ylabel("Query")

    for j in range(i+1, len(axes)):
        axes[j].axis("off")

    plt.suptitle(title, fontsize=18)
    plt.tight_layout()
    plt.show()


# Show First Layer Head Maps
show_all_heads(enc_attn[0], "Encoder Self-Attention (Layer 1)")
show_all_heads(dec_sa[0], "Decoder Self-Attention (Layer 1)")
show_all_heads(dec_ca[0], "Decoder Cross-Attention (Layer 1)")
```

What the Code Does

1. **Tokenizes the input sentence**

   The sentence is broken into tokens and indexed for the model.

2. **Passes it through a Transformer layer**

   Instead of just outputting the result, we also capture:

   - **Attention weights** for **all heads**.

3. **Extracts Attention Weights**

   For a sentence of length *N*, each head produces an **N × N** matrix.

   - Rows = *Query positions* (the token doing the attending)
   - Columns = *Key positions* (the token being attended to)

4. **Visualizes Each Head**

We plot each head's weight matrix as a **heatmap**:

- **Brighter areas** = stronger attention
- **Darker areas** = weaker attention

This allows us to **see** which words influence which other words during understanding.

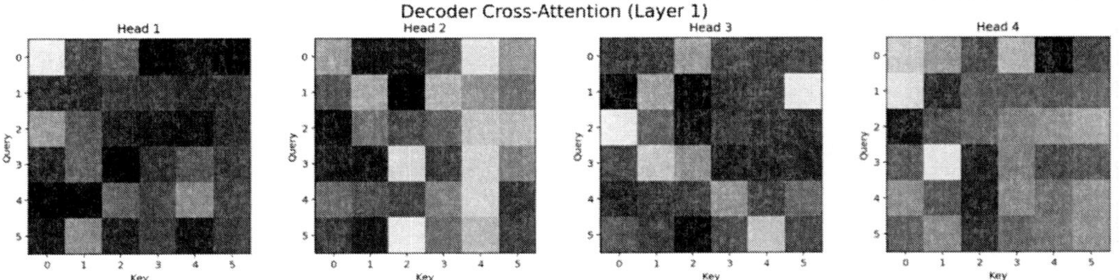

Illustration P6_Trans_4: Transformer

Master said, "Sam, think of this like a council of observers.

Each observer (head) watches the conversation from a different angle.

One notices subtle emotions.

Another watches grammar.

Another watches the context across distance.

Together, they form a *complete understanding.*

This is why Transformers became state-of-the-art."

Text Generator

Master said, "Apeksha, this work is a journey of transforming raw text into structured understanding, and then into new, meaningful expression.

First, we begin by *listening* to the text.

The PDF is opened, and its words are gently extracted.

The noise is removed — line breaks, irregular spacing, and symbols that do not serve a meaning are smoothed away.

The text becomes a continuous river, ready to be learned from.

Next, we craft the **vocabulary** — the language the model will think in. We count every word, and from the most frequent ones, we create our dictionary. Alongside these, we include special symbols:<BOS> — the breath before a sentence

<EOS> — the silence after meaning completes

<UNK> — the unknown

<PAD> — the quiet space used for alignment

The text is then translated into numbers — tokens — for a machine to understand only patterns, not letters.

We now shape the training data.

We do not teach the model one word at a time, but in *sequences of thought* — windows of 60 tokens.

Each sequence begins with <BOS> and ends with <EOS>, so the model learns when to begin speaking and when to conclude gracefully.

Then, we construct the **Transformer** — a structure of attention.

Unlike older models that read only left to right, the transformer observes relationships among *all* words simultaneously.

It sees language not as a chain, but as a *web* of meaning.

- The *Embedding Layer* gives each word a voice.
- The *Positional Encoding* tells the model where each word stands in a sentence — for meaning is not only in the word, but in its *place*.
- The *Transformer Layers* refine understanding through attention —letting the model decide which words matter most to one another.
- The final layer converts internal understanding back into language we can read.

- **Example P5 – U5 – D8**

GRU

```
import pdfplumber
import re
```

```
import torch
import torch.nn as nn
import math
from tqdm import tqdm
from collections import Counter
import torch.nn.functional as F

# ===================== DEVICE =====================
device = torch.device("cuda" if torch.cuda.is_available() else "cpu")
print("Using:", device)

# ============= LOAD & CLEAN PDF =====================
pdf_path =
r"C:/Users/User/mraj4/Documents/Optimum6/documents/Relationship.pdf"

def load_pdf(path):
    text = ""
    with pdfplumber.open(path) as pdf:
        for page in pdf.pages:
            page_text = page.extract_text()
            if page_text:
                text += " " + page_text

    text = text.lower()
    text = text.replace("\n", " ")
    text = re.sub(r"[^a-zA-Z0-9,.!?;:()'\- ]", " ", text)
    text = re.sub(r"\s+", " ", text).strip()
    return text

raw_text = load_pdf(pdf_path)
print("PDF Loaded. Characters:", len(raw_text))

# ================ VOCAB BUILD =====================
def build_vocab(text, vocab_size=8000):
    tokens = text.split()
    counts = Counter(tokens)
    most_common = counts.most_common(vocab_size - 4)

    idx2word = ["<PAD>", "<BOS>", "<EOS>", "<UNK>"] + [w for w, _ in
most_common]
    word2idx = {w:i for i, w in enumerate(idx2word)}
    return word2idx, idx2word

word2idx, idx2word = build_vocab(raw_text, vocab_size=8000)
vocab_size = len(idx2word)
print("Vocab Size:", vocab_size)

def encode(text):
```

```
    return [word2idx.get(w, word2idx["<UNK>"]) for w in text.split()]

def decode(tokens):
    return " ".join(idx2word[t] for t in tokens)

tokens = encode(raw_text)

# ====================== DATASET ======================
seq_length = 60
BOS = word2idx["<BOS>"]
EOS = word2idx["<EOS>"]

def create_sequences(data, seq_len):
    xs, ys = [], []
    for i in range(len(data) - seq_len - 2):
        seq = [BOS] + data[i:i+seq_len] + [EOS]
        xs.append(seq[:-1])
        ys.append(seq[1:])
    return torch.tensor(xs), torch.tensor(ys)

X, Y = create_sequences(tokens, seq_length)
X, Y = X.to(device), Y.to(device)

print("Dataset:", X.shape)

# ====== TRANSFORMER LANGUAGE MODEL ================
class PositionalEncoding(nn.Module):
    def __init__(self, d_model):
        super().__init__()
        pe = torch.zeros(5000, d_model)
        pos = torch.arange(0, 5000).unsqueeze(1)
        div = torch.exp(-math.log(10000) * torch.arange(0, d_model, 2) / d_model)
        pe[:, 0::2] = torch.sin(pos * div)
        pe[:, 1::2] = torch.cos(pos * div)
        self.pe = pe.unsqueeze(0)

    def forward(self, x):
        return x + self.pe[:, :x.size(1)].to(x.device)

class TransformerLM(nn.Module):
    def __init__(self, vocab_size, d_model=128, n_heads=4, num_layers=4):
        super().__init__()
        self.embed = nn.Embedding(vocab_size, d_model)
        self.pos = PositionalEncoding(d_model)
        layer = nn.TransformerEncoderLayer(d_model, n_heads, 512, batch_first=True)
        self.transformer = nn.TransformerEncoder(layer, num_layers)
        self.fc = nn.Linear(d_model, vocab_size)
```

```
    def forward(self, x):
        x = self.pos(self.embed(x))
        out = self.transformer(x)
        return self.fc(out)

model = TransformerLM(vocab_size).to(device)

# ===================== TRAINING =====================
optimizer = torch.optim.Adam(model.parameters(), lr=1e-3)
criterion = nn.CrossEntropyLoss()

epochs = 30
batch_size = 64

print("\nTraining Started...\n")
for epoch in range(epochs):
    total_loss = 0
    for i in tqdm(range(0, len(X), batch_size)):
        xb = X[i:i+batch_size]
        yb = Y[i:i+batch_size]

        optimizer.zero_grad()
        logits = model(xb)
        loss = criterion(logits.view(-1, vocab_size), yb.view(-1))
        loss.backward()
        optimizer.step()
        total_loss += loss.item()

    print(f"Epoch {epoch+1}/{epochs} Loss: {total_loss:.4f}")

torch.save(model.state_dict(), "soul_transformer.pt")
print("\n Training Complete. Model Saved.")

# ========== GENERATION (Stable Top-K + Repetition Control) ======
def generate(prompt, max_tokens=80, temperature=1.0, top_k=40,
repetition_penalty=1.15):
    model.eval()
    tokens = [BOS] + encode(prompt)
    x = torch.tensor(tokens).unsqueeze(0).to(device)

    for _ in range(max_tokens):
        logits = model(x)[0, -1] / temperature

        # Repetition penalty
        for token in set(x[0].tolist()):
            logits[token] /= repetition_penalty

        # Top-K
```

```
        values, indices = torch.topk(logits, top_k)
        probs = F.softmax(values, dim=-1)
        next_token = indices[torch.multinomial(probs, 1).item()].item()

        x = torch.cat([x, torch.tensor([[next_token]], device=device)], dim=1)

        if next_token == EOS:
            break

    text = decode(x.squeeze().tolist())
    return text.replace("<BOS>", "").replace("<EOS>", "").replace("<PAD>", "").strip()

# =============== SAMPLE OUTPUT =====================
print("\n---- SAMPLE GENERATION ----\n")
print(generate("each child", max_tokens=120, temperature=1.1, top_k=50))
```

Output:

Output
each child been successful in path to so to success and then, be smart enough to help that will require get to solve problems that the relationship between parent should roles in a way to success as parents, have ever evolving technology to be responsible, set have a lack of respect and resources. sometimes, kids have a better understanding of

Training begins.

The model reads the text again and again — **30 epochs** — each time adjusting itself to reduce the difference between its prediction and the true next word.

This is how memory forms.

Once trained, we ask it to *speak*.

We give it a prompt — a seed of meaning.

The model continues the thought, selecting each next word based on learned probability.
But to maintain richness and avoid dull repetition, we shape the generation:

- **Temperature** controls creativity — low is safe, high is expressive.
- **Top-K** keeps only the most meaningful next-word choices.

- **Repetition penalty** prevents the model from echoing the same words again and again.

Thus the machine responds not as a mirror, nor as a recorder of text — but as a **new voice** formed from all that it has read.

PART FIVE

DAY EIGHTEEN

Unit 5 - Lesson Four

The Heartbeat of Understanding

"Self-attention is the quiet dialogue within — where every word listens to every other, creating harmony in meaning, as consciousness listens to itself."

– Shree Shambav

Master said, "Akshatha, when we speak of *Attention*, we are speaking of how meaning is found. Not by reading words one after another, but by understanding which words matter to each other.

A sentence is not merely a line — it is a *constellation*.

Attention is the act of seeing the stars **in relation**, not in isolation."

☐ Understanding Attention in Transformers

Before transformers, language models were built using **RNNs** and **LSTMs**.

These models processed text sequentially — one step at a time — making them slow and limited in understanding long-range relationships.

Then came the revolutionary paper:

"Attention Is All You Need" (Vaswani et al., 2017)

This paper said something bold:

We no longer need recurrence.

We only need attention.

The Transformer architecture removed:

- Recurrence (like RNNs/LSTMs)
- Convolutions (like CNNs)

And replaced them with **only:**

- **Self-Attention Layers**
- **Feedforward Layers**

Silent Attention — The Essence

Master continued:

"Silent Attention is the unseen listening.

Before the model speaks, it *observes* the relationship between all words **at once**."

In a sentence:

On Friday, the judge issued a sentence.

- *judge* tells us *sentence* is legal, not grammatical.
- *issued* strengthens that meaning.
- *the* gives grammatical role clarity.

When interpreting a *sentence*, the model **selectively pays attention** to:

Word	Importance
judge	High

issued	High
the	Medium
on, Friday, a	Low

This selective relevance is **Self-Attention**.

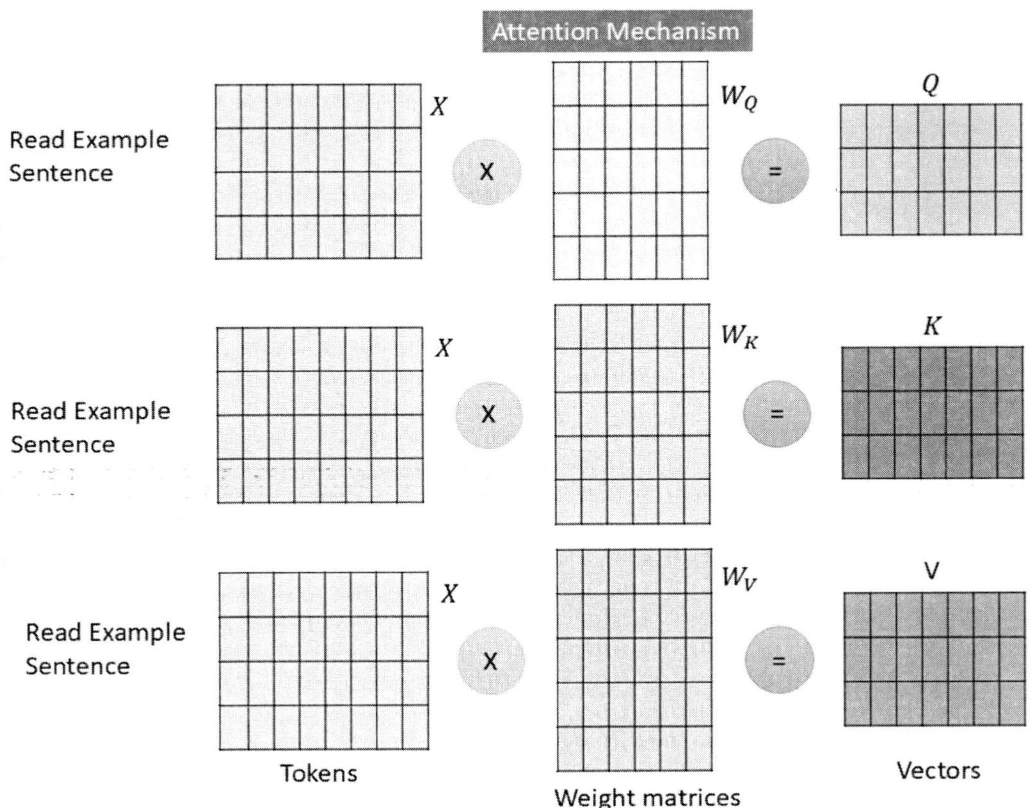

Illustration P6_Trans_6: Attention

Self-Attention: How a Sequence Attends to Itself

Each token (word) is represented as a vector.

From each vector, we derive **three new vectors**:

Vector	Purpose	Weight Matrix
Q (Query)	What am I looking for?	(W_Q)
K (Key)	What do I contain?	(W_K)
V (Value)	What information do I offer?	(W_V)

Attention Score Computation

For each token **x**:

1. **Dot product:**

   $Q_x \cdot K_y$

   (How relevant is token y to x?)

2. **Scale:**

   Divide by $\sqrt{d_k}$

   (Prevents scores from exploding)

3. **Softmax:**

   Convert scores into probabilities (attention weights)

4. **Weighted Sum:**

   Combine Value vectors according to these weights

5. **Contextual Update:**

   Add results back to the original token embedding

This updates each token according to **context**, not position.

Cross-Attention vs Self-Attention

Type	Used In	Query From	Key/Value From	Purpose
Cross-Attention	Enc-Dec Transformers	Decoder	Encoder	Understanding *between* sequences (e.g., translation)
Self-Attention	Both Encoders & Decoders	Same sequence	Same sequence	Understanding *within* a sequence

Cheng et al. (2016) first introduced **Intra-Attention**, later known as Self-Attention.

This led directly to:

- **BERT** (Encoder-only → Reading, Understanding)
- **GPT** (Decoder-only → Generating, Writing)

Autoregressive Self-Attention (GPT-style)

GPT models generate text one token at a time, ensuring they cannot *see the future* in the sequence.

This is done by applying a **causal mask**:

```
Token can only attend to tokens before it.
```

Thus, the model becomes a *storyteller.*

Why Transformers Are Powerful

Master smiled:

"A transformer does not merely process text.

It **reasons** with connections."

- It understands long-range meaning.
- It learns language relationships deeply.
- It scales naturally with data and compute.

Attention allows the model to **contextualize** every word using **every other word**.

This is why modern models:

- Write poetry
- Translate languages
- Solve reasoning tasks
- Generate meaningful stories

Because **they do not remember —They *understand.***

Master said:

"Language is not linear, Akshatha. Meaning is relational.

The Transformer sees what we often miss —**the connections between words, thoughts, and moments.**

This is why attention is not merely a mechanism. It is a *way of perceiving reality*."

Master said, "Akshatha, now that the *spirit* of Attention is understood, let us illuminate it mathematically.

For true comprehension is born when *intuition meets equation*."

Intuition: Self-Attention with Formulas

Consider an input sequence of **T tokens**.

Each token is represented as a vector of dimension **d**.

$$X = \begin{bmatrix} x_1 \\ x_2 \\ x_T \end{bmatrix} \in R^{T\times d}$$

Step 1 — Create Queries, Keys, and Values

Each input token vector x_i is projected into **three new spaces**:

$$Q = XW_Q$$

$$K = XW_K$$

$$V = XW_V$$

Where:

- $W_Q \in R^{d\times dk}$
- $W_K \in R^{d\times dk}$
- $W_V \in R^{d\times dv}$

Thus:

Symbol	Meaning
Q	*What this word wants to find*
K	*What this word offers*
V	*The information this word carries*

Step 2 — Compute Attention Scores

For every pair of tokens i and j:

$$\text{Score}(i, j) = Q_i \cdot K_j^T$$

This creates an **attention score matrix**:

$$\text{Scores} = QK^T$$

Step 3 — Apply Scaling

The dot products grow large when d_k is large.

To stabilize gradients:

$$\text{ScaledScores} = \frac{QK^T}{\sqrt{d_k}}$$

Step 4 — Softmax to Convert Scores into Weights

$$\text{AttentionWeights} = \text{softmax}\left(\frac{QK^T}{\sqrt{d_k}}\right)$$

Softmax ensures:

- Values are between **0 and 1**
- Rows sum to **1**
- Represents *how much each token attends to others*

Step 5 — Weighted Sum of Values

$$\text{Output} = \text{AttentionWeights} \cdot V$$

This produces a new representation where each token is **context-aware**, updated by contributions from the entire sequence.

Complete Scaled Dot-Product Attention Formula

$$\text{Attention}(Q, K, V) = \text{softmax}\left(\frac{QK^T}{\sqrt{d_k}}\right) V$$

☐ Multi-Head Attention

In transformers, attention is computed *multiple times in parallel*:

$$\text{head}_h = \text{Attention}\left(Q\,W_Q^{(h)},\ KW_K^{(h)},\ VW_V^{(h)}\right)$$

Then the heads are concatenated:

$$\text{MultiHead}(Q, K, V) = \text{Concat}(\text{head}_1,\ldots,\text{head}_H)W_O$$

Where:

- H = number of heads
- W_O = output projection matrix

This allows the model to:

- Capture **multiple types of relationships**
- Understand context **from different perspectives**

☐ Autoregressive Mask (for GPT)

To prevent the model from seeing *future tokens*:

$$MaskedScores_{ij} = \begin{cases} \dfrac{Q_i K_j^T}{\sqrt{d_k}} & if\ j \leq i \\ -\infty & if\ j > 1 \end{cases}$$

Softmax then ignores future positions automatically.

Summary Table

Stage	Formula	Meaning
Linear Projections	($Q = XW_Q$), ($K = XW_K$), ($V = XW_V$)	Create search, identity, and message vectors
Scores	(QK^T)	Measure token-to-token relevance
Scaling	$\frac{QK^T}{\sqrt{d_k}}$	Prevent large gradients
Normalization	softmax (.)	Convert to importance weights
Context Mix	weights V	Update each token by others
Multi-Head	Concat(heads)	Learn multiple relational patterns

Attention is not merely computation. It is the art of **knowing what matters**."

Master smiled gently, "Akshatha, now we will *see* attention — not just as symbols — but as numbers flowing and transforming meaning."

☐ Numeric Worked Example of Scaled Dot-Product Self-Attention

Let our sequence contain **3 tokens**:

$$X = \begin{bmatrix} x_1 \\ x_2 \\ x_3 \end{bmatrix}$$

Assume each token is represented by a **2-dimensional embedding**:

x1 = [1,0], x2 = [0,1], x3 = [1,1]

We define small weight matrices:

$$W_Q = \begin{bmatrix} 1 & 0 \\ 0 & 1 \end{bmatrix}, W_K = \begin{bmatrix} 1 & 1 \\ 1 & 1 \end{bmatrix}, W_V = \begin{bmatrix} 1 & 0 \\ 0 & 1 \end{bmatrix}$$

Step 1 — Compute Q, K, and V

$$Q = XW_Q = X \Rightarrow Q = \begin{bmatrix} 1 & 0 \\ 0 & 1 \\ 1 & 1 \end{bmatrix}$$

$$K = XW_K = \begin{bmatrix} 1 & 0 \\ 0 & 1 \\ 1 & 1 \end{bmatrix} \begin{bmatrix} 1 & 1 \\ 1 & 1 \end{bmatrix} = \begin{bmatrix} 1 & 1 \\ 1 & 1 \\ 2 & 2 \end{bmatrix}$$

$$V = XW_V = X \Rightarrow V = \begin{bmatrix} 1 & 0 \\ 0 & 1 \\ 1 & 1 \end{bmatrix}$$

Step 2 — Compute Attention Scores = QK^T

$$QK^T = \begin{bmatrix} 1 & 0 \\ 0 & 1 \\ 1 & 1 \end{bmatrix} \begin{bmatrix} 1 & 1 & 2 \\ 1 & 1 & 2 \end{bmatrix} = \begin{bmatrix} 1 & 1 & 2 \\ 1 & 1 & 2 \\ 2 & 2 & 4 \end{bmatrix}$$

Step 3 — Scale Scores

Since $d_k = 2 \Rightarrow \sqrt{d_k} = 2 \approx 1.41$

$$\frac{QK^T}{\sqrt{d_k}} \approx \begin{bmatrix} 0.71 & 0.71 & 1.41 \\ 0.71 & 0.71 & 1.41 \\ 1.41 & 1.41 & 2.83 \end{bmatrix}$$

Step 4 — Softmax Row-wise

Softmax turns each row into probabilities.

Example for first row:

softmax [0.71, 0.71, 1.41]

Exponentiate:

$e^{0.71}=2.03$, $e^{1.41}=4.10$

Sum:

2.03 + 2.03 +4.10 = 8.16

Thus:

⇒[0.25, 0.25, 0.50]

So the final **Attention Weights**:

$$\text{Attention} = \begin{bmatrix} 0.25 & 0.25 & 0.50 \\ 0.25 & 0.25 & 0.50 \\ 0.25 & 0.25 & 0.50 \end{bmatrix}$$

(Notice: All tokens attend similarly in this example.)

Step 5 — Weighted Sum to Compute Output

Output=Attention·V

$$= \begin{bmatrix} 0.25 & 0.25 & 0.50 \\ 0.25 & 0.25 & 0.50 \\ 0.25 & 0.25 & 0.50 \end{bmatrix} \begin{bmatrix} 1 & 0 \\ 0 & 1 \\ 1 & 1 \end{bmatrix} = \begin{bmatrix} 0.75 & 0.50 \\ 0.75 & 0.50 \\ 0.75 & 0.50 \end{bmatrix}$$

Final Output Token Representations

y1 = y2 = y3 = [0.75, 0.50]

Meaning of the Result

Every token's representation now carries:

Component	Represents
0.75	shared meaning from *"word 1"* and *"word 3"*
0.50	shared meaning from *"word 2"* and *"word 3"*

Even without recurrence or convolution, each word is **learned from all others**.

Master said, "John, let us understand the code slowly — not as instructions to a machine, but as the unfolding of attention itself."

In this demonstration, we are showing how **Scaled Dot-Product Attention** works using a small, clear numeric example in **PyTorch**.

We begin with:

- A set of **token embeddings** → representations of words in vector form.
- Three **weight matrices**:
  - W_x → W_q (Queries)
  - W_x → W_k (Keys)
  - W_x → W_v (Values)

These matrices transform the input embeddings into three different roles:

Example P5 – U5 – D9

Attention Mechanism – Scaled Dot-Product Attention

```
import torch
import torch.nn.functional as F

# We work with CPU
device = torch.device("cpu")

# Suppose we have 3 tokens and each token embedding = 4 dims
# (This is the same numeric example as before, just now in PyTorch)

X = torch.tensor([
    [1.0, 0.0, 1.0, 0.0],  # Token A
    [0.0, 1.0, 0.0, 1.0],  # Token B
    [1.0, 1.0, 0.0, 0.0],  # Token C
], device=device)

print("\nInput token embeddings (X):")
print(X)

# Weight matrices (learned in training, but we define them manually here)
W_q = torch.tensor([
    [1., 0., 1., 0.],
    [0., 1., 0., 1.],
    [1., 0., 1., 0.],
    [0., 1., 0., 1.]
], device=device)

W_k = W_q.clone()  # for simplicity, use same weights
W_v = torch.eye(4, device=device)  # Identity → V = X (for clarity)

# Compute Q, K, V
Q = X @ W_q   # (3,4)
K = X @ W_k   # (3,4)
V = X @ W_v   # (3,4)
```

```
print("\nQuery vectors (Q):")
print(Q)

print("\nKey vectors (K):")
print(K)

print("\nValue vectors (V):")
print(V)

# Step 1: Compute raw attention scores = Q @ K^T
scores = Q @ K.T        # (3,3)

print("\nRaw attention scores (QKᵀ):")
print(scores)

# Step 2: Scale by sqrt(d_k)
d_k = Q.shape[-1]
scaled_scores = scores / torch.sqrt(torch.tensor(d_k, dtype=torch.float32))

print("\nScaled scores (QKᵀ / sqrt(d_k)):")
print(scaled_scores)

# Step 3: Softmax over last dimension → attention weights
attn_weights = F.softmax(scaled_scores, dim=-1)

print("\nAttention Weights (softmax):")
print(attn_weights)

# Step 4: Weighted sum of Values
output = attn_weights @ V   # (3,4)

print("\nFinal Output (Attention * V):")
print(output)
```

Logical Flow of the Code

1. **Token Embeddings**

   We start with vectors representing words.

   These are our **inputs**.

2. **Linear Transformations (Q, K, V)**

   We multiply the input vectors by weight matrices:

$$Q = XW_q, \; K = XW_k, V = XW_v$$

This gives different perspectives on the same tokens.

3. **Compute Attention Scores**

   We compare each Query with every Key:

Scores = QK^T

This measures **similarity** between tokens.

4. **Scale the Scores**

   To keep values stable during training:

   Scaled = $\frac{scores}{\sqrt{d_k}}$

Output:

```
Output

Input token embeddings (X):
tensor([[1., 0., 1., 0.],
        [0., 1., 0., 1.],
        [1., 1., 0., 0.]])

Query vectors (Q):
tensor([[2., 0., 2., 0.],
        [0., 2., 0., 2.],
        [1., 1., 1., 1.]])

Key vectors (K):
tensor([[2., 0., 2., 0.],
        [0., 2., 0., 2.],
        [1., 1., 1., 1.]])

Value vectors (V):
tensor([[1., 0., 1., 0.],
        [0., 1., 0., 1.],
        [1., 1., 0., 0.]])

Raw attention scores (QKᵀ):
tensor([[8., 0., 4.],
        [0., 8., 4.],
        [4., 4., 4.]])
```

```
Scaled scores (QKᵀ / sqrt(d_k)):
tensor([[4., 0., 2.],
        [0., 4., 2.],
        [2., 2., 2.]])

Attention Weights (softmax):
tensor([[0.8668, 0.0159, 0.1173],
        [0.0159, 0.8668, 0.1173],
        [0.3333, 0.3333, 0.3333]])

Final Output (Attention * V):
tensor([[0.9841, 0.1332, 0.8668, 0.0159],
        [0.1332, 0.9841, 0.0159, 0.8668],
        [0.6667, 0.6667, 0.3333, 0.3333]])
```

5. **Softmax → Attention Weights**

   We convert similarities into probabilities:

   $$\alpha = \text{softmax (scaled)}$$

6. **Weighted Sum of Values**

   The final output is:

   $$\text{Output} = \alpha V$$

This means **each token rewrites itself** by borrowing information from other tokens —but only in the *proportion* of how relevant they are.

☐ Multi-Head Attention

Master smiled gently and said, "Akshatha, self-attention taught us how a word looks to the others.

But *multi-head attention* teaches us that a word does not look at the world in only one way."

Why Multi-Head Attention Was Needed

When we compute self-attention once, we obtain **one** representation of context. This is like asking a person:

"Tell me what this sentence means."

But meaning is not singular.

The sentence holds **grammar**, **tone**, **emotion**, **role**, **tense**, **relationships**, and **intent** — *simultaneously.*

Self-attention with a **single set of Q, K, V** can only learn **one pattern of significance**.

So the Transformer says: *"Let me let the sentence attend to itself* ***in multiple distinct ways*** *at once."*

This is **Multi-Head Attention.**

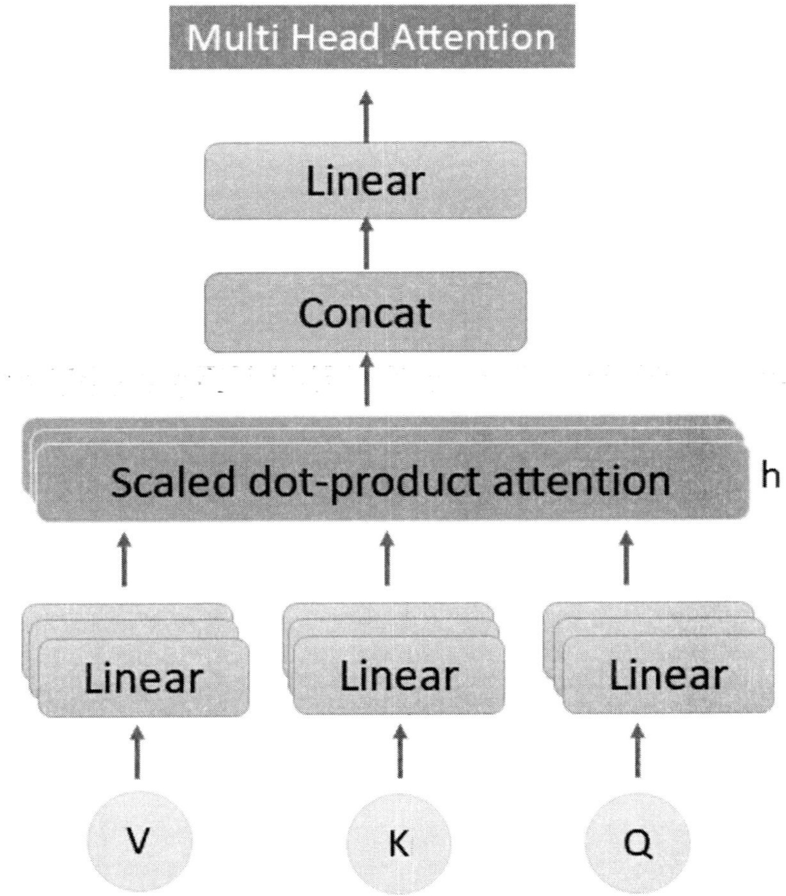

Illustration P6_Trans_7: Attention

How Multi-Head Attention Works

1. Suppose each token is a vector of size **d_model**.
2. We choose **h heads**.
3. We **split** each token embedding into **h smaller vectors**, each of size:

$$d_k = \frac{d_{model}}{h}$$

4. For **each head**, we have **separate** W_Q, W_K, W_V matrices.

So instead of one attention process, we have **h parallel attentions**:

headi = Attention(Q W_Q^i ,KW_K^i, VW_V^i)

Each head learns **a different perspective**:

- One head might capture **long-range grammar**
- One learns **emotional cues**
- One tracks **subject-verb agreement**
- One specializes in **names or entities**

Each head is like a **different specialist** sitting inside the model.

After Computing All Heads

We **concatenate** all attention outputs:

MultiHead (Q, K, V) = Concat ($head_1$, $head_2$, ..., $head_h$) W_O

Where W_O is a final learned projection.

This brings all perspectives **back into one unified representation**.

Metaphorical Understanding

Master said, **"Akshatha, consider a simple sentence:**

'The bank will not open until Monday.'

How do you understand the word *bank*?

- **Head 1** considers *financial institutions.*
- **Head 2** considers *river banks.*
- **Head 3** watches *verbs vs. nouns.*
- **Head 4** checks *weekday schedule context.*

Each head forms **a hypothesis**.

Then, all heads share their understanding.

Thus, the model decides:

This bank refers to a financial institution.

Meaning emerges **not from one viewpoint**, but from **the harmony of many.**

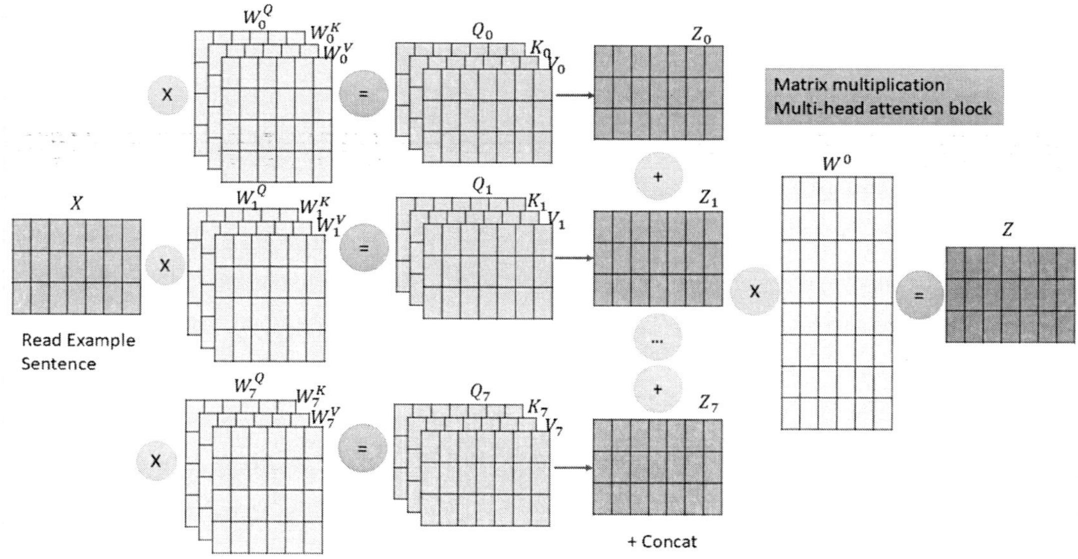

Illustration P6_Trans_9: Attention

Why This Matters

Because language is **multi-dimensional.**

One head sees **structure,**

another sees **emotion,**

another sees **relationships,**

another sees **patterns of time**…

Multi-Head Attention allows the model to **think in layers**, like human intuition.

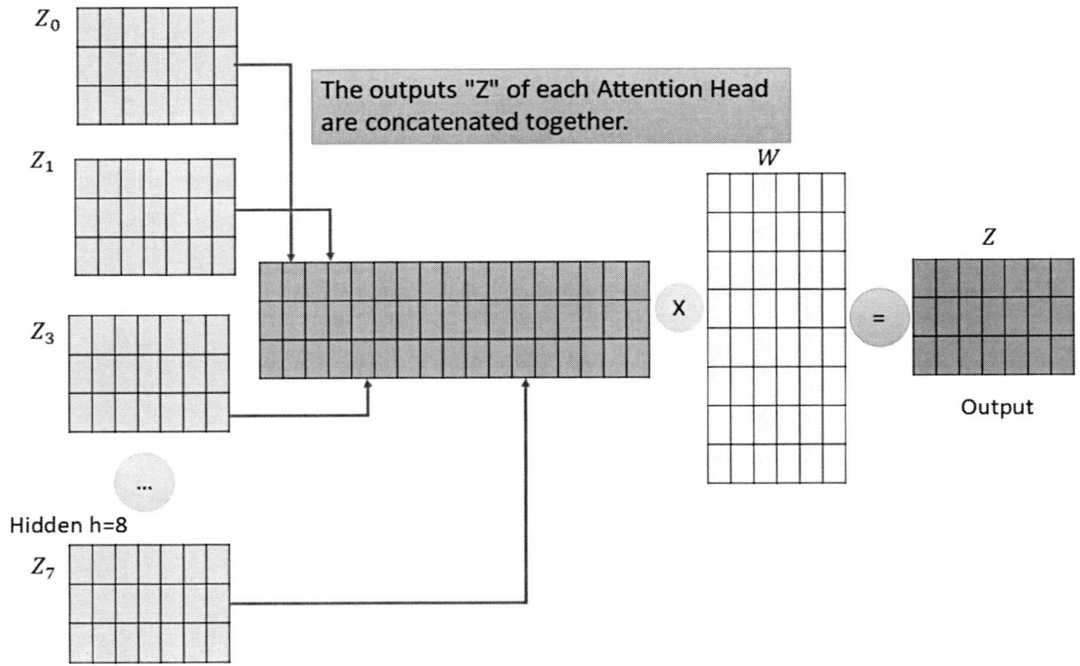

Illustration P6_Trans_8: Attention

Multi-Head Attention in Generation

When the final attention layers finish their work:

1. A **linear projection** maps the final representation to **logits** over the vocabulary.

2. A **softmax** converts logits → probabilities.

3. The model **chooses the next token**.

Then repeats.

And repeats.

And repeats.

This is how GPT-style models **generate text word-by-word**, like thought unfolding.

Master said, "Self-attention is awareness.

Multi-head attention is *perspective.*

And when awareness meets perspective — meaning arises."

☐ Intuition: Mathematical

Master said, "Akshatha, let us *see* multi-head attention in numbers — not theory alone, but a small, concrete computation you can follow and run. We will compute two attention heads in parallel, show their attention weights, the head-wise outputs, then concatenate them into the final output."

Setup (what we will use)

- Sequence length T=3 (three tokens).
- Model dimension $d_{model} = 4$.
- Heads $h = 2$ → each head dimension $d_k = d_{model}/h = 2$.
- Input token embeddings $X \in \mathbb{R}^{3x4}$

$$X = \begin{pmatrix} 1 & 0 & 1 & 0 \\ 0 & 1 & 0 & 1 \\ 1 & 1 & 1 & 1 \end{pmatrix}$$

We will define each head's linear maps so that head1 operates on the *first two* components and head2 on the *last two* components (this keeps the arithmetic simple and transparent).

Head 1 projection matrices (4×2)

These simply select the first two dimensions:

$$W_Q^{(1)} = W_K^{(1)} = W_V^{(1)} = \begin{bmatrix} 1 & 0 \\ 0 & 1 \\ 0 & 0 \\ 0 & 0 \end{bmatrix}$$

Applying these yields $Q^{(1)}, K^{(1)}, V^{(1)} \in \mathbb{R}^{3x2}$

$$Q^{(1)} = K^{(1)} = V^{(1)} = \begin{bmatrix} 1 & 0 \\ 0 & 1 \\ 1 & 1 \end{bmatrix}$$

Head 2 projection matrices (4×2)

These select the last two dimensions:

$$W_Q^{(2)} = W_K^{(2)} = W_V^{(2)} = \begin{bmatrix} 0 & 0 \\ 0 & 0 \\ 1 & 0 \\ 0 & 1 \end{bmatrix}$$

Applying them gives $Q^{(2)}, K^{(2)}, V^{(2)}$ (note they are identical in numeric form to head1 because of our chosen X):

$$Q^{(2)} = K^{(2)} = V^{(2)} = \begin{bmatrix} 1 & 0 \\ 0 & 1 \\ 1 & 1 \end{bmatrix}$$

Per-head attention computation (head 1 — identical arithmetic for head 2)

1. **Raw scores** $S^{(1)} = Q^{(1)} K^{(1)^T}$

$$S^{(1)} = \begin{bmatrix} 1 & 0 \\ 0 & 1 \\ 1 & 1 \end{bmatrix} \begin{bmatrix} 1 & 1 & 2 \\ 0 & 1 & 1 \end{bmatrix} = \begin{bmatrix} 1 & 1 & 2 \\ 1 & 1 & 2 \\ 2 & 2 & 4 \end{bmatrix}$$

(You can verify by dot-products of rows.)

2. **Scale** by $\sqrt{d_K} = 2 \approx 1.414$:

$$\widetilde{S^{(1)}} = \frac{S^{(1)}}{\sqrt{2}} \approx \begin{bmatrix} 0.707 & 0.707 & 1.414 \\ 0.707 & 0.707 & 1.414 \\ 1.414 & 1.414 & 2.828 \end{bmatrix}$$

3. **Softmax row-wise** to get attention weights $A^{(1)}$:

Compute softmax of first row [0.707,0.707,1.414]:

- $e^{0.707} \approx 2.028$, $e^{1.414} \approx 4.113$
- Sum = 2.028+2.028+4.113=8.169
- Probabilities ≈ [0.248, 0.248, 0.503].

With symmetry, the (approx.) attention matrices become:

$$A^{(1)} \approx \begin{bmatrix} 0.401 & 0.198 & 0.401 \\ 0.198 & 0.401 & 0.401 \\ 0.248 & 0.248 & 0.503 \end{bmatrix}$$

(Rows sum ≈ 1.0 — minor rounding differences possible.)

4. **Weighted sum**: $O^{(1)} = A^{(1)}V^{(1)}$.

Using $V^{(1)}$ rows [1,0],[0,1],[1,1], compute each output row:

- Row 1:

0.401[1,0] + 0.198[0,1] + 0.401[1,1] = [0.802, 0.599]

- Row 2:

0.198[1,0] + 0.401[0,1] + 0.401[1,1] = [0.599, 0.802]

- Row 3:

0.248[1,0] + 0.248[0,1] + 0.503[1,1] = [0.751, 0.751]

So:

$$O^{(1)} \approx \begin{bmatrix} 0.802 & 0.599 \\ 0.599 & 0.802 \\ 0.751 & 0.751 \end{bmatrix}$$

Because of our choices, **head 2 gives the same numeric outputs** $O^{(2)} = O^{(1)}$.

Concatenate heads and final projection

Concatenate along last dimension (for each token):

$O = \text{Concat}(O^{(1)}, O^{(2)}) \in \mathbb{R}^{3x4}$

So token-wise outputs become:

Row 1: [0.802, 0.599, 0.802, 0.599]

Row 2: [0.599, 0.802, 0.599, 0.802]

Row 3: [0.751, 0.751, 0.751, 0.751]

Finally, a learned matrix W_O (shape 4×4) projects this concatenated vector back to d_{model} = 4. If W_O were identity (for illustration), the final outputs equal O above.

Summary (intuition)

- Each head computed attention on a different subspace of the embedding (first two dims vs last two).
- Each head produced its own context-aware vectors $O^{(i)}$
- Concatenating the heads gives a richer representation that captures *different types of relationships* simultaneously.
- The final linear projection mixes those perspectives into the token's new representation.

Example P5 – U5 – D10
Transformer – Multi Head
import torch import torch.nn.functional as F torch.set_printoptions(precision=3, sci_mode=False)

```
# Input embeddings (3 tokens, 4-dim)
X = torch.tensor([
    [1., 0., 1., 0.],
    [0., 1., 0., 1.],
    [1., 1., 1., 1.]
]) # shape (3,4)

# Head projection matrices (4 x 2) as described
Wq1 = torch.tensor([[1.,0.],[0.,1.],[0.,0.],[0.,0.]])
Wk1 = Wq1.clone()
Wv1 = Wq1.clone()

Wq2 = torch.tensor([[0.,0.],[0.,0.],[1.,0.],[0.,1.]])
Wk2 = Wq2.clone()
Wv2 = Wq2.clone()

# Compute Q/K/V for head 1
Q1 = X @ Wq1   # (3,2)
K1 = X @ Wk1
V1 = X @ Wv1

# Compute Q/K/V for head 2
Q2 = X @ Wq2
K2 = X @ Wk2
V2 = X @ Wv2

print("Q1:\n", Q1)
print("K1:\n", K1)
print("V1:\n", V1)

# Attention function (scaled dot-product)
def scaled_dot_attention(Q, K, V):
    d_k = Q.size(-1)
    scores = Q @ K.T                    # (T,T)
    scaled = scores / (d_k ** 0.5)
    weights = F.softmax(scaled, dim=-1)  # row-wise
    out = weights @ V                   # (T, d_k)
    return out, weights

O1, A1 = scaled_dot_attention(Q1, K1, V1)
O2, A2 = scaled_dot_attention(Q2, K2, V2)

print("\nHead 1 attention weights A1:\n", A1)
print("\nHead 1 output O1:\n", O1)

print("\nHead 2 attention weights A2:\n", A2)
print("\nHead 2 output O2:\n", O2)
```

```
# Concatenate heads -> (3,4)
O = torch.cat([O1, O2], dim=-1)
print("\nConcatenated output O (3x4):\n", O)

# Final projection W_o (identity for demo)
W_o = torch.eye(4)
final = O @ W_o.T
print("\nFinal output after W_o (here identity):\n", final)
```

Output:

```
Output
Q1:
 tensor([[1., 0.],
        [0., 1.],
        [1., 1.]])
K1:
 tensor([[1., 0.],
        [0., 1.],
        [1., 1.]])
V1:
 tensor([[1., 0.],
        [0., 1.],
        [1., 1.]])

Head 1 attention weights A1:
 tensor([[0.401, 0.198, 0.401],
        [0.198, 0.401, 0.401],
        [0.248, 0.248, 0.503]])

Head 1 output O1:
 tensor([[0.802, 0.599],
        [0.599, 0.802],
        [0.752, 0.752]])

Head 2 attention weights A2:
 tensor([[0.401, 0.198, 0.401],
        [0.198, 0.401, 0.401],
        [0.248, 0.248, 0.503]])

Head 2 output O2:
 tensor([[0.802, 0.599],
        [0.599, 0.802],
        [0.752, 0.752]])

Concatenated output O (3x4):
```

```
tensor([[0.802, 0.599, 0.802, 0.599],
        [0.599, 0.802, 0.599, 0.802],
        [0.752, 0.752, 0.752, 0.752]])

Final output after W_o (here identity):
 tensor([[0.802, 0.599, 0.802, 0.599],
        [0.599, 0.802, 0.599, 0.802],
        [0.752, 0.752, 0.752, 0.752]])
```

Master said, "Akshatha, notice the power: each head sees a different *facet* of the same token. When their views are combined, the model's knowledge of context becomes richer than any single view alone."

☐ Additive Attention

Master said, "Apeksha, you have understood the *what* of attention. Now let us understand the *why* — the purpose, the evolution, and the subtlety behind each form of attention."

He continued gently:

1. The Birth of Additive Attention — *Bahdanau et al., 2014*

Before Transformers, **machine translation** was performed with **Encoder–Decoder RNNs**:

- The **encoder RNN** reads the source sentence (e.g., French).
- The **decoder RNN** generates the translation (e.g., English), one word at a time.

However, one problem emerged:

The meaning of an entire sentence had to be compressed into the *last hidden state* of the encoder.

This is like asking someone to read a **full paragraph** and summarize it in **one breath** — and then use *only that memory* to translate everything.

This led to **information loss**, especially for **long sentences**.

Bahdanau's Insight

"Not all words in the source sentence are equally relevant to each translated word."

So:

- At each decoding step (each word of the output sentence),
- The decoder **selects** which words in the input should influence its next output.

This selection is performed by **Additive Attention.**

Additive Attention — Step-by-Step

Let:

- Decoder hidden state at time *t* → **Query**: q_t
- Encoder hidden state at position *i* → **Key**: k_i

But **q** and **k** do *not need to be the same dimension.*

So we first align them into a shared representation.

Formula (Additive / Bahdanau Attention)

$$e_{t,i} = v^{T} \tanh(W_q q_t + W_k k_i)$$

- W_q → learns how to view the query.
- W_k → learns how to view the key.
- v → learns how to score the alignment.

Then apply softmax to convert alignment scores into probabilities:

$$\alpha_{t,i} = \frac{\exp{(e)_{t,i}}}{\sum \exp(e)_{t,j}}$$

Finally, create the **context vector**:

$c_t = \sum_i \alpha_{t,i} \, k_i$

This **context vector** is what the decoder uses to choose the next word.

Intuition

- If **Wq(q)** and **Wk(k)** *point in the same direction*, tanh outputs strong activation → large score → high relevance.
- If they are unrelated → score is low → low attention.

Why Additive Attention Was Powerful

- **Does not require Query and Key to have the same dimensions**
- Works well for challenging translation tasks between languages with **different word order** (e.g., Hindi ↔ English).

But there was a limitation:

It required a separate feedforward network for every attention scoring step — **slow** for large datasets.

☐ Dot-Product Attention — Luong et al., 2015

Luong simplified and accelerated Bahdanau attention.

Formula (Dot-Product / Multiplicative Attention)

$e_{t,i} = q_t^T$

Then softmax:

$\alpha_{t,i} = \text{softmax}(e_{t,i})$

Context vector:

$$c_t = \sum_i \alpha_{t,i} \, k_i$$

Benefits

1. **Very fast** — computed with a single matrix multiplication.
2. **Easy to parallelize** — modern GPUs love matrix multiplications.

Limitation

- Requires **q** and **k** to have the **same dimension**.
- For very large vector sizes, dot-products become **too large**, which destabilizes training (softmax saturates → gradients vanish).

☐ Scaled Dot-Product Attention — Vaswani et al., 2017

The authors of *"Attention Is All You Need"* introduced a simple but crucial fix:

$$\text{Attention}\,(Q, K, V) = \text{softmax}\,\left(\frac{QK^T}{\sqrt{d_k}}\right) V$$

W

hy Scale?

If key/query vectors are large:

- Dot products become huge,
- Softmax outputs become extremely peaked,
- Gradients become tiny → training becomes unstable.

Dividing by dk keeps values in a stable range.

This single scaling trick made training **deep and wide Transformer models possible**.

Significance

The attention mechanism in Transformers allows:

1. Parallel Processing

No recurrence → tokens processed simultaneously → **huge speed improvements**.

2. Capturing Long-Range Meaning

Words far apart in sentences can influence each other directly.

Example:
In the sentence:

"The **judge** issued a **sentence**."

The meaning of *"sentence"* depends heavily on *"judge"*, even if separated by words.

3. Scalability

Transformers power:

- GPT models
- BERT
- LLaMA
- Almost every modern LLM and diffusion model

They scale from:

- Small classroom experiments →
- To models with **hundreds of billions of parameters**.

Master said, "Apeksha, remember — attention is not merely a formula.

It is the model learning where meaning lives in language.

Bahdanau taught the model to *focus*.

Luong taught the model to *focus efficiently*.

Vaswani taught the model to *focus powerfully, globally, and in parallel.*

And that, is how language was awakened in machines."

☐ Grouped Query Attention (GQA)

Master said, "Sam, let us now understand one of the most important evolutions in the attention mechanism used in today's large language models — Grouped Query Attention (GQA). To appreciate GQA, we must first understand why it emerged."

Understanding the Context

In the original **Multi-Head Attention (MHA)** mechanism, *each attention head* has:

- Its **own Query projection**
- Its **own Key projection**
- Its **own Value projection**

So, if a model has *h* heads, it learns *h* different sets of Query, Key, and Value vectors.

This allows great expressive power because each head can specialise:

- One head may learn grammatical structure,
- Another may track long-range dependencies,
- Another may understand the semantic tone.

But this comes at a cost:

- High memory usage (storing h sets of keys and values)
- Slower inference during text generation
- Larger KV cache during autoregressive decoding

When models reach **billions of parameters**, these costs become enormous.

How Multi-Query Attention (MQA) Works

Master continued, "In order to solve this problem, researchers asked — *Do we really need a separate Key and Value for every Query head?* Thus came **Multi-Query Attention**."

In **MQA**:

- Each head still has its **own Query projection**
- But **all heads share a single Key and Value projection**

So:

Queries: Q1, Q2, Q3, ..., Qh (h unique)

Keys: K (shared)

Values: V (shared)

Benefits of MQA

- **Memory reduction:** KV cache becomes ~h times smaller.
- **Faster inference:** Less data movement; GPU memory is used efficiently.
- **Higher batch sizes possible:** Useful for training speed.

But… the cost

- **Loss of expressive richness.**

  Since multiple heads share the same Key and Value, they lose the ability to focus on different semantic relationships independently.

Thus:

MQA is efficient, but less intelligent.

And MQA **cannot be easily applied to pretrained models** — one must train from scratch.

How Grouped Query Attention (GQA) Works

Master raised his hand gently and said:

"Now comes the elegant middle path — **Grouped Query Attention**."

Instead of:

- One Key-Value pair shared across *all* heads (MQA),

  or

- Each head has separate Keys and Values (MHA),

GQA divides heads into groups.

Each group shares its own Key and Value set.

For example:

If there are 16 heads and 4 groups:

Group 1: Q1-Q4 share K1, V1 Group 2: Q5-Q8 share K2, V2 Group 3: Q9-Q12 share K3, V3 Group 4: Q13-Q16 share K4, V4

This achieves a Balance

Mechanism	**Key-Value Sets**	**Speed**	**Expressiveness**	**Notes**
MHA	h	Slowest	Best	Expensive for large models
MQA	1	Fastest	Weakest	Must train from scratch
GQA	g (1 < g < h)	Near-fast	Near-rich	Best tradeoff

So:

- **GQA is as accurate as MHA**, almost.
- **GQA is almost as fast as MQA.**
- **GQA can be applied to existing pretrained models** (via *uptraining*).

Thus, **GQA became widely adopted**:

- Meta LLaMA 2 & LLaMA 3
- Mistral 7B
- Granite 3.0
- Many modern inference-optimized models

Why GQA Matters

Master said, "GQA is not merely a technical trick — it reflects a deeper principle."

Principle

Wisdom is efficiency without loss of depth.

A model must look at language from multiple perspectives (multiple Query heads), Yet, it must recall knowledge efficiently (group-shared Key and Value heads).

GQA preserves:

- **Multiplicity of interpretation**
- **Efficiency of storage and computation**

This is why modern LLMs speak fluently, reason well, and still run fast on real hardware.

In Summary

Feature	Multi-Head Attention (MHA)	Multi-Query Attention (MQA)	Grouped Query Attention (GQA)
Keys/Values	Unique per head	Shared across all heads	Shared per group of heads

Performance	Slowest	Fastest	~Fast like MQA
Accuracy	Highest	Lowest	~High like MHA
Training	Standard	Must train from scratch	Can convert pretrained models
Use in Modern LLMs	Older models	Rare	Standard in new LLMs

Master smiled and said softly, "Sam, when you understand *why* the structure changes, you no longer memorize architectures — you see the intelligence behind their evolution."

PART FIVE

DAY EIGHTEEN

Unit 5 - Lesson Five

Encoding Thought, Decoding Meaning

Master said, "Akshatha, when we speak of *Attention*, we are speaking of how meaning is found. Not by reading words one after another, but by understanding which words matter to each other.

A sentence is not merely a line — it is a *constellation*.

Attention is the act of seeing the stars **in relation**, not in isolation."

☐ Encoder–Decoder

Master said, "Nikash, let us now understand—slowly and clearly—how an Encoder–Decoder model reads the world and then speaks back, and why positional encoding is the secret ink that preserves the order of thought."

1. The Encoder–Decoder as Reader → Interpreter → Storyteller

Imagine a scholar (the **encoder**) reading a long, sacred manuscript. The scholar underlines important phrases, summarizes pages into marginal notes, and produces a compact dossier — a map of meaning. A second scholar (the **decoder**) uses that dossier to write a new text (a translation, summary, or answer). But the decoder does not simply copy: at each step, it consults the dossier and decides which parts of the source matter *right now*. That consultation is **attention**.

- **Encoder** = reads and **summarizes** (produces context-rich representations for every source token).
- **Decoder** = generates one token at a time, repeatedly **consulting** the encoder's summary (via *cross-attention*) and its own prior outputs (via *masked self-attention*).

2. Concrete Flow — Step by Step (with intuition)

Input Embeddings

Each source token is converted into an embedding vector x_i. This is its "voice" in high-dimensional space.

Positional Encoding added

Because the transformer processes tokens in parallel, we add position vectors p_i to each embedding so the model knows *where* a token sits:

$$\tilde{x}_i = x_i + p_i$$

Now each vector says *what* the word is and *where* it is.

Encoder Layers (Self-Attention + Feed-Forward)

Each encoder layer lets every token look at every other token (self-attention), producing context-aware vectors. Repeated layers refine the dossier.

Per layer: $\text{EncOut} = \text{FFN}(\text{MultiHeadSelfAttn}(\tilde{X}))$

After the encoder finishes, for each source position i, we have a rich vector h_i summarizing the token in its full source context.

Decoder (Masked Self-Attn → Cross-Attn → FFN)

For generations, the decoder does three things per layer:

A. **Masked self-attention** over tokens already generated (prevents peeking ahead — causal).

B. **Cross-attention**: queries come from decoder states; keys/values come from encoder outputs H = $\{h_i\}$. This lets the decoder ask: *which parts of the source should influence my next word?*

C. **FFN** and normalization to produce the next hidden state.

The decoder repeats this for each token generated.

Output Projection + Softmax

The decoder's final vector for the last position is projected into vocabulary logits and normalized by softmax to yield next-token probabilities.

3. Attention Equations — Encoder–Decoder with Masks

Scaled dot-product attention (basic block):

$$\text{Attention}(Q, K, V) = \text{softmax}\left(\frac{QK^T}{\sqrt{d_k}}\right) V$$

Masked/causal attention used in decoder self-attn:

$$\text{MaskedAttention}(Q, K, V) = \text{softmax}\left(\frac{QK^T}{\sqrt{d_k}} + M\right) V$$

Where matrix M has $-\infty$ (or a very large negative number) in positions corresponding to *future* tokens, so softmax assigns them zero weight.

Encoder–Decoder (cross) attention: decoder queries Q (from decoder states), encoder keys/values K, V (from H):

$$\text{CrossAttn}(Q, K, V) = \text{softmax}\left(\frac{QK^T}{\sqrt{d_k}}\right) V$$

This yields a context vector for the decoder at each time step.

4. Positional Encoding — Why and How

Why it matters.

Order changes meaning. Transformers process tokens in parallel and therefore must be explicitly told "who comes first," otherwise "Allen walks dog" ≈ "dog walks Allen." Positional encodings inject this ordering.

Sinusoidal positional encoding (Vaswani et al.) — deterministic, infinite-length-friendly:

For position pos and dimension index i:

$$PE_{pos,\,2i} = \sin\left(\frac{pos}{10000^{2i/d_{model}}}\right)$$

$$PE_{pos,2i+1} = \cos\left(\frac{pos}{10000^{2i/d_{model}}}\right)$$

- Even indices use sine, odd indices use cosine.
- Lower dimensions vary slowly (long wavelengths) — capture coarse position; higher dimensions vary faster — capture fine position.
- Benefit: The model can generalize to unseen sequence lengths and compute relative position information via linear operations.

Learned positional embeddings.

Alternatively, learn a position vector per index. Simple and often effective, but it lacks easy extrapolation beyond trained length.

RoPE (Rotary Positional Encoding) — conceptually: rotates token subspaces by an angle dependent on position; encodes relative positional information more naturally and helps very long context windows.

5. Intuition: How Positional Encoding changes attention

- Two tokens close in position receive similar positional vectors. After adding to embeddings, their dot products tend to increase — attention between nearby tokens rises.

- Conversely, distant tokens get more different position vectors, so positional bias may reduce their attention unless the content strongly signals relevance.

Thus, positional encoding gives the transformer a *geography* of the sentence: which neighborhoods are near, which are far, and how to weigh them when reading.

6. End-to-End Example (short)

Translate: source = *"le juge a rendu son verdict"* → target (English).

- Encoder reads French words in parallel, but positional encoding tells it the order. Self-attention forms vectors where *"juge"* and *"verdict"* strongly relate.
- Decoder at step where it must produce "judge" forms a query from its partial output; cross-attention then assigns high weight to encoder positions corresponding to *"juge"* and *"verdict"*, drawing context for a correct translation.
- Masked self-attention prevents the decoder from seeing words it will yet generate.

7. Final analogy — an orchestra and a conductor

- **Encoder** = orchestra rehearsing the entire score (source): every instrument hears every other instrument and builds a rich, synchronized interpretation of the piece.
- **Positional encoding** = the conductor's beat and tempo markers — tell musicians *when* to play.
- **Decoder** = soloist improvising on stage: at each bar (token), the soloist listens to the orchestra (cross-attention), but can only hear what has been played previously in the solo (masked self-attention). The result is a new, coherent performance derived from the original score.

8. Practical notes & tips

- For **generations**, always use **causal masking** in decoder self-attention.

- For **sequence-to-sequence tasks** (translation, summarization), use encoder–decoder cross-attention so the decoder can focus on relevant source parts.
- Use **sinusoidal** when you want extrapolation; **learned** when training length is fixed and you prefer slightly better empirical performance; choose **RoPE** or relative encodings for very long contexts.

Master said, "Nikash, the encoder compresses the world into a map of relations; positional encodings annotate that map with where things are; the decoder reads the map piece by piece, consulting the parts that matter most through attention. Together they let a machine read, understand, and then answer — as if transforming the manuscript into a new, living text."

Example:

Master said, "Nikash, let us walk through the code with clarity.

We are building a **miniature Transformer** — just enough to understand how **self-attention** and **cross-attention** work inside the **Encoder–Decoder** framework."

Creating the Causal Mask

```
def causal_mask(seq_len):

mask = torch.triu(torch.ones(seq_len, seq_len), diagonal=1)

return mask.masked_fill(mask == 1, float('-inf'))
```

This creates a **triangular mask** used in the **decoder** so that:

- The model can *only look at past tokens*
- Future words are **blocked** (replaced with $-\infty$ so softmax ignores them)

This ensures **causal (left → right) generation**.

Multi-Head Attention Module

```
class MultiHeadAttention(nn.Module):
```

This class:

- Takes **queries (Q)**, **keys (K)**, and **values (V)**
- Splits them across **multiple attention heads**
- Performs **scaled dot-product attention**
- Then recombines the heads into the final output.

The important line:

```
scores = (Q @ K.transpose(-2, -1)) / math.sqrt(self.dk)
```

This computes **how much each word should attend to every other word**.

Encoder Step

encoder_input = torch.randn(1, 3, 8)

encoder_output = encoder(encoder_input, encoder_input, encoder_input)

The encoder:

- Applies **self-attention** to the input sentence.
- Learns relationships between the **input tokens themselves**.
- Produces **context-rich representations** (the *encoder memory*).

Example P5 – U5 – D11

Encoder → Decoder with Masked Self-Attention + Cross-Attention

```
import torch
import torch.nn as nn
import math

torch.manual_seed(0)
```

```
# ----------------------------
# Helper: Create a causal mask
# ----------------------------
def causal_mask(seq_len):
    mask = torch.triu(torch.ones(seq_len, seq_len), diagonal=1)
    return mask.masked_fill(mask == 1, float('-inf'))

# ----------------------------
# Multi-Head Attention Module
# ----------------------------
class MultiHeadAttention(nn.Module):
    def __init__(self, d_model=8, num_heads=2):
        super().__init__()
        self.d_model = d_model
        self.num_heads = num_heads
        self.dk = d_model // num_heads

        self.Q = nn.Linear(d_model, d_model)
        self.K = nn.Linear(d_model, d_model)
        self.V = nn.Linear(d_model, d_model)
        self.out = nn.Linear(d_model, d_model)

    def forward(self, q, k, v, mask=None):
        B, Tq, _ = q.shape
        _, Tk, _ = k.shape

        # Transform
        Q = self.Q(q).view(B, Tq, self.num_heads, self.dk).transpose(1, 2)
        K = self.K(k).view(B, Tk, self.num_heads, self.dk).transpose(1, 2)
        V = self.V(v).view(B, Tk, self.num_heads, self.dk).transpose(1, 2)

        # Scaled dot-product attention
        scores = (Q @ K.transpose(-2, -1)) / math.sqrt(self.dk)

        if mask is not None:
            scores = scores + mask  # mask future tokens

        weights = scores.softmax(dim=-1)
        out = (weights @ V).transpose(1, 2).reshape(B, Tq, self.d_model)
        return self.out(out)

# ----------------------------
# Encoder
# ----------------------------
encoder = MultiHeadAttention()

# Dummy input: 3 words → embedding dim 8
```

```
encoder_input = torch.randn(1, 3, 8)
encoder_output = encoder(encoder_input, encoder_input, encoder_input)  # self
attention
print("Encoder Output:", encoder_output.shape)

# ----------------------------
# Decoder
# ----------------------------
self_attn = MultiHeadAttention()
cross_attn = MultiHeadAttention()

decoder_input = torch.randn(1, 4, 8)  # decoder sees 4 tokens (predicting next step)
mask = causal_mask(decoder_input.size(1)).unsqueeze(0).unsqueeze(0)  # (1,1,4,4)

# Step 1: Masked self-attention (decoder does NOT see future tokens)
decoder_self = self_attn(decoder_input, decoder_input, decoder_input, mask)
print("Decoder Self-Attention:", decoder_self.shape)

# Step 2: Cross-attention (decoder attends to encoder outputs)
decoder_cross = cross_attn(decoder_self, encoder_output, encoder_output)
print("Decoder Cross-Attention:", decoder_cross.shape)
```

Output:

```
Output
Encoder Output: torch.Size([1, 3, 8])
Decoder Self-Attention: torch.Size([1, 4, 8])
Decoder Cross-Attention: torch.Size([1, 4, 8])
```

Decoder Step

a) Masked Self-Attention

decoder_self = self_attn(decoder_input, decoder_input, decoder_input, mask)

The decoder attends **only to past decoder tokens** because of the **mask**. This ensures autoregressive prediction, word-by-word.

b) Cross-Attention

decoder_cross = cross_attn(decoder_self, encoder_output, encoder_output)

Here:

- The **decoder's queries** look at the **encoder's keys and values**

- This is where the decoder **asks the encoder for meaning**.

This step lets the decoder **use the input's understanding** to decide what word to generate next.

Essence:

Component	**Purpose**
Encoder Self-Attention	Understands the input sentence and relationships within it.
Decoder Masked Self-Attention	Generates output step-by-step without seeing the future.
Decoder Cross-Attention	Consults the encoder's understanding to produce correct output.

Master said:

"The encoder forms **meaning**. The decoder reveals the meaning **one token at a time**. Masked attention ensures discipline; Cross-attention ensures wisdom."

☐ Autoencoder

Master said, "Apeksha, to understand an **autoencoder**, imagine we are sculptors of knowledge.

When we look at a stone, we do not memorize every grain of sand.

We seek the *shape*, the *essence*, the *inner form* hiding inside it.

An autoencoder does something similar with data."

What Is an Autoencoder?

An **autoencoder** is a **neural network** that tries to learn the **essence** of the input data:

The Encoder compresses the input into a **smaller representation**.

The Latent Space is the *bottleneck* — the compressed, distilled essence.

The Decoder reconstructs the original input from that compressed essence.

Input→Encoder→Latent Space→Decoder→Reconstructed Output

The goal is:

Reconstruction Output ≈ Original Input

The network trains itself by **minimizing reconstruction error**, e.g., mean squared error (MSE).

$$\text{Loss}=||x - \hat{x}||^2$$

Where:

x = original input

$\hat{x}$ = reconstructed output

The Latent Space — The Hidden Essence

The **latent space** is the *compressed inner representation* of the data.

It contains:

- Only the most essential patterns
- The axes of variation that define the data

The latent space is where:

- Faces differ by expression
- Music differs by rhythm

- Speech differs by tone

It is the place where the **soul** of the data resides.

Why Is This Powerful?

Humans do this constantly.

When you look at someone's face once, you do not memorize every pixel. You store:

- The curve of the jaw
- The softness of the eyes
- The feeling they carry

From this **compressed internal representation**, you can recall the entire face later.

This is **exactly** what an autoencoder learns to do.

Key Uses of Autoencoders

Task	**Purpose**
Data Compression	Store only the essential structure.
Image Denoising	Remove noise while preserving detail.
Anomaly Detection	Detect things that *do not fit* normal patterns.
Face Recognition	Identify identity from compressed features.
Representation Learning	Automatically learn meaningful features.

Autoencoder vs. Encoder–Decoder

Master said, "Not all who have an encoder and decoder are autoencoders."

Characteristic	Autoencoder	Encoder–Decoder (e.g., Seq2Seq, U-Net)
Input vs Output	Same (reconstructs input)	Different (transforms meaning)
Training Type	Unsupervised / Self-supervised	Supervised (needs labeled targets)
Purpose	Learn the essential structure	Convert input to a desired output
Example Use	Denoising an image	Translating English → French

In short:

- A **U-Net** *labels pixels* → supervised learning
- A **Seq2Seq** model *translates language* → supervised learning
- An **Autoencoder** *recreates the input* → self-supervised learning

Master said, "An autoencoder teaches the mind how to see the world not as it appears, but as it truly is beneath the surface.

It does not memorize the leaf.

It understands the **pattern of leafness**.

And from that understanding, it can recreate."

Master said, "Akshatha, to understand *how* autoencoders work, we must first realize **what problem they are trying to solve**.

Autoencoders are designed to **learn the essence of data**—to separate the *signal* from the *noise*. They do this by forcing information to pass through a **narrow gateway**, the *bottleneck*. Whatever survives this bottleneck represents the core, the underlying structure—the **latent representation** or **latent space**.

Let us walk through the journey of data inside an autoencoder:

The Encoder — The Art of Compression

The **encoder** takes the input and **compresses** it.

Imagine you have a 1000-dimensional image (a vector of pixel values).

The encoder gradually reduces it to perhaps **64 dimensions**.

This reduction is not random.

It is *learned*, meaning the encoder identifies **which patterns truly matter** for reconstruction.

Each successive encoder layer has **fewer neurons** than the previous one:

```
Input → 512 → 256 → 128 → 64 (Bottleneck)
```

This shrinkage forces the network to **prioritize important structure** and discard trivial or redundant information.

This act of compression is **the discovery of latent variables**: internal, hidden axes that describe the data more fundamentally than raw pixels ever could.

The Bottleneck — The Essence of the Data

The bottleneck layer holds the **latent space representation**.

This is not merely a compressed version of the input — it is a **conceptual encoding.**

For example, if the input is images of handwritten digits (like MNIST), the bottleneck might learn things like:

- Stroke thickness
- Curvature styles
- Angle of slant
- Symmetry

These features are **not explicitly programmed** into the network.

They *emerge* naturally because they are the patterns required to reconstruct the input accurately.

This is why autoencoders are considered a form of **self-supervised learning**:

the **input itself** is the teacher.

The Decoder — The Art of Reconstruction

Now the compressed latent code is sent to the **decoder**, which tries to **rebuild the original input**:

```
64 → 128 → 256 → 512 → Output (same size as input)
```

The decoder gradually **expands** the representation, restoring details to match the original form.

How well the reconstructed output matches the input determines the **reconstruction loss.**

A common loss is **Mean Squared Error (MSE)**:

$$\text{Loss} = \frac{1}{n} \sum_i (xi - \hat{x})^2$$

Where:

x = original input

$\hat{x}$ = reconstructed output

The goal of training is to **minimize this loss**, improving the encoder and decoder weights.

Why the Bottleneck Works

The bottleneck **forces the network to learn structure**, not memory.

- If the bottleneck is *too large*, the model may **memorize** the input → **overfitting**.

- If the bottleneck is *too small*, the reconstruction will be poor → **underfitting**.

Therefore, the **code size** is a crucial hyperparameter.

Why Not Use PCA Instead?

PCA (Principal Component Analysis) can also reduce dimensions, but PCA is **linear**.

Autoencoders can learn **non-linear** relationships:

- Curved manifolds
- Complex textures
- Human-like patterns in speech or images

This makes autoencoders much more powerful for **real-world data**.

Variants Tailored for Different Purposes

Different autoencoders adjust this structure:

Autoencoder Type	Key Purpose	Special Feature
Denoising AE	Remove noise	Train on noisy → reconstruct clean
Sparse AE	Find minimal activations	Encourages neurons to be mostly inactive
Convolutional AE	Process images	Uses CNN layers, preserves spatial structure
Variational AE (VAE)	Generate new data	Learns *distributions*, enables sampling

VAEs turn the bottleneck from a *point* into a *probability distribution*, enabling **creative generation** of new data (faces, voices, art, etc.).

When the Decoder is No Longer Needed

Sometimes, after the encoder learns the latent representation, the **decoder is discarded**.

The encoder can now serve:

- As a **feature extractor**
- As a **dimension reducer**
- As the backbone of another model

This is similar to how the **discriminator trains the generator** in GANs.

Master said, "Autoencoders teach us a profound principle, Akshatha:

To understand anything deeply, we must distill it to its essence. The truth reveals itself only when the unnecessary is removed.

Just as the autoencoder learns what to keep and what to let go, so too must the mind learn to filter noise from reality."

Master said, "Sam, to truly understand the different kinds of autoencoders, we must first see the tension at the heart of their design.

An autoencoder always faces a **duality**:

- It wants to **preserve** the essence of the data (to reconstruct it).
- Yet it must **forget** enough details to avoid mere memorization.

How the autoencoder resolves this tension defines its type."

Undercomplete Autoencoders — Simplicity and Constraint

These are the **purest** and most basic autoencoders.

- The **encoder compresses** input into a low-dimensional bottleneck.
- The **decoder expands** it back to the original dimension.

- The bottleneck enforces **forced forgetting**.

Only truly important features can pass through.

Input→(Encode)→Bottleneck→(Decode)→Reconstruction

If this bottleneck is **too large**, the autoencoder will simply learn the **identity function**:

$\hat{x} = x \Rightarrow$ Useless

If the bottleneck is **appropriately small**, the autoencoder must learn **meaning.**

Strength: Simple, effective for dimensionality reduction.

Weakness: If encoder/decoder networks are too powerful, the model will *still* cheat and simply copy the input.

Thus, undercomplete autoencoders are **limited**—they work only when the architecture is carefully constrained.

Regularized Autoencoders — Constraining the Mind, Not the Shape

Regularized autoencoders modify **how learning happens**, rather than relying only on bottleneck size.

These models introduce **penalty terms** that *shape the learning process*, helping them:

- Resist overfitting
- Learn more *meaningful* latent features
- Handle more complex data without collapsing into identity mapping

There are three major forms of regularized autoencoders:

a) Sparse Autoencoders (SAEs) — Few Neurons Speak

Sparse autoencoders do **not** reduce the number of neurons.

Instead, they limit **how many neurons may activate** at once.

This means:

- Many neurons exist
- **But only a few are allowed to "fire"** for any given input
- Each neuron learns to detect a **specific, distinct structural feature**

This creates feature detectors that are **specialised**.

The sparsity constraint is often imposed with:

- **L1** regularization
- **KL** Divergence

KL Divergence Intuition

KL divergence measures **how different** two activation distributions are:

$$\text{Penalty} \propto D_{KL}(\text{Desired Activation} \,||\, \text{Actual Activation})$$

We tell the network:

"Most neurons should stay quiet.

Speak only when you have something important to say."

Thus, sparse autoencoders produce **interpretable, structured latent spaces**.

b) Contractive Autoencoders — Learning What *Doesn't* Change

Where sparse autoencoders reduce *activation*, contractive autoencoders reduce **sensitivity**.

They penalise the network when small input changes cause big representation changes.

This is done by applying a penalty to the **Jacobian matrix** of encoder outputs with respect to inputs.

$$\text{Penalty}=||J||_F$$

Where:

J = Jacobian

$||\cdot||_F$ = Frobenius norm

This makes the learned representation **stable**, **robust to noise**, and biased toward **core structure**, not decoration.

These autoencoders **learn meaning that survives disturbance**—like recognising a face despite lighting changes.

c) Denoising Autoencoders — Learning to See Truth Through Noise

Here, the input is **intentionally corrupted** (e.g., adding Gaussian noise).

- The autoencoder receives the *noisy* input.
- But it is trained to output the **clean** version.

Corrupted Input→Autoencoder→Clean Reconstruction

This forces it to learn a **robust, noise-invariant structure**.

This approach became the foundation for powerful generative models like **Stable Diffusion**, where the model learns to **reverse noise → structure**.

Variational Autoencoders (VAEs) — From Learning to Creating

VAEs do something profoundly different.

They do not learn **a single latent code**.

They learn **a distribution** in latent space.

For each input:

Encoder produces μ and σ

During training and generation:

$Z = \mu + \sigma \cdot \epsilon, \epsilon \sim N(0,1)$

This is the **reparameterization trick**, which allows gradient-based learning while sampling.

Why this is powerful

Because the latent space is **continuous**, we can:

- Interpolate between representations
- Generate **new** samples that resemble training data
- Produce infinite variations naturally

VAEs are **generative models**, not just reconstructive.

Master paused and said, "Sam, every variation of the autoencoder is a different philosophical stance on the question:

What is essential?

The undercomplete autoencoder says: *Essence lies in compression.*

The sparse autoencoder says: *Essence lies in selective attention.*

The contractive autoencoder says: *Essence lies in what does not change.*

The denoising autoencoder says: *Essence lies beneath corruption.*

And the variational autoencoder says: *Essence is not a point, but a landscape.*

To understand learning, Sam, is to understand what we choose to keep—and what we let go."

☐ **Use Case – Autoencoder**
Master smiled and said, *"Akshaya, let us look at the autoencoder not as a machine, but as a storyteller — one who knows how to shorten, restore, and even imagine worlds."*

The **core principle** is this:

An autoencoder takes something large and full of detail, **passes it through a narrow doorway** (the bottleneck), and then tries to **rebuild it**.

To pass through the doorway, it must decide what part of the story is essential, and what can be forgotten.

This act of **intentional forgetting** is not a weakness — it is *wisdom.*

From it, three great abilities arise:

- It captures the main patterns.
- It ignores irrelevant noise.
- And if modeled probabilistically, it can **create** new examples that feel real.

Everything else we discuss springs from these three capacities.

1. Data Compression

What it does:

An autoencoder learns to represent high-dimensional data using a compact code — often far smaller than the original. This compressed vector stores only the most essential information needed to reconstruct the input.

Why it works:

During training, the encoder is forced to funnel the input through a **bottleneck** (a lower-dimensional layer). Because it must still reconstruct the original data, it learns to preserve only the **most important and informative features**, discarding redundancy and noise.

The decoder then learns the *inverse* mapping: how to expand this compressed code back into something resembling the original.

Analogy:

Imagine giving a long, detailed story to a poet who must distill it into a few short, powerful verses. Those verses are not the whole story, but they capture its soul. Later, a storyteller who knows the poetic style can expand those verses back into a full narrative. The "story" may not be word-for-word identical, but the meaning is preserved.

The encoder is the poet; the decoder is the storyteller.

The latent code is the poem — compact, essential, expressive.

Concrete Example:

- A **1024 × 1024 image** has over **1 million pixels**. A convolutional autoencoder can compress this into a **64–512-dimensional latent vector**, drastically reducing storage and transmission cost — useful in embedded systems, wireless video, medical imaging pipelines, etc.

Practical Tips:

Use **convolutional architectures** for images to preserve structure and achieve high-quality compression.

Choose the latent vector size carefully:

- Smaller latent space → higher compression, lower detail
- Larger latent space → better reconstruction, lower compression

Evaluate quality using image metrics such as **PSNR (Peak Signal-to-Noise Ratio)** and **SSIM (Structural Similarity Index)** rather than just pixel-wise error — these correlate better with human perception.

2.Dimensionality Reduction & Feature Extraction

What it does:

The autoencoder transforms high-dimensional input (like an image with thousands of pixels or a long time-series) into a compact, meaningful representation — a *feature vector* — that captures only the most important information. This compressed vector can then be used as input to other models, replacing raw data.

Why it works:

When the network is forced to pass information through a smaller bottleneck, it naturally learns to discard noise, redundancy, and irrelevant detail. Only the features essential for reconstructing the input survive this compression. Interestingly, these essential features are often the *same* ones that are most useful for tasks like classification, clustering, or prediction.

Analogy:

Imagine a skilled storyteller who hears a long, chaotic tale and retells it in just a few precise sentences — not losing the meaning, only the unnecessary clutter. The "bottleneck" is like the storyteller's skill: what remains is essence, clarity, and structure. Later, any listener can rebuild the full story from those sentences — but now the core message is easier to work with.

Concrete examples:

- Instead of training a classifier directly on raw images (pixel arrays), train an autoencoder first, then use the **encoder's output** as features in the classifier. This drastically improves performance, especially with limited labeled data.
- For **time series forecasting**, encode sequences using a CNN or RNN-based encoder; feed the latent representation into a prediction model. This filters out noise and focuses on underlying patterns.

Practical tips:

- If the downstream task has labels available, **fine-tune the encoder** along with the classifier — this aligns the features with the real target task. (This is a form of *transfer learning.*)
- To **understand** what the autoencoder has learned, use visualization techniques like **t-SNE or UMAP** to map latent vectors into 2D. Clusters or patterns that emerge will tell you what structure your data *actually* contains.
- Keep the bottleneck neither too small (which loses real structure) nor too large (which leads to memorization). Tune gradually.

3. Anomaly Detection (and Fraud Detection)

What it does:

An autoencoder first learns what *normal* data looks like. Later, when it encounters something that *doesn't fit* that learned pattern, it struggles to reconstruct it — resulting in a **high reconstruction error**. This error becomes a signal for an anomaly or fraud.

Why it works:

During training, the autoencoder sees only *normal* examples.

It therefore learns the **latent structure** — the smooth manifold — of typical behavior.

Anything that *deviates* from this distribution lies **off the manifold**, meaning the decoder does not know how to rebuild it accurately. The result is a distorted or inaccurate reconstruction, which we detect by measuring reconstruction loss.

Analogy:

Imagine a skilled calligrapher who has practiced writing standard scripts for years. They can reproduce familiar characters effortlessly. But if handed a symbol from an unfamiliar language, their pen hesitates, the lines wobble, and the result looks unnatural. The distortion reveals the unfamiliarity.

The autoencoder is that calligrapher.

Normal data is the script it knows.

Anomalies are foreign symbols that cannot be rewritten cleanly.

Concrete Examples:

- **Industrial Monitoring:** Train on *normal vibration or temperature sensor readings* from a machine. When the machine begins to wear down or malfunction, the signal shifts. The autoencoder's reconstruction error spikes → early fault detection.
- **Financial Systems:** Train on *legitimate* banking transactions. Fraud patterns often differ subtly (transaction timing, merchant type, amount sequence). These appear as outliers → high reconstruction error → flagged for review.

Practical Tips:

Choose **robust reconstruction metrics**, such as:

- Mean Squared Error (MSE)
- Cosine distance in latent space
- Learned discriminator scores (if using adversarial autoencoders or VAEs with critics)

Use a validation dataset with known anomalies (if available) to set **thresholds** for flagging events.

Denoising autoencoders improve robustness by training the model to ignore minor, harmless variations (e.g., sensor noise) while still detecting meaningful deviations.

4. Image / Audio Denoising & Inpainting

What it does:

It **cleans** corrupted input data — removing noise, restoring missing details, or reconstructing damaged regions. In denoising, the autoencoder learns to map *noisy → clean*. In inpainting, it learns to **fill in gaps** in images or audio so they appear natural and continuous.

Why it works:

During training, the model learns the structure of the **clean, underlying data manifold** — the true shapes, textures, tonal patterns, and continuity. So when a corrupted input is fed in, the autoencoder does not try to copy the noise; instead, it **projects the input back toward the closest clean version it has learned**.

Analogy:

Imagine a sculptor restoring a weathered statue. They have spent years studying the original style — the curve of the jaw, the folds of the garment, the balance of proportion. When part of the statue is cracked or missing, the sculptor does not replicate the damage. They rebuild what ***should*** *be there based on knowledge of form and harmony.*

The autoencoder is that sculptor — it restores what belongs, not what happened.

Concrete Examples:

- **Denoising low-light photos:** Grainy night shots can be mapped to clean, sharper versions.

- **Removing background hiss in audio:** Speech signals are recovered while ambient noise is suppressed.
- **Image inpainting:** Filling gaps from damaged or cropped images (e.g., restoring old film scans).
- **Removing minor artifacts in MRI or satellite imagery** to aid clearer interpretation.

Practical Tips:

Preserve spatial structure:

Use **U-Nets** or **convolutional autoencoders** so the decoder can reconstruct fine textures and edges.

For small noise:

Standard reconstruction loss (MSE / L1) works well.

For large missing regions or artistic realism:

Combine reconstruction loss with:

- **Perceptual loss:** Compare high-level features using a pretrained model (e.g., VGG features).
- **GAN loss:** Add an adversarial discriminator to ensure outputs look *plausible* rather than merely *close* in pixel space.

Augment training data with controlled noise:

This improves generalization and robustness.

5. Image Reconstruction / Colorization / Super-Resolution

What it does:

Rebuilds or **enhances** images when information is missing or degraded. This includes:

- Adding **color** to grayscale images,

- Restoring **fine detail** in low-resolution pictures,
- Reconstructing missing visual channels or regions.

Why it works:

When the input passes through the encoder, the latent code doesn't store raw pixels — it stores **structure and meaning**: shapes, contours, textures, and spatial relationships. The decoder then uses this **semantic understanding** to **recreate** the missing or higher-resolution details in a way that looks natural and coherent.

Analogy:

Think of a skilled painter who has studied human portraits for decades. Even if shown a rough pencil sketch or faded photo, they recognize the intent — the curve of the cheek, the light in the eyes — and can paint the full, lifelike version. They don't copy pixels; they ***recreate essence****.*

An autoencoder works the same way: it learns the **form**, then fills in the **details**.

Concrete Examples:

- **Colorization:** Convert black-and-white photos -> naturally colored images.
- **Super-resolution:** Convert a blurry low-res image -> sharp high-res output.
- **MRI / CT reconstruction:** Refine medical scans from compressed/sparse measurements.
- **Restoring old photographs** where parts are faded or washed out.

Practical Tips:

Use convolutional or U-Net style autoencoders to preserve spatial details and textures.

Combine multiple loss types for realism:

- **Reconstruction loss (L1 / MSE):** Ensures overall structure is correct.
- **Perceptual loss (feature-space loss):** Ensures outputs look *visually* realistic, not just pixel-similar.
- **Adversarial loss (GAN loss):** Encourages sharp, high-frequency detail and natural textures.

Avoid too small a latent space — losing too much information leads to unrealistic or overly smooth outputs.

6. Generative Modelling (VAEs & AAEs)

What it does:

Enables the creation of **entirely new**, yet **realistic** data samples—images, molecules, music, handwriting—by **sampling** from a learned latent space and decoding back into the data domain.

Why it works:

A **Variational Autoencoder (VAE)** doesn't just compress data; it learns a **smooth, continuous probability distribution** in the latent space.

It outputs not just a code, but parameters **(μ, σ)** describing a distribution from which we sample:

$$z=\mu+\sigma\cdot\epsilon,\ \epsilon\sim N(0, I)$$

This encourages the latent space to be **organized**, **interpolatable**, and **meaningful.**

So, points close in latent space represent similar real-world patterns.

An **Adversarial Autoencoder (AAE)** replaces the KL divergence with a **GAN-style discriminator** that forces the latent codes to match a desired distribution. Instead of explicitly computing μ and σ, it **learns to "shape"** the latent space through adversarial pressure.

Analogy:

Imagining the latent space as a well-arranged library:

The encoder acts as a librarian who learns how to **file** similar concepts on nearby shelves (similar faces grouped, similar molecule shapes closer).

The decoder is the storyteller who, when handed one of these "book codes," can **reconstruct** (or invent) the full story again.

In VAEs, the librarian organizes the shelves **neatly by rule** (using μ and σ).

In AAEs, the librarian organizes the shelves **by judgment**, guided by a discerning critic (the discriminator).

Concrete Examples:

- **Faces:** Generate novel human faces that didn't exist before.
- **Molecules:** Explore chemical spaces to propose new drug candidates.
- **Music / Speech:** Create new melodies or voices that mimic the style of a training dataset.
- **Style Interpolation:** Morph one face into another smoothly by walking through latent space.

Practical Tips:

VAEs trade off between **reconstruction quality** and **latent disentanglement.** Use **β-VAE** (weighted KL term) to tune this balance:

$$\mathcal{L}_{VAE} = \text{Reconstruction Loss} + \beta \cdot \text{KL Divergence}$$

AAEs can produce sharper results but require **careful discriminator balancing** to avoid mode collapse (all outputs look the same).

To improve realism:

- Combine **reconstruction + perceptual + adversarial loss**
- Use **diffusion models or autoencoder-based decoders** for high-fidelity detail.

When generating samples:

- Sample $\mathbf{z} \sim \mathbf{N(0, I)}$ for diversity.
- For interpolation, **interpolate in latent space**, not in pixel space, for smooth transitions.

7. Representation Learning for Downstream Tasks

What it does:

Learns **compact, meaningful embeddings** that capture the *essence* or *semantics* of the data. These embeddings can then be reused for tasks like **clustering, similarity search, classification, recommendation, and retrieval**.

Why it works:

By being forced to reconstruct the input from a **compressed bottleneck**, the encoder naturally learns to **ignore noise and irrelevant detail**, while preserving the **core structure** that defines the data.

This distilled representation is often exactly what downstream tasks need — a **clean signal** rather than raw complexity.

Analogy:

Imagine giving someone a complex story. Instead of remembering every word, they remember the key idea.

The **encoder** is the mind summarizing the story into a **clear concept**, and the **embedding** is that summary — compact, powerful, and reusable. This is why embeddings often **generalize well** across tasks.

Concrete Examples:

- **Content-Based Image Retrieval**: Store encoder embeddings; retrieve the most similar images by comparing latent vectors.
- **Semantic Search**: Text autoencoders (or Transformers trained with reconstruction) create embeddings that reflect meaning, not just surface form.
- **Classification**: Instead of feeding raw pixel grids or waveforms into a classifier, feed the learned latent vectors — giving faster, more stable learning.
- **Time-Series State Encoding**: Encoders turn raw signals into smooth state representations suitable for forecasting or control.

Practical Tip:

If labeled data exists, use **semi-supervised learning** by combining:

- **Reconstruction loss** (to preserve core structure)
- **Supervised loss** (to encourage class separation)

This results in embeddings that are **both informative and discriminative.**

$$\mathcal{L} = \mathcal{L}_{\text{recon}} + \lambda \cdot \mathcal{L}_{\text{supervised}}$$

Also, visualize and evaluate the learned latent space using **t-SNE** or **UMAP** to ensure meaningful clustering patterns emerge.

8. Pretraining & Transfer Learning

What it does:

Uses autoencoders to pretrain model parameters on large amounts of unlabeled data, providing a strong initialization for tasks where labeled data is limited.

Why it works:

Pretraining allows the encoder to learn stable and generalizable representations that capture essential structure in the data. When fine-tuned on a smaller labeled dataset, the model starts from a "knowledge-rich" state rather than random initialization, leading to faster convergence and better performance.

Concrete example:

Pretrain an autoencoder on thousands of unlabeled medical scans to learn anatomical feature representations. Then, fine-tune the encoder part on a small labeled dataset to classify disease types. This improves accuracy and reduces overfitting compared to training from scratch.

Practical tips:

Ensure the pretraining dataset is from a similar domain as the downstream task (domain alignment matters).

Experiment with **layerwise pretraining** (train one layer at a time) or **joint fine-tuning** (fine-tune all layers together).

During fine-tuning, use a **lower learning rate** for pretrained layers to preserve useful structure and avoid catastrophic forgetting.

9. Clustering & Disentanglement

What it does:

Autoencoders can learn latent representations where similar samples group naturally (clustering) or where different generative factors (e.g., pose, color, style) are represented independently (disentanglement). Variants like **VAEs** and **β-VAEs** explicitly promote this separation of factors.

Why it works:

The latent bottleneck forces the model to encode only the most essential underlying structure. Regularization (especially the KL term in VAEs) encourages the latent space to be smooth and factorized, making distinct factors of variation easier to isolate and manipulate.

Concrete example:

In a face dataset, different latent dimensions may correspond to attributes such as **smile intensity**, **head rotation**, or **lighting direction**. Adjusting a single latent dimension allows controlled transformation of that specific attribute while leaving others unchanged.

Practical tips:

- Increasing the **β value in β-VAE** encourages stronger disentanglement but can reduce reconstruction fidelity—adjust β to balance separation vs. clarity.
- To verify disentanglement quality, use metrics such as **MIG (Mutual Information Gap), DCI Disentanglement Score,** or **FactorVAE Score**.
- If clustering is the main goal, apply **k-means** or **Gaussian Mixture Models** directly on latent vectors rather than pixel space—it yields more meaningful groupings.

10. Scientific & Domain-Specific Applications

What it does:

Autoencoders learn compact, structured representations of complex real-world signals—such as molecular graphs, climate fields, genomic patterns, or physics simulations.

Why it works:

By compressing high-dimensional scientific data into a lower-dimensional latent space, the model captures the *underlying physical or semantic structure*. These latent variables can then be manipulated for **analysis, simulation, optimization, or discovery**.

Concrete examples:

- **Molecular design:** Encode molecular structures into latent vectors, explore the latent space, then decode to generate new molecules with desired chemical properties.
- **Climate & physics:** Compress massive simulation outputs into compact embeddings for faster forecasting or scenario testing.
- **Biomedical imaging:** Remove noise or reconstruct high-resolution scans where acquiring full data is expensive.

Practical tips:

Impose domain constraints directly in the **decoder or loss function**, such as:

- Chemical validity rules (valence, bond constraints) for molecules
- Conservation laws (mass, energy, charge) for physical systems

Consider **graph-based autoencoders** for molecules or networks, and **spatial U-Nets** for climate and medical imaging.

When interpretability matters, apply **latent space regularization** or factorization to align latent dimensions with known physical variables.

☐ Practical Implementation Notes & Best Practices

1. Match the architecture to the data domain

- **Images:** Use convolutional encoders/decoders or U-Nets to preserve spatial locality.
- **Sequential data (text, audio, signals):** Use RNNs, GRUs, LSTMs, or Transformers for temporal/semantic structure.
- **Tabular / low-dimensional data:** Fully-connected (MLP) autoencoders are sufficient and more efficient.

2. Prevent trivial identity learning

Autoencoders can simply copy inputs unless regularized. Helpful forms of regularization include:

- **Denoising:** Add noise and train to reconstruct the clean signal.
- **Dropout or weight decay:** Improves generalization.
- **Sparsity penalties / contractive penalties:** Encourage meaningful feature extraction rather than memorization.

3. Choose losses aligned with the goal

- **Pixel-wise fidelity:** MSE, L1
- **Perceptual similarity:** Perceptual (VGG feature-based) loss
- **Realism/texture fidelity:** Adversarial (GAN) loss
- **Image quality evaluation:** SSIM, PSNR (for reconstruction and super-resolution)

4. Tune the latent space intentionally

- Too **small** a latent dimension → information bottleneck → *underfitting.*
- Too **large** → trivial identity mapping → *no useful representation learned.*
- Depth of encoder/decoder controls expressiveness; increase capacity gradually.

5. Monitor training metrics holistically

- **Reconstruction loss over train/validation** to detect overfitting.
- For **VAEs**, monitor KL divergence terms and latent variance distribution.
- For **representation-learning use cases**, evaluate encoder features on **downstream tasks** (e.g., clustering, classification).

6. Ensure stability in sampling-based models

- **VAEs:** Use KL weight annealing, β-VAE schedules, or free-bits to avoid posterior collapse.

- **Adversarial-based autoencoders (AAEs):** Use gradient penalties (e.g., WGAN-GP), balanced generator/discriminator training, and tuned learning-rate schedules.

7. Ethical and safety considerations

Autoencoders, especially generative variants, can produce **convincing synthetic content**. Use responsibly:

- Add **watermarks or provenance metadata** when generating realistic outputs.
- Ensure compliance with **domain and privacy constraints**, particularly for medical or personal data.

☐ Common Pitfalls and How to Avoid Them

1. Identity Mapping (No Meaningful Representation Learned)

Problem: When the encoder and decoder are too powerful and the bottleneck is too large, the model simply learns to copy the input → no true feature extraction.

How to fix:

- Reduce latent dimensionality (stronger information bottleneck).
- Add regularization: sparsity penalties, dropout, denoising, or contractive loss.
- Monitor whether latent codes correlate with meaningful structure (e.g., via t-SNE/UMAP).

2. Blurry Reconstructions in VAEs

Problem: VAEs optimize pixel-wise reconstruction + KL regularization; this encourages smooth, averaged outputs rather than sharp details.

How to improve sharpness:

- Add **perceptual loss** (compare features in VGG space, not pixels).
- Add **adversarial loss** (VAE-GAN / VQ-VAE-GAN style).
- Use **hierarchical or autoregressive decoders** to capture fine textures.

3. Mode Collapse in Adversarial Autoencoders (AAEs / VAE-GAN hybrids)

Problem: The generator/decoder produces limited diversity, collapsing to a few similar outputs because the discriminator overpowers training.

Stabilization strategies:

- Use **WGAN-GP** (gradient penalty) or **R1 regularization** on the discriminator.
- Tune learning rates; often discriminator should not learn too fast.
- Increase batch diversity or use **mini-batch discrimination** layers.

4. Unreliable Anomaly Detection Scores

Problem: Autoencoders may treat small, irrelevant variations (lighting, noise, compression artifacts) as anomalies, and miss subtle but important deviations.

How to address:

- Normalize or standardize input to reduce nuisance variation.
- Use **robust error metrics** (e.g., SSIM loss, cosine distance, feature-level error instead of raw MSE).
- Validate with known anomaly examples to set realistic detection thresholds.
- Consider **Denoising AEs** or **Contrastive / Self-supervised approaches** for more stable embeddings.

What an Autoencoder Teaches Us

Master said, "An autoencoder is like a sage who has lived long and listened deeply.

Give them a long story, and they will not repeat it word for word—they will **distill** it into a proverb.

In that proverb, only the essence remains: the meaning, the pattern, the truth that matters.

And when the time comes to tell the story again, the sage expands the proverb back into narrative form—never identical, yet faithful to the spirit of what was once spoken.

But remember: the **nature of the summary** depends on what you ask the sage to preserve.
If you demand too much detail, the lesson is cluttered and shallow.

If you demand too much compression, the meaning dissolves and the story loses its soul.

Thus, mastery lies in shaping the bottleneck—in choosing **what must endure** and **what can be let go.”**

PART FIVE

DAY Nineteen

Unit 5 - Lesson Six

The Dawn of Generative Intelligence

"From the struggle of remembering in RNNs to the clarity of attention in Transformers, the journey mirrors human evolution — from effortful recall to effortless awareness."

– *Shree Shambav.*

Master said, "Roopa, by now you have understood that the attention mechanism liberated neural networks from the chains of sequential dependence. But what truly revolutionized modern AI was the rise of large Transformer models—architectures that did not merely *process* information but learned to *think* in structured, contextual ways.

Large Transformer Models

Model	Direction	Purpose / Core Strength
BERT (Bidirectional Encoder Representations from Transformers)	Bidirectional	*Understanding* — excels at reading and comprehending text, extracting context from both left and right directions. Ideal for classification, sentiment analysis, and question answering.
GPT (Generative Pretrained Transformer)	Unidirectional	*Generation* — reads from left to right, predicting the next word step-by-step. Excels at writing, storytelling, reasoning, and conversation.

T5 / BART (Text-to-Text Transfer Transformer)	Encoder-Decoder	*Transformation* — reformulates tasks into a unified format: "text → text." Excels at translation, rewriting, summarization, and question answering.

When the Transformer framework emerged, it became a **universal blueprint** for understanding and generating language, sound, and even images. But within this family, three main lineages evolved, each reflecting a distinct way of perceiving and creating meaning.

Why T5 Holds a Unique Place

Master continued, "T5, the *Text-to-Text Transfer Transformer*, arrived as a philosophical simplification of NLP. Instead of creating a separate model for every task—translation, summarization, classification—it taught the model that *everything is a transformation of text.* Translate this → that.

Summarize this → that.

Classify this → that.

It unified the entire field under a single paradigm of **input → output**, demonstrating that the essence of intelligence lies in understanding transformation itself."

Applications of Transformer Models

The Transformer's brilliance lies in its **universality**—its ability to generalize across data types and domains.

Natural Language Processing (NLP)

Transformers now power every major NLP task:

- **Machine Translation** (e.g., Google Translate)
- **Text Summarization** (e.g., news digests, report condensation)

- **Named Entity Recognition** (identifying people, places, organizations)
- **Sentiment Analysis** (understanding emotion and tone in text)

Speech Recognition

Transformers process **audio as sequential embeddings**, learning how sound patterns map to words. Modern speech-to-text systems like **Whisper** or **wav2vec** employ Transformer-based encoders to achieve near-human transcription accuracy.

Computer Vision

When applied to images, Transformers learn **visual attention**. Models like **ViT (Vision Transformer)** interpret images not as pixel grids but as sequences of "visual tokens." This enables object detection, image classification, and even **image generation** when combined with diffusion models.

Recommendation Systems

Transformers power **contextual recommendation engines**, understanding long-term patterns of user behaviour to predict preferences across movies, music, or shopping platforms.

Text and Music Generation

Transformers like **GPT**, **MusicLM**, and **Jukebox** generate coherent text and music compositions—proving that creativity, too, can emerge from structured pattern learning.

Modern Applications of Transformers

Master said, "Today, the Transformer architecture stands as the foundation of modern AI. What once began as a research innovation now orchestrates systems that millions use daily."

Examples of Real-World Systems

- **ChatGPT (OpenAI):** Powers conversational AI through large-scale Transformer-based language modeling.
- **Google Search (BERT / RankBrain):** Understands the meaning behind search queries rather than matching keywords.
- **Machine Translation:** Neural translation engines (e.g., Google Translate, DeepL) rely on encoder-decoder Transformers.
- **Voice Assistants:** Models like Alexa, Siri, and Google Assistant use Transformers for both understanding and generation.
- **Medical NLP Systems:** Transformers analyze clinical notes, pathology reports, and research papers to extract insights and aid diagnosis.

The Evolution of Thought

- **Limitations of RNN / LSTM / GRU** — The struggle with long-term dependencies.
- **Introduction to Attention** — The spark that allowed networks to "focus."
- **Self-Attention Mechanism** — The heart of contextual understanding.
- **Encoder-Decoder with Attention** — The dialogue between comprehension and expression.
- **Transformer Architecture** — Parallelized intelligence without recurrence.
- **BERT, GPT, and T5 Families** — The branches of understanding, generation, and transformation.

Real-World Applications — The flowering of AI into every domain of human activity.

Master said, "The Transformer is not just a model—it is a new way of perceiving intelligence itself.

It attends, not remembers. It relates, not recalls.

And in doing so, it teaches us that understanding is not in the sequence of words, but in the *relationship* between them."

The Rise of Large Language Models (LLMs)

Master said, "Roopa, once the Transformer architecture matured, something extraordinary happened:

Researchers began to scale it.

Not modestly, but **to a scale previously unimaginable**."

Where older neural networks grew slowly in capability, Transformers revealed a profound insight:

When you scale the model (parameters), the data, and the compute together— the intelligence does not merely increase; it *emerges*.

This was not a linear growth. It was a **phase change**— like water becoming ice, or steam becoming cloud.

These models are called **Large Language Models (LLMs)**.

What Makes a Model 'Large'?

Master continued, "Size here refers not to physical space, but *capacity to represent relationships*."

Concept	Meaning
Parameters	The internal adjustable weights that encode knowledge.
Training Data	The text, audio, images, or code that shape understanding.
Compute	The energy and processing used to discover patterns.

Early models had millions of parameters.

Modern LLMs have **billions**, even **trillions**, enabling deeper conceptual abstraction.

This scaling allowed models to:

Infer meaning

- Generalize structure
- Generate reasoning steps
- Maintain extended context
- Express creativity

Until at last, the models began to **sound like us, think with us**, and, in many ways, **think through us**.

Why Scaling Works — The Emergence Principle

As models grow:

- They learn **syntax → semantics → reasoning** in natural progression.
- They begin to represent **ideas**, not just words.
- They internalize **common sense**, patterns of logic, and social narrative.

Emergent abilities arise:

- Understanding humor, metaphor, and nuance
- Recognising intent
- Following multi-step reasoning
- Writing original text with style and emotional rhythm

This is why large models *feel intuitive.*

They are not memorising language —they are **modeling the probability structure of thought**.

Examples of LLMs

Model	Type	Strength
GPT Family (OpenAI)	Decoder-only Transformer	Text generation, reasoning, conversation
PaLM / Gemini (Google)	Decoder and multimodal	Reasoning, tool use, cross-modal understanding
LLaMA (Meta)	Research-focused LLM	Lightweight, efficient, open training research
Claude (Anthropic)	Safety-focused LLM	Long-context reasoning, instruction stability

Each represents a philosophical direction:

- **GPT** focuses on creative emergence.
- **Claude** focuses on aligned reasoning.
- **Gemini** focuses on multimodal integration.
- **LLaMA** focuses on accessibility and open study.

Capabilities of LLMs Today

- **Conversation & Dialogue** - Understanding intent and producing fluid, human-like responses.
- **Structured Reasoning** - Solving problems, proving statements, writing code.
- **Knowledge Synthesis** - Summarising books, analysing research, forming insights.
- **Creative Expression** - Poetry, stories, music lyrics, emotional tone crafting.
- **Multimodal Understanding** - Interpreting images, audio, diagrams, and equations.

LLMs have become general reasoning engines.

Master added gently, "With power comes responsibility. An LLM is a mirror polished with data.

If the world's voices feed it, the world's virtues and vices both appear.

So we must guide how these models are trained, interpreted, and applied.

The intelligence is emergent — but wisdom must be intentional."

Summary:

This section traces the evolution of sequence modeling from early recurrent neural networks (RNNs) to modern Transformer-based architectures. We begin by understanding the limitations of RNNs and LSTMs—specifically, their difficulty in capturing long-range dependencies and the inefficiency of sequential processing. This leads to the emergence of the Attention mechanism, which allows models to selectively focus on relevant information regardless of distance. We examine different forms of attention—spatial, temporal, self-attention, global, local, hierarchical, memory-based, and multi-head—and understand how each addresses different structural needs in data.

We then explore the Seq2Seq encoder–decoder framework and see how Transformers replace recurrence with Self-Attention, enabling parallel computation and better context understanding. Key components—Positional Encoding, Multi-Head Attention, Feed-Forward Networks, and layered Encoder–Decoder blocks—are explained, along with variants like Mini and Full Transformers, MQA (Multi-Query Attention), and GQA (Grouped-Query Attention).

The section concludes by introducing latent space representations, where data is compressed into meaningful abstract features. We examine how different autoencoder families—Sparse Autoencoders, Contractive Autoencoders, and Variational Autoencoders (VAEs)—learn these representations and enable tasks like compression, denoising, generation, and structural understanding.

This forms the conceptual foundation for understanding large language models and generative intelligence.

What Next:

The upcoming series of Optimus will explore The Philosophy of Scale and Emergence, revealing how intelligence arises not merely from individual components but from the relationships, interactions, and thresholds among them. We will examine how models grow in capability as their scale increases, leading to emergent behaviors that were never explicitly programmed. The series will also cover Multimodal Transformers capable of seeing, hearing, and speaking; LLMs and Retrieval-Augmented Systems (RAG); Generative Adversarial Networks (GANs); AI Agents that act autonomously; and the expanding field of Multimodal AI, including advanced AI image generation.

P5-U5-L1- 6 - Practice Question

1. What is the main limitation of RNNs in sequence modeling?
2. How do LSTMs improve upon RNNs?
3. Why were Transformers introduced?
4. What is the key innovation in the Transformer architecture?
5. What does the Attention mechanism compute?
6. Write the basic Attention formula.
7. What is Self-Attention?
8. What is Spatial Attention?
9. What is Temporal Attention?
10. What is Global Attention?
11. What is Local Attention?
12. What is Multi-Head Attention?
13. Why scale the dot product in Attention by $\sqrt{d_k}$?
14. What is Positional Encoding used for?
15. Write the sinusoidal positional encoding formula.
16. What is the role of the Position-wise Feed Forward Network?
17. What does the Encoder do in a Transformer?
18. What does the Decoder do in a Transformer?
19. What is Seq2Seq?
20. How does a Mini-Transformer differ from a Full Transformer?
21. What is Multi-Query Attention (MQA)?
22. What is Grouped Query Attention (GQA)?
23. What is Latent Space?
24. What is an Autoencoder?

25. What are Sparse Autoencoders (SAEs)?
26. What are Contractive Autoencoders?
27. What are Variational Autoencoders (VAEs)?
28. What is the VAE loss function?
29. Why include KL Divergence in VAEs?
30. How are Transformers different from RNNs?

PART SIX

APPENDIX

"Every layer in a deep model is like a layer of consciousness, refining perception, transforming raw input into the poetry of understanding."

– Shree Shambav

APPENDIX A
Online Resources

Online resources:

The supplementary materials for the book can be accessed online at:

Setup instructions:

The setup instructions provided here are the same as those in the book but include clickable links to all the components. If you encounter any difficulties during the setup process, please consult this resource.

Updates:

Python, like any other language, undergoes continuous updates and changes. We maintain a comprehensive collection of updates, so if you encounter any issues, please check this resource to see if the instructions have been changed.

Data:

The book provides some sample raw data for running the programs, but you can also create your own samples using various file formats such as Excel, CSV, or JSON.

Practice questions:

You are encouraged to allocate ample time to work on the exercises independently. If you encounter any challenges and cannot proceed, consult this reference link.

Exercises and assignments:

While it's important to try the exercises on your own, you might encounter difficulties that prevent you from making progress. If that happens, you can find solutions to most of the exercises online. We encourage you to dedicate sufficient time to working on the exercises independently before seeking help.

Cheat sheets:

You can also find a wide range of cheat sheets online covering major concepts, which you can download and use for quick reference.

Errata

Despite our efforts to ensure the accuracy of our content, errors may still occur. If you come across any errors in the book, whether in the text or the code, please report them to us. Your feedback will not only aid in enhancing future editions of this book but also assist other readers in avoiding potential frustrations.

Advance material:

Advanced material is provided for those seeking further insights into the subject. Beginners may choose to skip the advanced section at the outset.

Reference links:

Activities	**Sheets**	**Links**
Login	Signup/Login page	https://www.shambav.org/artifacts/signup.php
Practice question	With the answer sheet	https://www.shambav.org/artifacts/optimum-python-series-6
Exercises, Assignments	With answers	
Quiz	Quiz answers	
Data	Data Sheet	
Supplementary	Advanced material	
Instruction	Setup instruction	
Advance materials	Programs, tricks, assignments, mini projects, issues	
Cheat sheets	Major concepts	

APPENDIX B

Practice Question

Answers to the Practice question

Part 1: Deep Neural Network - ANN

P1-U1-L1-5 - Practice Question

1. What is Deep Learning?

Deep learning is a subset of machine learning that uses neural networks with multiple layers to automatically learn complex patterns from data.

2. What is the role of TensorFlow in deep learning?

TensorFlow is a deep learning framework that provides tools to build, train, and deploy neural network models efficiently.

3. How does Keras relate to TensorFlow?

Keras is a high-level neural network API that runs on top of TensorFlow, making model building simpler and more user-friendly.

4. What is a Neural Network?

A neural network is a system of interconnected nodes (neurons) that process information in layers to learn patterns.

5. What is Forward Propagation?

Forward propagation is the process by which input data moves through the network to produce output predictions.

6. What is Backward Propagation?

Backward propagation updates weights based on the error by moving backward through the network using gradients.

7. What is Gradient Descent?

Gradient descent is an optimization method that adjusts weights to minimize the loss function.

8. What is Stochastic Gradient Descent (SGD)?

SGD updates weights using one or a few training samples at a time, making learning faster and more dynamic.

9. What is Mini-batch Gradient Descent?

Mini-batch gradient descent divides the dataset into small batches, balancing speed and stability.

10. What is the Chain Rule used for in neural networks?

The chain rule helps compute gradients during backpropagation by linking derivatives across layers.

11. What is an Epoch?

An epoch is one complete pass of the entire training dataset through the neural network.

12. What is a Loss Function?

A loss function measures how far the model's predictions are from the correct values.

13. What are Weight Initialization Techniques?

Weight initialization techniques define how initial weights are set to ensure stable and efficient learning.

14. What is an Activation Function?

An activation function introduces non-linearity, enabling the network to learn complex patterns.

15. Name some common Activation Functions.

Common activation functions include Sigmoid, ReLU, Tanh, and Softmax.

16. What is a Perceptron?

A perceptron is the simplest neural network with one neuron used for binary classification.

17. What is a Multilayer Perceptron (MLP)?

An MLP consists of multiple layers of neurons, enabling learning of more complex patterns.

18. What is a Learning Rate?

The learning rate determines how much the weights change during training updates.

19. What is Hyperparameter Tuning?

Hyperparameter tuning is the process of selecting the best training settings—like learning rate, batch size, and number of layers.

20. What are Adagrad and RMSProp?

Adagrad and RMSProp are optimization algorithms that adapt learning rates for faster and more stable training.

Part 2 - CNN

P2-U2-L1 - Practice Question

1. What is a Convolutional Neural Network (CNN)?

A CNN is a deep learning model designed to automatically extract spatial features from data, commonly used in image processing. It uses convolutional layers to learn patterns such as edges, textures, and shapes.

2. Why are CNNs effective for image-related tasks?

CNNs reduce the number of parameters by sharing weights and capturing local relationships. This makes them efficient and capable of recognizing visual patterns even when images vary in size or appearance.

3. What is the role of the Convolution Layer in a CNN?

The convolution layer applies filters over the input to detect features like edges and shapes. It learns these patterns automatically during training.

4. What is the difference between Convolution and Cross-Correlation in CNNs??

In convolution, the filter is flipped before sliding, while in cross-correlation, it is not. CNNs practically use cross-correlation, but we still refer to it as convolution.

5. What is Valid Cross-Correlation?

Valid cross-correlation performs filtering without padding, meaning the output is smaller than the input. It focuses only on regions where the filter fully overlaps the input.

6. What is Full Cross-Correlation?

Full cross-correlation adds padding around the input so the filter can cover all positions. This results in a larger output size than the input.

7. What is Backpropagation in CNNs??

Backpropagation calculates gradients of the loss with respect to weights and updates them to reduce error. It is the core learning process of neural networks.

8. What is the purpose of Optimization in CNNs?

Optimization adjusts model weights to minimize the loss function. Popular optimizers include SGD, Adam, and RMSProp.

9. What is Binary Cross-Entropy Loss used for?

Binary Cross-Entropy measures the error in binary classification tasks. It compares model predictions with the actual labels to improve accuracy.

10. What does the Sigmoid Activation Function do?

Sigmoid squashes input values to a range between 0 and 1. It is commonly used for binary classification outputs.

11. What is the Pooling Layer in CNNs?

The pooling layer downsamples feature maps to reduce size and computation. Max pooling is the most common and selects the strongest activation.

12. How does Pooling help reduce overfitting?

Pooling generalizes features by focusing on the strongest signals and ignoring small variations. This makes the model more robust and prevents memorization of noise.

13. How do CNNs boost robustness in learning?

By sharing weights across spatial regions and using pooling, CNNs learn consistent patterns even in the presence of noise or variation.

14. Why are fewer parameters beneficial in CNNs?

Fewer parameters reduce memory usage and training time, making the model faster and less prone to overfitting compared to fully connected networks.

15. Where are CNNs commonly used?

CNNs are widely used in image classification, object detection, facial recognition, medical imaging, and video processing.

Part 3: NLP

P3-U3-L1-5 - Practice Question

1. What is the difference between NLU, NLP, and NLG?

NLP is the overall field of enabling computers to process human language.

NLU focuses on understanding meaning, intent, and context.

NLG focuses on generating natural language output that sounds human-like.

2. Define Text Preprocessing and explain why it is needed.?

Text preprocessing cleans and standardizes raw text before analysis. It removes noise and inconsistencies, improving model accuracy and performance.

3. What is Tokenization in text processing?

Tokenization breaks text into smaller, meaningful units like words or subwords. This makes text easier for algorithms to analyse and represent.

4. How does Lowercasing contribute to text normalization?

Lowercasing converts all characters to lowercase to maintain uniformity. It prevents the model from treating “Apple” and “apple” as different words.

5. What is the purpose of Stopword Removal?

Stopword removal filters out very common words like “the,” “is,” and “and.” This allows the model to focus on more meaningful and content-rich words.

6. Explain the difference between Stemming and Lemmatization.

Stemming trims words to a rough root form, sometimes producing non-words

Lemmatization returns words to their valid dictionary base (lemma) using context.

7. What is Text Normalization, and where is it used?

Text normalization converts text into a standard, uniform form.

It is used in chatbots, search engines, voice assistants, and sentiment systems to improve understanding.

8. Define Bag of Words (BoW) representation.

BoW represents text based on word occurrence counts in a document.

It does not consider grammar, context, or word order.

9. How does TF-IDF improve upon BoW?

TF-IDF down-weights commonly used words and up-weights rare but meaningful words.

This helps highlight key terms that distinguish documents.

10. What are N-grams, and why are they useful?

N-grams are sequences of N consecutive words (e.g., bigram = 2 words, trigram = 3 words).

They capture local word context and improve understanding of phrase-level meaning.

11. What are Syntactic Features in NLP?

Syntactic features describe the grammatical structure of a sentence, such as word order and sentence patterns.

They help the model understand how words relate structurally within a sentence.

12. What are Semantic Features, and how do they differ from syntactic features?

Semantic features capture the meaning and context of words and sentences.

Unlike syntactic features, they focus on what is being said, not just how it is structured.

13. What is POS Tagging, and why is it important?

POS Tagging assigns parts of speech (noun, verb, adjective, etc.) to each word.

It helps machines understand grammar roles, enabling better parsing and meaning extraction.

14. Explain One-Hot Encoding in the context of text data.

One-hot encoding represents each word as a vector where one element is "1" and the rest are "0."

It is simple, but it does not capture semantic relationships between words.

15. What problem does Word Embedding solve?

Word embeddings convert words into dense vectors that carry meaning. They solve the problem of one-hot encoding not capturing relationships or similarity.

16. Compare CBOW and Skip-gram models in Word2Vec.

CBOW predicts the target word from surrounding context words

Skip-gram predicts surrounding words from a target word and performs better on smaller datasets.

17. What is the main idea behind GloVe embeddings?

GloVe uses global word co-occurrence statistics to create meaningful word vectors.

It learns word relationships from the entire corpus, not just local context.

18. How does fastText differ from Word2Vec?

fastText represents words as combinations of character n-grams.

This allows it to handle rare words and even understand unseen words.

19. What is meant by Pre-Trained Embeddings?

These are embeddings that have already been trained on large text corpora.

They allow users to reuse learned language knowledge instead of training from scratch.

20. What is ELMo, and what makes it different from Word2Vec?

ELMo produces contextualised word embeddings that change based on sentence meaning.
Word2Vec gives static embeddings that stay the same regardless of context.

21. Define BERT, and explain why it is called bidirectional.

BERT is a transformer-based model that learns context from both the left and right sides of a word.

It is bidirectional because it reads sentences in both directions simultaneously.

22. What are contextual embeddings?

Contextual embeddings change based on the sentence or phrase in which a word appears.

They reflect different meanings of the same word in different contexts.

23. What is the purpose of Doc2Vec?.

Doc2Vec creates embeddings for entire documents instead of individual words.

It helps in tasks like document similarity, categorisation, and retrieval.

24. How is RoBERTa different from BERT?

RoBERTa is an optimized version of BERT trained on more data and for a longer time.

It removes some training constraints, resulting in stronger performance.

25. What is DistilBERT, and why is it used?

DistilBERT is a smaller, faster version of BERT created through model distillation.

It retains most accuracy but is lighter and more efficient for deployment.

26. What is the role of Corpus in training NLP models?

A corpus is the collection of text on which models are trained.

More diverse and larger corpora lead to richer language understanding.

27. Why is Vectorization essential for machine learning algorithms in NLP?

ML models can only process numbers, not raw text.

Vectorization converts text into numerical form so algorithms can learn patterns.

28. Explain how embeddings capture the semantic meaning of words.

Embeddings place words in a vector space where similar meanings lie close together.

This allows the model to understand relationships such as king - man + woman ≈ queen.

29. Give an example of how NLP is used in everyday applications.

NLP powers tools like Google Search, voice assistants, and email spam filters.

It helps machines interpret and respond to human language.

30. Describe how NLU is used in chatbots or virtual assistants.

NLU helps the system understand user intent and extract key information.

This enables the chatbot to reply meaningfully instead of just matching keywords.

Part 4: RNN | LSTM | GRU

P4-U4-L1-3 - Practice Question

1. What is a Recurrent Neural Network (RNN)?

An RNN is a neural network designed to handle sequential data by using past outputs (hidden states) along with current inputs to make predictions.

2. Why are RNNs used for sequence data?

Because they maintain memory of previous time steps, allowing them to learn patterns across sequences.

3. What is a hidden state in RNNs?

It is the memory representation that carries information forward across time steps.

4. What is RNN Unfolding?

It refers to representing the RNN across time steps like a chain, showing repeated cells for each input in the sequence.

5. What is BPTT (Backpropagation Through Time)?

A version of backpropagation used to train RNNs by unfolding them across time and computing gradients for each time step.

6. What is the Vanishing Gradient Problem?

When gradients become extremely small during training, it prevents the network from learning long-term dependencies.

7. What is the Exploding Gradient Problem?

When gradients become excessively large, causing unstable weight updates and divergence during training.

8. What is a One-to-One RNN Model?.

A simple model where one input corresponds to one output (e.g., image classification).

9. What is a One-to-Many RNN Model?

One input leads to multiple outputs over time (e.g., image captioning).

10. What is a Many-to-One RNN Model?

A sequence of inputs produces a single output (e.g., sentiment classification).

11. What is a Many-to-Many RNN Model?

Sequences in and sequences out (e.g., machine translation).

They help the model understand how words relate structurally within a sentence.

12. What does LSTM stand for?

Long Short-Term Memory.

13. Why were LSTMs introduced?

To solve the RNN's vanishing gradient problem and enable learning of long-term dependencies.

14. What is the Cell State in LSTM?

It is the long-term memory pathway that carries information across time steps.

15. What are Gates in LSTM?

Mechanisms that control how much information is added, removed, or retained in the cell state.

16. Name the three LSTM gates.

Forget gate, Input gate, Output gate.

17. What is the Forget Gate responsible for?

Deciding what information to discard from the cell state.

18. What is the Input Gate responsible for?

Controlling what new information to store in the cell state.

19. What is the Output Gate responsible for?

Determining the next hidden state (output).

20. What is a Bidirectional LSTM?

A model where LSTMs process the sequence in both forward and backward directions to capture the full context.

21. What is a Stacked LSTM?

An architecture where multiple LSTM layers are placed on top of each other to learn hierarchical patterns.

22. What is a GRU?

A Gated Recurrent Unit, a simplified version of LSTM with fewer gates and no separate cell state.

23. What are the main gates in a GRU?.

Update Gate and Reset Gate.

24. How do GRUs differ from LSTMs?

GRUs merge memory and hidden states into one and use fewer gates, making them faster to train.

25. What does the Update Gate control in GRU?

How much past information should be carried forward.

26. What does the Reset Gate control in GRU?

How much past information to forget.

27. What is a Bidirectional GRU?

A GRU that processes the sequence in both forward and backward directions.

28. What is a Stacked GRU?

Multiple GRU layers are stacked together to increase model depth and learning capacity.

29. When would you choose GRU over LSTM?

When training speed and efficiency are more important, and the dataset size is moderate.

30. When would you prefer Bidirectional Models?

When context from both past and future tokens is needed (e.g., text classification, translation).

Part 5: Attention | Transformer

P5-U5-L1-6 - Practice Question

What is the main limitation of RNNs in sequence modeling?

RNNs struggle with long-term dependencies due to vanishing and exploding gradients.

How do LSTMs improve upon RNNs?

LSTMs use gates (input, forget, output) to regulate information flow and retain long-term memory.

Why were Transformers introduced?

To overcome the sequential processing bottleneck of RNNs and better capture long-range dependencies using attention.

What is the key innovation in the Transformer architecture?

The Self-Attention mechanism, allows each token to weigh the importance of other tokens in the sequence.

What does the Attention mechanism compute?

It computes a weighted sum of value vectors based on similarity between queries and keys.

Write the basic Attention formula.

Attention (Q, K, V) = softmax $(\frac{QK^T}{\sqrt{d_k}})$ V

What is Self-Attention?

Self-Attention is attention applied within the same sequence, allowing tokens to relate to each other.

What is Spatial Attention?

It focuses on relationships across spatial dimensions (e.g., in images).

What is Temporal Attention?

It focuses on relationships across time steps in sequences (e.g., speech or time-series).

What is Global Attention?

It considers the entire sequence when computing attention weights.

What is Local Attention?

It restricts focus to a fixed window or neighbourhood region..

What is Multi-Head Attention?

Multiple attention layers run in parallel, learning different representation subspaces.

Why scale the dot product in Attention by $\sqrt{d_k}$

To avoid large values that make softmax unstable.

What is Positional Encoding used for?

To provide Transformers with order information, since they process tokens in parallel.

Write the sinusoidal positional encoding formula.?

$PE_{pos,\,2i} = \sin(\frac{pos}{10000^{2i/d_{model}}})$

$PE_{pos,2i+1} = \cos(\frac{pos}{10000^{2i/d_{model}}})$

What is the role of the Position-wise Feed Forward Network?

It transforms each token independently with non-linearity to enrich representations.

What does the Encoder do in a Transformer?.

Encodes input sequences into contextual representations.

What does the Decoder do in a Transformer?

Generates output sequence step-by-step while attending to encoder outputs.

What is Seq2Seq?

A framework mapping an input sequence to an output sequence using encoder–decoder models.

How does a Mini-Transformer differ from a Full Transformer?

It reduces layers, attention heads, and model dimensions for efficiency.

What is Multi-Query Attention (MQA)?

Uses multiple queries but shared keys and values to reduce computation and memory.

What is Grouped Query Attention (GQA)?

Queries are grouped to share keys and values partially—a compromise between MQA and Multi-Head.

What is Latent Space?

A compressed representation capturing core features learned by a model.

What is an Autoencoder?.

A neural network that compresses data (encode) and reconstructs it (decode).

What are Sparse Autoencoders (SAEs)?

Autoencoders with sparsity constraints to force useful feature learning.

What are Contractive Autoencoders?

They penalize the sensitivity of the encoder output to input variations to improve robustness.

What are Variational Autoencoders (VAEs)?

They learn a probability distribution in latent space and generate new samples by sampling.

What is the VAE loss function?

Loss = Reconstruction Loss + KL Divergence

Why include KL Divergence in VAEs?

To ensure latent space follows a known smooth distribution (usually Gaussian)..

How are Transformers different from RNNs?

Transformers process sequences in parallel, while RNNs process sequentially.

APPENDIX C

QUIZ

Part 1 – DEEP LEARNING | ANN | PERCEPTRON

1. Which of the following best describes an Artificial Neural Network (ANN)?
A. A rule-based system B. A network of interconnected nodes that learns patterns C. A predefined mathematical equation D. A hardware circuit

2. What is the perceptron mainly used for?
A. Regression B. Binary classification C. Clustering D. Dimensionality reduction

3. Forward propagation in a neural network refers to:
A. Updating weights using gradients B. Passing inputs through the network to get outputs C. Randomly initializing weights D. Resetting bias terms

4. Backpropagation is used to:

A. Compute output
B. Adjust weights based on error
C. Convert text into tokens
D. Remove stopwords

5. Which function measures prediction error during training?

A. Filter
B. Activation function
C. Loss function
D. Gradient

6. What does Bias do in a neuron?

A. Removes noise
B. Shifts the activation function output
C. Reduces model size
D. Performs pooling

7. The Sigmoid activation function outputs values between:

A. $-\infty$ to $+\infty$
B. 0 to 1
C. -1 to 1
D. 0 to 10

8. ReLU activation is preferred because:
A. It is linear and easy B. It reduces vanishing gradient issues C. It always outputs negative values D. It does not require training

9. Gradient Descent is used to:
A. Initialize layers B. Minimize the loss function C. Remove bias D. Apply regularization

10. In CNNs, a convolution operation primarily helps to:
A. Flatten the image B. Detect local features C. Generate labels D. Remove outliers

11. Cross-correlation differs from convolution because:
A. It flips the filter B. It does not flip the filter C. It changes stride length D. It increases the number of neurons

12. Valid cross-correlation means:
A. Padding is added B. No padding is added C. Output size is larger than input D. Output is always zero

13. Full cross-correlation means:
A. No padding B. Padding is added to include all partial overlaps C. Kernel is flipped D. Kernel is unchanged

14. What does a Pooling Layer do in CNN?
A. Converts text to embeddings B. Reduces spatial dimensions C. Performs weight updates D. Adds bias

15. Max Pooling selects:
A. The smallest value in the region B. The average of values C. The largest value in the region D. The last value only

16. Binary Cross-Entropy Loss is typically used for:
A. Regression tasks B. Binary classification tasks C. Clustering tasks D. Image compression

17. CNNs reduce overfitting using:
A. Larger filters B. Dropout and data augmentation C. Increasing output size D. Removing pooling layers

18. Which layer in CNN extracts high-level features?
A. Input layer B. Convolution layer C. Pooling layer D. Output layer

19. A deep neural network is defined as a network with:
A. One hidden layer B. Multiple hidden layers C. No hidden layers D. Only output layer

20. The main purpose of optimization algorithms (like SGD, Adam) is to:

A. Increase dataset size
B. Reduce training time
C. Minimize loss and update weights efficiently
D. Convert images to grayscale

Part 2 - CNN

1. Which layer in a CNN is responsible for detecting features like edges and textures?

A. Fully Connected Layer
B. Convolutional Layer
C. Output Layer
D. Dropout Layer

2. Which operation in CNN reduces the spatial dimensions of feature maps?

A. Normalization
B. Pooling
C. Activation
D. Gradient Clipping

3. Which pooling method selects the maximum value from each region?

A. Average Pooling
B. Sum Pooling
C. Max Pooling
D. Feature Pooling

4. Which function is commonly used in the last layer of binary classification using CNN?
A. ReLU B. Tanh C. Sigmoid D. Softmax

5. What does Backpropagation do in CNN training?
A. Initializes weights B. Updates weights by computing gradients C. Removes noise D. Stores feature maps

6. Binary Cross-Entropy Loss is mainly used for:
A. Multi-class classification B. Regression tasks C. Binary classification D. Clustering

7. Which of the following best describes Valid Cross-Correlation?
A. Output is larger than input B. Output size equals input size C. No padding is applied **D.** Excessive padding is applied

8. Which component helps reduce overfitting in CNNs by simplifying feature maps?

   A. Pooling Layer
   B. Convolution Layer
   C. Output Layer
   D. Sigmoid Layer

9. What makes CNNs more efficient than fully connected networks for images?

   A. They use fewer parameters by sharing filters
   B. They require more memory
   C. They remove feature extraction
   D. They study pixels individually without patterns

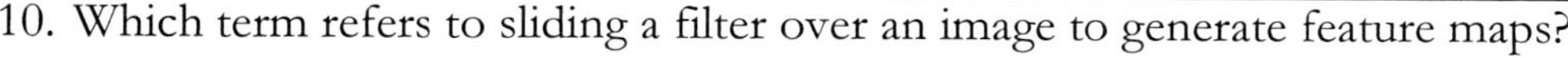

10. Which term refers to sliding a filter over an image to generate feature maps?

   A. Pooling
   B. Cross-Correlation
   C. Noise Reduction
   D. Dropout

Part 3 – NLP

1. Which field focuses on enabling computers to understand and work with human language?

   A. NLP
   B. Computer Vision
   C. Robotics
   D. Compilers

2. Which part of NLP deals specifically with understanding the meaning behind text?
A. NLG B. NLU C. OCR D. Data Mining

3. Which component of NLP focuses on generating human-like text responses?
A. NLU B. ASR C. NLG D. POS Tagging

4. Which process converts unstructured text into tokens (words or subwords)?
A. Parsing B. Tokenization C. Lemmatization D. Segmentation

5. What is the purpose of removing common words like the, is, and of?
A. Stemming B. Stopword Removal C. Parsing D. Chunking

6. Which technique reduces words to their base dictionary form?
A. Stemming B. Lemmatization C. Parsing D. POS Tagging

7. Which representation assigns each word a vector of 0s and 1s with a single 1?
A. TF-IDF B. Word Embedding C. One-Hot Encoding D. Bag of Words

8. Which model captures meaning by placing similar words closer in vector space?
A. Word Embedding B. BoW C. Stopword Model D. Bigram Model

9. Which Word2Vec model predicts a target word from surrounding context words?
A. Skip-Gram B. CBOW C. GloVe D. fastText

10. Which embedding technique captures subword information to handle rare or misspelled words?

A. CBOW
B. Skip-Gram
C. fastText
D. BoW

11. Which model is known as a bidirectional transformer for deep contextual understanding?

A. Word2Vec
B. TF-IDF
C. BERT
D. Doc2Vec

12. Which representation considers word meaning based on context, not fixed vectors?

A. Static Embeddings
B. Contextual Embeddings
C. One-Hot Encoding
D. POS Vectors

13. Which model is a distilled, smaller, faster version of BERT?

A. GPT
B. fastText
C. DistilBERT
D. RoBERTa

14. Which technique represents a document instead of individual words in vector space?
A. Word2Vec B. Doc2Vec C. One-Hot Encoding D. Parsing

15. Which NLP component is vital in chatbots to correctly interpret user queries?
A. NLG B. NLU C. Data Mining D. Computer Graphics

16. Which step in text preprocessing converts all characters to the same case for consistency?
A. Tokenization B. Lemmatization C. Lowercasing D. Parsing

17. Which representation method gives higher weight to rare but important words in a document??
A. Bag of Words B. One-Hot Encoding C. TF-IDF D. Stemming

18. Which type of feature relates to sentence structure and grammar?
A. Semantic Features B. Syntactic Features C. Contextual Embeddings D. One-Hot Encodings

19. Which model improves BERT by training with more data and removing the Next Sentence Prediction task?
A. Skip-Gram B. ELMo C. RoBERTa D. GPT

20. Which approach is commonly used for understanding user intent in Virtual Assistants?
A. NLG B. NLU C. OCR D. ASR

Part 4 – RNN | LSTM | GRU

1. Which of the following best describes a Recurrent Neural Network (RNN)?
A. A network that processes inputs independently B. A network that remembers previous outputs through hidden States. C. A network used only for image processing D. A network that cannot handle sequential data

2. What problem commonly affects standard RNNs during training?
A. Overfitting B. Vanishing gradient problem C. Memory overflow D. High bias

3. Which training method is used for RNNs?
A. Gradient Clipping B. K-Means C. Backpropagation Through Time (BPTT) D. Max Pooling

4. Which RNN structure is used for sentiment classification?
A. One-to-One B. One-to-Many C. Many-to-One D. Many-to-Many

5. What is the main purpose of LSTM networks?
A. Reduce model size B. Solve the vanishing gradient problem C. Remove hidden states D. Increase the number of parameters

6. Which component in LSTM carries long-term memory?
A. Hidden State B. Cell State C. Output D. Input Gate

7. Which gate in LSTM decides what information to forget?
A. Input Gate B. Output Gate C. Forget Gate D. Update Gate

8. . Which gate in LSTM controls what new information is stored?
A. Input Gate B. Reset Gate C. Output Gate D. Memory Gate

9. What does a Bidirectional LSTM do?
A. By using multiple binary classifiers B. By averaging all classes C. By combining KNN and SVM D. By using a single classifier for all classes

10. What is a Stacked LSTM?
A. LSTM with no hidden state B. Multiple LSTM layers placed one after another C. LSTM used for images D. LSTM that contains no gating

11. What is the main difference between LSTM and GRU??
A. GRU is slower B. GRU does not have a separate cell state C. LSTM has fewer gates D. GRU has three gates

12. Which gates exist in a GRU??
A. Input and Forget Gates B. Reset and Update Gates C. Forget and Output Gates **D.** Memory and Decision Gates

13. Which gate in GRU controls how much past information is retained?
A. Reset Gate B. Update Gate C. Forget Gate D. Output Gate

14. Which gate in GRU decides how much previous state to ignore?
A. Reset Gate B. Input Gate C. Output Gate D. Forget Gate

15. Why are GRUs computationally faster than LSTMs?
A. They have no hidden state B. They have fewer parameters C. They run on GPUs only D. They use no activation functions

16. Which model is best when future context is required?
A. Unidirectional RNN B. Dense Network C. Bidirectional RNN/LSTM/GRU D. CNN

17. Which architecture is used for Machine Translation (seq → seq)?
A. One-to-One B. One-to-Many C. Many-to-One D. Many-to-Many

18. In text generation, what is commonly used?
A. Many-to-One B. Many-to-Many C. One-to-Many D. One-to-One

19. What advantage does Stacking RNN/LSTM/GRU layers provide?
A. Lower accuracy B. Faster inference only C. Better hierarchical feature learning D. Removes sequential dependencies

20. When should GRU be preferred over LSTM?
A. When the dataset is very large B. When memory and training speed are priorities C. When no sequences are involved D. When only images are analyzed

Part 5 – Attention | Transformer | seq2seq

1. What problem does Self-Attention solve in sequence modeling?
A. Storing data on disk B. Capturing long-range dependencies C. Reducing dataset size D. Eliminating training time

2. Which model architecture introduced the Self-Attention mechanism?
A. CNN B. RNN C. Transformer D. GAN

3. Why do RNNs struggle with long sequences?
A. They use too many parameters B. They process sequences in parallel C. They suffer from vanishing gradients D. They do not support text input

4. What does the term "Query" represent in the attention mechanism?
A. Feature normalization B. The vector seeking relevant information C. Positional information D. Training loss

5. . What is the purpose of Positional Encoding in Transformers?
A. To sort tokens alphabetically B. To provide order information to the model C. To reduce model size D. To increase randomness

6. Which attention type focuses only on nearby tokens in a sequence?
A. Global Attention B. Local Attention C. Branch Attention D. Multi-Head Attention

7. Multi-Head Attention allows the model to:
A. Ignore irrelevant tokens B. Create multiple parallel attention computations C. Train without a GPU D. Remove positional encoding

8. In the Transformer architecture, the Encoder mainly:
A. Generates the final output sequence B. Converts input into contextualized representations C. Removes irrelevant words D. Compresses images

9. What is the role of the Decoder in a Transformer?

A. Predicts the next token using encoder output
B. Normalizes embeddings
C. Removes duplicate words
D. Reduces sequence length

10. Which type of attention shares Keys and Values across multiple Query heads?

A. Self-Attention
B. MQA (Multi-Query Attention)
C. GQA (Grouped Query Attention)
D. Hierarchical Attention

11. The basic Attention formula includes which key operation?

A. Matrix division
B. Dot product of Q and K
C. Gradient clipping
D. Weight decay

12. Sparse Autoencoders encourage what behavior in neurons?

A. Always activating
B. Never activating
C. Activating minimally and selectively
D. Random activation

13. Variational Autoencoders differ from standard autoencoders because they:
A. Do not compress data B. Model latent space as a probability distribution C. Only work on images D. Do not reconstruct input

14. Contractive Autoencoders improve robustness by:
A. Increasing model size B. Penalizing sensitivity to input changes C. Removing training loss D. Using only one hidden layer

15. Seq2Seq models consist of which main components?
A. Tokenizer and Decoder B. Query and Key networks C. Encoder and Decoder D. Classifier and Regressor

APPENDIX D

QUIZ

ANSWER

Part 1 – DEEP LEARNING | ANN | PERCEPTRON

1. Which of the following best describes an Artificial Neural Network (ANN)?
Answer: B

2. What is the perceptron mainly used for?
Answer: B

3. Forward propagation in a neural network refers to:
Answer: B

4. Backpropagation is used to:
Answer: B

5. Which function measures prediction error during training?
Answer: C

6. What does Bias do in a neuron?
Answer: B

7. The Sigmoid activation function outputs values between:
Answer: B

8. ReLU activation is preferred because:
Answer: B

9. Gradient Descent is used to:
Answer: B

10. In CNNs, a convolution operation primarily helps to:
Answer: B

11. Cross-correlation differs from convolution because:
Answer: B

12. Valid cross-correlation means:
Answer: B

13. Full cross-correlation means:
Answer: B

14. What does a Pooling Layer do in CNN?
Answer: B

15. Max Pooling selects:
Answer: C

16. Binary Cross-Entropy Loss is typically used for:
Answer: B

17. CNNs reduce overfitting using:
Answer: B

18. Which layer in CNN extracts high-level features?
Answer: B

19. A deep neural network is defined as a network with:
Answer: B

20. The main purpose of optimization algorithms (like SGD, Adam) is to:
Answer: C

PART 2 CNN

1. Which layer in a CNN is responsible for detecting features like edges and textures?
Answer: B. Convolutional Layer

2. Which operation in CNN reduces the spatial dimensions of feature maps?
Answer: B. Pooling

3. Which pooling method selects the maximum value from each region?
Answer: C. Max Pooling

4. Which function is commonly used in the last layer of binary classification using CNN?
Answer: C. Sigmoid

5. What does Backpropagation do in CNN training?
Answer: B. Updates weights by computing gradients

6. Binary Cross-Entropy Loss is mainly used for:
Answer: C. Binary Classification

7. Which of the following best describes Valid Cross-Correlation?
Answer: C. No padding is applied

8. Which component helps reduce overfitting in CNNs by simplifying feature maps?
Answer: A. Pooling Layer

9. What makes CNNs more efficient than fully connected networks for images?
Answer: A. They use fewer parameters by sharing filters

10. Which term refers to sliding a filter over an image to generate feature maps?
Answer: B. Cross-Correlation

PART 3 NLP

1. Which field focuses on enabling computers to understand and work with human language?
Answer: A

2. Which part of NLP deals specifically with understanding the meaning behind text?
Answer: B

3. Which component of NLP focuses on generating human-like text responses?
Answer: C

4. Which process converts unstructured text into tokens (words or subwords)?
Answer: B

5. What is the purpose of removing common words like the, is, and, of?
Answer: B

6. Which technique reduces words to their base dictionary form?
Answer: B

7. Which representation assigns each word a vector of 0s and 1s with a single 1?
Answer: C

8. Which model captures meaning by placing similar words closer in vector space?
Answer: A

9. Which Word2Vec model predicts a target word from surrounding context words?
Answer: B

10. Which embedding technique captures subword information to handle rare or misspelled words?
Answer: C

11. Which model is known as a bidirectional transformer for deep contextual understanding?
Answer: C

12. Which representation considers word meaning based on context, not fixed vectors?
Answer: B

13. Which model is a distilled, smaller, faster version of BERT?
Answer: C

14. Which technique represents a document instead of individual words in vector space?
Answer: B

15. Which NLP component is vital in chatbots to correctly interpret user queries?
Answer: B

16. Which step in text preprocessing converts all characters to the same case for consistency?
Answer: C

17. Which representation method gives higher weight to rare but important words in a document?
Answer: C

18. Which type of feature relates to sentence structure and grammar?
Answer: B

19. Which model improves BERT by training with more data and removing the Next Sentence Prediction task?
Answer: C

20. Which approach is commonly used for understanding user intent in Virtual Assistants?
Answer: B

PART 4 – RNN | LSTM | GRU

1. Which of the following best describes a Recurrent Neural Network (RNN)?
Answer: B

2. What problem commonly affects standard RNNs during training?
Answer: B

3. Which training method is used for RNNs?
Answer: C

4. Which RNN structure is used for sentiment classification?
Answer: C

5. What is the main purpose of LSTM networks?
Answer: B

6. Which component in LSTM carries long-term memory?
Answer: B

7. Which gate in LSTM decides what information to forget?
Answer: C

8. **.** Which gate in LSTM controls what new information is stored?
Answer: A

9. **What does a Bidirectional LSTM do?**
Answer: C

10. What is a Stacked LSTM?
Answer: B

11. What is the main difference between LSTM and GRU?
Answer: B

12. Which gates exist in a GRU?
Answer: B

13. Which gate in GRU controls how much past information is retained?
Answer: B

14. Which gate in GRU decides how much previous state to ignore?
Answer: A

15. Why are GRUs computationally faster than LSTMs?
Answer: B

16. Which model is best when future context is required?
Answer: C

17. Which architecture is used for Machine Translation (seq → seq)?
Answer: D

18. In text generation, what is commonly used?
Answer: C

19. What advantage does Stacking RNN/LSTM/GRU layers provide?
Answer: C

20. When should GRU be preferred over LSTM?
Answer: B

PART 5 Attention | Transformer+seq2seq

1. What problem does Self-Attention solve in sequence modeling?
Answer: B

2. Which model architecture introduced the Self-Attention mechanism?
Answer: C

3. Why do RNNs struggle with long sequences?
Answer: C

4. What does the term "Query" represent in the attention mechanism?
Answer: B

5. . What is the purpose of Positional Encoding in Transformers?
Answer: B

6. Which attention type focuses only on nearby tokens in a sequence?
Answer: B

7. Multi-Head Attention allows the model to:
Answer: B

8. In Transformer architecture, the Encoder mainly:
Answer: B

9. What is the role of the Decoder in a Transformer?
Answer: A

10. Which type of attention shares Keys and Values across multiple Query heads?
Answer: B

11. The basic Attention formula includes which key operation?
Answer: B

12. Sparse Autoencoders encourage what behavior in neurons?
Answer: C

13. Variational Autoencoders differ from standard autoencoders because they:
Answer: B

14. Contractive Autoencoders improve robustness by:
Answer: B

15. Seq2Seq models consist of which main components?
Answer: C

APPENDIX E

CHEAT SHEET

NEURAL NETWORKS & DEEP LEARNING

PART 1: THE RISE OF NEURAL NETWORKS – ANN | PERCEPTRON | TENSORFLOW

Concept: ANNs mimic the human brain with interconnected neurons for pattern learning.

Perceptron: Basic linear classifier; foundation of neural logic.

MLP (Multi-Layer Perceptron): Adds hidden layers to model complex, non-linear patterns.

Learning Process:

- *Forward Propagation* → Generates predictions.
- *Backward Propagation* → Updates weights via Gradient Descent to minimize error.

Activation Functions: ReLU, Sigmoid, Tanh → Introduce non-linearity.

Optimizers: Adam, RMSProp, SGD → Accelerate convergence.

Frameworks: TensorFlow & Keras → Simplify model design, training, and deployment.

Goal: Build efficient neural architectures with solid mathematical grounding.

PART 2: FROM PIXELS TO PATTERNS – CNN

Core Idea: CNNs recognize spatial features in images through local connectivity.

Convolution Layers: Filters detect features like edges, shapes, and textures.

Pooling Layers: Reduce dimensionality while retaining essential features.

Activation: ReLU for non-linearity; Softmax/Sigmoid for classification.

Loss Function: Cross-Entropy → Measures prediction error.

Regularization: Dropout, Batch Normalization, Data Augmentation → Prevent overfitting.

Applications: Image recognition, object detection, medical imaging, autonomous systems.

Goal: Transform raw pixels into intelligent pattern perception.

PART 3: THE DAWN OF LANGUAGE INTELLIGENCE – NLU | NLP | NLG

Domains:

- *NLP* → Text structure & processing.
- *NLU* → Understanding meaning, sentiment, and intent.
- *NLG* → Generating human-like responses.

Preprocessing Steps: Tokenization, Normalization, Stopword Removal, Lemmatization.

Encoding Methods: Bag-of-Words, TF-IDF, Word Embeddings.

Embedding Models: Word2Vec, GloVe, BERT → Capture contextual meaning.

Applications: Chatbots, translation, summarization, sentiment analysis.

Goal: Enable machines to understand and produce language naturally.

PART 4: THE EVOLUTION OF MEMORY IN MACHINES – RNN | LSTM | GRU

RNN: Processes sequential data; captures temporal dependencies.

Challenge: Vanishing Gradient limits long-term memory.

LSTM: Introduces gates (Input, Forget, Output) → Maintains long-term context.

GRU: Simplified LSTM with fewer parameters; faster training.

Techniques:

- *BPTT (Backpropagation Through Time)* for sequence learning.
- *Bidirectional/Stacked* RNNs for deeper context understanding.

Use Cases: Speech recognition, text generation, sequence prediction.

Goal: Embed memory and sequence awareness into models.

PART 5: FROM RNNS TO TRANSFORMERS

Problem Solved: RNNs struggle with long-range dependencies and parallelization.

Attention Mechanism: Allows focus on important parts of input sequences.

Transformers: Replace recurrence with Self-Attention and Positional Encoding.

Key Components: Multi-Head Attention, Feed-Forward Layers, Encoder–Decoder Architecture.

Variants: Mini/Full Transformers, MQA (Multi-Query), GQA (Grouped Query).

Latent Representations: Autoencoders (Sparse, Contractive, Variational) compress knowledge efficiently.

Applications: Language models, generative AI, vision transformers.

Goal: Achieve scalable intelligence through context-driven learning.

Quick Summary:

- **ANN** → Foundation of neural logic.
- **CNN** → Vision and spatial understanding.
- **RNN/LSTM/GRU** → Memory and sequence modeling.
- **Transformers** → Contextual, scalable intelligence for modern AI.

TESTIMONIALS

Optimum – Python – Ultimate Guide for Beginners – Series 1

"Optimum - Python Series I" provides readers with a roadmap to Python mastery, thanks to Shree Shambav's expertise and guidance. The book's structured learning path, clear explanations, and practical examples make it easy to grasp even the most complex concepts. Whether you're a beginner looking to learn the basics or an experienced coder seeking to expand your skill set, this book has something for everyone. I highly recommend it to anyone interested in Python programming!

Optimum – Exploring Data Structures and Algorithms – Series II

As a Python programmer looking to deepen one's understanding of data structures and algorithms, I can confidently say that Optimum – Exploring Data Structures and Algorithms – Series II is one of the best resources I've come across. Whether you're just starting or you're already experienced with Python, this book is an indispensable guide for anyone who wants to master both the fundamentals and the more advanced aspects of programming.

Optimum – Unleashing the Potential of Data Science with Libraries Series III

Shree Shambav's "Optimum – Python Power Series III" turns the vast world of Python libraries into a clear and structured path toward mastery. From NumPy to Scikit-learn, every chapter builds confidence and insight, making it a must-have for learners and professionals alike in the age of intelligent data.

Optimum – Unleashing the Potential of Data Science with Machine Learning Techniques Series IV

An extraordinary fusion of clarity, depth, and practicality. Shree Shambav transforms complex machine learning concepts into an engaging, intuitive learning journey that empowers readers to think like data scientists. A must-read for anyone seeking to master Python's true potential in the evolving world of data science.

ACKNOWLEDGEMENTS

To my grandfathers, grandmothers, mothers, fathers, aunts, uncles, neighbours, sisters, brothers, friends, and teachers, they poured in endless moral stories, retellings of Ramayana, Mahabharata, Puranas, Upanishads, and so on.

My teachers, neighbours, and kindred souls. Who provided us with a stage to perform wonderful Puranic stories and were gracious enough to acknowledge our efforts.

The artists and translators of epics have served as a source of inspiration, invigorating our spirits, making these works accessible, and enabling us to grasp the profound depths and deeper dimensions they contain.

I also cherish the stimulating conversations; I had with my wonderful mothers, Punitha Muniswamy and Uma Devi.

Our family's youngest member, Aadhya, who always overwhelmed me with questions, inspired this book.

I would likewise prefer to express gratitude to Mr Sivakumar, Mrs Roopa Sivakumar, Mr Akshaya Rajesh, Ms Akshatha Rajesh, Ms Apeksha Prabhu, Mr Akanksh Prabhu, Mr Nikash Sarasambi, and Mrs Spoorthi Nikash for their valuable inputs.

I must thank Mr Rajesh, Mr Savan Prabhu, Mrs Revathi Rajesh, Mrs Rajani Sarasambi, and Mrs Manju Reshma, who encouraged me and often suggested writing a book. Their unwavering belief that I had something valuable to offer kept me going during my writing sessions.

Love you all,

Shree Shambav

www.shambav.org

shreeshambav@gmail.com

BOOKS BY – AUTHOR

Printed at Repro India Ltd.